THE PACIFIC COAST AND
THE SANTA FE TRAIL

Copyright by Fred Harvey

ALSO BY STEPHEN FRIED

THING OF BEAUTY
The Tragedy of Supermodel Gia

BITTER PILLS
Inside the Hazardous World of Legal Drugs

THE NEW RABBI

HUSBANDRY

APPETITE FOR AMERICA

BANTAM BOOKS

NEW YORK

APPETITE FOR AMERICA

HOW VISIONARY

BUSINESSMAN FRED HARVEY

BUILT A RAILROAD

HOSPITALITY EMPIRE THAT

CIVILIZED THE WILD WEST

STEPHEN FRIED

Published in the United States by Bantam Books,
an imprint of The Random House Publishing Group,
a division of Random House, Inc., New York.

BANTAM BOOKS and the rooster colophon are
registered trademarks of Random House, Inc.

Fred Harvey logo is used by permission of
Xanterra Parks & Resorts, Inc.

LIBRARY OF CONGRESS CATALOGING-IN-PUBLICATION DATA

Fried, Stephen
Appetite for America : how visionary businessman Fred Harvey built a railroad
hospitality empire that civilized the Wild West / Stephen Fried.
p. cm.
Includes bibliographical references and index.
ISBN 978-0-553-80437-9
eBook ISBN 978-0-553-90732-2
1. Harvey, Fred.   2. Restaurateurs—United States—Biography.
3. Fred Harvey (Firm)   4. Cookery, American.   I. Title.
TX910.5.H34F75 2009
647.95092—dc22
[B]   2009047790

Printed in the United States of America on acid-free paper

www.bantamdell.com

2 4 6 8 9 7 5 3 1

FIRST EDITION

Book designed by Barbara M. Bachman

To Mom and Nana,
who taught me the comforts
of food, home, and family;
and to my traveling companion
in life, Black Bart

Fred Harvey? Do you know the name? If not, then your education has been much neglected . . .

Fred Harvey set a standard of excellence! . . . He has been a civilizer and a benefactor. He has added to the physical, mental and spiritual welfare of millions. No sermon can equal a Fred Harvey example—no poet can better a Fred Harvey precept. Fred Harvey simply kept faith with the public. He gave pretty nearly a perfect service . . .

The kind of business a man builds up is a reflection of himself— spun out of his heart. Man, like Deity, creates in his own image. I take my hat off to Fred Harvey, who served . . . so faithfully and well, that dying, he yet lives, his name a symbol of all that is honest, excellent, hygienic, beautiful and useful.

—Elbert Hubbard, renowned
American orator, philosopher, and
author of the early twentieth century

Wild buffalo fed the early traveler in the West and for doing so they put his picture on a nickel.

Well, Fred Harvey took up where the buffalo left off.

For what he has done for the traveler, one of his waitress's pictures (with an arm load of delicious ham and eggs) should be placed on both sides of every dime. He has kept the West in food—and wives.

—Will Rogers

RADIO INTERVIEWER: "How do you feel today, Mr. President?"

HARRY TRUMAN: "Fine. I just had breakfast, and I always feel fine after having a meal at Fred Harvey's. That's a 'plug' and I won't get paid for it, but I like the food anyway."

CONTENTS

WHO THE *HELL* IS FRED HARVEY?

⅁⅂

O N THAT SPRING NIGHT IN 1882, THE DRUNKEN COWBOYS RID-ing through northern New Mexico could have been forgiven for squinting in disbelief at the sight of the Montezuma Hotel. It did appear to be a hallucination.

The Montezuma was one of the most astonishing architectural creations in America—although perhaps most astonishing was its location. It was nestled in a gorgeous middle of nowhere, in the foothills of the Sangre de Cristo Mountains six miles outside of Las Vegas, New Mexico, an old Santa Fe Trail town that the railroad had only recently connected to civilization. The largest wood-frame building in the United States—some ninety thousand square feet, with 270 guest rooms—the Queen Anne–style Montezuma featured a dining room that seated five hundred, a casino, a breathtaking wine cellar, eleven bowling alleys, a billiard hall, and an immense therapeutic bathing facility offering six different kinds of baths and douches, so patrons could fully experience the medicinal powers of the underground hot springs.

The service at the Montezuma was brilliant, with staff imported from the best hotels in New York, London, Chicago, and St. Louis. And the cuisine was amazingly ambitious. The food combined the expertise of classically trained chefs from the restaurant capitals of the world with fresh regional American ingredients—fruit, vegetables, and shellfish, as well as delicacies like green turtles and sea celery harvested by pearl-diving Yaqui tribesmen—to which few other kitchens in the country had access, and which most chefs wouldn't come to fully appreciate for almost another century. Open for only a few weeks, the resort was already attracting dukes and princesses and presidents, who quickly booked passage on the Atchison, Topeka & Santa Fe, the upstart railroad whose newly laid tracks were the only way to get there.

In front of the Montezuma was a large park, exquisitely landscaped with shade trees and rare flowers, planted in three train-car loads of imported sod and topsoil. At the center was a huge fountain, flanked by lawns for tennis and croquet, an archery range, and even a zoo, where the deer and the antelope literally played. The free-form park was illuminated, as was the building itself, by thousands of gaslights fed by the hotel's own generating station.

So when "Red John" and his men approached on horseback that evening, they couldn't believe their bloodshot eyes.

The cowboys rode first to the park, where they hollered and shot their guns in the air while galloping across the manicured bluegrass and graveled walks. The commotion could be heard throughout the hotel, from its grand entranceway to its cavernous main dining room. There it reached a tall, slim man in his mid-forties, with a perfectly groomed Van Dyke beard, deep, cautious eyes, and senses that were always cocked. He tried to ignore the noise and enjoy his dinner, but soon threw down his linen napkin and rose abruptly from his cane-backed chair.

The man was dressed fastidiously in a dark blue suit with a waistcoat and dangling watch fob, the formal uniform of a Victorian gentleman from his homeland of England. But he walked quickly, with the nervous energy of America, drawing the attention of the dining room staff and some of the guests as he passed.

By the time he left the dining room, the cowboys had dismounted and were running riot through the hotel. He could hear them in the billiard hall, where they were taking target practice with the Indian relics and curios displayed above the bar, and shooting the tops off the private-label liquor bottles on the sideboard.

"Boys, put up your guns!" the Englishman called out, striding into the room.

"Who the *hell* are you?" Red John yelled.

"My name is Fred Harvey," he replied. "I run this place. And I will not have any rowdies here. If you don't behave like gentlemen, you can't stay here and you can't come again. Now put up your guns and take a drink with Fred Harvey!"

Although he had been in America for thirty years, Fred still retained his British accent, which made some Westerners titter.

But as the cowboys laughed, cursed, and taunted him, and hotel guests started gathering, he walked over and grabbed Red John by the collar. In a single motion, the fastidious Englishman yanked the dusty desperado over the bar and pinned him to the floor.

"You mustn't *swear* in this place," he told the stunned cowboy.

There was a moment of silence—and then Red John told his men to stand down.

"Fred Harvey is a *gentleman,* boys," he declared, brushing himself off. "I say, let's have those drinks."

When the drinks were done, they were served a midnight breakfast as well—the breakfast for which Fred Harvey was becoming famous. The freshest eggs and steak available in the country, shipped directly from farms in refrigerated train cars. Pan-size wheat cakes stacked six high. Quartered wedges of hot apple pie. And cup after cup of the best damn coffee these cowboys had ever tasted in their lives.

Red John and his men never made trouble at the Montezuma again.

But they still wanted to know, as did more and more people across the country:

Who the *hell* is Fred Harvey?

MORE THAN A CENTURY LATER, I am peering over the lip of the Grand Canyon in my pajamas at five o'clock in the morning. And I'm wondering the same thing.

As the sun slowly illuminates the canyon walls, I am reminded of why there is substantial literature just explaining why words cannot describe what I'm seeing. But as I turn away from the canyon, I take in another sight—less awe inspiring but in many ways equally intriguing, because it was created by man, by Americans, and plunked here on the very edge of the Divine Abyss.

It is El Tovar, the rustically majestic hotel that has afforded me the luxury of rolling out of a plush bed at sunrise, shuffling in my slippers down a carved oak staircase, and stepping outside to have the Grand Canyon pretty much to myself. El Tovar is, arguably, the most in-demand hotel in the world: Most of the guest rooms are booked up more than a year in advance, and an astonishing number of trips are planned around their availability.

El Tovar is also one of the last places where Fred Harvey lives on. The founder of the family business that created this hotel—and America's first hospitality empire—he still symbolically oversees every detail of its daily life, from his moody portrait hanging in the main lobby, next to where the maître d' arrives each morning at six thirty to greet the throng of tourists queued for the renowned breakfast-with-a-view. In the painting, he looks formidable and, frankly, a bit anxious, a clenched fist protruding from his black waistcoat.

Most visitors to the Grand Canyon don't have an inkling of why the Englishman in this portrait matters, or how he changed America. They are not aware that there was a time, not that long ago, when Fred Harvey was one of the most famous and intriguing men in the country—"a food missionary," as one prominent New York critic called him, on a quest to civilize the United States one meal at a time. They don't know that his waitresses—the legendary Harvey Girls—were the first major female workforce in America, allowing single women for the first time to travel independently, earn a decent living, and, over time, help settle the American West. They don't know that his restaurants, his hotels, and his Harvey Girls were once so much a part of American culture that in the 1940s his legend spawned a best-selling novel, and then an Oscar-winning MGM musical starring Judy Garland at the height of her career, which had the whole country singing along with her about the joys of exploring America "On the Atchison, Topeka, and the Santa Fe."

I was similarly unenlightened when I first encountered the Fred Harvey saga during a visit to the Grand Canyon in the early 1990s. I discovered him, as so many others have, in a sepia-toned photo in a hotel brochure. But then I started tripping across pieces of his story and his legacy in travels all over the country, although mostly in the areas that, as a born-and-bred Easterner, I think of as America's "better half": the Southwest and the Midwest (which was originally the West, or at least the western frontier). Over the years, Fred Harvey has become something of an obsession, because it seems that the more I learn about him, his family, his business, and his world, the more I understand about my homeland, and how it came to be. Seen through the prism of the Harvey family saga, the late 1800s—a period many of us slept through in high school history class—become a powerful, riveting drama of a great nation expanding and uniting, one steel rail at a time. And the formative years of the "American Century" take on a different meaning.

So, who the hell *was* Fred Harvey?

An Englishman who came to America in the 1850s, he built a family and a career and then, in his early forties, started a revolutionary business feeding train passengers in the Wild West along the Santa Fe railroad. While he died famous and wealthy, he was also a curiosity—a man out of time—because at the height of the Gilded Age, he became something much better understood today: the founding father of the American service industry. That's why his story and his methods are still studied in graduate schools of hotel, restaurant, and personnel management, advertising, and marketing. He is especially popular in the buzzwordy fields of "branding" and "brand extension," because "Fred Harvey" was actually the first widely known and respected brand name in America, established years before Coca-Cola.

"Fred Harvey" is also the name of the company he founded. Not Fred Harvey Inc. or The Fred Harvey Company. Just Fred Harvey. Why that is turns out to be one of the great untold family business sagas in American history—a tale not just about one brilliant, driven man and his empire but also about his largely unsung son Ford, who actually ran the company far longer than his father, but who stayed out of the spotlight so the public would think famous Fred was still alive, an ingenious marketing device. Because of Fred and Ford Harvey, this innovative family business played a crucial role in American culture from the post–Civil War era all the way through World War II.

Fred Harvey ran all the restaurants and hotels along the country's largest railroad, the Santa Fe between Chicago and Los Angeles; went on to serve the nation's cross-country drivers on Route 66, the first superhighway; and even played a vital role in the formative, thrilling, and scary years of the airline business—because Fred's grandson Freddy was an original partner in TWA with Charles Lindbergh and Henry Ford.

Fred Harvey's "eating houses" were prototypes of the disparate dining experiences that characterize American eating: They had formal, sit-down dining rooms (in which even cowboys were expected to wear jackets), attached to large casual dining areas with long curved counters (the genesis of the classic American diner), attached to take-out coffee and sandwich stands (the original Starbucks). Yet this curious English-man turned out to be more than just a brilliantly successful manager of hotels and restaurants and a true Horatio Alger story come to life (during the time when Alger actually was writing those stories). He created the first national chain of restaurants, of hotels, of newsstands, and of bookstores—in fact, the first national chain of *anything*—in America.

But unlike the chains of today, the Fred Harvey system was known for dramatically *raising* standards wherever it arrived, rather than eroding them. It turns out that being a fast-food nation was originally a good thing.

At its peak, Fred Harvey had over sixty-five restaurants and lunch counters, sixty dining cars, a dozen large hotels, all the restaurants and retail shops in five of the nation's largest railroad stations, and so many newsstands and bookshops that its prepublication orders regularly affected national best-seller lists. For many years, before highways and telephones and broadcast media connected the nation, there was only one thing that linked major cities as disparate as Chicago, Dallas, Cleveland, Kansas City, Los Angeles, St. Louis, and San Francisco, as well as small towns as far-flung as Needles, California; Joplin, Missouri; Raton, New Mexico; Purcell, Oklahoma; Rosenberg, Texas; and Chanute, Kansas. In each locale, the place to have dinner on a special occasion or simply a miraculous cup of coffee anytime was a Fred Harvey restaurant.

Fred Harvey was Ray Kroc before McDonald's, J. W. Marriott before Marriott Hotels, Howard Johnson before Hojo's, Joe Horn *and* Frank Hardart before Horn & Hardart's, Howard Schultz before Starbucks. And from the moment in 1878 when he lured the top chef at Chicago's vaunted Palmer House to run his first high-end restaurant and hotel—in a refurbished fleabag in Florence, Kansas, a town so small that the population often doubled when the Santa Fe train pulled into the station—Fred Harvey's managers and chefs became some of the first hospitality heroes of America. When the son of Kaiser Wilhelm stayed at La Fonda, the legendary Fred Harvey hotel in Santa Fe, he was thrilled to discover in the kitchen Chef Konrad Allgaier, who had cooked for his family in Germany.

Fred Harvey was also Walt Disney before Disneyland. He and his partners at the Santa Fe played a huge role in the development of American tourism as we know it. Fred Harvey was largely responsible for the creation of the Grand Canyon as the country's premier natural tourist attraction, as well as the development of the mythic Southwest and what grew into the National Park System.

Fred Harvey was also the most important driving force in the early appreciation and preservation—and, to some, exploitation—of Native American arts and culture. Most of the Indian art and crafts now on display in the world's major museums were originally owned by Fred Harvey. And much of the silver and turquoise jewelry that we think of as indigenous was commissioned, and in some cases even designed, by the Fred Harvey company to sell in its myriad gift shops. Fred Harvey was also the first company to embrace Native American and Spanish-American imagery in architecture and design, inventing what is now known as "Santa Fe style." Many of the best-known paintings and photos, and much of the best writing about the Southwest and the West, were originally commissioned or enabled by Fred Harvey.

The restaurants and hotels run by this transplanted Londoner and his son did more than just revolutionize American dining and service. They became a driving force in helping the United States shed its envy of European society and begin to appreciate and even romanticize its own culture.

"More than any single organization, the Fred Harvey System introduced America to Americans," wrote a historian in the 1950s.

And it's just as true today. Because, whether we know it or not, we still live in Fred Harvey's America.

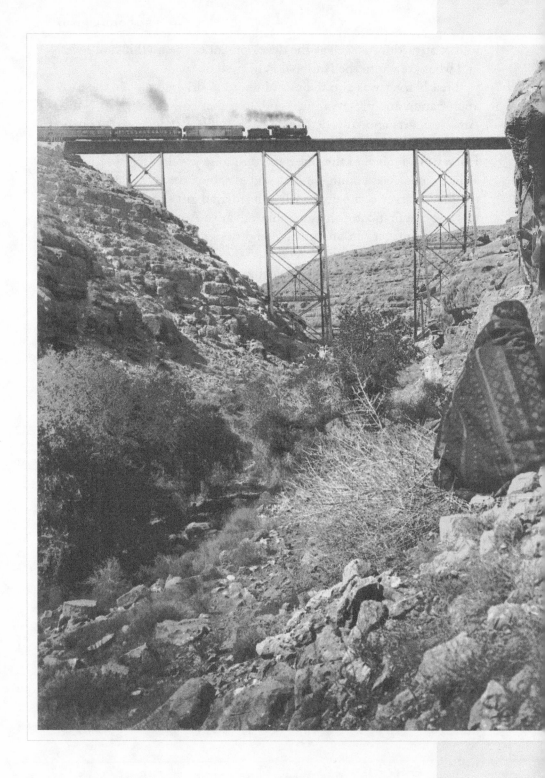

PART ONE

—

FRED
DISCOVERS
AMERICA

(AND VICE VERSA)

1853–1901

ATLANTIC & PACIFIC TRAIN, CROSSING THE CANYON DIABLO BRIDGE IN NORTHERN ARIZONA BETWEEN WILLIAMS AND WINSLOW, NOT LONG AFTER FRED HARVEY TOOK OVER ALL THE EATING HOUSES ON THIS SANTA FE SUBSIDIARY IN 1887, EXTENDING HIS CHAIN TO CALIFORNIA; INSET, FRED HARVEY, 1863 PORTRAIT

CHAPTER 1

POT WALLOPER

⊒⊑

WHEN PEOPLE WONDERED WHERE ALL HIS PASSIONATE AM-
bition came from, Fred Harvey never mentioned his father's failure.

But he never forgot being eight years old, in the muggy midsummer
of 1843, when the legal notice appeared in the *Times* of London. His father, Charles, a struggling thirty-two-year-old Soho tailor, was being
called before the Bankruptcy Court on Basinghall Street—a grand
Victorian building where the undoing of businessmen's lives had become public entertainment for those who couldn't afford tickets to the
theater or the serialized novels of young Charles Dickens.

On July 12 at 11:00 a.m., Charles Harvey appeared before Mr. Com-
missioner Evans, the senior judge. He was preceded by Samuel Polack,
a Newport woolen draper, and waiting to see the judge after him was
Abraham Harris, a slop seller in Tower Hill. Luckily, Fred's father was
merely declared "insolvent," so his creditors could pick over only what
he had earned and bought in his thirty-two years. If he had been declared "bankrupt," all his future earnings would have been garnisheed
as well.

While the difference meant a great deal to his father, the shame was
the same for Fred Harvey, his mother, Ann, and his two younger sisters, Eliza and Annie. The Harveys were officially paupers. They had
never been rich, living in rented flats first on Great Marylebone Street
in London's West End—an enclave of merchants and craftsmen near
All Souls Church, where Fred was baptized—and then in a similarly
hardscrabble section of Soho, at 16 Lisle Street. But they had always
gotten by. Now they had to start over financially, and the strain on his
parents' marriage was apparently too great. According to family lore,
his mother periodically ran off "with a coachman," and by the time

Fred was a teenager, he appears to have been living with his widowed Aunt Mary on Tottenham High Street. Mary Harvey had her own business and did well enough to have a servant to help with her three children.

Fred would later tell family, friends, and journalists that he left his homeland for America in 1850 at the age of fifteen. It was a good story with a nice round year, but the March 1851 London census shows him still living with his Aunt Mary. It appears he actually sailed to New York when he was seventeen, in the late spring of 1853. He told a colleague he left to avoid being drafted, as Great Britain was already fighting in Burma and was about to join the Crimean War. But, like many Londoners who came to New York that year, he was also seeking opportunity.

New York was holding the first world's fair on U.S. soil, the Exhibition of the Industry of All Nations. It was an Americanized version of the first world's fair *anywhere*, London's Crystal Palace Exhibition, which had drawn over six million visitors to the 990,000-square-foot exhibition hall in Hyde Park in 1851. New York decided to build its own Crystal Palace on 42nd Street between Fifth and Sixth avenues, in what is now Bryant Park, and was expecting a similar rush of tourists. On Fred's voyage, many of the first-class passengers were coming to see New York's Crystal Palace. Fred and his mates down in steerage simply hoped the world's fair would improve their chances of finding good jobs.

With only two pounds in his pocket, Fred began looking for work the moment he disembarked. Steamships from Europe moored at the Hudson River piers on the lower west side of Manhattan, as did the ferries from New Jersey. And just across from the pier was the Washington Street Market, the largest meat and produce market in America, offering provisions from farms hundreds of miles away, as well as those still operating in Manhattan, on the verdant land that would become Central Park.

The Washington Street Market reeked of *everything,* from freshly butchered animals and just-plucked vegetables to the overripe aromas of garbage—especially the heaps of shells from New York's favorite fast food, oysters. A two-story, block-long horn of plenty, with rows of dangling carcasses reaching all the way to the high ceilings, it served as the fresh-food mecca for New York's housewives, private cooks, and professional chefs alike.

And for those who worked in the food business, there was only one place to eat in the market: Smith & McNell's restaurant at Fulton and Washington, whose owners used the market as their larder and refrigerator. Originally a "coffee and cake" shop, Smith & McNell's had recently expanded into one of the most reasonably priced full-service restaurants in New York, open twenty-four hours and offering the best of the day's harvest, catch, and slaughter, prepared without adornment. Meals ended with every man's digestive pleasure—the best cigar he could afford.

Fred Harvey likely ate his first American meal at Smith & McNell's, as did so many others who entered New York at the Hudson River piers. And soon he was working there, starting at the bottom as a "pot walloper"—a dishwasher. He learned the restaurant business from Henry Smith and Tom McNell, who had strong ideas about fresh ingredients, handshake relationships, and the redemptive power of cash. Smith and McNell were legendary in the market for their quirky business practices. They refused to keep written records of any sort, and they did not believe in credit. At the end of each day, they settled their accounts and divided their profits.

There was a lot to learn at Smith & McNell's because it was really two restaurants: On the bustling main floor, you could get a hearty, filling meal for fifteen cents ($4.31)* while upstairs was a fancier dining room for wealthier patrons expecting prime cuts and a more refined gustatory experience. Some customers never aspired to eat upstairs: Long after he became a celebrated scientist, Thomas Edison would bring business associates to Smith & McNell's main floor for the deeply comforting apple dumplings and strong, fresh-brewed coffee, which had once been all he could afford.

Young Fred Harvey had chosen an ideal time and location for his culinary education. The American restaurant business was not even a quarter century old; it had been born just fifteen blocks across town from Smith & McNell's, on the other side of the financial district. There, in 1830, the legendary Delmonico's morphed from just another coffee and pastry shop into the first full-service restaurant in the United States. New York, like other major American cities, had always

---

* All dollar amounts in this book are followed in parentheses by their approximate value today. These figures are based on consumer price index comparisons using the handy "MeasuringWorth calculator" developed by economists from the University of Illinois at Chicago and Miami University.

had hotels that fed their guests from a set menu, as well as oyster bars, coffeehouses, and carts for quick, modest fare. But the idea of eating in a full-service restaurant—where patrons could order what they wanted from a broad and varied menu, à la carte—was still novel.

Restaurants had existed in France for some time, but in British culture, which still heavily influenced life in America, dining in a public place was considered uncivilized, gauche. The success of Delmonico's in the 1830s heralded a new chapter in American dining. With its authentic French cuisine and choice American beef—all served with its signature potatoes, grated into long strands and then oven baked with butter, Parmesan, and a touch of nutmeg—Delmonico's became the country's gold standard for dining out.

Fred spent eighteen months in New York, working his way up at Smith & McNell's from pot walloper to busboy, waiter, and line cook, while soaking up the trends of the country's most delectable city. During that time, he learned that his mother, Ann, had contracted tuberculosis. Since he couldn't afford to go back to visit her in England, he decided to have a portrait made so she could at least see he was doing well. He went to the Spread Eagle Daguerreian Gallery on Chatham Square, where photography innovator R. A. Lewis captured the earliest known image of him. In the daguerreotype, Fred's hair is dark, longish, and wavy; he sports the first of many styles of facial hair to come, this one a beard that extends sideburn to sideburn under his chin without ever encroaching on his slightly chubby face. He has a warm, reassuring smile, and his eyes are wide, as if mesmerized by all he is seeing around him in New York.

FRED'S MOTHER HELD on for six months in a sanitarium in Wolverhampton, before dying in August 1855 at the age of forty-eight. Not long after her death, he sailed for New Orleans, the culinary capital of the South. As soon as he arrived, he knew it wasn't for him. He was "concerned about trying to make a living, which was difficult in New Orleans, and he was appalled by the slavery that surrounded him on all sides," his great-grandson recalled being told. "He also became convinced there would be a war between the states, and he wasn't at all interested in serving in a 'Southern army'—especially after avoiding service in his own country."

Soon after, he headed up the Mississippi to St. Louis—where they were still at least debating the issue of slavery—and got a job in the bustling, smoky business district adjacent to the piers on the river's western bank. He worked at the Butterfield House, where the hotel's owner, Abner Hitchcock, became his friend and mentor—and later his sponsor when he applied to become a U.S. citizen. On July 27, 1858, Hitchcock served as a witness when twenty-three-year-old Fred Harvey took the oath renouncing his allegiance to Queen Victoria and declaring his loyalty to the United States and its Constitution.

Fred soon struck out on his own, taking over the Merchants Dining Saloon and Restaurant at 10 Chestnut Street. It was a plain three-story building just a half block from the docks, not far from the original Anheuser brewery—Busch hadn't yet married into the first family of American beer—and the house where young Samuel Clemens stayed with his brother when he came off the river. (Today, the location is almost directly under the famed St. Louis Gateway Arch.) He had a partner in the business, William Doyle, a thirty-eight-year-old Irish immigrant, who ran the saloon while Fred concentrated on the dining room. The Merchants Dining Saloon, reportedly quite popular, was on the first floor, and Fred lived upstairs in one of the twenty-four rooms that were rented out to travelers, transients, and his own staff. Doyle, his wife, and their four children lived next door.

At that time, St. Louis was the North of the South, the South of the North, the West of the East, and the East of the West, in every way a microcosm of where the country had been and where it was going. And Fred's restaurant was right in the center of it all. Next door was the city's main telegraph office, where every piece of news first arrived. Across the street was the local headquarters of the Republican Party, which opposed slavery. Right around the corner were several slave traders, with a large sign out front that read, "Negroes Bought Here."

Within a year, Fred had done well enough to let his partner, Doyle, and cook Dickson Brown run the restaurant while he visited England. He sailed from New York on the steamship *Africa* in October 1859, and when he returned several weeks later, he brought his father and his younger sister Eliza with him.

Fred also came back with a wife—a blond Dutch woman in her mid-twenties named Ann, about whom little is known. The whole family lived in the rooms above the restaurant. Fred's father visited for just a few weeks, but Eliza decided to stay, after meeting another recent British immigrant, bookkeeper Henry Bradley, whom she soon married.

Fred and Ann found out they were going to be parents in the summer of 1860. While business was still strong, Abraham Lincoln had just been nominated by the Republican Party, and tensions between North and South were rising before Fred's eyes. St. Louis, a key border city, was as far south as Lincoln's supporters ever campaigned.

By the time Ann gave birth in late February 1861, and Fred was able to hold their son, Eddie, in his arms, America was a different place. While Lincoln was in Washington being sworn in as president, a convention was meeting a few blocks from Fred's restaurant to decide whether Missouri would secede from the United States. It was a crucial decision, because control of St. Louis and its arsenal could mean control of the Mississippi River. When the convention voted *not* to leave the Union, Missouri's defiant secessionist governor set up his own Confederate military camp in the north of the city.

Fred's prosperous business lasted only a few more weeks. It effectively ended, like so much of normal life in St. Louis, on May 10, the day of the infamous St. Louis Massacre. After Union troops bloodlessly captured the governor's camp, hundreds of civilians gathered to watch the men of the vanquished pro-secession militia being led through town. When a skirmish broke out between Union soldiers and taunting onlookers, the troops panicked, firing into the crowd in front of Fire Co. #5 and killing twenty-eight civilians, including women and children. There was a brief truce after the incident, but it fell apart just weeks later; Union leaders took control, and Governor Jackson fled, calling for fifty thousand men to defend the city against Lincoln's troops.

By then, Fred Harvey had come to see himself, first and foremost, as a businessman—politics, like religion, was important but too divisive, bad for business. When asked for his political views, he was known to chuckle and say, "I'm for whoever wins." But he could not remain neutral on the subject of slavery, which he felt was wrong. He got into a violent argument with his partner, who was a Confederate sympathizer, and, not long after, discovered that Doyle had run off to join the secessionist army. He took with him every penny the two men had saved, over $1,300 ($32,774).

In reality, the Merchants Dining Saloon and Restaurant was probably doomed anyway. Martial law was declared in St. Louis, and steamboat traffic from the South on the Mississippi was severely restricted. No business that relied on river travelers could survive.

By the summer of 1861, Fred Harvey found himself a penniless twenty-six-year-old with a wife and baby to support. Not only had he become his father, but he had lost everything at a younger age. And in St. Louis, the city that had embraced him for five years and where he became an American, he suddenly felt like the ultimate outsider—a Yankee and a foreigner.

CHAPTER 2

THE LAST TRAIN STOP IN AMERICA

BEFORE FRED LOST HIS RESTAURANT, ONE OF HIS FAVORITE regular customers was Captain Rufus Ford, a veteran boatman who lived upriver in Quincy, Illinois, but often stopped in during his regular runs between St. Louis and St. Paul. Ford had become successful in the 1850s skippering "packet boats"—regularly scheduled steamships carrying people, goods, and mail—on the upper Mississippi. During his years as captain of the lavish one-hundred-berth ship the *Die Vernon,* he held the record for the fastest trip between St. Louis and St. Paul making all stops: only eighty-four hours.

Now in his late forties, Captain Ford had been telling Fred about the company he had recently started—a packet boat business farther west, on the other side of the state. There was a new railroad across the northern part of Missouri, connecting the eastern border at Hannibal to the small, bustling western river town of St. Joseph. The owners of the new Hannibal & St. Joseph Railroad had hired Ford to set up a packet boat service along the untamed Missouri River—allowing people and goods to cross, continuing on to Omaha and points farther west.

At the time, nobody could have imagined what a valuable route it would soon become. But then came the prospect of war, which brought railroad construction around the country to a screeching halt, leaving the East fairly well served from the Atlantic Ocean to just beyond the Mississippi, but nothing else in North America except a handful of small, isolated railroads in California, Oregon, and Texas. Suddenly the H&SJ—nicknamed the "Horrible & Slow-Jolting" for its rickety tracks and frequent derailments—mattered far beyond Missouri. And little "St. Joe," as locals called the town, was now the end of the line: the last train stop in America, the westernmost point on the entire eastern railroad system.

So the town quickly became famous nationwide for a burgeoning new industry: the mail.

The U.S. government made St. Joe the hub for the entire nation's transcontinental mail—which, after being sorted there, headed farther west on stagecoaches or packet boats. The city was also the end point for the Western Union wires from the East, which is why, in April 1860, it became home to the fabled Pony Express. St. Joe was the starting gate for the mad tag-team gallop to the West Coast by riders who responded to ads calling for "young, skinny, wiry fellows not over 18; must be expert riders willing to risk death daily; orphans preferred."

When the Civil War started, the H&SJ was so important that Ulysses S. Grant's first assignment for the Union army was to guard it. But in September 1861, it was attacked; the Platte River Bridge that the H&SJ crossed just before reaching St. Joseph was sabotaged, and an entire train, with over one hundred passengers aboard, flipped over and fell thirty feet into the water, killing seventeen and injuring dozens of others.

In such a challenging business environment, Captain Ford needed all the help he could get to keep his packet boats running on time. And he knew his friend Fred needed a job. So they made a deal, and the young Harvey family moved to the tiny postal boomtown of St. Joseph: population 8,932, one-eighteenth the size of St. Louis.

Fred quickly learned about life on the silty, temperamental Missouri River, "the Big Muddy," which was prone to freezing every winter, indiscriminately flooding or drying out every summer, and generally presenting endless challenges to Captain Ford's packet boats. There were passengers to feed and entertain—many of the boats had impressive restaurants and saloons—as well as cargo to care for and schedules to meet. It was a demanding and intriguing business, which showed Fred a world—worlds, actually—he had never seen living in two of America's largest cities. The Missouri River was the border between the fast, new, hulking trains, billowing with smoke and soot, and the squeaky stagecoaches and horse-drawn carriages—and the Missouri packet boats shuttled back and forth between the future and the past. Messages came into the Western Union station in St. Joseph using the fastest technology known to man, and left in the satchel of a Pony Express rider on horseback.

Life along the Missouri was full of such fascinating, dizzying extremes. There were also plenty of risks, including disease, and soon Fred became gravely ill, diagnosed with typhoid fever. There were no effective treatments available, and he came close to death. His recovery was slow, and he was lucky to be working for a friend, Ford, who was so patient. Yet while he survived the worst of the typhoid, it wreaked permanent havoc on his body, especially his gastrointestinal system. In a photo taken of him after his recovery, he appeared to be a different man—alarmingly gaunt, even a bit haunted, with chin whiskers dangling beneath his flat-lined, expressionless mouth. His wavy hair was combed forward on the sides and swept up in the front, in an attempt to obscure his receding hairline and widow's peak. He looked as if he had been riding packet boats on the River Styx.

By the time Fred finally returned to work, life in the fast-paced world of St. Joe had changed dramatically. The Pony Express had shuttered its stables after only eighteen months in business. Its demise was blamed on Western Union's historic new telegraph line from St. Joseph all the way to Sacramento; it was completed on October 24, 1861, enabling telegrams to be sent instantaneously from sea to shining sea. But in fact the Pony Express had been doomed for some time. It wasn't a business so much as a publicity stunt, meant to help its financially strapped parent company—the Central Overland California and Pikes Peak Express—snare from another firm the $1 million ($25.2 million) government contract to handle *all* the stagecoach mail delivery to the West. While the Pony Express lost money, as expected, the service attracted huge national press attention, and papers regularly published news stories "from California by the Pony Express." But after the government decided not to fire its current carrier, the Butterfield Overland Mail Company, the challengers were grateful for any excuse to put the Pony Express out to pasture.

Regardless of the new telegraph capabilities, letters were still the main form of communication, so the operation of the St. Joseph post office remained vital to war-torn America. As Fred's strength returned, he went back to work for Captain Ford and even took on a second job—because Ann was pregnant again and they would need extra money. He was hired as a government postal clerk in February 1862, and soon found himself involved in an experiment that proved much more important than the Pony Express: the nation's first traveling post office.

Since the United States began postal service in 1776, mail was allowed to be sorted only when it reached a local post office. But Fred's boss, assistant postmaster William Davis, convinced his government bosses to let him test a specially equipped train car on which mail could be sorted en route. Fred was assigned to the project, and the new mail cars were first tested in late July 1862 along the Hannibal & St. Joseph.

The railroad had grown even more "Horrible & Slow-Jolting" as the war limited supplies and materials for proper repairs. There were no more of those breakneck runs from the early days of the Pony Express, which one roadmaster fondly recalled because "it simply rained hogs. The engine would hit them, knock them in the air and pass them before they struck the ground." But the H&SJ could still be a pretty wild ride. Fred and his fellow mobile mail clerk, John Patten, were glad their boss had thought to have iron rods attached to the ceiling of the car so they could hang on.

Once the kinks were worked out, though, the postal-sorting car was a huge success, dramatically reducing the time it took to get mail to California. It became the prototype for how the mail continues to be delivered to this day, the model for the national Railway Mail Service.

With his postal service job and his ongoing work with the packet line, Fred was developing a sense of safety and security again. Even though the Civil War was raging, there had been no violence in St. Joe since the tragic Platte River Bridge sabotage, and the conflict's main effect on life in St. Joseph was to provide steady business.

He and Ann could feel cautiously optimistic about bringing another child into the world. Charles Harvey, named for Fred's father, was born on October 6, 1862. Like his older brother, he had blue eyes and tufts of curly blond hair. He was apparently a healthy baby, but there were complications with the delivery, and Ann became gravely ill.

At that time, almost one percent of all births in America resulted in the death of the mother, mostly from puerperal fever or unstoppable bleeding. In the fall of 1862, Ann Harvey became part of those tragic statistics. She was only twenty-seven years old.

WITH AN INFANT and a twenty-month-old to care for, Fred had little time to mourn. He had learned some things over the years as a businessman—important jobs, he knew, should not remain unfilled.

So, despite his grief, after being widowed for only four months, he married again.

His new wife was Barbara Sarah "Sally" Mattas, the eldest child of a large working-class family recently emigrated from the town of Pilsen in Czechoslovakia, first to Montreal and then to St. Louis. Just nineteen years old—eight years Fred's junior—Sally Mattas was a lively, diminutive woman with big, pinchable cheeks, kind gray eyes, and a sturdy build. She had been working in St. Louis as a seamstress, spending much of her time helping her mother take care of a brood of five young children.

Little is known about how Fred met Sally, because he purposely fictionalized their past for the sake of his children. He even went so far as to write a fake wedding date in the Harvey family Bible to make it appear that Sally had been Eddie and Charley's mother. In fact, the couple actually married on February 20, 1863, at the St. Joseph courthouse. According to their marriage record—only recently discovered, in a weathered, handwritten St. Joseph city ledger—ex officio Justice of the Peace M. L. Harrington officiated at the ceremony.

Fred first got to know Sally in St. Louis, where she may have been a waitress in his restaurant. But how they came to be married in St. Joseph is unclear. Perhaps he had been fond of her in St. Louis and returned for her after being widowed; or she may originally have been hired to help Fred with his children and saw her role in his life mushroom over those challenging months. Either way, there was some economic aspect to their union, because Sally's family was in desperate straits. Her father, Martin, a day laborer, had volunteered at the age of forty-one to fight for the Union with the Second Regiment of the Missouri Infantry. He served for a year and was discharged with a battle-related disability and pneumonia—and he was on his deathbed when Sally married Fred.

It was hardly an ideal way for a young couple to start their life together: more like a desperate business deal than a love connection. Still, it was a *good* deal. And within the confines of those staid Victorian times, Fred and Sally developed a certain affection for each other. Somehow, they made it work.

In the great tradition of celebrated Americans who started out in the mail room, Fred was able to parlay his time aboard the H&SJ postal-sorting car into a position with the railroad itself: as a sales agent for passenger tickets. It was a job better suited to his talents, and to the contacts he had already made working with Captain Ford's packet boat business. Even with the war raging in the East, the H&SJ was doing a small but steady business carrying passengers on trains that, for the most part, existed to transport the mail and other freight.

Fred sold passenger tickets for the H&SJ from St. Joseph for over a year, developing a reputation that caused railroad executives to take notice. In early 1865, he was offered a better job as a sales agent for the North Missouri Rail Road, a sister line of the H&SJ. But the North Missouri insisted he relocate. In anticipation of the war ending, everyone realized that St. Joseph, Missouri, wasn't going to be the last stop on the railroad too much longer. The North Missouri wanted Fred to work from Leavenworth, the first city on the Kansas side of the river, and the one most likely to be the first connected to the East when the war was over and railroad construction began again.

Leavenworth was only fifty miles downriver from St. Joseph. But in many ways it seemed like another country.

CHAPTER 3

A GENTLEMAN AMONG
THE BLEEDING KANSANS

⌐⌐

EVEN THOUGH LEAVENWORTH, KANSAS, SITS AT WHAT IS AL-
most the exact center of the United States, in 1865 it was still considered the last major outpost of civilization. Although Texas, Nevada,
California, and Oregon had already achieved statehood, since the 1830s
the contiguous United States had pretty much ended at Fort Leavenworth and the western bank of the Missouri River. The fort served as
the quartermaster station for all American military posts in the West.
And while the fort was a city unto itself, a separate civilian city with
a population of twenty thousand had grown up just south of its main
gates. A company town for the businesses of defending, exploring,
and exploiting the West, it was essentially the capital of the American frontier.

Leavenworth was rough, bustling, and bristling. One of Fred's best
friends described moving there from an eastern city as the greatest feeling of freedom he had ever known. "Herds of buffalo still roamed the
plains," he recalled. "Indians huddled on the street corners. Army officers rode back and forth to the jangling of swords and buckles."

In its utter diversity—ethnic, economic, sociological—Leavenworth
was a frontier metropolis that saw itself becoming, if not a New York
City for the Wild West, then at least the next St. Louis. It had a large
black population, which had already established three churches; in
fact, Fort Leavenworth would be home to one of the nation's first two
black cavalry units, the "Buffalo Soldiers." There was a growing Jewish community that founded the first synagogue in Kansas, and a large
German population, many of whom worked in local breweries. And
the Indian tribes living nearby, most notably the Pottawatomie, were in

town regularly. With thousands of troops moving in and out of the fort, Leavenworth was constantly playing host to high-spending soldiers. It boasted some two hundred saloons and brothels, and attracted its share of criminals and ne'er-do-wells, tossed out by the army or tossed off boats where the pier met downtown.

Leavenworth's wide dirt streets had gas-lit, wood-planked sidewalks teeming with new businesses, two- and three-story brick buildings with long awnings and large block-letter signs. Looming over Delaware Street was a massive cast-iron eagle, perched on the roof of the Hershfield & Mitchell watch and jewelry shop. From the eagle's beak dangled a huge clock in the shape of a pocket watch.

The historic center of town was the Planters' House, a four-story redbrick building that served as the city's finest hotel and restaurant. Planters' was originally envisioned as a riverside luxury spot for the city's pro-slavery politicians and businessmen. But when Kansas declared itself a free state before the Civil War, the hotel's owners realized it would be bad for business to remain so partisan.

Many new cities in the West were settled almost entirely by politically or religiously like-minded people. Leavenworth was different—its only common bond was frontier business, a shared desire to make money from a fort that took orders from whoever ran the government in Washington. So the hotel maintained separate bars and bartenders in the basement for those on either side of the slavery debate, just far enough apart that patrons couldn't spit on one another.

The Planters' House became an epicenter of the political divisiveness and border-war violence that earned the state its nickname: "Bleeding Kansas." And its signature customer was Leavenworth's over-the-top mayor, Daniel Read Anthony, who was willing to go to any length to win an argument, especially about slavery. Several years back, when he owned one of the local newspapers, Anthony had shot and killed a rival editor who criticized his antislavery politics and derided his honor. He successfully pleaded self-defense, earning a reputation as a "pistol-packin' pencil pusher" and ushering in a new era of extreme journalism in American frontier newspapers.

While Dan Anthony would later become better known as the brother of his suffragette sibling Susan B. Anthony, he was, in 1865, arguably the most powerful man in Leavenworth. When he took his regular table at the Planters' House, he always had twin six-shooters in his holster—in case anyone wanted to talk politics.

Like many city hotels, Planters' also served as a place of business for traveling salesmen. It was even commonplace for physicians to take out advertisements in the local papers announcing they were temporarily setting up shop there: "Dr. J. J. McBride, the great King of Pain, is in the city at the Planters' House, room No. 11. Can tell any person their disease without asking questions." These out-of-towners competed with local healers like Drs. Birge & Morey, whose ads promised cures "in all chronic diseases, such as Sore Eyes, Deafness, Cancers, Dyspepsia, Lungs, Female Complaints, etc., etc."

Fred decided his ticket counter should be in the Planters' House—the previous agent had sold train tickets from a bookshop—so he rented office No. 3 on its well-trafficked lower level. And in early February 1865, he loaded his family onto a packet boat to Leavenworth, where he moved them into a modest rented house on Pottawatomie Street, just a block from the river and down the street from his new office.

Sally spent her days at home caring for their two small boys, four-year-old Eddie and two-year-old Charley, both of whom had wavy blond hair, deep blue eyes, and wary grins. If anyone noticed the obvious differences in coloring and facial features between a dark-haired eastern European mother still learning English and her Nordic-looking children, they had the good manners not to say anything.

Fred set out to make an immediate impression in the business community, as the *Leavenworth Conservative* hailed his arrival: "The men of Leavenworth will be glad to hear of this most excellent appointment. Mr. H is a man of extensive railroad and steamboat experience . . . He is well and widely known as a thorough, competent and efficient business man, and a most agreeable gentleman. All who entrust business to his hands will receive perfect satisfaction."

The Harveys arrived in town just as the Civil War appeared to be finally wearing down. The slaves had been freed, Lincoln had been reelected, tentative peace talks had begun. And Fred and Sally, like America itself, felt a sense of renewal and hope.

Unfortunately, that feeling lasted only a few weeks. A scarlet fever epidemic swept the nation at the end of February, and Eddie and Charley both fell ill, their tongues turning the white strawberry color that every parent feared. Soon their tongues went red, their skin became rashy and changed texture—first sandpapery, then so flaky that Sally could peel off layers of their palms. Today, the boys would be cured with a dose of antibiotics, but in 1865 they didn't stand a chance.

Charley died at 2:00 a.m. on Thursday, March 2. Although he was quickly buried at Greenwood Cemetery, Fred and Sally waited before scheduling a public funeral service; they were too busy trying to keep Eddie alive. At the end of March, they finally put a death notice in the *Leavenworth Times* inviting their new "friends and acquaintances" to the house for a service for Charley—which was conducted while Eddie lay in his room, barely clinging to life. He died nine days later, at 9:00 on a Sunday morning.

As the Harveys struggled with the emotions of burying their second child in two weeks, the nation's psyche was being whiplashed from hope to despair. On the day Eddie died, Confederate general Robert E. Lee surrendered to Union commander Ulysses S. Grant at Appomattox—the official beginning of the end of the Civil War. But then, five days later, on Good Friday, Abraham Lincoln was shot in the head during the final act of a farcical British play about boorish Americans. He died the next morning, becoming one of the last and most resonant casualties among the 620,000 killed in America's war against itself.

SEVEN MONTHS AFTER Fred and Sally buried their boys, a peculiar item appeared in the city news section of the *Leavenworth Daily Times.* It could easily have been missed, surrounded by larger stories about a government sale of nine thousand horses at Fort Leavenworth, a local production of the popular abolitionist drama *The Octoroon,* several crimes involving stolen coats, and the 1865 equivalent of a weather and traffic report for an unpaved world: "The mud on the streets yesterday was horrible. It is seldom worse."

The item said that Fred Harvey had returned to town from St. Louis, and noted offhandedly, "He looks happy." It didn't say why.

While it may have seemed odd for the newspaper to comment on his mood, it wasn't surprising. There was something about Leavenworth's new railroad agent that lured people into his drama. With a brow that looked furrowed even when he smiled, and a certain earned intensity in his deep-set blue eyes, he appeared to have already survived a lifetime of heartache. And he was only thirty.

Local newspapermen had gotten to know Fred because they relied on him: As agent for the major railroad in Missouri, he was the first to get the incoming papers from the East, which he hand delivered to editors each morning as a courtesy. They had noticed his change of disposition and assumed he was just feeling refreshed after an extended vacation—"three weeks rustication" in St. Louis. But it turned out he was elated for a different reason.

Sally had just entered her second trimester of pregnancy. She was beginning to show.

With a baby coming, Fred sought a second job. He had become especially chummy with the staff at the *Leavenworth Conservative*, who saw that he was not only a smart businessman but an avid newspaper reader. He was offered a position selling ads and subscriptions as the paper's General Business Agent. He started just before Christmas 1865.

And three months later, Sally had a son. They named him Ford Ferguson Harvey, to honor Fred's enduring friendship with Captain Rufus Ford. Around the house, they called him "Fordie."

Fordie made his debut later that year at the Leavenworth County Fair—at the baby show, or what the newspaper referred to as a "large display of matrimonial fruits." He was one of "twelve specimens of incipient man and womanhood" chosen to be displayed among the prize livestock and vegetables. According to reports, the babies attracted "an immense crowd and elicited numerous remarks, complimentary and otherwise."

The baby show was just one of many ways Fred and Sally were becoming more active in the life of Leavenworth. Fred joined a Masonic lodge, and the couple started to be seen more and more often at the city's cultural events. They became regulars at Chaplin's Opera House, where melodramas like *Camille* alternated with Saturday matinees of *Uncle Tom's Cabin.*

The Harveys climbed quickly in Leavenworth's twin social scenes. The town itself had a whirlwind of civilian entertainments, parties, and celebratory dinners, at which they became friendly with Dan Anthony—whose sister Susan B. was often in town visiting—and Colonel James Abernathy, who owned a large furniture factory. There was also a large and well-developed military society within the walls of the fort, with an active calendar of events for officers and their families. The Harveys were popular in that crowd as well.

In fact, Fred Harvey enjoyed inhabiting two worlds. In a town where the mayor carried six-guns, Fred appeared to be quite the English gentleman. He dined like a Londoner: a light breakfast of toast and tea, his main meal at lunch, a low tea with lemon at 4:00 p.m., followed by high tea with meat at 7:00. Many of his friends were British. Leavenworth itself had quite a few expatriate civilians and visiting military men, and there were large enclaves of Brits in St. Louis and other cities he was starting to frequent for business. Yet while he identified with certain British ideals of honor and decorum, Fred was becoming the very model of a modern American striver, known for his ambition and determination.

The Harveys enjoyed having people over to their home in the evenings to play cards, listen to music, or read aloud—Shakespeare was a favorite—into the wee hours. But everyone knew that at precisely eleven o'clock, Fred would stand up, snap his waistcoat taut, and announce he was going to bed. His guests were encouraged to stay and play as long as they liked—and often did. Sally was happy to keep the party going; after growing up in relative poverty, she couldn't get enough of being a lady who entertained.

BECAUSE THEY HAD grown so fond of Leavenworth, Fred was particularly sad to realize that they might have to move, because the city was probably doomed. Civic leaders were claiming it wasn't true, that there was still hope. But even though he was just a ticket seller, Fred had absorbed enough about the higher echelons of the railroad business to know that the cause had already been lost. The city wouldn't die—it would always be a fine place to live. But its grand scheme to become the next great transportation hub, the next St. Louis, was going to fail.

The railroads had, literally, decided to go another way.

As the first city established in Kansas, and the home of the most important military base in the West, Leavenworth had naturally expected to be the first city with train service. That was part of the reason Fred moved there. But there were a lot of factors involved in when and how a city got connected to the railroad.

It was especially important to be on the "High Iron," industry slang for a railroad's main trunk line. A city's future depended on whether it was on the High Iron or merely served by a smaller branch line.

Fred understood how cities got trains. Adventure capitalists created companies that asked the government for long, skinny stretches of land so they could lay tracks along them. At the same time they went to the cities or counties along the route to persuade them to float bonds to pay for the construction—and for engines, cars, and stations. Since railroads never shared tracks or depots, cities were involved with multiple deals at the same time, each one a complex negotiation and a race against time and money. A lot of the deals fell apart.

In Leavenworth's case, they had *all* fallen apart, and the town's leaders—many of whom were now Fred's friends—watched in dismay as much smaller Kansas towns, like Lawrence and Topeka, got train service first.

Leavenworth had once come close to snagging the biggest railroad deal in the country, spending over $4 million ($88 million) lobbying in Washington to ensure the High Iron of the nation's first transcontinental railroad came right through the city and the fort. It was during the nationwide competition for the right to build a railroad from the Missouri River all the way to the Pacific, which pitted three different companies, and three different routes, against one another. But in 1862 the Lincoln administration chose the route championed by the Union Pacific—which ran two hundred miles to the north of Leavenworth, through Omaha. The route was a straighter shot from Chicago and more likely to remain sheltered from Civil War battles.

The city's next best hope was that the first railroad bridge over the Missouri River, connecting Kansas to the eastern train system, would be built there, making Leavenworth the major regional hub. In fact, the decision about that bridge was actually being made by Fred's boss.

The railroad he worked for, the Northern Missouri, was part of "the Joy System"—a loose conglomeration of regional railroads controlled by Detroit lawyer James F. Joy. While less well-known than the tycoons who were buying up railroads and railroad stock in the East— Jay Cooke, Jay Gould, Andrew Carnegie, Cornelius Vanderbilt, J. P. Morgan—Joy was the most powerful railroad magnate on the western frontier, starting out with the Michigan Central and eventually controlling major lines in Illinois, Iowa, and Missouri.

Unfortunately, Joy wanted to build his bridge and his hub thirty miles downriver from Leavenworth, in a sparsely populated area called "City of Kansas" on the Missouri side and Wyandotte on the Kansas side. Joy wanted this not because it made more sense but because it made more sense *for him*. He owned land in Kansas that would benefit if the bridge was built in this largely undeveloped area—which would come to be known as Kansas City.

Leavenworth had a strong advocate in Kansas's powerful U.S. senator James H. Lane. Indeed, Lane had a vested interest in seeing the railroad bridge built there because he was also president of the proposed Leavenworth, Lawrence & Fort Gibson Railroad. But just before the bridge bill was to be debated in Washington, Lane took a controversial stand during the argument over "reconstruction" of the South; he crossed party lines and became the only Republican to support the plan of Lincoln's successor, Andrew Johnson, a plan that was considered too conciliatory to the South and weak on civil rights. Lane's Senate colleagues, the so-called Radical Republicans, turned on Johnson (and later impeached him). They also turned on Lane, who had a history of mental illness. He suffered a complete breakdown in the summer of 1866 and shot himself.

He died ten days later, but before his successor was named—in fact, before he was even buried—the funding bill for James Joy's bridge at Kansas City was hurriedly proposed on the Senate floor and passed. It would be years before his "Hannibal Bridge" was built—everything in railroad construction took an enormously long time—but the map of Kansas, and of the American Midwest, had now been redrawn. All the young railroads being built in Kansas would use Kansas City as their main eastern hub instead of Leavenworth.

Still, in November 1866, the city did get some train service at last—but just a minor branch line. The Kansas Pacific—the local division of the company chosen to build the transcontinental railroad, the Union Pacific—laid tracks between Leavenworth and Lawrence, where passengers could change trains onto the High Iron to go east to Kansas City, or west through Topeka all the way to Fort Riley and Junction City.

Leavenworth had finally joined the modern world. And Fred Harvey was no longer a railroad ticket seller in a city without trains.

CHAPTER 4

RAILROAD WARRIOR

⊐⊏

W HILE HIS FRIENDS IN LEAVENWORTH WERE CRUSHED TO
get only a branch line, Fred saw the new train solely as a business opportunity. He immediately changed the name of his business at the
Planters' House to "Central Railroad Ticket Office" and advertised
through tickets to New York, Boston, Washington, and "all points in
the United States and Canada." He also began training a young man to
replace him day to day in Leavenworth, so he could start using the
train to broaden his business horizons. He arranged with his bosses at
the Joy System to sell passenger tickets in Kansas for all their railroads,
including the Chicago, Burlington & Quincy, which was the dominant
line out of Chicago. And he informed the publisher of the *Leavenworth Conservative* that he could now solicit ads for the paper all over
the state—and anywhere else the trains could take him.

Fred Harvey turned himself into a railroad warrior. He began traveling relentlessly not only in Kansas but in Missouri, up to Chicago,
and eventually all the way east to New York. He sold the West to East-
erners and the East to Westerners, along the way making numerous
friends and business associates—which, to him, were pretty much the
same thing. Soon he hired a second young man to work with him on
the road so they could canvass cities more quickly and efficiently, making collections on newspaper ads and dropping off ticket vouchers.
Then, as business improved, he hired even more traveling employees so
he could be represented in more places. The most dependable of this
group was a young man from Leavenworth named William "Guy" Potter, who took his mentorship with Fred very seriously.

Within a year, Fred was so successful as a traveling salesman that
his clients started giving him healthy advances just to keep their part of

his well-divided attention. In 1868, his bosses at the *Leavenworth Conservative* offered him a contract paying an annual advance of $3,000 ($47,000)—about fifteen times the average per capita income in the nation.

It was a good deal, but Fred had been learning a lot about negotiating during his travels. He was bolder now, more self-assured, and he understood how American businessmen thought. He had learned, as one friend put it, "how to ask for things . . . You should have seen Fred when he was building up. He used to ask for *everything*! He asked and kept on asking—-and finally got it." But he asked in such a way that all parties involved felt they were getting more.

Even as he was shaking hands with the publishers of the *Conservative* to clinch the deal, he was—according to a handwritten account of the meeting in his datebook—already angling for something else.

"Once I've sold an ad for you," he asked, "would you mind terribly if I solicited for another paper in another town, one that doesn't compete with the *Conservative*?"

The clients thought about this for a moment. It was a request both audacious and completely logical, as long as Fred could be trusted.

"Well," said one of the owners, "I guess as long as you don't neglect us. I just want to do what's right."

So, with another handshake, he was also free to sell ads for the *St. Joseph Herald,* the *Kansas Farmer,* and several other publications. And none of them ever regretted it. "Fred Harvey was the best newspaper solicitor I ever knew," said his boss at the *Conservative.*

Fred went on to develop similarly complex and fruitful arrangements with the railroads and the adjoining packet boat lines. Several of them put him on monthly retainer because he brought in so much business. The deals weren't all as big as the one with the *Conservative*— the Missouri River Packet Line, for example, paid him only $40 ($625) a month—but it all added up.

Fred kept track of all his deals in a bulging brown leather wallet with his name embossed in gold on its well-worn front. Inside was a datebook, a sleeve for his cash, and, tucked into the innermost flap, a hidden treasure to remind him that there was more to life than business. It was a small card he and Sally had printed up for their son's first Christmas season. It showed two cherubs kissing beneath a full moon and, below them, the words "Happy New Year, Fordie Harvey."

The datebooks he carried had a standard format, a full page for each day, but Fred would use the same book for several years. Sometimes he would write short descriptions of his business day, including reports on the weather and how hard he had worked. ("Still in Pittsburgh, worked very faithfully this morning in trying to get ads, but could do nothing. Weather very mild.") He also noted whenever he got a letter from Sally, and whenever he gave her money (in ledger form, "Wife, $5" or "Mrs. Harvey, $10"). But often he communicated with himself by jotting down lists—not every day, but rather when the listing spirit moved him. He crammed a month's worth of household expenses—pew rental fees, payments to the "servant" and the "washerwoman"—onto one page. He made lists of newspaper ads and train tickets for which he was owed a commission, business expenses to submit to his assorted employers, and moneys owed to his assorted employees. He kept track of the loans he made—including the money he gave to his perennially broke sister and brother-in-law in St. Louis, which he knew he would probably never see again. And he kept tabs on his investments.

With so much free time spent on the trains and in hotels, Fred read voraciously. He devoured newspapers, magazines, and books, "not for mere pleasure or pastime," according to one admirer, "but for the acquisition of profound knowledge." But he also read with an eye toward finding new business opportunities.

He wanted every penny he made to work for him. He invested in real estate and made private mortgage loans. He even made one foray back into the restaurant business—a silent partnership in the American House in Ellsworth, Kansas, a resilient young cattle town just reached by the railroads. The popular hotel and restaurant was right on Ellsworth's "Snake Row," the raucous part of town frequented by Wild Bill Hickok.

In the summer of 1868—when Fred's investment in the American House peaked—Hickok was running for sheriff of Ellsworth, hoping to cash in on his newfound fame. An article about Hickok in *Harper's New Monthly Magazine* caused outrage in the West because of its wild claims about the many hundreds of men he had gunned down. In response to the furor, he gave another interview to set the record straight, telling the *St. Louis Democrat* he had killed "considerably over hundred men," but never "without good cause." The stories became the cornerstone of Hickok's legend, and one of the earliest examples of national media hype about cowboys. Yet despite all his celebrity, Wild Bill lost the election, and soon moved on from Ellsworth. As did Fred, once his investment of $4,485.22 ($70,100) was repaid with interest.

FRED'S STAMINA AS a railroad warrior was all the more astonishing given his uncertain health. While he was energetic and driven, his bout with typhoid as a young man had left him less than robust, and he had been excused from the draft during the Civil War because of "physical disability." He suffered from a variety of chronic ailments of the gut and head, referring to his main problems as "neuralgia" and "headaches," although it was never clear whether he was talking about migraines, or a form of nerve pain in his body or extremities, or what today would be called clinical depression. Perhaps all three.

He suffered frequently from insomnia during his train rides— although he was probably not alone in that. The trains were extremely noisy, but the engines threw off so much smoke and soot, and the moving cars kicked up so much dust that passengers were left with a no-win choice: Either leave the windows open and deal with the smoke and dirt or close them and survive the stultifying heat and stale air. Still, Fred fell ill more often than others, and would lose entire days of work lying in a hotel bed waiting for his misery to lift. And, being Fred, he kept a running tally of his sick days in his datebook. ("Started out this morning but had to return in consequence of being sick," he wrote one day in Cincinnati, "have been in bed all day sufferd [*sic*] very much with my head. Weather mild.")

He tried all sorts of remedies—including many of the patent medicines for which he sold newspaper ads—and he was forever jotting down recommendations for new cures. His datebooks were peppered with notations to try a "linimint" made with "equal parts spirits of camphar, oil of peppermint, fluid extract of bella donna," or "podophylium 60 g, letandrin Sanguinnat . . . and pure caryenne, each 30 grams," which would be made into "60 pieces with a little soft extract of mandrake or dandelion." He also consulted numerous doctors and near-doctors, including a "spiritualist" in Chicago.

But nothing provided long-term relief, and he came to see his toils as his treatment as well as his torment. "His nervous disposition made it almost imperative to load himself with work," one family member observed. "Yet this very excess of work . . . made him more nervous, setting up a vicious cycle."

Actually, there was a new medical theory concerning Fred's condition. Dr. George M. Beard, a prominent young New York physician, published a study in the *Boston Medical and Surgical Journal* in April 1869 about a revolutionary new diagnosis. He called it "neurasthenia" or "nervous exhaustion," and said its victims experienced not only fatigue, headaches, and neuralgia but anxiety, depression, and impotence. His theory was that neurasthenia was caused by depletion of the energy reserves of the central nervous system in the brain or the spinal cord, comparable to the way anemia depleted blood. Neurasthenia, he claimed, caused "more distress and annoyance than all forms of fever combined, excepting perhaps those of a malarious origin. Fevers kill, it is true, while these neuroses do not. But to many, death is by no means the most disagreeable of the many symptoms of disease."

The ambitious thirty-year-old doctor had come to believe his new illness primarily plagued the wealthy and successful, whose problems, he said, were being ignored by medical science. "The miseries of the rich, the comfortable and the intelligent," he lamented, "have been unstudied and unrelieved." Beard also believed that neurasthenia was "a disease of . . . modern civilization, and mainly of the 19th century and of the United States." But it wasn't just that the illness was more commonly found here. He suspected the country itself might actually be *causing* the symptoms.

"It cannot be denied that in America there are climatic conditions and business and social environments to the influence of which the nervous system is peculiarly susceptible," he wrote, "especially if complicated with evil habits, excesses, tobacco, alcohol, worry, or special excitements." The problem was that "competitive anxieties [are] so intensified in this country" that they led to a pathological "worry of business and professional life."

Because of this epidemiological anomaly, it wasn't long before Beard's critics, as well as critics of American life in general, started to joke that maybe his disease should be called something else.

Perhaps what people like Fred Harvey had, they said, was a case of "Americanitis."

CHAPTER 5

OPPORTUNISTIC SPONGE

꒐꒑

THE MORE SUCCESSFUL FRED BECAME, THE MORE HIS WORK KEPT him away from home. So in the summer of 1869, he decided to take his wife and three-year-old Fordie along on a business trip. They left on the Hannibal & St. Joe, changing trains in Quincy, Illinois, for Chicago, where they stayed at his regular hotel, the Briggs House, and went to the theater together. On a detour to Battle Creek, Michigan, they visited Fred's old friend and mentor from St. Louis, Abner Hitchcock, who delighted the family with a trip around town in his buggy. And then Fred picked up his regular route around the Great Lakes, Detroit, Toledo, and Cleveland, continuing through to Buffalo. The family had planned a short visit there on the way to Boston, but found the luxurious, leafy breezes and the overflowing bowls of fresh berries in Buffalo so addictive that a few days at Mrs. Oliver's boardinghouse— just a short walk from Lake Erie—became a week and then another.

Enchanted by nature, workaholic Fred actually found himself pressing a flower between two pages of a "magic copying ink" book— an early form of carbon paper he used to make duplicates of his business letters. "I think Buffalo is one of the best places I ever was in," he wrote to a friend back home. "The weather is splendid. Fruit is very plentyful here. Strawberries, raspberries and cherries, 5–6 cents a quart. Can't you pick up and come down and lend us a mouth?"

But while he enjoyed this idyllic quality time with his family, this was supposed to be a business excursion. Sally wanted to stay a little longer at Mrs. Oliver's, so Fred got back on the train alone. He headed first to Rochester, then to Seneca Falls. He spent a fruitless day canvassing clients in Albany and Troy—berating himself in his notebook, "did nothing"—and then continued on to Boston, where a client took him to see the gargantuan new wooden coliseum erected for the recently held National Peace Jubilee. A multiday concert to benefit Civil War widows and orphans, the event was the brainchild of impresario Patrick Gilmore, who wrote "When Johnny Comes Marching Home" and produced extravaganzas known for their absurd number of performers. The coliseum had seating for fifty thousand, and plenty of room for Gilmore's thousand-piece orchestra and ten thousand choral singers. The highlight of the Jubilee was a performance of Verdi's *Il Trovatore* featuring, at just the right moment, one hundred Boston firemen clanging anvils.

Five days later, Fred returned to Buffalo for the weekend and then took the overnight train to New York City. He stayed at French's, a hotel for men only, situated next door to the *New York Times* building and across the park from City Hall. French's had become something of a symbol for ambitious New York businessmen after being featured in several of Horatio Alger's novels of young men striving for their piece of the American dream. The basement bar had its share of scuffles, and it wasn't uncommon to see a newspaper report of a suicide in one of the utilitarian guest rooms. Still, the hotel was a perfect headquarters for the work Fred needed to do in New York.

Indeed, he was doing quite well on this particular visit, sending back orders for a variety of patent medicine ads that hawked products like "Dr. Wolcott's Vinegar Bitters" and "Phelps' Nasal Douche"—as well as troubleshooting customer complaints. "I see you have not yet changed the type of the Gargling Oil ad," he wrote to one publisher, enclosing a copy of the font the clients demanded before they would pay. He was also concerned about mix-ups on the ads for Professor Holloway's pills and ointment. He wanted to make sure that the ads for the pills (made from aloe, ginger, and soap) alternated weekly with the ads for the ointment (beeswax and lanolin). The company was also to be billed for the ads featuring a new lozenge form of "Mrs. Winslow's Soothing Syrup," a product that actually *did* do something, since its active ingredient was morphine.

As Fred was preparing to leave New York after five successful days and head to Philadelphia, he received a telegram at French's at 1:00 p.m. It said he was needed in Buffalo immediately.

Fordie was ill. Terribly ill. In fact, he could be dying.

Fred checked out of his hotel, hailed a horse-drawn cab to take him to the New York Central station at 30th Street and 9th Avenue, and bought a ticket on the sleeper for the 6:30 p.m. train to Albany, which continued on through to Buffalo, an eighteen-hour trip. The train pulled out twenty minutes late and, after escaping the gritty city limits of New York, began its sunset trek along the eastern shore of the Hudson River, past West Point Military Academy and the towns where Washington Irving imagined a headless horseman riding through the night and Rip Van Winkle sleeping through the Revolutionary War. After midnight, the train turned west along the Mohawk River through the Allegheny Mountains, arriving in Buffalo around noon.

The doctor said three-year-old Fordie had "the Gastrick Feaver" and was worried that it could turn into typhoid. Sally and Fred were in agony because his fever wouldn't break. They waited through an unbearable twenty-four hours until his temperature finally started to drop. Still, even after the doctor told them Fordie would probably be fine, Fred was so unnerved that he remained in Buffalo with them for a week, catching up on his correspondence and doing some shopping: He ordered a handsome new buggy for Sally and then wrote home asking a friend if he could help him find a horse that would be a "bargain" and also "one that will be safe for my wife to drive." They even took a little trip to Niagara Falls.

And then Fred went back on the road again. Leaving Fordie and Sally in Buffalo, he returned to New York, then continued on to Philadelphia, Pittsburgh, Chicago, and St. Joseph, and stopped briefly at home in Leavenworth before heading back east. On the way he made sales calls in Hannibal, Missouri; St. Louis; and then Chicago again before taking a twenty-one-hour train ride to fetch his well-rested family.

By then, Sally and Fordie were more than ready to go home, the three weeks they expected to be away having stretched into two months. They boarded an overnight train to Chicago and five days later pulled in to the Kansas Pacific terminal in Leavenworth at mid-afternoon. They were home, alive and well. For Fred and Sally, that was nothing to take for granted.

OVER THE NEXT FEW YEARS, the Harveys had another child—a daughter, Minnie—and Fred's business steadily expanded. He bought his family a four-bedroom house on the corner of Second and

Linn, just a short walk to his office at Planters' House and the bank of the Missouri River. He could now afford to keep a live-in staff of two: William, the general servant, and Maggie, the cook and housekeeper, were both teenagers from Kentucky. And he continued to send money to his sister Eliza and her family in St. Louis.

Fred took a new job with a larger railroad on the Joy System: The Chicago, Burlington & Quincy—"the Burlington"—made him General Western Agent for freight. It was a position with much more responsibility than his old job, but he and his small group of employees would work only west of the Mississippi. So he stopped selling newspaper ads in the East, and instead spent his time crisscrossing the West—which had expanded enough that what he had once known as the frontier was now being referred to as "the *Mid*west."

Wherever the High Iron of a western railroad was extended, or new branch lines were added, Fred was there canvassing or collecting. He peddled the railroad's services to farmers, ranchers, miners, manufacturers—anyone with large-scale shipping needs, no matter how challenging. He arranged for the shipping of vast quantities of hay, corn, wheat, millet, potatoes; live chickens, hogs, cattle, or sheep; meats, freshly butchered or cured; wool and pelts; copper ore, salt, oil, coal, ice, explosive powder; lumber to build entire towns, fifty or sixty train-car loads at a time; enough railroad ties to traverse entire counties.

There was even a big business in shipping bones—primarily the bones of all the buffalo that had been slaughtered for hides, sport, or national security. The government believed the best way to keep Americans safe from Indian attacks was to wipe out the herds they depended on to live, so it was not uncommon for people just to shoot them at random. In places like Hutchinson, Kansas, buffalo bones were collected from the prairies, brought to the depot to be sold for $6 to $8 a ton, and then hauled east to be made into fertilizer or bone china.

And Fred Harvey was there to quote the best price and make the best deal. "We accept the proposition," he wrote of one transaction, "on [the] condition that the bones are thoroughly dry and free from bad smell."

It was a profitable business, and he was very good at it. Adept at making offers and business decisions quickly, he had an uncanny ability to assimilate the dynamics of new markets no matter how obscure or esoteric, and to remain a gentleman no matter how ungentlemanly the enterprise. While the financial institutions of the East sold money and bonds to one another, Fred Harvey was working on the front lines of the essential American economy: raw materials, agriculture, goods, and services. And as he watched the ebb and flow of hundreds of western businesses, he paid close attention to best practices and worst practices, gentlemen and scoundrels, the value of trust and the relentlessness of the cycles. He loved to listen to businessmen complain about their problems as much as brag about their successes. And he soaked up everything.

"Fred was like an opportunistic sponge," recalled one of his great-grandsons. "He fed on others' talents and he exploited these people as he concurrently, not subsequently, learned from them. He asked many questions, and always pressed for practical solutions as they invented wheel after wheel."

Since it was more important than ever that he appear to be represented in many places at once—and he had come to expect to lose a certain amount of time to his medical problems—Fred worked hard to maintain his small crew of salesmen and assistants. While he did his best to keep the ambitious men he trained, he understood that he couldn't stand in the way when one of them was ready to go out on his own. So he always kept an eye out, in Leavenworth and on the road, for the next enterprising young man who could help him.

He built relationships all over the West: sales agents from competing railroads, ranchers, farmers, miners, small manufacturers, the staff at his regular hotels. In every town he had colleagues with whom he ate and drank—always in moderation—and buddies who would take him hunting: He had become pretty good with a shotgun.

His closest friend, however, was in Chicago, an eccentric and self-delighted shipping executive named Captain Byron Schermerhorn. "The Captain," as Schermerhorn referred to himself—only half-jokingly—was nothing like Fred. He was bombastic and egotistical, with playful eyes, a round face, and a mustache and goatee that were long and unruly—completely the opposite of Fred's clipped and perfect Van Dyke. A member of a prominent family in upstate New York, Schermerhorn had served in the Civil War as part of the Twenty-first New York Volunteers, which fought against Stonewall Jackson—indeed, Jackson's troops had captured Schermerhorn in Upton Hill, Virginia, although he managed to escape. He also fought against Robert E. Lee at the Second Battle of Bull Run. After the war, he left the military and became successful in the express delivery business in Chicago. But he was a poet at heart, writing and illustrating endless volumes of satiric verse that he loved reading aloud to anyone who would listen.

The Captain was one of the few people who could make Fred really laugh. Over drinks and cigars, Fred would even sit through Schermerhorn's recitations of his fifty-two-page epic of the absurd, "The Stale Trout," an illustrated poem about a Civil War veteran who decides to mail "smelly fish" to various people around town, including his former superior officer. (Much hilarity ensues, including a *Monty Python*–esque exchange by two Norwegian servants trying to describe the stink.)

EVERY TIME THE TRAIN lines lengthened, Fred's horizons expanded even further. In the spring of 1869, the Union Pacific finally completed building the nation's first transcontinental railroad. It was considered the greatest technological achievement in American history and the turning point for the country—over seventeen hundred miles of track laid through challenging terrain between Omaha and Sacramento. Like everyone else in his industry, Fred was amazed by the accomplishment and its immediate impact on commerce. There was now a practical way to move people and goods all the way across America.

The only hitch was the Missouri River. There was still no bridge over the Big Muddy at Omaha, and it would take the Union Pacific several more years to build one. So, for the first two years of the new railroad, it wasn't really transcontinental at all; when they reached the Missouri, passengers and freight had to be brought across by ferries or barges. And when the river froze, they crossed by whatever means necessary—sometimes temporary tracks were laid across the ice.

The Union Pacific bridge at Omaha wasn't completed until 1872. By then, the Hannibal Bridge at Kansas City had also been built, so trains were finally free to traverse much of the country. Railroad companies were laying tracks as fast as the rails could be forged and the wooden ties cut, turning the nation into a huge board game, building not only to provide needed transportation but also, in many cases, to block competitors.

As the railroads consolidated and grew in the go-go postwar economy, their stocks were increasingly controlled by a small group of powerful eastern financiers who all sat on one another's boards, slapped one another's backs, and smoked the best cigars. But the railroad industry's unprecedented power carried equally unprecedented risks.

In the early fall of 1872, Fred started noticing that in every city he visited, the local papers carried bigger and bigger stories about a financial scandal involving the builders of the transcontinental railroad. Union Pacific executives were accused of looting profits from the transcontinental railroad through a questionable company they created and gave a foreign-sounding name: Crédit Mobilier. Not only did this company receive no-bid contracts to build much of the railroad, but several members of Congress who voted on train funding were allowed to buy Crédit Mobilier stock at bargain rates. No criminal charges were ever filed, and only two of the congressmen were even censured, but the Crédit Mobilier scandal spooked European investors—who were the ones who owned most of America's railroad stock.

Much of the concern focused on Philadelphia-based financier Jay Cooke, whose investment banking firm had helped Lincoln finance the Civil War by selling war bonds and who, in peacetime, became incredibly powerful by underwriting railroad development. Cooke's current obsession was building his own transcontinental railroad, a train line directly to the Pacific Northwest. He attempted to float $300 million ($5.6 billion) in government railroad bonds to build his new line. But when rival financier J. P. Morgan thwarted Cooke's efforts at financing, European investors became even more nervous—and they started dumping all of their American railroad stocks.

Jay Cooke's brokerage company declared bankruptcy on Thursday, September 18, 1873, triggering a worldwide financial panic and a Black Friday sell-off on Wall Street. On the following Monday, the New York Stock Exchange did not open—the first time in its history that the exchange had ever halted trading. It remained closed for ten days, and when it reopened, the market had lost so much of its value that the country was plunged into a depression. Tens of thousands of businesses failed.

"Bubbles Bursting," screamed the front-page headline in the *Chicago Tribune*.

Train stock prices dropped nearly 60 percent, and more than half of the nation's railroad owners were forced into bankruptcy. Fred's boss,

James Joy, was one of the hardest hit, and the Joy System unraveled. Luckily, the Chicago, Burlington & Quincy, which signed Fred's paychecks, remained stable enough to avoid receivership.

And even with the railroad companies in receivership, the trains still ran. In fact, Fred's Midwestern territory was initially spared the worst of the national economic collapse because its primary industry was agriculture, not high finance. In Leavenworth, it was business almost as usual for the Harveys—Fred traveled, and Sally raised their growing family. In December 1873 they had another child, a daughter, Marie, whom they called May.

Yet Kansas was visited by its own disaster the following summer—a plague of grasshoppers that descended on the landscape like sheets of black rain. They were first spotted on July 1, 1874, moving slowly eastward across the state. Not only did these "Rocky Mountain locusts" devour every county's crops in a matter of days, but they ate the wool off live sheep, the clothes off people's backs, and anything made of wood, including paper, lamp shades, even the handles on tools. At times, the grasshoppers even stopped the trains: Several inches thick on the ground, they rendered the tracks too slimy for the locomotive wheels to get any traction.

In his travels across Kansas, Fred saw people raking up piles of live grasshoppers, or using plows or sheets of metal smeared with tar as makeshift "hopper dozers," or mixing the insects into the cement for the foundations of new buildings—and all anyone could do was laugh at the absurdity of the situation. While the plague was devastating, the humor helped them get through. Kansans developed an even greater resolve to overcome the nation's economic woes and their own agricultural nightmares, reassuring one another that 1875 would be a great year, a landmark year.

CHAPTER 6

SAVAGE AND UNNATURAL FEEDING

⊐⊑

As FRED HARVEY'S FORTIETH BIRTHDAY APPROACHED, HE WAS faced with the realization that while he was by any measure a successful man, he still had a burning desire to achieve on a grander scale. It couldn't really be called a midlife crisis, because most American men didn't live past their early fifties. Technically, Fred had already reinvented himself for midlife back when he married Sally and started selling for the railroads. But he yearned for a third act. For inspiration, he would re-read a list of "Maxims for Business Men" he had clipped from the newspaper and pasted on the front of his datebook:

> NEVER FAIL TO TAKE A RECEIPT FOR MONEY, AND KEEP
>   COPIES OF YOUR LETTERS.
> DO YOUR BUSINESS PROMPTLY AND BORE NOT A BUSINESS
>   MAN WITH LONG VISITS.
> LAW IS A TRADE IN WHICH LAWYERS EAT THE OYSTERS
>   AND LEAVE THE CLIENTS THE SHELLS.
> CAUTION IS THE FATHER OF SECURITY.
> HE WHO PAYS BEFORE-HAND IS SERVED BEHIND-HAND.
> IF YOU WOULD KNOW THE VALUE OF A DOLLAR, TRY TO
>   BORROW ONE.
> NO MAN CAN BE SUCCESSFUL WHO NEGLECTS HIS
>   BUSINESS.
> DO NOT WASTE TIME IN USELESS REGRETS OVER LOSSES.
> SYSTEMATIZE YOUR BUSINESS AND KEEP AN EYE ON LITTLE
>   EXPENSES—SMALL LEAKS SINK GREAT SHIPS.
> AN HOUR OF TRIUMPH COMES AT LAST TO THOSE WHO
>   WATCH AND WAIT.

WORD BY WORD WEBSTER'S BIG DICTIONARY WAS MADE.
SPEAK WELL OF YOUR FRIENDS—OF YOUR ENEMIES SAY
    NOTHING.
IF YOU POST YOUR SERVANTS ON YOUR AFFAIRS THEY WILL
    ONE DAY REND YOU.
BE SILENT WHEN A FOOL TALKS.
GIVE A FOOLISH TALKER ROPE ENOUGH AND HE WILL
    HANG HIMSELF.
ROTHSCHILD, THE FOUNDER OF THE WORLD-RENOWNED
    HOUSE OF ROTHSCHILD & CO., ASCRIBED HIS SUCCESS
    TO THE FOLLOWING:
    NEVER HAVE ANYTHING TO DO WITH AN UNLUCKY MAN.
    BE CAUTIOUS AND BOLD.
    MAKE A BARGAIN AT ONCE.

Still, while the Rothschilds, the emperors of European investment banking, certainly represented an international standard of financial achievement, the businessmen Fred envied were closer to home. And nobody loomed larger than Pullman.

George Mortimer Pullman was just a few years older than Fred and had come to the Midwest to seek his fortune around the same time. But he was now a millionaire many times over, his name synonymous throughout the world with luxury train cars for sleeping and dining.

Pullman had grown up in Albion, New York, and after showing little aptitude for cabinetmaking, his father's trade, he went into the family's side business—which was moving buildings. Literally. He moved some buildings to help with the expansion of the Erie Canal and then relocated to Chicago, where his technique made him famous. In the late 1850s, it was becoming clear that much of Chicago was slowly sinking, the muddy ground along Lake Michigan turning into not-very-quicksand. Most buildings needed new foundations, which meant either moving them somewhere else on massive rollers or just lifting them temporarily so new structures could be created underneath.

The Matteson House hotel was the largest building anyone had ever tried to lift in Chicago, measuring some eighty by ninety feet, as well as the most prominent, sitting at the corner of Dearborn and Randolph, arguably the most valuable block in town. Since Pullman knew the owner, he was able to beat out local contractors for the job. And in late March 1859, the city watched in amazement as the twenty-eight-

year-old Pullman, with his chubby cheeks and manicured beard, or-
chestrated a massive industrial ballet. He had eight hundred screw
jacks placed under the building and then had eight hundred workmen
crank the jacks, simultaneously, a quarter turn at a time, on his whistle
commands.

This performance lasted for ten days. At the end of the process, the
building was five feet off the ground—which allowed new piers and a
basement to be built beneath it—and George Pullman was in business.
Over the next year, his company helped lift an entire Chicago block of
buildings (the job so delighting onlookers that shops reported dramatic
increases in sales while their premises were elevated) and eventually
was hired to lift the massive Tremont Hotel from its one-acre plot.

But, while raising buildings was a good business, Pullman had another enterprise in mind. Just before moving to Chicago, he had taken
a train from Buffalo south along Lake Erie to Westfield, New York, to
visit family and got a chance to experience the latest innovation in railroad service: the first generation of sleeping cars. He paid $1 ($26.98)
for a bed and discovered that the cars were like rolling tombs—the
berths were stacked three high, and when the unventilated cars were
heated with stoves, "the atmosphere was something dreadful," he recalled.

During the trip, which was mercifully only sixty miles, he lay awake
in his cramped upper berth dreaming up ways to build a better sleeper.
He struck up a friendship with an executive at the Chicago, Alton &
St. Louis Railroad who allowed him to experiment on some old cars.
The first one debuted in 1859 and was remarkable primarily for its innovative top bunk, which could fold flat up against the ceiling when
not in use. He continued to tinker with a dozen more retrofitted cars
over the next several years—interrupted by a foray to Colorado to try
his hand at gold mining—and after the Civil War he unveiled his first
sleeper built from scratch.

The Pioneer—actually, the "Pullman Pioneer" because his name
became part of the sales pitch—was longer and higher than any previous train car, and was so luxuriously appointed that it was as if he had
taken a fine Victorian mansion and put it on cushioned wheels. The
finishes on the wood-grain interiors were so lustrous that trainmen
started referring to private cars, and the fancy people who rode in
them, as "varnish."

The Pullman sleeper was an immediate sensation, not only because of its opulence—the murals on the ceilings, the chandeliers, the marble countertops in the bathrooms, and the exotic carpeting (on which no man would consider spitting)—but also because of its technical wizardry. There were various patentable contraptions that allowed the berths to be easily transformed into seating or storage space during daylight hours, and the ventilation system let in fresh air while keeping out the dust and cinders.

By the time Pullman decided to incorporate his company in 1867—a relatively new way of setting up a business, already popular with the industrialists whose ranks he was joining—he had built four dozen of these sleepers and had launched his first "hotel cars," which had drawing rooms and round-the-clock full-service kitchens. But the more luxurious cars he built, the more he realized there was a huge problem with his enterprise.

The railroads did a poor job taking care of passengers. They were good at laying and maintaining track, buying and maintaining cars, handling boxcars. But there was a reason that trainmen often joked "freight doesn't complain." Passenger service was terrible, and railroads did not have the kind of staff needed to take care of wealthier customers. Train conductors did not make good butlers or waiters. So Pullman decided to staff all his own cars and not use railroad employees at all; the extra fare Pullman passengers paid went to him, not to the railroads. His cars were like rolling hotels—attached to the trains, yet separated from them.

Pullman also decided that his new staff should be exclusively black. His porters quickly became the first major workforce of free black men in the country, eventually forming the foundation for America's black middle class. This did not necessarily reflect any particular progressiveness on Pullman's part. Some historians believe he chose to hire black men primarily because they were cheap and available—and because he and his white customers didn't regard them as full-fledged human beings. Since porters might be around white women disrobing or white men stumbling drunk back into their berths—perhaps from someone else's—Pullman wanted an employee, according to one scholar, "whom passengers could regard as part of the furnishings, rather than a mortal with likes, dislikes, and a memory." He hired only the most dark-skinned men and, especially in the early years, left them largely nameless—they were often referred to as "boy" or generically as "George." That said, this was still one of the best and best-paying jobs for black men in the country. So the opportunity to be a "George" was highly coveted, and the Pullman service on the trains was uniformly excellent.

As his business grew, Pullman went into partnership with the industrialist Andrew Carnegie, which assured him greater access to capital and the two biggest contracts in the world of trains: He was hired to build all the sleepers not only for the Pennsylvania Railroad, one of the dominant lines in the East, but also for the Union Pacific's new transcontinental railway. By the 1870s, the Pullman name had become synonymous with traveling in comfort.

YET THERE WAS ONE area of the passenger service business that eluded Pullman, and that was food. Pullman built fine dining cars—the first one was called The Delmonico, with menus created by chefs from that renowned restaurant—but they weren't nearly as successful as his sleepers. It wasn't his fault. At that time there were still no vestibules allowing passengers to walk between cars, so one couldn't go to the dining car while the train was moving or leave it after eating until the train stopped at a station. While moderately popular on shorter eastern rides, dining cars were considered impractical for longer-distance trains.

This meant that even the most "varnished" of Pullman's passengers still had to rely on the restaurants at train stations—which were, by and large, dreadful. The *New York Times* had recently bemoaned the situation:

> If there is any word in the English language more shamefully misused than another, it is the word "refreshment" as applied to the hurry scurry of eating and drinking at railroad stations . . . Directors of railroads appear to have an idea that travelers are destitute of stomach; that eating and drinking are not at all necessary to human beings bound on long journeys, and that nothing more is required than to put them through their misery in as brief a time as possible. It is expected that three or four hundred men, women and children . . . can be whirled half a day over a dusty road, with hot cinders flying in their faces; and then when they approach a station and are dying of weariness, hunger and

thirst, longing for an opportunity to bathe their faces at least before partaking of their much-needed refreshments, that they
shall rush helter-skelter into a dismal long room and dispatch a
supper, breakfast or dinner in fifteen minutes. The consequences
of such savage and unnatural feeding are not reported by telegraph as railroad disasters, but if a faithful account were given of
them, we are afraid they would be found much more serious
than any that are caused by the smashing of cars, or the breaking down of bridges.

Fred Harvey knew this all too well. In his years riding the rails, he had
probably eaten more stomach-turning depot meals and stayed in more
filthy depot hotel rooms than anyone else in America. He knew there
was a reason the food was called "grub" and the hotels "flea-bags." It
was a special kind of hell to have tasted the best of the restaurant and
hotel business from both sides of the counter—as a manager and a
patron—only to be trapped in the hospitality-challenged American
West before the invention of effective antacids.

It wasn't that the rest of the country was eating all that much better. "American cookery is worse than that of any other civilized nation,"
declared Chef Pierre Blot, the Julia Child of post–Civil War America,
who ran a popular French cooking academy in Manhattan and was
beloved for his best-seller *What to Eat, and How to Cook It.* Ironically,
in a nation that was becoming the world's largest producer of food, few
cooks had access to fresh ingredients or the slightest idea what to do
with them. West of the Mississippi, the food was particularly distressing. Almost everything was prepared with canned or preserved ingredients, and given the scarcity of even rudimentary refrigeration, eating
fresh meat could be life threatening.

But the worst food in town was always served at the railroad "eating houses"—which were spaced roughly every one hundred miles,
since that was how long a locomotive could go before it needed a stop
for fuel and water. Depot eating houses not only had lousy food and
skimpy portions but also didn't give passengers any *time* to eat. Food
preparation was often deliberately dragged out so diners wouldn't be
able to finish—or sometimes even start—their meals before the half-
hour meal break was over. As soon as the caboose was out of sight,
restaurant employees would scrape the uneaten food back into con-
tainers to be served to their next unsuspecting victims. For those who

couldn't afford one of these horrid sit-down meals, there were vendors who worked the platforms or came through the cars selling overpriced, skimpy sandwiches and wizened fruit from handcarts. They were called "butchers."

While the first generation of travelers out west had put up with these culinary indignities, Fred Harvey believed that the next wave would not and should not. He suspected there was money to be made if he could just figure out a way to dependably deliver palatable food at fair prices without any bait and switch. The railroads certainly weren't going to solve the problem. Even though ridership was increasing and the economy was recovering from the 1873 depression, the rail companies were still too strapped for cash to invest in food service. The railroads had made George Pullman rich with sleeping cars and dining cars that they could easily have built and managed themselves. It was only a matter of time before somebody got "railroad rich" by running good depot restaurants.

In fact, Fred was certain it was possible to serve the finest cuisine imaginable along the train tracks in the middle of nowhere. In the early days of eastern railroading, there was a legendary eating house along the Pennsylvania Railroad, the Logan House hotel in Altoona. As a young traveling salesman, Fred had often eaten at this homey Delmonico's of trackside dining.

And he also had seen the photos, read the menus, and heard the stories about the most ambitious trackside meals ever served in America. They were the highlight of "The Grand Excursion," the greatest promotional junket and gustatory extravaganza in the young nation's history.

Back in the fall of 1866, when the Union Pacific tracks from Omaha reached the 100th Meridian in south-central Nebraska—a contractual milestone that allowed the railroad to exercise the rest of its land grant and build all the way to California—everybody who mattered in the government and the train industry was invited to celebrate at the newly established end of the line. More than two hundred dignitaries, elected officials, and captains of industry—along with their wives and families—were brought by train to the Missouri River. Back then it was still unbridged, so they traveled by packet boats up to Omaha, where they met the new trains.

Fred heard from his old pal Captain Rufus Ford—whose packet boat the *Colorado* was one of many hired for excursionists—that the level of wining and dining on the river was unprecedented. The on-board dinner menu offered over sixty different entrées, including braised bear in port wine sauce, baked pike in oyster sauce, two kinds of tongue (beef and buffalo), two kinds of antelope (steaks with a sherry wine sauce, or larded with sauce bigarade), stuffed calf's head, filet of beef with Madeira sauce, rabbit potpie, quails on toast, and chicken salad "young America style." There were also more than two dozen desserts, including English plum pudding with white sauce, meringues with peaches, vanilla bonbons, cranberry tartlets, ladyfingers, apple pie, and pyramids of macaroons. But while the menus on the boat were sybaritic, it was the food service and entertainment during the excursionists' ride through the Nebraska wilderness that made hospitality history.

In the middle of a prairie—where most rail men would have been happy sleeping under the stars and dining on a fresh buffalo steak seared on the hot front grill of the engine—the Union Pacific set up a lavish tent city, with hay mattresses and buffalo robes for the guests, and imported a feast that would be expected only in the best hotels of New York, Chicago, London, and Paris. For after-dinner entertainment, the railroad hired one hundred Pawnee Indians to perform their colorful war dance. In reality, it was all rather tame, one observer said, noting the visitors were "only too glad to know that the Indians were entirely friendly, and catering only for the amusement of the company, instead of being enemies, dancing and gloating over their scalpless bodies."

Yet the next morning, as they awoke to the terrifying sound of Pawnees on the warpath raiding the camp, the excursionists were no longer so sure of their safety. When the guests began shrieking more loudly than the Indians, their hosts let them in on the joke. Those marauding Pawnees were also on the Union Pacific payroll, hired to *fake* an attack.

An especially sumptuous breakfast was served straightaway.

Then, as the sated excursionists headed back toward Omaha, they were given one last spectacular scene to remember. A prairie fire, with flames extending in an unbroken line for fifteen miles, had been set deliberately—just for their entertainment.

Historians would later note that the hugely popular Wild West Show of William "Buffalo Bill" Cody, a Leavenworth native, was basically a traveling version of the theatrics staged by the Union Pacific for the Grand Excursion. In fact, some of those same Pawnee Indians, unable to return to their tribal ways after the trains came through, ended up working in Buffalo Bill's show.

So as Fred Harvey traveled through the West, eating one ghastly meal after another, he couldn't help but think of the exquisitely comforting food of the Logan House in Altoona and the trackside victual indulgence of the Grand Excursion and wonder if such culinary magic shows could have regularly scheduled performances in the West.

CHAPTER 7

THEY'LL TRY ANYTHING

⊐⊏

FRED DIDN'T WANT TO GIVE UP HIS LUCRATIVE DAY JOB, SO HE
first explored the railroad food business with a partner: Colonel Jasper
"Jepp" Rice, the longtime owner of the Planters' House in Leavenworth, who had been his landlord and friend for a decade. They started
a company, Harvey & Rice, and got themselves hired to handle the
food service at three eating houses along the Kansas Pacific where Fred
had endured particularly loathsome meals.

None of the eating houses were anywhere near Leavenworth. The
closest one was in Lawrence, thirty-four miles away. The next was four
hundred miles west, on the opposite side of the state, in the cattle town
of Wallace, where Rice also owned a herd. And the third was still another hundred miles beyond that, in Hugo, Colorado, nestled among
the rich mountain mining towns on the way to Denver. Despite these
distances, Fred wasn't an absentee manager. During much of the year,
he was in these towns as much as he was at home, traveling at an ever
more grueling pace. On any given day in any western city where there
was exploding growth, Fred Harvey seemed to have just arrived or was
just leaving, his visits well documented in the pages of the small-town
newspapers cropping up all over the West.

Still, he had to place an enormous amount of trust in his new eating house managers: Not only did they represent him to patrons, but
they were empowered to sign his name to all correspondence and orders. Since he still had several young men working for him on the road
doing collections for railroad freight orders, he simply elevated some of
his best workers to the eating house positions. Loyalty, trustworthi-
ness, and the ability to instill confidence in people were more important to him than restaurant experience. He could teach them what they

needed to know, making up new rules and guidelines for them as situations presented themselves. One day he made a note to himself: "Shall I make a deduction [discount] for Indians and paupers?"

The managers kept track of everything they did in handwritten logs that he could inspect when he visited. And Fred did as much of the ordering himself as possible.

One of the biggest challenges in the eating houses was keeping up with the incessant demand for cigars—which apparently were more important to western diners than food, especially way out in cattle country. It was not uncommon for Fred to order several thousand cigars at a time for each house—Golden Crowns, small and large, Londres Grandes, Graciosas, and, for the Wallace House, lower-priced Conchas. One bill for six thousand cigars to stock three eating houses came to $433.50 ($8,983). And one of the manager's most important jobs was always keeping Fred personally apprised of the cigar inventory.

Because he was suddenly ordering so many provisions, Fred used the opportunity to get cigars and delicacies for himself and his friends, especially Byron Schermerhorn back in Chicago. He started writing notes to himself: "Send Schermerhorn prairie chickens [a type of grouse once plentiful in America], black tail dear, buffalo meat," or "Send Ball some white fish."

NOT LONG AFTER they took over the three eating houses, Fred and Jepp Rice realized something: They really hated being business partners. Each thought the other wasn't pulling his weight, and the Kansas Pacific wasn't easy to work with: The railroad agreed to help pay for shipping materials to the houses, but only by refund, for which Fred had to painstakingly invoice them for every last cigar and prairie chicken. He agreed to honor the contract, but soon started looking for an opportunity to strike out on his own with another railroad.

He spoke first to his bosses at the Chicago, Burlington & Quincy, telling them about the great potential he saw in their eating houses in Illinois, Missouri, and Kansas. They weren't interested, but suggested he talk to someone at one of the smaller, newer railroads, the upstart Atchison, Topeka & Santa Fe.

The Santa Fe—as it was known—was still pretty much a wannabe railroad, with a scant 560 miles of track in Kansas, 65 miles in Colorado, and about a mile and a quarter in Missouri. But it did have a reputation for a certain kind of frontier thinking that was unusual among the conservative, eastern-owned railroad companies.

"They'll try *anything*" is what people in the train business said about the Santa Fe, with a mixture of respect and incredulity.

This was, after all, the first rail line with a station in the gunslinging town of Dodge City, Kansas, where Wyatt Earp had just recently arrived to help keep the peace. Its passengers were known for gleefully firing their pistols and rifles out the train windows. Started by Cyrus Holliday, a lawyer from central Pennsylvania who came west in the 1850s to seek his fortune in railroads, the AT&SF was originally just the Atchison & Topeka, with a mission to link those two Kansas towns, some sixty miles apart, by laying tracks along the section of the Santa Fe Trail that already connected them for stagecoaches and carriages. But Holliday's railroad got a new name and an extremely ambitious new end point during the Civil War, when the government started giving out larger land grants; its executives dreamed of building along the trail all the way to Santa Fe, New Mexico, itself, replacing the entire stagecoach business, and then taking advantage of that city's historic role as the hub for trade from Mexico. Because the AT&SF route covered so much barren, virgin American ground, the railroad became known for aggressively "seeding" the land around its tracks, luring new settlers from the eastern states and all over the European continent with discounted train tickets, inexpensive acreage, and even "loans" of seed that farmers could repay after harvest (as long as they used the Santa Fe for shipping).

The plague of grasshoppers in 1874 had almost done in the Santa Fe, since its fortunes were so closely tied to agriculture. But the railroad had held on, and things were now looking up, because the Kansas wheat harvest of 1875 had turned out to be a great success.

Fred knew the superintendent of the Santa Fe, Charlie Morse, from when he worked in Nebraska for a different railroad. The two men decided to try a project together. The Santa Fe had a twenty-seat lunchroom on the second floor of its Topeka depot. It was a much smaller space than any of the eating houses Fred was managing for the Kansas Pacific, but Morse assured him he could run it exactly as he pleased.

True to form, Fred negotiated a superb deal for himself. Not only did he get the space rent free, but he convinced the Santa Fe to cover all the utilities (which in those days were heat, gas, coal, and ice) and throw in free transportation for his eating house provisions and his employees. As landlord, the railroad also covered the major "back of the house" equipment expenses like the ovens, ranges, sinks, and iceboxes. Fred still had to pay for the food itself, labor, and any upgrades to the "front of the house"—furniture, linens, dishes, stemware, and silverware. But after that, he could keep any profits.

He would, however, need to impress more than the passengers and crew from the five Santa Fe trains stopping at Topeka daily. While the railroad was based in Boston, its main operations office was across the street from the Topeka terminal. So Fred Harvey's meals would have to delight Charlie Morse and all the other top brass on a regular basis.

The two men shook hands on the deal—there was no written contract—and Fred sprang into action. He sent for his wife, Sally, as well as one of his most trusted employees from over the years, Guy Potter. Together, they scrubbed the small second-floor lunchroom from top to bottom and then replaced all the dishes, silverware, and stemware. Fred arranged with the Santa Fe and purveyors as far away as Chicago, St. Louis, and Boston to have fresh meat, produce, and specially roasted coffee brought in by train, rather than relying on what was available nearby. Potter agreed to become the manager.

When they opened for business in January 1876, Fred was there as the first customer came through the door. It was not a Santa Fe executive at all but rather Shep Smith, a nineteen-year-old rookie train fireman still waiting for his first mustache to fill in. Smith would later vividly recall Fred approaching him as he sat on one of the swiveling chairs along the long curved counter.

"Have some coffee, Shep," Fred said. "It's the first I've made. Tell me if it's any good."

Shep tried a steaming cup and declared it excellent. "Your coffee's good, Harvey," he said between sips, "but your place is too small. Three men would crowd it, and you have to climb a long flight of steps to get up here."

"Right-o," Fred replied, "but I'm going to make the coffee and food so good that the boys will come, no matter how far they have to walk."

Smith ordered a sandwich and a piece of the apple pie he saw cooling on the counter. They sliced him a wedge that was nearly a quarter of the pie and placed it before him. Smith cut through the flaky crust with one of those brand-new forks, stabbed himself a generous bite, raised it to his mouth. And, *damn,* it was good.

The opening of Fred Harvey's lunchroom in the Santa Fe depot in Topeka would later be touted as a major turning point in culinary history, perfectly timed for the beginning of America's centennial year. There is an oft-repeated story that the lunchroom was such an overnight success that the railroad feared western migration itself might be halted because nobody wanted to go past Topeka once they had tasted Fred Harvey's food. But in fact, success did not come quite so quickly or easily.

The Santa Fe lunchroom did get a nice little write-up in the *Leavenworth Times* on January 5, 1876, describing the eatery as "the neatest, cleanest dining hall in the State, everything bran [*sic*] new. The crockery, cutlery and silver-ware of the choicest patterns, and the table supplied in the best of style. It was a luxury to set down to such a table. A man who takes such pains to serve the public ought to be rewarded with liberal patronage." The paper didn't mention the owner—just Leavenworth's own Guy Potter behind the counter. But since Fred was now working for three different railroads that were competing bitterly for business in Kansas, perhaps that was just as well.

AS THE SUMMER OF 1876 approached, the nation was caught up in the celebration of the hundredth anniversary of the Declaration of Independence and the founding of America. Many people flocked to Philadelphia for the Centennial Exhibition. That world's fair would be remembered mostly for the products that debuted and were popularized there: the telephone, the electric light, the typewriter, and soda pop. But at the time, the exhibition signaled that America not only had survived its civil war but was on its way to becoming an international power. In fact, one immediate economic impact of the Centennial Exhibition—which attracted some ten million visitors to Philadelphia—was that America's traditional international trade deficit reversed itself for the first time.

The big celebration was on the Fourth of July. Amid the military parades, the Declaration of Independence was read aloud from the steps of the building at 6th and Chestnut streets where it was originally signed. Immediately afterward, Susan B. Anthony strode to the podium and read aloud her "Declaration of Rights for Women," while a friend held a parasol over her head to block the midday sun.

But the nation's self-congratulatory mood suffered a major setback several days later, when the newspapers reported what had happened to George Custer's troops in southeastern Montana Territory. At Little Bighorn, Custer and all 225 of his men had been killed while attacking a camp of Sioux and Cheyenne under the formidable command of Chief Sitting Bull and Crazy Horse.

In the eastern press coverage of "Custer's Last Stand," there was no question that the Indians were villains and an American hero had been felled. Where the Harveys lived, however, the issue of Little Bighorn was more complicated; in Leavenworth, Custer's legacy was more ambiguous, and "the Indian Question" was still a question.

The Harveys knew the Custers, who had lived on and off at the fort for years and were active on the city's social scene. So they were well aware that Custer had once been court-martialed in Leavenworth for deserting his command, taking seventy-five soldiers to work on his own personal business matters, and then ordering the execution of three "supposed deserters" who were shot without a trial.

And the "cause" for which he and his troops had given their lives at Little Bighorn was also controversial. The government had sent Custer to roust the Sioux out of the Black Hills, where gold had been discovered. But that land originally had been *given* to the Indians in a treaty. It was only after the economic downturn that Washington had decided to take it back, by force if necessary.

In Leavenworth, there were powerfully mixed feelings about the government's Indian policy. The fort was still the place from which troops were deployed for the "Indian Wars," and many of the casualties—including those from Little Bighorn—were buried in Leavenworth's national cemetery. Tribal leaders were often incarcerated at the fort prison. And there was certainly a great deal of bigotry. But people in Leavenworth saw "friendly Indians" on the street every day, mostly from the large and peaceful Pottawatomie reservation nearby. Fred and many others did business with the local tribal leaders through Enoch Hoag, the government's superintendent for Indian Affairs in Kansas.

In fact, Indians were sometimes among the many customers trying out the new and improved Santa Fe eating house in Topeka. Not long after Little Bighorn, a group of ninety-six Sioux stopped for lunch. Local newspaper coverage of the event wasn't particularly kind:

> People were a little disappointed upon seeing them, for all expected to see them in their war costume, with their bloody tomahawks and dripping scalping knives . . . Upon arriving at the depot a number of bucks with tin buckets made a break for the eating house where they got hot coffee and returned to their cars, where they partook of their frugal meal, which consisted of boiled beef without seasoning, and coffee. They gorge themselves when they eat. They all eat out of the same pan and drink coffee out of the same can. This is the reason they are not allowed to go into hotels to eat. They don't know how to behave themselves . . . However, a few of the "big injuns" were allowed the privilege of setting at the white man's table. Messrs. Spotted Tail, Red Dog and Fast Bear were taken to the railroad eating house, where they partook of double rations. They got away with everything set before them, in fact, everything that was within reach. They exhibited some of the traits of a human by using knives and forks, and blowing their coffee to cool it. They also mopped their mouths with napkins which they forgot to put in their pockets after using.
>
> Mr. Tail understood the uses of the knives and forks. He held the piece with the fork while he severed it with the knife, and with his fingers he placed the largest piece on the knife and dumped it into his mouth. Mr. Dog wiped off his gooms with his tongue after eating enough for three big men like John Carter. But old pap Bear gave the crowd away. After getting up from the table he reached over and grabbed up all the apples he could hold in his big hands, which were about four apiece, probably under the sweet impression that he was stealing them.

The reporter was particularly outraged by the way the local women interacted with the Indians. "Some of the ladies at the depot considered it a great honor to grasp these dusky murderers of the plains by the hand," he wrote. "Red Dog was so struck with the beauty of a lady there that he returned to the room to get a look at her."

While it was possible to encounter diners of almost any ethnicity and occupation at Fred's lunchroom in Topeka—Russian Mennonites on their way to start farms, Chinese laborers heading west to lay tracks, German Jews hoping to start businesses in the new towns, veterans of both sides of the Civil War, cowboys, and Indians—it didn't mean that everyone got along. Sometimes the only thing they all agreed on was Fred Harvey's coffee.

CHAPTER 8

SUITED TO THE MOST EXIGENT OR EPICUREAN TASTE

FRED MANAGED THE LUNCHROOM IN TOPEKA FOR NEARLY TWO years—while still overseeing three eating houses on the Kansas Pacific—before doing any further business with the Santa Fe. The Harveys had another child, a son, who was named after Fred's best friend: Byron Schermerhorn Harvey. (The Captain returned the favor by naming one of his daughters Fredericka, but she died in infancy.) And Fred continued selling freight for the Burlington line. But then he became intrigued, as did so many in the western railroad business, when the AT&SF suddenly became much more aggressive, and much more appealing.

In 1877, the Santa Fe rustled much of the western cattle business and, in the process, reinvented Dodge City as the fabled locale we know today. Dodge had already peaked as a center for buffalo hunting, and the stakes in local poker games were not what they used to be. But before the 1877 roundup, the Santa Fe built large cattle pens and a livestock shipping center at its Dodge City station—which was a hundred miles closer to where the cattle actually grazed than the livestock pens of the powerful Kansas Pacific. The Santa Fe also cut shipping prices, and suddenly many cattlemen driving their herds up from Texas switched railroads.

This turned Dodge City, almost overnight, into a raucous center of commerce—and the most dangerous new outpost in the Wild West. It also inspired a popular joke of the day. A train conductor approaches a drunken old prospector sprawled out over several seats and asks where he's going.

"To hell, I guess," the prospector replies.

"OK, that'll be 65 cents," the conductor says. "Get off at Dodge City."

In the aftermath of this cattle business coup, the Santa Fe announced a bold front-office move that rocked the industry. The railroad poached one of the most talented young executives in the business from the Chicago, Burlington & Quincy to become the new general manager of the AT&SF.

William Barstow Strong was an ambitious, dynamic railroad man with piercing eyes and a beard only a beekeeper could love. Every strand of hair emanating from his face had been left to grow straight down until it reached his collarbone. It was a bold statement even during the bad-hair years of the late nineteenth century, but he was a bold man. Fred had been friendly with him for years, since Strong had worked at several of the lines on the Joy System. Two years younger than Fred, Strong had grown up in Vermont and Wisconsin, got started in railroads as a station agent and telegraph operator, and was considered one of the most underappreciated executive talents in the business. Now he was getting his big break.

By hiring Strong, the Atchison, Topeka & Santa Fe signaled that it would no longer be content as just another successful regional line. Its leaders hoped to extend the railroad—which currently ran from Kansas only as far as La Junta, Colorado—not just to Santa Fe, New Mexico, but all the way to the Pacific, competing with the other big transcontinental players. But unlike those players, who had gone from business heroes to "robber barons" after the 1873 market crash, the Santa Fe planned to be the white hat in western railroading, building without scandals or government subsidies of any kind. They would be the good guys, the independent railroad, and they thought Strong was the man who could take them to that next level.

He immediately laid out plans to aggressively expand the AT&SF west, through Colorado to the Pacific. And within days of his arrival at the Santa Fe's main operations office in Topeka, Fred Harvey was there negotiating with the railroad to take over more eating houses in Kansas—starting with Florence, the most important restaurant and hotel on the line.

Florence was the primary meal stop for AT&SF passengers in eastern Kansas and also attracted sportsmen, since the hunting and fishing nearby were spectacular. Taking over the operation there was complicated because the Santa Fe, as an experiment, had actually sold its eating house and depot hotel to a local entrepreneur, rather than leasing it. The railroad had the right to replace him but only if he was bought out. And at the moment, the Santa Fe was cash poor, because every dollar was being spent on new tracks in Colorado.

Strong told Fred he could run the Florence eating house and hotel, but only if he laid out all the money himself to purchase the building and its contents—the price was $5,275 ($117,448), more than half of his life savings. The Santa Fe promised to buy the Florence building back, and to let him manage it rent free like Topeka, when conditions improved. It was a huge gamble for Fred, who was accustomed to seeking leveraged comfort in more conservative investments. But William Strong had a way of daring associates to be great.

STRONG LED BY FEARLESS EXAMPLE. He stunned the railroad world by ambushing the Raton Pass—which was considered by many to be the single most important and strategic mountain pass in the West. It was, at the time, clearly the best way to get a train from Colorado—where the Rockies made construction a nightmare—to California. And there was only room for one company to build train tracks over the pass, which had always been the Santa Fe Trail route through the treacherous Sangre de Cristo Mountains from Colorado into New Mexico, but in recent years had become America's quirkiest toll road.

The Raton Pass was actually privately owned by an odd bird named Richens "Uncle Dick" Wootton, who had bought the mountain land and improved the old trail, digging out and leveling sections by hand. He and his wife lived in a small hotel he built high up on the Colorado side of the pass, right next to where he had slung a locked chain across the trail. He made his living by charging $1.50 per stagecoach or carriage, twenty-five cents per horseman, and a nickel a head for livestock to cross over. Indians, Mexicans, and posses chasing horse thieves passed for free.

Several railroads wanted to control the Raton Pass, but Strong's main competitor was the feisty Denver & Rio Grande. In fact, the D&RG intercepted and decoded cables that Strong sent to his chief engineer telling him it was time to go make a deal with Uncle Dick. So on February 26, 1878, there was a showdown. Both railroads had teams on the same train to El Moro, Colorado, the tiny town closest to the pass. The Santa Fe engineers kept a low profile during the ride, and when the train pulled in to the station well after dark, they lagged behind their competitors until they saw them check into the depot hotel for the night. Then they bolted into action, hiring a carriage and horses to head off into the pitch-black to ride twenty bumpy miles to Uncle Dick's hotel. When they got there, a teen dance was in full swing, and Uncle Dick was about to call it a night. But they were able to keep him awake long enough to talk him into a handshake deal allowing the Santa Fe to build along his pass.

They agreed to work out the details later because the process of grading—digging out a rail bed so the wooden ties and steel rails would lie flat—had to begin *immediately* in order to solidify their legal claim to the pass. Quickly, they hired a ragtag group of teenage boys from the dance, and in the dead of night this motley crew hiked up the mountain carrying lanterns, shovels, and picks to mark off the route that the train tracks would take.

After the Santa Fe crew had been working for half an hour, the D&RG engineers and their large grading team arrived, hoping *they* could make a deal with Uncle Dick. When they found out that the Santa Fe had beaten them to it, several members of the crew pulled out pistols. But eccentric Uncle Dick made it clear that not only was the Santa Fe first, but he liked them better anyway. Somehow the dispute was settled without a shot being fired.

Six weeks later, however, plenty of shots were fired when the railroads clashed again at the Royal Gorge, a canyon cut by the Arkansas River east of Pueblo, which was crucial for building through to Denver, an alternative route to the Pacific. This time, when the Santa Fe team got to the site first, the D&RG brought a small army to fight them. Strong countered with a militia of his own.

He wired Bat Masterson, the sheriff of Dodge City, to hire one hundred of his meanest friends to come fight for the railroad, even sending a special Santa Fe train to pick them up. Each side dug bunkers and built forts to protect workers not only from gunfire but all manner of guerrilla tactics: Boulders would come rolling down at workmen, temporary bridges got blown up, and large pieces of equipment kept falling, mysteriously, into the gorge.

The fighting went on for over a year in Colorado and even in Washington, D.C., where the legal issues involved were heard by the

U.S. Supreme Court. But eventually, the D&RG was beaten by a force even more formidable than William Strong—the volatile equity markets in the East. The railroad went into receivership. The cowboy brawl at the Royal Gorge of Colorado was eventually settled in a fancy financial office in Boston. It was, after all, just business.

WHILE STRONG FOUGHT his battles in Colorado, Fred took over the depot hotel in Florence, Kansas, and soon received his first review. The *Florence Herald* reported that the new proprietor "has no cards and we don't know his name—but he sets a square meal all the same. Everybody takes breakfast and supper there."

For a restaurant where the food had previously been inedible, that was a rave. Yet Fred, emboldened by the daring of his bosses at the Santa Fe, wanted to try something more ambitious, almost absurdly so. He decided to turn the Santa Fe depot in Florence—a town of eight hundred that no travelers would *ever* visit unless they had to—into a boutique hotel, a destination restaurant. For that, he needed a big-city celebrity chef.

William H. Phillips first made his mark on the culinary world by feeding 500,000 people during the centennial celebration in Philadelphia. The effusive chef—known for charming customers with what one London paper called his "beaming, rubicund, jolly British face"—accomplished this feat as food manager of The Globe, a massive hotel erected alongside Fairmount Park for the tourism onslaught of 1876. Originally trained at the Cardiff Arms in Wales, he currently held one of the top jobs in the hotel world, running the food service at the Palmer House in Chicago.

That was where Fred Harvey first met him, and made the preposterous suggestion that he quit and come to Kansas.

Fred lured Bill Phillips to Florence with the same inducements still used today to entice chefs to leave large institutions for improbable specialty ventures: the promise of a large salary and the freedom to create an oasis in his own image. Together, they began inventing the standards of cuisine, efficiency, and hygiene that Fred Harvey would impose throughout the West.

The two English-born restaurant men immediately upgraded the table settings by ordering Irish linens from Belfast, china and stemware from London, and silver plates from Sheffield. The hotel's dinner menu was also dramatically rethought, creating special meals of ambitious fish and game dishes that brought European cooking styles to the vast varieties of meats and produce available only in rural America. Phillips let it be known that he would pay top dollar to local fishermen, hunters, and farmers for the best of their catch and harvest. And hotel guests who came to hunt and fish—the woods were filled with grouse and quail, the rivers and lakes teeming with black, striped, and spotted bass, pike, carp, buffalo fish, and catfish weighing up to one hundred pounds—were encouraged to allow Bill Phillips to prepare them their own personalized feasts.

The first major press coverage of the resurrected Florence depot hotel—beyond the praises of the local *Herald*—appeared in London. A sporting newspaper called *The Field* had an American correspondent, Samuel Nugent Townshend, who roamed the West seeking ecstatic experiences in shooting, fishing, and eating, and then filing ludicrously overwritten reports under the pseudonym "St. Kames." He was so taken by the cuisine and comforts of Fred's new hotel that he kept inventing excuses to revisit Florence.

When he had traveled on the Santa Fe the previous year, "the management of the refreshment rooms . . . was shocking," Townshend wrote. But now that Fred had taken over and installed Bill Phillips, the food was "splendid," with fish and game breakfasts, dinners, and suppers that were "marvels of luxury and neatness . . . suited to the most exigent or epicurean taste." He would often find himself in another western city, in a cramped hotel room with "a nasty bed," wondering if it was possible "to reach Florence and our compatriot Phillips in time for breakfast."

While in Florence, Townshend spent some time chatting with Fred about hunting. Fred was respectable with a shotgun and an able horseman. As his son Fordie got older—he was now twelve—Fred often took him bird hunting, and they did some fishing as well. But Fred did have his concerns about the addictive nature of the sport. He told Townshend about the jocular retiree "Uncle Joe" Irwin, whom they had hired to take hotel guests out hunting and fishing. While it was all well and good that Uncle Joe could regale guests with the story of how he caught 202 pounds of bass in one day, the only reason the old man needed the job was that he had squandered his considerable earnings and acumen.

"In the midst of the most intricate and urgent business," Fred explained, "he would never sacrifice a good day's shooting or fishing, hunting or boating. And this brought him to ruin."

The Florence depot hotel quickly became so successful that its rooms were constantly sold out. Since it was only a hundred miles from the main office in Topeka, Santa Fe executives brought their wives and clients there. Locals were so enthralled with the food that they were able to overcome their annoyance at train passengers receiving preferential treatment. While the restaurant was open to the public, all service to local customers was put on hold whenever a Santa Fe train approached, which happened five times a day, sometimes on schedule, sometimes not. The number of train passengers planning to eat in the dining room or the lunchroom was telegraphed ahead from the previous station, and their places were set for them before the train arrived. If too many local people were dining at the time, some were asked to give up their seats; the others had to wait until the passengers had eaten before being served.

Local patronage was important, but above all else the trains had to be fed.

Fred was so impressed by how quickly Bill Phillips made a major impact on his business that he decided to give him a contract and a share of the profits. The deal reportedly made Phillips the best-paid man in Florence, earning more than even the local bank president.

With Phillips in place, Fred expanded the Florence hotel and restaurant even further, adding not only more dining space but also offices, hotel rooms, and large "sample rooms" where traveling salesmen could show their lines to local customers. He also gave the place a proper name; instead of the Santa Fe depot hotel and eating house, it would now be known by the more elegant appellation "The Clifton." Fountains and a new sign were installed out front; inside were luxuries Florentines had yet to enjoy—even indoor plumbing.

"Every Tuesday and Friday, the ladies of Florence can have use of the bath rooms at The Clifton Hotel," the *Herald* proudly announced. "This will be a luxury which will be duly appreciated. All other days the bath rooms are open to gentlemen."

CHAPTER 9

COWBOY VICTUALER

L AKIN, KANSAS, WAS ONE OF MANY DUSTY WESTERN TOWNS willed into being by the arrival of the railroad. In fact, it was one of the first in which the Santa Fe acknowledged its creationist powers, naming the hamlet after one of its employees, D. L. Lakin, who ran the department that sold the land on either side of the Santa Fe's tracks.

While The Clifton Hotel in Florence got most of the attention, Fred was also transforming another Santa Fe depot hotel way out west in Lakin, the last stop beyond Dodge City before reaching the Colorado border. The Lakin hotel didn't have the same epicurean ambitions as Florence, but it still featured excellent service, imported table settings, and consistently good, fresh food, making it the best place to eat and sleep in the Wild West.

The Lakin depot hotel quickly became Fred's western home away from home. He even had family working there, his niece and nephew from England. His sister Annie had visited America with her children after her marriage to Charles Baumann, a Swiss count, went sour. When twenty-one-year-old Charles and his seventeen-year-old sister, Florence, decided they wanted to stay in the United States, Uncle Fred gave them both jobs.

In Lakin, Fred also got involved with ranching, a business that had intrigued him since he first started working with cattlemen as a freight agent. He found a herd for sale called the XY: ten thousand head of cattle with an "XY" brand on the left side and a signature cropping of the left ear. He spent $4,000 ($89,000) for a one-quarter interest in the herd, and an option to purchase the rest. But he decided to use that option for a more inventive investment in his own future. He reached out to William Strong at the Santa Fe and offered his boss the chance to be his partner in the deal.

Fred had become wiser in the ways of the train industry. He understood that if he wanted to play the game at a higher level, it couldn't hurt to be in business with his bosses. While the Santa Fe was considered one of the more scrupulous of the railroads, its executives were not above getting a taste of a side venture.

Soon Harvey and Strong were partners in the XY herd, along with another well-placed Santa Fe executive who was invited to buy in. They were looking forward to being ranch owners—as close as three guys who wore waistcoats and watch fobs would come to being cowboys. Strong even wrote excitedly to Fred about the prospect of coming west so he could watch "the round-up" of his own cattle.

FRED ENJOYED LAKIN so much that in the summer of 1879, he brought his family there and invited the entire town out for a Fourth of July picnic.

Fred and Sally's family had grown. They now had five children: Ford, Minnie, May, Byron, and a brand-new baby daughter, Sybil. Besides the kids, three servants, and a rotating cast of dogs in the house and horses in their small stable, they had Sally's mother, Mary Mattas, living with them now. The tiny Czech woman still spoke little English, but she communicated her love for her grandkids in other ways, such as praying for each of them in front of their bedroom doors each night.

The whole family came along on the trip to Lakin, as well as Sally's younger sister Maggie from St. Louis, who, at twenty-three, was more than ready to find a husband.

Fred chose Chouteau's Island for the Fourth of July picnic, which was hosted by him and Sally and catered by his hotel. Prominent politicians, businessmen, and ranchers from all over southwestern Kansas flocked to the lovely spot in the Arkansas River, a Santa Fe Trail landmark since the early nineteenth century, when a small band of trappers were said to have held off an attack by several hundred Pawnees.

The very young town of Lakin did not yet have an American flag for the celebration, so a group of local ladies volunteered to make one.

Led by Mrs. Carrie Davies—a housekeeper at Fred's hotel and the wife of rancher "Wild Horse" Davies—they hand stitched the stripes and all thirty-eight stars. On the day of the event, the entire Davies clan proudly rode together, on horseback and in coaches, behind their flag bearer, C. O. Chapman. His mettle was tested, however, when the section of the Arkansas River they needed to ford to reach Chouteau's Island turned out to be deeper in the middle than expected. Suddenly Chapman and his horse were completely submerged. He was barely able to hold the flagpole above his head until someone could rescue it—and then him.

Among the guests at the picnic was Colonel R. J. "Jack" Hardesty, one of the richest ranchers in the West. Hardesty lived in nearby Sargent, but his cattle, branded with a half circle over a lazy *S*, grazed farther south in "No Man's Land," the thirty-four-mile stretch that had remained unclaimed when Texas declared statehood in the 1840s and later became the odd little panhandle of Oklahoma. (The town of Hardesty, Oklahoma, was named for him.)

The Kentucky-born Hardesty had made his first fortune going west to mine in the 1860s, and he invested that money, including $10,000 ($252,000) worth of gold he claimed to have carried in his belt, in Texas cattle. He had a reputation for being a gentleman rancher—his cowboys knew better than to swear in front of him—and a generous host. Hardesty often sponsored grand parties: His Christmas ball in Dodge City was considered *the* social event of the year. But except for his golden retriever, Tick, he was alone at age forty-six, one of the most eligible bachelors west of the Mississippi.

Until he met Fred Harvey's sister-in-law Maggie Mattas.

After the picnic, everyone went home to change for the July 4th gala at the Lakin depot hotel, for which a band was imported from Pueblo. As the ball began, Fred and Sally Harvey were asked to lead the Grand March. At one point in the evening, Sally saw her petite sister dancing with muscular Jack Hardesty—who looked every bit the western gentleman in his full beard, Stetson hat, and highly buffed cowboy boots—and knew that Maggie had finally met a man who would change her life the way Fred Harvey had changed hers.

Only months later, the couple was married at the Harveys' home in Leavenworth. They moved into a fine new house in Dodge City, just a block away from the town's most infamous tourist attraction—the

Boot Hill Cemetery, where all the desperadoes from the early days were allegedly buried with their boots on.

WHEN THE SANTA FE asked Fred to expand into a fourth eating house, in La Junta, Colorado, he decided it was time to end his involvement with the competing Kansas Pacific. This meant finally admitting that he and his old friend Jepp Rice should formally dissolve the languishing partnership that had so strained their relationship over the past few years. It also meant that Fred was walking away from a steady source of income, but he had many others: He was still General Western Freight Agent for the Chicago, Burlington & Quincy, and he had money coming in from the Santa Fe eating houses, the XY ranch, his investments in real estate and private mortgages, and other deals he was juggling.

So, on a Thursday in early October 1879, Fred strode around the corner from his Leavenworth office to the redbrick building of the First National Bank, where he waited in line to see his regular teller. Fred handed the young man one last deposit of $1,398.91 ($31,100) for Harvey & Rice and then told him to close out the account.

"Give me half," he told the teller, "and place the other half to the personal credit of Rice. Here and now, the firm of Harvey & Rice ceases to exist."

Fred also moved his growing XY herd closer to the Santa Fe tracks. He and his partners bought huge tracts of land, consolidating two of the biggest ranches in southwestern Kansas and adding a horse farm. Their XY range now spread over four thousand square miles, bounded in the north by the Arkansas River and the Santa Fe railroad near Lakin and Garden City, extending down through the Oklahoma Panhandle and into Texas, where it was bounded in the south by the Canadian River, not far from Amarillo. This made the XY ranch almost as big as the state of Connecticut. (It also meant that Fred Harvey owned what later became the town of Holcomb, the site of the infamous Clutter murders that inspired Truman Capote's *In Cold Blood*.)

During roundup time, there were often more than two hundred cowboys roaming Fred's land, looking for XY cattle or others that had strayed from nearby herds. At night there would be huge campouts where cowboys would drink and share stories, some of which may have even been true. They howled over the yarn about young Eli "Romeo" Hall, who turned in two rustlers, "Longtoed Pete" and "Cross-Eyed Swiggett," for stealing Fred Harvey's cattle, and then turned down the $1,000 ($22,265) reward because Hall said he would rather just have a job on the Harvey ranch.

Ironically, even though Fred now owned several thousand head of cattle, they did not provide him easier access to meat for his restaurants. Since the West had few slaughterhouses and scant refrigeration, cattle were still being shipped live on railroad cars back to Chicago or Kansas City to be butchered. So, the farther out his eating house chain extended, the harder it was to find dependable local sources for the amount of beef he needed. This was a considerable problem, since most of his patrons had become accustomed to eating steak for breakfast, lunch, and dinner. One of the dramatic touches Bill Phillips had initiated in his dining rooms was to have the headwaiter emerge from the kitchen holding a large silver platter of sizzling steaks high in the air, which he served to each customer himself.

Fred made a deal to buy beef for all his locations—and, in so doing, may have invented the practice of large-scale centralized purchasing for national restaurant chains. He chose Slavens & Oburn, the oldest and most successful meatpacking firm in Kansas City, and ordered an entire year's worth of tenderloin steaks at twelve and a half cents ($2.78) per pound. For the first ninety days, he committed to buying at least 15,600 pounds of steaks—a minimum of 1,200 pounds of steaks per week. He would then see if he needed more than that.

With this single steak order, Fred dramatically improved dining west of the Mississippi. Before his arrival, few Westerners had ever been served pink meat. They didn't know quite how to react. One story circulated about a cowboy who was served his first Fred Harvey tenderloin—rare—and didn't know whether to eat it or to brand it.

"I've seen many a critter be hurt worse than that and get well," he quipped.

CHAPTER 10

VIVA LAS VEGAS

LAS VEGAS, NEW MEXICO—THE ONLY LAS VEGAS THAT AMER-
icans knew at the time, since the one in Nevada didn't exist until
1905—had already been transformed once by cutting-edge transportation. It had been an important stagecoach stop on the Santa Fe Trail
since the 1830s, and grew even larger when it was annexed by the
United States after the Mexican-American War, its population an unusual mix of immigrants from Mexico and, later, from Germany and
China.

But nobody in Las Vegas was prepared for the impact made by the
first Santa Fe railroad trains coming over the Raton Pass in the summer of 1879. Within weeks, the best and worst of the Wild West began
migrating there from Dodge City. "Doc" Holliday, the infamous desperado dentist, even moved there from Dodge to set up a practice.

Dr. John Henry Holliday had trained in Philadelphia at one of the
nation's first dental schools (now part of the University of Pennsylvania) and was practicing in Atlanta in the early 1870s when he contracted tuberculosis. He came west hoping the climate would be
curative, and when his hacking cough did not endear him to patients,
he found he could make a much better living using his other natural
talent—gambling. To defend himself, he learned how to shoot a six-
gun, and found his medical training came in handy when deciding
where to plunge a knife.

While he had done much more gambling and fighting than den-
tistry in Dodge City—knocking out more teeth than he ever fixed—
Doc Holliday saw the new train to Las Vegas as a chance to give his
dental practice one last try. As a backup, he also opened a saloon. And

it wasn't long before Holliday killed his first Las Vegan. He got into a fight with a local gunslinger named Mike Gordon, who didn't know any better when Doc Holliday asked if he wanted to step outside and settle their differences. Holliday told him to start shooting whenever he was ready. Within seconds Gordon lay dead on the street with three bullets in his belly.

When the lynch mob came for the trigger-happy dentist, he decided that maybe Las Vegas wasn't the best place for him after all and hightailed it back to Dodge. But other shady characters like Holliday kept pouring into Las Vegas. The crime rate grew so alarming that a group of men, calling themselves "Vigilantes," took out an ad in the local paper, addressed to "Murderers, Confidence Men, Thieves":

> The citizens of Las Vegas have tired of robbery, murder, and other crimes that have made this town a byword in every civilized community. They have resolved to put a stop to crime, [even] if in attaining that end they have to forget the law and resort to a speedier justice than it will afford . . . The flow of blood must and shall be stopped in this community, and the good citizens . . . have determined to stop it, if they have to HANG by the strong arm of FORCE every violator of the law in this country.

Fortunately, none of this deterred many law-abiding citizens from pouring into Las Vegas as well. They found a town with a growing merchant community and a vigorous sense of itself and its place in the West, which was reflected in its lively newspapers. The *Las Vegas Optic* was especially opinionated and often spit-take funny, romanticizing even the creepiest aspects of western life. Its stories were sometimes picked up by national newspapers and clearly inspired the writing style of the dime novels that later popularized legendary gunfights. It was the Las Vegas papers that renamed William Bonney—a local boy gone bad, who had grown up outside of nearby Roswell—Billy the Kid and turned him into the first rock-star bandit. ("We are informed that a purse of three thousand dollars has been raised to effect the recapture of The Kid," the *Optic* reported one Tuesday. "Here is an opportunity for some daring man to engrave his name upon the roll of dead heroes.")

Fred was asked to establish a temporary restaurant in Las Vegas before the Santa Fe had even built a proper depot, so he had his staff work out of three old Santa Fe cars parked on a rarely used side track. One veteran railroader remembered them as "the worst-looking boxcars . . . the company and Harvey could scare up . . . [but] when travelers entered the big side door . . . they gasped with wonderment at what met their gaze. The walls were shiny with fresh paint in the gaudy Indian colors, the tables were spread with heavy milk-white Irish linen and napkins the size of pillow slips, the silverware shone like a French plate mirror, the clean clear glass goblets were filled with ice and nice clear water, and on the tables were large vases filled with wonderful fresh flowers."

But Fred Harvey and the Santa Fe had bigger plans for Las Vegas than retrofitted boxcars, or even another conventional depot eating house. They wanted to cash in on a growing trend in the hotel business: health tourism.

For years, eastern doctors had been sending patients west in the hope that tuberculosis and other illnesses could be cured merely by being in the sunshine and fresh air. (The Stetson cowboy hat, that mainstay of western apparel, had been invented by one such health tourist: John B. Stetson, who came up with the idea while recuperating out west, and revolutionized his family's Philadelphia hat business.) In addition to the therapeutic climate, doctors had a lot of faith in the healing waters of mineral springs.

Six miles north of Las Vegas, in the foothills of the Sangre de Cristo Mountains, there were naturally occurring hot springs that had long been believed to have curative powers. In the 1840s, the U.S. Army had even treated soldiers from the Mexican-American War at the Las Vegas Hot Springs, building an adobe hospital and bathhouse that remained in use until the Civil War. It was reopened in the late 1870s, with a new Hot Springs Hotel and a bathhouse in which the hot mineral water was piped into long, coffin-like metal tubs. Among the guests at the Hot Springs Hotel was Jesse James, who spent a relaxing week there in the summer of 1879 and was reportedly joined for dinner on the evening of July 27 by Billy the Kid.

Within weeks after the first Santa Fe train pulled in to Las Vegas station, the AT&SF bought the Hot Springs and all the land and buildings around them for $102,000 ($2.3 million). The railroad took over the small Hot Springs Hotel, but also set to work planning a massive new facility: one of the nation's first grand health resorts—part spa, part sanitarium. The project was soon wildly off schedule and over budget. Since the AT&SF was having so much success with Fred Harvey's management of its depot properties, Strong asked him to step in and manage the existing hotel while helping oversee the construction of the new resort, which was to be called the Montezuma. When it was completed, Fred's company could run that, too.

The Montezuma project was a huge commitment. It would be bigger and more ambitious than all the properties Fred was managing combined. There was also irony and risk in the idea of a health resort being run by a man struggling with his own chronic illness, a man who could put on a brave face in business situations but was privately still keeping tally in his datebooks of how many days he lost to headaches or neuralgia, and compulsively scribbling down new treatments he wanted to try and medical books he wanted to read.

But the Montezuma was an opportunity Fred could not pass up. The Santa Fe was rapidly building farther west into New Mexico and would want more depot eating houses as the tracks were completed. Besides, Strong had done so well as general manager of the railroad that the board of directors in Boston had decided to elevate him to president of the Santa Fe. If Fred did not commit fully to the fast-growing railroad, he knew Strong could find someone else who would.

Fred, now in his mid-forties, decided to take the big gamble. He gave up his lucrative day job with the Chicago, Burlington & Quincy and devoted himself to turning his four eating houses into a hospitality empire along the Atchison, Topeka & Santa Fe.

DURING THE NEXT YEAR and a half, Fred basically commuted between Leavenworth, Kansas, and Las Vegas, New Mexico. The trip was more than eight hundred miles and took at least three days each way. It was a stunning ride across America's better half, but like any commute, it was exhausting, life-sucking. Fred would ride through the gloriously flat state of Kansas, stopping only to scrutinize his eating houses. He liked to hop off the train while it was still rolling into the station, so he could dash ahead and do a quick inspection before the passengers got off.

When he strode into one of his eating houses, the waitstaff was already standing at attention behind fastidiously set tables in the main dining room or curved wooden counters with spinning stools in the lunchroom. They were poised awaiting the ceremonial gong, which the headwaiter would take out onto the train platform and strike to let passengers know the dining areas were open. It was a dramatic flourish Fred had borrowed from the Logan House in Altoona, the trackside eating house he had so admired as a young railroad warrior.

At the sounding of the gong, the staff was to begin serving dozens of full-course dining room meals—with all the trimmings and table-side preparations, including handmade salad dressings—and just as many hundred flawless lunchroom meals, all within thirty minutes exactly. It was an Olympian culinary feat that had to be repeated, as if effortlessly, every time the train rolled into each of his locations.

During his inspections, Fred stalked through the rooms of his eating houses, peering everywhere and running his hand across random surfaces. If he found anything out of place—a crack, a crease, or the mere smudge of a partial fingerprint—he grabbed one of those costly linen tablecloths and yanked it as hard as he could, sending eight complete place settings flying and shattering on the spotless floor.

"You know better than this," he would say in his clipped British accent, and then withdraw to the manager's office, while the staff scrambled to clean up the mess and reset the table, the headwaiter still poised on the train platform with his mallet in the air, awaiting word that it was safe to bang the gong.

After the long, level ride across Kansas, the train began the climb into Colorado—where Fred stopped to inspect his house at La Junta—and then continued west to Pueblo before heading due south, with the Rocky Mountains visible out the window to his right. At Trinidad, the engine was changed because the ride up into the mountains to the Raton Pass was the steepest and toughest in all of American railroading and required maximum steam. The Santa Fe had commissioned the most powerful engine ever built from the Baldwin Locomotive Works in Philadelphia to make the roller-coaster climb; it was engine #2403, nicknamed the Uncle Dick. As the engine chugged high into the Sangre de Cristo Mountains, Fred could see sections of the old Santa Fe Trail alongside the tracks. At the very top of the Raton Pass, an elevation of almost eight thousand feet, the train slipped into a pitch-black tunnel, almost half a mile long through solid rock and only slightly wider than the cars themselves. He could actually stick his hand out the window and touch the rough-hewn wall.

Just as his eyes adjusted to the dark, the railroad car emerged from the tunnel, and he was confronted with a view of the biggest sky imaginable. From the peak of the Raton Pass, he could see mountains and valleys, forests and deserts, and even several different weather systems hovering over the astounding landscape.

The first stop on the other side of the pass was Raton itself, a small mining and ranching town, and from there it was literally all downhill to Las Vegas. By the time he arrived, he was often so depleted that he spent the next day in a hotel bed—where the ever-nosy *Optic* invariably would report he was holed up sick. And then he would get back to work.

There was so much to do in New Mexico. Besides the Montezuma health resort up in the mountains outside of Las Vegas, the Santa Fe was building a new trackside hotel and eating house right in town while rapidly grading land and laying tracks westward to Albuquerque and south to Mexico. In 1881, with construction still lagging at the Montezuma, the railroad wanted Fred to open three more eating houses in New Mexico.

Ironically, there was *not* going to be a Santa Fe eating house in the railroad's namesake city, Santa Fe. For reasons that were never entirely clear—some combination of the terrain and the local politics being too challenging—the AT&SF bypassed the capital of New Mexico. Instead, its tracks ran some twenty miles *south* of Santa Fe, stopping at the hamlet of Lamy on their way to Albuquerque.

The railroad did build a small branch line that connected Santa Fe to the High Iron at Lamy—and with that, its twenty-year mission to replace the old Santa Fe Trail with train tracks was completed. But Santa Fe, suddenly no longer a major transportation hub, was left to rethink and reinvent itself.

Fred opened a small eating house in the new Lamy depot in 1881 and took over the trackside restaurant and hotel in Raton, the Mountain House. He also set up operations in the dusty new depot in Deming, a tiny town just thirty miles from the Mexican border.

The Deming house was particularly difficult to manage. The location was incredibly isolated, and the few people there were either railroad workers, miners, or criminals on the lam. Almost from opening day, the Deming eating house was repeatedly robbed at gunpoint.

Actually, Fred was trying to establish order and civilization in New Mexico during a time that would later be looked upon as a watershed moment for guns and gunslinging in America. In the course of just a few months, two of the most legendary dramas in cowboy history unfolded in or near the cities where he was working. Billy the Kid, already sentenced to hang for murder, killed two prison guards and escaped, heading first to Las Vegas, where the newspapers carried so many stories of sightings that it seemed as if the sheriff was the only one who *hadn't* seen him. Finally, after two months, he was tracked down to a house in Fort Sumner, New Mexico, by the hard-bitten sheriff of Roswell, Pat Garrett. The twenty-one-year-old outlaw was killed by a single shot that pierced his heart, and in death he became as famous worldwide as he had been in Las Vegas. The shooting was covered in newspapers all over the United States and Europe, and several books were immediately published about the life of "the Kid," including one by Sheriff Pat Garrett himself: *The Authentic Life of Billy, the Kid, the Noted Desperado of the Southwest, Whose Deeds of Daring and Blood Made His Name a Terror in New Mexico, Arizona, and Northern Mexico.*

Only months after Billy's death came the "Gunfight at the OK Corral" in Tombstone, a small mining town just across the Arizona border from the Deming eating house. Sheriff Wyatt Earp, his deputized brothers Morgan and Virgil, and Doc Holliday had a showdown with five unruly cowboys who reportedly were "parading the town for several days, drinking heavily and making themselves obnoxious"— and then refused to surrender their weapons to the lawmen. Thirty seconds and thirty bullets later, three of the cowboys lay dead, a fourth was wounded, and the other had run away. Within days the gunfight was front-page news across the country. "Daring Desperados," the *Leavenworth Times* headline blared, "Three Cow Boys Bite the Dust."

In the middle of all this romanticized Western gun drama, the president of the United States was shot in Washington in early July. James Garfield survived, but one of the bullets was lodged so deeply that it could not be found—even by Alexander Graham Bell, who was enlisted by the White House to invent some sort of magnetic metal-detecting device. The president seemed to be recovering over the next few weeks, but then succumbed in mid-September at the age of forty-nine. While his wife claimed he died peacefully, it was later revealed that he had suffered horribly, his medical care from the nation's best doctors nearly as hazardous as the shooting itself. Along with high doses of quinine and morphine, and frequent sips of brandy, he was treated with calomel, a diuretic later banned as toxic because its active ingredient was mercury. But the most likely cause of the president's torturous demise was the doctors' inability to remove the bullet and close his wound. Originally three and a half inches, the wound was probed so many times by the germy fingers of so many physicians that by the time Garfield died, it was almost twenty inches long, deeply infected, and festering.

FRED CONTINUED TO HAVE troubles in Las Vegas. The doctors at the Hot Springs Hotel—increasingly anxious for the big new Montezuma to be done so they would have more paying patients—were at each other's throats. The Santa Fe had hired a shiny new Harvard-trained physician, William Page, but he clashed with local favorite Dr. N. J. Pettijohn, who had roots in the Las Vegas community. According to accounts in Page's diaries, the two constantly quarreled over patients. One day they got into a screaming match over which one of them was treating Mrs. Charles Bush, a New Orleans socialite.

"If you do not stop talking to her, I will *fix* you!" Pettijohn yelled. "I believe you to be a god-damn old *fraud*!"

"I *know* you to be such!" Page shot back to the "scoundrel."

Actually, employee unrest was a problem for Fred all over New Mexico. He had Bill Phillips come down from Florence to help—still running the hotel there, the jolly British chef had now become Fred's culinary adviser for the entire chain—but nothing seemed to work. New Mexico was a much wilder West than he and the railroad had ever experienced, and the old Santa Fe Trail towns resisted the changes brought by the railroads. In Kansas and Colorado the railroads created many of the communities, but in New Mexico the AT&SF was going into old cities and literally replacing the centers of town. In fact, the area around the Santa Fe depot in Las Vegas was called New Town. Local residents had a love/hate relationship with the railroads, and Fred's restaurants, so visible a symbol of what the trains brought to town, were often the targets of local frustrations. Competing restaurant owners resented Fred because they knew he got better, fresher ingredients than they did—and paid less for them, because the railroad waived his freight charges. There were often break-ins at the eating houses or the parked refrigerator cars: not for cash, but to steal those gorgeous aged steaks.

Some customers also resented the dress code Fred was instituting in his eating houses: While almost any outfit was allowed in the lunch-rooms, men had to wear jackets (which were provided if they didn't have one) in order to eat in the main dining rooms. In dress-casual New Mexico, this rule was particularly rankling.

More than ever before, Fred was finding out he had his share of enemies—who were all too happy to run to their friends at the local newspapers whenever they heard about difficulties at his restaurants. One day the *Las Vegas Optic* reported histrionically that Fred was los-ing control of his entire operation:

"Eating Establishment Excitements: Whooping It Up in Sad Shape for a Well-Known Hotel Proprietor," the headline blared on September 12, 1881.

"Fred Harvey . . . is having a terrible time of it and seems to be gaining an unsavory reputation," the *Optic* went on to explain, noting that the manager and night clerk at the Las Vegas depot hotel had quit, and at the Hot Springs Hotel, Fred had "acted so outlandishly 'off' " that his manager there was also leaving.

In Deming, not only had Fred fired the manager; he reportedly heaved him out the front door and onto the train platform, "and the dining room equipment followed after him in quick order." The mer-curial Englishman was also blamed for the "grub" in Deming being so poor that "the beef stake was fairly alive with little crawling things commonly called maggots." He was accused of "a lack of proper deco-rum," and the *Optic* hoped "for the sake of his reputation, that things will run smoother in the future and that his name will not be contam-inated by town talk, as it has been."

Fred immediately contacted the paper to tell his side of the story, and the next day, under the headline "Harvey Heard," he explained that the trouble was "incited by chronic howlers," and it was only a question of whether he or his employees would "dictate management of the houses." He made it clear that the employees were fired because they were incompetent and had disobeyed orders. "It's no easy task to operate hotels in New Mexico, so far distant from each other," he said.

"But I believe I have the ability to get along with detrimental circumstances about as well as the next fellow. And that's all."

Still, keeping his staff in line remained difficult. Several days after the news stories, he visited the new hotel doctor seeking treatment for "a blow on the right temple." The injury was caused by a servant opening a door into Fred's head. It was charitably described in the physician's log as "accidental."

CHAPTER 11

WE ARE *IN* THE WILDS,
WE ARE NOT *OF* THEM

BACK IN KANSAS, SALLY AND THE CHILDREN WERE HAVING A
hard time with Fred's absences. They had become accustomed to his
periodic travels as a freight agent, but looked forward to the long
bonding times at home between trips. Now he was gone more than
ever, and returned more enervated than they had ever seen him.

"Papa, when are you coming home?" his daughter Minnie, now ten,
wrote to him in Las Vegas. "Mama cried all day Sunday because you
was not home."

He was missing important milestones in his family's life, not just
birthdays, anniversaries, and school pageants, but other memorable
moments. Cities across the country were just starting to offer rudimentary home phone service, but Fred wasn't home the day the Harveys
got their first telephone in the dining room. He was also away when
Leavenworth finished installing its first electrical generator, and for the
first time electric lights were visible in a few commercial buildings.

Ford was already away at prep school in Racine, Wisconsin. Fred
had missed the tail end of his eldest son's childhood. It even fell to Sally
to send Ford off with words of wisdom, as she inscribed his photo
album: "Desire not to live long, but to live well; How long we live, not
years, but actions tell." And the other kids were growing up largely
without their father.

By now, Sally had grown accustomed to attending Leavenworth social events alone. Her biggest distraction was playing cards, especially
euchre. The game was all the rage across the country, a form of light
gambling acceptable even in religious communities, the shift from
poker to euchre a sign of becoming more "civilized." Euchre was so

wildly popular in Leavenworth that the society columns were beginning to read like sports coverage, reporting not only what people wore to card parties and what they ate but who took the prizes in the "progressive euchre" tournaments. Sally played in those, but also had other housewives over for more casual games, and perhaps a drink or two.

Fred did manage to get home for major holidays, though, and these were warm and memorable. The Harveys traditionally celebrated Christmas with Byron Schermerhorn's family, and they always had a raucously good time. The younger children would go wild together: Schermerhorn's daughter Nell would never forget little Byron Harvey shouting down to Sally, "Mother, make the girls put some clothes on! They're running all over upstairs without any."

Fred's Christmas gift from his best friend would be a barrel of pure corn whiskey, which was put out in the stable and siphoned into bottle after bottle during the visit. After a few drinks Byron would start making jokes about Fred's dogs. He got along fine with Charlie, the elderly King Charles spaniel with halitosis, but he was scared to death of Fred's Old English bulldog Crib, which was descended from a famous bullbaiting dog of the same name. He claimed that if he ever met up with Crib outside of the Harveys' yard, "I'd certainly cut off one of my arms and throw it to him."

In fact, one year Byron conspired with Fred's neighbors to lobby for the dog's exile. He arranged for almost half of Leavenworth to have their servants carry identical holiday messages over to the Harvey home.

"If you will remove that bulldog from the front steps," each handwritten note read, "we would like to call on you."

JUST AFTER CHRISTMAS 1881, Fred walked briskly over to his bank to offer his favorite teller, twenty-two-year-old David Benjamin, a position that would change both of their lives.

Cherubic, charming, and quietly assertive, with wire-rim glasses, black hair parted just off the middle, and a neatly trimmed mustache, Dave was bright and ambitious and, much to Fred's delight, loved talking about their common homeland, Great Britain. The Benjamin family had left London when Dave was young, relocating to Leavenworth, where they became cornerstones of the large local Jewish community centered at Temple B'nai Jeshurun, the first synagogue in Kansas. Dave was the eldest of three close brothers, who by their teens were already impressing business leaders in Leavenworth. As Dave worked his way up at the First National Bank of Leavenworth, where Fred Harvey and other prominent men sought his counsel, his middle brother, Alfred, was becoming a protégé of one of Fred's closest friends, Colonel Abernathy, in his large furniture business. The youngest brother, Harry, was a rising attorney at the prominent Leavenworth firm of William C. Hook and Lucien Baker.

Fred came to Dave's window and made a withdrawal. While passing currency through the steel bars at his station, they started to chat.

"Do you really plan to be a banker for your entire life?" Dave would later remember Fred asking.

"Yes, sir, I have always intended to be a banker." It had, in fact, been Dave's childhood dream.

"Lots of bookkeeping experience?" Fred asked.

"Lots of it."

"I need a good general accountant for my business. I think you would like that better than a bank."

"Yes," Dave said, surrendering his dream for a better one without a moment's hesitation. "I think I would."

Fred no longer had much of a business presence in Leavenworth; he had long ago sold his ticket operation there, and just maintained a small office in the Hannibal & St. Joseph depot. His books had been kept by a railroad accountant at the Santa Fe general office in Topeka, J. J. Blower, but he knew it was time he had his own business manager, somebody to oversee the numbers for his growing chain the same way that Bill Phillips in Florence was overseeing the food.

He also knew that with all the time he was spending away from his family, especially now that Ford was away at college, it might help the situation if he had a trusted associate in Leavenworth. Dave could not only do his books, he could help him stay in better touch with Sally and the kids when he left civilized Kansas and returned to the pistol-packing patrons of the Southwest.

AFTER SEVERAL GRUELING weeks back in New Mexico in early 1882, Fred appeared to have finally made some progress at the Hot Springs

Hotel. The *Optic* reported that "things are now in such a shape that the guests are beginning to murmur, because they have nothing to grumble about."

With the construction at the Montezuma looking as though it might actually come to an end soon, both the railroad and the local physicians began publicizing the place, especially the curative powers of the hot springs. The water itself was frequently analyzed by different experts, and each time a new element was found, it was added to the list at the top of the letterhead and on all the promotional materials. One day a visitor, Professor Hally, announced that "the waters are especially adapted to the ailments of the left kidney." But the resident physician, Pettijohn, went a step further. According to the *Optic,* he claimed the waters "will cure anything from a sore thumb to unrequited love. He even goes so far as to say that three straight drinks of the water per day will keep a man on good terms with his mother-in-law."

After inspecting the Montezuma, Fred headed back east for a cross-country shopping spree, picking out furnishings, cookware, dishes, silver, and stemware for his new hotel dining room. He also visited his favorite hotels in St. Louis, Chicago, and New York and shopped for staff, pulling aside chefs, concierges, maître d's, waiters, and housekeepers he liked to let them know of the wonderful opportunities at the Montezuma. In Boston, he met with the corporate executives at the Santa Fe office there, which also gave him a chance to spend time with his favorite coffee purveyors, Caleb Chase and James Sanborn—later known just as Chase & Sanborn—who roasted a special blend that was being used in all of Fred's restaurants.

As the last touches were being put on the Montezuma, the railroad built a six-mile branch line from town so that guests could be brought by Santa Fe train all the way from the Midwest to the front entrance of the new hotel. And on the morning of Sunday, April 16, 1882, several dozen well-dressed men and ladies took their places in four lavishly appointed Pullman cars at the Kansas City station. Among the passengers were Sally Harvey, the Harveys' close friends Colonel and Mrs. Abernathy, Elizabeth Custer (George's widow), and Kansas City meat magnate S. B. Armour and his wife. They were joined along the way by well-known Mexican-American politician and businessman Don Miguel A. Otero and editors from newspapers in Chicago, Cincinnati, Kansas City, Topeka, and Leavenworth.

Also on the train was that inevitable, junket-loving American correspondent for *The Field,* Samuel "St. Kames" Townshend, who over the years had become good buddies with Fred Harvey and Bill Phillips. Townshend was part of the in-train entertainment, as he and a half-dozen other guests amused themselves by putting on a "sacred concert . . . in which all the familiar camp meeting melodies were grandly rendered," according to the *Optic.* "The singing was kept up until 11 o'clock and there was little sleep in any of the Pullmans until it subsided."

When the guests arrived at the new Montezuma hotel depot, they were met by a flock of bellmen who whisked away their bags, leaving them to stroll leisurely across the Gallinas River footbridge and along a small path from which the hotel was barely visible for the trees. Then, suddenly, the massive 270-room, four-story wooden structure loomed on their left—and when they were done staring, a turn to the right revealed a broad, lush park with fountains, footpaths, lawn tennis courts, archery ranges, even a miniature zoo.

That evening, there was a banquet in the main dining room, a forty-by-seventy-foot hall with floor-to-ceiling windows topped with stained-glass transoms. It was lit by eight massive crystal chandeliers, each with four gas jets, and adjoining it was a separate serving room equipped with carving tables and built-in steam to heat the trays.

The feast began with bluepoint oysters, followed by a consommé of green sea turtle—made from turtles harvested in the Gulf of Mexico and kept alive in a man-made pool outside the hotel. Then came an array of succulent dishes: fresh California salmon and mountain trout; spring lamb with French peas; tenderloin of beef with truffles and stuffed tomatoes; sweetbreads braised with mushrooms; pâté; asparagus with butter sauce; deer with currant jelly and watercress; and broiled teal duck. The dessert spread included Queen's pudding; lemon, coconut, and apricot pies; various jellies; Muscatine ice; California fruits; and a dazzling array of cheeses.

And after the meal, of course, came the toasts, dozens of them. The first ones were "to the press . . . men of brains, energy and education" whose words were disseminated by "the greatest and grandest medium through which intelligence is conveyed to a civilized world." There were similarly effusive toasts "to the railroads"—which William Strong and the assembled Santa Fe brass accepted warmly—and "to the doctors." This included not only the physicians caring for hotel guests but the Montezuma's special medical friends around the globe who presumably would be prescribing the hot springs "cure" and New Mexico's healing climate. They went on to toast the great territory of New Mexico and the American hotel industry.

And then they raised their crystal glasses one last time, with all eyes turned to a proud but depleted Fred Harvey. He acknowledged their accolades with a pursed smile and eyes full of weary relief.

"Entertainment is the soul of my business," he said, "and I can only hope that we have so satisfied everyone here tonight that they know they can always expect a courteous reception here at the Las Vegas hot springs."

And with that, the dining hall was cleared of tables, Professor Helms' Famous Fourth Cavalry Orchestra set up and sounded the Grand March, and the Montezuma Ball was under way. While there were only fourteen numbers listed on the printed dance card, the frolicking started at 9:30 p.m., and the band was still keeping "feet in a bustle" until sunrise.

Fred, however, had retired early, long before his usual bedtime of 11:00 p.m., and the next morning was unable to leave his room, or even get out of bed. The *Optic*, which sometimes appeared to be receiving more medical information about high-profile patients than the patients got themselves, reported that Fred was "dangerously ill . . . no visitors are admitted to his room today." Fortunately, he recovered within a day or two, because the hotel was booked solid.

MANY OF THOSE reservations were the result of a new American social phenomenon: group tours called Raymond Excursions. Organized in major cities by the Boston-based Raymond & Whitcomb vacation company, they were the latest thing in leisure travel.

England's famed Thomas Cook travel agency had made its name booking European Grand Tours, which cultured people were expected to take at least once. They were both a travel experience and a social one, since it was common for groups who had "Grand Toured" together to remain close friends, hold lavish reunions, and even privately publish accounts of their journeys.

Raymond & Whitcomb had started out organizing regional trips—a group from Boston, New York, Philadelphia, or Washington would travel together to Niagara Falls or even the coal country of western Pennsylvania, which was considered an exotic tourist attraction. But now the hot Raymond Excursion was the grand tour of America, back and forth across the country over fifty-nine days, for an all-expenses-paid fare of $450 ($9,777).

A group of 150 Raymond "excursionists" had left the Boston area on Pullmans two weeks before and arrived at the Montezuma on April 21, 1882, at six in the evening, in time for dinner and perhaps a soak in the mineral baths. They were off the next morning—Montezuma porters complaining about their meager tips—and headed south to Deming, where the Santa Fe met the Southern Pacific, whose tracks hugged the Mexican border across Arizona into southern California. From there, the Pullmans carrying the Raymond excursionists continued north to visit Yosemite and later stay at the only western resort in the same league as the Montezuma: the Del Monte, which the Union Pacific had built in Monterey. Finally they connected with the transcontinental railway heading east through Nevada, Utah, Wyoming, and Nebraska, crossing the Missouri River, and returning to civilization. As they headed home, other groups of Raymond excursionists were already departing from Boston and Philadelphia to become American grand tourists.

The Montezuma attracted all kinds—the well, the "worried well," and the truly ill—from America, Europe, South America, even Asia. One of its first celebrated international guests was British army officer Captain Henry John Brinsley Manners, the eighth Duke of Rutland. When Captain Manners arrived, he immediately announced his intention "to live on the grounds in a tent, in the manner of the wild, free trappers and hunters of the region."

Fred did his best to talk the duke out of it.

"Captain Manners," he said, "while it is true we are *in* the wilds, we are not *of* them."

When Manners insisted, Fred let him pitch a tent, but only under two conditions. The captain had to take his meals in the main dining room—and, like all the other men, wear a jacket while eating. He also had to answer nature's call in the hotel's handsomely appointed bathrooms, and not among the bluegrass and shade trees they had labored so diligently to grow in New Mexico.

After the hotel had been open for six months, Fred hosted a group at the Montezuma who were on a junket to Mexico—organized by the

Santa Fe and his former employers at the Burlington, and led by his friend and fellow Burlington freight agent Edward Payson Ripley. In fact, Fred met the train in Pueblo and rode with the large group of agents from railroads all over the country down to Chihuahua—or "Che! Wah! Wah!" as the dozens of jovial excursionists called it. The entire trip was documented by journalist George Street, who was voted the group "historian" and made it very clear in his account how much the large group of men enjoyed meeting captivating dark-eyed "señoritas"—including several dozen local women who came onto their private train to tour the luxurious Pullmans. Fred had to laugh as the men literally tripped over themselves rushing to offer guided tours.

Some excursionists decided to stay one night in a Mexican hotel, rather than in their Pullman berths, and had quite an adventure: Several of them went out to a local casino and then found themselves locked out of the inn, so they had to sleep on park benches. Others who stayed in the hotel slept with their clothes and boots on, their money and prized belongings in their pockets, because the doors had no locks and the windows were wide open.

They were all relieved when the train returned them to New Mexico so they could luxuriate in Fred's hospitality at the Montezuma, where "adjectives fail to express the excellence of the dinner" and the railroad agents danced all night with "as fair partners as ever graced a ball-room." At 2:00 a.m., the orchestra ended with "Home Sweet Home," and as they left, several members of the group broke into a rousing rendition of "Good Night Ladies." The next morning, they got a complimentary visit to the bathhouses for Turkish baths, Russian baths, mud packs, and other treatments they had never even considered, let alone tried. They walked through the baths wrapped in sheets and then were shown into their individual rooms, where they sat on small stools and the doors closed behind them. Then:

> a thousand jolts of hot water suddenly strike you like needles, from all directions . . . and the boiling process begins. You gradually feel yourself melting away, and wonder how much of you will be left to take home to your family; but before you are entirely evaporated, the attendant makes his appearance, asks you how you feel, just to see if whether you can speak yet, opens the prison door and leads you to the next room. There you are put through a course of spouts. Hot and cold water are fired at you

alternately; you are laid on a marble slab, drenched with soap-suds, scrubbed with a brush until you think that the able-bodied attendant has mistaken you for a pine floor, shampooed until your skin is as smooth as the marble slab you are lying on, spanked with a paddle or some other weapons till you are sore; your joints are all pulled, twisted and bent, dislocated and re-set, and after being drowned once or twice more you are rubbed down with dry towels, taken into a warm room and put to bed, where you may stay till you have recovered and feel well enough to get up and dress. Going again in to the open air, you feel like a bird, fly across the bridge, prance around the balcony, and then enjoy the best and biggest breakfast you have ever had.

After breakfast, some of the excursionists went hiking in local ravines or watched Indian women wash their clothes in one of the bubbling hot springs. Others remained at the hotel, chatting with the ladies in the parlor or retiring to the basement to play billiards or try their hand at the bowling alleys. There was yet another banquet that night, and they departed in the morning. Fred took the train with them as far as Raton and bid them farewell, but the group had a hard time getting his hospitality out of their minds. They voted to create an association to commemorate their ten days together, and meet for dinner once a year. They named it the Montezuma Club, and after electing officers, and drafting a resolution thanking the Santa Fe railroad, they broke into song, ending with their war chant:

"Che! Wah! Wah! Hurrah! Hurrah! Hurrah!"

CHAPTER 12

HARVEY GIRLS

Wᴴɪʟᴇ ᴛʜᴇ Mᴏɴᴛᴇᴢᴜᴍᴀ'ꜱ ʟᴀʀɢᴇ, ᴡᴇʟʟ-ᴛʀᴀɪɴᴇᴅ ꜱᴛᴀꜰꜰ ᴡᴀꜱ earning accolades, Fred's problems were mounting all over New Mexico. One day, he received a wire from his manager in Lamy, requesting help after a "gang of gamblers and confidence men" had taken over the town and robbed all the Santa Fe employees. Actually, the thugs were now ordering all their meals at the Santa Fe eating house and then refusing to pay. When the manager finally got up the nerve to tell the men he wouldn't serve them anymore, they pulled their guns and told him to get out of town.

Fred arrived in Lamy on the next train, accompanied by his scariest-looking employee in Las Vegas: John Stein, the hulking cashier at the Montezuma. They were sitting in the restaurant the following morning when a dozen desperadoes entered, demanding to eat. When refused service, they asked for the manager.

Fred approached them. "What do you want with the manager?" he asked.

"We want to hang him," they said.

"Well, I hope you won't do that, because he's a good manager and I need him to run the place. However . . . I don't need *him*," he said, turning his gaze to the massive Stein, "and you can hang him as often as you like. But as long as he's *alive*, you pay for your food or you don't stay."

Big John Stein stared at the men, unblinking, until they tossed some money on a table and left. Then he and Fred had breakfast and waited for the eastbound train to take them back to the Montezuma.

By this point, Fred was no longer surprised by the holdups; a certain number of Santa Fe trains and depots were always going to be robbed, it was just the cost of doing business. But what he could not abide were the continuing racial problems he saw at his new eating houses.

Western restaurants commonly hired black men as waiters and bus-boys. But many cowboys were former Confederate soldiers who had fled the South because they could not imagine living in peace among freed slaves. The cowboys' prejudice against black workers was often more extreme than any tensions they had with Indians—whom they at least feared, and sometimes grudgingly respected.

The truth was that Fred Harvey's black male waiters in New Mexico got little respect and often lived in fear. They had every reason to believe that, at any time, they might need to defend themselves against their own customers.

"A colored waiter at the Depot dropped a huge revolver from his hip pocket to the floor of the dining hall at the supper hour last evening," the *Optic* reported. "It is being discovered daily that hotel waiters are a persecuted class, and to keep off their enemies they are required to pack big guns around with them."

In the early spring of 1883, Fred received word of a drunken fight among the beleaguered all-black waitstaff at his eating house in Raton. The manager reportedly told Fred there had been a midnight brawl and "several darkies had been carved beyond all usefulness." There was also a more elaborate version of the story circulating, in which the intoxicated waiters had not only fought each other with knives and guns but accidentally shot and killed a Mojave spectator. Tribal leaders were supposedly demanding the life of a waiter in return. When told the shooting was accidental, the Indians declared they "would be satisfied to shoot one of the Harvey waiters by accident."

Fred jumped on the next train to Raton. He was traveling with young Tom Gable, a family friend from Leavenworth whom he had watched grow up. The Gables and the Harveys lived on the same block of Linn Street; Fred had been friendly with Tom's late father, Barnabas, a successful farmer, and Sally was still very close to his mother, Mary. Fred had known Tom as smart and able from the time he started working in the Leavenworth post office as a teenager. Now thirty-one, with a wife and a baby, Tom had let Fred know he had ambitions of finally leaving Leavenworth, and hoped there might be a place for him in the eating house business.

In Raton, Tom watched in fascination as "old Fred lit like a bomb," instantly firing the manager and the waitstaff. As Tom would later re-call it, Fred then turned to him and said *he* should become the new manager in Raton and move his young family there.

"I had no restaurant experience," Tom said, "but one did not argue with Fred Harvey."

The two of them talked about how the situation in Raton might be improved, and Tom insisted he would take the job only if Fred would let him try something completely different. He wanted to replace all the black male waiters with women—but not local women. He wanted to import young white single women from Kansas. He thought they would be easier to manage, less likely to "get likkered up and go on tears."

It was a radical idea. Still, one of the things Fred relished most about management was acting on the brainstorms of his employees. He had always hired some female servers for less hostile locations—his houses for the Kansas Pacific had a few waitresses, and so did the original Santa Fe eating houses, starting with The Clifton Hotel in Florence. One of the original waitresses there had been Matilda Legere, a sixteen-year-old from Belgium, who never forgot the first thing Fred Harvey ever said to her: "Don't throw the dishes so hard or you'll break them." In fact, as early as 1880, when Lakin, Kansas, was still the "far West" for the Santa Fe, there were young women on the waitstaff, including Fred's niece, Florence.

Still, while female servers may have worked in Kansas, it was considered far too dangerous to have single women waiting on tables in forward positions in New Mexico. There were, according to the old joke, "no *ladies* west of Dodge City and no women west of Albuquerque." But that was exactly why Tom Gable believed Fred should try it. He thought the move could have a positive, calming influence, first and foremost on the men working at the eating house and the train depot but also, perhaps, on the customers as well. The women could help alleviate racial tensions, and maybe even make the cowboys a little more gentlemanly.

They would also be a welcome addition to the community, because the West was desperate for women. Recent stories in the *Omaha Bee* and the *Laramie Boomerang* had bemoaned "The Scarcity of Women Out West," citing data from the recently tallied U.S. census. Overall, there were one million more men than women in the United States. While the eastern states had "large excesses of females," the farther west one traveled, the more the numbers painted a man's world, and a lonely man's world at that. Some of the western states had a two-to-one "surplus of males."

Fred agreed to let Tom Gable try his idea. They sent cables back to Kansas—where Sally, Tom's mother, Mary, and his wife, Clara, and Dave Benjamin and his wife, Julia, started reaching out to local single women who might agree to be trained by Fred Harvey for a good-paying job.

"And that," Gable later explained, "is how I brought civilization to New Mexico. Those waitresses were the first respectable women the cowboys and miners had ever seen—that is, outside of their own wives and mothers. Those roughnecks learned manners!"

AMONG THE FIRST HARVEY waitresses with the courage to serve in Raton was Minnie O'Neal, a beautiful eighteen-year-old from Leavenworth whose father worked on the railroad. When she first showed interest in the job, her mother forbade it—waitressing, especially out west, was not an occupation for a "good girl." But then her parents separated, and the family suddenly needed the money. Fred was offering $17.50 ($388) a month, plus tips—decent pay, especially considering that he was also offering to provide room, board, and transportation.

Leaving home for the first time in her life, Minnie took the train from Leavenworth to New Mexico, stopping along the way for meals at Fred Harvey eating houses, where she began to understand what would be expected of her. After three days on the train, she was treated to the roller-coaster ride over the Raton Pass and then the big sky of New Mexico, until the brakes brought the train to a shrieking halt at the Santa Fe depot in Raton. It was a small, two-story red building in the middle of a mountainside frontier town of wood-frame saloons, stores, and houses.

The moment Minnie arrived, Tom Gable laid out the rules he and Fred were developing. She would live with the other waitresses in a dormitory attached to the hotel, and they had hired a female live-in chaperone to keep a watchful eye on them. They had to be in bed by eleven o'clock—except on Friday nights, when the eating house sponsored a town social. That was the only time Minnie was allowed to be seen in the hotel in street clothes. Otherwise, she was required to wear a uniform: a plain black long-sleeved, floor-length woolen dress with a just-short-of-clerical "Elsie" collar, along with black shoes and stockings. To complete the outfit, she would wear a starched white apron from neck to ankle, which had to be changed immediately whenever the slightest spot showed. Her hair was to be kept plain and simple, preferably tied back with a single white ribbon. Makeup was forbidden: The house manager would take a damp cloth and wipe it over each girl's face to make sure. Minnie had to be dressed this way during her entire waitressing shift—twelve hours a day, at least six days a week—and whenever an off-schedule train arrived in the middle of the night.

She also had to sign a contract that Fred had drawn up, requiring her to remain on the job, and stay single, for at least six months. If she made it that far, she would receive a vacation with free train travel anywhere on the Santa Fe, after which she could be invited to return for another six-month tour of duty.

Minnie ended up working at the Raton eating house for a full year, and during that time became friendly with two of the restaurant's best customers—Stephen Dorsey, a former Arkansas senator, and his wife, who had relocated to a cattle farm near Raton. Eventually, the Dorseys asked Minnie to leave the Harvey eating house and come work for them in their thirty-five-room stone mansion. This was a bit unusual—Fred's main problem was losing waitresses who decided to marry Santa Fe trainmen or local ranchers. But Minnie didn't remain single much longer. She fell for the foreman at the Dorsey ranch, George Washington Gillespie. They married and raised five sons.

FRED WAS IMPRESSED with Tom Gable's experiment, and quickly moved to adopt it for his entire eating house chain. Feminist scholars would come to see this decision in 1883 as a crucial turning point for American women. There had been only one other significant female workforce in the country—the female mill workers in Lowell, Massachusetts, from the 1820s through the 1840s. But those mill laborers were often exploited, and had never enjoyed anything like the kind of freedom and empowerment that came from leaving home and reinventing themselves in a new place.

To men working and living in western towns, however, Fred's decision meant only one thing: a steady supply of single, personable, and often comely young ladies being brought in by rail. They gave this unique group of working women a nickname:

Harvey Girls.

It wasn't long before Harvey Girls became a predominant daydream of men who worked or traveled in the West. They wrote songs and poems about Harvey Girls, told jokes about Harvey Girls, imagined what went on in the Harvey Girl dormitories. It was a new kind of populist male fantasy for the democratized American West.

Tom Gable's Harvey Girl brainstorm arrived at a perfect time. Just as he was training his first waitresses in Raton, the Santa Fe was asking Fred to expand his operation dramatically. Four new eating houses were being added in Kansas—Arkansas City, Newton, Hutchinson, and Wellington—and a fifth had changed locations. (The Lakin hotel was taken apart, board by board, and rebuilt forty miles farther west in Coolidge.) And five more houses were being built in New Mexico: Albuquerque, Rincon, San Marcial, Vaughn, and Wallace.

Fred needed to hire and train a lot of good people *quickly*. Up to this point, he had mostly hired local people in each town; now he could shift the entire operation over to waitresses from the East, who would be found through word of mouth or print advertising and interviewed in Leavenworth, Kansas City, or even Chicago. He could train them in his more established eating houses, transfer them wherever they were needed, and house them on-site so his managers could count on them showing up for work. This concept was almost unheard of in the restaurant and hotel business, which was still almost completely local. A hotel might bring in a chef or maître d' from another city—the way Fred had imported Bill Phillips—or share staff with a seasonal resort. But nobody was running quality restaurants in so many locations, or importing regiments of trained servers.

Fred's idea, however, was very much in keeping with the way the two most powerful forces in the frontier West—the railroads and the military—trained and managed people. In fact, after a while, his employees began referring to themselves as being "in the Harvey Service" because there were many similarities to the military. When recruited, potential Harvey Girls often felt honored to have been chosen for the training. They were put through a kind of culinary boot camp. Those who couldn't handle all the pressure and the rules were quickly discharged—if honorably, with train tickets home. Those who flourished under the system lived like an elite feeding force. While many left after their first six-month tour of duty, those who stayed a year had the Harvey Girl equivalent of a medal pinned to their chests: a large silver brooch with a number, which changed each year to indicate how long they had served.

TO MAKE SURE this Harvey Service had a proper headquarters, Fred had Dave Benjamin move from Leavenworth to Kansas City, where he rented a cramped one-room office in the annex building next to the Union Station (where the city's main telegraph center and all the major express delivery companies were also located). Dave's first hire in Kansas City was his younger brother Harry, who had been working part-time for Fred while trying to develop a law practice—advising on legal matters, but also helping with the boss's correspondence because "Mr. Harvey," while possessing a brilliant and daring mind for business, had absolutely dreadful handwriting.

Although Dave had started as little more than a bookkeeper, two years later Fred had him running the day-to-day operations for the entire chain—now more than a dozen different locations spread out over eleven hundred miles between Topeka and the western border of New Mexico. The Kansas City office became the communications hub of the company. It was also the central clearinghouse for the large amounts of cash generated by the eating houses. From the very beginning in Topeka, it was not uncommon for each house to generate at least $250 ($5,200) in pure profit each month. Many of them made much more—enough so that in locations that were less profitable, as long as the managers were doing a good job, they were told to maintain standards even if it meant running deficits. There was more than enough money to go around.

Dave blossomed as a right-hand man. He had an intuitive understanding of his boss's vision and ambitions, and a nonjudgmental appreciation for his weaknesses. Fred was brilliant at hiring, inspiring, and firing people; his instincts and taste were impeccable, his honor beyond reproach. But he could be a little scary, a little over-the-top in his demands. He was once described by an admirer as "one of those keen-eyed, stern and few-worded humans who use a cold exterior to hide a double-size heart." But not everyone saw the heart. Fred also still relied on his own memory too much. While he expected his employees to keep exacting records, he was still haphazardly scribbling lists in his datebooks.

More important, Fred was obsessed with something he called "maintaining the standard." It was a phrase he repeated constantly to his staff, a challenge to always strive for excellence. But to some degree, they were still *inventing* the standard.

Fred had become close to the editor and publisher of the powerful Chicago-based *National Hotel Reporter,* F. Willis Rice, through whom he was getting friendly with many of the giants in the hospitality industry, including Potter Palmer of Chicago's Palmer House and George Boldt of the Bellevue-Stratford in Philadelphia (and later New York's Waldorf-Astoria). Fred learned "their secrets of success," the trade paper later reported, "and from his gleanings, combined with his creative genius, developed the Fred Harvey system."

He wanted there to be a "Fred Harvey way" of doing *everything.* And Dave began creating elaborate systems to put Fred Harvey's demands and dreams into memo and manual form, making "the standard" easier to understand. He combined what he knew about accounting procedures with what he was learning about how the railroads did business: From his vantage point in Kansas City Union Station, he could see the way the various roads published intricate rules and procedures—constantly updated—for everything that happened on the train, in the depot, even out on the tracks, and how they circulated copies to all personnel. But while the railroad manuals and memos were often mechanical, robotic, Fred Harvey's systems—as interpreted and codified by Dave—tried to predict human nature as well, and incorporated issues of professionalism, loyalty, even morality. Although Dave was Jewish and Fred Episcopalian, they found common ground in what their faiths could teach employees (and bosses) about doing the right thing and giving perfect service. As they began distributing memos and manuals, the advice they offered was often quite wholesome and even philosophical, like one list of "Fundamentals" that went to everyone in the expanding Harvey System:

FUNDAMENTALS

1. Have a Sincere Interest in People
2. Like all your Daily Contacts with Guests
3. Radiate Cheer and Make Guest feel at Ease and at Home

4. Remember "Travel Follows Good Food Routes"
5. Keep Well Informed and Updated on the Condition, Origin and Season of different Supplies, and the Serving of Same
6. Be Human and Be Yourself
7. Courtesy and a Smile Pay Dividends
8. Real Service is Without Discrimination
9. <u>Preserve</u> or <u>Create</u>—Never Destroy
10. Tact is an Asset and HONESTY is still a <u>Virtue</u>

At other times, the advice in the company edicts was more practical, like this sign that hung in the early Harvey employee housing:

> EMPLOYES ARE REQUESTED NOT TO SCRATCH MATCHES, DRIVE NAILS OR TACKS, OR IN ANY OTHER WAY MAR THE WALLS OF THEIR ROOMS.
>
> NO RUBBISH OF ANY KIND MUST BE THROWN IN THE TOILETS.
>
> BATH TUBS MUST BE THOROUGHLY CLEANED BY EMPLOYES AFTER USING.
>
> LOUD TALKING AND LAUGHING IN ROOMS AND HALLS SHOULD BE AVOIDED.
>
> EMPLOYES MUST BE IN THEIR ROOMS BY 11:00 O'CLOCK P.M. UNLESS GIVEN SPECIAL PERMISSION BY MANAGER TO REMAIN OUT LONGER.
>
> ROOMS MUST BE KEPT IN TIDY CONDITION AND WEARING APPAREL MUST BE KEPT IN ITS PROPER PLACE.
>
> CLOTHING OF ALL EMPLOYES MUST BE NEAT AND CLEAN AT ALL TIMES.
>
> EXPECTORATING ON FLOORS IS POSITIVELY FORBIDDEN.
>
> THE PURPOSE OF THE ABOVE RULES IS TO BRING ABOUT A TIDY AND HOMELIKE CONDITION IN YOUR ROOMS AND WE REQUEST YOUR CO-OPERATION SO THAT THE DESIRED RESULTS WILL BE BROUGHT ABOUT.
>
> —FRED HARVEY

The Harvey System had rules for everything. All the eating houses baked and hand sliced their own bread, and every slice had to be three-eighths of an inch thick. Tap water in each of the houses was tested regularly for alkali levels—if these were too high, water had to be brought in on a train car from elsewhere to make the coffee. Orange juice had to be hand squeezed only *after* it was ordered; if a pitcher of recently squeezed juice was found in the icebox, someone was going to be fired. Once Bill Phillips, now the system-wide chef, had the recipe for a new dish exactly the way Fred liked, it had to be followed exactly, without deviation, for every serving at every restaurant. The menus in the restaurants were also systematized so that passengers wouldn't be offered the same dishes and specials at every stop.

Yet Fred did not want this centralized system to quash creativity and ambition, so he encouraged the chefs and managers at the eating houses to be innovative as well as entrepreneurial. If they heard about a good deal on local fruit, vegetables, meat, or fowl, they were encouraged to buy not only for their eating house but for all the others. The fresh ingredients would be loaded into the next Santa Fe refrigerator car—in a compartment that only fellow Harvey chefs could open with a special key—and were sent on down the line. Besides keeping the menus lively, this also led to some of the first wide-scale migration of regional American ingredients and preparations, for which the eating houses became known along with more traditional Continental and British fare.

Fred also created exacting systems for serving, the best known of which was the "cup code." Harvey Girls didn't write down a customer's beverage order. Instead, they repositioned the cup at its place setting so that when the "drink girls" descended on the table, they knew exactly what to pour. For coffee, the cup was left in its saucer. For milk, it was flipped and put on the table next to the saucer. For iced tea, the flipped cup was leaned against the saucer. There were also three possible variations for hot tea: The flipped cup was placed on the saucer and, depending on which direction the handle was pointed, the customer wanted black, green, or orange pekoe.

The cup code was just one of many practices designed to wring every excess second out of the thirty minutes the railroad allotted for a meal stop. There were even intricate rules about what Harvey Girls were to do when they had nothing to do. When not actually serving, they had to attend to the large coffee urns that were the most visible symbol of Fred Harvey's culinary commitment. The urns always had to be perfectly shiny. But, more important, at a time when most eateries in the West brewed coffee once a day and reheated it over and over,

Fred Harvey's urns were very publicly emptied every two hours and then refilled with freshly ground coffee shipped directly from Chase & Sanborn in Boston.

During the rest of their free time, the Harvey Girls were expected to be seen polishing the silverware, every piece of which had Fred Harvey's name etched on the handle. When asked for the secret of how shiny everything was in his restaurants, Fred said, simply, "We *concentrate* on it."

At the beginning of each workday, Fred wanted to know everything that had happened at each of his eating houses the day before. How many eggs and steaks had been eaten, how many pounds of butter and slices of bread, how many of each brand of cigars had been smoked? Also, how did each employee behave, who was having personal problems, who was ready to be promoted, who needed to be transferred or fired? It was a level of interest and detail that most American businesses would not bother to consider for another century, with the help of computers. Dave figured out ways to collect that information for Fred in the mid-1880s, before most places had telephones or electricity, using a complex maze of telegraphed daily reports and letters.

Dave also developed a unique Fred Harvey–only telegraph code so that nobody, including Santa Fe employees, could translate their messages. Fred always carried with him a handwritten codebook to which Dave's brother Harry would routinely add new entries.

Still, even with all the reports, the only way to fully enforce the increasingly complex Harvey System was to keep making unscheduled inspections. There was now often some kind of warning when Fred was about to arrive on one of his "surprise" visits. His employees developed a little secret code of their own; word would come over the telegraph wire from the eating house Fred had just left: "sack of potatoes due on the next train" or "a tornado is coming." Tales of his legendary inspections were passed on from Harvey Girl to Harvey Girl, the retellings often as effective as the actual smashing of dishes and yanking of tablecloths.

Managers circulated Fred stories like biblical teachings. The parable of "The Crank" was one of their favorites.

One day an eating house steward was complaining to Fred about a serially dissatisfied customer.

"There's no pleasing that man," said the steward, "he's nothing but an out and out *crank*!"

"Well, of course he's a crank," Fred shot back. "It is our business to please cranks. *Anyone* can please a gentleman."

IT IS NO WONDER Fred was obsessed with maintaining standards; he lived in a world with so few of them. There were still no real standards of hygiene or medical care. In America's largest industry, the railroads, standards were still amazingly diffuse. Companies didn't share tracks or, in most towns, depots, so they had different ways of doing almost everything. They didn't all lay their tracks the same way or even the same distance apart. While a standard gauge—the distance between the two rails—was emerging (it was four feet eight and a half inches), many railroads ran on narrower or broader gauge.

And, most amazingly, in 1883 they still hadn't agreed on a standard of time.

America had always been considered too vast to have standardized time. Each city and town determined time by when the sun rose and set *there,* so clocks in Philadelphia were set four minutes behind clocks in New York. When the railroads began connecting these cities and needed a way of creating schedules, each used the time at its headquarters as the "standard time" throughout its entire system. Consequently, up through the 1880s, America had fifty "time zones," each controlled by a different railroad. Train stations had multiple clocks—not showing the time in various parts of the nation or foreign capitals, as they do today, but rather the slight differences in time between nearby cities.

England had recently adopted a national standard time based on the meridian that went through Greenwich. In the United States, however, there was vehement opposition to standardizing time—due to a mixture of civic pride, a desire to maintain a truly local reality, and a resistance to being told what to do by the government. But in 1883, the major railroad companies all agreed to devise a simpler system of timekeeping, utilizing a plan created by the editor of the *Travelers' Official Railway Guide,* William F. Allen. He proposed four time zones, based on the time at the 75th meridian, which runs through Philadelphia, the 90th, which runs through St. Louis and New Orleans, the 105th, which runs through Denver, and the 120th, which runs just west of Los Angeles.

On October 11, 1883, at the Grand Pacific Hotel in Chicago, representatives of all the major railroads ratified the plan. Across the country, Sunday, November 18, was deemed "The Day of Two Noons," when every clock in the country was reset. The fact that this new national standard of time was put into place by the railroads, and not the government, gave a fair indication of who was really running the country.

CHAPTER 13

LIKE A HOUSE AFIRE

FRED WAS AMAZED BY HOW QUICKLY HIS EATING HOUSE BUSINESS had grown and how lucrative it had become. He knew that flawless service and fresh ingredients would be a revelation in the West, that the act of providing freshly brewed coffee any time of the day or night was enough to get him elected mayor in most towns. The Santa Fe was still primarily an ambitious regional rail line connecting Kansas, Colorado, and New Mexico—it was far from a major player in the railroad business. But he was already making a small fortune.

His personal profits from the eating houses alone were now more than $50,000 ($1.1 million) a year. That was after *all* expenses, and at the time there were no federal, state, or local taxes, personal or business. His company didn't own any real estate—the railroad had bought back the hotel in Florence—and he refused to incur any other significant debt. Taking a lesson from his very first bosses in America at Smith & McNell's in New York, he paid for everything immediately with cash, never asking for credit and never extending it to anyone else. So the company's profits were all cash—and all his.

He plowed some of it back into the eating house business, and did some investing in conservative stocks and bonds. He also made private loans, often to people who were far wealthier than he was but whose fortunes weren't quite as liquid. It was a little like the maître d' at a pricey restaurant lending tip money to his best customers, but Fred had long since accepted the social and class oddities that came with making a lot of money in the nascent service industry.

Much of his money, however, was invested in the cattle business, which he had grown to love. He always stopped at the ranch during eating house inspection trips, to check up on his cowboys and his cattle, and often sent Dave, too. Owning the XY herd made Fred feel like a genuine American frontier entrepreneur, and raising cattle in western Kansas also had the feel of a family business, especially now that he and his brother-in-law Jack Hardesty shared winter grazing land on New Mexico's Cimarron Range. Fred enjoyed spending time with his brother-in-law, which was a good thing, because Sally was always looking for any excuse to visit her sister Maggie—especially after the Hardestys named their baby daughter, Sallie, after her.

Fred's partners in the cattle business found they didn't share his delight in ranching, so he offered to buy them out. The XY had doubled in size to twenty thousand head of cattle, plus thousands of horses and valuable grazing land. The partners' value to Fred had also increased. William Strong now ran the railroad, and the other partner, C. W. Smith, had become a Santa Fe vice president—so it was important that everyone feel good about the deal. Fred offered to pay each of them $50,000 ($1.1 million), more than twelve times what they originally invested five years before, and more than he had ever gambled on any investment in his life. He paid the first $11,000 ($244,000) in cash; the rest was paid by auctioning "all marketable fat cattle" in the herd and then giving his partners all the proceeds. Within sixteen months, they were paid in full.

Not long after buying out the herd, however, he decided to move it because the cattle industry in western Kansas was coming under fire from families staking out farms along the Arkansas River. Farmers and cowmen had mutually exclusive dreams of the American West. The farmers, many of whom were brought to Kansas by the Santa Fe with promises of cheap land and free seed, did not appreciate cattle trampling through their crops—nor did they want their sons to grow up to be cowboys. The railroads had spent a great deal of money attracting both ranchers and farmers, and controlled more than enough trackside land for both. Since it was easier to ask a cattleman to graze his herd elsewhere than to move a farm, the railroad encouraged ranchers like Fred Harvey to shift their operations farther west. Fred negotiated a deal to buy 100,000 acres of grazing land in Colorado, near the town of Granada, for $70,000 ($1.5 million) and moved the XY herd there. This made the farmers in western Kansas so ecstatic that for years afterward they actually taught their kids a little song about the departure of Fred's crew: "It was the tenth of May, God bless the day, when the XY cowboys went away."

THE MOST VISIBLE sign of Fred's newfound wealth was the home he bought his family in Leavenworth—a stately mansion on a hill at the corner of 7th and Olive streets, one of the most fashionable sections of town. It was just down the street from the lavish home of bank president and Kansas Central Railroad executive Lucien Scott, who was so excited about being the first person in Leavenworth with an indoor shower that he had the plumber leave all the pipes exposed so his bathroom would cause the maximum sensation.

The new Harvey house was built of locally mined cream-colored limestone in the Second Empire style. It had twelve large rooms and seven fireplaces, multiple porches and Gothic dormers, and intriguing masonry work along the roof and around the entrances, including a carved lion's head in the archway of the front door. Each window in the house was equipped with fully retractable wooden shutters, and every doorway had a delicately etched transom window. The dramatically curved main staircase began with an elaborately sculpted newel post topped with a large wooden acorn—which looked as if it were almost daring one of the Harvey children to knock it off. The mansion also had a two-story carriage house, stables, and more than an acre of land for the kids and dogs to romp over.

Fred bought the house from Harvey and Mary Rush, who owned the major wheat mill in Leavenworth and one of the largest grain elevators in the West. (Their main competitor across the river, the R. T. Davis Mill Company in St. Joseph, was the birthplace of Aunt Jemima's self-rising pancake mix.) Fred paid $24,956 ($565,000) for the house itself, and Sally so loved the way Mary Rush had decorated the place that they also bought much of the furniture and draperies.

The house had expansive living, dining, and cooking areas on the first floor, and bedrooms for Fred, Sally, the children, and Sally's mother on the multilevel second floor. Most of the third floor, however, was Fred's domain. He kept an office up there, next to the billiard room. He also had a large library space, which he needed because his collection of books had grown enormous over the years, and he continued to devour volumes on history, medicine, politics, art, virtually *any-thing*. His shelves contained everything from *Hill's Manual of Social and Business Forms: A Guide to Correct Writing*—the businessman's bible, with copies of every form and style of letter imaginable—to several volumes of the complete works of Shakespeare, bound volumes of the *Illustrated London News*, a popular British parody of Samuel Pepys's diary called *Manners and Customs of Ye Englishe*, works of Keats, Poe, Fielding, Coleridge's epic *Rime of the Ancient Mariner*, and nearly a dozen different Bibles.

BUSINESS WAS WONDERFUL everywhere except at the Montezuma, which had become a huge problem, a Victorian white elephant. During a recent visit to the hotel, Dave had reported back to Fred in utter disbelief: "There are not even 20 at the Montezuma," he lamented, "and people going there to stay a month only remain a day or two."

The reason was unclear. It could have been the location, but many felt the Montezuma had an image problem. The Santa Fe had apparently been far too successful advertising the health resort as an actual medical facility—so everyone assumed it was full of really sick people. One *Optic* writer noted that the public seemed to believe the hotel was filled with "men without noses and ears and otherwise horribly disfigured from disease." It proved hard to convince people that most of the guests were perfectly healthy tourists—and that the "invalids" were generally not contagious.

Then, on the bitterly cold Thursday morning of January 17, 1884, Kittie Philbin thought she smelled smoke.

Kittie was the most popular housekeeper at the Montezuma, and had been preparing for weeks to take her first vacation since the hotel opened. Everything she owned was packed in her suitcases, including her life savings of $600 ($13,600), which was hidden beneath her clothes. The housekeeping staff had just finished eating lunch when an explosion was heard throughout the hotel and smoke started rising from underneath the main lobby. The fire alarms were sounded, and Kittie rushed through the corridors knocking on as many doors as she could, hurrying everyone out into the frigid winter air. Since the Montezuma was barely one-quarter full, with only sixty-two guests sprinkled among its 270 rooms, everyone was able to escape safely.

All the hydrants were frozen shut, but that probably didn't matter. The largest wood structure in the country, the Montezuma was a veritable tinderbox. And no building could have survived the freak accident in the hotel's volatile lighting system—which employed vapor from a large pool of naphtha (a crude form of petrochemical today used mostly by fire jugglers and campers with portable stoves) mixed with forced air to fuel the jets. Since naphtha was full of impurities, there were traps under the main lobby of the hotel that periodically had to be emptied of highly flammable gunk. Two men emptying the traps that day were working by the light of a small "spirit lamp"—a precursor to the oil lamp that also burned volatile liquid. Vapors from the gunk in the traps caught fire, and the workmen panicked and ran—leaving the system to explode in flames fueled by the naphtha.

The resulting inferno, according to the *Optic,* "required a whole dictionary of adjectives to describe." With the guests out of danger, volunteer firefighters reportedly spent most of their time trying to save, or loot, the contents of the wine cellar—leaving the birds and animals in the hotel's aviary and zoo to roast alive. One hotel historian joked that "enough liquor was 'liquidated' at the scene of the fire to have quenched the blaze had it been properly applied." It took less than forty minutes for the entire structure to burn to the ground. All that remained were two charred chimneys.

Fred did not rush to visit the ruins of the Montezuma. While the hotel had been an amazing opportunity and had given his company a major boost in national credibility, its creation had bled him dry emotionally and physically, and its management was bleeding him and the Santa Fe dry financially. There would be an insurance settlement, and the Santa Fe immediately hired the rising Chicago architecture firm of Burnham & Root to redesign the hotel. (Daniel Burnham was already claiming the Montezuma had been built in the wrong place.) But the railroad would have to find someone else to direct the rebuilding. It would not be Fred.

In the meantime, he wanted to make sure his best hotel employees did not feel abandoned. It was the right thing to do and also good business. He immediately sent a telegram to Kittie Philbin.

"Come to my home," it said, "it is yours also."

Three days after the fire, Kittie was on a train headed for Kansas with $60 ($1,360) in her pocket. The other housekeepers at the Montezuma had taken up a collection to help replace her life savings.

AS FRED'S BUSINESS GREW, he became even more reliant on his protégé Dave Benjamin, who was empowered to make decisions in Fred's absence and oversaw all day-to-day operations from the Kansas City office—for the eating house business as well as the ranch. As Dave's star rose, Fred's original partner in the restaurants, food czar Bill Phillips, decided it was time to move on. It may have been jealousy: Dave, a much younger man, was given a deal similar to his, with a one-eighth share of the company's growing profits, and enjoyed Fred's trust. But most likely, the problem was that Fred's business with the Santa Fe had grown in a different direction than Phillips had hoped. A longtime city hotel man, he had been most interested in grand, unique properties like the Montezuma. But Fred's future was clearly in medium-size depot eating houses and hotels.

Some time after the Montezuma burned, the name of Bill Phillips suddenly disappeared from news stories about Fred's company. The job of culinary czar for the growing chain was given to thirty-five-year-old Victor Vizzetti, whom Fred and Dave considered the best young chef in the system. They had found him at the Clarendon Hotel in Leadville, Colorado, where he was a line cook, and started him in the kitchen at their smallest eating house in Wallace, New Mexico—where he quickly became known, in Dave's words, for serving "the best meal on the road." He was also a workhorse—when they had staffing problems at western eating houses, he would sometimes be called upon to cook meals at two houses on the same day, hopping the express trains back and forth.

Vizzetti was British born but Italian in ancestry, and had trained in Italy. He immediately began importing Italian chefs, and some Germans as well, making the staff more international and the cooking even more diverse. Up to this point, restaurants had typically brought foreign chefs to America to re-create classic European and British cuisines. But Fred and Vizzetti were equally interested in Americanizing certain international dishes—as well as the more distinctively regional dishes so that they were more palatable to a broader range of eating house patrons. The best cuts of meat and chicken were used to make stews and other dishes normally created from lesser cuts or left-overs. Authentically exotic spices were used, but toned down a bit.

Fred also brought his buddy Byron Schermerhorn into the business full-time. The Captain had been running the Brink's Chicago City Express, mentoring the founder's son as he built what was to become one of the best-known businesses in America: the Brink's Armored Car company, forever synonymous with secure delivery of cash and valuables. Fred now hired Byron as a full-time personnel manager for all the eating houses—a position requiring almost constant travel—and gave him a small piece of the company's profits.

In fact, Byron's deal was similar to Dave's—although nobody would mistake the two top executives. Dave was solid; Dave was trustworthy; Dave would take a bullet for Fred Harvey. Byron was the boss's oddball friend whom the employees more or less endured. Even the press found him difficult. During Byron's visit to Las Vegas after his promotion, the *Optic* said he "reigns over all the employees of Fred Harvey and governs them with a meek and lowly hand . . . This person has a big heart, a large head and feet in proportion. If he don't like this item, we are glad of it."

ALTHOUGH FRED HAD now built an excellent team, he was not certain how much longer he would be well enough to lead it. His health, cyclically precarious, was not improving, and he had to be realistic about his age: He would soon be fifty, then an age that, for most Americans, was the beginning of the end. So he felt forced to make a painfully difficult decision.

He told his son Ford that he would have to quit college and start learning the business.

Ford had grown into a fine young man—bright, clever, passionate, and almost too good-looking to be a Harvey, with his wavy brown hair, strong cleft chin, and engaging, wide-set brown eyes. One family friend called him "the handsomest and most glamorous person I ever saw," and he never hid his bone-dry wit, even signing his five-year-old sister's autograph book "your Crass old brother, Ford." Now in his second year at Racine College in Wisconsin, he was winning award after award for his academics and enjoying the chance to explore nearby

Milwaukee and Chicago. The last thing he wanted to do was to quit school. But his father insisted.

Fred claimed he wanted Ford to learn the business from the bottom up. But he had another agenda as well, because he didn't send his son down to Kansas City to take a menial office job. Instead, he made Ford move back to Leavenworth and shadow him every day—at work as well as at home. While this was certainly an opportunity for the young man to learn his father's ways, it was also an excuse to have another Harvey man in the house in case, as Fred worried, his poor health left him incapacitated.

So while his younger sister Minnie was away at boarding school in the East, Ford found himself, at age nineteen, trapped in his parents' new house in Leavenworth with the kids—two younger sisters and a kid brother—his non-English-speaking grandmother, and a pack of aging dogs.

CHAPTER 14

ACUTE AMERICANITIS

As the headaches and neuralgia worsened, Fred found himself caught in the crippling cycle of chronic illness—even when he felt well, he was anxious about when the symptoms would return. It was not uncommon for him to lie in bed at night, his body clenched in anticipation of the next attack. He was especially nervous on trips to large cities. "I have been looking for the Neuralgia all the time since I have been here," he wrote Sally from New York, explaining why he couldn't stay there long. "I am very confident I would have Neuralgia here for every thing is on the rush all the time."

Yet Fred somehow managed to visit the office in Kansas City every few days, and he continued to take periodic inspection trips across Kansas, Colorado, and New Mexico. If anything, his illness made him more demanding, more irritable, and more obsessed with cleanliness, hygiene, and order. It sometimes seemed as if his neuralgia, dyspepsia, and headaches were turning him into that "crank" whom Fred Harvey employees were always taught they had to please.

Dr. George Beard, the nation's leading expert on neurasthenia, had some new ideas about treating patients like Fred. He still prescribed some of the popular medicines of the day—strychnine, phosphorus, and arsenic (all now known to be poison)—and recommended that nerves be recharged by "general electrization," which involved standing wet and naked on a charged copper plate while a wet, charged sponge was wiped across various parts of the body. (Fred never mentioned receiving this treatment, but given his endless searching, it seems likely he tried it.)

In the early 1880s, however, Beard published three books in five years that turned his novel medical observation into a sweeping diagnosis not only of his patients but of nearly every aspect of modern life in the United States. People had once jokingly called this disease Americanitis; he now fully embraced that concept, officially renaming the illness "American Nervousness" and explaining that "the greater prevalence of nervousness in America is a complex resultant of a number of influences, the chief of which are dryness of the air, extremes of heat and cold, civil and religious liberty, and the great mental activity made necessary and possible in a new and productive country under such climatic conditions." Beard went on to implicate an encyclopedic list of possible stressors, which ranged from the intense beauty and sophistication of American women (which had "no precedent, in recorded history") to the strain of long railroad trips ("it would seem that the molecular disturbance caused by traveling long distances, or living on trains as an employee, would have an unfavorable influence on the nervous system").

So it came as no surprise that the fashionable new treatment for neurasthenia—and all other nervous disorders—was simply to *leave* America and all its sickening energy.

British scientists and social observers—whose writings Fred often read—took Beard's analysis and ran with it. "The lank and shriveled Yankee" is merely "a desiccated Englishman," wrote one British commentator, who claimed that his own son had visited the United States, and "during his short absence, he had grown thinner and taller, lank-jawed and sallow, displaying all the characteristic symptoms of what I cannot refrain from calling acute Americanitis."

In addition to advising they leave the country, Beard recommended that wherever patients went, they do almost nothing. "Many years ago I observed that nervous patients were better on Sundays, when they did nothing, than on other days," he wrote. "There are patients who need to make every day a Sabbath—to have sixty, or ninety, or more, consecutive days of rest." He also suggested isolation from family members, business associates, or friends—depending on

> the character of the friends themselves . . . if they are unduly emotional, superstitious, and demonstrative; if they constantly burden and weary . . . with oppressive talk and attention, then removal may be indispensable . . . When such cases are taken

out of these really hostile influences, and carried in any direction and kept resolutely apart from those who know and love and pity them, they are so far delivered from one of the worst possible exciting causes of functional nervous disease, and an opportunity is given for the forces of nature and medication to work together without friction toward recovery.

Beard expressed some reservations about this treatment. "I doubt whether there is any medicine which is more indiscriminately used than travel," he wrote, "especially in the form of a trip to Europe." And some of his treatment regimens were mutually exclusive. While recommending the "rest cure" for some patients, he railed that too many others wasted their lives resting; what they needed was the "work cure," or some combination, guided by the gut instinct of physicians. Still, his work offered a compelling scientific case that neurasthenics should flee the country.

It is unclear if Fred actually met with Dr. Beard or was being treated by a local physician well versed in this cutting-edge, and later largely discredited, literature on American Nervousness. But he obviously decided that the only way to stop his suffering was to leave his family, his business, his friends, and his adopted country to pursue the "rest cure" in England. He was certainly not alone in seeking questionable treatments available only to the railroad rich: Financier Jay Gould had an entourage that included a personal physician, a French chef who could prepare his special dainty diet of "ladyfingers and other featherweight pastry," and even a "traveling cow" (which rode in the baggage car) because he had been prescribed large quantities of fresh milk. Still, a medical decision this extreme was startling, especially given that the last time Fred had visited England, for several weeks in the summer of 1883, he returned feeling just as sick as when he left.

But now he would go away for as long as it took to feel better. In the late spring of 1885, he booked passage on the newest Cunard ocean liner, the *Etruria*, sailing from New York City on the Fourth of July, and arranged to stay in England for at least three months.

BEFORE FRED LEFT, there was a small party at the house to celebrate his fiftieth birthday. It was a low-key affair. Even Byron Schermer-

Fred in New York City (1) around 1853, and in St. Louis (2) early 1860s after losing his restaurant there and becoming ill working on Missouri River packet boats; Charlie and Eddie Harvey (3), Fred's sons with his first wife, Ann; Barbara Sarah "Sally" Mattas, Fred's second wife (4); downtown Leavenworth (5), where Fred set up a railroad ticket office in 1865.

1

2

4

3

5

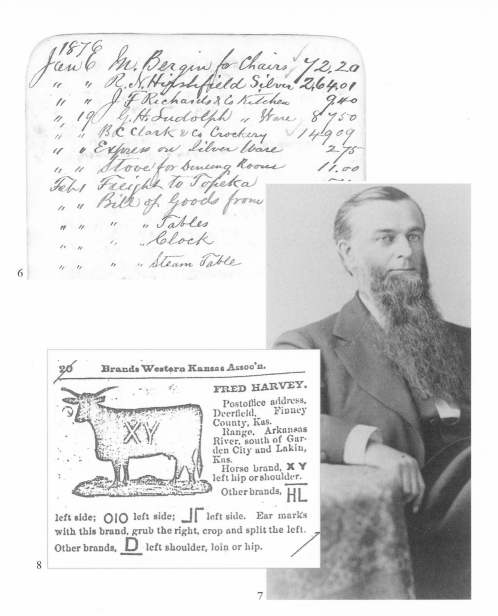

1876

Jan 6 M. Bergin for Chairs 72.20
" " R. N. Hirshfield Silver 2,64.01
" " J F Richards & Co Kitchen 9.40
" 19 G. H. Sudolph " Ware 8.750
" " B & Clark & Co Crockery 14909
" " Express on Silver Ware 2.75
" " Stove for Dining Room 11.00
Feb 1 Freight to Topeka
" " Bill of Goods from
" " " " Tables
" " " " Clock
" " " " Steam Table

6

20 **Brands Western Kansas Assoo'n.**

FRED HARVEY.

Postoffice address, Deerfield, Finney County, Kas.

Range, Arkansas River, south of Garden City and Lakin, Kas.

Horse brand, **X Y** left hip or shoulder.

Other brands, HL

left side; O¦O left side; ⅃⌐ left side. Ear marks with this brand, grub the right, crop and split the left.

Other brands, D left shoulder, loin or hip.

8

7

Byron Schermerhorn (1), Fred's best friend; Jepp Rice (2), Fred's initial partner in railroad eating houses on the Kansas Pacific in 1875; their Wallace, Kansas, dining room (3), in the earliest known picture of a Fred Harvey restaurant; Fred's photo business card (4); Topeka depot of the Atchison, Topeka & Santa Fe (5), where Fred took over the second-floor lunchroom in early 1876; page from Fred's datebook (6) showing purchases for new Topeka house; AT&SF president William Barstow Strong (7), who encouraged Fred's eating house chain; ad in cattle publication (8) for Fred's XY herd, in which Strong was an investor.

1

3

2

4

5

6

7

8

9

10

Santa Fe depot hotel in Florence, Kansas (1), the ambitious prototype for Fred's chain, although most of the eating houses looked like this one in La Junta, Colorado (2); the oldest known piece of signature china (3); the fabled Montezuma hotel (4) outside of Las Vegas, New Mexico, the health resort that made Fred's career (and nearly destroyed his health); Fred and Sally portraits (5, 6) in the early 1880s as they became more prosperous; early photos of Harvey Girls—who replaced male waiters system-wide after a racial incident in Raton, New Mexico, in 1883—in Hutchinson, Kansas (7), Syracuse, Kansas (8, 9), and in one of the many romanticized images they inspired (10).

1

My dear Son Byron
I hope that You
Will always Speak
the truth — Under no
Consideration ever
Tell a lie
your father
Fred H. Harvey
Jan 20/87

2

3

4

5

❖ Dave Benjamin (1), Fred's former Leavenworth bank teller, who became his second-in-command based in Kansas City; Fred's hand-written advice (2) to his youngest child, Byron, age ten; heir apparent Ford Harvey and his teen sweetheart, Josephine "Judy" Blair (3), after they married in 1888, the same year Fred Harvey/Pullman dining cars (menu, 4; diners, 5) debuted on the Santa Fe's new "airline" from Chicago to Kansas City; the Arkansas City Harvey House surrounded by "boomers" awaiting the signal for the 1889 Oklahoma land rush (6); Ford (7) holding his first child, Katherine "Kitty" Harvey; Edward Payson Ripley (8), the new Santa Fe president who helped rebuild the railroad after its bankruptcy during the 1893 Depression and convinced ailing Fred (9) to let Ford and Dave run the business.

1

2

St. Louis Union Station (1), part of Fred Harvey's dramatic expansion in the 1890s into its first big-city operations (and into the postcard business)—other locations included Chicago Dearborn Station (2, lunchroom), Le Grande Station in Los Angeles, and, in San Francisco, restaurants on boats the Santa Fe ran between its Oakland depot and the Ferry Building; the Castañeda (3) in Las Vegas, New Mexico, became the prototype for the large Mission-style trackside Fred Harvey resorts the Santa Fe built all over the Southwest; it immediately became famous when Teddy Roosevelt and his Rough Riders (4) held their fabled 1899 reunion there; Fred—at home, in what is believed to be his last photo (5)—got to watch his company's rebirth, but often from a sickbed.

3

4

5

horn's poem—he wrote and recited one for every occasion—was sobering, almost fatalistic, ending with the stanza:

> Fred, time's clock strikes again, Fifty years have been tolled
> The hands travel fast and our bodies grow old
> But our hearts younger grow as our faith we extend
> Toward home and reunion in world without end.

Fred took the train to New York and found the *Etruria* docked at Pier 40 in lower Manhattan, where he had arrived in America over thirty years earlier. The Irish-built ship was huge, five hundred feet long, fifty-seven feet across, with two large red smokestacks and three main sails. It held 550 first-class passengers, and another 960 in intermediate and steerage, and was considered the fastest ship on the Atlantic, usually able to make the crossing in just over six days.

Early on Independence Day 1885, the *Etruria* pulled away from the pier and moved slowly south past Bedloe's Island. Fred could see wooden packing crates sitting on its shore, over two hundred of them in various sizes.

Each crate held a piece of the Statue of Liberty. This cargo had arrived from France two weeks earlier, but couldn't be opened because there was no place to assemble it. After nearly a decade of delays, the French had finally completed the statue and its unique internal framing, but the Americans responsible for building its pedestal had not yet raised the money for it. Publishing magnate Joseph Pulitzer had recently committed the editorial page of his paper, the *World,* to guilting Americans into donating the $100,000 ($2.3 million) required. In the meantime, the crates sat on the shore of Bedloe's Island, an odd vision of packaged liberty.

It was a lovely day for sailing. The sky was fair, and the morning temperature, which Fred complained had been unseasonably cold, rose into the comfortable mid-seventies as they headed out to sea. Sally had asked Byron Schermerhorn and the children to write letters that Fred could read once he was at sea, hoping to cheer him up.

When he opened the note from his youngest daughter, Sybil, pressed flowers fluttered into his lap. She couldn't think of what to say, she explained in her large, looping script, so she enclosed some flowers from a bouquet he had once given her.

Byron Schermerhorn, never at a loss for words, sent three densely handwritten pages:

As you read I can see the tear trickle down, salty tears, from the ocean of heart that many have fathomed.

We shall all be with you for we are:
Never alone awake or asleep
For fancied forms around us creep
While retrospective fingers sweep
        Chords sweet or sad
Absent loved ones living or dead
Linked to our souls by memory's thread
Keep by our side with noiseless tread
        Companions still
Evoked the voice, the form, the face
Imagined near in mental space
Our arms are outstretched to embrace
        But no—we must wait
Sail away, and may the water that bears you safely away from us all bring you back well and happy to our hearts.

> With warmest Love
> Captain

As a postscript, Schermerhorn scribbled, "Don't hesitate to telegraph for me to come at once to London if you need me."

SEVERAL WEEKS AFTER Fred departed, Sally and the children went to visit the new Montezuma. The architects from Chicago had completely redesigned the hotel, moving it a half mile, changing its shape to an L, and giving it a stunning five-story cupola and observatory. Inside, the main lobby had a massive Gothic Revival fireplace, Art Nouveau light fixtures, and gloriously detailed wood paneling on the walls, the vaulted ceiling, and all around the front desk.

It was the first building in New Mexico with fully electric lighting. And this time, the architects promised, the Montezuma was "absolutely fireproof."

The Harvey family stayed in one of the hotel's majestic three-room suites, and basically had the run of the place. This was in part because, as the *Optic* noted, "Mrs. Harvey has lots of old friends around the hot springs." But the truth was, there weren't many other patrons vying for the staff's attention.

A week after his family arrived in Las Vegas, Fred was sitting in a London hotel room when he received a wire from his office in Kansas City with shocking news.

The Montezuma had burned to the ground. Again.

The Saturday night fire was apparently triggered by an electrical short in a storage room near the observatory, which sent flames down the elevator shaft and then outward through the ceilings. It burned slowly enough to allow all the guests to be evacuated, and many of the furnishings were saved by moving them out onto the veranda—the roof of which was kept doused with water. But, reportedly, the fire hoses were not long enough to reach the main source of the flames, and it was a total loss.

Fortunately, Sally and the children escaped unharmed. Sally's jewelry, initially reported missing, also turned up when, according to the *Optic*, a young man named Gould "found a handful of diamonds and jewelry belonging to Mrs. Fred Harvey, and returned them to her." Fred immediately cut short his health retreat and headed home on the *Etruria*, a voyage that shaved three and a half hours off the world's record for crossing the Atlantic. The trip from Queenstown to Sandy Hook took only six days, five hours, and thirty-one minutes.

Upon his arrival in Las Vegas, the *Optic* reported he had "regained much of his failing health by the rest and recreation abroad." When he left four days later, headed back east to Kansas City with Ford to catch up on business, the *Optic* reported he was "very much better and feels youthful again."

Unfortunately, these assessments were overly optimistic. While Fred did return to work in the fall, by Christmas he was already planning to go back to England for his health. He sailed in February 1886 and stayed abroad for seven months, keeping in touch by telegram and mail. Dave was left in charge of the company's unadorned offices in Kansas City Union Station—which now had ten employees—and the growing Fred Harvey eating house chain: twenty locations, each with a manager, a chef, at least a half-dozen Harvey Girls, and ten or more other employees.

Dave was also left in charge of the unsentimental education of young Ford Harvey, who was about to turn twenty and was still living at home, though he was spending more time in the Kansas City office.

At a muscular five foot ten, he was taller and more broad shouldered than Fred, but Ford was clearly his father's son, right down to his manner of speech. Although he had never spent a day outside of the United States, the young Harvey spoke with a clipped, slight British accent, pronouncing schedule "shed-ule," process "proe-cess," and been "bean."

Ford was a quick study, although it was sometimes hard for Dave and the other executives not to treat him like a kid—especially since their boss still did. Fred would even send Ford homework assignments from Europe.

During his medicinal stay in London, Fred also took the Grand Tour of Europe. After buying some Italian bronzes, paintings, and photographs for the house, he wrote to Sally from the Hotel Belle Due in Munich that he wanted "Ford and the children to study up on" the historical themes of the images. "I would also like them to read up on Rome and Pompeii so that they will understand the photographs when I get home." Sally was instructed to tell Ford to find a copy of *The Last Days of Pompeii,* the very popular historical novel by Edward Bulwer-Lytton (whose work is largely forgotten today, except for the aggrieved first line of his novel *Paul Clifford,* which begins, "It was a dark and stormy night").

Ford couldn't help but roll his eyes. The same father who had made him leave college was now sending him a syllabus.

His real education, however, was out on the rails. He would accompany Dave, Byron Schermerhorn, or Victor Vizzetti on their inspection trips, and each would try to teach him something different about the eating house business—and the world. Byron would regale him with his philosophical insights about the human condition, Dave would instruct him in matters of money and finance, and Victor was a walking culinary encyclopedia. Each of them also knew how to scare and dare the staff of an eating house—to stand in for Fred Harvey and invoke his wrath, like a mother warning, "Wait until your father comes home."

But while Ford was learning how to unnerve eating house employees, he was also learning how to talk to them. Most Fred Harvey employees had once been in the same position as their customers: far from home and yearning for creature comforts, friendly faces, the great big bear hug of America.

Ford was also absorbing the culture of railroads. He was learning everything from who did what—on the train and in the depot—to why and when an engineer blew his train's whistle. (A mile or so before any road or path crossed the tracks, there was a sign telling the engineer to sound his whistle as a warning, because by the time he could see something or someone on the tracks, it was impossible to slow down and stop without risking the lives of everyone on the train.) He was also learning how the railroad companies were organized, and where Fred Harvey fit into the Santa Fe system.

While Dave did a creditable job explaining the train business, Ford did have another mentor: Santa Fe president William Strong, who had become one of the most powerful executives in America. Ford had known Strong since childhood, initially just as his father's friend but later as someone who could offer advice on the kind of American higher education Fred never had. It was no coincidence that the prep school and college Ford attended in Wisconsin—before Fred summoned him home—were located not far from the Strong family estate, Partridge Farm in Beloit.

Ford regarded Strong as something of an uncle. So, when all hell broke loose in the railroad business in 1887, he got a chance to watch Uncle Bill duke it out with the biggest names in American business, as well as the president of the United States.

GROVER CLEVELAND WAS the first Democrat to be elected president since before the Civil War. He had run on a promise to clean up the railroads, which were so unnerved by his election that they panicked. Fearing that the bonanza of government land grants for railroad construction would soon end, the companies submitted absurd numbers of last-minute requests for additional land—and, by doing so, assured that their worst fears were realized.

Since the beginning of the Civil War, the government had given away almost one-tenth of all the land in the entire continental United States to the railroads to encourage construction and development. Most of these land grants were in the central and western states, where the railroads now controlled over 30 percent of the land. In the weeks before Cleveland took office in 1885, nearly 700,000 additional acres were turned over to railroad companies—even though some of those railroads existed only on paper. Outraged, Cleveland ordered a massive investigation of the land grant system, and the railroads were forced to return about 81 million acres.

Next, the president began looking into whether the federal government—which was still relatively weak—had the power to regulate the railroad business. He found his answer in a legal dispute over $27 ($637) in train shipping charges that reached the U.S. Supreme Court in 1886 and changed American history. *Wabash, St. Louis & Pacific Railroad Company v. Illinois* was a case about why a company shipping thirteen tons of corn from Illinois to New York paid $27 less than a company shipping thirteen tons of "oil cake," a residue used in feed and fertilizer. While conceding that charging different prices for the same weight was unfair, Wabash lawyers challenged the right of the State of Illinois to regulate interstate shipping rates at all. In October 1886, the Supreme Court agreed with them, ruling that states did not have jurisdiction over interstate commerce. The federal government did.

The Act to Regulate Commerce was quickly pushed through Congress, and when President Cleveland signed it in early 1887, he basically added a fourth branch to the American system of government—the federal regulatory agency. It was a major turning point in the very concept of a truly federal government and a truly United States.

The law would later lead to an alphabet soup of initialed entities—everything from the Food and Drug Administration to the Office of Homeland Security. But its first practical application was the creation of the Interstate Commerce Commission, which Congress established that year, urging a crackdown on the railroads that began with their pricing.

Before *Wabash*, railroad fares looked a lot like airline fares today—they were lowest on routes where there was a lot of competition and, on any given train, besides freight being hauled at different prices, there were passengers who had paid different fares for identical trips. The railroads also had a controversial practice called pooling, which was a form of collusion that kept prices high but stable; the companies agreed to divvy up "pooled" receipts and traffic in areas where their services overlapped, ensuring that competition wouldn't drive down rates.

Under the new Interstate Commerce Commission, pooling was declared illegal, as was charging different prices for identical passenger tickets or freight shipments. But without pooling, the railroads immediately went wild trying to undercut one another, and the Santa Fe was no exception. In fact, the one-upmanship became so intense that one Sunday not long after the ICC was created, the fare from Kansas City to Los Angeles actually fell to *one dollar* ($23.35)—a $26 ticket with a rebate of $25. On that day, it was cheaper to ride across the country than to stop for two Fred Harvey meals along the way.

In the chaos of this new economics of railroads, William Strong believed that only a few of the strongest would survive. He felt he was left with no choice—his Santa Fe had to get much bigger and more powerful very quickly, or it would be swallowed by Jay Gould and the other big eastern financiers who were still the power players in the industry.

Strong formulated bold new plans to expand the Santa Fe all the way from Chicago to California—and he summoned Fred Harvey home from Europe. They needed to discuss the future.

CHAPTER 15

TRANSCONTINENTAL FRED

꧁꧂

DURING THE PREVIOUS TWO YEARS, FRED HAD BEEN OVERSEAS more than he had been home. He had taken three long trips to England and the Continent, usually returning to Leavenworth in the fall, staying through Christmas and New Year's, and then sailing back. He occasionally had visitors in England, friends or business associates, but never his wife or family. His role in their lives was reduced to whatever happened during those few months at home. His youngest son, Byron, would always remember going to a parade with his father where they played a game counting white horses (when they reached one hundred, he got a $5 half-eagle gold coin) and the advice Fred wrote to him in an album before leaving the year he was eleven: "My Dear Son Byron, I hope that you will always speak the truth—under no consideration ever tell a lie."

Most of the family relationships, however, were carried on by international mail; Fred wrote home often, and was never subtle in his disappointment when he did not receive individual letters from his wife and children. "Well, Ma," he wrote during one long stay in Europe, "I hope you and the children are well . . . I have not heard from Minnie, May, Byron or Sybil for some time. Kiss them all for me and tell them to write. Say to them the letters I write you are intended for them as well."

Fred was able to spend so much time away because his business was relatively stable. It had not grown any easier to maintain the standard at twenty different eating houses; Harvey Girls were getting married at a dizzying pace; managers and chefs would leave to run their own hotels and restaurants. But the scale of such pressures had grown predictable, as had the strong cash flow and the low overhead.

But now everything was about to change. The Santa Fe system, which for Fred basically ended in Albuquerque, was going to be extended all the way to California—immediately. Strong had once hoped to build new, wholly owned tracks to the Pacific, but President Cleveland had put an end to the land grants. So the Santa Fe consolidated two railroads it half owned: the Atlantic & Pacific, which ran from the Rio Grande at Albuquerque across northern Arizona to the California border; and the California Southern, which started where the A&P ended in Needles, California, and went all the way to San Bernardino, with connections to Los Angeles and San Diego.

In May 1887, the Santa Fe began offering its own through service from Kansas City to Los Angeles. To further "brand" this cobbled-together route, Strong announced that the Santa Fe would now be featuring its signature "Meals by Fred Harvey" all the way to California.

This meant that Fred had to take over the wretched eating houses along the new desert route, each one at a more sun-scorched, godforsaken location than the last. There were eight of them, starting at Coolidge, New Mexico, about a hundred miles west of Albuquerque, continuing across northern Arizona through Winslow and the area that would become Flagstaff, and ending in Mojave, California, about a hundred miles north of Los Angeles.

It was a trying ride. One Santa Fe railroadman recalled, "the people who made the long trip in those days were the real dyed-in-the-wool travelers, the kind that wore caps with a visor at both ends and a bow on the top, loud checkered Sheppard plaid English suits, spats; many with monocles, some with canes and, of course, the crooked stem English bulldog pipes . . . The passengers were not in any good humor, for they were hot, dusty, hungry and none too well pleased with the country and its accommodations."

Overnight, these new eateries doubled the geographic breadth of Fred's empire—and quintupled his headaches. They were all dumps, managed by Stackpole & Lincoln, a California firm that had briefly run the eating houses well, until a series of disastrous fires forced it into receivership.

When Fred took his first train ride to survey the eight new eating houses, they made him sick. Literally. When he got to the sixth house— in Barstow, California, the town named for his friend William Barstow Strong—he had such a severe attack of neuralgia that he remained in bed there for two days before turning around and heading home.

The deal for Fred to take over the houses was formalized and reported on the front page of the *Los Angeles Times*. But nobody reported just how risky a deal it was. Unlike his previous arrangements with the Santa Fe, where the railroad built depots and gave him the space, Fred had to buy out the Stackpole & Lincoln leases as well as their equipment and furniture, even though he knew it would all have to be replaced. (Dave was dispatched to execute the buyouts: "With the aid of sheriffs or of railroadmen," one magazine described, "he took possession of one place after another, striking the best bargain he could with the proprietors.") Since the eating houses were so distant from each other—and from Kansas City—he would also have to set up a western satellite office, which Byron Schermerhorn agreed to run from Riverside, California. All this would require nearly $100,000 ($2.33 million)—more than twice as much as he had invested in the eating houses up to this point.

After the deals were made, eight new managers and chefs were selected from the staffs of existing eating houses to oversee the remodeling and staffing of the dining rooms, lunchrooms, and kitchens. By now, Fred had decided that all positions of authority should be filled from within; as tempting as it was to hire seasoned managers from other restaurants or hotels, the only way to maintain the standard was to elevate and challenge loyal employees already well versed in the company ethos.

New furniture was ordered, and Fred left immediately for Europe to buy everything else needed to quickly make these houses Harvey-worthy. In New York, he was joined by his daughter Minnie, who for her sixteenth birthday was given the honor of being the first family member to accompany him to England. She saw where Fred had grown up in London, and he took her to Wolverhampton to visit his mother's grave. Then he left her with his sister Annie while he went shopping.

His first stop was Belfast, where he bought one thousand linen tablecloths and three thousand oversize linen dinner napkins. Then he went to Sheffield, where he ordered hundreds of "Fred Harvey" signature place settings. Crossing the Channel, he traveled to Bordeaux to buy wines for the restaurants, and to Limoges for porcelains. Everything was shipped back to the States and then carried by train to the eating houses in Arizona and California.

Fred gave his new managers a month to get set up before he returned for his first inspection of the transcontinental Harvey System. He was not pleased.

In Kinsley, Kansas, he scribbled angrily in his datebook, "Girls flirt with traveling Men . . . have run of the store room. Cashier should be changed." In La Junta, Colorado: "Cooking poor, Tables have 71 inch cloth that should have 84 or 87 inch cloth." In Coolidge, New Mexico, he found the "pastery poor, coffee poor, House generally poor."

But the worst was Williams, Arizona, one of the towns from which intrepid explorers were beginning to set out for what was then called the "Grand Cañon of the Colorado." There he was appalled to see sewage from the bathroom on the kitchen floor.

"Very bad," he wrote in his datebook. "House not satisfactory. Worthless manager."

After ten years of running eating houses, Fred found it amazing how much work there was still to be done, how many tablecloths still to be yanked.

AS SOON AS THE Santa Fe reached California, William Strong turned to face the siege of Chicago. He laid tracks from Kansas City east across Missouri, through the southeastern corner of Iowa, crossing the Mississippi at Fort Madison, and then across Illinois all the way to Chicago's oldest downtown train station at Dearborn and Polk streets, a Romanesque brick and pink granite building with a grand twelve-story clock tower. By doing this, he put his railroad in direct competition with all the big Midwestern lines that had previously provided the Santa Fe with much of its business, carrying freight and passengers as far as Kansas City.

Some thought him foolish to challenge his best business partners, many of whom were also his close friends. But he believed it was the only way. One railroad dominated the route between the East and Chicago, the mighty Pennsylvania Railroad. And he believed one railroad would eventually dominate from Chicago west. He wanted it to be the Santa Fe.

The new route was referred to as an "airline" between Chicago and Kansas City, because it had very few stops and the trip was fast—only twelve hours. To call attention to it, Strong built what the press called "the handsomest trains in the world." The first-class cars had

mahogany walls and high-back sofa seats with plush maroon upholstery and gold piping; the sleeping cars were done in a Louis XV motif
with bronze hardware, antique oak, and peacock blue silk upholstery;
the parlor car, finished in elaborately carved oak in a Moorish design,
had a smoking room and a separate reading room with a library, a writing desk, and movable wicker settees. All the interior trimmings were
silver plated, and even the brake handles were solid bronze.

Besides the visual splendor, the train was a mechanical marvel.
Each car had its own self-sustaining electrical system—with a revolutionary new laborsaving device, "switches, so that the light can be
turned on and off at will"—and was heated using steam from the engine instead of the old-fashioned wood-burning heaters located in
each car.

The train also incorporated the latest innovation in railroading,
"vestibules." George Pullman had finally figured out how to allow train
passengers to walk from car to car in safety. He had invented and
patented the first working vestibule, a flexible, sturdy covered platform
through which people could pass while the train was moving. And
there was a special incentive for passengers to walk through this
train—because its dining car was making culinary history.

The nation's two greatest names in passenger comfort and service
were collaborating for the first time. George Pullman designed and
built the dining car, with its sensational state-of-the-art metal-clad
kitchen, and Fred Harvey designed the sumptuous menu and provided
the staff to cook and serve it.

The dining car walls and furnishings were hand-carved French antique oak. There were private dining areas, as well as a wine room and
a buffet room. On the menu were bluepoint oysters, followed by consommé, and then tender young chicken halibut with fine herbs, spring
lamb with mint sauce, sweetbreads sautéed with mushrooms, or teal
duck, served with new potatoes in cream, sweet potatoes au gratin, or
potato croquettes. For dessert, there was English plum pudding with
brandy sauce, strawberries in Neapolitan cream, and various cakes and
cheeses. There were five wines to choose from, after-dinner cognac,
and, of course, a generous assortment of the finest cigars. Dinner was
prix fixe at $1 ($23).

The train made its inaugural run on May 1, 1888. It was the crown-
ing achievement of William Strong's career, and he bet everything he
had on it. The Santa Fe had doubled in size in just the past two years,

laying three thousand miles of new track and upgrading every rail and tie on its existing tracks. It was now the largest railroad in the world. To accomplish all this, Strong had run up a massive debt of $65 million ($1.5 billion), but the investment seemed to be paying off.

His new service from Chicago to the Pacific—featuring "Meals by Fred Harvey"—was such a runaway success that rumors began circulating in the financial press that the Santa Fe was not going to stop there. They said Strong would build or buy tracks all the way to New York, riding in with his white-hat philosophy to take on the robber barons and clean up America's railroads.

JUST THREE WEEKS after the triumphant debut of the new transcontinental Santa Fe train, the Harvey family had a more personal milestone: Ford got married. The event seemed perfectly timed as a celebration of the official end of his four-year apprenticeship—just as the company had doubled in size and its possibilities seemed limitless. It was also the culmination of a great Leavenworth love affair.

When Ford first started dating Josephine "Judy" Blair, the daughter of prominent attorney General Charles W. Blair, there were a lot of raised eyebrows in Leavenworth society. The Blairs lived in the Piety Hill neighborhood on the north side and were "old money," which in Leavenworth meant they had been wealthy for at least twenty years. The Harveys were clearly among the south-side nouveau riche. Judy— a handsome young woman with melancholic, compassionate eyes and thick hair she wore pulled back in a loose bun—was the youngest of four wealthy daughters, and Ford was the only one of the Harvey children who *hadn't* been born into wealth.

The courtship of Ford and Judy had been tempestuous, and the younger Harvey children had watched it like an entertaining parlor drama. Periodically, one of the Blairs' servants would show up at the Harvey home on Olive Street, returning all of Ford's letters and presents to Judy. Then Bean, the Harveys' coachman, would be dispatched to Piety Hill to return all of Judy's letters and presents to Ford. After they made up, the servants would cross paths again, bringing everything back. As the relationship became more serious, some of the fights were probably about religion: The Harveys were Episcopalian, and the Blairs were Catholic.

Now they were finally marrying. Ford was twenty-two and couldn't wait to move out of his parents' house; at twenty-one, Judy was also more than ready. Ford agreed that Judy would raise their children as Catholics, but since he didn't want to convert, they couldn't be married in her family's church. Instead, the wedding was at the Harveys' church, St. Paul's Episcopal, on May 19, 1888, and it was the social event of the year. The front pages of all the Leavenworth newspapers overflowed with descriptions of the gowns, the food, the guests, and the floral motif: snowballs in May, accented by roses of all types and colors. The wedding dinner at the Blair mansion was prepared by Werner, the famous Chicago caterer, who served "a menu comprised of all imaginable delicacies."

After the wedding weekend extravaganza, the newlyweds did the fashionable thing—they took the new Santa Fe vestibule train to Chicago, where they honeymooned at the Palmer House. Then they took the new train back to Kansas City, where their things had already been moved into their new home. It was within walking distance of the Fred Harvey office in Union Station, in an upscale residential neighborhood, with a name apt for the heir to a family business dedicated to perfectionism.

It was called Quality Hill.

CHAPTER 16

BITING THE HAND

T HE SANTA FE HAD BEEN WARNED AGAINST COMING INTO CHICAGO; even William Strong's closest friends told him he was laying track too close to the sun. For the first few months, it looked as if he had proved his critics wrong. But it soon was clear he had badly miscalculated how hard it would be to earn back the millions he had spent expanding the Santa Fe from Chicago to Los Angeles. He also misjudged just how far his competitors would cut prices to make his life miserable.

Now that the government didn't allow pooling to stabilize prices, nobody knew how to stop passenger fares and shipping rates from bottoming out. The rates for shipping cattle or dressed beef would be cut in half overnight, then in half again. Passenger rates started to include all kinds of rebates and inducements. The Santa Fe lost one big party traveling from Iowa to California when a competing road offered "a private car and free beer all the way." In less than six months, the Santa Fe went from being the darling of the financial markets to a possible takeover target for financier Jay Gould, who owned the competing Missouri Pacific but had made so much money financing other railroads that there was a constant threat that he would destroy, or buy, anything in his path.

When the Santa Fe announced it needed to borrow millions to make ends meet, financial markets became wary. "Unless confidence is restored in some way," the *Chicago Tribune* reported, "a great slaughter of stock is predicted." Within weeks, the *New York Times* was reporting on its front page that Strong was in New York, huddled in a conference room with Gould trying to figure out a way to stabilize freight rates or consolidate the competing western railroad companies before they drove each other out of business. There were rumors the Santa Fe might go into receivership.

Just after Christmas, in the year that was supposed to be the most triumphant and satisfying of his career, William Strong announced he might resign as president of the Santa Fe. While his health was blamed, everyone knew he was being pressured by board members who wanted a more fiscally conservative strategy, among them financier Oliver Peabody, whose Boston brokerage house, Kidder, Peabody, handled the Santa Fe's bonds.

Suddenly Fred Harvey's empire was in grave danger. He still had nothing but a handshake agreement with the railroad. That had been fine for all these years, because the hands he shook belonged to friends. But if William Strong was forced out, the railroad could snatch his entire eating house business away at a moment's notice.

In the meantime, the fare wars hurt Santa Fe ridership, and eating house business was off. Fred returned to England for his health, but as he sat in the guest bedroom of his sister Annie's house in London reading letters and telegrams from home, he was antsy—and often bored out of his mind.

"I almost wish sometimes some business matter would call me home," he wrote to his wife in March 1889, as the Santa Fe board pondered Strong's fate. "When I am feeling well, as I do now, I hate to be loafing around London. Ford and Benjamin both write me that business is very dull and that we still continue losing money. This I do not fret about, however, for were I home, I could not alter that."

Fred was finally summoned home by Strong, in mid-April, to discuss the future of his eating house chain. His ship arrived in New York on April 22, a day when many of his employees were more focused on an extraordinary drama unfolding outside the Harvey eating house in tiny Arkansas City, Kansas.

Nearly 100,000 people were descending on the town in southeastern Kansas, all of them waiting for the biggest land giveaway in American history. Fred's depot hotel was filled to capacity, people were camped on the streets, and there were four miles of tent cities leading all the way to the border between Kansas and what is now Oklahoma but was then called Indian Territory (because the government had forced the major tribes of the Southeast to relocate there in the 1830s). As Harvey Girls tried to serve the endless stream of customers, they would occasionally peer through the venetian blinds of the dining room to watch the spectacle. The streets teemed with panhandlers, con men, patent-medicine salesmen, and anxious boomers brandishing pistols and whiskey bottles.

The government was opening Indian Territory to white settlers at exactly noon on April 22—and because the Santa Fe controlled the major rail line through the territory and into Texas, it was coordinating with army battalions out of Fort Leavenworth to make sure everything went smoothly. The trains pulling out of Arkansas City that morning were so packed, they looked like "giant centipedes with hundreds of arms and legs and heads sticking out everywhere," according to one eyewitness. They left every fifteen minutes, carrying thousands of homesteaders to Guthrie, where many of them leaped out of train windows or climbed through roof ventilators to jump off and dash to open plots first.

By day's end, as Fred was checking in with his office from New York, the land rush had finished, and his manager in Arkansas City was trying to restore some normalcy. Over 1.9 million acres had been claimed. There were now more than ten thousand people living in Guthrie who hadn't been there the previous day. Almost all of them had arrived on the Santa Fe.

WILLIAM STRONG AGREED to go quietly: He would be routinely voted out of office at the next board of directors meeting. Before he left, however, there was one more thing he wanted: a last-minute reprieve for Fred Harvey. The two old friends secretly met and negotiated a deal that would finally give Fred a written contract, committing the Santa Fe to let him manage its eating houses for at least the next five years. On May 1, 1889, they signed an agreement that formalized the thirteen-year-old handshake deal. It also appears Strong arranged for a secret cash payment to his friend's company—equal or close to the $100,000 ($2.4 million) Fred had recently been forced to invest in the new western eating houses—which may have been kept quiet to avoid the scrutiny of the Interstate Commerce Commission.

Within months, Strong was out. His successor, Allen Manvel, was brought in from the St. Paul, Minneapolis & Manitoba Railroad because of his reputation for fiscal restraint. Hired to reverse what were seen as Strong's excesses, Manvel considered Fred Harvey and his operation to be an unnecessary extravagance. He couldn't believe the railroad had let Strong make an eleventh-hour deal protecting the Harvey restaurant and hotel franchise.

However, since he couldn't cancel the contract, the Santa Fe's new president tried to make Fred's life miserable by exploiting what he believed to be a loophole in the agreement. Strong had given Fred exclusive control of Santa Fe restaurants and hotels west of the Missouri River; there was no mention of dining cars, since at the time the railroad had only a couple of them, servicing the "airline" between Chicago and Kansas City. Manvel decided he would buy dining cars for his western trains and stop making thirty-minute meal stops at depots with Harvey eating houses. His excuse was that he wanted to cut travel times on competitive western routes.

Manvel quietly fired Fred from the dining car service on the Chicago-to-Kansas City train, and the Santa Fe ordered a fleet of new dining cars to be built, which the company announced it would run itself.

Fred was outraged. So was George Pullman, who believed that if Harvey didn't control the Santa Fe dining cars, then *he* should. Pullman reportedly threatened to sue the railroad, but then pulled back. Fred consulted with his local lawyer, William Hook, and they decided to hire a high-powered Chicago attorney, George Washington Kretzinger, a former railroad general counsel who had argued in front of the U.S. Supreme Court, to represent his interests. Kretzinger's negotiations with the railroad continued for more than a year. While they argued, the railroad waited to deploy its new dining cars in the West, so it was nearly business as usual for the Harvey eating houses—except that Dave Benjamin and Ford Harvey were changing roles and taking on more responsibilities.

Now that Ford was married and living in Kansas City, he spent almost every day with Dave, who remained Fred's second-in-command. Dave was only eight years older than Ford, but the gap was significant. He was thirty-three, long married with two children, and already well established as a businessman and budding civic leader. In his personal life, he and his siblings were becoming active in Kansas City's expanding Jewish community—particularly his brother Alfred, who now had a position similar to Dave's with Fred's friend Colonel Abernathy, whose furniture company had also relocated there from Leavenworth.

Ford and Dave had been in an unusual situation for some time.

Both had grown up revering Fred Harvey, whose success and vision had brought them wealth and prestige. Now they were in the same plush foxhole together, faced with the complex dynamics of family business. Dave had to respect Ford not only as the boss's son but as someone who was one Fred health crisis away from becoming *his* boss, too. Yet Ford still looked up to Dave, in part as the older brother he never had but also as a substitute for the father he didn't see very much. It was not surprising that when Ford marked his adulthood with facial hair, he grew a full mustache like Dave's rather than copy his father's Van Dyke. But it was also a sign of the times: As American men became more civilized, they preferred to be less hairy.

Dave and Ford shared one other thing: They were the only ones who realized the full impact of Fred spending so much time away from his family and his business. While he still made all the major decisions—many via coded telegram from England—it was amazing how many day-to-day choices each of them was making for, or rather *as,* Fred Harvey.

Ford was gaining confidence in his increasing independence. He no longer needed a mentor to travel with him to inspect the eating houses or the ranches. Mostly, he took the long train rides only with his assistant, Tim Cooper, the company's first black office employee—who had started as a messenger for the bookkeeper and worked his way up.

While the daily pressures of handling the eating house business were unchanged, emotions ran high at the Kansas City office as Fred's lawyer wrestled with the Santa Fe's attorneys. Everyone knew what was at stake: At any moment, they could go to war with the railroad or be forced to close the entire Fred Harvey system overnight. The fear could be seen in the telegraph codes that Dave added to Fred's pocket cipher book whenever the boss left for England—to cover every possible worst-case scenario. According to the cipher book, the word "Quandary" meant "Indications are that Company are getting ready to put [dining] Cars on the road but can get nothing official," "Quarrel" meant "Mr. Manvel declines to delay the matter until you can get back."

And "Quench" meant "Kretzinger advises us to bring suit at once." When Fred read that word in a telegram he received in London at the end of July 1891, he immediately booked passage back to the United States. As he sailed home on the *City of Paris,* his lawyers filed suit against the railroad with which he had risen to greatness.

FRED HARVEY V. AT&SF RR CO. was the talk of the railroad industry and the restaurant business. People had been wondering for years just how Fred Harvey did it, how he ran what were essentially marketplace restaurants in remote, arid locations using a train refrigerator car as his greengrocer. While the Fred Harvey name was well-known, Fred himself was a mysterious figure—"a peculiar character," according to the *Chicago Herald*, who "always keeps his whereabouts a secret, and is liable to jump from a train at one of his eating houses at any moment and without warning." He did not like people knowing his business. Now his relationship with the railroad was national news, splashed across the pages of major newspapers in New York, Chicago, and Los Angeles.

The papers were especially taken by Fred's frontier saga, which they gobbled up like any great cowboy yarn. His lawsuit told the story of how, for the past fifteen years, he had run his company "at great risk and loss and with many disadvantages," because his eating houses were "frequently invaded by desperate desperadoes" and "constantly menaced by incursion of hostile Indians and infested by gamblers and other dangerous and lawless persons." His employees were "subjected to indignities" and often found themselves at the wrong end of a gun, driven from the eating houses "and at times from the town at the point of revolvers."

The lawsuit revealed the full scope of Fred Harvey's very private business. He now ran Santa Fe eating houses, lunchrooms, and hotels in twenty-four towns across five states. He had a huge cattle ranch in Granada, Colorado, where he had also started raising milk cows and chickens for his eating houses. And he had recently bought a second farm in Emporia, Kansas. He had four hundred employees and an annual payroll of nearly $250,000 ($6.1 million). He was serving five thousand meals *a day*. He had a lot to lose.

But Fred was well connected in Chicago. He had many prominent friends there, and he had comped meals and hotel rooms for many a Chicago politician and businessman venturing out to see the West. His attorney was also influential, and they were able to find a sympathetic judge. The day after the lawsuit was filed, a temporary injunction was issued against the Santa Fe. The railroad challenged it, but the judge denied the appeal and made the injunction permanent.

The railroad appealed again, claiming that the local courts had no jurisdiction and the Interstate Commerce Commission should get involved in the case. That challenge was also denied. The judge left it to Fred and Santa Fe president, Allen Manvel, to work out their differences. In the meantime, the railroad was not allowed to replace Fred Harvey meal stops with dining cars.

It was an embarrassing defeat for the Santa Fe. The largest railroad in the world, with reported annual earnings of nearly $25 million ($610 million) and stock valued at over $200 million ($4.9 billion), was being held hostage by its small, privately held food concessionaire. The caboose was wagging the train.

CHAPTER 17

THE BIGGEST CATERED LUNCH
IN AMERICAN HISTORY

ꋟꋟ

EVERYTHING FRED HAD BUILT SEEMED IN DANGER OF FALLING apart. Relations with the Santa Fe continued to deteriorate, business was stagnant, and, adding to the strain, the Harvey family suffered a devastating loss. Byron Schermerhorn died suddenly in California at the age of fifty-six, leaving a wife and two teenage daughters. Fred received the news in New York, just before heading to Washington, D.C., to lobby several senators with railroad backgrounds for support in his battles with the Santa Fe.

He took some consolation in memorializing his friend, arranging to have a collection of Schermerhorn's poems typeset and published in a handsome hardcover book. But the grief was exceedingly difficult to process: Best friends for over two decades, they had spent the past few years preparing for what would happen when Fred, inevitably, died first.

Soon, however, there was some joyful news. Ford's wife, Judy, gave birth to a baby girl, Katherine—who was nicknamed Kitty—in July 1892, and the next Fred Harvey generation had begun.

The baby came just as Fred, Dave, and Ford were starting to formulate backup plans for their business—other ways to deploy what had grown into a veritable army of loyal employees—since the disputed contract with the Santa Fe was set to run out in less than two years. Thinking big, they put in a bid for the largest job in U.S. culinary history—the catering contract for the Columbian Exhibition, the world's fair to be held in Chicago to commemorate the four hundredth anniversary of Columbus reaching America. Its success was a matter of civic pride and national honor, since Americans had made a decidedly anemic showing at the last world's fair in Paris, where they couldn't compete with the French exhibit: the Eiffel Tower.

Fred had some "ins" at the Chicago world's fair. He had known architect Daniel Burnham—the driving force behind the fair and the mastermind of the urban fantasy of a classical "White City" in the middle of gritty Chicagoland—for years, since he redesigned the Montezuma. And Fred had several other friends on the ways and means committee, which was stacked with Chicago railroad executives. So nobody was surprised when Fred's company was selected as one of two finalists for the massive job, along with the catering department at Chicago's Wellington Hotel.

Instead of holding a bake-off for the contract, the committee decided to have the two companies audition together—by serving the biggest catered lunch in American history. It was the grand finale of the "Dedication Day" ceremony in October 1892—which, because of endless delays, was the only event of the world's fair that actually took place during the anniversary year of Columbus's voyage. In fact, the lunch was served in two of the only buildings in the White City that were actually finished, in part to placate creditors and doubters. After President Benjamin Harrison read a proclamation, there was a parade to the fairgrounds, followed by performances, speeches, and lunch. The caterers were charged with preparing and serving a sit-down meal for 4,500 invited guests in one building and then providing "a nice lunch" for everyone else who attended the parade, regardless of the number.

Ford made a bet with his father over how many of those "nice" lunches they would have to serve. He wagered a hundred Imperial cigars that it would be more than 100,000, a bet Fred recorded on one of the Leavenworth Bank scratch pads he carried in his jacket pocket.

The sit-down lunch was in the Manufacturer's and Liberal Arts Building, a massive Corinthian-style structure that covered forty-five acres and required sixty tons of paint to make it white enough for the White City. The service for the meal was as complex and precise as any major military operation. There were 120 waiters, and 6 chefs who did nothing but brew fresh coffee: 150 gallons of it. All the other food was prepared ahead of time: 9,000 sandwiches of assorted meats, 120 gallons of chicken salad, and, for dessert, 300 pounds of cake, 80 fruit custard tarts, and 80 wine-jelly rolls, all presliced.

Sixty thousand people showed up for the public lunch, so Ford lost the bet. They dined in the Electricity Building, at rows and rows of tables that would have extended a mile and a half if laid end to end. There were 350 waitresses serving eight tons of ham sandwiches, 240,000 doughnuts, and 120,000 cups of coffee. Just outside the kitchen, the fifteen-hundred-member children's choir who had sung during the ceremony ate sandwiches and bananas.

The lunch was a great success and received high praise from the directors of the fair. Since Fred Harvey and the Wellington Hotel caterers had worked so well together, they decided to team up to bid on the multimillion-dollar contract to feed the entire world's fair. The *Chicago Tribune* reported that they were expected to get the job.

But at the last minute a well-connected New York firm was allowed to put in a competing bid. In the shoot-out of underbidding, Fred lost the single biggest job of his career. It wasn't until six months later, however, that he discovered just how great a loss it really was—for as the entire American economy went into free fall, the Chicago world's fair was virtually the only place left in the country where business was any good.

MOST AMERICANS TODAY have never heard of the Panic of 1893, and the subsequent four-year financial bottoming out that many economists still believe was every bit as bad as the Great Depression of 1929. That's probably because in 1893 the economy didn't succumb to a single huge heart attack, but was instead devastated by a series of strokes over many months.

Only weeks after Fred lost that catering contract, Jay Gould, who was believed to be the richest man in the world, died of tuberculosis at the age of fifty-six. His death in December 1892 was not a surprise, and elaborate preparations had been made to prevent a negative impact on financial markets. Unfortunately, Wall Street soon was rocked by a series of company failures in industries as diverse as railroading, banking, and rope making, all of which put more pressure on what was considered a glaring weakness in the nation's monetary policy: Gold reserves were being depleted to artificially prop up silver prices for western miners.

The first visible symptom of the economy's ill health was the bankruptcy of the Philadelphia & Reading Railroad in February 1893. It wasn't an especially large railroad, and was considered a chronic underachiever, but it left millions in unpaid debt and sent a signal that other struggling railroads might not survive.

Five days later, Fred's combative boss at the Santa Fe, Allen Manvel, died. He was only fifty-five, but had been suffering from Bright's disease, a then-untreatable kidney ailment, and his death raised the specter that the Santa Fe was in financial trouble as well.

In the late spring, the World Columbian Exhibition opened in Chicago to great fanfare (even though many of the exhibits still weren't finished, including the first-ever Ferris wheel). But while there was glee at the fairgrounds—and Fred's eating houses along the Santa Fe route were packed to and from Chicago—much of the country was in a panic. Two days after the fair began, there was a massive sell-off on the New York Stock Exchange, and one of the most-traded companies—the National Cordage Trust, a combination of twenty-five rope and cord manufacturers that controlled 80 percent of its market—went bankrupt. Cordage yanked the rest of the market down with it, setting off further panic selling and bank failures across America.

Many called on Grover Cleveland—who was president again, after being voted out of office in 1888 and then reelected in 1892—to respond to the financial disaster. But the president had just been diagnosed with oral cancer, and to keep his condition out of the papers, he disappeared on a "fishing trip" when he was actually having major surgery to remove part of his upper jaw—an operation that was performed on a yacht floating off Long Island Sound to maintain the ruse. As he recuperated, the economy seemed to do the same, until the Erie Railroad declared bankruptcy on July 25. Two days later, banks across the country announced they would not allow large cash withdrawals, leading to widespread hoarding of currency and even more bank failures. Congress acted to change the controversial law that had depleted the nation's gold reserves. But the move came too late—and it also caused the silver markets to crash. While employment estimates for the volatile time period vary, economists agree unemployment had at least doubled by summer's end, and perhaps tripled. At least one million Americans were out of work, and the number kept climbing.

The world's fair, however, continued to attract visitors; the Ferris wheel, with cars as big as Pullmans, was finally up and running, causing a sensation. It seemed as if the fairgrounds at Jackson Park were the only place in America shielded from the failing economy. By October, nearly twenty-seven million people had paid admission to see the fair, a number equal to roughly half the population of the United States.

As the fair wound down, the railroad industry was rocked by the news that the Union Pacific, which had built the first transcontinental railroad, was going bankrupt.

The Santa Fe managed to hold on, largely due to the efforts of its chairman of the board, George Magoun. A powerful international investment banker, Magoun was the American representative of Baring Brothers bank in England—which controlled most of the Santa Fe's foreign-owned stock. He was trying to buy some time for the railroad, which had run out of money to make payroll and was facing a $5 million ($123 million) interest payment due on the first of the year.

By November 1893, Magoun was under enormous pressure. Besides the Santa Fe's problems, he was a major player in the difficult reorganization of the failed National Cordage Trust—and he was struggling with his own health, which had been ravaged by diabetes. In late December, George Magoun died at the age of fifty-three.

As Christmas Eve approached that year, the worst yet in the American economy, fifteen somber, well-dressed men crossed a platform at St. Louis station at 2:00 a.m. to board a special private train—consisting of an engine, a baggage car, and one Pullman coach—headed for Little Rock, Arkansas. When they arrived the next day around lunchtime, they took carriages to the U.S. Court of Appeals for the Eighth Circuit, filing into the chambers of Henry Clay Caldwell, the last judge appointed by Abraham Lincoln.

They emerged at 5:30 p.m. with the sorrowful news. The Atchison, Topeka & Santa Fe—a railroad that in its thirty-four years had gone from being a local laughingstock to the largest, most expensive, and, unfortunately, most indebted carrier in history—was no more.

More than one hundred American railroads failed in 1893, as did five thousand U.S. banks and ten thousand other companies. Unemployment reached double-digit figures and kept rising. The devastation was evenly distributed between the cities and the countryside.

As Americans wondered why this was happening to their country, a relatively obscure academic paper was published in the *Proceedings of the State Historical Society of Wisconsin*. Prepared for the World Columbian Exhibition by historian Frederick Jackson Turner, the paper examined the role of the frontier in U.S. history. Turner boldly suggested that frontier spirit—and the drive farther and farther west for free land—was what defined America and Americans. And he dared to wonder aloud what would become of the United States now that there was no more frontier, nowhere else to expand.

It is "to the frontier the American intellect owes its striking characteristics," wrote Turner:

> That coarseness and strength combined with acuteness and inquisitiveness; that practical, inventive turn of mind, quick to find expedients; that masterful grasp of material things, lacking in the artistic but powerful to effect great ends; that restless, nervous energy; that dominant individualism, working for good and for evil, and withal that buoyancy and exuberance which comes with freedom—these are traits of the frontier . . . Since the days when the fleet of Columbus sailed into the waters of the New World, America has been another name for opportunity, and the people of the United States have taken their tone from the incessant expansion which has not only been open but has even been forced upon them. He would be a rash prophet who should assert that the expansive character of American life has now entirely ceased . . . the American energy will continually demand a wider field for its exercise. But never again will such gifts of free land offer themselves . . . What the Mediterranean Sea was to the Greeks, breaking the bond of custom, offering new experiences, calling out new institutions and activities, that, and more, the ever retreating frontier has been to the United States directly, and to the nations of Europe more remotely. And now, four centuries from the discovery of America, at the end of a hundred years of life under the Constitution, the frontier has gone, and with its going has closed the first period of American history.

While the validity of Turner's "frontier thesis" would be discussed for decades to come, there was no question that the year it was published, at the height of the worst depression in American history, it was a scary prognosis.

MUCH TO FRED, FORD, AND DAVE'S AMAZEMENT, the Panic of 1893, while destroying businesses all over the country, probably saved their company. It was clear before the stock market collapsed and the railroads went bankrupt that the Santa Fe was planning to dump Fred Harvey as its eating house concessionaire when the contract ran out in mid-1894. Fred probably would have retired with his substantial savings, and Ford and Dave would have looked for new jobs. Instead, the Santa Fe's receivers welcomed Fred back with open arms. They were dealing with engineers, brakemen, conductors, and switchmen who had not been paid in months, so Fred's arrangement, which didn't cost the railroad any cash, was the least of their concerns. Instead of firing him, the receivers were thrilled to extend his contract indefinitely—or at least until the reorganization was complete.

Yet business remained challenging. In addition to the financial crisis, 1894 turned out to be a year of freak occurrences. The weather went biblical. The winter storms were among the worst in recorded history. A massive belt of snow and sleet buried so much of the country that there were actually snowball fights on the streets of Tucson, Arizona. Fred lost many head of cattle to the unrelenting cold.

After the freeze came a big spring thaw, heavy rains, and massive flooding, especially near the Rocky Mountains. AT&SF railroadmen working in Pueblo, Colorado, watched in disbelief as the Arkansas River—which flowed past the depot—kept rising and rising until it flooded its banks, carrying in its torrent everything from the carcasses of horses, sheep, cows, and dogs to hundreds of homes torn from their foundations.

And then, just as the western rivers were receding, the workers in George Pullman's plant went on strike in May 1894. Within weeks, they triggered a monumental national work stoppage—and turned Pullman into the most hated man in working-class America.

Pullman had created a "company town" not far from Chicago where his employees built customized cars for his many American and European railroad clients. But the residents of tiny Pullman, Illinois, were outraged when their wages were cut in response to the depression. Their wildcat strike closed Pullman's plant, but he refused to negotiate with his workers. Then the new American Railway Union, over 100,000 members strong, held its long-planned first annual convention in Chicago. The union's president, Eugene V. Debs, convinced his members to call for a boycott of all trains carrying Pullman cars until Pullman himself agreed to negotiate with his employees. Within a week, the front-page headline of the *New York Times* proclaimed the work stoppage the "Greatest Strike in History."

While Chicago was the epicenter of the strike, the hardest-hit railroad was the Santa Fe. Union protesters halted trains in every station between Illinois and California. When local law enforcement proved ineffectual, U.S. marshals were sent to ride the trains and protect the depots. On Independence Day 1894, President Cleveland ordered troops into the stations.

Just weeks before, a group of wealthy businessmen from Michigan and California had met at Fred Harvey's eating house in Williams, Arizona, for a banquet to kick off their hunting and camping trip to the Grand Canyon. They dined on diamondback terrapin soup, frogs' legs, brook trout, spring chicken cutlets with asparagus, tenderloin of beef, orange fritters à la crème, meringue pies, sabayón custard, and bottle after bottle of champagne and claret.

Now that same Williams depot was a war zone. Strikers had removed some tracks near the station, causing one of the engines to run aground. In nearby Winslow, a company from the army's Whipple Barracks was camped on the railroad right-of-way near the Harvey House, with sentinels posted all around the depot.

At Las Vegas, New Mexico, a Santa Fe train from San Francisco with 250 passengers on board was taken hostage by union protesters. The travelers weren't even allowed to cross the picket line surrounding the depot to go into town to buy food. For the first few days, there was enough in the eating house refrigerators for the cooks and Harvey Girls to feed everybody. Then, with no resolution in sight, Dave Benjamin sent a wire from Kansas City telling them to serve just two meals a day. A week passed with the train still captive, so Dave got permission from the Santa Fe to let his chefs rummage through the freight cars trapped at the depot for food. When protesters announced their intention of running the Pullman porters out of town at gunpoint, soldiers helped the train pull out of the Las Vegas station. But when it arrived at Raton, the protesters there held the train for another two days.

There were riots at train depots across the country. American troops were ordered to shoot civilians. In Chicago, seven strikers were killed and dozens more injured while hundreds of train cars were destroyed. Several of the White City buildings from the world's fair were torched. Eugene Debs and other American Railway Union officials were arrested, charged with ignoring a federal injunction to stop striking, because the work stoppage was interfering with interstate commerce and the delivery of the U.S. mail.

After eleven harrowing days, the Pullman strike finally ended and train travel resumed. The issues raised by the strike, however, did not go away. Outraged by the actions of the government and the railroads, a young lawyer at the Chicago & North Western Railway, Clarence Darrow, quit his job to switch sides and represent Debs and the union. They lost the criminal case, and Debs spent a year in prison, but Darrow also challenged the right of the government to file an injunction and bring in troops to stop the strike—and that case went all the way to the U.S. Supreme Court. In May 1895, the high court ruled against Debs and Darrow again, in a unanimous decision to "ensure the general welfare of the public."

BY THE SUMMER OF 1895, the economy was starting to show signs of recovery. Fred, now back in England, was feeling well enough to entertain company at his small hotel in the Putney section of London. He even wrote to Ford that he might welcome a visit from "mamma"—his wife, Sally, who had never come to England with him.

Among Fred's guests that summer at 23 Carlton Road was J. J. Frey, recently hired by the receivers of the Santa Fe to be general manager during the corporate reorganization. He had come all the way from Chicago to discuss a touchy subject. The railroad now wanted Fred to manage the very dining cars they had built to drive him out of business.

Fred entertained the executive lavishly—he is "having a very good time here, certainly he has received a great deal of attention," he wrote to Ford—and they talked for the better part of two days. Frey found out that no matter how sick he had been, Fred Harvey still knew how to ask for everything. Because it was impossible to break even on dining cars—railroads ran them as loss leaders—he insisted the Santa Fe reimburse him 25¢ ($6.61) for every meal served that cost more than a quarter: prix-fixe meals at that time being 75¢ ($19.84). Fred also claimed, as his lawyers had during the lawsuit, that the addition of dining cars would render some of his eating houses superfluous, impossible to run even at an acceptable loss. So he wanted the railroad to agree, in writing, to make him whole for the value of any depot restaurants or hotels he would have to close.

J. J. Frey left England several days later to tour the Continent for three weeks before heading back to talk to his superiors. If they agreed, it would almost seem as if all the legal battles and heartaches of the past seven years had never happened. Almost.

CHAPTER 18

LET THE BOYS DO IT

I N THE LIFE OF A FAMILY BUSINESS, THERE IS NO PERIOD MORE perilous than when the specter of succession arises—and begins to haunt every major decision, every minor decision, every conversation, and, ultimately, every fleeting glance. That period can last a week, a year, a decade, or sometimes forever. But once it starts, almost anything can happen.

By the mid-1890s, Ford and Dave had to be honest with themselves. They had been acting as "Fred Harvey" almost as long as Fred Harvey himself. In the day-to-day world of the company, Fred Harvey had transcended mere mortality to become a watchful, powerful entity, equally capable of benevolence or vengeance. He had become the corporate father-figurehead, a management tool used to keep employees focused on the high aspirations of the company and the dire consequences of mediocrity. And the more often Fred was away, pulling strings from behind the curtain, the more his mystique grew, not unlike a fictional character soon to be created in Kansas: the Wizard of Oz.

On January 24, 1896, Ford and Judy Harvey had a second child, a son they named Frederick Henry Harvey—"Freddy." As sixty-year-old Fred Harvey held his namesake in his wiry arms, it was clearer than ever that the time had come to make a decision about succession. Ford was a different kind of executive than his father—less nervously demanding and more quietly commanding, able to motivate calmly with a raised eyebrow and subtle turn of phrase rather than a smashed plate. And he was more than ready to lead. Yet, like so many sons in family businesses, he didn't know how to broach the subject with his father without seeming disrespectful.

The new president of the Santa Fe, however, knew *exactly* how to do it.

Edward Payson Ripley prided himself on being blunt. He got away with it because he was extremely bright as well as exceedingly large. At fifty, Ed Ripley was still a towering presence; nobody doubted him when he boasted of having nine *Mayflower*-era blacksmiths in his family tree. Even his walrussy mustache was formidable. One newspaper described him as "massive of head and features, tall, broad, flat as an athlete at the abdomen; huge of chin, nose, and mouth; gray of eyes and leonine—a man, in short, as one would picture on a tremendous black horse, armor-clad, and carrying a heavy sword." His only physical weakness was his vision, but he refused to wear spectacles. So his disarming frankness was partly attributable to the fact that he often couldn't focus on people when speaking to them, and so couldn't see how they were reacting.

Fred had known Ed Ripley forever. They grew up in the business together—when Fred was general western agent for the Chicago, Burlington & Quincy, Ripley was its passenger and freight agent for the East—and they reconnected when Ripley, then a vice president at the Chicago, Milwaukee & St. Paul, sat on the steering committee for the Chicago world's fair. It was a pleasant surprise when Ripley was made president of the railroad—renamed the Atchison, Topeka & Santa Fe *Railway* after emerging from receivership—as it looked toward its future. Yet, because Ripley understood the Harvey family situation so well, his ascendancy also signaled the moment of truth.

Ripley went discreetly to his board of directors to find out how much leeway he had in determining his old friend's future. Would they consider letting him *fire* Fred and buy out his eating house business if Ripley decided it was in the best interests of the railroad? As he pointed out to the board, he didn't want to lose the Fred Harvey prestige if he could help it, but "we are under no obligation, moral or legal, to continue . . . as he has gotten rich out of the opportunities he has had." Ripley believed the railroad could make a handsome profit taking over the eating houses, and even suggested they could probably swipe Ford—whom he considered "an exceedingly capable man"—for a handsome salary.

But, luckily for Fred, the railroad was still reluctant to invest its own cash in the food-service business. The board told Ripley to make a new deal with the legendary restaurateur—although, this time, on terms more advantageous to the railroad. If Fred Harvey wasn't going to pay any rent, the railroad wanted a share, at least, of his profits.

Fred, ailing again, was already in England when the time came to negotiate, so the talks began without him, with Ford and Dave representing the company. As the deal-making became intense, Fred wrote to Ripley from London, lamenting that while he wished to return and get involved, the matter would have to wait until he felt better.

Ripley, however, wanted to deal with "Fred Harvey," the innovative American company, not Fred Harvey, the aging international health seeker. So he decided to do Ford—and ultimately Fred as well—a big favor. He took it upon himself to tell the old man it was time to retire.

Ripley initially dictated a rather formal response to Fred's letter, saying he was sorry to hear of his illness and didn't feel it was necessary for him to rush home, since "I do not think your interests are at all likely to suffer in the hands of your son."

When it came time to sign the typewritten letter, however, Ripley decided it needed a more personal touch. Below his signature, he handwrote: "FH, Stay til you feel like coming home. You have but one life to live and you have worked hard enough. Let the boys do it now."

And with that gesture, Ford Harvey was freed to seek his own greatness—which he chose to do, always, in the name of his father.

Over the next six months, Fred gave his son a broad power of attorney, and let him negotiate a new ten-year deal with the Santa Fe Railway to manage all its restaurants, hotels, and dining cars. The timing was perfect, because the U.S. economy was slowly starting to pull out of its rut like a creaky locomotive finally picking up steam.

While haggling with Ripley over the contract, Ford and Dave also made a subtle decision that forever changed the company's fortunes, and would later be seen as a turning point in the history of American business. They decided to avoid any public acknowledgment of the family succession.

It would have been traditional to mark the milestone by changing the name of the company to Fred Harvey & Son. (Or Fred Harvey & *Sons*, since Byron, currently studying at Yale, might one day want to join the business.) Instead, they chose to do just the opposite.

The name of the company would remain "Fred Harvey." Not "Fred Harvey Company" or "Fred Harvey, Inc." Just "Fred Harvey." The railroad would continue advertising its "Meals by Fred Harvey." At the restaurants and hotels, menus and other printed materials would make a point of noting "Your host is Fred Harvey."

The decision, while semantically tricky, was unambiguously brilliant. For the rest of Fred Harvey's life, and for decades afterward, patrons would feel as if they were being taken care of by Fred Harvey himself.

And, in a way, they were.

UNDER THE NEW DEAL with Ripley, Ford became the exclusive concessionaire for all depots and dining cars associated with the Santa Fe. The contract continued to give the company free rent, utilities, and transportation, but Ford now agreed to split his profits with the railroad at the end of each year—after every possible expense had been deducted. As for dining cars, Ford made the same deal his father had with the railroad's receivers: The Santa Fe agreed to reimburse Fred Harvey twenty-five cents for each meal served.

Ford also convinced Ripley to let him take over all the depot newsstands and gift shops for the Santa Fe. So, overnight, Fred Harvey became the dominant distributor of newspapers and periodicals west of the Mississippi. Ford now controlled newsstands stretching from Chicago to Los Angeles, as well as all the "butchers" who hawked reading material, snacks, and bag lunches to passengers by roaming the aisles or pushing their carts alongside the train to pass their goods up through the open windows. This also made him a major national player in a business near and dear to his father's heart: cigars.

These new contracts immediately doubled the number of cities with Fred Harvey eating houses—or "Harvey Houses," as they were coming to be called—since they included all the lines the Santa Fe had partnered with during the years when the railroad and the restaurateur were feuding. The new locations were on the St. Louis & San Francisco railroad, which was nicknamed the Frisco, even though its tracks ran from St. Louis to northern Texas, and the Gulf, Colorado & Santa Fe, which continued down through the Lone Star State to the Gulf of Mexico.

And since he was his father's son, Ford asked Ripley for one more thing: permission to start a side business, outside of the Santa Fe contract. He wanted to start bidding to run the restaurants and newsstands in the new "union stations" that were springing up across the nation. While Indianapolis and Kansas City had early union stations, most cities still had individual depots for each railroad and were in the process of making deals to begin building central terminals. The first of these was going to be in St. Louis, and Ford snared the contract to run its restaurants and newsstands.

St. Louis Union Depot turned out to be the largest and most glamorous railroad depot in the nation, and certainly the most architecturally eclectic—a mesmerizing jumble of strong colors and Romanesque style with sixty-five-foot-high barrel-vaulted ceilings in its Grand Hall and a Victorian train shed covering eleven acres, built at a cost of some $6.5 million ($172 million). For Ford and Dave, it was a daring leap forward into the company's largest market yet, its first major city. For Fred it was deeply nostalgic; he now owned one of the top restaurants in the city where he had first started, and first failed.

Soon Harvey Girls were serving the dishes that made Fred Harvey beloved in St. Louis, which came to include the Harvey Girl Special Little Thin Orange Pancakes, based on a recipe from the head vegetable cook's grandmother; the cream of Wisconsin cheddar cheese soup; the Plantation Beef Stew served over hot biscuits; and the chef's special sautéed cauliflower greens. In addition to new recipes, working in a big city meant new challenges: To help the numerous immigrants passing through the station who barely spoke English, Ford set up a separate side dining room with Harvey Girls who were multilingual.

The move into St. Louis also brought Fred Harvey a much bigger national profile because not long after Ford took over, St. Louis hosted the 1896 Republican National Convention. Harvey Girls were serving at some of the power meals that led to Ohio governor William McKinley's nomination to run against populist orator and ideologue William Jennings Bryan.

Besides all the expansion that happened almost immediately in 1896, Ripley had ambitious plans for the future. He was building new tracks between Los Angeles and San Francisco and expected that soon there would need to be Harvey Houses all over California. He also decided it was time for the Santa Fe to become much more aggressive about its passenger business, which had always taken a backseat to shipping. Just as the Santa Fe had always helped farmers, ranchers, miners, and manufacturers who would then use the railroad to ship their goods, Ripley now wanted to "seed" the passenger business. The Harvey "standard" of passenger care was a key to his strategy.

He started with grand personal gestures to demonstrate the Santa Fe's newfound love of its riders. When the fast, new all-Pullman train was put into service between Chicago and Los Angeles—with a special dining car menu of "good things from Mr. Harvey's plethoric larder," including bluepoints, fillet of sole à la Normande, sweetbread cutlets with French peas in Claret sauce, and tenderloin of beef with mushrooms—a uniformed boy greeted passengers at the halfway point in Colorado, presenting every lady with a bouquet of roses, carnations, and violets, and every gentleman an alligator wallet.

But Ripley's master plan was to build a chain of new trackside hotels along the Santa Fe route, big, beautiful destination hotels where tourists would be compelled to linger for several days. All these hotels would of course feature the fine food and impeccable service of Fred Harvey.

It sounded like quite a ride.

FORD DID HIS BEST to make sure that his father got to experience much of the excitement. When Fred was in England, he and his son exchanged letters and telegrams almost daily. They discussed everything from business strategy (Fred urged his son never to let his feelings "interfere with the strictest business principals [*sic*]") to what lovely gifts of European foodstuffs, liquor, and cutlery Fred could ship back to the States, so that Ford could shower the company's friends in high places with Harvey-style swag.

They wrote a lot about the family. Like all sick people, Fred was obsessed with everyone else's health. He worried about his wife—who he thought should eat better and drink fewer "spirits"—and especially their daughter May, who had always been somewhat sickly and was being told by doctors that she needed the "Alexander operation," a now-discredited surgery to "correct" the position of the uterus in women having menstrual problems.

They also corresponded about their mutual annoyance with some extended family members, whom Fred was about ready to disown. As he grew wealthier, his two sisters—Annie in London, Eliza in St.

Louis—and their children had become more and more demanding. After Eliza's son, George, solicited help yet again in a financial matter, Fred wrote to Ford, "The amount you gave him was quite enough & all I am willing to donate. That family has had enough, as well as my sister Annie's family. She never has appreciated what I have done for her children, so I am unwilling to do any more."

He and Ford also corresponded about the farm in Emporia, as well as the XY ranch out in Colorado, which they moved farther west yet again, closer to the La Junta depot. Fred reportedly sold his forty-five hundred acres in Granada for $200,000 ($5.3 million) to a syndicate from Bloomington, Illinois.

When Fred did return to the United States, he and Ford would often spend time together in Emporia, which was just a hundred miles from Kansas City. On a hill overlooking the 750-acre property, they had built a handsome fourteen-room home with the first indoor bathroom in the area. The property had several barns, as well as bunkhouses and carriage houses for staff and guests. Fred had bought it in 1890, as an experiment to see whether the company could grow some of its own corn and vegetables and raise some of its own beef and dairy cattle. They were now raising horses there as well.

The entire Harvey family tried to get to the Emporia farm for at least two weeks every summer, during which Fred and Ford did a lot of hunting and fishing. They were a familiar seasonal sight for Emporians. One ranch manager liked to tell the story of seeing father and son return after a particularly long day of hunting. He asked what they had gotten.

"Wet clothes and a hungry stomach" was Fred's reply.

In Emporia, Fred and Ford had become friendly with journalist William Allen White, the editor of the *Emporia Gazette,* who often dined at the Harvey depot restaurant with his wife. For years the Harveys knew him as a talented but provincial small-town newspaper editor, but in the summer of 1896 he suddenly became a player in national politics. A sarcastic editorial he had dashed off before leaving on vacation was discovered by the McKinley campaign and was so quickly and widely distributed that by the time White returned from his trip, he was famous.

The editorial, "What's the Matter with Kansas?" took potshots at the Populist Party of William Jennings Bryan, making fun of the idea that what Kansas needed was "fewer white shirts and brains, fewer men with business judgment, and more of those fellows who boast that they are 'just ordinary clodhoppers' . . . who hate prosperity and who think because a man believes in national honor, he is a tool of Wall Street . . . Whoop it up for the ragged trousers; put the lazy, greasy fizzle, who can't pay his debts, on an altar, and bow down and worship him."

The Republicans loved White's message that Middle America still needed a social and political elite. In return, they made him their homespun literary hero and invited him to help write their campaign platforms.

William Allen White's fame as "the sage of Emporia" grew rapidly. As he traveled more and more, Fred arranged for him to have a pass for free meals at his Santa Fe eating houses. It was a friendly gesture but also a smart one. White was already a big fan of Fred Harvey, and now he would occasionally pontificate in print, to his growing national audience, about the joys of Harvey House food—which he missed even when dining in the best restaurants in New York.

"The more one sees of the world," White wrote, "the more he respects Fred Harvey. He is the Great American Caterer."

IT WASN'T LONG before the Harvey Houses became a sensation in a new broad swath of America, starting in St. Louis, going across Missouri, down through Oklahoma and Arkansas, and all over Texas. (The Harvey newsstands extended even farther, into Tennessee, Mississippi, and as far southeast as Mobile, Alabama.) With all these new locations, the "civilizing" influence of Harvey Girls, fine food, and jacket-only dining rooms reached more of the country's rough patches. In one Texas town, the newspaper heralded the coming of Harvey Girls by noting that "no smirking, tip-seeking negro stands back of one's chair in a Harvey restaurant, figuring out just how much he will get for his minimum service. Emoluments are given in the realm of the Harvey girl as they were originally intended to be given—in appreciation of the service rendered and the attentive interest shown by the clever girls in white."

To fill the positions for all these new restaurants, the company went on a hiring spree for new Harvey Girls, promising good jobs, good pay, and, of course, the company's legendary marital prospects. One Harvey

Girl recalled being told, "We'll guarantee you a good railroadman for a husband." But she was also taught how to handicap desirability: "You learned that brakemen were a dime a dozen, engineers were good, but men in the communications department, like telegraphers, were *very* good."

The Fred Harvey training was brought to a new generation of young women—including all the inside jokes and hazing. When a new girl cleared the table after serving her first order of bluepoint oysters, it wasn't uncommon for one of the others to pull her aside and convince her she was expected to wash out those shells so they could be reused. Occasionally a kindly veteran would intercede to prevent the embarrassment—one remembered telling a rookie to take the clean shells, put them in her bag, and tell the other girls she had decided to start a collection.

As usual, the sudden influx of bright, single young Harvey Girls generated more excitement among men than women. "We caused a lot of jealousy among the local girls," recalled one Harvey Girl. "Sometimes after a dance where one or more Harvey Girls had been socializing with a lot of the local men, young women from [the town] would come into the lunchroom and find fault with everything we did—the toast was too brown, the eggs not the way they ordered them—petty things. We'd just grin and bear it."

The competition, however, was real. "You know, nearly every single unmarried man in [town] proposed to me!" recalled one Harvey Girl. "There were an awful lot of single men . . . I finally got engaged to a young man who was an engineer with the Santa Fe. His father was a big lawyer in Nebraska. We were engaged a few months . . . when he started to grow this mustache. He kissed me one night and that mustache made me mad. I asked him to shave it off—I told him I wouldn't marry him if he didn't. Well, he wouldn't shave it, so I gave him back his ring."

The newspapers started paying more attention to the impact of all these Harvey Girl marriages. William Curtis, a well-known Chicago journalist who covered the Southwest and Latin America, wrote:

> [Fred Harvey] is responsible for a great deal of the growth and a great deal of the happiness in this part of the country. He has done more than any immigration society to settle up the Southwest and still continues to provide wives for ranchmen,

cowboys, railway hands and other honest pioneers . . . and the successful results of his matrimonial bureau are found in every community. It must not be forgotten that a precedent for Mr. Harvey's enterprise was established by the first English settlers in America. Two cargoes of wives were sent out to the colonists of Jamestown by the Virginia Society in London and were sold to bachelor colonists for 120 pounds of tobacco per wife—while Mr. Harvey does not even charge a commission.

But to the wives of travelers who were already married, these hundreds of single Harvey waitresses represented something else entirely. *New Yorker* memoirist Emily Hahn, who spent one college summer working for Fred Harvey, recalled childhood scenes of her parents arguing about Harvey Girls:

When my father . . . traveled every year in the West, Harvey Girls stood for much the same thing as businessmen's secretaries often do today—they were hazards for stay-at-home wives. Harvey Girls were famous for looks as well as dexterity. Mother had half believed that my father was carrying on a flirtation with one of the young ladies, though even if he was it couldn't have amounted to much—a gallant remark or two thrown at her, as she rushed past, across the heavy railway china.

CHAPTER 19

ROUGH RIDDEN

AFTER FRED TURNED HIS PROXY OVER TO FORD, HE BEGAN TO finalize his will. And if he needed any lessons on how *not* to handle his estate, he had only to consider the example of George Pullman. In the years since the strike of 1894, Pullman's company had done well for investors, and he had been personally charitable. But in the public consciousness, the growing labor movement had successfully painted him as perhaps the worst boss in American history.

Pullman was never forgiven for allowing the entire country to be closed for business, and for letting so many be killed and hurt during the protests, simply because he didn't want to negotiate with his workers. His ideas about controlling life in his company town, long seen as "un-American," were eventually found to be illegal. While his workers may not have fully agreed with the characterization—especially the sleeping-car porters, who still had some of the best jobs available to black men—Pullman had become the prototype of the corporate businessman more concerned about his stockholders than his employees.

In fact, Pullman's reputation was so tainted that he decided to leave one last great invention as his legacy: a tomb impervious to desecration by his enemies. After he died in the fall of 1897, at the age of sixty-six, his body was placed in a mahogany casket lined with lead. After the funeral at Chicago's Graceland Cemetery, his coffin was wrapped in tar paper and then lowered into a pit thirteen feet long, nine feet wide, and eight feet deep, with eighteen inches of steel-reinforced concrete at the bottom. Once the coffin was precisely in place—it had to be equidistant from each wall within a fraction of an inch—it was encased in a one-inch layer of quick-hardening asphalt. Then the concrete floor, which was already set and cold, was warmed up so it would mesh better with the fresh concrete poured all around the encased coffin—which created a rim a half inch above the asphalt layer. Next, eight steel rails were laid across the casket and bolted together with two long iron rods. More tar paper was used to create a small space below the rails to prevent settling that might crush the casket, and then enough concrete was poured to cover the rails. Once this set, another entire day was spent pouring layer after layer of concrete, reinforced with metal sheeting. Finally, dirt and sod were placed on top of the concrete and myrtle planted in it so the grave would better fit in with the others around it.

But none of these fortifications could protect Pullman's family from the bombshell of his will. He disinherited his twin sons, one of them his namesake (whose fiancée immediately broke off their engagement). The bulk of his personal fortune—estimated at $7.6 million ($203 million)—went to his daughters, his wife, and a fund to build a retraining school for his employees. Leadership of his company was turned over to Robert Todd Lincoln, the late president's son, a lawyer who had been one of Pullman's right-hand men for years.

Pullman's sons didn't sue the estate, but others did, including his personal barber, who claimed unsuccessfully that he deserved one of the $500 ($13,389) bequests left to household servants because he had shaved the master every morning and acted as his "gazette," telling him the news of the day and "sundry funny anecdotes." Pullman's wife eventually decided to give her sons some of her money, but the entire affair was a front-page family fiasco.

Fred Harvey would have none of that. While he had admired Pullman as a young man, he had deliberately built his business to be the opposite of the Pullman Palace Car Company. He wanted Fred Harvey to remain a closely held, privately owned company with employees who felt as if they were part of an ever-growing extended family. He would leave his wife and children more than enough to live comfortably, but not in a way that might jeopardize his reputation as an exemplary boss forever devoted to maintaining the standard.

AS FORD'S NEW ROLE in the family business became clear, his sister Minnie decided she would like to be more involved. Minnie was now a cosmopolitan twenty-seven-year-old who had been living in New

York on and off since attending boarding school there. Smart, direct, and sometimes stunningly opinionated—a "tsk" always at the ready— she was a no-nonsense woman except when it came to her hats and her little dogs, which she fussed over like spoiled children. She had strong, handsome features and thick brown hair, which she usually wore pulled back, and both of her parents could see themselves in her face: She had her father's aquiline nose, her mother's cherubic cheeks. Unlike Ford, she had managed to escape from Leavenworth and develop a more independent relationship with her parents. Her father had always managed to spend quality time with her when he was in New York, and she would return home periodically to be with her mother, with whom she also sometimes traveled. As her parents grew further apart, she was sometimes their only point of contact.

Minnie had recently married a New Yorker, John Huckel. A tall, fit man with a closely trimmed beard, an eternally arched eyebrow, and a penchant for playful confrontation, Huckel grew up in a well-known Episcopalian clergy family—his father was the longtime rector at St. Ann's in Brooklyn. But, after graduating from Williams College, he chose publishing over the pulpit. He spent several years at Harper & Brothers, the nation's leading publisher of books and magazines (including *Harper's Weekly* and what was then called *Harper's New Monthly Magazine*), before becoming assistant publisher of the *New York Evening Post*.

When Minnie married John Huckel in the fall of 1896, it appeared they would live the charmed lives of New York socialites, "at home" on 91st Street and Columbus Avenue, with summers spent at the seaside resort of Spring Lake, New Jersey, or in Europe. But Minnie grew homesick, in part because of a health crisis that was kept hush-hush. Not long after marrying, she became pregnant with twins, but had an especially difficult miscarriage that left her unable to bear more children. Besides wanting to be closer to her family—especially Ford's children, Kitty and Freddy, whom she adored as her own—she had also acquired the Harvey fascination with the West. With Ford taking control of their father's company, she saw an opportunity to relocate closer to home, become involved with the business, and travel as well.

Minnie's upbringing made her realize there would be no way for her to have an official role at Fred Harvey. She had grown up listening to Susan B. Anthony—whose namesake niece, "Susie B.," had attended childhood birthday parties at the Harvey home—and had watched her father build an empire that made it possible for thousands of American women to have good jobs, even careers. But she knew there was a vast difference between hiring Harvey Girls and creating a place in the boardroom for a Harvey *Woman.*

Instead, she did what strong, resourceful women had been doing for centuries: She became a power behind the throne. She planted the idea in the head of her husband that living in Missouri wouldn't be so bad, and she nudged her father and brother to hire him. Eventually, she got her way. The Huckels moved to Kansas City, John went to work running the company's fledgling newsstand and retail division, and Minnie advised him on dealing with her family, and all their business.

IN 1898, AMERICA had a little war. It was one of those rare "short, winnable wars" that actually turn out to be both short and winnable—a few hundred Americans were killed, while the enemy lost tens of thousands of men. When the war was over, America was changed forever. Especially Fred Harvey's America.

Since the American frontier had now expanded all the way to the Pacific—everything between Canada and Mexico was part of the United States, with only the territories of New Mexico, Arizona, and Oklahoma awaiting statehood—there were many who felt the nation should start looking for a new frontier outside its borders. Cuba, a Spanish colony that was home to many American-owned sugar plantations, was especially tempting, and President McKinley was pressured to help Cuban revolutionaries push the Spaniards out. Most of that pressure came from the press, in particular publishers Joseph Pulitzer and William Randolph Hearst, both of whom were testing how far the media's muscles could be flexed.

In late January 1898, the U.S. battleship *Maine* was sent to Havana harbor. This incensed the Spanish minister to the United States, whose private letter lambasting President McKinley as "weak" and "a low politician" was leaked to the newspapers. When the *Maine* exploded and sank on the night of February 15, drowning more than 250 crewmen, it set off an explosion of patriotic fervor against the Spanish, who the newspapers claimed were responsible. America was pressured to declare war on Spain and soon established its first base as an imperial power—at Guantánamo Bay.

The impact of the war on the Santa Fe and Fred Harvey was immediate—suddenly they were transporting and feeding thousands of troops. Then Theodore Roosevelt, the thirty-nine-year-old assistant secretary of the navy, resigned his post to enlist and create a "cowboy cavalry" that would bring the best riflemen and horsemen of the American frontier—cowboys and Indians alike—together to defend the country. Roosevelt's western pedigree came from the years that he had spent at his ranch in the Badlands of North Dakota. Yet when it came time to recruit for his cavalry, he went right to the heart of Santa Fe country, choosing "dead shots" and "fearless fighters" primarily from New Mexico, Indian Territory, and Texas.

It was a great news story, which brought attention to the unsung (or at least under-sung) virtues of the Southwest and all the "true Americans" who lived there. And then the story got even better. Roosevelt's Ivy League polo-playing chums in the East insisted on lending their cultivated athletic and equestrian skills to the effort. Cowboys and preppies would charge side by side, led by swashbuckling Teddy Roosevelt.

The cavalry sounded like something concocted for the wildly popular Buffalo Bill show, which had been touring the country for fifteen years reenacting cowboy and Indian dramas. Its full name was "Buffalo Bill's Wild West and Congress of Rough Riders of the World," so the newspapers nicknamed the cowboy cavalry "Roosevelt's Rough Riders." Americans came to know these men the way they would later know the *Apollo* astronauts: They were heroes before they even did anything.

Ironically, the Rough Riders never got to ride in Cuba. The troopships had no room for their horses, so their famous attacks on Las Guásimas and San Juan Hill were actually done on foot. But they did win lopsided victories and suffered several dozen casualties.

The Spanish-American War lasted less than four months, and when Spain surrendered in early August, the United States had not only "freed" Cuba but had won for itself Puerto Rico, Hawaii, and Guam. America also made a deal to buy the Philippines from Spain for $20 million ($536 million) in a process McKinley called "benevolent assimilation." All in all, Spain lost over 50,000 men, and America lost only 2,446 soldiers, most of them having died from disease.

"A splendid little war" is how John Hay, then U.S. ambassador to England, described the conflict; one sailor on the U.S.S. *Oregon* reportedly saw it more as "a turkey shoot." Both would agree, however, that it served as an excellent debut for America as a world power.

Domestically, the war had a very different effect. Besides jump-starting the economy, it further united the United States. The experience of facing a common enemy—even a fairly weak one—was profound. It fostered a patriotism that was genuinely national and felt inextricably linked to and inspired by that "frontier spirit" of the Old West. It was a renewed version of the idealistic spark that historian Frederick Jackson Turner—whose work was still obscure, but was known to Roosevelt—wondered if the country might have lost forever.

The war also seemed to trigger the first of many cycles of Americans looking within—within the country, within themselves—to recapture that spirit of the frontier, that authentic "real America," as a way of counterbalancing the forces of modernity and urbanization. This translated into a postwar wave of interest in cowboys, Indians, and the Great Southwest.

To capitalize on this, the Santa Fe and Fred Harvey jumped at the opportunity to host the signature national event of the new frontiersmen: the Rough Riders' reunion. In the late winter of 1899, cities all over the country were jockeying for the right to host the reunion. Every state that had a resident Rough Rider wanted the event, and each one was convinced it could lure the key guest: Teddy Roosevelt, who had since been elected governor of New York. Civic leaders in Chicago, Kansas City, Oklahoma City, El Paso, Santa Fe, and Albuquerque were most vocal about getting the reunion, which was expected to draw huge crowds and the entire national press corps. Fund-raising and lobbying were well under way in all these cities when suddenly word spread that the Rough Riders had agreed to hold their reunion in . . . Las Vegas, New Mexico. And it just so happened that the Santa Fe had recently finished building a new kind of hotel there.

The Castañeda in Las Vegas was the prototype of the innovative, glamorous trackside resorts that Ed Ripley planned to build—for Fred Harvey to run—all along his new and improved Santa Fe. The hotel was a spectacular U-shaped Mission Revival–style mansion with lush gardens and a main entrance that faced the tracks, not the town, so passengers would feel more welcome, more at home, the moment they got off the train. And Teddy Roosevelt, his Rough Riders, and all the national press would be staying there. In one of the first instances of corporate sponsorship in history, the Santa Fe appears to have made a discreet deal to pay for all transportation and lodging if the event was held in its new signature Fred Harvey hotel.

That deal was most likely brokered by the railroad's first vice president, Paul Morton—a Roosevelt family friend from Nebraska whose father, J. Sterling Morton, had been Grover Cleveland's secretary of agriculture (and invented Arbor Day). Roosevelt, who was already thinking about the presidency, got an all-expenses-paid whistle-stop tour on the Santa Fe, commandeering Morton's plush private Pullman car—and Morton got a chance to shadow the newly minted American hero.

As the Rough Riders' train approached New Mexico, so did a huge thunderstorm, causing local flooding that washed out half a mile of Santa Fe track. But that could be repaired. The bunting catastrophe that befell downtown Las Vegas, however, could not. Every building in the city had been decorated with brightly colored streamers and ribbons, all of which were either blown away or soaked until the colors ran, leaving the houses and storefronts dripping red, white, and blue.

The tempest did not quash the enthusiasm of Las Vegans, however. When Roosevelt arrived at their depot, thousands were there to greet him, and he was "almost lifted bodily from his feet by the press of persons anxious to grasp his hand," according to the *Los Angeles Times*. The crowds followed him down the train platform as he and other Rough Riders kept serially saluting all the way along the main courtyard of the Castañeda hotel. There Roosevelt stood on the veranda, along with New Mexico's governor, Miguel Otero, and an entourage of Rough Riders, until he could salute and shake hands no more and headed into the hotel for some Harvey hospitality.

The restaurant at the Castañeda featured a large number of native southwestern dishes among the Fred Harvey favorites, including albondigas soup with beef and veal meatballs and enchiladas stuffed with chopped chicken, chilies, and olives, along with comforting classics like Fried Chicken Castañeda with fresh tomato sauce and French peas. For the Rough Riders' visit, the Harvey Girls wore special outfits. Angelica, the St. Louis firm that was now making all of Fred Harvey's uniforms, created a western version with long denim cowboy skirts and matching vests.

The next day there was a huge parade led by Roosevelt on horseback. As it began, he was handed the original regimental flag, which was badly torn and covered with powder burns.

"Boys, it doesn't seem much to look at now, does it?" he said, as a tear rolled down his cheek. "But it was worth a good deal to us on San Juan Hill."

Roosevelt departed early the next morning in his private railroad car, leaving his compatriots to enjoy a day of bronco busting, horse racing, roping, and games of the new national pastime—baseball. And as many of the Rough Riders were basking in their glory, with no further military plans except to attend future reunions, others talked about reenlisting. They wanted to finish the job they had started.

THE U.S. PURCHASE of the Philippines had not gone exactly as planned, and the two countries were now at war—America's first sustained imperialist war outside its own hemisphere. Over forty thousand American troops were already there, with no end in sight.

Not long after the Rough Riders' reunion, a small detachment from the U.S. 33rd Voluntary Infantry entered the remote Philippine town of Cabaranan on the island of Pangasinan. In one of the Nepa huts, Lieutenant Hugh Williams was surprised to discover a worn piece of silverware that immediately conjured images of home.

It was a spoon etched with the name "Fred Harvey."

Williams was utterly baffled as to how the spoon had gotten there, since his men were supposedly the first American regiment to set foot in Cabaranan. His best guess was that it had been picked up by one of the many soldiers who rode the Santa Fe to California, where they were shipped off to the Philippines. It had probably been taken from him in Manila by a rebel soldier who then fled to the remote island.

Williams sent the spoon back to the States. He thought Mr. Fred Harvey might like to have it. When it arrived, Sally Harvey had a leather case made for it, and displayed it in the dining room with the rest of her growing collection of silverware.

CHAPTER 20

THE CLUTCHES OF THE
GRIM MONSTER

ꟼ乚

THE FRONT PAGE OF THE SUNDAY *NEW YORK TIMES* CARRIED A distressing item, datelined London, on October 15, 1899.

"FREDERICK HARVEY ILL," the headline read. "He has just had an operation performed, and it is not certain he will recover."

Through more than a decade of illness, nobody had ever been entirely sure what was wrong with Fred Harvey. In 1899, however, he became much sicker, and he finally got a solid differential diagnosis. It came from perhaps the most renowned medical authority in the world—forty-six-year-old Sir Frederick Treves, London's master surgeon, who was revered in the medical journals for his daring procedures and well-known by the public for his treatment of Joseph Merrick, "the Elephant Man." While Treves had written about and taught many subjects, his main area of expertise was abdominal surgery. He was best known for his ability to dissect and remove blockages in the digestive tract and for his splendid appendectomies (which were quite surgically advanced, although his theory about letting a patient writhe in acute pain for five days before removing the appendix was later shown to be ridiculous—and often deadly). Given such high demand for his services, Treves had recently resigned his long-standing staff position at the London Hospital and was now taking only wealthy private patients—who paid the outrageous price of 100 pounds ($13,014) to be operated on by the great surgeon.

Fred came to see Treves at the doctor's well-known consulting room at 6 Wimpole Street, and was diagnosed with colon cancer. This would be consistent with many years of untreated inflammatory bowel disease—ulcerative colitis, diverticulitis, or Crohn's disease—any one of which would be a reasonable explanation for some of Fred's chronic symptoms. (While an armchair diagnosis is unprovable, there is a very strong corroborative Harvey family history of colon cancer and digestive tract disease.) Treves had, in fact, written the textbook on colon cancer and its treatment, which was not wholly different than it is today—exploratory surgery leading to removal of tumors and a resection of the bowel. The difference was in the surgical production values.

Not only were the cutting and suturing extremely crude, but at that time Treves still thought his friend Dr. Joseph Lister's theories about maintaining "strict antiseptic precautions" were only for "enthusiasts" and "surgical ritualists" going to "strange and blundering extremes." He wore no gloves during surgery and chided the surgeon who made an "exquisite ceremonial of washing" and "parad[ing] his cleanliness." There were no drugs—such as antibiotics—to prevent infection, and Treves didn't believe in sterile dressings. He liked to dust wounds with iodoform, a crystalline yellow antiseptic powder with a sickly sweet smell, and leave them exposed to the hospital air. "The fact that the iodoform is swarming with micro-organisms may disturb the bacterially-minded surgeon," he said, "but it disturbs neither the wound nor the patient."

Not surprisingly, almost 40 percent of his patients died during colon resection surgery, and of those who lived, more than half were dead within a year. Only one patient had survived three years.

Ever resilient, Fred managed to survive the surgery—though just barely. Ford had come to England to be at his father's bedside and did his best to keep the family, and the newspapers, informed of the patient's condition. Two weeks after the procedure, the *Los Angeles Times* was reporting that Fred was still critically ill. In fact, some newspapers even reported he had died, prompting the *Santa Fe New Mexican* to run a corrective headline: "Fred Harvey Not Dead."

In letters home, Fred spared no detail of his suffering, describing the great pain in his bowels and the excretion of blood and mucus. He was now tethered permanently to a colostomy bag, and reported it was agony to urinate "even a teaspoonful." So his new physician, Dr. Harrison—Treves had left for South Africa to treat British soldiers fighting in the Boer War—had him catheterized with a rubber-tipped glass catheter every two hours through the night.

When his father's condition finally stabilized, Ford cabled to his younger brother, Byron—who had recently graduated from Yale—to come and relieve him so he could return to Kansas City and attend to business. Byron stayed for several months, but Sally did not come to visit. The correspondence between Fred and Ford suggests that Sally—who had been to the Continent the year before with Sybil and Byron—was herself too ill to travel such a long distance.

"I think if Mamma could make the voyage—say by Byron running over to New York to meet her there—it would be a good thing for her to do," Fred wrote. "At the same time, I would not have her come and endanger her health." Sally suffered from rheumatism and had apparently put on a great deal of weight. Fred had sent her a bicycle, the latest craze on both sides of the Atlantic, in the hope she would exercise. He also believed that in all their years away from each other, his wife had developed a drinking problem.

Fred was not sure he would ever be well enough to return to America, which had slipped into the twentieth century in his absence, yet "sometimes I feel hopeful of being able to see my loved ones again," he wrote to Ford in February 1900. In the meantime, he could hear their voices—and send them his—using the latest technological advance: Edison cylinder recordings. The cylinders, which predated flat discs as a recording medium, were made of tan wax and shaped like oversize toilet-paper rolls, about four inches high and two inches wide. The device used to record and play the cylinders looked like a sewing machine with a trumpet bell attached to it. Fred had one brought to his sickbed, and Ford got one for the family.

Some of the Harvey family's Edison cylinders contained mundane conversation, while others captured Fred in his worst moments. "The pain, Mother, *the pain*," he was heard moaning on one of them. To make sure nobody recorded over Fred's messages, Ford marked the boxes "Father's Voice."

In the spring, as the convalescence dragged on, Byron returned home and was replaced by Minnie, who sailed over with her husband. By May, Fred felt strong enough to travel back to America, though as a precaution he hired one of his physicians, a Dr. Montgomery, to return with him and be his full-time caretaker.

Landing in New York, they took the Pennsylvania Railroad to Chicago and then transferred to the Santa Fe at Dearborn Station, where there were now Harvey Girls serving meals. In Fred's absence, his company had taken over the station's large lunchroom—which was always packed with diners seeking Harvey comfort-food favorites and new signature dishes such as the delicately prepared Finnan Haddie, smoked haddock cooked with milk, cream, butter, and sliced potatoes.

ON MONDAY, MAY 28, 1900, Fred Harvey was brought by horse-drawn carriage to the Olive Street house he'd thought he would never see again. He spent a few peaceful weeks at home, during which he did little other than get up, dress, read, and perhaps take a short walk. In one of the last pictures ever taken of him, he looks comfortably ensconced in a plush chair with long dangling tassels at the bottom, intently reading the morning paper in his sitting room, surrounded by the tasteful paintings and sculptures and objects collected during his travels. His legs are crossed, with the top one cocked slightly; his face is much fuller and his beard almost gray, and he appears if not happy, then at least cozy.

When the weather grew too warm, Fred, Sally, Minnie, and Sybil took a vacation to Mackinac Island, a resort on Lake Huron, between Michigan and the Canadian border, which had become popular with the "railroad rich." But by summer's end, Fred's health had taken yet another bad turn, so instead of returning with his family to Leavenworth, he was moved to Chicago, taking up residence at the lakefront Chicago Beach Hotel along with his doctor, a nurse, and a servant who tended to him round the clock.

He allowed few visitors, just his children and most trusted employees. But the one he most desperately wanted to see was Ford. Ultimately, Ford was the only one who understood him, and the only one he understood. While he loved his other children dearly, they were children of privilege, children of the rich man he had become. Only Ford knew him way back when, and only Ford knew him now.

After Ford's initial visit, Fred wrote that it was "the first moment that I have felt anything like myself." Ford then sent his father a very moving letter, to which Fred quickly replied, "Your words and actions are always so tender that I cannot express to you what pleasure they give me. It is hard for others to appreciate my feelings. When I know there is nothing but constant pain and misery before me, *your* own health causes me more care than anything I know of."

While he was eager to see Ford again, Fred seemed ambivalent about a visit from his wife. "If you can impress upon her that I cannot stand the slightest worry or crossing, I would be glad to have her come up," Fred wrote to Ford. "I appreciate at times I can be unreasonable, but the agony that I am in makes me for the time not responsible. It does seem that after forty years she ought to be able to bear with me [for] another. But I can only repeat as I have so many times that to the best of my ability I have never failed to do my duty to my wife and children to the fullest extent. I constantly pray that the Almighty will give you all health and protect you from all evil."

JUST AFTER RETURNING HOME, Fred instructed his son to make certain discreet financial moves so the family might escape some taxes when he died. There was now a national income tax, and the federal government had recently levied a new estate tax to pay for the Spanish-American War, which took up to 15 percent of estates valued at over $1 million.

Fred decided he and his wife would make spontaneous, tax-evading "gifts" to the children, giving each of them $50,000 ($1.32 million). Since he didn't have easy access to $250,000 in currency, he gifted family members with stocks, bonds, even personal promissory notes, including several from loans he had made to some of Kansas City's wealthiest men when they were short on cash. Minnie was given two $25,000 notes from Charles W. Armour, a partner in one of the country's largest meatpacking plants and a contemporary of Ford and Dave's. Armour had borrowed the money from Fred over a four-week period.

Yet such moments of levelheadedness and estate planning on Fred's part would often be interrupted by well-meaning friends and relatives convinced they had found some miracle remedy. One day Ford received an urgent telegram, which his father had sent just before midnight, saying people were telling him to see a Chinese doctor they had heard about as a last-ditch attempt to cure his cancer. Fred wanted to do it, "unless mamma and you object," he explained.

Ford wired back that he *did* object, and followed the wire with a long letter explaining why. "The Chinese doctor is not a regular qualified physician," he wrote, and "it is a very grave question [whether] we can afford to cast aside the best educated brains and the most skilled hands of our own world in return for the advice of one man and that man of an entirely different race with entirely different methods than those in which we have been taught to believe." Ford also worried that the English physician who had been by Fred's side for six months might be outraged and quit. He urged his father to wait until he could come up to Chicago so they could discuss this further.

The next day, Ford was golfing at the Kansas City Country Club, when he received another urgent telegram from his father. "Have seen Chinese, am exceedingly anxious that you should come this evening . . . I feel very much encouraged. Come if possible."

But the Chinese treatment failed, so they consulted another Chicago doctor, Henry Favill, the family physician of hotelier Potter Palmer, whom Fred had known for years. Fred was heartened when Dr. Favill called him "the most sprightly invalid I have ever seen."

He felt well enough for a visit from his friend William Strong, who had taken several railroad posts after leaving the Santa Fe and then retired to his family farm in Wisconsin. The two men had carried on an active correspondence, and Fred had sent Ford and Dave to Strong for advice on many occasions. But the old chums hadn't seen each other much over the past few years, and Strong didn't know what to expect.

"It was a delightful surprise to see him appear and talk so naturally—so like himself," Strong wrote to Ford after the meeting. "It was hard, very hard to realize his real condition. It was a most painful thought that I might never again see him. It came to me as I left him . . . what a friend he had been and what his vacant chair would mean to me. In a business lifetime we meet but few such men, men capable of such loyalty and unselfish friendship. I pray he may live just as long as the pleasures of life exceed the pains of living."

Strong also wanted Ford to know how much he admired the way he was handling the pressures and emotions involved in caring for an ailing parent: "Your father spoke to me in such a tender manner of his children that it touched me deeply—your faithfulness will have its rewards. It comes daily, I know, in the fact that you are doing your duty with every true purpose of heart as a loyal son. God bless you."

FACED WITH THE prospect of losing his father, Ford relied on Dave Benjamin's counsel and support more than ever. They had grown closer over the years, especially after Dave's wife, Julia, died in her mid-thirties, not long after giving birth to their third child. He had since married again, but the loss, as well as Fred's worsening condition, had caused the two men to bond even more, the lines between work and life becoming even blurrier. Now in his early forties, Dave was arguably the most indispensable person in the sprawling Fred Harvey organization.

Which is why Ford was frantic when he disappeared suddenly on a routine business trip to Texas.

On the rainy morning of September 8, 1900, Dave was riding from Houston to the Gulf of Mexico when the train suddenly slowed to a crawl on the bridge over Galveston Bay. The water was frightfully high, with waves lapping just below the tracks, and it took the engine forever to inch across the trembling three-mile span. Once on Galveston Island, the train went only another two miles before it was forced to stop because the tracks were washed away. Eventually, another train came along to fetch them, bringing Dave and his fellow passengers fairly close to the Santa Fe depot, but that train's engine was also flooded by the rising tide. So they walked through rushing, waist-deep water the rest of the way, the men carrying the women and children, until everyone was safe at the station—a four-story Romanesque building with a tall observation tower.

As the water kept rising and the winds gusted up to thirty-five miles an hour, Dave, ever the determined Fred Harvey man, insisted on going back out to keep a business appointment nearby. The client wasn't there, so Dave optimistically rescheduled for an hour later and went back to the depot to call the Kansas City office. He sat in one of the second-floor offices overlooking the station's large rectangular main room, waiting for the rain to stop pelting the domed glass ceiling.

But before long, the water rose so high that the bay met the ocean, flooding the Fred Harvey lunchroom and forcing everyone upstairs. It crept higher for several hours, and then, at around 7:00 p.m., the wind began to wail, and the water suddenly rose four feet all at once. They were horrified to see the body of a drowned child among the debris floating through the station.

All communications to Galveston Island were down, so it was nearly twenty-four hours before Ford could get any news at all—and when he did, it didn't bode well. A train out of Houston, stuck six miles short of Galveston Bay, had reported that the prairie was strewn with hundreds of dead bodies. There was no word from Dave for two days, during which the death toll in Galveston rose to an estimated five thousand.

There was great relief at Fred Harvey headquarters when he finally checked in and let them know he was safe and unhurt. The way he did it was typically Dave. Calm, fearless, and matter-of-fact, he insisted to Ford, and later to reporters who wanted to know about his experience, that he had never been worried or felt he was in any real danger.

WHEN THE WEATHER in Chicago began turning its typical shade of raw, Fred came to Leavenworth to celebrate one last Christmas at home with his family and then headed to Southern California in pursuit of warmth and a new set of doctors. Santa Fe president Ed Ripley arranged for one of his private Pullman cars to pick up Fred, his personal physician, and his son Byron in Kansas City. Their destination was the Castle Green in Pasadena, a trackside resort that had become the winter home for the first generation of American snowbirds. They arrived just after the New Year, and rose petals were still blowing in the streets from the Tournament of Roses Parade.

By this time, California had become a major Fred Harvey state. The company was now managing dining rooms and lunch counters in ten different locations from San Diego and Los Angeles all the way up to San Francisco—which actually had two *floating* Harvey Houses. Since the Santa Fe didn't run directly into town—its tracks ended on the Oakland side of San Francisco Bay and passengers ferried over to the city—Ford and Dave opened eateries and newsstands on two ships, the *Ocean Wave* and the *San Pablo,* and were about to open a lunch counter and a newsstand in the gorgeous new Ferry Building on the Embarcadero.

Several weeks after Fred's arrival in Pasadena, the doctors acknowledged there was nothing more to be done. He wanted to die at home, so the railroad arranged for a private Pullman to take him back to Leavenworth. He was now so weak he had to be carried onto the train, and by the time the California Limited began its three-day journey back across Fred Harvey's America, the staff of every Santa Fe eating house and dining car knew that their leader was barely tethered to life.

The Limited did not make meal stops; it had a Harvey dining car, from which waiters brought chipped ice to moisten Fred's dry, cracking lips. But at each station where the train stopped to take on passengers, Harvey Girls, chefs, and busboys stood in silence, paying their last respects.

FRED HARVEY'S TRAIN pulled in to Leavenworth, which had just dug out after a huge, drifting snowstorm, on Sunday, February 3, 1901. He and Byron were brought by carriage to the house, where they were joined by the Kansas City Harveys—Ford and Judy and the grandchildren, eight-year-old Kitty and five-year-old Freddy, along with Minnie and John Huckel. Their youngest sister, twenty-one-year-old Sybil, who still lived at home, greeted them at the door. Sally Harvey and their other daughter, May, were on their way home from the hot springs in Arkansas.

Doctors told the family to expect the end at any moment, but Fred periodically regained consciousness. Initially, this was a pleasant surprise. But the longer he was awake, the more he felt the monstrous ache in his gut, and needed more morphine, which made him drift away again.

A few close friends were allowed to see him. Pistol-packing editor Dan Anthony was so moved by his visit that he rushed an emotional article into the *Leavenworth Times*: "Fred Harvey lies at the point of death at his home . . . surrounded by family, friends and everything wealth could procure, yet with all this, during the last three years there has never been a moment when Mr. Harvey has been in a condition to look at even the humblest little newsboy or bootblack without a feeling of envy . . . Since 1898, the man has been doomed . . . All over the world Mr. Harvey has fled in a vain and fruitless endeavor to escape the clutches of the grim monster, who is no respecter of persons, and whose visit is inevitable."

In the early afternoon of Saturday, February 9, 1901, Fred died with his family gathered around him. Ford, ever the dutiful son, did what his father would have expected of him. He took a few moments to shed a tear, hug his family, collect his thoughts—and then he called Western Union and started dictating telegrams to everyone who needed to know.

"Father passed away peacefully this afternoon," he said. "Stop."

All the pallbearers were longtime employees, led by Dave Benjamin. Fred was buried at Mount Muncie Cemetery, just outside of Leavenworth, in a grave that had to be dug through a five-foot snowdrift. The funeral was the largest in Leavenworth history, and the newspaper tributes across the country were elaborate and moving.

"Fred Harvey . . . has done more to promulgate good cooking—healthful, substantial, wholesome, digestible cooking . . . than all the cook books ever published," wrote William Allen White in his nationally read column in the *Emporia Gazette*. "Men who have eaten at Fred Harvey's eating houses have come home and insisted on having their meats broiled, not fried; their roasts roasted, not boiled; their potatoes decently cooked and their biscuits light.

"Fred Harvey was a greater man than if he had been elected to something. *The Gazette* will hereafter pay more attention to great men out of politics, and less to giving politicians free advertising."

Fred's will was made public several days later. It was, as Dan Anthony wrote in the *Leavenworth Times,* "in many ways . . . out of the ordinary." In fact, it was downright peculiar, but in a very modern, managerially brilliant way.

Fred decreed that for the next ten years his heirs should carry on as if he were still alive. During that decade, nothing was to be done to change the operation of his company in any way, and none of his possessions could be sold, split up, or even inventoried. There were no bequests of any kind to his wife or children, no money donated to charity, nothing set aside for his sisters, nieces, or nephews. His wife and family were to stay in their house and keep all the servants on. Ford and Dave were to continue operating the Fred Harvey eating houses and hotels, along with the two Fred Harvey ranches in La Junta, Colorado, and Emporia, Kansas, as if nothing had happened. After ten years, his wife and children would inherit everything, with half going to Sally and the other half divided among Ford and his siblings.

The amount they would eventually be sharing, according to a front-page story in the *Los Angeles Times* about Fred's estate, was estimated at $1.2 million ($31.3 million) but was believed "to be greatly in excess of that amount." There was also a life insurance policy paying his wife and daughters $35,000 ($914,515). But Fred's main objective was clearly to preserve the status quo. If his children wanted to make more money anytime soon, they were welcome to make it the way he and Ford always had—by working long hours in the family business. The same was true for his employees.

When confronted by Dan Anthony about what the unusual will meant, Ford said its message was clear: "[The business] will be conducted just as it was by my father. The name of Fred Harvey will be preserved and the present standard of the business maintained."

While the family was prohibited from making any changes in their father's business or home, there was one issue they felt needed to be addressed immediately. In the weeks after the funeral, they decided Fred's grave site simply would not do. The plot in Mount Muncie Cemetery—section 15, lot 68—was small and too far from the main road. Father would have expected something more prominent and more practical, easier to get to in bad weather.

So, several months after the funeral, Fred Harvey was disinterred. His coffin and headstone were moved to a tree-shaded plot on a hill just inside the main entrance. At the same time, the remains of his two sons Charley and Eddie were dug up from the Greenwood Cemetery across town, where they had lain since 1865. The boys were reburied next to their father.

Only then could Fred Harvey finally rest in peace.

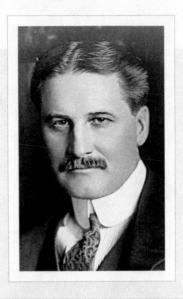

PART TWO

—

EXCEEDING
THE
STANDARD

1901–1948

CHAPTER 21

A LITTLE JOURNEY
IN THE WILDERNESS

⁌⁍

NINE MONTHS AFTER HIS FATHER'S DEATH, THIRTY-FIVE-year-old Ford Harvey stood at the edge of the Grand Canyon, gazing out over the most stunning vision of America's past and contemplating the future.

It was the last day of an enlightening and challenging expedition—by train, by stagecoach, on horseback, and on foot—that would mark the turning point in the development of the West and the way Americans view America. Everyone on this trip had been through the Southwest many times on business, but they all had always regarded the long, hot train ride as a journey across the turn-of-the-century equivalent of "the flyover states." Now, for the first time, they were feeling the soul of the Southwest.

Santa Fe president Ed Ripley and his wife, Frances, had invited his inner circle—Ford Harvey, first vice president Paul Morton, and several other top Santa Fe executives—to join them on a rugged adventure through some of the most beautiful, sacred, and controversial sites in Indian Territory. Their guide was Charles Fletcher Lummis, the self-appointed "Apostle of the Southwest," a Harvard-educated writer who had been publishing magazines and books about the West for years. A small, weathered man who had lost the use of his left arm after a stroke, Lummis was a brilliant and tireless promoter of Indian causes, of western environmental causes—and of himself.

Snagging him to lead the Ripley expedition was particularly impressive in late October 1901 because, to guide them, he had to blow off an invitation to the White House. Teddy Roosevelt, his Harvard classmate and longtime friend, had just become president under tragic circumstances. He had served as second-term vice president to William McKinley for only six months when an anarchist shot the president on September 6, 1901, at the Pan-American Exposition in Buffalo. When President McKinley died a week later, the forty-two-year-old Rough Rider became the youngest commander in chief in American history.

He summoned Charles Lummis to the White House, but was told his friend had too many deadlines to get there right away. In fact, Lummis decided that a weeklong walkabout with the top brass of the Santa Fe railroad might be more important to the southwestern causes he held most dear. So the new president would just have to wait until he had taken these powerful men and their wives on what he called "a Little Journey in the Wilderness."

Ford met up with the Ripley expedition in Albuquerque, where the Santa Fe had begun construction on the Alvarado—the second of its grand trackside hotels, and a much more elaborate undertaking than the Castañeda in Las Vegas. The new hotel was being designed by Charles Whittlesey, a protégé of renowned Chicago architect Louis Sullivan who had gone out on his own and then moved his family to Albuquerque to undertake commissions from the Santa Fe. In addition to the Alvarado, Whittlesey had designed the large new depot adjacent to it, with enough office space and housing to enable both the Santa Fe and Fred Harvey to use Albuquerque as the main terminal point for all their operations in the Southwest. The buildings featured the Mission Revival style—with dramatic archways, towers, and arcades, all with rough stucco walls—that was becoming the Santa Fe's distinctive visual signature.

Ripley's party had nearly twenty members. Besides Ford and Ripley's family—his wife, son, two daughters, a son-in-law, and a soon-to-be daughter-in-law—there were a half-dozen Santa Fe executives, some with their wives (although Judy Harvey had elected to stay home), as well as an artist, several stenographers, and a small army of porters and servants. Dressed in casual jackets, jodhpurs, and cowboy hats, the group boarded four private Pullmans near midnight and traveled west to the town of Cubero, where they watched the sunrise from their parked train cars and disembarked. Boarding horse-drawn wagons—although a few chose to ride saddle horses—they set out on the eighteen-mile trip south to Acoma Pueblo, the oldest continuously inhabited settlement in America and home to a small, independent Indian tribe called the Keresans. Their wagons wove through mesas, many of which had once been inhabited but were now just silent sentinels, guarding Acoma, which loomed in the distance.

Acoma Pueblo's stunning "City in the Sky" was nearly 370 feet above them—and looked even higher when Ford and the others realized there was no road up and they would have to climb a steep "stone ladder" to get there. At the top, they discovered the mesa was high enough to have its own weather: Uncharacteristic for New Mexico at midday, it was misty up there, making the seventy-acre plateau town— with an ancient monastery and many terraced houses—appear rather spooky. Out of the mist to greet them came Acoma's pueblo governor, Lorenso Lino, who wore a waistcoat, white shirt, tan hat, and a look of stolid resignation. He invited them to his home, where they all rested and enjoyed a big lunch.

Lino then invited the Ripley party to do some climbing down the scenic but dizzying "Split Trail"—with its rugged footholds and long drops onto wide boulders—and then back up the precipitous "Staircase Trail." The women, led by Mrs. Ripley, were brave enough to try the climb, but Ford and most of the other men chickened out. Instead, they spent the afternoon meeting other Keresan families, taking pictures, and buying Navajo blankets, prehistoric arrowheads cut from agate and obsidian, and bracelets and earrings made by Vicente, the pueblo's silversmith. When the climbers returned, Governor Lino ordered a ceremonial dance in their honor. Ford, Ripley, and the other visitors sat close to the dancers so they could capture every measured beat of the tombe drum, every step and chant. Above them, the Acoman families watched from their rooftops.

Everyone in the party was invited to stay over, but, again, Ford, Ripley, and most of the other executives demurred, heading back to sleep in the Pullman cars. Five of the women and three of the younger men remained in the pueblo overnight, and were treated to even more displays of big war dances and then, late at night, a very private performance in one family's home by their four-year-old son, dancing in what Lummis described as "a G-string," accompanied only by his father's quiet drumming. The next day, when everyone gathered at the train station, Ford and the others heard all about what they had missed.

Ripley's private train headed west to Thoreau, then the Santa Fe depot closest to the Navajo Reservation, which straddled the border between New Mexico and Arizona and had been carved out of land that the U.S. government forced the Navajos to leave during the Civil

War. In 1864, the Indians were led across New Mexico—in what became known as "the Long Walk"—to a government internment area at
Fort Sumner. Three years after the war ended, the government led
them back to where they had lived; though 3.5 million acres of the land
was given to them as a reservation, their society had been decimated.
Thirty years later, they were still trying to pick up the pieces.

The party slept in their Pullmans, parked on a side track at the
Thoreau depot. After breakfast, Ford was astonished by the scene outside their train car—a huge procession of wagons and saddle horses,
including a hundred-member Navajo escort party for their journey
into the reservation. This horse-drawn convoy had been organized by
their host for the next part of the journey: controversial relic hunter
Richard Wetherill, a former Colorado cattle rancher in his early forties
with a dark full beard, beady eyes, and an uncanny ability to spin tales
of things that he was the "first white man" to see or do. Wetherill was
the leader of the famous—and in some quarters infamous—Hyde Exploring Expedition, funded by a New York family whose fortune had
been made selling "Babbitt's Best Soap." He would be escorting them
for the sixty-mile trip to Chaco Canyon.

The spiritual center of the Navajo reservation, Chaco Canyon was
considered the earliest hub of civilization in North America, home of
the very first Indians—whom the Navajos referred to as Anasazi, "the
ancient ones"—before they spread out to the Four Corners region
where New Mexico, Arizona, Colorado, and Utah meet. Chaco was
also an archaeologist's dream, the site of some of the world's oldest and
best-preserved native ruins. That's why so many people were outraged
that the artifacts Wetherill discovered for the Hyde Expedition were
being removed and shipped to the American Museum of Natural History in New York—one of the epicenters of the growing national fascination with "ethnology," jump-started by the Indian exhibits at the
1893 Chicago world's fair. Wetherill had recently added to the outrage
by declaring that he should be able to *own* the sacred Indian grounds
he was excavating, and by submitting a homestead claim to the government. To stop him, politicians and scientists were attempting to make
Chaco Canyon a national park, and declare much of Wetherill's work
illegal. (He would later become a major reason the first American law
protecting antiquities was passed in 1906.)

With Wetherill and dozens of Navajos on horseback leading the
caravan, Ripley's party navigated mesas and the tortuously windy trails

down into the Cañon Agua Negra Chiquita, where they set up camp for lunch by the river, laying out large white blankets near a spray of bent trees that seemed to be bowing toward them. Afterward, the group posed for some photos—in which they look more like a bedraggled posse who have rescued some ladies from train robbers than high-paid railroad executives and their cosmopolitan wives—and then continued on for several more hours. They stopped for the night at Pueblo Pintado, where a camp with seven large tents had already been prepared by Wetherill's people. After supper, Ford and the others sang around the campfire in the pulsing star-shine, and then, as the moon rose, sixty Navajos did an entrancing dance.

The next morning, the sixth day of the ambitious expedition, they finally reached Chaco Canyon and proceeded to Pueblo Bonito, the largest and best-preserved ruin, where Richard Wetherill lived. Not only had he built a small shelter for himself in the ruins, but he was personally occupying some of the 180 rooms he had already excavated.

Whatever his crimes against archaeology and anthropology, Wetherill was a genius at exciting people about ancient Indian culture. He made a marvelous tag team with Charles Lummis, who was so lovingly obsessed with Indians that he could almost be forgiven for trying to draw attention to their plight by referring to them as "living ruins." Together, the two held Ford, Ripley, and their colleagues spellbound with their vivid descriptions of Indian history and customs. The excavated dwellings at Pueblo Bonito were absolutely breathtaking, and the stories Wetherill wove of what had taken place in these ancient rooms—many of which still had the wooden ceilings and lintels intact—brought Ford and the others a whole new understanding of these very early Americans and their lives. Wetherill also guided them through several other legendary Chaco Canyon sites he had excavated—Chettro Kettle, Pueblo del Arroyo, and Pueblo Viejo—before they decided to head back to the train, another long, rugged sixty-mile trip. On Sunday, October 27, the group reboarded their Pullman cars at Thoreau and headed west.

They stopped for a long leisurely supper at the Harvey House in Gallup, New Mexico, which was the closest Harvey location to the reservation—and very much looked it. The walls were decorated with fine Indian blankets, and there were pieces of turquoise and silver jewelry for sale at the checkout counter, next to the customary selection of candy, newspapers, and, of course, cigars. Back on the train, Ford,

Ripley, Paul Morton, and Lummis sat up late talking and smoking cigars—Lummis smoked four himself—as they crossed the Arizona desert under a full moon.

At Williams, they were diverted off the High Iron onto the new branch line the Santa Fe had built all the way to the rim of the Grand Canyon. And by doing so, they became among the first people ever to travel by train to the edge of forever.

WHILE THE GRAND CANYON had a rich life during the time of the Anasazi—who inhabited the rim and the caves and cliffs at the base—white people had long considered it a big pain in the neck: too wide to cross and far too long to circumvent. It was more than a mile deep, and big enough to easily fit the state of Rhode Island, all five boroughs of New York City, and Washington, D.C. The canyon was not really near anything—the closest town was twenty miles away—and could not be seen from a distance; it appeared completely without warning after a long journey through the dense pine Coconino Forest. For travelers on their way to somewhere else, it was the world's largest and most spec-tacular dead end.

"Ours has been the first and will doubtless be the last party of whites to visit this profitless location," wrote the first U.S. government representative to visit the canyon, Lieutenant Joseph Ives, after his trip there in 1857, "the region is, of course, altogether valueless . . . after entering it there is nothing to do but leave."

It was another decade before geologist John Wesley Powell con-vinced the fledgling Smithsonian Institution to fund the first expedi-tion down the Colorado River to explore and map the canyon. He led a harsh one-hundred-day trip, in which three of his eight men were killed by Indians and two of his four boats were destroyed, along with many of Powell's notes. But he returned two years later, and this time was more successful, painstakingly mapping, measuring, photograph-ing, and naming various canyon formations. In 1880, an expedition for the recently created U.S. Geological Survey, led by Powell's protégé Clarence Dutton, surveyed the canyon from the perspective that most visitors would eventually experience it—from the rim, particularly the South Rim, rather than from the bottom. Within a few years, daring tourists began arriving at the South Rim on horseback and in carriages.

Charles Lummis was one of those early tourists—visiting for the first time in 1885. He saw the local Indian tribes, the Hualapai and the Havasupai, already being pushed out by the U.S. government so that mining and logging companies might have their way with the canyon and its surrounding pine forests. As he explained to Ford, Ripley, and the rest of his rapt audience, the Grand Canyon was saved from the miners only because it proved too difficult to excavate, lacking veins rich enough to justify the risk and expense. Frustrated miners had to find another way to make money from the trails they had worked so hard to blaze, and realized that tourists would pay to walk them, and pay even more to ride them—on saddled mining burros.

The prospectors suddenly found themselves with new careers as guides and trail owners, some even turning their houses into primitive bed-and-breakfasts. In fact, when Fred Harvey took over the two Arizona eating houses closest to the canyon—in Williams and Peach Springs—in 1887, there was already regular stagecoach service from the depots to the canyon, and Harvey House managers often arranged trips for their more adventurous guests. One miner turned trail master actually built his own seventy-mile road from the railroad town of Ash Fork all the way to the South Rim, connecting to his trail down into the canyon.

The Santa Fe showed its first real interest in the canyon during the turbulent early 1890s, as the railroad was deciding what to exhibit at the Chicago world's fair. An AT&SF executive reached out to Thomas Moran, a renowned naturalist painter with a Moses-like beard who had brought his dramatic, Turner-esque palette to the American West. Congress had bought two Moran paintings to hang in the Capitol, one depicting what was then called the "Grand Canyon of the Yellowstone," in Yellowstone Park, Wyoming, and the other depicting the canyon in Arizona, then still referred to as "Grand Cañon of the Colorado," but seen from the North Rim. Both paintings illustrated views that were most easily accessible from the tracks of the Santa Fe's rival, the Union Pacific.

The Santa Fe offered Moran an all-expenses-paid trip—including two railroad employees just to haul his stuff around—if he would go to the South Rim, closest to AT&SF tracks, and create similarly iconic paintings. He could paint and stay there as long as he liked; in exchange, the railroad wanted a single canvas to display, just one. Although Moran's painting was never exhibited at the world's fair, the

railroad printed up thousands of copies of a handsome six-color litho-
graph and made it omnipresent. Framed lithographs hung in every
Santa Fe depot, as well as on the walls of schools, offices, and government buildings across the country. Prints were even given away as a
premium for subscribing to the *Los Angeles Times.*

Moran's painting from the South Rim became perhaps the single
most recognizable image of the American West. And with that single
act of Machiavellian art patronage, the fates of the Grand Canyon, the
Santa Fe, and Fred Harvey were inextricably linked.

BY THE TIME FORD HARVEY arrived with Ed Ripley's entourage on
a cloudy Monday morning at the end of October 1901, the South Rim
of the Grand Canyon was a bustling village of bearded white men and
their Indian employees. It featured a handful of rustic boardinghouses,
several profitable trails, and a little photography studio offering "instant" portraits that were ready by the time the tourists came back up
on their burros. By then, there were about two thousand visitors a year,
mostly in the summer. They all wanted a chance to see what naturalist
John Burroughs—on his recent first visit with his friend John Muir—
had called "the Divine Abyss," where one looks "into the earth as
through a mighty window or open door."

When Ford looked into the Divine Abyss, he realized that his life
was going to change forever. He was thirty-five years old and had been
working full-time, largely without a break, ever since he left college at
nineteen. He was a man possessed by his responsibilities—to his father, to his wife and children, to his employees, and, most recently, to
his widowed mother. A creature of routines, he woke up early each
morning so he could walk to work (in fact, he walked everywhere he
could, because he heard it was good for his heart), he went to bed at
precisely the same time every night, and even though his office was in
the train station, when he returned from a business trip, he always went
home first to have a meal before checking in at his office. He had no
distractions, no hobbies. When he went to a party or to the country
club to golf, it was invariably about business; when he traveled, it was
all business. What he longed for in his life was a passion—a passion of
his own, not one he inherited.

In the Grand Canyon, he was seeing something profound and unexpendable, a vision that would take more than a lifetime to absorb, a frontier that even the potent modernizing forces of America could not civilize. Although Ford belonged to a church, he had always considered himself a secular man. Gazing into the Grand Canyon, he realized he had found something sacred and mystifying.

Ford rejoined Ripley, Lummis, and the others, and the conversation turned to the hotel the Santa Fe was planning to build on the South Rim—a hotel that Ford would be running. But their discussion soon devolved into a huge fight, with Lummis arguing that the railroad men were plotting to defile the canyon.

"You want to put the hotel *on the brink*?" he cried incredulously.

Apparently, Ripley's architect, Charles Whittlesey—who had never actually been to the canyon—was designing a building with protruding porches and balconies that would jut out over the South Rim. The design would create dazzling views for hotel guests—and destroy the experience of an unimpeded vista for everyone else.

Lummis shouted at Ripley's vice president Paul Morton, who favored the site—two friends of Teddy Roosevelt's now going at it on the canyon's edge over the future of that edge. Eventually, Morton backed down, and Ripley agreed the hotel would be moved. Someone borrowed Lummis's camera to take a picture of him, Ford, and two other executives sitting serenely on the ground with their legs dangling over the rim. On the train back to Williams, Lummis rode in Ripley's car with Ford and the others. They talked a lot about the hotel, and Lummis was pretty sure they would honor the promise they had made at the rim.

But just to be certain, when he finally went to Washington to meet with Roosevelt, Lummis told the president all about the dispute—to ensure that Teddy would side with him if the issue ever came up again.

CHAPTER 22

THE FRED HARVEY
INDIAN DEPARTMENT

WHEN FORD RETURNED TO KANSAS CITY, HE WAS A CHANGED man. Like many who see the Grand Canyon and the Indian pueblos for the first time, he was in the throes of an inexplicable experience that he couldn't stop trying to explain.

His sister Minnie was thrilled. She had been fascinated by Indian culture since the first time her mother had taken her and her siblings to New Mexico. When Minnie's husband, John Huckel, the head of Fred Harvey's newsstand and retail operations, was off inspecting the Harvey Houses in the Southwest, he would sometimes buy objects for her from the Indians who appeared along the train platforms with exquisite pots balanced on their heads and rugs draped across their shoulders. And he often rode the branch line from Lamy into Santa Fe so he could shop downtown for curios for their collection.

Minnie now saw a look in her brother's eyes that she recognized: the rapture of the Southwest, the Land of Enchantment. So she and her husband started drawing Ford out about his experience, hoping to plant an idea in his head: Maybe his new fascination with all things Indian was a business opportunity for Fred Harvey.

Ford wasn't sure, but his sister was very persuasive. As one of their grandnephews pointed out, "Once Harvey women begin getting interested in something, the men are pulled along by the short hairs." Ford was intrigued enough with the idea to dispatch his sister and brother-in-law on a field trip to do some research. Their first stop was the Harvey House he had just visited in Gallup, New Mexico. It was "the Harvey way" to always promote from within—and Ford knew that the longtime manager in Gallup was some kind of genius when it came to Indian arts and crafts.

Herman Schweizer was like a character out of *Blazing Saddles*—a short, stocky, prematurely balding, cigar-chomping German-Jewish immigrant whose hobby was riding by horseback to Navajo trading posts and villages to buy or trade blankets, pottery, and jewelry. Schweizer had been running the tiny Harvey House in Navajo country for thirteen years; Fred Harvey himself had promoted him to manager when he was only seventeen, after an incident that became a company legend. At the time, Schweizer was just a cashier and had started collecting antique guns, displaying a few on the wall behind his register. One night a very tough freight train crew came into the lunchroom for coffee and pie, then tried to leave without paying. Schweizer crowned one of the men with a Fred Harvey signature silver sugar bowl, and pulled a gun on the others. They shut up, paid up, and got out—never realizing the gun was an unloaded antique that was just for display.

Schweizer, who never married, spent much of his free time in Ganado, Arizona, fifty miles northwest of Gallup, where there were a handful of trading posts run by non-Indians. At the trading posts, the Navajos swapped or pawned for necessities like coffee, grain, and fruit. As compensation for the Long Walk, the government had given them sheep and goats, but increasingly they were turning to their crafts as a way to earn money. The skills once reserved for creating Navajo religious and decorative items, as well as utilitarian pots, baskets, and rugs, were now cornerstones of their near-subsistence economy.

Schweizer learned everything he could about Indian art and culture, befriending the Navajos, who referred to him as *Hosteen Tsani*—"bald-headed man." He was one of the few non-Indian experts in Navajo blankets, baskets, pottery, and especially jewelry—which was quite bulky, made of heavy silver, and adorned with large stones.

And after many years running the Harvey House in Gallup, he had also become an expert in the tourist trade. There were two kinds of travelers, Schweizer explained to Minnie and John Huckel when they came to visit. There were those who appreciated authentic pieces and others who preferred something cheaper, more colorful, less substantial: Navajo Lite.

So while Schweizer always bought the best of the best for himself, he also started commissioning craftsmen to produce costume jewelry knockoffs—even going so far as to bring the Navajos thinner silver and smaller pieces of polished turquoise than they would normally use. Although he wasn't the first white man to ask the Indians to do this, he was the first to order and market such pieces in volume, to turn it into a serious business. When this Navajo Lite style went on to become what most Americans think of as typical "traditional" southwestern jewelry, Indian art experts had to admit that while the pieces were executed by Navajo artisans, the style itself was rightfully credited to this small, bald, quirky German Jew who worked for Fred Harvey.

Schweizer brought the Huckels to the reservation, where they visited trading posts and met Navajo artists. Minnie was impressed. She felt she could learn a lot from Schweizer, and liked the idea of the company having an in-house Indian art guru. Her husband, John, appreciated Schweizer's knowledge and commercial pluck, but he wasn't sure he actually *liked* him. While Huckel had excellent taste and strong marketing skills, he was still a fairly formal, stuffy Easterner. He had trouble adjusting to the multicultural casualness, intensity, and spontaneity of the Southwest that came so naturally to Schweizer.

Still, the friction didn't keep Minnie and John Huckel from working well with Schweizer. Over the next few months, they devised a plan for Fred Harvey to dive headfirst into the world of native art. They convinced Ford, who then convinced Santa Fe President Ripley, to let them take over the building that connected the new Albuquerque depot and the Alvarado, their new hotel, and turn it into the country's premier museum for Indian art and crafts. Schweizer assured them he could assemble a collection as good as anything on display at New York's American Museum of Natural History or the Field Museum in Chicago. But his display would be, like everything else about Fred Harvey, a marvel of efficiency—in a space not much larger than a big-city museum entrance hall, he could offer an in-depth ethnological experience that could be absorbed in less than thirty minutes, which is precisely how long the train stopped in Albuquerque.

The Indian museum was intended to be a nice little vanity project for the next generation of the Harvey family. Little attention was paid to what it would cost the company or whether it could ever break even. The goal was simply to strengthen the association between the Santa Fe railroad and the exotic culture of the Southwest, which some viewed as "America's Orient." But of course Schweizer and the Huckels also hoped they might ignite some public interest in the Indians of the

Southwest and help to elevate their status—since some travelers regarded them largely as panhandlers who surrounded passengers as they disembarked, hawking trinkets.

WITHIN SIX MONTHS, Schweizer and the Huckels had bought every private collection of Indian art and crafts they could find, but now didn't know quite what to do with the pieces in that big empty space in the Albuquerque train station. So they reached out to an improbable woman none of them had ever met—a thirty-three-year-old high school industrial arts teacher in St. Paul, Minnesota, who apparently had been recommended to the main office in Kansas City by a Fred Harvey cashier in San Francisco.

Mary Elizabeth Jane Colter was a tiny dynamo, a petite, formidable woman with full lips, long, thick hair she never let down in public, wide blue eyes that cataloged every detail, and calloused hands equally adept at fine detail drawing and bricklaying. She had a strong jaw—often used to bite people's heads off—and an almost religious belief in her own good taste.

"An incomprehensible woman in pants" was how one admirer described her.

One day in the summer of 1902, Colter was standing on the roof of her cabin in the woods outside of St. Paul, fixing a leak, when a Western Union boy arrived from town with a long telegram for her. In it, Herman Schweizer, whom she had never even heard of, told her to get on a train to New Mexico immediately. Fred Harvey needed her help with a new Indian museum.

Mary Colter had been entranced with Indian culture ever since she was nine years old and a family friend brought her drawings done by Sioux prisoners from the Battle of Little Bighorn. Colter's father died when she was seventeen, and she had to support her sickly mother and older sister, moving them with her to San Francisco so she could study architecture and interior design at the California School of Design. After she graduated, the family returned to St. Paul, where Colter taught school. She also began teaching herself metalwork and jewelry making, and got involved in the Arts and Crafts Movement. A post-Victorian design revolution, Arts and Crafts sought to topple the barriers between "high art," industrial design, and handicrafts; to elevate the skills of the architect, the interior designer, and the craftsman; and to take female artists more seriously. While the movement began in Europe, its impact was greater in the United States, which had yet to fully establish its own style of "high art"—but had plenty of native "primitive" art and design.

The Santa Fe and Fred Harvey had already shown their Arts-and-Craftiness by using vernacular architecture for the new hotels and depots. But while the railroad's architects could mimic authentic exteriors, they weren't sure how to handle the interior living spaces—which, if authentic, would be spare, minimalist, and fairly uncomfortable by Victorian standards.

Mary Colter was brought in to solve that problem. She arrived in Albuquerque to find a series of large rooms with rough adobe walls and concrete floors, nestled between the new depot and the new Alvarado Hotel. The museum space was entered through two adobe arches, which led to four linked display areas that ended with the door to Herman Schweizer's office—where he kept his "vault" of treasures.

Colter's job was to take these big empty rooms and turn them into rich, provocative environments that would narrate the entirety of the Native American experience while also showing the many exciting ways that native goods could be used in white people's houses—and in so doing to help rescue the fragile economy of the Southwest. What is amazing is how well she executed these impossible orders. The rooms she created were paradoxical: both entirely faux and deeply, richly authentic, crammed with genuine pieces of native art and crafts set amid pre-weathered, deliberately distressed beams, wooden floors, and brick fireplaces. She took the items that Indians were selling on train platforms and put them into context—a context of her own inspiration. While some of the ideas she used were already in the air at the time, they had mostly been expressed in exhibits at museums or world's fairs. Yet these rooms in Albuquerque felt intimate enough to live in every day—and, in fact, appeared as if someone fascinating had been inhabiting them for years.

This cross-cultural tableau of fantasy rooms marked the beginning of what we now refer to as "Santa Fe style."

Not surprisingly, it took a while to get passengers to fully appreciate the museum—or, as most people called it, the "Indian Building"—because they were so anxious to eat at the Alvarado.

"Herman stood in front of his Indian building *begging* travelers just to step in for a look," one of his colleagues recalled.

But when people finally did come in, they were astonished. Many of them wanted to know if they could buy the priceless pieces right off the walls and tables. Some wanted to purchase entire rooms. Before long, this little Harvey family vanity project looked as though it could be a sensation—and a moneymaker.

To keep up with demand, Schweizer continued to buy every collection he could find, and his private "vault" had to be expanded to house all the treasures.

"He just had room after room of these great artistic finds," recalls one family member who spent time in the vault. "The rooms had a musty, sweet smell, sort of an earthy smell, from all the dust on everything." While he was running a business as much as a museum, Indian art experts believe his buying sprees may have saved certain items—like the Navajo rug—from extinction. "Fred Harvey saw the value of this outmoded article when others less discerning were casting it aside for the new," wrote one authority on Navajo weaving.

Mary Colter returned to St. Paul to resume her teaching duties, remaining involved as a consultant. But within months, the world of anthropology was shocked when the eminent Dr. George Dorsey, curator at the Field Columbian Museum in Chicago, took a leave of absence to journey to Albuquerque, move into the Alvarado Hotel, and begin overseeing what was now being called the vaguely academic-sounding Fred Harvey Indian Department. Other academics soon followed. Wealthy physician-turned-anthropologist Dr. John Hudson—the husband of artist Grace Hudson—was paid to come and write about his own amazing basket collection, which was added to the displays.

Hudson wrote home to his wife raving about life at the Alvarado. His room, he said, was

> as handsome and inviting as any in the land. The mattress was so extraordinarily soft that really I lay awake in the bliss of realization of perfect comfort . . . Four or more trains pass here daily and they never fail to take advantage of the half hour stop to run into this little gem of a hotel and seem just like wondering, delighted children and I don't blame them, for everything is quaint and comfortable to the last degree. In front of the big

fireplaces are upholstered swings for four, swung by big chains from the ceiling and are delightful to sit in.

IT WASN'T LONG before Albuquerque had what felt like its own separate Santa Fe railroad trackside city. The main terminal point in the West for both the trains and Fred Harvey, the depot complex was home to more than a hundred railroad managers, accountants, and land agents. In addition to the flocks of new Harvey Girls in the 150-seat dining room and the twenty-four-hour lunchroom, there were Fred Harvey cooks, managers, hotel maids, clerks, accountants, and secretaries, as well as a huge laundry staff, who cleaned all the clothing, uniforms, and linen for five Harvey hotels and the entire Harvey dining car system—some five thousand pieces of laundry a day.

The most intriguing employees at the Albuquerque depot, however, were "the Harvey Indians." As the Indian Building grew in popularity, Schweizer and Huckel added another feature to their museum: actual Indians demonstrating their crafts. Schweizer reached out to the Hubbell Trading Post in Ganado, asking for help finding some Indians who would be willing to move away from home and live at the Alvarado. He offered to pay them double what they were getting for their creations on the reservation—as long as they agreed to be seen *making things* when the trains pulled in four times a day.

The whistle of an approaching Santa Fe engine was the work siren for the Harvey Indians—and as soon as the whistle of the departing train was out of earshot, their time was pretty much their own. Some took on second jobs around the hotel—cleaning and stocking shelves. Others did only what Schweizer was paying them for—to be Indians far from home, participating in what critics would deride as "staged authenticity" but many tourists came to adore.

The best-known Harvey Indian was Elle of Ganado—in Navajo, *Asdzaa Lichii'* (Red Woman)—a moonfaced, middle-aged member of the Black Sheep Clan who was believed to be one of the Navajos forced onto the Long Walk. She spoke no English, and communicated primarily through her gregarious husband, Tom of Ganado—*Naaltsoos Neiyéhé* (Mail Carrier)—from the Many Goats Clan. Tom, who spoke four languages, was very comfortable around non-Indians from his years carrying the mail between Gallup and the Hubbell Trading Post.

Elle was his eighth wife and the only one with whom he did not have children, which was part of the reason they could relocate from their village to a train platform. While Elle was an enormously talented weaver whose work was highly valued, Tom was an adequate silversmith at best. But he made up for it with charm: With his muscular physique, chiseled face, and flirtatiousness, he was popular with female customers, who loved him even when he taunted them to their oblivious faces.

NOT LONG AFTER she started working at the Indian Building, Elle of Ganado began weaving an extraordinary blanket. For days tourists watched as she sat at her loom, in the "authentic" alcove Mary Colter had created for her—twigs and branches hanging overhead, a large white drum topped with a fur pelt next to her stool, imported dirt covering the concrete floor, dusting the hem of her full-length skirt. And each day another level of the image would appear, for the rug took shape from the bottom up. First there were the stripes of a border, next white diamonds floating in a blood-red sea, and then a five-pointed star. Then text began to emerge—an upcoming date, then "Albuquerque," followed by the words "Commercial Club . . . Membership Card . . . Honorary." It wasn't until she wove "THE PRESIDENT" into the top line that it became clear what she was doing.

Theodore Roosevelt was on a breakneck two-month spring tour across the country. While it had been two years since he assumed the presidency, there were still many parts of America he had never visited: He hadn't yet set foot in the state of California, for instance, and despite all his travels through the nation's natural wonderlands he had never seen the Grand Canyon. Roosevelt's trip was much more than a whistle-stop tour; the most charismatic leader in a generation was meeting the people. With foreign immigration exploding, the country's population had more than doubled during Roosevelt's lifetime. There were now more than eighty million Americans; thousands upon thousands awaited him at every depot.

When the president's train arrived in Albuquerque just before 3:00 p.m. on May 5, 1903, five thousand people were there to greet him. He was whisked to a platform in front of the Alvarado, where he delivered remarks about irrigation and the future of the Southwest, and then was hustled to the Albuquerque Commercial Club, where he was presented with Elle's blanket. Late in the afternoon, his train pulled out of Albuquerque, and he settled into his Pullman for the overnight ride to the Grand Canyon.

When the president arrived at the Grand Canyon Railway the next day, a saddled white stallion awaited him. He charged up the hill through the tall, straight juniper pines, seeing nothing ahead but blue sky until he was almost upon it. When he beheld the Divine Abyss at last, he was, perhaps for the first time in his life, speechless.

"The only word I can use for it," he said finally, his voice dropping reverently to a whisper, "is *awful*... awe such as I have never before known. It is beyond comparison. It is beyond description."

High in the saddle, the president took a rousing twelve-mile ride along the South Rim with his old friend Charles Lummis and a group of local Rough Riders, all of whom had been recruited by the late Bucky O'Neill, an Arizona businessman who had been Roosevelt's most trusted officer in the Spanish-American War, before being killed by sniper fire. The O'Neills had a cabin on the South Rim, and Roosevelt never forgot how Bucky talked about his beloved Grand Canyon.

After the ride, the president spoke from the balcony of the Bright Angel Hotel, a two-story wooden building that looked like an old farmhouse a tornado had dropped ten feet from the edge of the canyon. Slatted wooden fences had been put up behind the hotel so guests didn't accidentally step off the back porch and fall to certain death. The audience of over eight hundred people was the largest group ever assembled at the South Rim. There were local politicians and New York newspapermen in suits, miners in dusty work clothes, Indians in full regalia, frontier wives, farmers, lumberjacks, hotel clerks, tourists, campers, and trail guides.

"I have come here to see the Grand Canyon," Roosevelt began, "a natural wonder which, so far as I know, is absolutely unparalleled in the world. I shall not attempt to describe it because I cannot. But I want to ask you to do one thing in connection with it—in your own interest and in the interest of the country. *Keep this great wonder of Nature as it now is!*" There was thunderous applause.

"I was delighted," he continued, "to hear of the wisdom of the Santa Fe railroad people in deciding not to build their hotel on the brink of the canyon." In fact, Roosevelt, Lummis, and others remained concerned that just the opposite was true, that the railroad still hoped to place its huge Fred Harvey hotel right out over the edge. The canyon was not yet a national park—it had been staked out and claimed by private individuals and companies like any other piece of federal land, and there was no easy way to stop the railroad from building where it wanted. So Roosevelt had to resort to the growing power of his own presence and the presidency:

> I hope you will not have a building of any kind—not a summer cottage, a hotel or anything else—mar the wonder of its grandeur, its sublimity, the great loneliness and beauty of the canyon. *Leave it as it is.* You cannot improve on it, not a bit. The ages have been at work on it, and man can only mar it. What you can do is keep it for your children and your children's children and for all who come after you, as one of the great sights which every American, if he can travel at all, should see.

And then, what had begun as a warning shot to the Santa Fe and Fred Harvey became one of Roosevelt's first major environmental addresses:

> We have gotten past the stage, my fellow citizens, when we are to be pardoned if we simply treat any part of our country as something to be skinned for two or three years for the use of the present generation. Whether it is the forest, the water, the scenery, whatever it is . . . make it of benefit not to the speculator who hopes to get profit out of it for two or three years, but handle it so it will be of use to the homemaker, to the man who comes to live here, and his children after him. Preserve them but *use* them, so they will not be squandered, they will not be wasted, and they will be of benefit to the Arizonans of 1953 as well as the Arizonans of 1903.

The president was supposed to make only brief remarks before accepting a gift from the governor of Arizona and handing out diplomas to the graduating class of Flagstaff High School. But he was caught up in the moment, moved not only by the canyon but by the largest turnout of Indians he had ever seen:

I want to say a word of welcome to the Indians here. In my regiment, I had a good many Indians. They were good enough to fight and to die, and they are good enough to have me treat them exactly as square as any white man.

There are a good many problems in connection with them. You have got to save them from corruption, save them from brutality. And I regret to say that at times we have to save them from the unregulated Eastern philanthropist. Because, in everything, we have to remember that although the worst quality [to have] is hardness of heart, I do not know that it does as much damage as softness of head.

All I ask is a square chance for every man—*give him a fair chance*. Do not let him wrong anyone, and do not let him be wronged. Help him as far as you can without hurting him in helping him, for the only way to help a man in the end is to help him help himself. Never forget that!

I believe in you. I am glad to see you. I wish you well with all my heart. And I know that your future will justify all the hopes we have.

The cheers went on for so long that the correspondent from the *Los Angeles Times* wondered if it was possible to have *too much* applause and adulation.

By late afternoon, the president was back on the train, headed to California, where he would visit Los Angeles and San Francisco for the first time and then conclude his journey with a camping trip in Yosemite with John Muir. But the impact of his thirty-six hours in New Mexico and Arizona was profound. Because of Roosevelt, the two cornerstones of Fred Harvey's Southwest—the Indian Building in Albuquerque and the Grand Canyon—were suddenly in the consciousness of most Americans.

Before Roosevelt's speech, people still talked about various "grand canyons" in the West. There was the Grand Canyon of Arizona, which some also called the Grand Canyon of the Colorado. And there was the Grand Canyon of the Yellowstone, which the Santa Fe's rival, the Union Pacific, used to market its proximity to that natural wonder.

But after Roosevelt's visit, America had only *one* Grand Canyon.

His rim-side statements were immediately tweaked so they would live on—in publicity and history—as the president proclaiming the

Grand Canyon "the one great sight that every American should see."
And exactly one month after his visit, northern Arizona's *Coconino Sun*
reported that the Santa Fe railroad had finally approved the plans for
the design and location of its fabulous new hotel. It was still going to
be in the pine forest east of the current Bright Angel Hotel, as had always been envisioned. But now it would be "further back from the
rim."

CHAPTER 23

TENTH LEGION

ᗡᑕ

On a typical morning at the fred harvey offices in kansas City, Ford met with his top executives—"the Tenth Legion," as he jokingly called them, after Caesar's elite fighting force. Clad in nearly identical gray suits, they sat discussing problems large and small throughout the sprawling Harvey System: anything from the specter of federal regulation of train depots, to the problem of pregnant Harvey Girls, to how it was that tiny toads found their way into all the coffee cups in Guthrie just before a seating—discovered only when scalding beverages were poured on them. Or sometimes the subject was a tiny price change in an indispensable provision—which, multiplied by several million meals a year, meant a considerable amount of money.

"Coffee has riz, two cents higher this morning—how much have we left?" Dave asked, his British accent and word placement still strong, as a rare visitor, a local reporter, listened in.

"Two cents a pound? That's going to set us back five thousand dollars, just about," said one of the legionnaires. "We're using twenty-five thousand pounds a month or more." Every year, Fred Harvey was now buying and serving some 6,480,000 eggs; 300,000 pounds of butter; 1,000,000 pounds of sugar; 2,000,000 pounds of beef; 600,000 pounds of chicken; 500,000 pounds of ham; 100,000 pounds of bacon; 150,000 pounds of lard; 100,000 pounds of turkey; and 60,000 pounds of duck. It also used seventy-five train-car loads of flour (about 3,000,000 pounds) and eighty-eight train-car loads of potatoes (about 2,800,000 pounds). All chased down with over 300,000 pounds of Chase & Sanborn coffee.

Another gentleman strode into the office, holding a package of dinner rolls. It was Victor Vizzetti, the company's culinary czar. "A fellow sent these from Hutchinson," he explained. "Says they're better than ours."

Ford and Dave stuck out their hands for samples while checking other reports piled in front of them.

"Here's a letter from a man in Washington who says they serve better olives in a hotel there than we do," Ford said. "How about it?"

"Look over there on that desk, Mr. Harvey," Vizzetti shot back. "I wrote immediately to that hotel and procured the brand when I heard about it. It's *exactly* the same olive we've been serving. I have one man on the West Coast who puts in all his time looking up the best olives and olive oil for us."

Ford picked up the jar of olives and examined it. "I guess that chap was carried away by the flowers and shaded lights and the music," he said with a shrug. "He just *thought* those olives tasted better." Olives were no small matter at Fred Harvey; Ford had recently sparked a huge controversy by admitting to *Pacific Fruit World* that he believed Italian olive oil was still better than anything made in California, which was why his chefs used it exclusively.

No matter how large the company got, every day at Fred Harvey headquarters started the same way—with a meeting of Ford's Tenth Legion. The group included Dave, John Huckel, Victor Vizzetti, Dave's brother Harry, A. T. Hilyard, the head of procurement, and Frank Clough, the book buyer for the newsstands. All of these men had known Fred Harvey personally, and had been promoted through the ranks by Ford and Dave. All of them understood the company's obsession with the needs of customers as well as employees, since any personal problem could quickly become a professional one.

And all of them, in the words of the reporter, knew "the multiplication table backward down to the division of a mutton chop. They juggle daily with reports and train routes and figures and maps and crop failures and markets until they can tell you the exact reason why there was a pint of sweet cream left over on a trip through the American Sahara until it soured enough to use for the salad dressing they served that terrible hot day the passengers didn't seem to care for hot meats."

Fred Harvey had been gone for three years, and the plan for how the company would run after his death had succeeded brilliantly. By not allowing any estate issues to slow or divert the family business, the Harvey System was riding a wave of renewed American prosperity and the rising fortunes of the Santa Fe Railway. In addition to the depot eating houses and lunchrooms in over sixty cities and towns, Ford and Dave were now running eight large, handsome trackside hotels the Santa Fe had built over the past few years—in Newton and Dodge City, Kansas; La Junta and Trinidad, Colorado; Clovis, Las Vegas, and Albuquerque, New Mexico; and Temple, Texas—and there were plans for many more. They also created large "commissaries" in Chicago, St. Louis, Kansas City, and several other cities that did food prep for all the dining cars and tested out recipes and new ingredients.

To fill the seemingly endless needs for fresh ingredients, Ford had established his own dairy farms and poultry facilities at Newton, Temple, and Del Rio, Arizona, which not only produced milk and dressed chicken parts but also made fresh ice cream. These also allowed the company to set new standards for safeguarding the nation's milk safety, following up on the suggestion of a well-known customer: "Frontier Doctor" Samuel Crumbine, a nationally known public health reformer who lived in Dodge City and had breakfast every day at the new Harvey hotel there, the El Vaquero. One morning, when Dave Benjamin was in the hotel, Crumbine pulled him aside and complained about how dangerous it was that milk was being stored in open jugs and pitchers, inviting bacteria. So Fred Harvey became one of the first companies in the nation to use only smaller milk bottles that could be sealed.

While the restaurants and hotels were his main focus, Ford was also taking care of the expanding Santa Fe dining car business, where he made a major personnel change that also helped solve the problem of where to put his twenty-six-year-old baby brother, Byron—whom he loved dearly, but generally considered to be spoiled and somewhat lazy. He sent Byron, who had been soaking up the culture in the Kansas City office, to Chicago as the family's representative in the Santa Fe dining car business. The dining car operation was completely separate from the eating houses, and was run very differently. The chefs and supervisors, as well as the servers (who, like the train stewards, were black men—there were no Harvey Girls on wheels), were managed by the Fred Harvey dining car office in Chicago. But they were paid by the railroad. The menus, ingredients, and service were absolutely Fred Harvey quality, but the operation was more of an interactive partnership with the Santa Fe than the eating houses and hotels were. And running the dining car business was more about schmoozing railroad executives and crunching the numbers than the kind of creative, bottom-up management Ford's people did from Kansas City. Byron, who had excellent people skills but limited executive moxie, was brought in as the "titular head of the dining car operation," according to one of his grandsons, "but in essence he was 'minded' by the senior supervisors who had actually been running that division. They were instructed by Ford to 'train' Byron, so he could become more than a figurehead leader."

"My father didn't know how to do *anything* when he went to Chicago," one of Byron's sons would later recall. "Some cheese company sent him a Roquefort cheese to try it out. He had somebody open it; he smelled it and told the guy to go out and bury it, it was rotten!"

Besides hospitality, Ford was moving the company more strongly into a new business—publishing. Taking the advice of his brother-in-law John Huckel—who always offered his own opinion as well as Minnie's—Ford increased the amount of space and attention allotted to books in their newsstand business. This turned the company's longtime book buyer, Frank Clough, a former Leavenworth neighbor of the Harveys who had started out as an eating house cashier, into something of a phenomenon in the publishing industry. Because of the company's expanding reach and his own proven instincts, he was now one of the few book buyers in America who could predict, or create, a best-seller.

But there was more to publishing than books. Ford was also investing in the country's hottest new communications medium: the picture postcard. He teamed with the new American powerhouse in the postcard business, the Detroit Publishing Company, which had cornered the market by securing the U.S. patent on the best new process for colorizing black-and-white photos and then partnering with America's preeminent outdoor photographer, William Henry Jackson, so they could make all his pictures into color postcards. Then Detroit benefited from a stroke of luck: In 1898 the U.S. government lowered the postage required on a card from two cents to one, and also began loosening restrictions on what could appear on the picture side as well as what could be written on the blank side. A partnership with Ford took Detroit Publishing to the next level. Not only did the Harvey System have a powerful distribution network, but the company owned a huge stockpile of photographs and was constantly taking more—all of which could be made into postcards. The two companies made an exclusive wide-ranging contract in 1904, and pictures of "Fred Harvey Indians," archaeological wonders, and southwestern life started appearing on postcard racks around the country. The two companies also explored other ways to profitably publish the images, everything from handsome books to sets of highly collectible gold-leaf Fred Harvey "Souvenir Playing Cards of the Great Southwest" with a different tinted photo on the face of each card.

Each time the company expanded, more businessmen around the country came to appreciate what a unique talent Ford was—how creatively he had taken what his father built and molded it into something so much larger and more complex while still maintaining the standard and, if anything, increasing the loyalty of employees and patrons. Yet there was something curious about the way Ford still refused to put his name on anything, and labored to maintain the illusion that his father was still alive. Every menu, every piece of promotional material, still ended with "Your host is Fred Harvey."

One Kansas City society columnist suggested Ford was "peculiarly lacking in personal ambition . . . Even his identity is obscure to the general public." But actually, he was every bit as ambitious as his father, which made his willingness to remain behind the curtain, and lead by powerful presence, that much more intriguing.

A handful of eastern entrepreneurs had seen Ford's vast operation and were trying to copy aspects of it. William and Samuel Childs had returned from a train trip west and started a small chain of "dairy lunch" cafeterias in their hometown of New York City. Two Philadelphia luncheonette owners, Joseph Horn and Frank Hardart, had taken the self-serve idea one step further and opened the first American coin-operated automat. At Horn & Hardarts, individual servings of cold foods were displayed behind rows of small chrome-plated doors, each with its own coin slot that only accepted nickels; hot foods were served at steam tables, except for wondrous hot chocolate, which flowed from a chrome-plated spout after your nickels dropped *clink* into the slot.

The cafeterias and automats represented the first steps toward a new kind of fast-food eating—prompted, in part, by the rising price of oysters from the polluted, overharvested waters around New York, which had finally eroded the mollusk's status as a staple for quick, easy meals. But the food at these new cafeterias and automats was generally much simpler than Fred Harvey's, and there was, by definition, no service. The Harvey System was the nation's gold standard for fine, fast, dependable, comforting food in cities large and small.

NO MATTER HOW FAR and wide the Harvey System spread, its heart and soul were still in Kansas City. Ford had managers in each Fred Harvey location, regional offices in New Mexico, California, and Texas, and a band of roving inspectors and auditors, but the entire business was still run by his Tenth Legion from their growing suite of low-profile offices on the second floor of the Kansas City Union Depot annex building. While the Harvey family saw the Southwest more and more as their home away from home, Kansas City was where they, and the company, lived.

In fact, Ford and Judy Harvey had become major players in the growth of the former "City of Kansas," which was starting to fulfill its dreams of being the next Chicago—the second city's second city. When they moved there as newlyweds back in the late 1880s, it had about sixty thousand residents and was just beginning to develop a distinctive brand of Midwestern urban life. But Kansas City was now one of the twenty-five largest cities in America. It had a population of over 165,000, and it was growing rapidly under the tough-love political leadership of city councilman James Pendergast, whose concrete company was involved in much of the new construction.

Ford and Judy Harvey had been part of Kansas City's young social set in the Quality Hill neighborhood and were founding members of the Kansas City Country Club. Now that their children were older—Kitty was eleven, Freddy, eight—and business was flourishing, they moved to the wealthy neighborhood near Hyde Park. They bought the spacious house at 3617 Robert Gillham Road that the late architect Henry Van Brunt, a protégé of Frank Furness's, had designed for his own family. Ford became increasingly active in the civic life of Kansas City, and his wife was a rising star of the social scene, known for her good works, great parties, and ambitious family travels.

The Harveys were especially involved with Catholic charity work. While Ford was still technically Episcopalian—although, lately, most of his religious experiences involved his awe at God's handiwork in the Southwest—Judy remained a devout Catholic. She had followed through on her promise to raise the children in her faith, and was deeply involved in Catholic social causes. Ford was fully supportive of the charity work she did, and gave generously, though always with characteristic discretion.

In a very cozy arrangement, Minnie and John Huckel would soon buy a house down the street from Ford and Judy's new home, so the Kansas City Harveys were together often—and had frequent visits from their mother and sisters, who took the train down from nearby Leavenworth. Dave Benjamin and his wife, Linnie, also bought nearby on Gillham Road.

So, Ford and the leaders of his Tenth Legion grew closer personally as well as professionally. And those who succeeded in the Fred Harvey Service understood the need to accept a similarly blurred line between work and private life. As one national magazine writer said of Ford, "His employees who do their work well are his friends."

The way they lived mirrored the way their employees lived, in more than seventy different outposts connecting more than half of America: from Chicago west across Illinois, Kansas, Colorado, New Mexico, and Arizona to California, and from Chicago south across Iowa, Missouri, Arkansas, and Oklahoma all the way down through Texas. In each city and town, whether there was just a lunchroom and newsstand or a new hotel with a staff of fifty or sixty, being in the Harvey Service meant living and working in close quarters with intense commitment. Fred Harvey people lived as if they were on small military bases where the strategies and tactics of hospitality were taken every bit as seriously as those of combat. As in all military operations, there were a large number of young, ambitious people looking to improve themselves during a short term of duty, a handful of lifers who had stayed on to be promoted up the ranks, and a townful of people who had gotten their discharge from the Harvey Service (honorably or not) and decided to make their homes where they were last posted. So they still came to eat in their old restaurants and participated in the social lives of the Harvey Houses like veterans: There were regular dances, plays, baseball games, sing-alongs, weddings, baby showers. The culture of Harvey people was so intense that they were given their own section in the Santa Fe railroad employee magazine, because they communicated in a language all their own.

TO KEEP IN TOUCH with his nearly seven thousand employees, and remind them—and himself—of the importance of their work, their loyalty, their integrity, and their ingenuity, Ford would sometimes dictate long conversational memos to be copied and circulated throughout the system. He also sent around copies of speeches he gave to trade groups about the company's successes and challenges, as well as typewritten versions of any newspaper articles mentioning Fred Harvey service.

While his father had primarily communicated through actions, Ford was learning the power of words. And he was using them to explain a business ethos that was adapted from his father's ideas and informed his own contemporary experience.

Ford could make an entire sermon out of an order of pompano.

[We] instruct our people always to *give the customer the benefit of the doubt*—which goes a step further, I think, than simply assuming that the customer is always right. It is not always so simple to satisfy a customer, even by giving the customer the benefit of the doubt. He may be *wrong*—and while we must satisfy him, if we leave him under the impression that he is right he may carry away a harmful impression.

We serve a good deal of pompano, for example, a highly flavored fish. Those who like it cherish this flavor. But, unfortunately for us, the customer who orders it may not know it. And then the chances are excellent that he calls the dining-car steward or the restaurant manager and complains that his fish is spoiled. Our man knows exactly what is up, of course. He knows further that his first job is to suggest some other dish which will suit the customer. But next comes the dilemma. Shall he, by keeping still, admit that his place is serving bad fish, and thus shake the customer's confidence in us? Or shall he offend the customer mortally by pointing out that the customer knows nothing about fish, else he would recognize the pompano as excellent?

It is a situation which calls for big-caliber diplomacy. About the only way out is for our men to pay extra attention to the customer throughout the rest of the meal, get the conversation around to fish and their peculiarities of flavor, and then—without letting the customer suspect he is doing so by intention—plant the idea that by reason of its unusual high flavor pompano is often unjustly suspected of taint. Such a job requires consummate tact. If we were able to score a bull's eye 50%

of the time, the State Department would recruit ambassadors exclusively from our employ!

Through his talks and writing, Ford was developing a running list of rules for businessmen—an unconscious update of those that Fred used to carry around glued to the front of his wallet when Ford was a baby, which was equally illuminating:

1. **Never buy a cheap thing:** Everything you buy, you in turn sell. If you buy the best, your customer gets the best.
2. **The best price is always the fair price:** You may be the first on the market in the morning, but the buyer who is always seeking his supplies at a price *under the market* will fail to secure preferential consideration.
3. **Concentrate your business in as few hands as possible:** When you have formed the right associations, "stick" unless convinced your confidence is misplaced, and in that case be careful to see that you hitch up right the next time.
4. **Loyalty is double barreled—if you want it, you must *be* loyal.**
5. **Plow your profits under:** At every point, our growth has been clearly in proportion to our willingness to be moderate in our immediate profit-taking for the sake of the fullest possible satisfaction of the customer. We have not always been so moderate as we might, but always we have paid more for the fun than it was worth. Now, anything above the normal in profits in any section of the business is taken at once as a danger signal and calls for investigation. Generally, we have found, it means that somebody has been cutting costs for a profit showing—without enough regard for profits in the long run.
6. **Be committed to complete customer satisfaction:** In every venture from the Topeka lunchroom on down, we have been assailed and assailed again with the most plausible reasons for doing things less well. Sticking to our commitment in spite of all sorts of inducements to depart from it has really counted for us.
7. **Hold constantly to a level of theoretical perfection:** Of course we are not unfailingly successful in having our policies carried out. Of course some of our people fail to hold to our

standards, some more often than others. But trying to attain perfection creates a process of natural selection that helps management with its purpose. If, unthinkably, I should direct our meat buyer to purchase second grade beef hereafter, I honestly believe that he would disregard the order. It is the same with all of our department heads and our buyers. Any one of our responsible executives under such circumstances would simply conclude that I had said something that I really did not mean, or that I had suffered a temporary aberration from which I would soon recover.

8. **Catch employees young,** or at least fairly inexperienced in your kind of business. We find we have a better chance with them that way than if we get them already trained by someone else.

9. **Always promote from within your own ranks:** We are firm about this. And it is not without a good deal of regret that we sometimes pass up the opportunity to add to our staff a particularly competent individual who has proved himself elsewhere. Our people recognize the opportunities that come to them because we will not hire a man for a responsible job if we can possibly fill it from within.

10. **Gradually and steadily expand,** so that we may make opportunities for the competent youngster who comes up from the ranks. If we did not expand, they might leave us.

11. **Always please the cranks:** Anything which suits a finicky customer is bound to be more than satisfactory to the great run of folks who take what is handed them without complaint. The unreasonable customer, by setting the standards to which we hold, has insured our pleasing the reasonable customers who would be satisfied with less. And the finicky customer is by disposition a talker. Take away any grounds for complaint, deprive him of his grievances, and he goes about the world praising you just as ardently as he would otherwise decry you.

12. **Never take yourself too damn seriously.**

CHAPTER 24

ON THE VERY BRINK OF
THE DIZZY GULF

B UILDING A NEW LUXURY HOTEL AT THE GRAND CANYON, SOME
sixty miles from a dependable source of fresh water, was, predictably, a
nightmare. The new hotel finally had a name: El Tovar, after Don
Pedro de Tovar, the Spanish conquistador who first told his boss, explorer Francisco Vásquez de Coronado, about this natural wonder,
leading to its "discovery" by white men in 1540. (They considered a
Coronado-related name, but all the good ones were already taken—the
most prominent being the popular Hotel del Coronado beachfront resort in San Diego.)

Construction on the building immediately fell way behind schedule, and Ford was getting nervous. He was accustomed to delays—after
all, he worked with the trains, so his life was all about delays and feeding people who were famished and cranky because of them. But the El
Tovar delays were different. This was not another trackside hostelry in
the middle of the desert or the prairie. This was the Ritz of the Divine
Abyss, a monument to the new American pastime of "sightseeing" and
a project whose progress the president of the United States, and the
entire nation, were watching.

There was also competition. The Union Pacific had decided to
build a similarly grand hotel in Yellowstone. Conceding canyon bragging rights, they were naming it after their geyser, the Old Faithful
Inn.

But for Ford, El Tovar had greater personal significance: It was the
Montezuma all over again. He never forgot what that hotel had done
to his father, to their family. He was fifteen years old when Fred had
basically left them for months at a time. Looking back, Ford could now

see that the Montezuma *made* Fred Harvey professionally but injured him physically and psychologically. He was never the same after that—never truly *well,* only "better" or "worse."

And while nobody liked to say it out loud, the Montezuma had been Fred Harvey's most colossal failure. In its third incarnation, the resort hotel had lost so much money that the railroad was probably wishing it would burn down again, since nobody would buy it. Most recently, the Santa Fe had attempted to capitalize on its friendship with the president to help convince the U.S. Army to accept the Montezuma as a gift, a fine mountainside convalescent home for soldiers. But the government wouldn't even take it for free.

Fred Harvey's business had recovered from the Montezuma because the disappointment had occurred early in his relationship with the Santa Fe, when they were still getting to know each other. But Ford was not so sure his partnership with the nation's largest railroad system could survive anything less than resounding success with El Tovar.

IN THE MIDST of these pressures, Herman Schweizer and the Huckels got some thrilling news. Because of the success of the Indian Building in Albuquerque, the territory of New Mexico was asking the Fred Harvey Indian Department to create its exhibit for the Louisiana Purchase Exposition, the 1904 world's fair in St. Louis. In less than two years, their little trackside museum had gained so much credibility that it was worthy enough to compete with the Smithsonian Institution and the other major museums of the world.

While their original big-name anthropologist had returned to the Field Museum in Chicago, he was replaced by one of the world's leading experts on the Hopi Indians, Henry Voth, who had spent ten years on the Hopi reservation in northern Arizona. As a Mennonite missionary, Voth had converted only six Indians to Christianity over an entire decade, but in the process he had been able to painstakingly document Hopi life and culture. While his methods were controversial—he photographed Hopi rites against the tribe's wishes—Voth was clearly the tribe's premier ethnographer. He had also amassed perhaps the world's greatest collection of Hopi art and artifacts, which had never been publicly displayed. They became the cornerstone of the Fred Harvey–New Mexico exhibit at the exposition.

There were dozens of elaborate Indian displays at the St. Louis world's fair, ranging from complete re-creations of Pueblo cliff dwellings to the tragic image of the infamous Apache chief Geronimo, a federal prisoner for eighteen years, sitting in a booth "whittling bows and arrows and selling his autographs for 10 cents each." Almost anywhere visitors walked, but especially down the fair's midway, "The Pike" (which is where the phrase "coming down the pike" originated), they would encounter native peoples in full regalia. There were daily snake dances and other slices of "living history," interspersed with more modern displays such as Marconi's new wireless telegraph technology, an early motion picture theater, the latest in automobiles, and the debuts of a "health drink" called Dr Pepper, as well as baked cones for eating ice cream.

While the Fred Harvey exhibit in room 111 of the Anthropology Building didn't attract quite as much attention as snake dances and ice-cream cones, it did win a number of prestigious jury awards: a grand prize for "best ethnological exhibit," another grand prize for "best aboriginal blanketry and basketry," and two gold medals. For a little museum run by a private company, it was a tremendous honor—not to mention great publicity.

In ethnology-crazed America, Fred Harvey was becoming the first name in the buying of Indian art and crafts. Word spread that any serious collector needed to make the pilgrimage to Albuquerque and talk to Herman Schweizer.

One of his most insatiable customers was William Randolph Hearst, who was hooked after seeing a Fred Harvey promotional display of Navajo blankets at the Auditorium Hotel in Chicago. Hearst, who was by then a congressman from New York as well as the owner of several powerful newspapers, insisted on buying several choice items right off the display—at a healthy discount. He became a regular at the Indian Building, since he often traveled on the Santa Fe express to and from California, but then he began writing or wiring Schweizer whenever the collecting spirit moved him, demanding that a selection of the finest items either be shipped to him immediately in California or be made available for perusal in his Pullman compartment so he didn't have to leave the train.

Hearst and "My Dear Mr. Schweizer," as he called him, developed a curious relationship. Not exactly friends, or even fellow collectors sharing the excitement of rare finds, they were more like a drug dealer and his richest addict, both respecting and detesting their mutual dependency. Schweizer understood Hearst in a way few did, in part because he often had to interact with Hearst's mother, who traveled with the publisher and shared his fascination with Indian art.

Before Christmas one year, Hearst and "the bald-headed man" had a big argument over some items that Mrs. Hearst had tried to buy during a visit to Albuquerque. When offered her son's usual 10 percent discount, she decided she could do better, and instead made Schweizer an absurdly low "offer for the lot"—$2,500 ($62,400) for seven fine blankets, a piece of Spanish tapestry, and a rare Acoma wedding dress.

Schweizer stunned her with a word she was unaccustomed to hearing: "No."

Hearst fired off an angry letter. In his three-page response, Schweizer did his best to pacify him, even enclosing an unusual silver Navajo ring as a peace offering. Hearst liked the ring, but still insisted Schweizer ship him all the items his mother coveted—at a big discount—and audaciously asked him to include a sampler of new blankets as well. In exchange, he claimed he would buy enough pieces to make it worth Schweizer's while, but also offered to sweeten the deal:

"If a little article in the newspapers any time would be of value," he wrote, "let me know on what lines you would like it prepared and I will see that it is inserted."

The stubborn pair continued negotiating through several more impassioned letters, before Schweizer made one final offer—which also provided an interesting insight into his way of doing business. He stuck to his guns and refused to give Hearst the discount his mother wanted—yet at the same time he sent an extra blanket as a personal gift, assuring them it was worth more than what they had hoped to save. The deal was made.

The irony of all this negotiating was that Hearst was notorious for ignoring his Fred Harvey bills. Schweizer and his boss, John Huckel, had numerous discussions and letter exchanges—all copied to Ford because of the delicacy of the matter—concerning the risks of trying to make the publisher pay his bills. Yet Hearst was relentless in demanding more and more.

"I will bet you two huge Mexican dollars that you haven't shown me your real treasures," he wrote. "Out with them now Mr. Schweizer or I shall feel that I am not being treated fairly."

IN THE LATE FALL of 1904, Ford went back to the Grand Canyon to oversee the end of construction at the South Rim. He slept in one of the rustic rooms at the old Bright Angel next door, which now looked like a run-down carriage house for his new hotel complex.

Regardless of the myriad delays and budget overruns, Ford was pleased with El Tovar. It was the ultimate Fred Harvey oasis, in every way honoring President Roosevelt's plea not to deface the canyon. It was an intriguing combination of styles and materials, a cross between a log cabin castle and a Swiss château, its dark wood floors, walls, and ceilings decorated with an occasional Indian rug or moose head. The long, narrow building had 125 guest rooms, and a massive square-helmeted turret rose above its three-story center staircase—an architectural feature that served to hide the water tower inside the roof, which would be filled several times a week with water carried to the canyon by railroad car. But its architecture, ultimately, was less impressive and surprising than the simple fact of its location—it was hard to believe that a luxury hotel could be built so far from civilization, and so close to the edge of the Divine Abyss.

Just across the circular driveway from El Tovar was a similarly counterintuitive structure, dreamed up by Mary Colter—a more ambitious version of the Indian Building at the Albuquerque depot. This time, she had convinced the Santa Fe and Fred Harvey to let her replicate an actual Indian building—a full-scale, brand-new, eight-hundred-year-old pueblo, authentic to the smallest detail, where the Indians who were hired to do art demonstrations and dances would actually live. Inspired by buildings in the nearby reservation city of Oraibi, it was called Hopi House.

Colter and Harvey ethnologist Henry Voth drove local workmen crazy trying to re-create perfectly imperfect surfaces, inside and out. Colter brought in an old wooden bench that had been dug out of a shiny denuded log, and insisted that every piece of furniture and support beam have the same weathered sheen, as if nature had been buffing them for centuries. There was, by design, hardly a straight line in the entire structure. The exterior was built of irregular slabs of Coconino sandstone, endlessly stacked until they created three towering stories, with tiny, slightly skewed rectangular windows. The cement floors were poured to resemble mud, and the walls were irregularly plastered like adobe. The sloping ceilings were made of peeled logs with smaller branches laid across them, and there were several working fireplaces whose chimneys were fashioned from new, old-looking clay pots with the bottoms freshly broken out. The native ambience was so "real" that one easily forgot the dim rooms were ingeniously lit with hidden electric lights.

The star attraction of the Hopi House was Nampeyo, the forty-three-year-old Hopi woman who was considered the most important native potter of her generation and had been featured at several world's fairs. Nampeyo agreed to become a "Fred Harvey Indian," living, working, and performing at Hopi House, along with her large family.

The cost of the two new buildings—trumpeted in the promotional materials because it was higher than the price of the Union Pacific's Yellowstone hotel—was $250,000 ($6.3 million). Another $50,000 ($1.3 million) was invested in stables for the horses that guests would ride along the rim and the mules on which they would descend into the canyon. While the railroad owned the buildings, Fred Harvey was responsible for buying, training, and maintaining the livestock, as well as running the on-site farms where fruits and vegetables were grown for the restaurant.

But El Tovar and Hopi House, while extraordinary, were not the main selling points. The first Santa Fe ads, which started running across the country well before the opening, promised nothing less than the chance "to see how the world was made . . . deep down in the earth a mile and more you go, past strata of every known geologic age. And all glorified by a rainbow beauty of color."

El Tovar made its debut on January 14, 1905—a soft opening in the dead of winter when the canyon often got an abundance of snow, so there would be plenty of time to work out the kinks before the anticipated throngs of summer. To manage the hotel, Ford brought back into the Harvey fold one of his father's favorite employees: Charlie Brant, the heavyset Russian immigrant who had been Fred's maître d' at the opening of the Montezuma. Trained at Delmonico's in New York and the St. Charles Hotel in New Orleans, Brant had left the Montezuma after the original building burned down, and went on to a distinguished career running hotels and private clubs in Chicago, Detroit, St. Louis, and Mackinac Island, Michigan. Now in his mid-fifties, he and his wife, Olga, were looking for one last great challenge in the hospitality business. Nothing could be more challenging than running El Tovar and becoming de facto mayor of the little tourism town growing at the edge of the canyon.

The large Fred Harvey staff immediately doubled the number of people living along the canyon. The influx of Harvey Girls was especially welcome. They represented more single women than had ever been seen in northern Arizona, and the tour guides and miners particularly enjoyed their regular Friday night socials, chaperoned by the large and formidable Miss Bogle, the housemother of the Harvey Girl dormitory. Miss Bogle always kept her eye on the Kolb brothers— Emery, Ellsworth, and Ernest—a randy trio who ran the local photography studio but were best known for their off-camera exploits with the ladies, which they referred to as "rimming," their code word for finding a secluded place along the canyon edge to make out. When Ernest Kolb danced too wildly and too close to a Harvey Girl, Miss Bogle would simply walk over, lift him up, look him in the eye, and say, "Stop your jiggling, you hear?"

Yet while everyone enjoyed the influx of Harvey Girls, there were deep suspicions about their boss. To this ragtag bunch of former miners and adventurers who had made nice little businesses for themselves, the arrival of Ford Harvey, who had enough muscle and money to buy and sell them many times over, was frightening. Ford wielded the full force of the Santa Fe, which had given him its complete proxy on the South Rim. Every entrenched small-time businessman there was either quaking in fear or preparing for battle—although, being pragmatic, they were also calculating their buyout prices so they would be ready when the inevitable offers came.

As the inaugural summer tourist season arrived, the first newspaper reviews were ecstatic. The *Los Angeles Times* called the hotel "magnificent":

> Reared upon the very brink of the dizzy gulf of the gorge, the view afforded the guests from its windows and balconies is something to live long uneffaced in the memory. One may flip the butt of his cigar from his chair on the veranda of the hotel down through space for a distance of more than 7000 feet, considerably more than a mile. He requires a field glass to the ground below his bed-chamber window. He cannot afford to be a somnambulist unless he carries a parachute strapped under his

arms. To live in El Tovar is like enjoying the sensation of occupying a room in the top floor of a hotel more than 400 stories high, or in the pinnacle of seven Eiffel Towers piled one on top of the other, but fortunately without the inconvenience of having to send to China for a bell boy every time one rings for water.

El Tovar and Hopi House drew more people to the Grand Canyon than had ever visited before. The hotel was crowded, and initial business was good.

But the same had been true of the first tourist season at the Montezuma, so Ford maintained his reserve. In fact, when he and Ed Ripley made the deal for Fred Harvey to run the Grand Canyon properties, Ford hedged his bet. Instead of just splitting the profits evenly with the railroad—as he was doing now at all the other eating houses and hotels—he took a smaller percentage of the profits and insisted that the Santa Fe guarantee Fred Harvey would be reimbursed for all net losses. Just in case El Tovar turned out to be another sinkhole.

CHAPTER 25

TRAINIACS

⌐⌐

IT WAS THE FASTEST AND MOST EXPENSIVE TRAIN RIDE IN HIS-
tory: Walter Scott, former Buffalo Bill sideman turned boastful gold
prospector, offered the Santa Fe $5,500 ($139,000) in cash for a private
locomotive and a chance to break the speed record from Los Angeles
to Chicago. But if he was going to do it, he wanted to make the wild
ride in style: His "Coyote Special" included not only a Pullman coach
but a fully stocked Fred Harvey dining car.

Chef Geyer, a Harvey veteran from Germany, was picked for the
assignment, and his wife was frantically trying to talk him out of it. She
reminded the chef he had four children at home and begged him "to let
some other man break his neck" on the swiftest train ride ever.

"Und I say to her," the chef reportedly explained, "if dot man in der
enchine [engine] can stand it to pull der train, I can stand it to ride behind him, yet."

As the Coyote Special pulled out of Los Angeles, the saltshakers
danced across the tables and cookware rattled on the steel kitchen
counters as Chef Geyer started preparing the first meal. Cost was no
concern, since Scott—known as "Death Valley Scotty" because of the
location of his gold mine—had agreed to pay an extra $1,000 ($25,240)
for the Pullman dining service. They started with caviar sandwiches—
because Scott regarded simpler canapés as "dude food"—and an iced
consommé. The diners were Scotty, his wife, and Los Angeles sports-
writer Charles E. Van Loan, who had been chosen to write onboard
dispatches for the Associated Press.

The first courses were going well until just before Needles, California, when the train hit a curve at sixty miles an hour. Everything on the

table went flying, leaving the diners grateful for the prescient wisdom of Chef Geyer for choosing a clear chilled soup.

After the dishes were removed from the table and the soup from the wall, the entrées were served as the train flew at speeds of seventy, even eighty miles an hour. Geyer called his special dishes "Porterhouse Steak a la Coyote, two inches thick and a Marvel of Tenderness," and "Broiled Squab on Toast, with Strips of Bacon au Scotty," and he served them with succulent stuffed tomatoes. For dessert, there was freshly made Fred Harvey ice cream with "colored trimmings," followed by a cheese plate, coffee, and, naturally, cigars.

Although no more food flew, there was one airborne Harvey waiter: During the delicate run through the curvy Glorieta Pass, near Pecos, New Mexico, he was hurled into a dining car window, smashing it with his shoulder.

After getting past the mountainous areas and into Kansas, the train barreled ahead at unheard-of speeds, peaking at 106 miles an hour. From the Dodge City Harvey House—while stopped briefly for fuel— Scotty wired President Roosevelt: "An American cowboy is coming east on a special train faster than any cowpuncher ever rode before; how much shall I break the transcontinental record?" The president didn't respond, but the press did, filing dispatches from each Santa Fe depot about whether Scott's train was running ahead of the record or behind. On July 11, 1905, at 11:54 a.m., Death Valley Scotty's Coyote Special pulled in to Dearborn Station in Chicago, after traveling 2,265 miles in just under forty-five hours—more than seven hours faster than the previous record.

The ride received enormous media coverage, as did Chef Geyer's gutsy performance. "Any man who can cook like that at sixty miles an hour," wrote one Kansas City reporter covering the trip, "is worthy of a place in the culinary hall of fame!"

Death Valley Scotty ended up becoming more famous for the record than for the gold mine he used to pay for it—which turned out to be a fraud, and the train ride an attempt to distract his investors. But the trip would forever be a highlight of the last golden age of the railroads, before government regulation altered their world forever.

Trains had been changing life in America for nearly fifty years, but it was just after the turn of the century that the railroad business reached its peak of economic and cultural influence, independence, and power. There were already several thousand gas-powered automobiles puttering around the country, and the Wright Brothers had already made their first airplane flight at Kitty Hawk. But in 1905, the nation's railroads dominated every aspect of national life as no industry ever had—and, in the estimation of some, no industry has since.

And each time the trains became faster, America seemed a little more intimate, more manageable, a nation paradoxically getting bigger and smaller at the same time.

In the first six years of the twentieth century, the Pullman company filled more orders for "private varnish"—each car costing at least $50,000 ($1.3 million)—than it had in the previous twenty years. There was great competition over the opulence of the decor and the technological perks: Some cars had working fireplaces, and a few even had pipe organs driven by steam from the engine. And those who didn't want the hassles of ownership could rent from the growing Pullman fleet.

For those who couldn't afford such luxuries, the train stations also provided a popular form of entertainment—as compelling and regularly scheduled as radio, movies, and television would come to be.

"It was a great deal to us kids, watching the trains come in," recalled one Midwestern woman who grew up to be a Harvey Girl. "Everybody in town did it, every single day. Mama showed us where to stand, and we'd go down there every afternoon after school and watch all the people and activities around the depot. There was one railroadman who knew us, and he'd take us into the Harvey House for some of their homemade ice cream. We were just little girls. There was nothing like it in the world, *nothing!*"

FORD'S BUSINESS WAS certainly surging with the railroads, and was only expected to get better as the Santa Fe built him more large hotels along the High Iron. But he had some major life decisions to make. The ten-year contract between the railroad and Fred Harvey—the last deal made while his father was still alive, and the one that Fred's will was written to protect—had less than a year to run, expiring in September 1906. At the same time, Ford and Ripley were both approaching milestone birthdays. Ripley, his walrussy mustache graying, was turning sixty, an age when most railroad executives considered retiring.

Ford was about to turn forty, the same age at which his father had rethought his life's goals and started the eating house business. And he was faced with a similar window of opportunity. When the contract ended, the promises he made to his father and the company—to honor the obligations made during Fred's lifetime—would all be fulfilled.

Ford and Ripley had been discussing the gravity of this moment. Ripley was extremely proud of what the railroad and Fred Harvey had been able to accomplish in the past ten years. But he also truly cared for Ford, almost as if he were another son: He had two of his own, but they were more interested in oil and steel than railroading. Ripley's relationship with Ford was special. He once wrote to him: "To be 'nice' to one's friends is comparatively easy—to be equally 'nice' to one's father's friends is a much rarer quality and one (among others) that has made you conspicuous . . . You cannot know the satisfaction a man of my age has in the friendship of one twenty years or more his junior."

Ford knew that if he chose to, he could parlay his success into a high-profile position in business or politics. He had watched his long-time colleague Paul Morton, Ripley's first vice president, leave the Santa Fe to join Roosevelt's cabinet as secretary of the navy and then take one of the top financial jobs in the world: president and chairman of the board of the Equitable Life Assurance Society, in New York. Ford had offers every day for Fred Harvey to take over management of top hotels and restaurants across the United States, Canada, and the United Kingdom, which would dramatically broaden the scope of his empire—and perhaps lessen his reliance on the Santa Fe. Or he could simply take all the money he had made, sell the company, and start over.

It was a tough decision because there were signs that the golden age of railroading could soon be coming to an end. Teddy Roosevelt was becoming increasingly aggressive about regulating the railroads—and *all* aspects of "big business." This included trying to "bust" the powerful New York–based financial trusts whose leaders—especially New York financier J. P. Morgan, along with heirs to the Rockefeller and Vanderbilt fortunes and railroad magnate E. H. Harriman, the so-called captains of industry—sat on the boards of most major railroads as well as the largest companies that shipped by rail. In 1903, Roosevelt signed the Elkins Act, which beefed up the power of the Interstate Commerce Commission and made it illegal for railroads to offer discounts on published rates. His attorney general also successfully prosecuted and broke up the Northern Securities Company, run by Morgan, Harriman, and John D. Rockefeller, which controlled a number of competing railroads in the Midwest and the West.

Now the Roosevelt administration was pushing through two more pieces of groundbreaking legislation to reinvent the power of the federal government to regulate business. One was a bill Ford Harvey very much supported: the Pure Food and Drug Act of 1906, which created the first national standards for the safety of food and the safety and efficacy of medicines. But the second act, passed the same week, made everyone in the railroad business crazy: The Hepburn Act gave the Interstate Commerce Commission unprecedented power to regulate and infiltrate almost every aspect of the industry. The bill allowed the ICC to actually change any shipping rates deemed not "just and reasonable." It forced the railroads to adopt standardized accounting procedures so their books could be easily examined by government inspectors. And it completely disallowed discounts or any other preferential treatment for better shipping customers. Under the new rules, the government could also regulate train terminals, express companies, and sleeping cars, which brought it uncomfortably close to being able to directly regulate Fred Harvey.

Ripley and his fellow railroad executives considered the Hepburn Act a disaster, an artificial and unhealthy drag on the industry through which America's economic lifeblood coursed. As the elder statesman of the American railroad business, he was outspoken about his belief that by keeping passenger and freight rates unnaturally low, the ICC would prevent the railroads from making enough money to maintain and improve train service.

The railroads "are being gradually strangled," Ripley wrote to the editor of the *Kansas City Star*, "and before long the people will realize that [they are] practically extinct—*then* they will be sorry, too late—and there will be nothing left but to take the roads over and run them under a Government Bureau, with what results can easily be guessed when we observe how Government transacts business."

As the deadline approached for Ford and Ripley to decide whether to make a new deal, they got yet another sign that business as they had known it might be over. One of the most important cities for the Santa Fe and Fred Harvey, and for the American economy, was nearly destroyed. On April 18, 1906, San Francisco—then the nation's ninth-largest city, behind New York, Chicago, Philadelphia, St. Louis,

Boston, Baltimore, Cleveland, and Buffalo—was hit by an earthquake registering 7.9 on the Richter scale.

Dave Benjamin was in San Francisco at the time, inspecting the Fred Harvey operation at the Ferry Building on the Embarcadero, so he was able to help direct the company's response to the worst natural disaster in the nation's history. He was awakened in his hotel room before daylight when the first tremor hit, and he was over at the Ferry Building—where the observation tower was left lurching to one side, its clock frozen at 5:15—assessing the damage by the time the aftershock occurred at 8:14 a.m., demolishing many of the structures already compromised.

Hundreds died instantly and thousands more over the next few days as fires raged and troops tried in vain to keep order. Droves of people huddled at the Ferry Building begging for food and shelter. The Harvey employees there did what they could to feed them with whatever was on hand, and the Santa Fe ran barge after barge of disaster victims across the bay to safety in Oakland. The U.S.S. *Chicago* was summoned via wireless telegraph—the first time the new technology was used in a major emergency—and helped to evacuate over twenty thousand people. The Ferry Building remained untouched by flames until the third day, when the winds picked up and the fire approached. The city's entire firefighting force was rushed there: It was arguably the most important structure still standing in San Francisco. After hours spent battling back the flames, officials finally declared the building safe.

"This is about the only time in this fire when the puny forces of man have been able to save anything," one *Washington Post* correspondent commented. "We have been the sport of the gods."

ONLY WEEKS AFTER the earthquake, in the summer of 1906, Ford finally decided that he would go ahead and renew his relationship with the railroad—tying his fortunes to Ripley's, and the Santa Fe's, for another ten years. He wanted to see just how far this quirky empire that he and Dave had built on the foundation of his father's standards could go.

Ford negotiated and signed a new ten-year contract for the eating houses, the hotels, the dining cars, and the retail business at newsstands and curio shops. And he made a separate ten-year deal for the Grand Canyon operation—which looked as though it might be a success after all.

Before the new Santa Fe contracts were executed, Ford and Dave put the finishing touches on the process of restructuring the company, incorporating it in the state of New Jersey under the name Fred Harvey. They also created another, smaller corporation, "Harvey Hotel & Restaurant Company" in Kansas City to handle extracurricular businesses like the restaurants in St. Louis Union Depot and Chicago's Dearborn Station.

Ford made himself president of both corporations. And he stopped asking himself if he should do something else professionally for the rest of his life.

This did not prevent him, however, from having a little personal midlife crisis. Several family members would later recall they heard he had a girlfriend. "He was a handsome devil," his grandnephew recalls, "and Minnie told me many women were crazy about him. I suspect that he could have had liaisons with high society friends and maybe even a love of long standing who was married."

Ford's marriage had turned out to be completely the opposite of his father's. He left town only for business while Judy traveled extensively, usually with the children: She took them all over Europe, often for long stretches. During one of their extended trips—when Ford was a "bachelor" for several months—handwritten notes marked "Personal" began arriving at his office, some by mail, others dropped off.

Ford had always received a lot of personal mail, because in his job he had to keep a lot of secrets. He was privy to a great deal of confidential business information about the railroads, the hospitality industry, and the civic affairs of Kansas City. It was impossible to run hotels catering to an affluent and celebrated clientele if you weren't able to keep their private needs private.

Still, starting in 1907, he received an awful lot of "personal" notes from a Mrs. John G. Camp of 17 Phelps Street in Kansas City, thanking him for all kinds of extravagant gifts—flowers, wines, gourmet foodstuffs, and other kindnesses. And when these personal notes were discovered, only very recently, by family members, they were found in an old black metal strongbox of Ford's—along with letters from his wife during the same time period.

It is unlikely Ford was having an affair with Mrs. Camp, a widow who was old enough to be his mother (and, in fact, signed her notes "Mother"). But he did seem to have an unusually close attachment to her, and sent her an awful lot of gifts—which were also enjoyed by her daughter, Rebecca, who was his contemporary. Rebecca Camp was the second wife of meatpacking heir Charles Armour, Ford's longtime social colleague in Kansas City; the couple had no children, and Rebecca's mother lived with them. It is curious that all these letters, written by Mrs. Camp on Rebecca Armour's stationery, were sent to Ford personally at the office and not to him and his wife at home—especially since the Armours knew the Harveys well.

The letters from Mrs. Camp began arriving not long before Judy Harvey took an extended trip to Europe, meeting up with Kitty, who spent much of 1907 studying in Italy. Over the next few years, the Camp letters would provide an interesting counterpoint to the ones Judy sent: the long, detailed missives that always began "My Darling" and were signed "Goodnight my precious love, your Jude" or "I want you so—your own devoted, Jude."

Judy wrote to Ford from the Waldorf-Astoria on the morning of their anniversary as she was about to leave the country: "I will be thinking of you darling as you read this and longing oh so ardently to be back in your dear arms again. God keep you safe." Several days later another note arrived—this one from Mrs. Camp.

THE FIRST YEAR of Ford's new contract turned out to be hugely challenging financially for the country. The stock market crashed twice in 1907, first in March and again in October. The second, more severe crash was triggered by a failed attempt by the founder of the United Copper Company to manipulate the market on his own stock, which took down with it the massive Knickerbocker Trust in New York. This instigated a run on the nation's banks—which at that time relied only on their own reserves. Many of them simply ran out of money.

To save the U.S. economy, Roosevelt was forced, ironically, to seek help from J. P. Morgan and the very captains of industry whose trusts he had been busting for the past few years. There was money in the federal treasury to rescue the failing banks, but no easy way to get the currency to them. Morgan, who was about to leave town on vacation, set up a command post in the library of his home and, along with other top financiers, basically invented a way to help banks cooperate so those with too much cash could help those with too little (laying the groundwork for what would later become the Federal Reserve system). Within three weeks, the crisis had been averted, Morgan left on his vacation, and the government went back to trust-busting.

Although the Panic of 1907 hurt the financial institutions of the East, Fred Harvey actually had its best year ever, with profits of over $243,000 ($5.7 million). But just after the banner year ended, Ford was faced with disaster. Early in the morning on Monday, January 13, 1908, an electrical fire started in the Kansas City Union Station annex building, where the Fred Harvey offices had been located for over twenty years, growing from one tiny room with a desk for Dave to a large suite. The annex also housed the post office, all the major express-package companies, the Pullman company, and the Railway Association YMCA. That morning, they all went up in flames. By the time Ford and Dave got there, firemen had already given up on trying to save their annex building, and were instead trying to keep the fire from consuming the entire Union Station complex.

The depot annex was a total loss. Thirty-five sacks of registered mail and thousands of packages were incinerated, and there was nothing left of the Fred Harvey corporate offices. Ford estimated the company's loss at more than $50,000 ($1.2 million), although much of what burned was irreplaceable.

Although the fire was devastating, it was the kind of event for which anyone associated with the railroad business—especially in the West—always had to be prepared. In the world of the Santa Fe, flames were an all too frequent occurrence. The railroad's insurance files were overflowing with fire claims: for bridges, depots, laundry facilities, sheds, Harvey Houses, hotels, anything made of wood. The Fred Harvey files, like all other business paperwork associated with the trains, were maintained in multiple copies for this reason and stored at the major Santa Fe railroad division points. This allowed easy remote access to files in the pre-fax world and also created a backup system.

Because Dave always maintained disaster contingency plans, the company was able to respond quickly after the fire and set up another office across town at the American Bank Building at 8th and Delaware, an eight-story structure with a handsome cut-stone arched entrance and a row of bowed-out windows above it. It would be Fred Harvey's "temporary" quarters—until Kansas City built the new Union Station complex that had been promised for several years.

All across the country, cities were looking to replace the disjointed stations from the first generation of railroading with grand union stations like St. Louis Union Depot and South Station in Boston. Many of the newer union stations were being designed in the European Beaux Arts style because of a social movement called City Beautiful, which claimed that urban blight could be combated architecturally if major public buildings were all big, white, and of classical design (like those in Chicago's White City). Washington, D.C.'s Union Station had recently opened, and New York was in the midst of building its new Pennsylvania Station. (This would be torn down in the 1960s, its facilities driven underground in order to create the new Madison Square Garden.) Every other major American city hoped to follow suit, erecting a fabulous classical station not only for the railroads but to anchor an entire new local transport system of trolley cars or even subways.

On September 27, 1908, Henry Ford's first Model T rolled off the production line in Detroit. But it was, at the time, just one more automobile—a machine that was, for most, as unfathomable an expense as buying your own Pullman car. The United States was still a country connected by tracks, not highways. Americans rode together, in trains.

CHAPTER 26

KANSAS CITY STARS

⌐⌐

IT WAS STILL HARD FOR FORD TO BELIEVE THAT HIS FATHER had been dead for ten years. But now, whenever he doubted it, there was a team of accountants at the Kansas City offices of Arthur Young, as well as his watchful brother and three sisters, ready to remind him that it was time to divide up Fred Harvey's estate. Many of them were in far different situations than they had been when Father died in 1901.

In many ways, Ford's two youngest sisters had never completely grown up. Sybil, the youngest, was still living at home in Leavenworth with her mother. She had never been a robust child, and even now, at thirty-one, it wasn't clear if she was taking care of her mother or the other way around.

While May had grown up sickly as well, she became strong enough to travel and attend private school, eventually moving to New York, where she married into a well-known, if not particularly well-to-do, family. In fact, her in-laws were rather infamous. She married the only son of New York's most tragic mayor, Abraham "Elegant Oakey" Hall, a brilliant attorney turned political patsy. Hall had been brought down by the 1870 "Boss Tweed" scandals—in which the Democratic Party machine that got him elected mayor also helped shady contractors defraud the city of over $75 million ($1.3 billion). He spent the rest of the century trying to prove he had been a dupe, not a crook.

May's husband, Herbert Hall—who was, like his father, called "Oakey"—had lost both his parents just before he met her in the late 1890s. He was a Williams College alum just like Minnie's husband, John Huckel, and May apparently fell into one of those "me-too" relationships that sometimes occur when a beloved older sister marries. Oakey Hall was twelve years her senior, a moderately successful commercial real estate broker and member of the elite New York Players Club. But he was haunted by his father's legacy, and the Harveys feared he was primarily interested in May for her money. Shortly after they married in 1902, she started requesting substantial advances on her inheritance. Oakey himself even asked Ford for a personal loan from the estate of $10,000 ($252,000). Still, since May adored him, the family more or less endured him.

Byron Harvey, on the other hand, married into a much sunnier family. His wife, Helen Daggett, was a lithe and lively Southern California girl who rarely missed an opportunity to prove that she could still do a handstand whenever family photos were being taken. Byron's father-in-law, Charles Daggett, was a prominent Kansas City lawyer who in the late 1880s had moved his family to Pasadena, where the Daggetts became one of the town's bedrock social families and cofounders of the Tournament of Roses Parade. Charles could actually take partial credit for starting the Rose Bowl, the nation's first postseason college football game, since the decision to inaugurate the contest was made during one of the years he was parade chairman. A powerful civic leader in Los Angeles, he devoted much of his time to the "Good Roads Movement," which tried to force state and federal officials to create better and perhaps even *paved* highways for all those new automobiles. Byron's mother-in-law, Mary Stewart Daggett, was a celebrated literary figure in Southern California. She published several well-received novels, and her fiction was sometimes serialized in the *Los Angeles Times,* which was owned by their society friends the Otis family.

Byron had married Helen Daggett not long after his father's death, and moved to Chicago when Ford arranged for him to work in the Santa Fe dining car division. The couple had three sons in quick succession, brought up in a stylish home in Lake Forest. Over time, Byron grew into a competent enough executive, although it was clear he did not inherit his father's drive or vision.

He and his family lived the good life in Chicago, although it appeared they harbored some insecurities about their social status. People always assumed that the Harveys were richer than they really were. The family business threw off an enormous amount of cash every year, but it didn't *own* things—factories, real estate—that were worth a lot of money and could appreciate in value. The company's main assets were its ethos, its quality control, its loyal, almost cultish employees, and its management contracts. Fred Harvey was like an oil well that would never gush: It constantly needed to be pumped. In Chicago and Pasadena, Byron and Helen were surrounded by people who had earned, or inherited, tens of millions.

As Ford saw it, his younger brother aspired to be one of the idle rich, but didn't seem to understand that he would always have to be one of the *working* rich.

With so much money now at stake, there was a lot of tension as Ford let his siblings know how Father's estate would be handled. With the full support of his mother, he ruled the company as well as the family, so none of his siblings was in a position to challenge his decisions. They were all inheriting significant sums, and when Ford announced a restructuring plan for the company stock, they realized they would be getting even more.

Fred's will left half of his assets—plus the family home on Olive Street and two smaller properties they owned in Leavenworth—to his wife, Sally, with the other half divided evenly among his five children. A detailed report of those assets had been prepared for each of them by accountants at Arthur Young; it was on legal-size ledger paper bound with a gray cover and held together by a red string. If they turned to page one, they saw that since their father's death, his assets had nearly quadrupled in worth. The Fred Harvey estate was now valued, very conservatively, at $2.6 million ($61 million). Each sibling inherited $261,239.76 ($6.1 million), and the rest went to their mother.

Before they got the money, however, there was the matter of the stock in the newly restructured Fred Harvey corporation. Ford had created a complex scheme to ensure that he kept complete control of the business. He also wanted to prevent his mother and sisters from having any ownership stake—because he believed strongly that women should not own stock in a company run by a man. Sally Harvey and her daughters were told they had to sell their shares.

Minnie, especially, was taken aback by this. She had been active in the business, but was also being forced to sell her shares—and to her own husband. The final indignity was that since John Huckel didn't have that kind of cash, she actually had to *lend him* the money to buy her own stock from her.

Byron was allowed to keep his shares, and buy some more from his mother (on an installment plan). But Ford was careful to ensure that his younger brother would never have the voting power to challenge his authority. Ford controlled most of the stock, with Dave the second-largest stockholder; Byron was a distant third.

To set the share prices, the company was valued at $1.5 million ($35 million), which made Dave uncomfortable; he knew Fred Harvey to be worth almost three times as much. But he was torn. As a trustee of the estate, he was bound to get as much for the company as he could, but in his new role as a part owner buying into the privately held stock, he didn't want to pay any more than was necessary. So he reluctantly agreed to the valuation.

The shares were issued and immediately sold—after which each of them had to sign ten copies of a seven-page document typed on onionskin paper bound with brass rivets. Sally signed first, in small tight lettering that represented her official farewell to her husband of forty-eight years. Then Ford stepped up and executed the dramatic, eccentric signature he had developed so people knew when he was signing something personally (most company correspondence was routinely hand signed "Fred Harvey" regardless of who wrote the letter). Dave was next, and with his signature he finally became a part owner of the company to which he had dedicated his unswerving loyalty for thirty years. Then came Byron, Sybil, Minnie, and May, followed by John Huckel and finally Dave's brother Harry, who was allowed to buy a few shares.

Ford signed one final time, as the president of the company—and with that, Fred Harvey's estate was finally settled. Ten years after his death, every debt was paid, every promise kept, his good name better than ever.

Ford Harvey had honored his father in a way almost unprecedented in American business. And the next generation was well on its way. His debutante daughter, Kitty, was about to have her coming-out party in Kansas City, and his son, Freddy, was headed off to prep school at St. Mark's in Massachusetts. From there, he was expected to go to Harvard and then, eventually, to inherit the business.

IN THE MONTHS after his father's estate was settled, Ford Harvey began to reveal himself to the public the way he had always been known to friends and colleagues. It started when he accepted a very high-profile position in Kansas City: Federal appellate judge William

Hook, who had been his father's lawyer and one of his pallbearers, appointed Ford to lead the reorganization of the city's bankrupt streetcar and elevated railway system. The job was a headache, but it did carry great political power—and came with one truly pleasing perk. When he and Dave walked to work together in the morning, Ford could now bring his Airedale along with him. And when he got to the office, he could send the dog back on a streetcar, where an attendant would make sure his new boss's pet got off at the right stop and trotted home.

The court-appointed job made Ford more of a public figure than he had ever been in his life. In his fifteen years of running Fred Harvey, his name had never once appeared on a menu, advertisement, or piece of promotional literature for his company. Now it appeared at the bottom of every display ad for the Kansas City transit system, every public filing. And the fact that he ran Fred Harvey—and that the "original Fred Harvey" had been dead for ten years—began to be acknowledged more frequently in the local newspapers.

When Ford realized that his company didn't collapse after he was revealed as the man behind the curtain, he started being more open with the press. He just made sure nothing too controversial came up in front of a reporter. Nobody needed to know, for instance, that President Taft, who weighed well over three hundred pounds, got himself stuck in one of the bathtubs at the Alvarado.

Ford was also raising his profile in Kansas City in other ways. He and his wife assumed a leading role in fund-raising efforts for a new hospital. Judy was also becoming even more immersed in Catholic charity work, and was developing a close working friendship with the new bishop of Kansas City, Thomas Lillis.

While some of Ford's new public persona represented a change in attitude, he was, after all, a businessman, and he was likely preparing for a deal. Kansas City was finally building its new Union Station, which would be one of the largest depots in the country, befitting a city that was now rising to its geographic imperative. After all, Kansas City was the dead center of the United States, the middle of the middle of America. With this new station, it would lay claim to being the nation's crossroads as well.

Ford wanted the station to be a national showcase for Fred Harvey. He also wanted to flex his muscles locally, sending a signal to any company trying to copy the Fred Harvey formula. There were several of these wannabe firms in Kansas City, primarily servicing railroads that

Ford had turned down when they begged him to manage their eating houses. The largest competitor was the Van Noy company, which was primarily a newsstand company with "butcher boys" on commission aggressively trolling the trains; however, it also managed the eating houses and hotels along the Missouri Pacific and the Illinois Central. A lower-budget operation than Fred Harvey, it was profitable, and the brothers who ran it—the "Van Noy Boys"—were well-known in Kansas City society. The city was also home to the John J. Grier company, which handled the Rock Island Railroad, and the Brown News Company, which managed restaurants in Texas and Louisiana for the Southern Pacific.

Ford made a deal for the Union Station that quickly put these competitors in their place. For the first time ever, Fred Harvey would control not only the dining facilities—"there won't be any better restaurant in America," a company spokesman promised—but all the retail stores and other services as well.

Everything in the new Union Station except the trains themselves would be operated by Fred Harvey. The designs for all the interior spaces would be done by Mary Colter, who after years as a freelancer had recently come to work for Fred Harvey full-time, joining the Tenth Legion at the Kansas City office as the in-house design and decoration guru.

Ford was a little nervous about expanding so extensively beyond their core business, but his brother-in-law John Huckel insisted they were up to the challenge. It wouldn't be like starting the Indian curio business at a location thousands of miles away. The new corporate offices of Fred Harvey would be right upstairs at the Union Station—like an observation tower—so they could watch over their new stores. Fred Harvey could use Kansas City as a kind of laboratory to test what the American public wanted.

And for the first time, the top brass at Fred Harvey would be able to have lunch every day in their own restaurant, served by their own Harvey Girls.

Ford knew his mother would love the new station restaurants. Still living in the family home in Leavenworth with her unmarried daughter, Sybil, Sally Harvey had grown heavy and weak over the past few years—but one of her remaining pleasures was lunch in Kansas City with Ford and Minnie. Unfortunately, she did not live to see the station finished. After a brief illness in the early summer of 1913, she died at home with her children at her bedside, just after breakfast on a Monday in late June, at the age of seventy-one. She was buried next to Fred in Mount Muncie Cemetery.

Ford mourned his mother very publicly, and for so long that it caused whispers in Kansas City society. He wore a black armband around his coat sleeve every day for over a year, prompting "Betty Ann"—who wrote the "Audacious Tattlings" column for Kansas City's weekly society newspaper, *The Independent*—to wonder aloud if it was good taste to make such a public display of bereavement for so long.

"Ford is in all things one of the most perfectly groomed men about town, a regular glass of fashion and mold of form, save in this one instance," Betty Ann opined. "I don't see why he does it." She suggested that if he insisted on remaining grief stricken, he at least switch to something more modest and appropriate, perhaps "an old-time hat band of somber crepe."

DAVE BENJAMIN KNEW the opening of the new Union Station, with its Fred Harvey corporate offices upstairs, was going to be hell. With so much hard work looming, he decided to take his wife, Linnie, on a vacation during the summer of 1914, before business matters became too stressful.

They chose the Grand Tour of Europe for their getaway—and they were having a pretty grand time, too, until Germany declared war on Russia on August 1. Suddenly the Benjamins found themselves trapped in Europe, along with what the State Department estimated were at least one hundred thousand other American tourists.

As France and Britain quickly joined the war, Americans abroad could no longer cash personal checks, traveler's checks, or letters of credit—so even the richest among them were effectively broke. Worse, they had no way of getting home. Of the hundreds of steamships Americans used to cross the Atlantic, only a handful actually flew the American flag. European-owned liners were needed for troops. Commodore and Mrs. Cornelius Vanderbilt soon figured out how to charter a private yacht—flying Old Glory—and went home to Newport, but ordinary well-to-do people like Dave and his wife were stuck. From the resort town of Rorschach, Switzerland, they headed to Zurich, then Lucerne, then Bern, seeking help at the American and

British consulates, as well as at the bank, the telegraph office, and the travel bureau.

Even Dave, the consummate emergency maven, didn't know what to do.

One American general said that he thought President Woodrow Wilson should negotiate a six-week truce on the North Atlantic so all American tourists could get home.

"Otherwise," he told the *New York Times*, "incalculable hardship will be imposed upon an army of innocent people whose only fault is that they should visit Europe as usual to spend countless sums of their good money."

Wilson, who had defeated both Republican president Taft and Teddy Roosevelt (who ran as an independent) in the 1912 election, held strongly to an isolationist policy to keep America from being sucked into the war. He arranged for an armored ship, the *Tennessee*, to sail to Europe hauling nearly $8 million ($178 million) in gold to rescue tourists. Part of the money was government aid, but most was from American banks so that the wealthier travelers could cash large checks.

Dave and his family were never in actual danger—there are worse places to be "trapped" than a hotel in the Swiss Alps—but they were stranded nonetheless. After a week of trying, they finally received personalized letters of passage from the U.S. envoy in Bern. With those documents, they were able to get to Paris, and then to England, where they arranged first-class accommodations on the *RMS Cameronia* out of Glasgow.

By the time they returned to Kansas City, they were sapped of any restorative powers from their "vacation," but there was no time to rest. Union Station was opening soon: They had only two months left to finish the new corporate offices, the new commissary to serve all the dining cars and eating houses (including massive humidors capable of holding three million cigars and five million cigarettes), the company's most ambitious dining facilities to date, and its first-ever Fred Harvey retail stores.

TO SET THE PROPER TONE for opening day in Kansas City, Ford had his assistant reach out to Shep Smith, who, at age nineteen, had been the first customer at the Topeka lunchroom in 1876. Smith was now a well-known engineer on the Frisco line, and Ford heard he had been chosen to handle the throttle on the first Frisco passenger train departing from the new Kansas City train shed.

"Tell Shep to come here with his family ahead of the opening tomorrow," Ford told his assistant. "He drank the first cup of coffee my father ever made for sale, and he shall drink the first cup of coffee ever served in the new Kansas City union station." In fact, the Smiths ate the first full-course meal served in the station, just before it opened to the public on Friday, October 30, 1914.

With battles raging in Europe, President Wilson agreed to take time from his busy day at the White House to push a gold button on his desk to cue the festivities in Kansas City. There is some debate about whether he actually pushed the button, as was widely reported at the time (an enterprising journalist later checked his secretary's logs and determined he wasn't there at the crucial moment). But the button was pushed, and the front doors of Kansas City Union Station opened to reveal an eighty-piece band playing "America the Beautiful." During the first twenty-four hours, over fifty thousand people came to see the building, a massive Beaux Arts structure spread over an eighteen-acre plaza. Mary Colter had designed a 200-seat lunchroom with brilliantly buffed black marble counters and swiveling cane-backed seats, a soda fountain decorated with Roman urns made by Tiffany in gold and silver, and a 152-seat dining room that was a model of elegance.

Ford had brought some of the top Harvey Girls from around the country to staff the Kansas City restaurants, which reportedly had 170 employees and kitchens that were

> equipped with the most improved paraphernalia for the cooking and serving of food. There are pots and pans of hammered copper, cauldrons for soup and beef *a la mode,* and a special stationary steam pot for boiling hams. Then there is a machine that peels potatoes by bouncing and rubbing them against a rapidly revolving cylinder. Every emergency in the way of odd appetites has been provided for. Should any guest enter the dining room who prefers his butter without salt, there is a ½-gallon glass churn on a shelf in one of the cupboards. Sweet butter may be had in three minutes by turning a small crank.

The menus were built around dishes that were already popular in other Fred Harvey eateries, plus some innovations, such as a curried chicken casserole with sherry, cream sauce, and Swiss cheese, and one Harvey Girl's favorite recipe for macaroni and cheese with oysters. On the first day they served over five thousand meals, and the rush of customers continued through the weekend. One newspaper noted with interest that "many Kansas Citians ate their Sunday dinner there"—since the idea of eating Sunday dinner in a restaurant was still unheard of in most parts of the country.

While the restaurants were a hit, it was the Fred Harvey retail stores that intrigued visitors. John Huckel had managed to create boutiques with selections as extensive as anything in Chicago or New York, but with friendlier, homespun Harvey service. There was a Fred Harvey perfumery, with scents from all over the world. There was a Fred Harvey drugstore, the biggest and best in town. There was a Fred Harvey toy store, since more families were traveling with children than ever before. There was a Fred Harvey gift shop with Indian curios.

And, after years of selling only a modest selection of the most popular books at newsstands, the company finally had a large full-service bookshop. It was open twenty-four hours and stocked thousands of titles on gorgeous wooden shelves. Any book they didn't have could be ordered and express mailed free of charge—or if you were heading west to stay at a Harvey hotel, it could be sent on the train and delivered to your hotel room. The store immediately became book buyer Frank Clough's test kitchen (and within months he had helped create a national best-seller: Gene Stratton-Porter's *Michael O'Halloran*, of which the Harvey System sold an astonishing 17,500 copies).

With the town's best restaurants and stores now located under one roof—and, in many cases, open around the clock—the train station took on a whole new role in expanding Kansas City. What had previously been merely a place to pick up, drop off, or feed passengers was now the city's new "downtown"—but *indoors*. In fact, it can be argued that the Fred Harvey retail and restaurant operation in Kansas City's Union Station was the nation's first true shopping center or indoor mall, where people could come by train or car and shop in a variety of stores. (It opened a full decade before the complex most historians call the first shopping center in America: the Country Club Plaza in suburban Kansas City, which was created by a social friend of Ford's, J. C. Nichols, to compete with Fred Harvey's Union Station shops.)

And on the second floor of the new station, Mary Colter had designed handsome offices for Ford, his Tenth Legion, and the large staff, in a style that combined Mission Revival woodcraft and downtown power office: high vaulted ceilings with dark crossbeams; wood-paneled walls that were, on closer examination, made from interlocking pieces; brass fittings; and subtle touches like the four small carved Indian heads inset in the stone fireplace in Ford's large corner office.

Ford worked at a large mahogany table desk, although he kept the antique rolltop from his father's study nearby: a Continental Biedermeier-style walnut desk, circa 1820. Hanging on the wall was a copy of the oldest Fred Harvey menu that survived the office fire—a dining car menu from 1888—and on his desk was a curious paperweight. There was a small metal plaque that read, "Fred Harvey, Topeka, Kansas, Founded 1876," and, behind it, a large wooden acorn that anyone who knew the Harveys well would recognize. It had once adorned the newel post on the stairway of the family home in Leavenworth, and was knocked off by one of the rambunctious children sliding down the railing.

CHAPTER 27

NATIONAL PARKING

⊒⊏

WHILE FORD HAD BEEN OBSESSED WITH THE GRAND CANYON
from the first time he laid eyes on it, he had no concept of how many
other people would come to feel the same way. But from its cautious
beginnings as an extreme-tourism attraction, the South Rim had blossomed into one of the most popular destinations in the world. Before
the train line opened to the canyon, about eight hundred intrepid visitors came every year. But the number of tourists grew exponentially
each year after El Tovar was finished. By 1911, more than thirty thousand people were visiting annually. Most came by train, although an
increasing number came by automobile. And occasionally someone arrived who was wealthy enough to do both.

When steel magnate Andrew Carnegie commissioned his own
Santa Fe train to the canyon for a handful of his closest friends, it included six private Pullmans—plus a special car just to haul his guests'
autos. This allowed Carnegie's party to motor along the South Rim—
where there was just a mile and a half of dirt road—and stop periodically to throw pebbles over the edge and wait to hear them strike far
below. (When Carnegie grew bored with this, he reportedly turned to
a nearby tourist and, treating him like his best golfing buddy, said,
"What a *bunker* this canyon would make! I should hate to have to
make it.")

Unfortunately, the Grand Canyon simply was not prepared for so
many visitors, and nobody was sure who should be responsible for improving conditions on the South Rim—the local businessmen, the railroad, the state government (Arizona had finally been admitted to the
Union in 1912), or the federal government. The debate quickly reached
the highest levels in Washington. And Ford found himself caught up

in the larger discussion about the future of America's national parks; he was a featured speaker at the groundbreaking conferences, starting in 1911, that led to the creation of the National Park Service in 1916. Even though the Grand Canyon wasn't yet a national park—a victim of political forces locally and nationally—the secretary of the interior, Walter Fisher, relied on Ford's advice and counsel. While much of the national park debate involved issues of conservation, wildlife, and forestry, in the new and vexing areas of hospitality and transportation nobody knew more than Ford.

"It would be exceedingly inappropriate," Secretary Fisher declared at the first national parks conference, "if we did not hear from Mr. Harvey."

Over the years, Ford cautioned the national parks stakeholders—everyone from foresters, politicians, park superintendents, hotel managers, and transportation executives to automobile enthusiasts and environmentalists such as John Muir—about the practical challenges of life and commerce inside a natural national treasure. His speeches always showed deep humility and a touch of humor. One year he began: "Gentlemen, you are not to blame for what you are about to suffer; neither am I. When honored by your chairman with an invitation to address you, I replied by letter that I was totally inexperienced in speaking and could not talk. His response was a telegram reading: 'Many thanks. Appreciate your willingness to speak.' "

There were, at that time, only thirteen national parks—all in the West, since the idea of federal oversight and protection started there. Lincoln recognized Yosemite in California as early as 1864 (although it was under state control until 1890) and Yellowstone became the first true national park in 1872, created on territorial land that later became parts of Wyoming, Montana, and Utah. The Grand Canyon and twenty other western sites carried the lesser designation of "national monuments"—with less government protection and funding, either by the Interior Department, the Agriculture Department, or the War Department. (Similar natural sites in the East were protected by the states.) Like the canyon, most of the parks and monuments had been settled by private companies or individuals, and connected to the world by the railroads. Now that people were traveling more—and the government was regulating the railroads more—it seemed clear that a federal agency with a proper budget was needed to oversee these protected areas, a true National Park Service.

NATIONAL PARKING   **235**

Ford argued forcefully that the federal government, and not the companies that held the hotel concessions, should be building the roads needed inside the national parks and monuments, because the roads were for everyone, not just hotel guests. When he failed to convince the Interior Department to fund the road he wanted along the South Rim, he got Ed Ripley and the Santa Fe to put up the $200,000 ($4.6 million) required to grade and pave a nine-mile stretch until it was, according to one Fred Harvey pamphlet, "wide, safe, dustless and level as a floor . . . a city boulevard in the wilderness . . . in places, there is a sheer drop of 2000 feet . . . yet you are as safe as in an easy chair at home."

Ford also urged the leaders of the national parks movement to always keep in mind the broad range of visitors. "All classes of people visit our national parks," he said. "Many do not care what they spend, or do not care what it costs if they get what they want. Others are not so particular what they get if it does not cost too much. They must all be taken care of." Besides economic differences, there were also all different kinds of tourists. Some were intrepid and adventurous, others quite the opposite.

"For the first class, the conventional sort of things would be rather objectionable," Ford explained. "His enjoyment would be that of the explorer; the sense of the unusual would appeal to him; and I must say that I think it is the higher sense. But the bulk of our visitors belong to the other class. They want comfort . . . [and] they have to be taken care of when they go to the Grand Canyon. There must be some sort of a program for those people; there must be something *conventional* for them to do. To expect them to seek their own entertainment and take care of themselves is to expect the impossible."

He did not, however, discriminate between the different kinds of visitors. In one memorable parks conference speech, he described a trip he and Freddy took to the canyon in which they tried to have it both ways—daring to travel by auto across Arizona, but also trying to assure all creature comforts, including separate cars for the servants and a chef.

"We took a Packard Forty-eight six-cylinder car for ourselves, with a driver, and a Cadillac Four with our bedding and camping equipment," Ford explained, "then we took a little Chevrolet car for our retainers . . . and were not to suffer any inconvenience or want if we could help it." But not long after they set out, heavy rains caused the Colorado River to flood one of the roads. When they tried to drive through, the two big cars were damaged so badly they were forced to leave behind their attendants, gear, and food and just take the Chevrolet "without anything except a little chap to drive us." They reached moonlit Mesa Verde at 3:00 a.m., slept in the car, and the next morning met a husband and wife camping nearby who offered them breakfast. When "the chap" wouldn't take any payment for the food, Ford offered to treat him to some gasoline—"he had a cheap little car of some sort"—at the local supply store, which he could just have billed to Fred Harvey.

"I thought that was too small a compensation for so welcome a breakfast," Ford said, chuckling, "but when I got the bill for the gasoline I changed my mind. He had purchased ten gallons at a dollar and a half per gallon, which made my breakfast bill $15 ($303)."

Ford also argued forcefully that hospitality services at each park should be controlled by only one company. "In my opinion, the hotels in each national park should be in one man's hands," he said. "He should not be there simply with a license to get as much money as possible, but should have a definite obligation and responsibility in the way of satisfactory service. It is no small undertaking to do this properly . . . A good hotel is a good hotel wherever operated, just as a good man is a good man wherever you find him . . . I think that is probably so of any business, but it seems to me to be more so in the case of a hotel—regardless of the fact that after a man has made a failure of everything else, he usually thinks he can run a hotel."

The idea Ford proposed of a "regulated monopoly" at each park was particularly appealing to Stephen Mather, the powerful Chicago industrialist who had become a champion of the parks (and was eventually named the founding director of the National Park Service). Mather, who had made his money in the borax business, was Ford's age, and they became instant friends and allies in park politics.

"Scenery is a splendid thing when it is viewed by a man who is in a contented frame of mind," Mather told one national parks conference. "Give him a poor breakfast after he has had a bad night's sleep, and he will not care how fine your scenery is."

FORD HAD LEARNED the hard way what happens at a park when hotels, trail guides, mule skinners, and photographers compete against one another. There had always been grumbling about Ford and his fancy hotel and his salaried Indians. ("You know how the Grand Canyon was formed?" went one popular joke on the South Rim. "Fred Harvey lost a nickel and started digging for it.") Now there were legal struggles: One old-timer, Ralph Cameron, who blazed and owned the popular Bright Angel Trail, was claiming he owned the mining rights to most of the tourist South Rim, including the land under El Tovar. Since Cameron had become a U.S. congressman, he also made trouble for Ford in Washington, and was one reason the canyon still wasn't a national park.

At the rim itself, there was sometimes open warfare over customers. "From the time a tourist arrives at the canyon he is continually harassed by crowds of livery solicitors and guides, who on many occasions have fought with pistols and knives over prospective customers," a U.S. Forest Service official told the *Washington Post,* claiming the poor visitors were forced to "dodge behind trees to escape injury."

The veteran manager at the Grand Canyon, Charlie Brant, did his best to keep peace with his competitors. But the truth was, Ford had tried to buy them all out—and when they wouldn't sell, he decided that Fred Harvey should create its own superior version of just about everything available at the South Rim. This meant offering better rides on better mules down a better trail, better tour guides with better tall tales, and a new rim-side photography studio (where the photographers were more interested in pictures than "rimming"). So, Ford actually had his own trail blazed down into the canyon, along an old Indian path that could be reached only by the Santa Fe's newly paved road. And the railroad commissioned two small buildings for which Mary Colter did the architecture as well as the interiors—tasty little projects she controlled completely, unlike the larger hotels, where she was still doing mostly interior decoration.

Colter built a new photography studio and postcard shop, near El Tovar, the Lookout Studio, a small stacked-stone building full of rudimentary telescopes that had short paths leading down along the canyon wall. Its location was chosen so that guests strolling from El Tovar would find it before reaching the older, renowned Kolb Brothers Studio.

And eight miles down the road from the hotel, at the summit of Ford's new trail into the canyon, Colter conjured a structure that appeared to have been sitting there, undiscovered, for decades—designed to look like the secret home of one of those "hermits" mythologized by the greatest Grand Canyon yarn spinners. She called it Hermit's Rest and, following the theme, named the new path down into the canyon Hermit's Trail. Colter modeled her hermit theme and back-story on an actual person—Louis Boucher, a scrawny old French-Canadian prospector who always rode a white mule with a bell around its neck—but the novel architecture was entirely her own. The building appeared to be constructed from haphazard chunks of the very same rock covering the ground, with a large, seemingly precarious chimney and a front porch made from stripped logs and tree trunks. Inside, the main room was a hermit's fantasy—more than half the space was taken up by an enormous fireplace big enough to stand in, an arched hearth contained within another twenty-foot-high arched hearth, with decades' worth of simulated soot and smoke damage. The furniture was carved from tree trunks, and on the stone floor in front of the fireplace was a bearskin rug with a roaring head.

When some of the first railroad employees saw Hermit's Rest, they didn't get it. The place was a mess, full of dirt and cobwebs.

"Why don't you clean it up?" they asked Colter.

"You can't imagine what it cost to make it look like this," she said, laughing.

Each year more tourists arrived at the Grand Canyon, and the competition for them became fiercer. In 1914, William Randolph Hearst bought one of the last remaining South Rim properties, the Grandview Hotel and its twenty-acre plot, and let it be known that he planned to build his own modern hotel there, "the most palatial and commodious in the entire West." He even floated the idea that he would establish residency there and run for senator from Arizona. Hearst never did anything with the Grandview, but adding him to the list of Ford's Grand Canyon adversaries certainly affected the chess strategy for control of the South Rim. And it set back still further the lobbying effort to make the canyon a national park.

Ford did have some powerful supporters on the national park issue. The Philadelphia-based editors of the enormously popular *Saturday Evening Post* even got involved, assigning one of the national magazine's best and liveliest writers, Irvin S. Cobb, to visit the canyon and do a long, illustrated travel piece. It was the first in a series called "Roughing It De Luxe," in which he updated Mark Twain's classic journal of "variegated vagabondizing" by riding the Santa Fe from

Chicago all the way to California. The articles were then published as a book, the entire first half of which covered Cobb's amusing experiences at the Grand Canyon. He was one of the first national writers to memorably describe the quintessential American experience of riding mules down a precarious rocky trail into the canyon:

> Down a winding footpath moves the procession, with the guide in front, and behind him in single file his string of pilgrims—all as nervous as cats and some holding onto their saddle-pommels with death grips. Just under the first terrace a halt is made while the official photographer takes a picture; and when you get back he has your finished copy ready for you, so you can see for yourself just how pale and haggard and wall-eyed . . . you looked. The parade moves on. All at once you notice that the person immediately ahead of you has apparently ridden right over the wall of the canyon. A moment ago his arched back loomed before you; now he is utterly gone. It is at this point that some tourists tender their resignations—to take effect immediately. To the credit of the sex, be it said, the statistics show that fewer women quit here than the men. But nearly always there is some man who remembers where he left his umbrella or something, and he goes back after it . . .
>
> Over the ridge and down the steep declivity beyond goes your mule, slipping a little. He is reared back until his rump almost brushes the trail; he grunts mild protests at every lurching step . . . You reflect that thousands of persons have already done this thing . . . [and] no serious accident has yet occurred— which is some comfort, but not much . . . Then something happens. The trail . . . takes an abrupt turn to the right. You duck your head and go through a little tunnel in the rock . . . and as you emerge on the lower side you forget all about your insurance papers and freeze to your pommel with both hands, and cram your poor cold feet into the stirrups . . . and all your vital organs come up in your throat, where you can taste them . . . You have come out on a place where the trail clings to the sheer side of the dizziest, deepest chasm in the known world. One of your legs is scraping against the ever-lasting granite; the other is dangling over half a mile of fresh mountain air . . . Then to you there comes the pleasing reflection that if your mule slipped and you

fell off and were dashed to fragments, they would not be large, mussy, irregular fragments, but little teensy-weensy fragments . . . only your mule never slips off!

It is contrary to a mule's religion and politics . . . to slip off . . . [although] my mule had one very disconcerting way about [her]. When she came to a particularly scary spot, which was every minute or so, she would stop dead still . . . then she would face outward and crane her neck over the fathomless void of the bottomless pit, and for a space of moments would gaze steadily downward, with a despondent droop of her fiddle-shaped head and a suicidal gleam in her mournful eyes.

AT THE TURN of the century, a group of western businessmen invented a slogan they thought would help equate tourism and patriotism: "See America First." As part of their campaign, they claimed that the United States was losing over $200 million ($4.4 billion) a year because Americans spent their tourism dollars in Europe.

But in 1915, with Europe at war, tourists suddenly had no choice but to "See America First." As a cartoon in the Santa Fe employee magazine pointed out, "Europe is Closed." And, amazingly, the war "closed" the Continent just as America was opening not one but two world's fairs—both of which were in key cities for Fred Harvey and the Santa Fe. San Francisco was hosting the Panama-Pacific International Exposition, a huge, traditional world's fair celebrating the recent opening of the Panama Canal while showcasing the recovery of the city since the earthquake. San Diego was hosting the Panama-California Exposition, a smaller, more regional fair focused primarily on the culture of the Southwest—and created primarily to capitalize on the millions of travelers expected to flock to California.

Ford had agreed that Fred Harvey would create a preposterously ambitious exhibit at each world's fair. In San Francisco, they were building a massive scale model of the Grand Canyon more than a city block long. For San Diego, however, they had something more astonishing in mind: a ten-acre, full-scale pueblo village where hundreds of Native Americans could actually live, work, and, most important, "be real Indians" for an entire year. For the Fred Harvey Indian ethnology buffs—Ford, Minnie and John Huckel, Herman Schweizer, and Mary Colter—it was the challenge of a lifetime.

Each exhibit had a budget of more than $160,000 ($3.5 million) and had been in the works for years, with the railroad planning a huge "two fairs for one fare" ad campaign. An artist had camped out in the Grand Canyon for two months, along with a Santa Fe escort, to make sketches for the massive panorama—to be viewed from a "deluxe coach" holding thirty to forty people at a time. For the San Diego exhibit, Mary Colter spent months doing sketches and paintings in the Kansas City office for Ford and the Huckels to ponder, before she built a wax model and then three different plaster models on the way to a final approved design. All the while, Herman Schweizer was down in Albuquerque laboring not only to get enough Indian crafts for both fairs but to hire enough Indians.

Although the San Diego fair was smaller, it was in many ways more important to the railroad and Fred Harvey. The Indian Village there was meant to right some of the wrongs that had been done to native peoples at previous world's fairs—where they had always been a main attraction, but were treated somewhat like freaks. The San Diego fair was being overseen by a new generation of southwestern ethnologists who were considered more sensitive to native peoples. By today's standards, some of their rhetoric still sounds appalling: Although Indians were now being referred to as "the first Americans," a considerable step up from "living ruins," they continued to be treated as primitives, noble savages. Still, even the harshest of contemporary scholars view some of the social scientists most closely associated with the San Diego fair as having their hearts (if not their ethnic politics) in the right place. They were led by archaeologist Edgar Hewett, a rising star in Santa Fe who was the director of the School of American Archaeology and ran the popular Museum of New Mexico.

Herman Schweizer had hired Hewett's protégé Jesse Nusbaum to oversee the construction of the village—which included two completely habitable pueblos and several other dwellings. Among those hired to live and work in the exhibit was Maria Martinez, a San Ildefonso Indian from outside of Santa Fe who would later be recognized as the re-inventor of one of the most beloved styles of Indian pottery: the stunning black-on-black matte earthenware that had been all but lost until it became her signature (and is widely copied to this day). It wasn't easy keeping the Indians on their faux-adobe reservation. Many grew homesick and existentially depressed. Maria made her black pottery, and her husband, Julian, did his best to resist taunting the white visitors who wanted him to "act Indian." But by summer, the Indians had been living in the village for five months, and many of them were fed up, looking to get out of their contracts. While they were being paid—for adults, $10 ($221) a week—some were terribly exploited: During the Fourth of July parade, for example, seven Indians were featured on the float of the Savage Tire Company. Later in the month, Taos Indians brought in by Fred Harvey created a huge controversy when they broke into the office of the New Mexico State Building and stole films that had been taken of them back home performing the "katsina dance" for the Fiesta de San Geronimo. They had asked a newsreel crew not to film certain rites, believing it would cast an evil spell on the tribesmen, but the cameraman did it anyway. Livid that the film was being shown at the fair, they were also convinced this was the reason for the terrible drought back at their pueblo.

Still, even with these controversies, the Indian Village exhibit at San Diego was considered a huge success, and the fair drew about four million people. While the San Francisco exposition drew five times as many visitors, the San Diego world's fair had a much longer-lasting impact on California and the entire Southwest. It was a turning point, a sign that the area had come of age.

THE CALIFORNIA FAIRS helped jump-start Southwest tourism—as did all the newspaper articles and books about trips to the fair that were published over the next year. One of the more interesting books was written by Emily Post, before she became the country's etiquette doyenne; in *By Motor to the Golden Gate,* she spent an entire chapter describing her visit to the Alvarado in Albuquerque, where she was regaled by Herman Schweizer on native lore—including why Indians ran away from tourists wearing violet ("the color of evil," he said). She also learned that even though the Harvey hotels, which she admired, now had many patrons who arrived by auto, rail passengers still got special treatment:

Stopping at the various Harvey hotels of the Santa Fe system, yet not being travelers on the railroad, is very like being behind the scenes at the theater. The hotel people, curio-sellers and Indians are the actors, the travelers on the incoming trains are the audience. Other people don't count.

For instance, you enter a tranquilly ordered dining-room. The head waitress attentively seats you, your own waitress quickly fetches your first course, and starts toward the pantry for the second, when suddenly a clerk appears and says "Twenty-six!" With the uniformity of a trained chorus every face turns toward the clock, and the whole scene becomes a flurry of white starched dresses running back and forth. Back with empty trays and forth with buttered rolls, radishes, cups of soup, like a ballet of abundance. You wonder if any one is going to bring your second course, but you might as well try to attract the attention of a hive of bees when they are swarming. Having nothing else to do you discover the mystic words twenty-six to be twenty-six places to set. Finally you descry your own waitress dealing slices of toast to imaginary diners at a far table.

Then you hear the rumble of the train, the door leading to the platform opens and in come the passengers. And you, having no prospect of anything further to eat, watch the way the train supper is managed. Slices of toast and soup in cups are already at the place, then in files the white aproned chorus carrying enormous platters of freshly grilled beefsteak, and such savory broiled chicken that you, who are so hungry, can scarcely wait a moment patiently for your own waitress to appear. You notice also the gigantic pots of aromatically steaming coffee, tea and chocolate being poured in everyone's cup but your own, and ravenously you watch the pantry door for that long tarrying one who went once upon a time to get some of these delectable viands for you.

"Will you have broiled chicken?" asks the faithless She you have been watching for, bending solicitously over a group of strange tourists at the next table. At last when the train people are quite supplied, your speeding Hebe returns to you and apologizes sweetly, "I am sorry but I had to help get train Number Seven's supper. They've eaten all the broiled chicken that was cooked, but I'll order you some more if you don't mind waiting twenty minutes."

By and by the train people leave, your chicken arrives and you finish your supper in commonplace tranquility.

With this dramatic increase in American leisure traveling—by train and by car—when Ford went to the next National Parks Conference, he announced that visitors to the Grand Canyon had increased fivefold in the past four years. In 1915, over 150,000 people had come to the Divine Abyss, more than had visited the three largest national parks, Yellowstone, Yosemite, and Glacier, combined. But he was incredulous that all his years of lobbying for national park status—supported by everyone from Ed Ripley to Teddy Roosevelt—had so far come to nothing.

"I have heard personally . . . about the fitness of the Grand Canyon . . . on different occasions from two Presidents of the United States, three Secretaries of the Interior, every United States Senator and Congressman I ever met who has been to the canyon, and innumerable distinguished men of letters and science and arts," Ford lamented. "And still [it] is not a national park and, as far as I know, there is no definite step, not even a bill before Congress today, to make [it] a national park."

Ford's lobbying was partly altruistic. The infrastructure of the South Rim simply could not accommodate this many visitors—it wasn't safe anymore for the tourists or the canyon. But he also had a business motive. The Grand Canyon had surprised everyone by becoming an enormous source of revenue for Fred Harvey—in fact, it was now the single most profitable location in the entire Harvey System, and the one with the most growth potential. Yet it was also the only location the Santa Fe couldn't guarantee Ford could keep; the railroad owned its buildings there, but it could never control the land under them.

The only way for Ford to keep his business at the canyon was if the government made it a national park and Fred Harvey made an exclusive deal directly with the new National Park Service. That way, even if the Santa Fe lost interest in the canyon, Ford could have the contract to feed and house all South Rim visitors.

He was lobbying everyone he knew in the government, trying to call in favors for all the free meals and comped hotel rooms that he, and his father before him, had given public officials. Ed Ripley was also working his contacts, and out of sheer frustration even tried putting a huge financial gun to the government's head. He publicly offered to make $1 million ($20.2 million) of improvements along the South Rim if Congress passed an authorization for national park status. When the bill failed, the offer was just as publicly withdrawn.

And as the war raged in Europe, America continued to bask in its isolationism, taking a good look at itself and liking what it was seeing. The U.S. population had just topped one hundred million, and the summer of 1916 was the best in the history of the country's tourism.

The editor of *National Geographic* magazine, Gilbert Grosvenor, declared that Americans had finally realized the treasures of the Old World were eclipsed by the splendors of the new:

> It is true that one finds more ancient culture in Europe . . . more splendid architecture . . . [and] better art. But in that architecture which is voiced in the glorious temples of the sequoia grove and in the castles of the Grand Canyon, in the art which is mirrored in American lakes, which is painted in geyser basins and frescoed upon the side walls of the mightiest canyons, there is a majesty and an appeal that the mere handiwork of men, splendid though it may be, can never rival.

CHAPTER 28

DARING YOUNG FREDDY
& HIS FLYING MACHINES

ᴎᴇ

Fᴏʀᴅ's sᴏɴ, ғʀᴇᴅᴅʏ, ʜᴀᴅ ɢʀᴏᴡɴ ғʀᴏᴍ ᴀ ᴄᴜᴛᴇ ʟɪᴛᴛʟᴇ ʀɪᴄʜ kid who wrote postcards home from Europe to see if his daddy would send him "the funny papers" into a dashing and daring young man. By the time he got to Harvard, he had a reputation for fearlessness, his life a seemingly endless game of chicken. He loved fast horses, fast boats, and fast cars: His classmates were awed by his breakneck drives between Harvard and Manhattan, a trip he regularly made in just four hours, averaging an unheard-of speed of sixty miles an hour. And he played his favorite sport, polo, as if every match were sudden death. When the family was at the Grand Canyon, he climbed where only eagles or idiots dared; in his sister's favorite picture of him, he was hanging by his fingertips from the canyon rim. Strong and lithe, with sleepy eyes and a trim mustache that made his face look older than his body, Freddy had complete trust in his physical strength and his instincts.

He was also fearless socially and sexually. With good looks and charm inherited from both of his parents, he was a well-known ladies' man whose name struck fear in the hearts of society parents with ripe daughters. According to one of his classmates and fellow jocks at Harvard, they might also have worried for some of their sons as well. Prescott Townsend, the Boston Brahmin who grew up to be one of the nation's earliest gay advocates, told his biographer that he lost his virginity to Freddy at Harvard.

"I was very frightened," Townsend recalled, but he said Freddy made him feel as if he were being welcomed into "a distinct brotherhood" so he didn't "ever feel guilty."

In 1917, America finally entered the war. Among the final straws were Germany's overtures to Mexico to join the conflict in January, and then the Russian Revolution in March, which undermined Russia's active support for the Allies. On April 6, America declared war on Germany.

Twenty-one-year-old Freddy Harvey dropped out of Harvard, where he was a junior, and enlisted, as did a great many of his classmates. Most signed up for the army or the navy. But Freddy was a "born flyer," in the lingo of the nascent field of flight instruction. So he joined the fledgling American Air Service, a precursor to the air force, which was just a small division of the U.S. Army Signal Corps. Like tanks, planes had never been used in combat before this "Great War." So while the European countries had been stocking up on planes and pilots for several years, America had barely started. When war was declared, the country had just two small airfields and 225 planes, not one of which was safe for combat. There were forty-eight officers in the air service, and only 1,330 men.

"We lacked men of experience; we lacked aviators of mature judgment; we lacked airplanes fit to fly against the Huns; and we lacked facilities for building them . . . The Air Service was a genuine expression of the 'American Idea' . . . splendid courage accompanied by a high degree of disorder," said one of Freddy's flight school colleagues, Hiram Bingham, the celebrated Yale professor who had led the expedition to the "lost" Peruvian city of Machu Picchu (and decades later helped inspire the daredevil movie archaeologist Indiana Jones). Bingham was more than twice the age of his fellow trainees, and recalled, "never in my life have I felt so old as I did during my two months of association with this brilliant group of young pilots."

Freddy was in the first class of volunteers trained after America joined the war—part of a group shipped off to Miami, Florida, where the government had commandeered a facility owned by America's premier plane manufacturer, Glenn Curtiss. It was as much a laboratory and testing range as a flight school, but there were planes to fly—at least one was always in service, and sometimes even three or four. Freddy was learning how to fly just as Glenn Curtiss himself was learning how to build better military aircraft, improving on his standard plane, the JN-4, known as a Jenny. So students and instructors discovered design and manufacturing flaws in new planes the hard way: in the air. It was not uncommon for propellers to break apart or spin off the plane in flight, forcing young inexperienced pilots to improvise landings. One time a new plane was sent up with wings that didn't exactly match. It went into a tailspin at fifteen hundred feet and slammed headfirst into the ground, its engine partially buried. Somehow, both instructor and student survived. After ten days in the hospital, they were back at the airfield hobbling around, anxiously awaiting a chance to fly again.

Freddy was a leader among this noisy bunch of pilots. After six months of training in Florida, he was commissioned as a lieutenant and put in charge of the 27th Aero Squadron, which was sent to Toronto to train with the British Royal Flying Corps. Soon thereafter he was appointed assistant officer in charge of Scott Field, the first air-training facility in the Midwest, just outside of St. Louis in Belleville, Illinois. It was named for Colonel Frank Scott, who only weeks before Freddy transferred there had become the first American flyer to die in a plane crash.

Just before Thanksgiving 1917, Freddy let his parents know he would be flying home for the holiday. A huge wooden cross, painted white, was placed on the polo field at the Kansas City Country Club, the site of so many of his athletic triumphs, as a landing marker. And on a blustery Friday afternoon, the Ford Harveys, along with two dozen family friends, could be seen standing alongside the polo field staring into the sky for nearly two hours. Finally, at about two o'clock, the crowd gasped and pointed as the small Curtiss biplane—painted army drab except for red, white, and blue crosses on the wings—materialized in the distance. It buzzed through the chill fall sky, touched down on the polo field, and rolled to a stop just in front of where Ford stood.

Young aviator Freddy hopped out "with as much calmness and aplomb as if he was stepping out of the train coming home from school," according to one account, and greeted his family and friends. With him was a fellow airman, Major Claude Rhinehardt.

"It's the greatest sport in the world," Freddy told the assembled throng, who peppered him with questions. "Frightened? Not a bit. I'm *blasé* to most of the scary part now. We averaged a hundred miles an hour several times, but if it had not been for some bad air currents and a lot of clouds that persisted in bothering us, we would have arrived here sooner. Hazardous? Well, sometimes you think so and then again you feel as safe as though you were on the ground. We traveled for the most part at a height of about four thousand feet and you feel pretty safe when you're this short distance from the ground."

He promised that if folks returned the next day, they would see a dazzling aerial show—a promise that appeared on the front page of the *Kansas City Star.* Several thousand patriotic adults and "wriggling youngsters" took him up on the offer, lining up all the way around the polo field at the country club the next afternoon. At the appropriate time, the crowd parted for Lieutenant Harvey and Major Rhinehardt, "two leather-rigged, behooded and begoggled figures," who the *Kansas City Times* claimed were also wearing spurs for effect. The pilots took turns putting the plane through a series of daredevil moves, spins, and loop-de-loops that had one fan in the audience crowing, "Those chaps do a flip with no more thought about the spectacular than you would have about asking the waiter for a clean spoon."

At one point the engine stopped in midair and the plane began to plunge—"a dead stick!" Freddy exclaimed—but it was quickly restarted and landed safely.

The event was big news in Kansas City society, where the *Independent's* breathless columnist Betty Ann reported that Ford was bursting with pride for his "very expert bird man . . . fearless to a fault and as at home in his high perch as on the floor of a dance hall." But the city's social arbiter admitted, "If I was the mother of a son who was a bird man I would never have a happy moment; no sophistries or would-be consolations or positive assertions that there was no danger would place or impress me, and I haven't a doubt that Mrs. Harvey feels the same way, but she is too good a sport to show it."

In fact, while Ford was proud of his son for enlisting—and becoming the first Harvey to ever fight for his country—he was, if anything, even more nervous about Freddy's flying than his wife. This was his only son, and the namesake future of Fred Harvey. Ford did his best to remain stoically optimistic, even after Freddy was appointed an officer in charge of flying at one of the most hazardous airfields in the country, the massive aviator training facility at Camp Taliaferro in Fort Worth, Texas. Over six thousand men, American and British, were trained there in just six months—and at such breakneck speed that thirty-nine men died in training.

Freddy became a legendary instructor in Texas. Flight students reverently referred to him and two fellow captains as "The Three Bombardiers."

SHORT OF SACRIFICING his son, Ford was willing to do anything to help the war effort. When America joined the fighting, Woodrow Wilson chose one rich and powerful man in each major city to lead the fund-raising drive for the American Red Cross. In Kansas City, the president appointed Ford.

Fred Harvey was also feeding tens of thousands of American soldiers a day as they traversed the country by train en route to their new training assignments. Kansas City Union Station became the primary crossroad for troops, who spent their layovers getting assistance from the famous Red Cross station in the main concourse, and enjoying discounted meals at the Harvey lunchroom across the way. Fred Harvey also had contracts to serve soldiers at many of its other locations: Ford had negotiated a rate with the War Department of sixty cents ($10.08) per meal. Sometimes the dining rooms would be reset for military feeding, all the tables lined up so as many soldiers as possible could be served. At other times the staff would prepare hundreds of hearty bag lunches to be quickly distributed through train windows. Former Harvey Girls were brought out of retirement to help serve the troops. And army officers from bases all over the Midwest and West besieged Ford to lend them Harvey chefs. Gus Burkett, the chef from the Emporia Harvey House, was now cooking for General Leonard Wood at Camp Funston, in Manhattan, Kansas, and Fredrick Sommers, a chef from the Kansas City Union Station, was cooking for the Thirteenth Engineers in Chicago.

In all, over 25 percent of the company's male employees had enlisted. Their hero, of course, was the founder's valiant grandson, Lieutenant Frederick Harvey.

Ford's influence in the war effort increased in December 1917 when President Wilson announced that the federal government would be taking over all the railroads. The secretary of the Treasury, William McAdoo—who was also President Wilson's son-in-law—was given the militarized title of "Director-General" of the new U.S. Railroad Administration.

While Santa Fe president Ed Ripley wanted nothing to do with the government takeover, his well-run railroad was clearly the model that McAdoo had in mind when building his team. The Director-General selected several Santa Fe men to help run the nation's trains during wartime: McAdoo's second-in-command was the former chairman of the Santa Fe's board Walker Hines, and one of Ripley's vice presidents was given the top position directing the nation's train traffic.

Ford was summoned to Washington to head the advisory board on how to feed America's troops and train passengers during wartime. After all, until the war started, Fred Harvey had been among the country's largest bulk purchasers of foodstuffs, and probably fed more people every day than any other entity in the nation.

Under Ford's leadership, all of the nation's dining cars were changed over from kitchens offering elaborate à la carte meals to simpler table d'hôte menus that could be used for private passengers or soldiers. There would be no more bluepoint oysters served on America's trains until the Germans were defeated.

AS A YOUNG COUNTRY that had never before been unified and mobilized coast-to-coast for war, the United States had never nationalized an industry before and didn't know exactly how to go about it. The takeover began congenially enough, with the Railroad Administration working with executives to make sure that military needs always superseded those of private passengers and freight haulers. When the railroads questioned how they would be reimbursed for all this military transport, a bill was passed that basically said, "Don't worry, we'll pay you back."

It was soon clear, however, that the hundreds of railroads needed more than government guidance and reassurance. Years of competition and federal regulation had created a system that was too unwieldy to operate smoothly. While western and Midwestern railroads like the Santa Fe were in pretty good shape and ran fairly efficiently, the trains in the East were not ready for the sheer volume of men and supplies that had to be moved quickly en route to Europe. The eastern tracks and cars required more repairs and upgrades than the railroads could afford, so backups in certain cities became endemic: The Pennsylvania Railroad was in particularly poor shape, and trains were forever being held up in its strongholds of Pittsburgh and Philadelphia.

Director-General McAdoo finally had to admit that Ed Ripley had been right during all those years: Government regulation was a big reason why the railroads hadn't been able to keep investing in new cars and better tracks. The Interstate Commerce Commission had forced them to keep passenger fares and freight rates absurdly low, and even with the recently mandated eight-hour workday, wages had not risen enough to keep those workers who hadn't enlisted from repeatedly threatening to strike.

Yet while McAdoo knew the government had helped cause these problems, he grew impatient when the railroads couldn't fix them. He was tired of arguing with executives about the best way to carry out his orders. So in May 1918, he took a drastic and entirely unprecedented step.

He announced that the U.S. government was summarily firing the president of every railroad in the country.

The presidents would be replaced with "federal managers" who worked for the government. Technically, all the executives were being "retired," although their companies could still pay them and rehire them after the war. Some were even appointed federal managers at a fraction of their normal peacetime salaries. However, in most cases, younger, more ambitious, and more cooperative executives—from within a company or, occasionally, from its competitors—were put in charge.

At the Santa Fe, Ed Ripley was hugely supportive of the war effort, but he had no interest this late in his career in starting to work for the government. One of his most able vice presidents, William Storey, was named federal manager, which also made him Ripley's heir apparent.

The new federal managers were forced to quickly standardize their railroads—doing away with competition, duplicate services, and individual corporate idiosyncrasies in all aspects of their operations. New standards were created for railcars, and the government ordered thousands of new ones. Ticket offices in railway stations were consolidated.

In order to avoid any labor unrest, the Railroad Administration gave railroad employees large across-the-board raises. For the first time ever, the government even mandated that female employees receive wages equal to men. To pay for the increases, the federal managers raised all passenger fares and freight charges. So, while the government was still promising that after the war, the railroads would get all their trains back in exactly the condition they had left them, this was already impossible. The entire economics of "working on the railroad" had been changed forever.

Most Americans today are more familiar with the changes and compromises made during World War II, because it lasted longer and is fresher in memory, than with the actions the government took during the first World War. But in many ways, what happened in 1917 and 1918 is far more significant and shocking. This was the first time major industries were impounded in the world's largest democracy. And quite a few individual freedoms were seriously curtailed as well.

The Temperance Movement used the war as a way to convince the government to pass a temporary "War-time Prohibition Act," which laid the groundwork for national prohibition. The 1918 law was sold as a way to help conserve grain and keep it from brewers—many of whom were German immigrants. If it kept the country's soldiers sober, and perhaps halted drinking in America altogether, that was just an added benefit.

In the name of "social hygiene," the government also became insidiously involved in trying to quash a sexual revolution. As young men poured into military facilities across the country, the government started to arrest and detain young women for being too attracted to the soldiers. As many as fifteen thousand women were incarcerated in "camp cities" because they could be "proven in federal court to be a menace to men in training." Many were accused of being prostitutes— and certainly some of them were. But a surprising number were detained for being "charity girls"—so enamored of men in uniform that they *charitably* surrendered themselves sexually to young soldiers headed off to war. Some were arrested even before they had sexual contact with fighting men. A study of the population of one Chicago detention center described "one immoral girl" who was arrested "for writing indescribably obscene letters to various soldiers with whom she was not personally acquainted," and another woman arrested in the middle of the night en route to visit a sailor she "was crazy about." She was diagnosed as "an ultra-emotional and excitable type, the offspring of an erratic and probably immoral mother. She had been permitted to read sensational novels and sex stories for years."

The entire effort was portrayed as a way to stop the spread of venereal disease among enlisted men—which, with no effective treatments, was indeed a serious problem. But the truth was, social reformers had been discussing for years what to do about young women who "forfeited their claims to the respect of the virtuous." The war was simply a welcome opportunity to enlist government support for criminalizing sexuality.

LATE ON A SUNDAY afternoon in the early summer of 1918, as thousands of passengers and soldiers in uniform rushed through the cavernous main waiting room of Kansas City Union Station, a powerful tenor voice rang out above the din.

O beautiful for spacious skies,
For amber waves of grain . . .

People stopped in their tracks and looked toward the east end of the complex, where the Red Cross booth sat below an illuminated scene of volunteers helping soldiers on a grave-strewn French countryside. The booth was being run by the usual flock of Red Cross volunteers—women from the Junior League, students from Westport High School, and a handful of Harvey Girls who were helping raise money during their break. Standing in front of them, however, was a middle-aged Hopi Indian chief in full tribal dress regalia.

For purple mountain majesties
Above the fruited plain . . .

The crowd quickly shuffled toward Chief Silvertongue, transfixed by his voice and his bearing.

America! America!
God shed his grace on thee,
And crown thy good with brotherhood
From sea to shining sea!

When he finished the verse, the entire concourse stood silent. So he began another verse. When that was done, the crowd still stood dumbfounded.

Then someone called out, "Let us *all* sing!"

And so they did, soldiers and Harvey Girls, adults and children, their voices soaring with almost religious exaltation:

O beautiful for heroes prov'd
In liberating strife,
Who more than self their country loved,
And mercy more than life.

America! America!
May God thy gold refine
Till all success be nobleness,
And ev'ry gain divine.

When the song ended, the throng remained in such a patriotic fervor that Chief Silvertongue led them in several others, and Red Cross volunteers found themselves deluged with contributions. Most people could afford only a dime or a quarter, but over the next several hours nearly nine thousand people made donations—including a regiment of soldiers who were passing through the station on their way to war.

It was the last day of the biggest National Red Cross campaign yet. The White House had set a goal of raising $100 million ($1.4 billion) in one week. Ford Harvey, Dave Benjamin, and John Huckel had worked furiously, sending their office employees, Harvey Girls, and family members out to canvass every train that came through the station, going window to window along the broad platforms until the stroke of midnight on Sunday. The quota set by the government for Ford's operation in Kansas City was $800,000 ($11.4 million). When they finished the tally early Monday morning, they realized they had doubled it.

OVER THE SUMMER, as his fellow flyers were sent overseas into combat, Freddy remained stateside, training pilots and flying in government air shows. His squadron's performance was the highlight of New York City's "loyalty parade" for Independence Day—in which more than seventy thousand foreign-born Americans, grouped by nationality or religion, proceeded in formation down Fifth Avenue in what was called "the greatest 'march for freedom' the world has ever known."

Freddy and Major Rhinehardt led a squadron of twenty-two planes that buzzed New York City, taking off from Mineola Field in Queens, hovering over Belmont Park, and then zooming across the Bronx before putting on a show just off Riverside Drive. Then they turned and flew low down Fifth Avenue, the pilots dropping leaflets with the words to "The Star-Spangled Banner." When the planes reached Madison Square and the Flatiron Building, they separated into three squadrons and veered off to fly amazing stunts all over Manhattan. There was even a pretend near accident over East 72nd Street—which was made more ironic when, at day's end, one of the planes did a nose-dive and crashed into crowded Van Cortlandt Park, with some two thousand spectators watching. (Reportedly, no one was hurt, although police immediately confiscated all cameras, destroying all negatives at the Kingsbridge Police Station.) The New York loyalty parade show was such a success that the government sent Freddy and Rhinehardt out in August to do a fourteen-city national tour.

Freddy finally received orders to ship out for Europe in September 1918, with the war still raging. His departure was delayed only because of a medical procedure: He had his tonsils removed. The twenty-two-year-old aviator probably didn't have tonsillitis; the operation was most likely done to prevent influenza, the deadly virus that had arrived with epidemic vengeance in the United States from the pestilent trenches of the war in Europe. Tonsillectomies and tooth extractions were among a handful of procedures believed to ward off the flu, along with inhaling chloroform and drinking Scotch whiskey. In some cities, people were being arrested for spitting or coughing.

Ford was in Washington when Freddy, who had been promoted to captain, got his orders. Besides Ford's Railroad Administration business, the lobbying for national park status for the Grand Canyon had reached a critical stage. He wrote to his brother, Byron, from Washington's New Willard Hotel that Freddy was "pretty miserable" after the tonsillectomy, and everyone else in the family was upset about his going to war. His wife and daughter, Kitty, were, "of course, depressed."

By the time Freddy sailed for France in mid-October, it was becoming clear even to the Germans that they would soon have to surrender. But the war was still on, and the risks remained high. On October 27, Freddy's Harvard classmate Hamilton Coolidge, who had been flying in Europe for six months and had survived more than a hundred missions and eight dogfights, was killed by a direct hit from an anti-aircraft gun while flying over Chevrières. His plane exploded on impact, and his comrades watched his body free-fall to the earth.

That week was one of the deadliest in American history, but not only because of the war. In Europe, some twenty-seven hundred American soldiers died in combat; but at home, during the same period, over twenty-one thousand people died of the flu. When the end of fighting was celebrated on November 11, Armistice Day, many people stayed indoors to avoid unnecessary contact, and those who dared to venture out to celebrate wore masks. It was not uncommon in major cities to see priests on horse-drawn carts rolling down the streets calling, "Bring out your dead!"

Freddy ended up being stationed at the Third Aviation Instruction Center at Issoudun in central France. He was there for only four months, but they were months that forever changed the country he had left behind. America endured an endless stream of funerals. The worldwide death toll for the war, over four years, was about 16 million; America lost about 100,000 men. The death toll for the flu pandemic, the worst of which took place during the last few months of the war, was at least *50 million* worldwide, with more than 675,000 lives lost in the United States. Together, the two calamities wiped out at least 3 percent, and perhaps as much as 6 percent, of the world's population. The final weeks of 1918 passed like one long global wake.

Just as the New Year began, the first great hero of the new American century, Theodore Roosevelt, died in his sleep of a coronary embolism at the age of sixty. When Congress came back into session in January, it passed his final piece of pet legislation at last. The bill to make the Grand Canyon a national park was approved and sent on to President Wilson for his signature. At El Tovar on the South Rim and in the Fred Harvey offices on the second floor of Kansas City Union Station there was a mixture of jubilation and relief.

Yet the Harvey family was also rejoicing for another reason: Freddy was coming home. And true to his seemingly charmed life—or perhaps his father's growing influence in Washington—he was unharmed. Freddy's flight-training colleague Hiram Bingham made a curious statement about why the young flyer hadn't seen combat. In his memoir of the air service, he claimed that Freddy "was so greatly appreciated that he was not permitted to go abroad" until the fighting had ended. It isn't clear whether the air service or his powerful father "appreciated" him too much to let him risk his life.

When Captain Frederick Harvey's ship pulled in to New York harbor in mid-February, America was in a state of national relief and grief.

But Freddy hadn't changed a bit. From a phone in the lobby of the Plaza Hotel, he called home and his sister answered.

"How are you?" he asked. "Where's Father?"

"I'm fine," she replied. "Father is in Washington."

"And where's Mother?"

"In New York," she said, "at the Plaza."

"So am I," he said, laughing. "Goodbye." He hung up and dashed off to find her.

Two weeks after his discharge, the news came from Paris that President Wilson, still trying to hammer out the details of the Treaty of Versailles, had taken time out to attend to some domestic business and signed the bill creating Grand Canyon National Park. Since no other company could make a serious bid for the contract to serve all the tourists at the canyon, it was only a matter of time before Ford made a deal with the National Park Service.

If Freddy had any thoughts about returning to Harvard to finish up his degree, the National Park bill ended them. His father wanted him home in Kansas City so he could begin basic training all over again. For the next few years, he would toil as an apprentice to traveling Fred Harvey supervisors. If he was going to assume command of Fred Harvey someday, he would have to start as a private.

ALTHOUGH THE WAR was over, the federal government did not immediately relinquish control of the railroads. And while the Santa Fe waited to get its trains back, Ed Ripley announced that he was stepping down as president. His protégé William Storey, who had been running the Santa Fe as federal manager, would take over, and Ripley would become chairman of the board, charged with helping oversee what was certain to be a rocky transition back to private control.

Hailed by the *New York Times* as America's "greatest living railroad man," Ripley planned to live full-time at his winter home in Santa Barbara, on Pedregosa and Laguna streets near Mission Park. His mustache now snow-white, he wanted to play a lot of golf, spend more time with his family, finish a book he was writing about California wild birds, stay active in the Santa Barbara Chamber of Commerce, and keep a hand in his pet project, the damming of the Colorado River to provide electricity to Arizona. (This was the lobbying effort that led to the construction of the Hoover Dam.) Mostly, Ripley planned to spend long, sunny Santa Barbara afternoons giving sage advice as the emeritus professor of railroads, the conscience of American big business.

Ford was looking forward to sharing some of those expansive afternoon chats. He had recently bought a splendid family vacation home in Montecito, several miles from the Ripley estate. It was called Arequipa, a ten-acre property with elaborate gardens that had been built in 1899 as a wedding gift for a prominent local couple. Its name—invoking a city in Peru—meant "yes, here" or "here, rest" in the South American native language Quechua.

Unfortunately, Ripley did not live to see the government return his beloved railroad to the company he had led for over twenty years, or to have those expansive chats with Ford. On a Wednesday afternoon in early February 1920, he rose after a light lunch and told his wife and daughter he was retiring to his bedroom for "a short siesta." Only minutes later, his daughter checked in on him and discovered that he was not breathing.

One of the biggest hearts in American industry had finally given out. And Ford Harvey had lost his closest friend and mentor in the railroad business.

CHAPTER 29

SOROPTIMISTAS

⊐⊏

Kansas city wasn't exactly as freddy had left it. For one thing, his high-society mother and sister now had . . . jobs. Actually, they had started their own little restaurant, the Tip Top Cafeteria. While doing volunteer work for the Red Cross during the war, Judy Harvey and her daughter, Kitty, had marveled at the growing number of working women in Kansas City and were upset that there was no place for them to get an inexpensive lunch. They decided it was time for the Harvey women to open their own eatery. To get it started, they asked each of their society friends to donate $60 ($747) and agree to prepare some of the food themselves in their own home kitchens— perhaps with a little help from their full-time cooks.

The ladies commandeered a suite of rooms on the top floor of the Altman Building (named for the grandfather of director Robert Altman, who was a successful Kansas City entrepreneur). The building was well-known in the financial district because businessmen frequented the Turkish baths in its basement and ladies loved its five stories of retail stores. On the sixth floor, the society women set up a lunchroom and a separate reading area, with books brought over from the Catholic Free Library, their partner in the project.

Society columnist Betty Ann covered the opening of Judy and Kitty Harvey's Tip Top Cafeteria as though it were bigger news than the peace talks in Versailles:

> Never in their wildest expectations did the women engineering the Tip Top Cafeteria expect to serve the crowd, the mob, the riot which swamped them when they opened the door . . . It

is odd the magic there is in a society woman's name. Had Mrs. Ford Harvey been some struggling, dependent soul trying to earn a living by serving meals to the hungry at moderate price, I'd wager a chicken ranch she would have gone broke. What was the actual result? Mrs. Harvey had so many pie-eaters and sandwich fiends pushing, crowding, scrambling to get inside this little food shop . . . that it looked like bargain day at the handkerchief counter.

Mrs. Robert Keith, with her cheeks as pink as roses, was behind the counter handing out ham sandwiches which were made, in plain sight, by Mrs. Harry Seavy. Mrs. Leo Stewart waited on the trade, as if she had never done anything else . . .

When the crowd became so great that clean dishes were at a premium . . . Mrs. J. C. Firth and Mrs. Francis Drage—honestly, they are the best-looking women—turned their hands into the dish pan and washed while [Kitty] Harvey and Mrs. Herman Brumback wiped. Mrs. Ford Harvey was on the floor most of the time and over it all presided.

The opening of the Tip Top also made the front page of the *Kansas City Star*, which was stunned by the image of society women "emptying garbage at a public cafeteria" and being ordered about by commoners, who got their attention by calling out, "Say girlie, bring me a fork, will you?"

While the Tip Top was an immediate hit, serving over two hundred working women a day, the ladies didn't have the slightest idea how to run a restaurant, and neither did the Catholic Library Association. After a week or so, Judy reluctantly asked Ford—who was one of the only men in town who patronized the Tip Top—to have Harvey chefs help her with the project. For this, he was lavished with praise by Betty Ann, who noted "the newspapers never get hold of the thousand and one contributions [Ford] makes to countless charities and indigent people, helpless mothers of little children, stranded men, erring girls, wayward youths and all the rest of the unfortunate; his heart never turns against them."

While the Harvey chefs made most of the food, the society women all continued working one lunch a week, bringing in homemade desserts and waiting on tables for "the girls employed."

The ladies of Kansas City loved being Harvey Girls for a day.

AS FOR THE CAREER Harvey Girls, they were flourishing in postwar America. Train service was getting back to normal, as was life in the Harvey restaurants and hotels. But the ranks of the Harvey Girls had been dangerously depleted by marriages to returning soldiers: Of the two thousand Harvey Girls employed in 1918, twelve hundred had reportedly quit since the war ended to become brides. So the company had to hire and train an army of new waitresses. And "Miss Steele," the woman who interviewed and chose new girls for the company, became something of a celebrity.

Alice Steele was a Kansas farm girl who had come to Fred Harvey as a file clerk in 1910 and worked her way up in the employment department until she became known as "the woman who hires the Harvey Girls." Unmarried, in her early thirties, and living with her niece—still "a girl herself," noted one story about her—she was a serious-minded woman with kind eyes, short black hair, and a photographic memory of everyone she met.

Being head of personnel for the entire Fred Harvey company was a remarkably important executive position for a woman. In fact, "Miss Steele" and "Miss Mary Colter" were among the highest-ranking women in corporate America. Steele's position made her a queen bee and role model for working women from all around the country who flocked to the office at Union Station in Kansas City—or to Chicago, when she held interviews there at the satellite Fred Harvey office—to get a chance at a good-paying job, travel, and chaperoned adventure. She was a combination of model agent, women's college recruiter, and pop sociologist, and nobody in the country better understood the experience of America's new working women.

Alice Steele embodied the cresting idea of "soroptimism"—knowing what was "best for women"—as Soroptimist Clubs began springing up all over the United States and Europe in the 1920s to support working women. It was no surprise when Steele became a charter member and a national leader in the Soroptimist movement, helping to recast the image of Harvey Girls for modern times. For thirty years they had been viewed as the most fetching, efficient, and available of young women. "The girls at a Fred Harvey Place never look dowdy, frowsy, tired, slipshod or overworked," raved one nationally known writer.

"They are expecting you—clean collars, clean aprons, hands and faces washed, nails manicured. There they are! Bright, fresh, healthy and expectant—Extra Choice!"

But now the newspapers were calling them "the smartest girls in the world."

Some of their stories were still laden with backhanded compliments, but they did show the changing appreciation for the role of working women nonetheless. "Today's girl is 'glorifying' her job," the *Kansas City Journal* rhapsodized in a profile of Steele. "The modern girl is less superficial and frivolous, has a deeper sense of responsibility, has more self-reliance and is surer and clearer in her thinking than the first women to invade the field long monopolized by men."

Steele explained that "when a woman comes to me applying for work, I never talk to her from [an] executive pedestal, but as one woman to another. I try to get an understanding of the outside conditions surrounding the applicant's life, so that if she enters our employ I can be more help to her in the future."

This allowed Steele to choose a perfect rookie assignment after a Harvey Girl finished her one-month unpaid training—or quickly make a change if she had guessed wrong. "A girl who is lonely in Chicago, for instance, and not at her best, may give ideal service in a little town where she soon makes friends with everybody," she noted. But others couldn't wait to get out of those little desert towns and work in larger cities—or at the Grand Canyon, which for many was the dream posting.

"We have many girls who are actuated by wanderlust," Steele said. "Sometimes girls realize that life in a stuffy office is not living at all."

It was, of course, hard to make more modern Harvey Girls follow the old company rules, such as the 11:00 p.m. curfew and the prohibition against dating fellow employees—especially in those cities where the women no longer lived exclusively in dormitories, but were also put up in rooms the company rented from private home owners. In time, Miss Steele started hearing more and more stories about Harvey Girls hiding relationships, and realized she would have to overlook such indiscretions by otherwise dependable, loyal employees—such as Joanne Stinelichner.

At the age of twenty-two, Joanne had emigrated from Germany during the war; she was living in Milwaukee taking classes to learn English when she and two friends, a beautician and a schoolteacher, went to Chicago for Harvey Girl interviews. "I was dressed real nice," she recalled, "with rosy cheeks and nice hair." They were all hired, but Joanne was the only one who stayed with the company, finishing her English education in the immersion course of working as a Harvey Girl in Hutchinson, Kansas.

She was later transferred to the Fred Harvey hotel in Syracuse, Kansas, where she fell for the chef, John Thompson. Luckily, both were friends of the night watchman at the Harvey Girl dorm, who never reported their late-night meetings to the manager. And when they decided to marry, Fred Harvey didn't want to lose them, so the ceremony was held in the manager's apartment, and they were allowed to live together. They were then transferred to the Harvey House in Waynoka, Oklahoma, where they soon had something else to keep secret from management: Joanne was pregnant. She kept it quiet in Waynoka and at their next posting in Galveston, but by the time they were transferred to Emporia, Kansas, some of her fellow Harvey Girls had figured it out.

"I worked up to the end of the ninth month," she recalled. "I was on the floor in Emporia, Kansas, when my water broke!" After giving birth, she continued working for Fred Harvey for years, her daughter, Helen, growing up among dozens of Harvey Girl surrogate mothers.

Joanne's career was one of many that showed Alice Steele the value of bending the rules. But occasionally, Miss Steele guessed wrong and made disastrous mistakes. The most infamous was Millie Clark, a Harvey Girl who became one of the best-known prostitutes in the Southwest, "Silver City Millie."

Millie grew up a headstrong orphan in Kansas City, bouncing around in foster homes until she found herself in front of a young local judge by the name of Harry S. Truman, who had just gotten into politics. (Like many local politicos, he was a regular at the Fred Harvey lunchroom in Union Station.) Judge Truman sent her to live with a Greek family who knew Alice Steele. Worldly beyond her years, fourteen-year-old Millie fooled Miss Steele into believing she was sixteen, the minimum age for Harvey Girls. She was desperate for the job, which would allow her to go west with her sister, Florence, who had tuberculosis.

Millie and Florence ended up in Deming, New Mexico, among the most dreaded first postings for Harvey Girls. It was one of the few original Fred Harvey locations that had never really flourished, remaining a desolate desert outpost. But there was still a small Harvey hotel there, primarily for railroaders, cowboys, and rookie Harvey Girls, who never forgot the large sign hanging over the door from the kitchen to the dining room. "Water, Butter, Ice," it read, reminding them to make sure that every customer had a full glass of ice water and three pats of butter at all times. And each pat of butter had to have a fork mark visible on the top, so no patron would fear it had been put on the plate with someone's dirty fingers.

Millie initially did well there. Since most of her salary went to pay for the nearby sanitarium that was caring for her sister, she quickly figured out how to use her charms, and her rapidly developing body, to get bigger tips. Flashing her toothsome smile, batting her wide blue eyes, she made a big production out of buttering a gentleman's toast, or putting cream or sugar in his coffee, asking him suggestively: "Is that *enough*?"

After six months at Deming, Millie received the standard Harvey Girl one-week leave and a train pass to the destination of her choice. She took her sister to El Paso, to another sanitarium, and soon decided to quit being a Harvey Girl. Her recommendation from the Harvey House helped her find work in El Paso, but as her sister's health-care costs skyrocketed, Millie couldn't make ends meet working two full-time jobs. So she started turning a few tricks on the side, eventually deciding to make it a career, first in El Paso and then in Carrizozo, New Mexico, where she worked in the well-known whorehouse of Madam Jenny. Eventually, she set up her own place in a nearby mining town, where she became known as "Silver City Millie," the infamous Harvey Girl turned madam.

THE MOST THOROUGHLY modern woman in the Harvey family was Kitty, Ford and Judy's daughter, who at the age of thirty was still fiercely single. In fact, the gossip columns had long since stopped speculating about her marital prospects, even though she had once been considered the most eligible young woman in Kansas City.

Almost everything else about the handsome, athletic socialite, arts enthusiast, nationally ranked golfer, and world traveler made the papers. There were her social engagements and good works in Kansas City, where she still lived with her parents and got good reviews for her appearances in local theater productions. There were her many sojourns to Chicago and New York, where she visited family and society friends, who would then join her on adventures of all kinds: anything from weekend excursions to the Kentucky Derby or the Hamptons to grand expeditions all through Europe. There were her frequent train trips to California, where she spent months at a time entertaining at Arequipa, the family's getaway home in Montecito.

And then there were Kitty's glorious journeys through the Southwest, where she was high society's most fearless, engaging, and witty tour guide, organizing groups to visit Santa Fe, Taos, and the nearby pueblos, or take rugged trips down into the Grand Canyon. She and her younger brother had been traveling in the Southwest since childhood—sometimes with their parents, sometimes by themselves, watched over by Harvey House managers and Santa Fe train conductors. They became extraordinarily close—in almost every photo of them, they seem to be sharing a private joke—and the Southwest was like their private paradise.

It was out west that Kitty Harvey seemed to feel most free, most like herself. In the city, she was always impeccably garbed in the latest silk dresses, elaborate hats, and darling shoes—much like her mother and Aunt Minnie, for whom she had great affection. But when hiking and camping in the Southwest, she wore a man's hat, jodhpurs, and boots, and a man's white shirt and tie. And she invariably traveled with an unmarried female companion.

There were plenty of single women in the Fred Harvey service who appeared to be of ambiguous sexuality—never married, rarely associated with men socially, just focused on working hard and taking care of their parents or siblings. Mary Colter was the best known of these women, and though she eventually became a feminist icon and, many presumed, a gay heroine, none of her biographers—including one who is gay himself—felt there was enough evidence to support such speculation.

Kitty Harvey, on the other hand, had such a clarity about her sexuality that most people had stopped pretending. The guessing ceased not long after her Kansas City debutante class decided to put on an evening of "Living Reproductions of Famous Paintings" as a fund-raiser for the Women's Guild of St. Paul's Church. One after another, her very eligible peers appeared dressed in Victorian fineries, re-creating portraits of lovely ladies ranging from "Miss Innocence" (posed holding a lamb) and "the Countess of Oxford" to Marie Antoinette.

Then the curtain opened, and there was Kitty Harvey, dressed as Joan of Arc, in full armor, brandishing a sword.

"Whether it was acting or that the character simply suited her," the *Kansas City Star* reported, "everyone agreed" it was an "inspired" choice. "Miss Harvey has a slight yet determined kind of figure and her face took just the expression one imagines on the Maid of Orleans as she listened to the message of St. Michael."

Kitty had two close female friends, both from prominent families, who were also resolutely unmarried. One was Harriet McLaughlin, the Chicago coffee heiress. Her grandfather was a coffee and tea importer whose company became known nationwide for McLaughlin's Manor House Coffee. Harriet's father, George, was president of Manor House—which was renowned in Chicago not only for its coffee but its advertising (the company sponsored local radio and, later, TV shows). And her uncle Frederic was a World War I hero who led the 333rd Machine Gun Battalion of the 86th "Blackhawk" Infantry Division. An avid sportsman and polo player, he went on to spend much of his inheritance buying the hockey team in Portland, Oregon, and moving it to Chicago. He renamed the team the Blackhawks and went down in hockey history.

Kitty's other close friend was Mary Russell Perkins, whose father was one of the nation's great early railroad executives. In fact, Charles Perkins was vice president of the Chicago, Burlington & Quincy Railroad during the 1870s, when Fred Harvey himself worked for the road. It was one of Perkins's managers who had turned down the young Englishman's idea for revolutionizing railroad eating houses, sending him off to make a deal with the Santa Fe. Mary's older brother was a Harvard-educated polo star who also became a major railroad executive.

It is likely that Kitty Harvey and Mary Perkins first met in Colorado Springs, where their families were both fixtures. The Perkins clan had such a gigantic estate there that when Mary's father died in 1907, she and her siblings donated to the city almost five hundred acres near the base of Pikes Peak for what became the Garden of the Gods park and nature center. And even though Kitty was seven years younger than Mary, she had been visiting Colorado Springs since she was very young; her Aunt Minnie and Uncle John Huckel had a vacation apartment at the Broadmoor resort, and there was a Fred Harvey eating house and hotel in the local train station.

As Kitty Harvey and Mary Perkins grew older, they saw each other mostly in California, where their family estates were just a few miles apart. They shared a passion for western art and culture. Kitty had been collecting for years. She was just a teenager when she bought her first drawing from a nine-year-old Hopi boy named Fred Kabotie, whom she met in Santa Fe after wandering away from her mother at an art show. Kitty bought a couple of his paintings with her allowance, and then arranged to send Kabotie paper and brushes if he would make her more, which she agreed to buy at the price of $1 per figure. She was initially surprised at Kabotie's contention that if so much as a character's finger showed, it should be counted as another figure. But this was all part of her education as a young investor (and it turned out to be a small price to pay when, years later, Kabotie became famous, his work collected by the Museum of Modern Art and the American Museum of Natural History).

Mary Perkins had a growing collection as well, but she was more fascinated with cowboys—she had briefly been married to one as a teen—and Indian fighters. Her passion was buying items that had belonged to George Custer.

Kitty and Mary's exploits were often covered in the *Los Angeles Times* society pages, which portrayed the couple as equally comfortable at Southern California garden parties (where Kitty drank Bloody Marys with extra hot sauce) and on fishing trips to Mexico. Both had been taught by their fathers to hunt birds, and they often went out shooting together.

"We'll warm their trousers," Kitty was fond of saying as the birds tried to fly away.

But mostly they just enjoyed each other's company. One of Kitty's younger cousins recalled a childhood visit to Arequipa where he sat and watched for hours as "the two ladies played cards and smoked and drank wine." In fact, Kitty and Mary allowed him to have a glass of wine, his first. He came downstairs the next morning not feeling very well.

"They just laughed," he said.

KITTY'S BROTHER, FREDDY, also kept company with formidable women, so it came as quite a shock when the society pages started linking him romantically with Betty Drage.

A tall, lovely swan-necked girl who was a gifted equestrian, Betty made sense for Freddy in certain ways. Her father was a former British Royal Horse Guard officer and a polo player, and her mother, heir to a major Midwestern grain brokerage, was a social phenomenon. Lucy Christie Drage was known as the first woman in Kansas City society to ever smoke in public, and had perhaps the most-sought-after taste in town—everyone asked for her advice when redecorating, and her opinion on clothes was always the final word.

And everyone knew what Lucy thought about her daughter's relationship with Freddy. She was appalled. Freddy Harvey was twenty-six. Betty was only *sixteen.*

When the society columns began speculating on "the rumor of pretty little Betty Drage's engagement" to a mysterious older man in Kansas City, Lucy Drage dispatched her husband, Frank, to take their teenage daughter immediately to Paris, where the nuns at a convent school could set her straight. Betty "got as far as the door" of the convent, according to the *Independent,* "but refused to go in." So Frank Drage hired her a tutor and didn't let her out of his sight.

Betty turned seventeen in Paris, where her father tried to get her interested in boys her own age, but to no avail. In early July 1922, the *Independent* reported that the trip had "failed to cure Miss Betty's symptoms" and the young woman was returning to Kansas City, where her family appeared ready to face the inevitable. In fact, not only was Betty going to marry Freddy Harvey, the dashing flyboy and polo star ten years her senior, but she wanted a wedding as soon as possible, the first order of business in the fall social calendar. So just seven weeks after announcing their engagement, they were married on a Thursday morning at the Cathedral of the Immaculate Conception. Because Betty was under eighteen, her father had to sign her marriage license for her.

As befitted the best-dressed family in Kansas City, the seventeen-year-old bride wore a floor-length gown of ivory panne velvet, with bodice and sleeves of Irish Carrickmacross lace, a matching cap with full tulle veil, and a court train of velvet lined with pale blue georgette. Her mother complemented her beautifully in a periwinkle blue crepe de chine dress and a striking brown hat trimmed with an ostrich feather.

Kitty was the maid of honor. Freddy's best man and groomsmen were mostly flying buddies, Bostonians he knew from the air service, along with his weekend pilot and polo pals from Kansas City and his cousin Byron Jr. After the ceremony, there was a lavish British-style breakfast reception and dancing at the Drage mansion, Stony Glen.

The wedding presents were "magnificent, with few duplicates," according to the *Independent*. "Besides the quantities of silver and glassware," there were "a full set of Wedgwood china, rare tapestries from Russian palaces, a ball watch set in onyx with a chain, several rare paintings in oil, antique furniture and a great chest of jams and preserves," as well as the signature gift for the "dry" 1920s—a huge silver tray with martini glasses and a large shaker.

"The clever bride wrote her notes of thanks for each gift as it arrived so she might at the last leave for her wedding trip with no task undone," the society page reported. Young Betty Drage simply could not wait to become Mrs. Freddy Harvey. Besides planning the wedding and their extensive honeymoon trip to Europe, she and her mother had chosen fabrics and furnishings for the new house Ford bought the couple, just around the corner from his own home. All the decorating was done while the newlyweds were away. When they returned, Betty's new life as a grown-up was perfectly in place.

The same was true for Freddy. He returned to a new home and a new executive position at Fred Harvey. But, perhaps more exciting, the airfield he and four aviation buffs had been building, the first in Kansas City and one of the first in the country, was open for business.

Within a few months of the wedding, Betty Ann reported in her Audacious Tattlings column, with even more incredulity than usual, that "the big white stork" would soon be visiting the young couple.

"It is rumored that lovely Betty Drage Harvey is joyously inspecting layettes," she said. "Perhaps Betty is buying them for doll clothes. It hasn't been long since she played with dolls."

Unfortunately, soon after, Betty lost the baby. It was the first—although given the abruptness of the wedding, it may actually have been the second—of many failed attempts to produce the next Fred Harvey.

CHAPTER 30

THE ROAR OF THE TWENTIES

AMERICA'S CITIES EXPLODED AFTER WORLD WAR I, BUSTLING and churning to the sound of ragtime becoming jazz and the spiritual becoming the blues, as the nation's two busiest train junctions, Chicago and Kansas City, became centers of cultural cross-pollination. While Chicago was larger, Kansas City was freer, because the leaders of the Democratic political machine—still dominated by the Pendergast family, cement magnates in their second generation of controlling the local economy—made it clear they had no intention of enforcing the rules of Prohibition (which went into effect on January 16, 1920) or any other rules they didn't like.

Fearless Freddy Harvey and his teenage bride, Betty, with her trendy flapper haircut and pouty lips, were stars in the new, youth-driven, all-hours social life of Kansas City. They cut a fine figure on any dance floor and held lavish parties. Freddy continued his daredevil exploits in the air and on the polo field—where his achievements, and occasional injuries, always made the papers. And, like everyone else in Kansas City, they might be found, at any time of the day or night, eating breakfast at the Fred Harvey restaurant in Union Station. Since it was open round the clock and was known for the most indulgent comfort food, the restaurant became a center for a diverse group of Kansas Citians whose days and nights ended at different times. Besides regular mealtimes, there were those who came after the theater to end their evenings, and then a younger crowd who came near midnight, their evenings just beginning. While Kansas City's burgeoning jazz and blues clubs—which were spawning the likes of Count Basie—were farther east, in the center of downtown, they were just a streetcar ride away from the place that most people had taken to calling "Harvey's."

If you were a close friend of Freddy and Betty's, you might even qualify to have Harvey's brought to you. Fellow polo player Frank Baker, whose family was powerful in the grain industry, had a bachelor pad downtown where he threw many elaborate dinner parties—all discreetly catered by the Fred Harvey chefs at Union Station. Sometimes the chefs sent live lobsters or fresh mountain trout, prairie chicken or venison, to be prepared in Frank's small kitchen, but often they just cooked all the food at the restaurant and it was delivered to the apartment by car.

SOME OF THE GLAMOUR of the Fred Harvey restaurants—not just in Kansas City, but all along the line—was generated by the more than occasional presence of movie stars dining among the locals. The Santa Fe was the preferred railroad to Hollywood, and had been since the first films were made there in 1910, by New York directors and actors seeking a place to shoot outdoors in the winter. The relationship between Fred Harvey and Hollywood was cemented in 1912, when directors D. W. Griffith and Mack Sennett stopped in Albuquerque on their way home from California, set up shop at the Alvarado, and made two silent pictures there in ten days. Griffith shot an Indian melodrama called *A Pueblo Legend.* Sennett directed his girlfriend, the budding young film comedienne Mabel Normand, in *The Tourists,* a slapstick comedy about sightseeing in which a tourist named Trixie becomes so engrossed with buying pottery at the Indian Building that she misses her train. To kill time, she and some friends visit a pueblo, where the "Big Chief" shows them around until "Mrs. Big Chief" gets jealous, and soon the "Indian Suffragettes" are on the "war-path," brandishing clubs. Trixie hides in an Indian blanket, but eventually she and her friends are chased back to the train, which the Indian "squaws" beat on with their clubs until it pulls away—with Trixie waving her handkerchief, smiling.

Neither picture went on to be taught in film schools. But movie people did get to know Fred Harvey and the Santa Fe, and they all realized the opportunity for cross-promotion. Some actors, directors, and executives preferred to keep a low profile while traveling, but others took full advantage of the exposure. In many ways, the railroad publicity machines were bigger and better established than those of the growing silent-film studios. The Santa Fe wanted to be seen as the railroad to the stars, who were only too happy to benefit from their relentless public relations efforts. So, it was no coincidence that when a well-known actor was riding toward any major Santa Fe city, a remarkably well-informed story about the trip would appear in the local newspaper.

"The biggest thrill I ever had was when William S. Hart, the famous western silent-movie star, came into the dining room," recalled a Harvey Girl from the El Garces in Needles, California. "He sat at one of my tables and when I served him he said, 'I'd like to stick you in my pocket and take you home and let you play with my ponies.' He patted me and left. I looked under the plate after the train had gone and found a silver dollar . . . Sometimes you'd get someone who was needy— Groucho Marx was like that. The coffee wasn't hot enough, the service not enough, nothing pleased him. We'd give those people special attention, but otherwise, everybody was treated the same."

Humorist Will Rogers was a frequent train traveler and a regular at many Harvey restaurants. "All the girls knew who he was and used to go and stand on the porch of the Harvey House to watch him perform in the street," recalls one Harvey Girl posted in Amarillo, Texas. "I became the Harvey Girl he always requested serve him. We became great friends. He'd call me by name when he came into the Amarillo dining room and then he'd say, 'Bring me some of that corn bread and red beans and some of those delicious ham and eggs!' Everybody knew what he wanted; and he'd get it, even at dinner time. He was a great favorite."

In fact, Hollywood columnists would learn to pump Harvey Girls for information about traveling stars. After hearing that Carole Lombard had just said goodbye to Clark Gable at the Santa Fe station in Los Angeles, a reporter asked a busy Harvey Girl to help him out with some fashion details.

"What's that Carole Lombard is wearing so I can tell my wife?" he asked.

"It's a beige dress," she said, hustling to clean away dishes.

"What kind of hat is that?" the reporter wanted to know.

"Listen, big boy," the Harvey Girl shot back. "I've got five hungry men here screaming for food. I'm busy. Get yourself another stylist."

While the motion picture business had been growing for some time, vying with theater and concerts to become the entertainment mainstay in cities large and small, the biggest postwar media explosion was on the airwaves. Commercial radio began to be viable in the early 1920s, which meant that companies were investing in broadcasting and families were buying huge living-room radios.

There was, of course, a Fred Harvey connection to this new business. Byron Harvey's brother-in-law John Daggett became one of the first major stars in radio broadcasting. He was known to listeners as far as KHJ radio's signal would carry—which, on most nights, was all the way to Chicago—as "Uncle John," whose "Children's Hour" was the last thing most kids remembered hearing before falling asleep. He came on at 6:30 p.m. and offered a gentle combination of musicians, actors, and comedy, before reading America's youngsters a bedtime story. Uncle John was also the station manager at KHJ—which was owned by the *Los Angeles Times,* where he was a reporter. The *Times* got into radio to extend the brand into a new electronic medium and reap whatever profits this new technology might be stealing from print.

At the height of his fame, Uncle John, then in his early forties, was married on the radio to a seventeen-year-old whose high school glee club had appeared on his show. His young wife, Marguerite Daggett, became a character on the show, "Pal O'Mine," but their marriage later imploded as famously as it began. During their front-page divorce, Uncle John accused his wife of having an affair with Michael Cudahy—the meatpacking magnate whose family had been friendly with the Harveys for decades—and she claimed he drank, cheated on her, and encouraged her to have sex with other men while he watched because he was too old to satisfy her.

It was the kind of scandal that the Harvey family had always successfully avoided. But for all their serious-mindedness in business, it was impossible to completely dodge the giddy media frivolity of the 1920s. One morning Ford Harvey was appalled to find in his morning mail a clipping from a front-page story in the *Los Angeles Examiner* with the headline "Diamond-Studded Toothbrush Stolen From Harvey's Daughter." The story claimed that "Fred Harvey's daughter" had been robbed while staying at the Plaza Hotel in New York, with bandits making off with $50,000 ($629,000) in jewelry and precious stones—including the bejeweled toothbrush. In fact, the robbed woman wasn't a Harvey at all; she was Kansas City socialite Dorothy Clendening, whom Ford and Judy knew from the country club, along with her husband, a prominent physician and medical writer. According to Ford, her closest connection to the Harveys was that he had called his friend Fred Sterry, who ran the Plaza, to make sure she got a nice room.

"Mrs. Clendening is a very dignified, attractive young matron who has no more idea of 'a diamond-studded toothbrush' than you or I," Ford wrote angrily to his brother, Byron, after seeing the clipping. "Many will form an erroneous and unfavorable opinion of the Fred Harvey family from this . . . [which] demonstrates how helpless we are against the misrepresentations of a newspaper reporter."

FORD WAS NO HAPPIER with the ongoing national coverage of the company's bizarre battle with an Oklahoma state official who decided that the long-standing policy of requiring men to wear jackets in Fred Harvey dining rooms was actually un-American—and had to be stopped. Campbell Russell, the excitable chairman of the state's corporation commission, went to the Harvey eating house in Purcell for dinner one hot August night, removed his jacket, and was stunned when the maître d' told him he needed to put it back on—or take his meal in the lunchroom, where the same food could be had à la carte in more casual surroundings. Russell refused to put on his jacket, so he was refused service.

Several days later, he called a public hearing of his commission—which controlled business practices in the state—to take sworn testimony on the coat rule, which had been in place, in states with climates as warm as Oklahoma, as far back as the 1880s, long before Fred Harvey eating houses even had electric fans. Besides calling in various Oklahomans for their opinions, the commission compelled representatives of the Santa Fe and Fred Harvey to come to Oklahoma City and testify. Ford sent Freddy to explain why the company had the rule, and how they provided loaner jackets free of charge to any man who didn't have one. The Santa Fe sent a vice president who challenged the commission's jurisdiction in the matter.

A week after the hearing, Campbell's commission declared that men absolutely *could* dine in Harvey eating houses in Oklahoma without jackets. Ford's lawyers immediately challenged the ruling in court.

Naturally, newspapers and radio commentators across the country had a field day.

Among the critics of the Fred Harvey jacket rule, the *Washington Post* called it "discrimination," and the *Chicago Tribune* said it exemplified the double standard of fashion between the sexes: "Women do as they please . . . [while] American men are the most conventionalized and most timid wearers of clothes in the world . . . [but] a man has not lost any of his citizenship rights if he has removed his coat." One Oklahoma paper went so far as to call the rule a conspiracy of "snobbery from England [against] the low brows of Oklahoma" and a " 'Jim Crow law' . . . aimed at whites only."

But many papers lambasted Campbell Russell for his "ruthless warfare" against the very "conventions of society." As one small-town editor said, it was only a matter of time before men would demand to dine without shoes and want to "take all the dogs and oxen in, too."

More amazing than the national outcry was just how long Ford Harvey had to fight in court over the jacket rule. The case dragged on for three years in the Oklahoma legal system, eventually ending up on the docket of the exasperated state supreme court. During the same week that a judge in Chicago was making legal history by deciding the sentences for Leopold and Loeb—whose lawyer, Clarence Darrow, had turned their sensationalized murder trial into a popular referendum on capital punishment—Oklahoma's chief justice, Neil McNeill, and his colleagues were stuck wrestling with the issue of whether men should wear coats in the dining room.

In a unanimous decision, the supreme court supported the Fred Harvey jacket rule:

> Unlike the lower animals, we all demand the maintenance of some style and fashion in the dining-room. Civilized society has developed the masculine attire from the breech-clout to the coat and trousers. Always a part of the masculine garb . . . [the jacket] is worn as an adornment to satisfy the conventions of society rather than for bodily comfort and protection . . . these conventions of society cannot be entirely ignored, without disastrous results . . . Man's coat is usually the cleanest of his garments, and the fact that he is required to wear a coat serves notice that decorum is expected and creates a wholesome psychological effect.

ACTUALLY, THE OKLAHOMA jacket battle was the least of Ford Harvey's problems with government regulation. Like everyone else in the restaurant and hotel business, he was searching for a way to replace the profits lost to Prohibition. Fred Harvey was not quite as dependent on liquor sales as other establishments. The company had started in Kansas—which had long been one of the drier states in the country, an epicenter in the national temperance movement, and the home of anti-liquor crusader Carry Nation—and had operated under earlier statewide Prohibition laws in Kansas and Oklahoma for years. In fact, Fred Harvey had always been positioned as a more family-friendly alternative to saloons.

Nonetheless, most of the Fred Harvey hotels and eating houses had featured extensive wine selections, as well as private-label Scotch imported from Ainslie & Heilbron and a private-label whiskey made by Old Forester in Louisville—all high-profit items. And nobody had expected Prohibition to remain in place for so long, or to be prosecuted so vigorously all across the country. Regular raids in major cities had led to the closing of some of the nation's most famous restaurants and hotels, especially when enforcement picked up on New Year's Eve 1923. Within the next six months, New Yorkers watched in shock as dozens of popular eateries were forced out of business, including Shanley's, Murray's Roman Gardens, and the Knickerbocker Grill. Eventually, even historic Delmonico's closed, after nearly a century as New York's best-known restaurant.

Many restaurants and hotels around the country tried to remain quietly "wet," by sneaking wine or spirits to customers. The most famous—and successful—was probably "21" in New York, which maintained not only a hidden wine cellar but an entire underground lounge for drinking. But Fred Harvey could not afford to take such risks.

Even before Prohibition, Fred Harvey was the only food-service company in the country being regulated by the federal government. It was under the constant scrutiny of federal regulators at the Interstate Commerce Commission, and Fred Harvey contracts at the Grand Canyon were entirely dependent on the good graces of the Department of the Interior. The company's considerable stock of wine and spirits had to be locked away or sold off. While hotel patrons surely overtipped bellmen to have them find liquor they might enjoy in the privacy of their rooms, Fred Harvey establishments could never have secret basement lounges. There was too much at stake.

So Ford tried to grow his business in different, nonalcoholic ways. He made a deal to run all the restaurants and retail spaces in the new Chicago Union Station—a handsome classical building with a stunning twenty-thousand-foot, five-story-high Beaux Arts Great Hall. When the new Chicago station opened in 1925, it featured a Fred Harvey drugstore and soda fountain, a perfumery, a toy store, a barbershop, a beauty salon, a twenty-four-hour bookstore, and no fewer than eight Fred Harvey eateries, from a huge formal dining room to a small sandwich-making operation next to the taxi stand for cabbies.

With its successes in St. Louis, Kansas City, and Chicago, Fred Harvey was sought out by other cities planning to build union stations. And not just traditional Santa Fe railroad cities. Ford was bidding on contracts for the new stations being planned in Los Angeles and Dallas, and was also considering the first major Fred Harvey operation east of the Mississippi, in Cleveland.

PROHIBITION ALSO FOSTERED the growth of other restaurants, which now had to innovate with food because they couldn't make money on liquor. Much of the growth was in chains, every one of which based its business on the models created by Fred Harvey. The first generation of largely self-service eateries, which began opening in major cities at the turn of the century—especially the Childs cafeterias and the Horn & Hardart automats—were now substantial chains in many eastern cities and widely copied. Major cities also had take-out bakeries for breads and dessert items once made mostly at home— which the Fred Harvey restaurants had always done for their local customers—and even catering shops that offered prepared entrées for takeout or delivery. As early as 1902, Levy's restaurant in Los Angeles was running this ad in the *L.A. Times*: "They're coming tonight and I haven't ordered a blessed thing for dinner. Why, of course, how absurd. I'll just order from LEVY'S what I want. What a relief. Telephone us when your friends drop in unexpectedly. We deliver direct from kitchen to table. Try our lucky number Main 2184."

By the 1920s, however, Americans were seeing the first wave of sit-down fast-food shops featuring signature hamburgers and frankfurters, sodas and ice cream. The first major hamburger chain was White Castle, which began in 1921 with four locations in Wichita, Kansas—where it competed with the Harvey House—and then spread into other Fred Harvey strongholds, Kansas City and St. Louis, before expanding into Minneapolis and many other Midwestern cities. The small, extremely shiny White Castles served small tasty burgers, and were able to overcome a long-held public fear of beef—left over from the Chicago meatpacking scandals—by stressing cleanliness (the interiors looked like gleaming white tile bathrooms) and even hiring young men to dress up as doctors and sit at the counters eating enthusiastically.

White Castle and the A&W Root Beer drive-ins (which started in Sacramento at around the same time) were among the first of the classic American fast-food franchise operations. It was a new and exciting business model that Fred Harvey had eschewed—although Ford was constantly getting offers to try it. The franchise chains expanded by selling local entrepreneurs the plans to open a look-alike facility of their own, and making them sign contracts to purchase signature foods. Some people bought multiple franchises; others used one to learn the business and then went out on their own. (The Marriott hotel chain, for example, had its origins in an A&W Root Beer stand that J. Willard Marriott and his wife started in Washington, D.C., in the 1920s, leading them to create their own drive-in company, The Hot Shoppes, and then hotels.)

Most of these new chains did not have the same level of service or food quality as the Harvey Houses—and their owners appreciated perhaps more than anyone the ability of Ford's restaurants to prepare and serve entire full-course meals in twenty minutes. But the burger joints and soda shops were spreading everywhere as America became a faster-food nation.

AS THE COMPANY GREW—it now had seven thousand employees in more than eighty cities—Ford was anxious to find a project to get Freddy more involved in the family business. Ford and his brother-in-law John Huckel were now well into their fifties, and Dave Benjamin was in his sixties and starting to spend more time on family and community matters.

In 1923, Dave's two brothers died within six months of each other. Harry, with whom he had been working at Fred Harvey every day for over thirty years, suffered a sudden fatal heart attack. Then Dave lost his brother Alfred, who had become one of the most widely admired men in Kansas City, the selfless leader of the city's first major Jewish philanthropic organization, United Jewish Charities, and a bridge between the fund-raising efforts of other religions. (Judy Harvey was often on the Catholic side of that bridge.) A rabbi and a Catholic priest presided at Alfred's funeral, and outside Temple B'nai Jehudah a mourner was overheard saying, "I would rather be Alfred Benjamin than anyone I know." Dave felt it was his responsibility to try to take Alfred's place in the philanthropic community, so he was devoting more time to good works.

Now approaching thirty, Freddy remained a young, restless soul, still too distractible and reckless for his father's comfort. When Ford got off the train in a Harvey town, he always went to the eating house first, just as his father had before him. But not Freddy: When his train pulled in, he was more likely to head off to the local airfield, hoping there might be a plane available for him to fly. He claimed he could get a better feel for a city by seeing it from the air. But his father knew there was only one way to get a feel for a city: You inspected the Fred Harvey kitchen, the dining room, the hotel lobby, you talked to the managers, the Harvey Girls, the maids. Flying, polo, fishing, hiking, all of Freddy's passions—these were the things you did to relax only *after* business had been conducted.

It was time for Freddy to grow up already. Ford loved his younger brother, Byron, who had matured into a charming and temperate husband, father, and socialite and was doing perfectly well in Chicago overseeing the dining car business. He even appreciated his brother's somewhat quixotic desire to design his own dining cars: Byron had received a patent for a diner car with the kitchen all the way at one end, instead of in the middle, which improved efficiency, but allowed passengers to enter only from one end. When the car debuted, it was heralded as the first new patent in dining car design since George Pullman's in 1865. Byron had a scale model of it made for his desk.

But, patent or no patent, Ford had no intention of ever letting his brother, Byron, run or own a controlling interest in the company. He was determined that his son, Freddy, would be the next Fred Harvey.

CHAPTER 31

SANTA FATED

🔲

I F FREDDY WAS EVER GOING TO SUCCEED IN THE FAMILY BUSI- ness, he needed his own Grand Canyon. It had to be a venture that meant as much to him as flying, with as much potential for the future of the company as El Tovar. And there was really only one place in the Southwest so magnetic and full of possibilities, yet largely unexplored and unexploited by Fred Harvey and the AT&SF. That was Santa Fe itself, which the railroad had left for dead in the 1880s when it replaced the old Santa Fe Trail but was still, to many, the most vibrant and inspiring town in the West.

Santa Fe had been the Harvey family's favorite place in the Southwest for decades, ever since Sally first took Ford and Minnie there as children. While the Grand Canyon was a glorious place to visit and gape, Santa Fe was a heavenly municipality where people lived and worked amid the grandeur of the big sky and the endless desert, the Indian and Mexican cultures and commerce infusing everyday existence. The oldest colonized city in North America, settled several years before the Pilgrims arrived at Plymouth Rock, Santa Fe had been a major commercial center for centuries, the hub for trade between Mexico and America. When the railroad bypassed it in 1880, Santa Fe was forced to do what so many American cities would attempt a century later after losing their manufacturing base—it reinvented itself as a place to visit, a getaway, an escape. It was becoming a haven for health seekers, artists, writers, archaeology buffs, nonpracticing cowboys and cowgirls, and, of course, tourists. Some saw it as a little Paris, a place where the light was also "just different"—but in a distinctly American way. In fact, as a response to the City Beautiful movement that was sweeping

America's urban areas, Santa Fe created its own nickname: "The City Different."

Santa Fe, more than any other place in the Southwest, already offered what the Grand Canyon had lacked: "something conventional," in Ford's words, for tourists to do. It had wonderful shopping, restaurants, and galleries in its small, soulful adobe downtown—which was kept soulful and adobe by a 1912 city plan urging architects to employ the Pueblo Revival and Territorial styles exclusively, so the city would always appear unified and in-scale. And every September the city celebrated Santa Fe Fiesta, which dated back to the 1700s and almost petered out in the late 1800s, but was reinvigorated after the world war—largely at the instigation of archaeologist Edgar Hewett, who had learned a few things about ethnological showmanship while working with Herman Schweizer, Mary Colter, and John Huckel at the San Diego world's fair in 1915. Hewett helped reinvent the Fiesta as a three-day celebration, centered around each of the major ethnic groups in New Mexico, with parades, street fairs, concerts, and art shows.

Fred Harvey had been booking side trips to Santa Fe for railroad passengers for over forty years, through all these changes. But while Ford and Minnie and their families visited often and had friends there, Santa Fe was, in many ways, the only place in the Southwest where they were still guests. All that was now about to change.

Ford had decided it was high time to open a hotel in Santa Fe. While it was a great opportunity for his son to have a pet project that didn't require being airborne, he had been persuaded to expand into Santa Fe by someone else: a rising star in the company, Major R. Hunter Clarkson. One of Ford's most flamboyant and opinionated managers in the Southwest, Hunter Clarkson was a decorated British officer—equally at home in a uniform or a kilt—who had turned his job as transportation manager at the Grand Canyon into a little empire. He was shuttling more than fifty thousand visitors a year around the canyon with military precision, but he had a dream. In his dream, there were fleets of automobiles and buses—"Harveycars" and "Harveycoaches"—taking tourists on adventures all across the Southwest. Not for a few hours like at the canyon, but for days, even weeks. They would go to the pueblos, they would watch the snake dances, they would see *real* Indians, not just Harvey House Indians. They would have unique American travel experiences, not unlike the one that had galvanized Ford in 1901.

In the West, tourists were commonly referred to by locals as "dudes." Hunter Clarkson believed that Fred Harvey could corner the entire dude market.

He came up with a catchy name for his scheme, the "Indian Detours," and even sought backing outside of Fred Harvey. He was married to the daughter of a Santa Fe vice president, and his plan also had the support of Santa Fe railroad advertising director Roger Birdseye, who at the time was the best-known member of the Birdseye family. (His brother Clarence had recently developed the first practical process for freezing food.) His plan was to start the auto tours in New Mexico with the hope of eventually extending them all the way across Arizona to the Grand Canyon. Santa Fe, and its scenic sister city to the north, Taos, were situated right in between the two largest Fred Harvey hotels in New Mexico—the Castañeda in Las Vegas and the Alvarado in Albuquerque—which made the "City Different" a perfect center point and staging area.

Just as Ford had once sent Minnie and John Huckel to Gallup to brainstorm the Indian curio business, he dispatched his son to Santa Fe, where he was to shop for a suitable hotel. Freddy found a property just off the city's main plaza, on the historic site of the old Exchange Hotel—the actual end of the old Santa Fe Trail. A relatively new hotel had been built on the site, but its investors had already run out of money.

Ford arranged for the railroad to buy the hotel, and it was quickly overhauled to make it sufficiently Harvey-worthy for the 1926 tourist season: New staff was brought in from other Harvey locations, the dining rooms got new linens, silver, and stemware, every surface was repainted. The only thing they kept was the name: La Fonda.

In addition to taking over the hotel, Fred Harvey ordered a large fleet of cars and buses that were so lavishly appointed they were referred to as "Pullmans on wheels." Freddy and Hunter Clarkson also arranged to buy out one of Santa Fe's leading tour operators, Erna Fergusson, the energetic docent of Indian country.

Besides her passion and knowledge, Fergusson had the only all-female tour guide staff in town. They became the prototypes of a new kind of Harvey Girl: the "Indian Detours Courier." The Couriers were expected to be much better educated and more "refined" than Harvey Girls—bright, attractive college students, preferably bilingual in Spanish and at least one other idiom. They were given an enormous amount of historical material to memorize, from scripts and manuals created by the company. Erna Fergusson did much of the writing (and later became a well-known author of lively travel books for Knopf), but the company brought in other writers. The aging Southwest advocate Charles Lummis wrote some of the Courier materials, repurposing old stories from his magazines. Mary Colter and Herman Schweizer also created some of the manuals, bringing the amassed knowledge of over twenty years in the Fred Harvey Indian Department.

While the inaugural team of twenty Couriers faithfully memorized all the material in the manuals during their monthlong training, they did stage a revolt against the outfits chosen for them: men's shirts, riding breeches, high-laced boots, and straight-brimmed hats. The college girls urged the company to costume them in more stylishly feminine attire, and new uniforms were quickly tailored in Albuquerque. They featured velveteen blouses in jewel colors and elaborate squash-blossom necklaces; the skirts were dark with a walking pleat, accented with a silver concha belt, and they could wear either walking shoes or boots. There was also a soft-brimmed cloche hat with a silver thunderbird symbol—a copy of an image Herman Schweizer had once sketched at an Indian ruin. Except for the hat, the Courier uniform quickly became a look that tourists wanted to emulate, and to this day many female visitors to Santa Fe are delighted to return home with their own updated version of this outfit.

The first group of detourists arrived on May 15, 1926. An editorial in the Albuquerque paper optimistically predicted that the Indian Detours would bring fifty thousand visitors a year to the state's three major cities—which was almost as many people as lived in those cities combined.

FORD'S WIFE, JUDY, was preparing for her annual midsummer trip to the West, accompanied, as usual, by Kitty and Mary Perkins. While their excursions always ended at the family home in California, on the way they liked to find new places to explore and shop. Since the debut season of the Indian Detours was already in full swing, they decided to visit Santa Fe and do some private detouring of their own.

Before departing on July 14, Judy Harvey did what she had always done before leaving town—she went to Mass and received Communion. Afterward, she visited the bishop of Kansas City, Thomas Lillis, in his residence to say goodbye for the summer. Bishop Lillis was pleased that she was so excited about her trip, but as always he looked forward to her return. With her generous donations of time, money, social networking, and energy, she made his life, and the life of Kansas City, much easier.

The three women left Kansas City in a private Santa Fe railcar, which they rode to Trinidad, Colorado, where they were met at the Fred Harvey hotel, the Cardenas, by one of the plush new Harveycars and a private driver. They drove over the Raton Pass and then enjoyed a scenic route through northern New Mexico that train travelers never saw, hugging the base of the majestic Sangre de Cristo Mountains until reaching Taos Pueblo. From there, they drove down a breathtaking mountain pass—now called the Taos High Road, but back then the *only* road. When they reached downtown Santa Fe, an entire team of La Fonda bellmen were bucking for the privilege of carrying the bags of the boss's family.

The next morning, the Judy Harvey party was properly fussed over during breakfast at La Fonda before riding, with their own private driver and Detours Courier, about forty miles to the Santa Clara Pueblo to visit the Puye Cliff Dwellings. As a younger woman, Judy had taken vigorous trips with her children, including a camping trip into the Grand Canyon with Kitty and a group of her friends not long before the war. At fifty-nine, however, she was no longer in good enough shape to keep up with her athletic daughter. To reach the Puye Cliff Dwellings—seven hundred roomy niches carved into a two-hundred-foot-high volcanic ridge—visitors had to walk up a steep, rough trail. Judy gamely tried to keep pace with Kitty and Mary. But then she started to feel faint.

The next thing Kitty knew, her mother was having a massive stroke. They were hours away from medical care.

As soon as Ford heard the news, he summoned the family physician, and they boarded a private car on the next Santa Fe train. By the time they reached La Fonda on Tuesday morning, Freddy had already arrived and was with Kitty at their mother's bedside. Judy was being treated with stimulants in a desperate attempt to bring her back to consciousness, but nothing helped. By Wednesday evening, her kidneys were failing. After staying up with her all through the night, Ford emerged from the hotel suite bleary-eyed at 5:30 a.m. with the painful news that his wife of thirty-eight years had died.

Word spread rapidly through La Fonda as well as in the town, where the Harvey family had many friends. Everywhere they went, in the hotel or on the street, someone approached to express sympathy. The railroad arranged for two special cars to carry the body and the mourning family back to Kansas City as quickly as possible. Bishop Lillis issued a heartfelt statement about his friend, whose faith "was as simple as that of a child." He could not believe that after seeing her just a week before, when she appeared to be in the best of health, he was now writing her eulogy.

Three days later, Judy's casket was carried into St. James Roman Catholic Church, escorted by a Girl Scout "guard of honor" made up of representatives from all the various troops across the city that she had supported. Bishop Lillis gave a moving eulogy, mirroring the editorial about her that appeared in the *Kansas City Star*.

"Seldom has a woman not in public life had so wide an acquaintance and so broad an influence," the paper wrote, and then quoted Robert Louis Stevenson: "So long as we love, we serve; so long as we are loved by others, I would almost say we are indispensable."

Ford was beside himself with grief. His friends knew that while he was stoic and patient in business matters, he didn't believe in hiding his emotions concerning death. They remembered how long and intensely he had grieved for his father, and later his mother. Given how close he was to Judy, and how unexpectedly she had been taken, there was no telling how long he would mourn.

THE INDIAN DETOURS became so popular so quickly that La Fonda's fifty-five rooms were not sufficient. The overflow of guests were booked into other downtown hotels, although some spent the night in nearby Lamy, where Fred Harvey had a small depot hotel, El Ortiz. When that filled up, the railroad would arrange for multiple Pullman cars to be parked at Lamy, as an expandable trackside hotel with all the amenities.

Mary Colter was told to start planning for a dramatic expansion of La Fonda. Besides the Indian Detourists arriving by train, Ford believed the hotel would soon need to accommodate a new and growing breed of motoring tourists.

They would arrive on U.S. Route 66, the government's first transcontinental "highway," which became the most popular and romanticized route from Chicago to Los Angeles, the "Mother Road" for exploring and traversing the American West. Route 66 officially opened only six months after the Indian Detours, on November 11, 1926 (along with the rest of the fledgling federal highway system). The largely unpaved road went from Chicago to St. Louis, then southwest into Oklahoma and northern Texas, crossing into New Mexico near Tucumcari. From there, it pretty much followed alongside the Santa Fe tracks all the way to California, with one major deviation. Unlike the railroad, Route 66 came directly into downtown Santa Fe, just as the original Santa Fe Trail had. Motorists pulling off Route 66 found themselves less than a block from the entrance to La Fonda.

CHAPTER 32

A WONDERFUL LIVE TOY
TO PLAY WITH

AFTER THAT SUCCESSFUL FIRST SUMMER OF THE INDIAN DE-
tours, both Fred Harvey and the Santa Fe railroad began investing
even more heavily in southwestern tourism. They also dramatically increased the use of Indian imagery to brand their companies—which
they had been doing piecemeal for many years, ever since railroad advertising manager William Haskell Simpson started a nationally distributed Santa Fe Railway calendar in 1907, featuring original paintings
and drawings of Native scenes. An increasing number of top artists in
Santa Fe and Taos—many of them transplanted realists from New
York's Ashcan School who wanted to paint something other than ash
cans and gritty urban scenes—supported themselves in their cowboy
Bohemia by doing illustrations for magazines, the railroad, and Fred
Harvey.

In the fall of 1926, the Santa Fe started a faster daily train service
that cut the ride between Chicago and Los Angeles by more than five
hours, to just under sixty-three hours total—"only two business days."
Previous high-end trains always used names employing words such as
"special" or "limited," but this new train was simply called "the Chief,"
and all its advertising featured a stylized drawing of a powerful, looming Indian leader.

For the inaugural run of the Chief, the cast of the new MGM
Western *War Paint* rode between Chicago and Los Angeles in costume. While the Union Pacific and the Southern Pacific started competing fast train service the same day, their ceremonies and photo ops
featured only executives and starlets christening engines with cham-

pagne bottles. (During Prohibition, champagne bottles could be broken, as long as nobody drank.) The Santa Fe ceremony featured young Chief Yowlachie, one of the stars of *War Paint,* in full headdress.

Even as they agreed to let the railroad use them as promotional tools, the professional Indians were debating the dilemmas of marketing "noble savagery." The performers who participated in the debut of the Chief were the same ones trying to organize Indians in Hollywood to lobby for fairer treatment and better parts. They didn't want to be stereotyped—but if this was going to happen anyway, they wanted to at least make certain that all Indian roles were played by actual Indians. Thirty tribes with members in the movies—bolstered by the dozens of Indians brought in from Wyoming to make *War Paint*—came together to form a loose Native actors' union, the "War Paint Club." Chief Yowlachie was a leader of the group and performed at its first public fund-raiser: a "pow-wow" held on the set of the film.

This love/hate relationship with the marketing of Indian imagery and rituals extended to the artists who painted the pictures, and even to the tourists. While outsiders had been visiting Indian pueblos for decades, the runaway success of the Indian Detours—and the omnipresent advertising for the auto tours—brought many more people to see the snake dances and buy curios, and it became a lightning rod for national attention to the issue of exploitation. This was exacerbated by all the artists and writers drawn to Santa Fe and Taos, who had their own mixed feelings about being ethnological tourists.

Author D. H. Lawrence was a perfect example. Spirited to New Mexico in the mid-1920s by Mabel Dodge, the wealthy artist collector who moved her high-society salon from Greenwich Village to Taos, Lawrence went to see the snake dances like everyone else. He promptly wrote a magazine essay about how horribly exploitative it was: "The Southwest is the great playground of the white American . . . [and] the Indian, with his long hair and his bits of pottery and blankets and clumsy home-made trinkets, he's a wonderful live toy to play with. More fun than keeping rabbits, and just as harmless." Then, a week later, Lawrence wrote another, better-known essay about the beauty and profundity of the very same dance. It was the quintessential experience of the self-loathing tourist—fascinated and repelled by the pueblo dances and the way they were marketed, outraged by tourism without really acknowledging that he, too, was a tourist.

As more creative people came to visit Santa Fe and Taos, or to live there, these mixed feelings received more artistic and well-written expression—especially after the 1927 publication of novelist Willa Cather's *Death Comes for the Archbishop*, which was set in Santa Fe, invoked many of her experiences there, and made many Americans want to visit. (Georgia O'Keeffe arrived not long after and quickly became part of the artistic and communal life of the area: She socialized with the Harveys in Santa Fe, and her picture appears in family photo albums from that time.) But there were an equal number of well-known detractors who felt the Indian Detours were exploiting, and possibly even destroying, the "last vestiges" of the "real America" they were selling.

Ashcan School painter John Sloan did a wickedly satirical etching after his detour, depicting eight earnest Indians trying to dance surrounded by a dozen big Harvey buses and hundreds of distracted, well-dressed tourists, some lined up at a nearby Harvey buffet.

The great cartoonist W. E. Hill made one of his beloved full-page illustrated journals for the *Chicago Tribune* titled "The Great Southwest." Under his drawing of a fetching Courier guide, he wrote:

> Indian detour couriers are smart girls. A Girl guide taking a party of inquisitive tourists on a sightseeing trip must have her geology, zoology and languages right at her tongue's end. She must know enough about geological formation to be able to point and say, "Look! That's a mountain." And she must have a smattering of Mexican and Spanish so that when visiting an Indian pueblo, she will be able to say, "Why, Manuelito, aren't you ashamed to charge two dollars for that!"

Under a drawing of well-dressed society ladies exploring cliff dwellings near Santa Fe, he wrote:

> Mrs. Mosher and Mrs. Haverstraw are discussing a certain problem that sooner or later a tourist taking the Indian detour trip just has to face. "What," asks Mrs. Mosher, coming up from the deserted kiva, "are you going to do about the courier girl when you leave? She's a college graduate, you know, and I should hate to offend her by offering her money. Besides, this courier tells me she's cousin to an Earl!"

And under a drawing of a very uncomfortable little Indian girl, he wrote, "Indian child being coaxed, to no avail, by a lady tourist who wants a snapshot."

But, love them or hate them, the Indian Detours quickly became a popular cultural touchstone, the closest thing America had to Disneyland in the 1920s. Even though they were still a relatively small part of Ford's empire—and, while successful, still not all that profitable—they brought a disproportionate amount of attention to the entire Fred Harvey experience. A flurry of well-known America writers chimed in on their Harvey House exploits. F. Scott Fitzgerald complained in his 1927 journal, "It takes so long to get to California, and there were so many nickel handles, gadgets to avoid, buttons to evoke, and such a lot of newness, and too much of Fred Harvey so when one of us thought we had appendicitus [sic] we got out at El Paso."

Humorist Will Rogers, on the other hand, said he couldn't get enough of Harvey food. In his syndicated "daily telegram," he wrote:

> Wild buffalo fed the early traveler in the West and for doing so they put his picture on a nickel.
>
> Well, Fred Harvey took up where the buffalo left off.
>
> For what he has done for the traveler one of his waitress's pictures (with an arm load of delicious ham and eggs) should be placed on both sides of every dime. He has kept the West in food—and wives.

During this same year, the young food writer M. F. K. Fisher was having a transformative experience in a Fred Harvey dining car during her first-ever train ride. She was nineteen at the time, traveling on the Chief with her beloved Uncle Evans, and she would later claim her meals on the trip triggered the first stirrings of her career as America's premier culinary scribe. Uncle Evans, who rode the Santa Fe often, was a lifelong Fred Harvey fan. "The only test of a good breakfast place is its baked apple," he told his niece. "The Harvey girls never fail me." She went on to describe the experience:

> Uncle Evans knew where to ask the dining-car steward to put things like live trout, venison, fresh corn, melons. They were served to him at our twinkling, snowy little table in the restaurant car, at noon and at night, and I paddled along happily in the

small sensual spree my uncle always made of his routine travelings. I probably heard and felt and tasted more than either of us could be aware of.

One time when he looked at me over his menu and asked me whether I would like something like a fresh mushroom omelet or one with wild asparagus, and I mumbled in my shy ignorance that I really did not care, he put down the big information sheet and for one of the few times in my life with him, he spoke a little sharply. He said, "You should never say that again, dear girl. It is stupid, which you are not. It implies that the attentions of your host are basically wasted on you. So make up your mind, before you open your mouth. Let him believe, even if it is a lie, that you would infinitely prefer the exotic wild asparagus to the banal mushrooms, or vice versa. Let him feel that it matters to you . . . and even that *he* does!

"All this," my uncle added gently, "may someday teach you about the art of seduction, as well as the more important art of knowing yourself." Then he turned to the waiter and ordered two wild asparagus omelets. I wanted for a minute, I still remember, to leave the dining car and weep a little in the sooty ladies' room, but instead I stayed there and suddenly felt more secure and much wiser—always a heady experience but especially so at nineteen. And I don't believe that since then I have ever said, "I don't care," when I am offered a choice of any kind of food and drink. As Uncle Evans pointed out to me, I either care or I'm a dolt, and dolts should not consort with caring people.

CHAPTER 33

POISED FOR TAKEOFF

As MUCH AS YOUNG FREDDY HARVEY WAS EXCITED ABOUT HIS role in the company's Santa Fe expansion, his head was still in the clouds. While Ford kept urging him to cut back on his flying—wasn't polo dangerous enough?—Freddy kept telling his father that America's future was in aviation. In fact, a proper airport was being built in Kansas City—right in town, not far from Union Station. He would be able to take off whenever he wanted.

By the spring of 1927, Freddy's obsession with planes no longer seemed so unusual. All over America, people were becoming fascinated with aviation as pilots announced they intended to fly across the Atlantic and finally claim the Orteig Prize. Back in 1919, Raymond Orteig, a Frenchman who owned two major hotels in New York, offered $25,000 ($311,131) to anyone who could fly nonstop between New York and Paris. A pair of flyers was poised to try the flight from France: socialite Captain Charles Nungesser, a highly decorated World War I flyer whose many broken bones were rumored to have been replaced with platinum, along with his one-eyed navigator, Lieutenant François Coli. There were three other American pilots jockeying for the prize. Two were similarly well-financed war heroes; the third was a bold young mail-plane pilot from St. Louis named Charles Lindbergh.

Freddy knew Lindbergh from the air corps—the young flyer had attended a two-week reserve officers camp in Kansas City in 1925, where he impressed Harvey and his fellow aviators by flying brilliantly and single-mindedly, refusing to drink, smoke, or even joke around with the others. Freddy had also known Lindbergh's backers for years—they were the wealthy members of the flying club in St. Louis, the closest major club to his own group in Kansas City. Lindbergh had been giving flying lessons to prominent St. Louis banker Harry Knight, who in exchange helped him put together a syndicate to raise the money to build a new plane for him—the *Spirit of St. Louis*. Their hope was that if Lindbergh made it across the Atlantic alive, his flight would bring attention to aviation in their hometown.

St. Louis was desperately in need of some good news. Like many cities along the Mississippi, it had been ravaged by the monumental flood that spring, which broke 145 levees between Missouri and Louisiana and became one of the worst natural disasters in the country's history. More than twenty-six thousand square miles of land were flooded, killing 246 people and displacing 600,000 more, many of whom had to live in squalor in refugee camps; 41,487 buildings were destroyed, 162,017 homes flooded, and over $100 million ($1.2 billion) in crops and farm animals were lost. The Mississippi Delta needed *something* to boost its spirits.

As Lindbergh and his two American rivals prepared their planes on Long Island in early May, word came from France that Nungesser and Coli were already airborne. Like all aviators, Freddy was riveted to the front-page coverage of the flight, which began gleefully but soon turned tragic when the French plane vanished. It was never heard from again, and no wreckage was ever found.

Lindbergh, undeterred, waited only for the weather to clear, and at 7:52 on Friday morning, May 20, 1927, he took off. With nothing for company but four sandwiches and two canteens of water, he flew thirty-five hundred miles, without stopping, in just under thirty-four hours. When he touched down at Le Bourget field in Paris, more than a hundred thousand cheering people were waiting there to greet him.

Charles Lindbergh became the biggest overnight celebrity the world had ever known. His fame literally redefined fame. *Time* magazine invented its "Man of the Year" cover feature just to honor him.

To capitalize on that fame—and use it to further the cause of aviation—Lindbergh and his plane were immediately sent on a propeller-stop tour of every state in the Union, underwritten by Harry Guggenheim, the thirty-seven-year-old heir to the family mining and smelting fortune. Like Freddy, Guggenheim became obsessed with planes while flying in the war, later convincing his father to donate $3 million ($36 million) of the family's riches to create a fund for the promotion of aeronautics. In three months, Lindbergh flew the *Spirit of*

St. Louis to over ninety American cities. He delivered nearly 150 speeches, rode in some thirteen hundred miles of parades, and took dozens of rich and influential people on plane rides, including Henry Ford, Will Rogers, and pretty much any celebrity, businessman, or government official considered important for the future of air travel.

Freddy Harvey was one of those influential passengers. In April 1928, Lindbergh came to Los Angeles to test a new four-seat plane that the Lockheed company had designed for delivering airmail. (Even though it was still unclear how passenger service might work in planes, the air transport business was already soaring.) Lindbergh met in California with his St. Louis friend and backer, Harry Knight, and they invited Freddy along for the test ride. Since the plane was brand-new, it was suggested that they wear parachutes just in case. The two passengers strapped on their chutes; Lindbergh had to be talked into it. They took off, ascended sharply, came down for a bouncy landing, and then took off again, buzzing the airfield before landing. Afterward, the three of them sat in the plane for a long time, talking about how it handled, before adjourning to a lunch stand where they had sandwiches with Lockheed executives and swapped aviation gossip.

After lunch, Lindbergh flew Freddy and Harry Knight from Los Angeles to Carpinteria Air Field near Santa Barbara, where they were met by a flock of Montecito debutantes, all of whom wanted to ride with "Lucky Lindy." He squired them, three at a time, in the new plane. "Thirty-Six Girls Bragging of Air Trips," read one of the *Los Angeles Times* headlines the next day.

For Freddy, however, the trip was both pleasure and business. Knight's brokerage firm in St. Louis was assembling a group to start the nation's first cross-country air passenger service. Since passenger planes couldn't fly in the dark—they had no lights, nor did the airfields—there was only one way to use the power of flight to speed up travel from coast to coast. The planes would fly as far as they could during daytime, and the passengers would travel by train at night, to be picked up the next morning by yet another plane. This way, the trip from New York to Los Angeles could be accomplished in just two days, instead of the three required by train—but it also would require the partnership of railroads to succeed.

A month after Freddy flew with Lindbergh, the *Wall Street Journal* announced the creation of Transcontinental Air Transport (TAT), which brought together many of the biggest names in transportation and finance. The plane business was represented not only by the Wright Brothers and Glenn Curtiss but by Henry Ford, since Ford Motors was now also in the aircraft-engine business. The brokers were led by Blair & Company, the Wall Street firm that handled much of the Rockefellers' money.

There were only two rail industry partners in the venture. One was the mighty Pennsylvania Railroad, which bought 20 percent of the company. The other was Fred Harvey—both the company and Freddy personally. While the Santa Fe agreed to be the rail line for TAT passengers in the West, its executives felt it would be a conflict of interest to invest in an alternative form of transportation. Freddy, of course, couldn't *wait* to be a major player in the airline business. He wanted the first meals served in the air to be Fred Harvey meals. He wanted the first servers on planes to be Harvey Girls.

The company raised some $5 million ($63 million) in start-up capital from its founding partners. It is unclear whether Freddy convinced his father to put up company money for this investment or used his own funds, since he had recently inherited more than $100,000 ($1.2 million) from his mother's estate. But according to the *Wall Street Journal* announcement of the deal, there were only two private investors in the group that bought the original stock. One was railroad magnate William Vanderbilt. The other was Freddy Harvey.

A few days later, Charles Lindbergh announced he had joined the company and would map out the route for the fourteen-passenger Transcontinental Air Transport planes. From that moment on, few used the company's cumbersome moniker. They just called it "the Lindy Line."

"Air travel in the U.S. is soon to emerge from the spasmodic era of the thermos bottle, the cheese sandwich and the leather jacket," *Time* magazine crowed, reporting that the price of the trip would be comparable with first-class rail travel: about $375 ($4,713) from coast to coast, only $40 ($503) more than the train.

Time made special note of the safety features that would "comfort nervous passengers." The planes wouldn't fly at night, and the treacherous Allegheny Mountains, known as the "Hell Stretch"—the Bermuda Triangle of early aviation—would be crossed by train only in both directions.

IT WAS A VERY good time to be Ford and Freddy Harvey. Only weeks after the announcement of Fred Harvey's alliance with the nation's first major airline, the GOP descended on Kansas City for its national convention. The Republicans, who had controlled the White House for most of the 1920s, came to the Midwest to praise themselves for five years of small government and "Coolidge Prosperity." And since President Coolidge declined to run again, the GOP planned to elect his cabinet member Herbert Hoover. It was a backslapping, good-time convention, steeped in the self-congratulatory spirit of a decade well done.

And the Harveys were Kansas City's finest hosts. The Fred Harvey restaurants and stores in Union Station were packed. Ford entertained Republican bigwigs on the greens and fairways of the Kansas City Country Club. The *Washington Post* reported that the first big golf game of the convention pitted Ford and another local business leader against Campbell Slemp, the former Virginia congressman currently serving as President Coolidge's personal secretary, and legendary protectionist senator Reed Smoot of Utah, chairman of the finance committee and a powerful friend of the National Park Service. Ford knew better than to win. He and his partner were roundly trounced.

Freddy did his entertaining on the polo field, where his Kansas City Country Club team hosted the first-ever GOP polo tournament. Squads competed from all over the country, including a foursome from Akron's Chagrin Valley Hunt Club that featured the sons of tire magnate Harvey Firestone, who never missed a match.

But the biggest news in the tournament was a team fielded by Will Rogers—who shared Freddy's addictions to polo and flying. Rogers was well-known in Hollywood for having his own personal polo field, and he was the first major celebrity to completely embrace air travel, flying to engagements on mail planes if necessary, no matter how troubling the weather. To get to Kansas City that week, for example, he had flown a Western Air Express mail plane that crash-landed in Las Vegas, Nevada, breaking its right wheel on touchdown and flipping over on its back. With only a few cuts and bruises, Rogers got back on the plane after the wheel was fixed and flew through harsh winds to

Cherokee, Wyoming, where he refueled. But during takeoff, the plane hit a gopher hole that snapped a strut, so he had to stop and wait for a *new* plane to arrive from Cheyenne before continuing to Kansas City.

Will Rogers was feeling particularly fearless, because his popularity had reached heights never before imagined even in Lindbergh's America. A cover story in the May 31, 1928, issue of *Life* magazine announced that he would be running for president, the candidate of the "anti-bunk" party. The mock candidacy was simply an excuse for him to cover the presidential campaign for *Life*, but like all the best faux politicians and fake newsmen who followed, Rogers attracted more popular interest than the election.

By night, Will Rogers filled the Shubert Theater in downtown Kansas City with his wildly popular one-man show. But by day, he played polo, leading a team of his native Oklahomans called the Will Rogers Cowboys. Freddy was a star for the hometown favorites, the Kansas City Country Club Blues, and their teams finally met on the fifth day of the tournament.

Freddy scored the first goal, but Rogers's team scored the next three. The match remained close until the comedian's *horse* kicked in a goal, bringing a broad grin to his face. After that, Rogers went on a scoring spree, finishing with eight goals, the last one from sixty yards out.

In between the polo and the parties, the Republicans nominated Hoover, who had served as Coolidge's secretary of commerce for the past seven years. He was considered a safe choice. Besides being pro-business, he was a well-known humanitarian—the government's point man during the Mississippi flood—and his wife was poised to become the first First Lady with a college degree. Hoover was fully expected to win in a landslide that fall, and to keep America's economic motor running for years to come.

ON A THURSDAY afternoon not long after the Republicans left town, Freddy phoned the house to see if his wife needed anything.

"Something *terrible* just happened!" Betty screamed, holding the receiver in her left hand because her right was dripping with blood.

Freddy rushed home with the police detective in Union Station, Edward Boyle. They found twenty-three-year-old Betty "prostrated from fright," with a bloody knife wound above her wrist and several other superficial cuts.

Betty said that not long after the servants left for the day, there was a knock at the front door. She opened it a crack—leaving the chain bolted—and saw a well-dressed young man with a Van Dyke beard, heavy eyebrows, a high forehead, and a sallow complexion that made her wonder if he might be on drugs. Before she could think, he reached in through the crack, grabbed her arm, and put a knife to her wrist, ordering her to let him in.

She told police that when she refused, he slashed her arm. So she opened the door.

"I want your jewel box and I want it quick," he said.

"I have no jewel box," she cried.

According to the police report, the intruder then picked her up and carried her upstairs, where he forced her to lie on her bed, but only after a struggle during which she received several more defensive cuts on her arms.

"Now, tell me where that jewel box is or I'll cut you to death," he said.

Betty gave him the two diamond rings she was wearing and told him he could have anything else, if he would just leave. He looked at the rings and threw them aside.

"Those are *nothing!*" he growled. "I want the *Harvey jewels!*"

Apparently, in the public's imagination, there was a treasure chest of priceless gems—perhaps including that diamond-studded toothbrush—passed down by Fred Harvey to his heirs.

Betty said that when she insisted all she had was the jewelry in her dresser, the thief jumped on top of her, pressing the knife to her throat. It was at that very moment, she said, that Freddy called home. The ringing phone startled the thief, who released her immediately and fled.

Since several details of her story, as reported, sound more than a little implausible, it is unclear whether something less ominous—or more ominous—actually took place. But Freddy didn't hush it up. He publicly demanded an investigation.

"I am furious and aching to lay my hands on the fellow," he told one reporter. "Of course his moustache is shaved off by now so he'll be hard to find. But I only hope I'll be able to get at him a few minutes some time."

Police never caught the intruder, and the media coverage eventually died down. But what Freddy described as "the unnerving of my wife" had a lasting impact. Doctors started making frequent house calls to 3533 Locust Street, and Betty took a long time to bounce back. Her wounds were superficial, but the trauma was not—especially since she had been obsessing about her health and her body for some time before the attack. In the six years she and Freddy had been married, she had been desperate to have a child. But it just wasn't happening.

She was also struggling with the breakup of her parents' marriage. Several months after she was attacked, her father took one of his periodic trips to England—and never returned. To keep up appearances, her parents pretended that they were maintaining some kind of long-distance romance because he needed to be in England for business. Her father did breed horses there, specializing in mounts for big fox hunts that sometimes included the royal family, and her older brother later joined him in the business. But the Drages' marriage had long been over.

Unfortunately, before he left, Betty's father had spent most of her mother's substantial inheritance. So Lucy Drage—the proud, stylish heir to what remained of the Christie grain fortune—found herself alone and forced to do something she never dreamed would be necessary: She had to get a job. Society ladies in Kansas City had been asking her for design advice for years, so she decided to open a shop. She would help her friends redo the interiors of their mansions and redesign their gardens.

Because she didn't have enough money left to finance such a shop, she was forced to ask for help. Freddy co-signed a bank loan for his mother-in-law, and also lent her some start-up money himself.

WHEN HERBERT HOOVER was elected in November, 1928 was shaping up to be what financial writers would dub "the greatest year in the history of Wall Street"—and 1929 was projected to be even better. The railroads and the nation's manufacturing industries were at their absolute peak, and some of the newer businesses were coming on strong. With more road building, automobile sales continued to climb, and a new mobile culture was emerging. The business of mass entertainment was being revolutionized by the proliferation of radios—driven by the

Just weeks after the first Santa Fe train arrived at the Grand Canyon in the fall of 1901 (1), Ford (2) took a rugged tour through the Southwest with railroad president E. P. Ripley and other top executives (3); they began at their sprawling new Alvarado Hotel complex at the Albuquerque depot (4), toured Indian villages and ruins, and ended at the lip (5) of the Grand Canyon—where Ford (top left), Southwest historian and friend of Teddy Roosevelt Charles Lummis (top right), and Santa Fe executives argued about how close to the edge the railroad would build its new hotel.

1

2

3

4

5

❖ Fred's eldest daughter, Minnie, and her husband, John Huckel (1), convinced Ford to open an Indian exhibit at the Alvarado, curated by longtime employee and "Harvey anthropologist" Herman Schweizer (2, at Mesa Verde) and designed by the young, unknown architect Mary Colter (3). The "Indian Building" (4) was supposed to be a little museum, but soon turned into a huge tourist attraction (5)—featuring weaver Elle of Ganado (second from right)—and a profitable Indian art business, with customers including William Randolph Hearst. Teddy Roosevelt (6) at the Grand Canyon in 1903, where he gave one of his first important environmental speeches—partly to warn the railroad about the location of the Fred Harvey hotel. El Tovar (7, from a distance; 8, front entrance; 9, Carl Moon portrait of Harvey Girl in summer uniform) opened there in 1905, as did Mary Colter's "Hopi House" (10).

1

2

3

4

5

Kansas City Union Station (1) was the company's most ambitious project when it opened in 1914, since Fred Harvey ran not only the restaurants but all the retail stores from its new corporate offices on the second floor. The station was heavily used during WWI—for which Ford's son, Freddy (2), enlisted as a pilot in the fledgling Air Corps. After the war, more than half of the Harvey Girls quit to marry returning soldiers, so the staff was rebuilt system-wide with a new generation of modern "working women" in more modern uniforms (3, 4, 5) and many new cooks (6) as well. Perhaps the most modern Harvey Girl was Ford's unmarried daughter, Kitty, seen here in Kansas City (7) and in Indian Gardens at the Grand Canyon (8); in 1925, at the height of the roaring twenties, the new, all-Fred Harvey Chicago Union Station opened (9).

1

FredHarvey

2

3

6

4 & 5

7

THE HARVEY PLANE, SMASHED AGAINST A BOULDER.

8

9

10

11

12

La Fonda Hotel in Santa Fe (1) as it looked when Fred Harvey took it over in 1926 for the Southwest "Indian Detours," attracting tourists from all over the world so that it soon had to be dramatically expanded; the new Fred Harvey logo (2), designed (presumably by Mary Colter) from the founder's actual signature; the last portrait of Ford Harvey (3) before his shocking death, from the flu, in 1928, which left the company's future in dispute between his brother, Byron (4), who wanted to control the firm and move it to Chicago, and his sister Minnie (5), who insisted it stay in Kansas City—so Freddy and Kitty (6), who inherited the controlling shares, could one day run it; La Posada in Winslow (7), Ford's last dream project and Mary Colter's masterpiece; the first airborne Fred Harvey meals (8) are served on a Transcontinental Air Transport flight; Albert Einstein (9) and his wife visit the Grand Canyon in 1931 (Herman Schweizer at left); some of the last pictures of Freddy, under a plane wing (10), and his wife, Betty (11); photo of the crash site (12).

✦ Kitty (right) with girlfriend Mary Perkins in California (1) after being forced to sell her controlling shares of the company; Mimbreño table setting Colter designed for new Super Chief (2); troops overwhelming Harvey Girls in the new Los Angeles Union Station restaurant (3), a scene replayed across the country; Byron and his sons (from left, Daggett, Stewart, Byron Jr.) (4); Judy Garland as Harvey Girl (5); Elizabeth Taylor (6) posing with box of Harvey Girl candy, one of many Fred Harvey-branded products.

wide appeal of shows like *Amos 'n' Andy,* which premiered on the *Chicago Daily News*'s radio station WMAQ in March 1928—and the technological breakthrough of "talking" motion pictures. While Al Jolson's *The Jazz Singer,* which had some isolated sound sequences among the traditional title cards, had come out the year before, it wasn't until 1928 that full-length "talkies" were released by Hollywood, starting with the Warner Brothers gangster film *Lights of New York.*

It was also a heady time for Fred Harvey, because the 1920s had turned out to be the decade when Americans discovered how much they liked *other* people's cooking. With women working, nightlife booming, and Prohibition still forcing innovation in prepared food (to make up for lost liquor sales), the number of restaurants in the United States had grown astronomically in the past ten years.

Fred Harvey remained the most admired and copied restaurant and hotel system in the country, although the Childs cafeteria chain now had more locations, with over one hundred cafeterias, primarily in New York and other eastern cities. Unlike Fred Harvey, Childs owned some of its own real estate and directly leased the rest—and given its pricey downtown locations, the rent alone on 125 leases cost the company $48 million ($603 million) annually. To pay for this overhead, the Childs brothers took the family business public, allowing the firm to raise enormous capital for expansion. Unfortunately, it also cost them their company. In the fall of 1928, the board of directors, now largely controlled by DuPont and Standard Oil money, began to expel all of the original Childs brothers from leadership positions.

When Ford heard stories like this, they reinforced his conviction that he had been right to keep Fred Harvey private. And nobody could argue with the results of remaining family owned. By the fall of 1928, he was running twenty-five hotels, forty sit-down restaurants, fifty-four lunchrooms, and the newsstands and gift shops in eighty cities along the Santa Fe. He was also running all the restaurants, soda fountains, and retail stores in union stations in Chicago, Kansas City, St. Louis, Houston, Wichita, Galveston, and Fort Worth, as well as luxury hotel operations at the Grand Canyon and in Santa Fe. He was serving over twelve million meals a year.

The Harvey hospitality empire had just celebrated its fiftieth anniversary and was uniquely poised for the future. By controlling the Santa Fe depots and dining cars, Ford had exclusive access not only to all the train passengers but to the drivers along the new Route 66—

which still hadn't been paved, but was already one of the most popular rides on the new federal highway system. And because Freddy had helped position the company at the forefront of the air passenger business, they could one day vie for control of restaurants and retail stores in airports.

Fred Harvey had no appreciable debt. Ford had favorable long-term contracts with the nation's largest railroad, major union stations, and the U.S. government, and owned arguably the most recognizable, beloved, and marketable name in the hospitality industry.

"How large can such a business grow?" Ford asked, in a mission statement he sent out to every one of his seven thousand employees. "Is it possible to keep on expanding indefinitely a business where everything centers around good-will, and where the good-will itself is dependent upon doing each component part of the job in a way which is considerably above the average of generally accepted standards? . . . Frankly, we do not know."

But he was anxious to find out.

CHAPTER 34

FORD HARVEY HAS A COLD

ON A CHILLY FRIDAY IN EARLY DECEMBER, THE WORD PASSED
from desk to desk through the bustling offices on the second floor of
Kansas City Union Station:

"Ford Harvey has a cold."

His nose was stuffy, and he felt a bit feverish as he sat at his desk in
the elaborately wood-paneled corner office. As he kept feeling worse,
he walked over to the large brass National Regulator Company thermometer mounted on the wall to see if the heat had been turned up too
high. But the temperature in the room was fine. He stayed at the office
for a meeting about the endlessly delayed construction at La Fonda—
for which Indian Detours chief Hunter Clarkson had come all the way
from Santa Fe. Then he headed home and went to bed.

An influenza epidemic had been sweeping the West for weeks.
While the flu of 1928 didn't appear to be deadly, like the 1918 pandemic,
it spread almost as quickly and in an unusual way. It was one of the first
flus to ever begin in California and move west to east across the entire
country.

The first outbreaks were reported in November in San Francisco,
where Ford's colleague William McAdoo, the former Treasury secretary who had run the railroads during the war, was an early victim.
Senator Hiram Johnson of California was also stricken, unable to even
get out of bed to vote in the presidential election. Students at several
Bay Area schools and colleges became ill, and many classes were
canceled—but sporting events were still played shorthanded, spreading
the illness.

The flu traveled to Los Angeles, appearing not long after Stanford
played USC. It descended on Hollywood and closed down many

movie productions. Buster Keaton, Hoot Gibson, Clara Bow, and Loretta Young were among the first actors reported ill. Almost everyone recovered within a week or two, although there were a handful of deaths when the flu developed into pneumonia. Veteran stage and film character actor Edward Connelly, at sixty-eight the longest-running studio player in Hollywood, who had made over sixty pictures for MGM, died after a brief bout. So did a forty-two-year-old Santa Ana grammar school teacher named Fannie Hasty, who got it from her students before officials closed her school.

The city health officer in Los Angeles announced that he would arrest anyone with the flu who didn't stay home.

Since Fred Harvey had large operations in San Francisco, Los Angeles, and San Diego, the flu affected the Harvey System rapidly. An early outbreak was reported in Prescott, Arizona, which was on the Santa Fe branch line to Phoenix. The virus also traveled by train along the railroad's High Iron, as well as the lines of its western competitors, with outbreaks in Idaho and Utah.

By the Friday afternoon that Ford Harvey went home sick— insisting on taking the streetcar, as he always did, instead of a taxi, even though it was freezing outside—the hot zone of the epidemic had reached the dead center of the United States. The army announced a quarantine of Fort Riley in Kansas, not far from the original Fred Harvey eating house in Topeka.

The surgeon general was reporting that while 200,000 Americans had influenza, Kansas and Missouri were currently the hardest hit. He also stressed that this flu was a much "milder variety" than the one that had decimated the country a decade before. It was *not* a "killer flu," he insisted. Patients just needed to "go to bed and stay there."

This was exactly what Ford Harvey did. He hired nurses to take care of him around the clock so he could remain in bed—Inez Meek and Minnie KreienKamp were on duty during the day, with Sylvia Terrell covering the nights—and his physician, Dr. Comingo Griffith, stopped by regularly to see him. And he still felt well enough to make phone calls. He stayed in touch with Dave and John Huckel at the office, spoke to Freddy and Kitty, who were both out at the family home in California, and took calls from Hunter Clarkson as soon as he got back to Santa Fe. When he wasn't on the phone, Ford listened to the radio: He had just leased a high-tech system, the Majestic "all-electric" radio with the "Dynamic speaker."

Ford was a sixty-two-year-old man in robust health. He had walked nearly two miles to work every day for years. The local papers, which always covered the health of Harvey family members, reported that he was "progressing satisfactorily." There was no reason for concern.

But after three days in bed, Ford suddenly became gravely ill, with chest pains and labored breathing. Fearing pneumonia, the doctor sent a sputum sample to Duncan Laboratories in town, so it could be injected into specially bred mice that were being used to test for and "stage" pneumonia. The early stages, Types I and II, were believed to respond to an antigen made of horse blood serum, although the foreign proteins in the treatment were known to make many patients sicker.

Ford was given the horse blood antigen, and an oxygen tent was delivered to the house so he could breathe easier. The Fred Harvey drugstore at Union Station sent over an analgesic balm to spread on his chest, along with eucalyptus oil, to clear his congestion.

On Tuesday, as his condition worsened, several top physicians were summoned—including renowned clinical cardiologist James B. Herrick, arguably the world's leading expert on coronary artery disease, who was rushed down from Chicago. Ford had apparently consulted with Herrick previously—most likely because the cardiologist was one of the earliest proponents of walking as a way of preventing heart disease. (Herrick was the first to ever diagnose a myocardial infarction in a living patient, and he later went on to co-found the American Heart Association and discover sickle-cell anemia.)

Word of Ford's deteriorating condition leaked to the press. "Ford Harvey Nears Pneumonia Crisis," read the headline in the *Kansas City Journal.* Doctors told the family that his condition was deteriorating. Yet it was still hard for anyone to believe that he might actually be on his deathbed. After all, he had been sick *for only six days.*

But on the seventh day, Ford's temperature surged past 103 degrees, and kept rising, no matter how much they tried to cool him with ice. He was delirious, his brain stewing in its own juices.

On the eighth day, at 9:30 in the evening, Ford Harvey died. Dr. Griffith recorded his last body temperature at 108 degrees.

FORD'S DEATH CAME as such a shock, its ramifications for the family and the company so unimaginable, that nobody knew quite what to do.

When his funeral began at 2:00 p.m. on Monday, December 17, Fred Harvey employees in over fifty cities and towns across the United States stopped working and remained silent for five minutes to remember their beloved boss. There was no eulogy at the service, and no press release from the company. It was left to a wordsmith who had watched Ford Harvey grow up to say the most poignant goodbye.

Only hours after his death, a telegram arrived from William Allen White.

"I have lost an old friend," wrote the Pulitzer Prize–winning journalist, "and the West has lost a commercial leader who is typical of all that the West holds fine: enterprise, imagination, courage, honesty, social vision and an understanding heart. His loss will be felt for years."

The chairman of Harris Trust, one of Chicago's largest banks, where Ford had been a board member, called him "the leading citizen of Kansas City . . . he won his place by a devotion to the finest principles of life in business and in his personal affairs."

The president of the Santa Fe, William Storey, who had known Ford for twenty-five years, described him as "a considerate friend, a lovable companion, a gentleman in every sense of the word. I feel a distinct personal loss that cannot be filled."

In tribute, the Santa Fe employee magazine reprinted one of Ford's favorite quotations, from Stanley Baldwin, the prime minister of England:

> All my life I have believed from my heart in the words of Browning: "All service ranks the same with God." It makes very little difference whether a man is driving a tramcar, or sweeping streets, or being Prime Minister, if he only brings to that service everything that is in him, and performs it for the sake of mankind . . .
>
> Four words of one syllable each are words which contain Salvation for this country and for the whole world, and they are: Faith, Hope, Love, Work. Faith in the people; Hope in the Future; Love for our fellowmen; and Work, and Work, and Work.

The magazine also published a painfully somber photo taken the day of the funeral in front of Kansas City Union Station, of Ford's friends and colleagues from Fred Harvey—members of the Tenth Legion, managers from California, Arizona, New Mexico, Kansas, Missouri, and Texas, even his old assistant from when he joined the company in the 1880s. Sixty-four men in trench coats, holding their hats and staring stunned at the camera, as if the photographer, instead of asking them to say "cheese," had just given them the worst news imaginable.

While Ford's death was a shock and a mystery, when the epidemic finally ended several months later, it was easy to see what had happened. The very week Ford got sick was when the influenza went from being relatively benign—mucusy, achy, and annoying, but survivable—to being lethal. When the Public Health Service later analyzed all the reports from its regional offices, it was clear that the flu had become deadlier and deadlier as the Christmas shopping season progressed. By year's end, health officials finally declared an all-out war, but without medicinal weapons they could only resort to increased fines for spitting and, in some cities, a ban on kissing and "all forms of petting."

Many people, including many celebrated patients, survived the illness: among them Charlie Chaplin, Ethel Barrymore, Jackie Coogan, Lon Chaney, Mrs. Cornelius Vanderbilt Jr., journalist Ida Tarbell, opera prima donna Ganna Walska, and, at the beginning of baseball season, Babe Ruth.

But more than a hundred thousand Americans did not survive. And unlike previous epidemics, which mostly struck in cities, this one killed in even the most remote territories: More than 10 percent of the entire Indian population of the Northwest was wiped out. The flu of 1928–1929 turned out to be one of the worst influenza outbreaks of the twentieth century, second only to the pandemic of 1918.

THE READING OF FORD's will was anxiously anticipated, but it was over before it really got started.

"In as few words as ever disposed of an estate of more than a million dollars, the will of Ford F. Harvey . . . was filed with the probate court today," said the *Kansas City Star*. The will, "one of the shortest ever filed," was only fifteen typewritten lines.

In the months before his illness, Ford had spoken to Dave and others about rewriting his will, because he knew it was woefully inadequate. He had drafted a temporary will after his wife's death, simply to remove her name from the list of his beneficiaries, but he forgot to update it. So, unlike his father's will, which laid out an elaborate ten-year plan to preserve the future of the company, the document Ford left consisted of only three short paragraphs, which said little more than that he left his entire estate to his two children, "share and share alike."

The estate included a large and diverse portfolio of municipal bonds—representing virtually every city on the Santa Fe, as well as others across the country—each worth between $5,000 and $25,000, and all 136 of them valued together at over $1 million ($12.6 million). There was another $75,000 ($943,000) in private mortgages he had given and cash deposits in banks. And then there were Ford's stocks: some $600,000 ($7.5 million) in blue-chip companies—as well as his large holdings in Fred Harvey. One useful aspect of owning a private firm was the ability to manipulate the price of its private shares. So for estate reasons, Ford's controlling share of Fred Harvey was computed to be worth an absurdly low $400,000 ($5 million)—even though he had paid $600,000 ($14 million) for it in 1911, and it was now worth at least twice that much. Ford also left two lavish homes—the mansion in Kansas City and the vacation house in Montecito, each filled with art and antiques—and two cars: a 1924 Lincoln and a 1925 Buick.

Kitty and Freddy Harvey had now lost both of their parents in two-and-a-half years. Their first Christmas without them was agonizing. To try to keep Father alive for one more holiday, Freddy arranged for the estate to go ahead and buy the Christmas present Ford had chosen for Kitty the last time he was in New York. It was a bronze statuette group by John Angel, a British sculptor gaining renown in America for his work creating the main figures for the Cathedral of St. John the Divine, under construction in upper Manhattan. The piece was called "The Treasure."

While Kitty and Freddy were close enough to negotiate their way through "sharing" the estate, the future of the company was more complex. From the time his father yanked him out of college at the age of nineteen because of a medical "emergency" that went on for nearly twenty years, Ford Harvey had spent his entire professional life planning for every imaginable possibility. For decades, Ford, Dave, John Huckel, and the executives they trained had maintained an almost maniacal level of preparedness. Even at the local manager level, while employees were never treated as if they were replaceable, they quit often enough that everyone on the staff was constantly being assessed for his or her ability to move up. So it was astonishing that Ford Harvey had not left exacting instructions for his own successor and the company's future.

Yet his general wishes were clearly known to Dave Benjamin and the Tenth Legion. They knew full well that Ford wanted his son to take over the business. Under no circumstances did he want his brother, Byron, to be put in charge.

Dave was initially offered the presidency of the company, but refused it. "A Harvey should always be the head man of the firm," he said, according to what he told his daughter, Gertrude, about the offer. But he did make a move to assure that the Harvey-in-charge would not be Byron: Dave sold his own Fred Harvey stock, the only major block not already in family hands, to Freddy.

Since Freddy and Kitty inherited their father's controlling shares of the eating house and hotel business, and Freddy also inherited Ford's 99 percent ownership stake in the profitable Harvey subsidiary that ran all the union stations, there was no question that Ford's children had control of the family business. But Byron wanted Ford's title and was the oldest male Harvey in the company, so a compromise was worked out.

Byron Harvey was named the new "president" of Fred Harvey, and an official announcement was made of his elevation. However, anyone who did business with the firm could see that this promotion was merely titular. Byron continued to live in Chicago, while the company's main offices remained in Kansas City Union Station. Ford's Tenth Legion continued to run the company day to day. While both Byron and Freddy were briefed on various decisions and situations, neither one was ready to lead the way Ford had.

So Byron could be the figurehead president until Freddy was ready to assume his birthright as the next Fred Harvey. After all, the company was in great shape—its next five years of moves already well choreographed by Ford—and the U.S. economy was at its absolute peak. If the Harvey System needed to remain at this cruising altitude for a while, what could possibly go wrong?

CHAPTER 35

FREDDY SPREADS HIS WINGS

AT THE AGE OF THIRTY-THREE, FREDDY HARVEY APPEARED prematurely mature but acted preternaturally young. With his thinning slicked-back hair, pencil mustache, and droopy eyes, he looked like an aging British movie star. Yet he maintained the stamina, taut athleticism, and occasional capriciousness of a man in his twenties, and his very American sense of adventure was growing.

Freddy's moment had arrived much sooner than expected. This was supposed to be the year he made his first real impression on the family business by finishing his two pet projects—the new hotel in Santa Fe, the largest in the company's history, and the nation's first transcontinental airline. Instead, he and Kitty now basically owned one of America's largest privately held companies. It would have been daunting had Freddy not been so constitutionally undauntable.

In the months leading up to the summer debuts of La Fonda and Transcontinental Air Transport, Freddy faced two more personal dramas. In mid-March, Mary Colter was nearly killed when the taxi she was riding in crashed headfirst into an oncoming streetcar in downtown Kansas City. She suffered serious back and hip injuries, and her face was badly cut by flying glass. While Colter was in Saint Luke's Hospital for weeks, it was only a matter of days before she was ordering her secretary, Sadie Rubins, to bring her all the updated plans for La Fonda so she could bark orders—by phone and by wire—to the architects, construction crews, and artisans in New Mexico.

While Colter recuperated, one of Freddy's closest friends committed suicide at the age of thirty-two. Rogers Crittenden, the never-married son of the former mayor of Kansas City, had been a country-club polo buddy of Freddy's, a groomsman at his wedding, and a fellow flyer who helped build the first local airfield. But just after turning thirty, Rogers fell into a deep depression, started seeing a psychiatrist, stopped flying, quit his job, and moved back home. When his parents went off to Europe for the winter, two male friends stayed at the Crittenden mansion to keep an eye on him. But on April 12, 1929, just before supper, Rogers was found in his childhood bedroom with a self-inflicted shotgun wound to the head. He left a sealed suicide letter, addressed only to his mother, which said he felt his life had been a failure. Freddy and several of their closest friends served as pallbearers.

Mary Colter finally recovered to the point where she could take the train to Santa Fe and personally shepherd the finishing touches on the new La Fonda—albeit from her wheelchair. The hotel reopened on June 15, 1929, just in time for Indian Detours season.

Colter designed the exteriors of La Fonda with a rising young local architect, John Gaw Meem, and together they created a combination of Pueblo and Spanish simplicity that brought new clarity to what became the Santa Fe Style. While Meem had designed a few homes using some of these ideas, La Fonda was the new architectural masterpiece of the City Different, a breakthrough in adobe architecture with soft, casually elegant lines interrupted only by windows and the exposed ends of the logs that vaulted all the ceilings. But while the outside was brilliantly simple, making a new building five stories high and a square block wide seem somehow intimate and approachable, the interiors were complex, color saturated, whimsical. Among the more surreal images were the ashtray holders, made of aged-looking iron bent into elongated jackrabbits. In fact, there were many other extraordinary, unexpected touches throughout: eight hundred pieces of handmade furniture; surfaces covered with paintings, murals, mosaics; a huge bouquet of copper pots dangling from a cantina wall. And there were fireplaces everywhere.

"You may not be able to get all these fireplaces in," Colter wrote to one of the managers of the La Fonda project, "but Mr. Frederick Harvey and I are crazy about fireplaces and want to have as many as we can!"

The food in the new La Fonda dining room was also spectacular, with chef Konrad Allgaier—who had cooked for Kaiser Wilhelm and in major European hotels—bringing his classical training to traditional New Mexican cuisine. His specialties included Chicken Lucrecio, a chili-roasted chicken with a garlic and almond gravy, beef empanadas with vanilla sauce, Chiles Rellenos à la Konrad, huevos rancheros, and heavenly fresh sopapillas.

La Fonda became an instant classic in American architecture and a monument to the kind of aesthetic coziness for which Fred Harvey was famous. Besides being packed with "detourists," it quickly became the center of life in Santa Fe.

"You never met anybody *anywhere* except at the La Fonda," wrote Ernie Pyle, the popular syndicated newspaper columnist, who lived in New Mexico, "you never took anybody to lunch anywhere else." French author Simone de Beauvoir would later call La Fonda "the most beautiful hotel in America, perhaps the most beautiful I've ever seen in my life."

WHILE OVERSEEING THE OPENING of La Fonda, Freddy was also in the middle of the national public relations blitz for the upcoming maiden flight of the Lindy Line. The newspapers, radio, and movie-theater newsreels were in a frenzy over the first transcontinental air-rail service, which would speed up life in the United States by shortening the time it took to cross the nation by an entire day.

Freddy's role in the publicity assault was to explain the challenging job of choosing food for air travelers with Fred Harvey "dietitians" in the Kansas City test kitchens.

"Airsickness is mental, to some degree," he told the *Kansas City Star.* "But with the plane riding nicely, the whole journey could be spoiled for the passengers by an inappropriate diet on board. The rich heavy foods in which one ordinarily indulges would be disastrous if eaten on an air journey."

He took great pains not to say what everyone was thinking—that he was trying to find foods that passengers were less likely to throw up. Given the small planes, unpressurized cabins, and sharp changes in altitude, most passengers were bound to experience some degree of airsickness—the treatment for which, at the time, was sucking on a slice of lemon.

Part of the reason for the public relations whirl was that TAT was running so far behind schedule that it now had competitors: Several other regional airmail carriers had cobbled together lesser and slower versions of what TAT was promising by partnering with different railroad lines. But none of the competitors had the star power of TAT, which was augmented on May 27, 1929, when Lindbergh wed Anne Morrow—whose father, Dwight, a partner at J. P. Morgan and the U.S. ambassador to Mexico, was a major player in aviation, having chaired the presidential commission that initiated the U.S. Army Air Corps. The marriage generated front-page stories around the globe, and was soon followed by the news that TAT had hired Lindbergh's friend Amelia Earhart, the thirty-one-year-old Kansan who was on her way to becoming the world's best-known female flyer. Earhart actually had another tie to the company: She had known Freddy Harvey, casually, for years, because she and Frank Baker, his Kansas City polo and partying buddy, had been childhood friends in Atchison.

Transcontinental Air Transport finally opened for business, simultaneously in New York and Los Angeles, during the July 4th weekend. Freddy flew out to L.A. by himself to attend the festivities at the new TAT air terminal in Glendale, stopping along the way to visit the Grand Canyon.

He continued on to Los Angeles, and was joined there the next day by Charles and Anne Lindbergh—who had spent the past few days flying into the western cities with TAT airports and enjoying Harvey hospitality at each stop. The Lindberghs were greeted by a crowd of thousands and then whisked away to a private reception held by Freddy and several other TAT officials. Among them was Eugene Vidal, a storied flyer and athlete who had been in the air corps with Freddy but went on to be an all-American quarterback at West Point, an Olympic decathlete, and then West Point's first aeronautics trainer before joining the nascent aviation industry as TAT's assistant general manager. The entire group was then driven to the Los Angeles office of California governor C. C. Young, where Lindbergh officially inaugurated the airline on both coasts simultaneously—in a sequence of events that brought to mind the popular syndicated cartoonist Rube Goldberg and the contraptions invented by his mad scientist character Professor Lucifer Gorgonzola Butts.

With a sheepish grin, Lindbergh pushed a button on the desk of the governor's office, which caused an electrical circuit to close at the local Western Union office, which sent a signal across the country to Pennsylvania Station in New York, where a light then flashed, signaling Amelia Earhart to break a bottle of champagne over the front of a TAT plane on display in the station and then lead her nine fellow passengers onto their special Pullman on the Pennsylvania Railroad's new "Airway Limited," which quickly pulled out of the station for its overnight train ride through the Alleghenies and on to Ohio.

When the train arrived in Columbus the next morning, it was greeted by Henry Ford and Harvey Firestone and a large crowd waiting to see these intrepid first-time cross-country flyers—who were not so much the astronauts of their era as they were the equivalent of the first civilians on the space shuttle. After the requisite hand shaking, speeches, and photographs, the group was escorted by male flight attendants—referred to as "couriers," like the Fred Harvey guides in the Southwest—to "Aerocars" that whisked them, and their luggage, to the runway.

The official TAT plane was a Ford Tri-Motor, which had three propellers and was affectionately nicknamed "the Tin Goose" because of its unusually long fuselage and rounded, birdlike tummy. The company had purchased a flock of ten; it also bought or leased airports in ten cities, and hired pilots and crews, along with seventy-two weather forecasters all along the route. Each plane could accommodate ten passengers, five on either side of a narrow aisle, in adjustable cane-backed seats with all the essentials: an individual reading lamp, electric cigar lighter, and ashtray. The windows, draped with brown velvet curtains, could be opened. There were heaters on the floor, but since they were not really powerful enough to combat the drastic changes in temperature, passengers were encouraged to hold on to their overcoats.

The plane made frequent stops—ostensibly to refuel, but mostly to make passengers feel there were regular safety checks. (Also, anyone too nervous to continue flying could get off and switch to a train.) From Columbus they flew to Indianapolis, landed, and then took off again for St. Louis, where the Fred Harvey lunch was brought on board so it could be served while airborne across Missouri, on individual aluminum tables with lavender linen tablecloths. The menu was freshly made sandwiches—chicken salad, egg salad, and cheese—along with a pickle, a piece of cake, an apple, a banana, and a choice of coffee or milk.

The Tin Goose landed in Kansas City and once more in Wichita before the flight ended in tiny Waynoka, Oklahoma. The previously obscure hamlet was now crawling with reporters, who wanted to see Earhart and her fellow passengers dine at the Fred Harvey eating house before boarding their Santa Fe Pullmans for the overnight train ride across Oklahoma and the Texas Panhandle. In the middle of the night, they passed another Santa Fe train coming in the opposite direction: It was carrying the first group of TAT passengers heading east from California. Since the tracks were so close together, the engineers and crew could actually wave to each other.

As the sun came up, Earhart's train pulled in to Clovis, New Mexico, just across the Texas border, midway between Amarillo and Roswell. They had a big breakfast at the Fred Harvey hotel there, the Gran Quivira, before heading for the Clovis airfield, five miles west of town, where two TAT planes awaited them: They had picked up several more passengers along the way.

The first plane took off without incident. But as the second taxied down the runway, a gust of wind caught one of its wings and threw the plane into a scary spin—which ended only when it skidded across a freshly plowed field and smashed into one of the airport hangars. The hangar windows shattered, sending glass flying. Nobody was hurt, and journalists were later told that the passengers "showed no concern" during the "slight" crash. One can only imagine how they felt as they were marched across the runway to a replacement plane, being assured that *this time* the takeoff would go smoothly.

From Clovis they flew across New Mexico to Albuquerque, and then on to Winslow, the most dangerous part of the flight because of the altitude needed to cross the mountains. Couriers handed out chewing gum, as well as cotton balls for passengers to stuff in their ears, but nothing could really prevent the ear popping. TAT executive Eugene Vidal's son—who grew up to be the controversial author Gore Vidal—was a passenger on one of the company's flights at the age of four, and would never forget his eardrums bursting and "blood trickling from my tiny lobes."

At Winslow, they were greeted by Lindbergh, who was there to personally pilot one of the two planes to California. They made one more stop in Kingman, Arizona, and then flew directly to the Grand Central Air Terminal outside of Los Angeles, where several thousand fans were waiting to be part of the historic moment—along with actress Gloria Swanson, who was just there for the photo op.

Earhart and her fellow passengers had traversed the United States in a scant forty-eight hours. But unlike previous cross-country speed marks, this one wasn't an experiment or a one-shot deal: It was to be a regularly scheduled miracle.

It was a glorious moment, bursting with the promise that, in the words of the TAT commemorative book, "American Aviation Shall Be Surpassingly Useful to Mankind." The American economy was at its screaming all-time high, and the nation had never before been so prominent economically or socially. While it would be some years before *Life* magazine publisher, Henry Luce, would proclaim the 1900s as "the American Century," by 1929 it already felt true—with many of the trends, dynamics, and frictions of that century already in place and in play.

Nowhere was this more clear than out west, where visitors jammed the Grand Canyon and other Fred Harvey tourist attractions as never before, yearning to "find America" and be part of that grand American experience.

It was the greatest summer ever in the history of Fred Harvey and the Santa Fe.

If only Ford had lived to see it.

CHAPTER 36

PAY NO ATTENTION TO
THAT CRASHING SOUND

⊐⊏

Aт the end of every summer, amasa mcgaffey left his home in northern New Mexico to meet a group of friends for an elaborate big-game-hunting expedition. He had traveled by train and more recently by car, but now his kids were urging the rugged fifty-nine-year-old to try the plane, since the two-month-old TAT service was so easily accessible from Albuquerque.

On the Tuesday after the long Labor Day weekend of 1929, McGaffey boarded the TAT plane *City of San Francisco* heading west, and met his fellow air passengers—who barely outnumbered the crew. This was not surprising. Much to the disappointment of Freddy and the other owners of TAT, people were more afraid to fly than they had anticipated. So many passengers were asking to get off at the next airport and switch to rails that critics joked that TAT really stood for "Take a Train."

Other nervous passengers did what they could to tough it out. The couriers loved to tell the story of the little old lady who got on the TAT plane in Los Angeles and immediately opened a dainty parasol over her head. When asked why, she said, "Young man, I'm shielding myself from God's wrath for defying the law of gravity."

McGaffey's fellow passengers that day included a shipping company executive from Boston, a paper salesman from Cincinnati, a woman whose husband and father both worked for the airline, and William Henry Beers, the editor-in-chief of *Golf Illustrated* magazine. Their plane took off from Albuquerque at 10:20 a.m., flying into the kind of passing storm that often makes its way across northern New

Mexico, and it was sighted by any number of people cruising over Gallup at around 11:30 a.m.

But the flight never arrived at Winslow.

Within a few hours, nearly every plane in the West—private, commercial, army, and navy—was buzzing over the area in search of the missing Ford Tri-Motor with "9649" on its wing. Search parties set out from towns all over New Mexico and Arizona. News of the missing TAT plane spread quickly across the country by radio and newspapers, especially after the airline offered a $5,000 ($63,000) reward for information leading to the discovery of the lost plane, and the parents of the young steward on board immediately offered to double it. By the next morning, more planes had joined the search, and more than five hundred New Mexicans were out scouring the countryside—Anglos, Hispanics, Indians from the nearby Navajo and Zuni reservations.

Freddy was probably one of the pilots searching from the air. But since TAT board members had been asked to keep a low profile until there was news—Lindbergh was in New York and was told to stay there and avoid the press—there was no mention of it in the papers.

After three days of fruitless searching, news came Friday morning that a plane had spotted four people on a high mesa, waving white shirts in what looked like a distress signal. Charles Lindbergh and his wife immediately took off for New Mexico to be there for the rescue. While they were en route, however, the airline determined that the "survivors" were just rural New Mexicans who were waving their shirts with excitement because they had never seen planes before.

The next morning, however, an airmail pilot did spot some wreckage near the southern peak of Mount Taylor, a volcanic mountain, sacred to the Navajos, about fifteen miles above the town of Grants. He took aerial photos of the site, which was about eleven thousand feet high, and brought them to Albuquerque, where the identity of the plane had been confirmed by late afternoon.

Since there were no trails to the crash site, the company search team—pilot Paul Collins, together with an intrepid vice president and an engineer—had to navigate through the woods in pitch darkness on packhorses, led by an Indian guide. A group of local police officers and national newspaper reporters trailed them through the dense forest, the temperature dropping as they climbed. At daybreak, the company search plane returned. Reporters were told that the pilot had orders to dive over the spot of the site—but this was a ruse. In fact, he had been told to dive at a sham location to lure the reporters away, then fly along the ledge and quickly pull up when he reached the actual site. So as the reporters and local police ran through the woods toward the decoy spot, Paul Collins led the airline's team to the actual site. Only one news photographer thought to follow them.

The scene was a horror show—all eight passengers had burned to death on impact. When the photographer started snapping pictures, Collins grabbed his camera and yanked out the film. He didn't want anyone *ever* to see what he was seeing. The pilots' charred bodies were found with their left hands fixed in front of their faces, shielding themselves from the impending impact.

It was an eerie image, but an apt harbinger for the airline—and, in fact, for the entire nation.

WHEN THE STOCK market reopened on September 9, 1929, the Monday after the bodies were discovered, there was a predictable sell-off in aviation stocks, depressing their prices. But the surprise was that railroad stocks, especially the Santa Fe, fell with them, leading the *Wall Street Journal* to speculate about "a Railroad Problem." Markets appeared to stabilize over the next few days, but three weeks later the stock market collapsed in its worst sell-off of the year. Some stocks then rebounded, but not TAT and the other aviation companies. Word was out that the government was investigating the crash and would call for the industry to be regulated by the dreaded Interstate Commerce Commission.

The airline tried slashing prices and added America's first regular in-flight movies, but nothing helped. Freddy's new business was floundering.

Luckily, the eating houses were having their best year ever, with the exception of San Marcial, New Mexico—and that was only because in late September the entire city was literally washed away in a flood. The Santa Fe station and Harvey House, deliberately built on the highest ground in the area, were the only structures not wiped out by the raging Rio Grande. Fifty-four people were trapped on the second floor of the Harvey hotel, where they huddled for hours until boats could rescue them. When the waters finally receded, the state declared martial law: Besides the town itself, fifty miles of Santa Fe track was unusable.

The railroad rebuilt the tracks, but decided to write off San Marcial as a total loss.

The city of fourteen hundred simply ceased to be.

Within three weeks, the same could be said for much of the New York Stock Exchange. On October 24, 1929—"Black Thursday"—the market lost over $9 billion ($113 billion) in the first two hours of trading, and the gallery at the exchange had to be closed to prevent a riot. The market caught its breath on Friday, but opened Monday morning even lower and kept falling, losing over 22 percent of its value—the worst one-day loss in American financial history. And on the next day, there was no rebound at all—not even what analysts call a "dead-cat bounce." Stocks fell another 12 percent, and the market lost another $14 billion ($176 billion) in value.

AT FRED HARVEY, the reaction to the stock market crash was the same as it was to everything else: business as usual. If the trains were running, there would be people to feed. Being a privately owned company, it had no stock that could plummet. While some family members might have lost money in the market, the only positive thing about Ford Harvey's death was that the lion's share of the family fortune—his estate—had been liquidated during the process of probating his will, so it was sitting in very safe U.S. government Treasury bills.

Many Americans still believed the country was, at worst, in a recession, a downturn, a correction. This was especially true in the Midwest and the West, where the regional economies were based more on livestock than stock, on wheat harvests rather than auto production.

Still, the staffs at Harvey Houses certainly noticed that some of their better-tipping local patrons had suddenly disappeared. "We had one customer from the Ford Motor Company," recalled a former Emporia busboy. "He had a special table where he sat with his paper every evening for several years . . . He knew all the Harvey Girls and he treated them very well. After the crash of '29 . . . he didn't come into the Harvey House anymore. I later saw him traipsing around Emporia in ragged clothes. For a long while, I didn't realize he was the same man."

Yet most Americans did not own stocks. There were few bank failures in the first year after the crash, and while unemployment did begin to rise, it was still under 9 percent through the end of 1930. So the Santa Fe and Fred Harvey saw no reason to deviate from what had carried them through decades of bumper crops punctuated by occasional bad harvests. They decided to continue with the ambitious plans they made before the market collapsed—in fact, the plans that Ford Harvey had made before he died.

Their biggest project together was a new train depot and hotel complex for Winslow, Arizona. They hoped to take advantage of the city's new TAT airport, where Lindbergh, Howard Hughes, and other well-known aviators were often seen. But Winslow was also prized for its location between the two cornerstones of the growing Harvey tourism empire: the Grand Canyon and the city of Santa Fe. Ford had been certain that a new luxury hotel in Winslow was the key to luring tourists to the Southwest for much longer stays, so they could enjoy extended adventures like the one that had first so inspired him in 1901.

Ford had also arranged for the company's biggest project ever *without* the Santa Fe. Fred Harvey had a deal to take over operations in the huge new union station in Cleveland, if it ever got finished.

So, in the months after the stock market crash, the company showed no fear or caution whatsoever. Work continued through early 1930 on the new hotel in Winslow and the new Cleveland Union Terminal as if nothing had changed.

And Freddy kept flying his planes.

One day he decided he absolutely *had to* try out a new single-engine plane that had just set the world speed record—especially since the vaunted Inland Sport was built by a company in Kansas, just a few miles from his office. He had his chauffeur, Franz Jawurek, drive him to the small Fairfax Airport, just across the river from Union Station, where the Inland planes were built and tested.

Freddy also insisted that his chauffeur fly with him in the two-seat plane. As they took off, however, Franz noticed a problem.

"You've lost a wheel, sir," he shouted into his boss's ear.

"Don't be silly," Freddy replied.

But Franz insisted. Aside from the fact that he could see that the wheel on his side was missing, there was someone down on the runway waving the wheel at them.

Freddy loosened his seat belt and had Franz reach over and hold the steering wheel, so he could look over the side. Not so silly after all. In fact, pretty scary, since the experimental plane had no radio.

The director of the small airfield alerted the Kansas City Municipal Airport to prepare for an emergency landing. Police and fire departments were summoned, and since there was no way to contact Freddy, somebody at Kansas City Municipal found a spare wheel that they could wave at him from their runway, too.

Instead, Freddy decided to turn around and attempt an acrobatic landing at the little airfield. He came in low, on an angle, urging the single-engine plane to land teetering only on its one good wheel. Then, keeping the plane precariously balanced, he stalled the engine at precisely the right moment, so that it slowed, rolled a few feet, looped a little loop, and then came to rest with its nose tilted neatly to the sky. Neither the passengers nor the plane was damaged.

"F. H. Harvey in a Thriller," read the headline in the next day's *Kansas City Star*. While some senior executives surely wrung their hands that their young boss still took such risks, they had to admit he had a gift for heroic antics.

IN THE THIRTY YEARS Mary Colter had been working for Fred Harvey, she had convinced Ford and his brother-in-law John Huckel, her day-to-day boss, to let her build some pretty outrageous things—by talking about them in a way that made them seem not outrageous at all, but inspired and essential. She helped design an absurdly tiny boutique hotel in Lamy, New Mexico—just ten rooms, a little dining room, and a patio—that she knew would delight Minnie and John, and others for whom nearby Santa Fe was too crowded. She designed a hardscrabble lodge and cabin hotel for the *bottom* of the Grand Canyon: Phantom Ranch, which was the harshest assignment in the Fred Harvey system—the small staff had to remain at the very bottom of the canyon for one or two weeks at a time—but offered one of the most unique perspectives in American tourism. These special projects were also the company's way of compensating Colter for the less glamorous responsibilities of her job: making interior decorating decisions for every shelf and surface in the Harvey universe, the endless memos about whether to paint or paper certain walls in the guest rooms in Wellington, Kansas, and then the additional memos about precisely which color would make them more "homelike and livable."

But Colter had never been granted the kind of freedom she was given for La Posada, the new hotel in Winslow. The building became Ford's going-away present to her, and hers to him: It was a project he adored, because it embodied all the disparate passions he, his sister Minnie, and his children had shared with Colter during her unique career with them.

When La Posada opened in May 1930, it was clear that Colter had conjured her most eccentric structure ever. It was a faux-Spanish hacienda purposely designed to have a kind of architectural multiple personality disorder—it wasn't supposed to match *itself*. She invented an elaborate backstory to explain why the eclectic building appeared to have been designed by unrelated architects over many decades— and not by a petite Midwesterner in her sixties, entertaining herself in a Kansas City office. According to Colter's made-up legend, La Posada was first built in 1869 as a Spanish immigrant's ranch home, and was added to over the years—until his heirs decided to sell the estate to the railroad. That was why some parts of the sprawling La Posada compound were authentic Spanish design, while others seemed miscellaneous—one hallway and courtyard, which supposedly connected two "older" buildings, actually had exposed cinder-block walls.

Seen from Route 66, the hotel looked traditionally Spanish, with stucco walls and orange clay roof tiles. The entrance from the train tracks, however, was entirely different. With its picket fence (featuring subtly wavy posts), its improbable lawn of thick green grass, and its modest doorway into the lobby, La Posada appeared to be not a depot hotel but a very inviting private residence. It was the clearest architectural depiction ever of Fred Harvey's original concept of a trackside home away from home. The home just happened to have six dining rooms, seventy-five guest bedrooms, tennis courts, stables, and gardens that bloomed in the middle of the desert.

The original mid-six-figure budget for the hotel was considered extravagant by the railroad even *before* the stock market crash. When the costs actually topped $1 million ($12.9 million) in the months just after the financial meltdown, Santa Fe executives did their best to grin and bear it.

"Congratulations on the new building, La Posada," read the telegram they sent to Fred Harvey on its opening. "Hope income exceeds estimates as much as building costs did."

THREE MONTHS AFTER La Posada opened, Fred Harvey made what many considered its boldest move yet—into Cleveland, Ohio, its first location east of the Mississippi and its first city with absolutely no ties to the Santa Fe. The new Cleveland Union Terminal was the brainstorm of the railroad-rich Van Sweringen brothers, who were responsible for creating Shaker Heights, one of the country's prototypical upscale suburban communities. The terminal (now called Tower City Center) was ten years in the making and required the destruction of a thousand city buildings, followed by an excavation so preposterously ambitious that it was said to be second only to the digging of the Panama Canal. Rising above the sprawling new station, which covered seventeen acres, was the dramatic fifty-two-story Terminal Tower, which Clevelanders could boast was the tallest building in America outside of Manhattan.

By the time the Union Terminal was finally completed in August 1930, the Van Sweringen brothers' personal fortune—estimated at over $3 billion ($38.7 billion)—had been decimated by the crash, and they didn't even attend the grand opening. But their station attracted nationwide attention. It also provided a stunning introduction to the world of eastern railroads for Fred Harvey.

Ford had arranged for the company to run all the new terminal's restaurants: the English Oak Room for fine dining, a huge lunchroom with Belgian marble floors and walls of inlaid oak and ebony that could seat seven thousand, a tearoom, and a soda fountain. John Huckel's division also controlled more than 175,000 feet of retail space, including a large drugstore operation, a barbershop, a toy shop, a men's haberdashery and a women's clothing store, a bookstore, and all the newsstands.

The New York–based book publishing world was especially intrigued—and a little frightened—by this new Fred Harvey operation in Cleveland. The trade magazine *Publishers Weekly* sent a correspondent to do a big article about how the company's book business, run by longtime Tenth Legionnaire Frank Clough for three decades, had become an innovative powerhouse. Now that Clough's operation was moving eastward, *PW* wanted to know how the Fred Harvey stores did what many other booksellers could not: successfully service consumers of best-selling novels while also capturing the market for more serious readers of nonfiction and classics.

Besides offering the kind of obsessive customer service usually found only in high-end restaurants—and centralized buying in Kansas City, with volumes shipped by airmail—the Harvey bookstores were full of marketing ingenuities. *PW* marveled at the way Clough displayed books on slanted bookshelves that were "really the fronts of drawers holding duplicate stock, and each one pulls out without effort, so no storage space is lost." It was also impressed by the way Fred Harvey turned so many corners of the train station into bookselling spaces, with more popular titles also available at every newsstand and a complete selection of children's books at the toy store.

"If America is to have chain bookshops," *Publishers Weekly* proclaimed, the model that "chain builders must study is the Harvey chain."

While Cleveland was a great new opportunity for Fred Harvey, it was more important as a possible gateway to the East—which had many large new union stations that could benefit from Harvey management. The mighty Pennsylvania Railroad had withdrawn from the Cleveland project and was still using its old station, but its archrival in the East, the New York Central, was a major owner of the new Union Terminal. If the Cleveland experiment proved successful, it was not hard to imagine Fred Harvey one day running the restaurants and stores in the New York Central's historic home: Grand Central Station on 42nd Street in New York City.

THROUGHOUT THE ECONOMIC crisis of the Depression, the Grand Canyon remained crowded. In the entire Harvey System, it was the only destination where the number of visitors actually *rose* during those years. And no Grand Canyon outing received more attention than the day Albert Einstein arrived.

In December 1930, Einstein left Germany to spend the winter at the California Institute of Technology. It was a prescient time to flee—Adolf Hitler's Nazi Party had just enjoyed its first significant showing in a national election. Einstein and his wife, Elsa, first sailed to New York, where he celebrated Hanukkah with a huge throng at Madison Square Garden and later gave a speech calling for brave men to resist war and refuse military service. Even if only 2 percent did so, he said, it would make a huge difference; pacifists nationwide began wearing buttons that said "2%."

When Einstein lectured at Caltech, he exhorted young scientists not to let their work be used to wage war:

> Why does this magnificent applied science, which saves work and makes life easier, bring us so little happiness? Because we have not yet learned to make sensible use of it . . . Instead of freeing us in great measure from labor that exhausts spirituality, it has made men into slaves of machinery . . .
>
> Just consider a quite uncivilized Indian, whether his experience is less rich and happy than that of the average civilized man—I hardly think so. There lies deep meaning in the fact that children of all civilized countries are so fond of playing Indians.

Within days, Einstein was at the Grand Canyon "playing Indian" himself. He was met there by a contingent of Hopi Indians—who Einstein assumed were local natives, not realizing that most of them worked for Fred Harvey. Herman Schweizer was also there, both to meet the renowned scientist and to act as a translator, since Einstein was still more comfortable speaking German. So Schweizer became part of the most famous photo opportunity in canyon history. The Hopi presented Einstein with a headdress, which he wore as he posed in front of Hopi House in a suit and tie but with a goofy kid grin—brandishing a peace pipe in one hand and holding the tiny hand of a little Indian girl with the other.

During the visit, Einstein was made an honorary chief of the tribe. But the Hopi weren't sure what to name him.

"What's his business?" one of the Harvey Indians asked.

"He invented the theory of relativity," Schweizer replied.

"All right, we'll call him 'Great Relative.' "

CHAPTER 37

LOAVES AND FISHES

⊒⊏

As THE DEPRESSION DEEPENED, THE HARVEY HOUSES TOOK on a new role in economically ravaged America—they became known as the softest touches in the West, the places where impoverished locals and drifters went in search of a free meal. It was company policy never to let anyone who couldn't afford to pay leave hungry. Many begged for food at the back door and were pleasantly surprised to get sandwiches, fruit, bread, and coffee. Others came in through the front door.

Bob O'Sullivan, who later became a well-known travel writer, never forgot the hot, dusty fall afternoon in Albuquerque when he was a second grader and his family had to rely on the kindness of strangers in Harvey Girl uniforms. His mother was driving him and his eleven-year-old sister—with all their belongings stacked high against the backseat windows—to California, where they hoped to meet their father and make a new start. The O'Sullivans had arrived in Albuquerque expecting that $25—several weeks' pay—had been wired to them at the Railway Express office. But when his mother walked out of the office in tears, Bob knew the money hadn't arrived. As she pulled on her driving gloves, the children asked if they could still get something to eat.

She hesitated.

"Of course we can," she said finally. "We have to, don't we?"

She drove along the railroad tracks to the Alvarado and led her children into the dining room. There were few customers there, but lots of delicious aromas, and every surface was gleaming. When a smiling Harvey Girl approached them, her puffed sleeves and starched apron rustling, Bob's mother pulled her aside and whispered something. The waitress walked to the kitchen and returned with a man wearing a suit, to whom his mother also whispered. Then they were led to a table, where Mrs. O'Sullivan began to order sandwiches for the kids and just a cup of coffee for herself—until the man in the suit interrupted her.

"Why don't you let me order for you?" he said, and proceeded to tell the Harvey Girl to bring hot soup, then the beef stew, mashed potatoes, bread and butter, and coffee for the lady. He asked the children if they wanted milk or hot chocolate.

"Yes, sir," they both said.

"Milk *and* hot chocolate for the children," he continued, "and some of the cobbler all around. Does that sound all right?"

"Will that be all?" the waitress asked.

"Oh," the man said, "and these people are the guests of Mr. Fred Harvey."

Bob saw his mother mouth the words "Thank you."

The taste of that stew would stay with him his entire life. As would the memory of what happened when they finished eating. His mother pushed what few coins she had left toward the waitress, who pushed them back with a smile.

"Oh, no, ma'am. You're Mr. Harvey's guests," she said, placing two bags in front of them. "And the manager said I was to wrap up what you didn't eat, so you could take it along."

"But we cleaned our plates," young Bob blurted out. His sister sighed and looked at him as if he were the dumbest person in the world. Then the Harvey Girl started giggling, followed by his mother and then the kids.

In the car, Mrs. O'Sullivan opened the bags, and found them filled with more food than they had eaten for dinner.

"What's in them?" Bob asked.

"Loaves and fishes," she replied, shaking her head in amazement. "Loaves and fishes."

THE ONLY WAY the company could afford to maintain such standards of quality and generosity, however, was if cuts were made elsewhere. And so, for the first time in its fifty-four-year history, Fred Harvey started removing some links from its vast chain. This was done in ways so subtle that residents of the affected communities barely noticed at first. By the end of 1930, all the small-town Harvey Houses along the old Frisco line—between St. Louis and central Texas—had been turned back to the control of that railroad. In some places, the Frisco then hired the entire Harvey staff and tried to keep serving pretty much the same food—and people continued to call them Harvey Houses or "the old Harvey House." But the Harvey System no longer included Tower Grove, Cape Girardeau, Springfield, Monett, and Joplin, Missouri; Francis, Hugo, Sapulpa, Vinita, and Guthrie, Oklahoma; Fort Scott, Kansas; Fayetteville, Arkansas; and the lunchroom in Birmingham, Alabama. The next year, Fred Harvey left two more Texas towns, Cleburne and Gainesville, and also three older Santa Fe locations, Wellington and Chanute, Kansas, and Merced, California. And then, in 1933, Fred Harvey abandoned some of its oldest Santa Fe railroad locations: Arkansas City, Kansas, the site of the land rush; Trinidad, Colorado; Rincon, New Mexico; and Kingman, Arizona. In California they closed Mojave and Bakersfield, the lunchroom at the San Diego station, even the floating ferry restaurant on San Francisco Bay. They shuttered more eating houses in Oklahoma and Texas—including Purcell, Canadian, Sweetwater, and Fort Worth Union Station—leaving only the larger operations in Waynoka, Oklahoma; and Galveston, Houston, Temple, Brownwood, Slaton, and Somerville, Texas.

Since many people in these towns had been eating either breakfast or lunch at their Harvey House every day, and dined there on Sundays and special occasions, the departure of Fred Harvey left an enormous social and gastronomic void. It was like the closing of a small military base, with thirty or more years of history as an eating place, meeting place, and a business that brought hundreds of new employees to town who stayed and settled down.

Equally painful, hundreds of Harvey employees in Santa Fe cities, who had always thought of themselves as having the most stable jobs in town, were suddenly displaced. Some of the male employees—chefs, managers, busboys—were able to be reassigned to the Harvey dining car service, but that was a completely different world from the eating houses. The hours were much longer, the train rides endless.

"Those were tough times," recalled one Harvey Girl whose husband, an eating house manager, was transferred to the dining cars. "He would be gone for eight days and was then home for two . . . It was a very hard job for my husband but he never complained." Dining car staffers were really more employees of the railroad than of Fred Harvey, so their colleagues were a much tougher, unionized group. There were also no Harvey Girls on the trains. So the coed balance of the restaurants was replaced by a situation much like the one that led to the Harvey Girls being invented: an all-male staff with a certain amount of racial friction, cooped up together in a rolling tin can for hours on end.

Young writer Adam Clayton Powell, Jr. would marvel at the amount of responsibility Fred Harvey gave to black dining car employees during the Depression: "My waiter informed me that the entire car was not only staffed but also run by Negroes," he wrote in the *Amsterdam News*. "Here I was in the heart of the Texas Panhandle—cracker land—with the ace diner in complete charge of Negroes. Weren't these white folks a-scared? Why didn't one of them die of fright?... [Actually] the amount of criticism has been negligible . . . The hillbillies and prairie folks who have never seen a diner before pass out when a Negro tells them to sit here or there . . . The regular traveler takes this in stride."

The decisions to close the eating houses were probably made by executives at the Santa Fe, not Fred Harvey, and many of the closures were only coincidental to the failing economy. In a way, they had been envisioned for years—ever since Fred Harvey started competing against itself by running the dining cars as well as the eating houses. In fact, some of the smaller depot restaurants had survived solely because some train passengers still preferred them—for nostalgic reasons, but also because their prices were slightly lower. But trains were becoming faster—steam engines were getting more powerful, and the first diesels were on the way. More and more trains had Fred Harvey dining cars. So it was becoming harder for the railroad to justify making long meal stops and maintaining so many unprofitable eating houses.

One tough decision, however, did fall to Byron and Freddy. No matter how much they adored the Indian Detours and the entire culture that had grown up around them, that business, even with all its popularity, had never broken even. Now it was deeply in the red—and these were Fred Harvey losses, not shared with the railroad. So they decided to get out of the Indian Detours business. They kept La Fonda, but the Indian Detours company itself, including all the buses and Harveycars, the Courier outfits and guidebooks, was sold at a huge loss to its founder, Hunter Clarkson.

It was no longer possible for the Santa Fe and Fred Harvey to keep pretending the Depression was a temporary situation. That was especially true as it became clearer that the tariffs of the Smoot-Hawley Act of 1930—championed by the same Republican senator who had golfed with Ford during the convention—not only had failed to protect the U.S. economy but apparently did just the opposite; the tariffs were blamed for exporting the Depression overseas and further dragging down the world's financial markets.

Herbert Hoover was voted out of office, replaced by the Democratic governor of New York, Franklin Roosevelt, who had built a national political coalition with the help of two powerful Westerners: William McAdoo and William Randolph Hearst. Roosevelt's election and his "New Deal" offered some faint hope as he took office in March 1933.

But while the new president helped jump-start financial markets, he could not control the weather. As if the nationwide Depression were not enough, the Great Plains began experiencing droughts, devastating farmers in the heart of Santa Fe country. The railroad, which had to keep lowering fares and freight charges to compete, watched its operating revenue erode by half in the four years after the crash. Even more startling, its net income fell from $61 million ($767 million) to just $3.7 million ($61.5 million). The president of the Santa Fe, William Storey, resigned in exasperation and disgust.

WHILE THE ECONOMY CRUMBLED, Mary Colter and Herman Schweizer drove the back roads of the Southwest, searching for one more burst of inspiration. Now in their early sixties, they had aged into a feisty and odd pair of friends. Neither had ever married—their only sustained passion was work. Together they had recast America's view of Indians and Indian culture, and created some of the nation's most intriguing institutions and buildings. But with everything in their worlds so uncertain, it seemed this could be their last hurrah. Schweizer was growing nervous that the company would force him to sell off the Indian artifact collection he had spent over thirty years buying and curating. And Colter didn't know how much longer the company would need her, with all the Harvey Houses closing. So, this building they had her researching for the Grand Canyon had to be special, resonant.

The single most breathtaking spot on the South Rim of the canyon was called Desert View, some twenty miles east of El Tovar. From there, visitors could see twenty to thirty unimpeded miles of the canyon and the Colorado River—and, if they were lucky, they could also watch the greatest weather show on earth, the lightning storms that regularly barrel through the canyon, followed by gleaming rainbows. The National Park Service had paved a scenic road along the canyon's edge to connect Desert View with El Tovar and the main entrance to the park. Colter's task was to create something that would improve the experience of one of the world's greatest vistas.

She decided to build her own Indian "ruin" of a watchtower, some five stories high, with its own "kiva," the rooms Pueblo Indians used for sacred rituals. To research it, she made repeated visits to every similar building still standing in northern Arizona and New Mexico. Sometimes she would insist on being taken up in small planes, to get that perspective. But mostly, she and Schweizer had a driver take them around. The two of them would sit in the backseat bouncing as the car traversed the treacherous, dusty roads and paths. They also camped out for days at a time, hiking and sketching or photographing ancient structures.

When it was finished, Colter's watchtower appeared on the horizon like a huge Stone Age silo, a gravity-defying seventy-foot-high pile of indigenous rocks with irregularly shaped window openings positioned haphazardly around each floor. In fact, one of the windows was designed to appear as if it were falling apart, with a fake masonry crack clearly visible in the exterior wall. Yet the building was actually as steady as a skyscraper—beneath the authentic stone exterior was a steel-girder frame.

While kivas are usually underground, Colter had hers built as the first-floor entrance, with huge square windows and a remarkable ceiling crafted from concentric circles of stripped logs. This led to the Hopi Room, which evoked the Hopi Snake Dance with an altar, paintings on the walls, and a sand painting on the floor preserved under glass. From there, visitors passed into the silo's astounding interior, crammed with paintings like a conical Southwestern Sistine Chapel, which one architecture writer would describe as

> a balcony-ringed, cave-like column of space that rises three stories and surrounds one with an enthralling display of colors and folk images. A phantasmagoria of abstract architecture and art,

it is a romantic, even mystical creation whose imagery suggests a fusion of modern paintings—Klee and Chagall come most immediately to mind—freed from their frames and spread onto the crudely modeled walls and ceilings.

Above that rose two additional floors, more open, with stairways corkscrewing along the outer walls (in a design likely invoked decades later by Frank Lloyd Wright's Guggenheim Museum in New York) until a visitor reached the fifth-floor observatory, the "Eagle's Nest." It was the highest point on the entire South Rim, more than seventy-five hundred feet above sea level.

Colter sweated so many details—down to editing every stone—that when the Watchtower was nearly completed, she sat down and wrote a hundred-page booklet for the Fred Harvey canyon guides so they could properly appreciate and explain it. She enclosed a letter apologizing for "the bulkiness of this manual" and assuring them that they weren't "expected to learn it by heart," but she also noted that she would not stand for anyone rattling off her hard-won insights in "parrot fashion." If they didn't talk about the Watchtower with the same passion she had, Colter threatened, "I won't love you any more!"

When the Watchtower was finished, Colter was told what she already suspected. It would be her last building for a while—and perhaps her last building for Fred Harvey ever.

CHAPTER 38

HEIR RAISING

SINCE FORD'S DEATH, DAVE, JOHN HUCKEL, AND THE OTHER top executives had been shuttling back and forth between Kansas City and Chicago so that both Byron and Freddy could feel as if they were weighing in on decisions. But to a large degree, Ford Harvey's company was still running itself. It proved to be an impressively self-sustaining machine—built to last, even with all the cutbacks, and still the envy of any businessman who owned, or dreamed of owning, a chain of restaurants, hotels, retail stores, anything. But it could not continue indefinitely without new, strong leadership.

Both Uncle Byron, a proper English-style gentleman in his mid-fifties, and Freddy, his dashing thirtysomething nephew, had lived fairly cushy lives provided to them by Ford and his Tenth Legion. So it was not really surprising that neither of them had aggressively grabbed the reins. Any conflict between them remained understated, as British as the family's roots, a battle not of corporate fisticuffs but of raised eyebrows and reserved asides at family gatherings. Yet everyone in the family and at the top levels of the company knew that eventually only one of them could truly be in charge.

Besides the closings, a few small adjustments had been made in the business: A new company logo was developed using a stylized version of Fred Harvey's own signature, prices were lowered to respond to hard times, the union station restaurants opened stand-alone retail bakeries. But Dave was semiretired and John Huckel was nearing retirement age. And neither Byron nor Freddy had stepped up to offer long-range strategic plans; they seemed to have more faith in the railroad than in themselves.

"In the 1930s, it was the common belief among the Harveys that as long as the Santa Fe remained viable, so would Fred Harvey," recalled one of Byron's grandsons. " 'People will always require rail transportation,' they always said. Rather like the Pukka Sahibs' belief in the same time period that the British Empire would be eternal—that it was too big and important to end."

BYRON HAD NEVER done anything at Fred Harvey but manage the dining cars, so his knowledge of the inner workings of the core family business was considered limited. Also, he was still viewed as too nice, too genteel, to be a hard-core top executive. He would even joke about his own lack of business toughness, always delighted to retell the story of the black dining car waiter coming to his office expecting to be disciplined.

"Charlie," he recalled saying, "put yourself in my position. If a waiter came to you with a report that wasn't very good, what would *you* do?"

"Well, Mistah Haahvey," Byron would recount, mimicking a stereotyped black dialect, "I'd do just like you always do . . . I'd put my feet up on my desk and smoke a big black cigaaah."

Yet Byron was close to the railroad top brass in Chicago, and he had been waiting for decades to prove that his older brother, Ford, had been wrong about his leadership abilities. He wanted control for himself, but also for his sons, who were now out of college and slowly working their way up in the family business.

He and his wife, Helen, had raised their three sons—Byron Jr., Stewart, and Daggett—in a Lake Forest mansion on five and a half acres, a two-story brick Georgian building with thirteen rooms, five baths, stables, a conservatory, and apartments for the gardener and chauffeur. When the boys were away at boarding school and later at university, Byron would often write to them collectively, dictating from behind his large wooden table-desk. The letters always began "Dearest Boys" and talked about prep school or Ivy sports, family matters, and money. ("I am enclosing the dividend checks from American Steel Foundries stock. Don't spend all of yours at once.")

Byron Jr., who inherited some of his mother's spunk, theatricality, and good looks and briefly considered a career in acting, went to Stanford and then apprenticed at the Palmer House in Chicago and the Fred Harvey office in Kansas City before coming to work with his father in Chicago. Stewart, the middle brother, was the rebel Harvey. An athletic rabble-rouser, he barely survived St. Mark's, and got by at Yale for a while largely because he was a good football player. But when a foot infection ruined his chances to make the varsity team, he started spending too much time drinking and playing poker—badly. He eventually flunked out, which was particularly embarrassing because his precocious and studious younger brother, Daggett, had actually skipped a year and was in his same class at Yale, getting honors.

One night Stewart simply drove off in a secondhand Model T, and nobody saw or heard from him for ten months. During that time he did various jobs—sold cars in Port Arthur, Texas, swabbed decks and put out fires on an oil tanker—and finally decided to return to the family business, where he showed promise. But he struggled with what he later understood were alcoholism and manic-depressive illness, and his brothers often looked out for him. On his twenty-sixth birthday, Stewart received a telegram from his older brother, Byron: "Trust you will have [a] very happy birthday dear boy and that you are enjoying your work. Be sure you are getting lots of exercise so you will not gain too much weight. Am depositing $5000 [$71,000] to your credit at First National Bank as little birthday gift."

In 1931, Byron Jr. and Stewart married within three months of each other. Byron married Kathleen Whitcomb, an heiress and aspiring actress of some talent who had trained at the Goodman Theatre. Her grandfather had started a major Chicago locomotive manufacturing firm and later moved west, where he founded the city of Glendora, California. Stewart, in turn, married Laura Hotchkiss Cornell, a fiery Hunter College–trained artist who lived in Santa Fe, where she was studying with the prominent painter Randall Davey. The couple met when Stewart was making an inspection of La Fonda.

Within a year, both sons made their father, Byron, a grandfather. But when it came time to name those two baby boys, all familial hell broke loose.

Stewart and Laura wanted to name their son after the company's founder, a Fred Harvey for a new generation. The idea was immediately torpedoed by their Aunt Minnie—in the first of many signs that the Kansas City Harveys and the Chicago Harveys were going to fight over the future of the family and its business.

In the years since Ford's death, Minnie Harvey Huckel had developed into the family matriarch. She was Fred's eldest living child, and the one who had been closest to Ford. Her husband, John, was the senior executive at the Kansas City office, but she no longer had to make her opinions known through him; she now enjoyed the complete loyalty of her beloved niece and nephew, Kitty and Freddy, who also voted most of the company stock. So Minnie wielded a great deal of power. Sharp-tongued and forbidding, she made any seat her throne, her twin Pekingese perched on her lap, yapping and snapping. She had a sense of humor about her dogs—she and her sister Sybil had once staged a high-society dog wedding, complete with canine gowns and pearls, at her summer home in Colorado Springs. Yet she was deadly serious when it came to breaches of family protocol.

Minnie insisted that the right to pass on the founder's name belonged solely to Freddy, the Kansas City heir apparent. After ten years of trying, he and Betty were still hoping to have a baby. It simply would not do for the Chicago Harveys to try to steal the birthright of Ford Harvey's only son.

Of course, Minnie had her own issues with Freddy—as did Kitty, who looked forward to a day when she could advise her brother as he ran the company. Both were bothered by Freddy's presumption that whatever he needed to know would simply rub off from working around the older executives, and that he didn't really need to learn *everything* about the business because there would always be plenty of smart people around to advise him. They were annoyed that he was pushing forty and still didn't seem to grasp the concept of working all day, every day. But despite all this, Freddy was the only candidate to be the family's Kansas City savior. His legacy had to be protected.

So Minnie and Freddy both told Stewart—who was working at the Kansas City office at the time—that he needed to find another name for his baby. Since he felt a certain allegiance to the Kansas City Harveys, he quickly acquiesced and named his son Stewart Jr.

But three months later, when Byron Jr.'s son was born in Chicago, he openly defied Minnie by naming his baby Frederick Henry Harvey III. A birth certificate with the name was issued at Passavant Memorial Hospital at Northwestern University.

At that point, Minnie had a long talk with Byron Sr., who even at age fifty-five was still her kid brother. While nobody ever found out what they "discussed," a new birth certificate was issued several days later, and the baby was renamed Byron Harvey III. To avoid Byron gridlock at family events, he was called Ronny.

And just to make certain there was no question in the family that the Kansas City Harveys would produce a namesake heir, Freddy's wife, Betty, arrived in Chicago several weeks after the birth certificate was changed—and announced to the society columns that she was in town to find a male baby.

"Mrs. Frederick Harvey Here 'Shopping' for Baby Boy to Adopt," read the headline in the *Chicago American*. The gushy article, which described Betty as "breathtakingly lovely" and "almost unbelievably beautiful"—in the same sentence—explained that since "no ordinary baby would do . . . the process of finding just the right one has been quite difficult." Apparently, adoption had already become quite competitive by the early 1930s. Betty "found a cunning pair of twin boys at one clinic, but before she could quite adjust her plans for twin beds in the nursery, some other couple who had an option on them snapped the twins up and carried them off."

After sizing up the "Chicago baby market," Betty returned to Kansas City and gave Freddy a full report on her "shopping tour." And then they flew to Santa Barbara in his new plane, which the paper said was "his pride and joy."

As for the baby—well, they would just have to keep shopping.

IN THIS GAME of family chess, the Chicago Harveys soon made a surprising countermove. Byron Sr. announced he was doing something unprecedented in the company's fifty-seven-year history: He was moving the company into a new business that had nothing to do with the trains, and would be opening sophisticated urban restaurants with no Harvey Girls. He and his oldest son had agreed to run five new Fred Harvey restaurants, all located in the Straus Building (now called the Metropolitan Tower), a glamorous skyscraper at the corner of South Michigan Avenue and Jackson Boulevard that overlooked Grant Park and Lake Michigan. The new restaurants were only a few blocks from where Chicago's long-awaited Century of Progress International Exposition—the 1934 world's fair—was slated to open in a few months.

Little is known about Byron's decision, but there are certainly hints in the newspaper coverage that the family was far from united concerning the new restaurants. The announcement in the *Chicago Tribune* barely mentioned the Kansas City home base of the company or its executives. The *Kansas City Star* story, on the other hand, barely mentioned Byron, instead explaining rather awkwardly that Freddy and John Huckel were in Chicago "to cooperate with other officers of the company." Between the lines, it was clear that Byron's decision was causing a good deal of family friction.

If Byron was making a mistake, there was nobody left to talk him out of it. Dave Benjamin was the last voice of reason who had known Fred and Ford well and could remain above the fray of family fighting—and he was no longer actively involved in day-to-day business. He had cashed out his shares, and while he was still technically a vice president, he spent most of his time raising money for charity. He focused on poverty and Jewish causes. "I try to follow the teachings of Judaism," he said, "by helping my brother, and I don't think that help should be limited to my Jewish brother." He was also active in the nascent YM-YWHA movement, which would eventually create Jewish Community Centers all over America. He saw them as havens for "those who can't afford the more expensive form of Jewish clubs." On his recent seventy-fifth birthday, he had been presented with an oil portrait of himself by the board of United Jewish Charities.

Just two weeks after the announcement of the new, non–Harvey Girl restaurants in Chicago, Dave Benjamin was in the news. The *Kansas City Journal-Post* reported that the serially providential business leader—"who has had his share of harrowing experiences" and had just recently "enjoyed a talk with his colleagues" about them—had survived yet another natural disaster. He and his wife were visiting Los Angeles when the city was rocked by an earthquake on March 10, 1933, registering 6.3 on the Richter scale. More than a hundred people were killed, thousands were injured and homeless, and there was over $40 million ($643 million) in property damage. But, as the *Journal-Post* headline read, "David Benjamin Telephones Calmly as Earthquake Showers Plaster."

Ironically, only weeks later, Dave took ill in the safety of his own home, after playing cards on a Sunday night with his wife, his spinster sister, Fanny, and one of his sons. The game broke up just before 11:00 p.m., and ten minutes after his guests left, Dave said he didn't feel well and excused himself. When his wife went to check on him a few minutes later, she found him in the bathroom clutching his chest, dying from a massive heart attack.

Dave Benjamin was buried that Wednesday morning, and his pall-bearers were all close colleagues from the Kansas City office, led by Freddy. Later that day, in Chicago, there was an event he would have been sorry to miss. Some twenty-five thousand Jews marched on Grant Park, just across Michigan Avenue from the new Fred Harvey restaurants. They were there to protest the Nazi persecution of Jews and to demand that the Century of Progress exposition ban Germany's chosen envoy to the world's fair. Adolf Hitler, who had recently seized control of the German government and was now chancellor, apparently planned to send Dr. Joseph Goebbels as his nation's goodwill representative to the exposition.

The next day, as the Benjamin family mourned, Century of Progress officials announced the Germans would not be coming to the Chicago world's fair after all.

IN THE WEEKS leading up to the fair, Byron unveiled his new restaurants in the Straus Building. But the media and the public were considerably more interested in an utterly delightful side venture that Fred Harvey had undertaken on the fairgrounds: the first restaurant just for kids, the Toy Town Tavern.

The Century of Progress exhibition had an entire separate fair for children: the "Enchanted Island," featuring amazing amusement rides, engaging street performers, and a special library where many of the world's top children's authors served as resident storytellers. There was also a kid-friendly theater, with productions running nonstop from 10:00 a.m. to 10:00 p.m. every single day.

And in the middle of this colorful chaos was the Harvey Toy Town Tavern, a sleek, curved one-story building with twenty-foot-high windows, revealing an interior decorated with a smorgasbord of colorful storybook images. The chandeliers were dangling dollhouse villages and castles, the walls were painted floor to ceiling with circus images, witches on broomsticks, and life-size cows jumping over the moon. The Toy Town Tavern even had its own kid-friendly, limited-edition china pattern, with hand-painted images of Mother Goose rhymes, professorial elephants teaching French grammar, and bon vivant rabbit couples out for a stroll. The decor was designed with the help of renowned puppeteer Tony Sarg, the Jim Henson of his day, who was also a prolific and beloved illustrator and had invented the first whimsical balloons for the Macy's Thanksgiving Day Parade in 1928. (Sarg also designed and built the first mechanical animations for Macy's Christmas windows.)

When the Chicago world's fair opened in May 1933, there was cautious optimism about its chances for success in the harsh economy. The most recent Summer Olympics, which were held in Los Angeles because no other city in the world would bid on them during the economic crisis, had been something of a disaster; nearly half the countries that normally competed could not afford to send their athletes to the games, and the president did not even attend.

Yet the Century of Progress exposition was surprisingly successful. Over a hundred thousand people arrived each day. While many traveled by car, the train stations were packed with tourists—and since Fred Harvey ran all the restaurants and shops in Chicago Union Station, and the restaurant in Dearborn Station, where the Santa Fe trains came in from the West, its capacity was pushed to the limit. For the first time in years, redcaps were working up a sweat juggling luggage, and Harvey Girls were busy juggling customers.

The mood in the restaurants was especially festive, because after thirteen "dry" years patrons could legally order a beer or a glass of wine. One of President Roosevelt's first acts when he took office in March had been to sign a bill legalizing the manufacture and sale of light wines and low-alcohol beer, and the ratification process for a full-scale constitutional amendment legalizing all liquor was under way.

Because all the Fred Harvey union stations feeding into Chicago were surging with world's fair business, Kansas City Union Station was more crowded than usual on the morning of Saturday, June 17, as seven federal agents tried to hustle murderer and train robber Frank Nash through the terminal without attracting attention. He had recently been recaptured after escaping from prison; a car was waiting outside to take him back to jail in Leavenworth—where a new federal penitentiary had been built near the fort.

When the men reached the black sedan in the crowded parking lot, the agents shoved Nash into the backseat, where he raised his cuffed hands and then ducked—a signal to three gangsters lying in wait with machine guns. One of them yelled, "Let 'em have it," and they opened fire, a dense spray of bullets pelting the car and everyone near it. The gunmen—led by the infamous Charles "Pretty Boy" Floyd—rushed to the car to get their friend, but when they opened the door, they saw that Nash, and everyone else, was dead. As they raced out of the parking lot in a dark Chevrolet sedan, a Kansas City cop fired at them, but they got away—leaving four federal agents dead and two more critically wounded.

The "Kansas City Massacre" immediately became priority number one for the fledgling federal Bureau of Investigation and its ambitious young leader, J. Edgar Hoover. The massacre investigation would become the turning point for federal law enforcement, bringing Hoover's agency a much wider national mandate than ever before—for the first time, his agents were allowed to carry firearms and countermand local police—and leading directly to the creation of the modern FBI.

At the Fred Harvey lunchroom in Union Station, however, the massacre was just one more Depression-era drama for the Harvey Girls to gab about with their regular customers. They all howled when retelling the story of what happened in the restaurant right *after* the shooting. Their manager, Walter Rouzer, had missed the entire incident, but when he heard about it ten minutes later, he came running excitedly into the lunchroom, slipped at the entrance, and slid across the floor on his belly. It looked like a movie slapstick routine, and from then on they called him "Wild Dash Rouzer."

AS PRESIDENT ROOSEVELT'S first year in office came to an end, hopeful Americans looked for any sign that the nation was headed into recovery. Instead, in the spring of 1934, it started raining dirt.

At Harvey Houses all over Kansas, the exhaustively manicured front lawns were disappearing under dust that had fallen from the sky. On St. Patrick's Day, the dirtstorm reached Kansas City, causing the temperature to plummet from a balmy sixty-eight degrees to well below freezing in six hours. Soon it was sleeting dirt and then snowing dirt. Freddy watched in disbelief from the corner office he had inherited from his father.

Weathermen called it a "freak storm," but then it happened again. In some Midwestern towns, the dust drifted so deep that it covered the snow fences; in rural areas, snowplows were used to remove sand and dirt from roads.

In early May, Chicago was shrouded by a cloud of dirt so large that airplanes had to be rerouted, because even at ten thousand feet they couldn't get above it. Some twelve million pounds of dust were swept into Greater Chicago by the windstorm in just over twenty-four hours—four pounds for every man, woman, and child. And then the black cloud moved east across America, in a five-hundred-mile band hugging the Great Lakes, at a rate of sixty to a hundred miles an hour. The next morning, it descended on New York City during rush hour. The sun's rays were so distorted that Manhattan was cast in an obscure half-light, which observers likened to a partial solar eclipse.

When it was over, the topsoil that made America's Midwest the most abundant source of grain in the world was gone—dried out and loosened by summers of drought and improper crop rotation—and the "Dust Bowl" era had begun. It decimated American agriculture and triggered one of the largest migrations in the nation's history—nearly half a million people driving, riding, hitching, walking, hopping freight trains west. They came from Oklahoma, the Texas Panhandle, Missouri, Kansas, and New Mexico, mostly by Santa Fe trains or on Route 66.

Their migration put the remaining Fred Harvey hotels and eating houses under even more pressure to feed the hungry. For several years, Harvey Girls, chefs, and busboys had seen firsthand the more urban devastation of the Depression. But now the Dust Bowl was destroying the rural economy as well, and an entirely new group of Americans were begging at the Fred Harvey eating houses along their route to the "promised land" of California.

One Santa Fe conductor never forgot a scene he witnessed at the Purcell, Oklahoma, station, when railroad police, "bulls," were trying to chase hobos away from the trains. "The thirty-six freight train was pulling out of Purcell and the hobo caught the boxcar and was trying to climb across the rods," the conductor recalled. "He slipped and fell. The wheels cut off both of his legs at the knees. They called in a doctor and gave him some shots and . . . put him on a stretcher in the baggage room where he waited for the southern freight train from Oklahoma City to take him to a hospital."

He recalled the hobo said only one thing:

"Did they get them both?"

Someone told him, "Yeah."

CHAPTER 39

GREAT EXPECTATIONS

ᴵF THE DEPRESSION MADE LIFE MORE DIFFICULT FOR ANY OF THE
Harveys personally, it certainly didn't show. As a private company, their
business dealings did not get much coverage unless they sought it—so
nobody reported when the new restaurants in the Straus Building lost
money or mentioned how many Harvey locations had closed since the
crash. As public people, they were still society-page stars.

The Byron Harveys entertained grandly, and each year Helen Harvey's name appeared on Chicago's best-dressed list. The family's place
in society was elevated, and assured for years to come, when Daggett—
now a practicing attorney and the only young Harvey not in the family business—became engaged to one of Chicago's most illustrious and
desirable debutantes: Jean Cudahy Wilhelm, the granddaughter of
meatpacking magnate Edward Cudahy.

In Kansas City, the exploits of Freddy and Betty Harvey always
made news. They threw lavish parties and fund-raisers for major arts
charities—especially the new William Rockhill Nelson Gallery of Art
(now the Nelson-Atkins Museum of Art), created by the trust of the
late *Kansas City Star* publisher. The Harveys and the Huckels also
helped the museum create its Indian art collection by selling items from
the company vault in Albuquerque (which made Herman Schweizer
extremely nervous).

Freddy and Betty were among the world's first "jet-setters"—even
before there were actually jets. "One day while zooming above the Missouri clouds, Betty suggested dinner at the Chateau Frontenac in Que-
bec," *Mademoiselle* magazine reported. "Fred likes Creole cooking, so
he held out for Antoine's in New Orleans. After going round and

round on the subject, they put it up to the wind. A sudden gust blew them South, and New Orleans won."

The couple was also known for their obsessions with their pets. They had a pair of purebred black dachshunds, Samson and Susanna, that Betty had carried back with her on the ship from Europe as puppies, registering them in the U.S. branch of the "Tail Waggers Club"—which raised money for "less fortunate dogs"—immediately upon arriving in New York. All member dogs got a special round medal for their collars, which read, "Be a Tail Wagger and help your pals," and Betty also bought the puppies Tail Waggers monogrammed coats. She often took Samson and Susanna with her when traveling: In London, she got to know the king and queen of Norway because the royal couple spotted the dachshunds at Claridge's hotel and insisted on meeting their owner.

Once, when Susanna was pregnant, Freddy had her flown home from New York by his airline so the puppies could claim Kansas City as their birthplace. It is unclear whether Susanna came in a carrier, got her own seat, or sat on the lap of pilot D. L. Mesker, who was photographed holding her for the *Kansas City Journal-Post*. Local papers also ran editorial cartoons about the dog's flight and her pregnancy, and covered the birth. She produced only one pup—even their dog had fertility issues.

The society pages did not dare to hint that Freddy and Betty's marriage was anything but joy and frivolity. But some family members believed their life together was no longer so cheery. "I always wondered how well they were getting along, since I thought Betty was a little flirtatious," recalled one Harvey grandson. "They fought a lot," said a great-grandson. "She was apparently a tigress of the first order."

As for Kitty, since she shuttled back and forth between the family homes in Kansas City and California, her exploits were well detailed in the society columns in both places. The *Kansas City Star* was fascinated by a monthlong "camping and wandering expedition" she and Mary Perkins took through the Navajo country in Arizona. (They chose such challenging, hazardous routes that three of their eight pack mules fell over the side of a narrow trail; one died.) And the *Los Angeles Times* often covered Kitty's life in Southern California, as she entertained more often at Arequipa.

The family estate had award-winning gardens, constantly upgraded by their gardener, who experimented with plants and flowers in the large greenhouse. The property had two large California Mission–style buildings and a small house for the staff. The main house featured large formal rooms, an industrial steel-clad kitchen, and an elevator; the family's art collections covered almost every available inch of wall space, with each room separated by theme. They contained everything from Native drawings and drums to antique six-shooters, Frederic Remington statues, and a painting of the Grand Canyon that Thomas Moran had signed "To my friend, Ford Harvey." Since Arequipa was almost ten miles from the ocean, Kitty followed the trend of other Montecitans and had a separate beach house built in the Sandyland beach colony. Mary Perkins built her own Sandyland cottage nearby.

EVEN IN ECONOMIC hard times, Fred Harvey restaurants did not lose their ability to dazzle those diners who could afford the culinary entertainment. In late October 1934, the flamboyant chef at Kansas City Union Station, Sylvester Bonani, invited one of his best customers, county prosecutor W. W. Graves, to indulge in a favorite dish of Henry VIII: He was going to crush him a duck.

A friend of the prosecutor's had brought freshly shot ducks to the Fred Harvey restaurant for preparation, and Chef Sylvester decided to re-create the classic dish. The ducks were roasted in the oven for just four minutes, then placed on silver platters and carried dramatically into the dining room. As the chef sharpened his carving tools, he called out, "Away my knaves . . . fetch me the duck press!" It was, according to the *Kansas City Post* food writer who attended the dinner, probably the only duck press in the region and one of the few in the country: a massive solid-silver contraption over two feet high with a large wheel on the top.

Chef Sylvester delicately sliced the breast meat and leg meat from the very rare ducks and placed it in a chafing dish. Then he put the uncooked carcass of one of the ducks in the press, turning the wheel until they could hear the bones crunching—followed by a trickle of blood and other juices dribbling from the silver spigot into the chef's saucepan. He then stirred in "many things . . . the maestro's secret"— the dish normally includes butter, cognac, and the ground and seasoned liver of the duck—and created a stunning sauce that was poured over the warming duck meat.

A half hour after the table-side ritual had begun, the prosecutor and his party were served. Awestruck at his own creation, Chef Sylvester thumped his chest in pride, whispering loudly enough for everyone to hear: "What a regal bite."

BY 1935, THE DEPRESSION seemed as if it might be starting to lift, in response to a barrage of economic innovations from Franklin Roosevelt's New Deal, which was entering its second phase. Some of the New Deal programs became permanent parts of the American economy, such as Social Security, the Securities and Exchange Commission, and the FDIC, which insured bank deposits. Others had lasting impact, like the Works Progress Administration, which among its many jobs programs created public art all across the country. And some were experiments that ultimately failed, including the price and wage controls attempted under the short-lived National Recovery Administration (NRA), an attempt to create a "code of fair competition" for each industry. While declared unconstitutional in 1935, some of the NRA rules lived on in the 1936 Robinson-Patman Act, which made "fair trade" the law of the land, prohibiting discount prices or rebates of any sort.

This very strongly affected John Huckel's division at Fred Harvey, which, like most major retailers, had always charged magazine publishers and candy manufacturers extra for preferential shelf placement. Until Robinson-Patman, companies just had to play hardball to avoid those payments: When the president of Chicago-based Mars candies was told what it would cost to make sure his Milky Way and Snickers bars got premium display at Harvey newsstands, he pulled fifty carloads of sugar and chocolate off the Santa Fe until the railroad pressured Huckel to relent.

Still, taken together, all of Roosevelt's economic initiatives appeared to be having an impact, and companies were beginning to respond. Both the Santa Fe and Fred Harvey started new projects with guarded optimism.

The railroad began investing in its future. Because of the dust storms in the Southwest, the Santa Fe decided it needed air-conditioning in its dining and passenger cars, and to keep up with the higher speeds that technology would make possible, the railroad ordered new diesel engines. To attract more travelers of all classes, the Santa Fe expanded its luxury services, but also beefed up its economy services. These upgraded trains, and the dining cars they required, were primarily handled through Byron's offices in Chicago.

In Kansas City, Freddy, John Huckel, and Mary Colter started spending much of their time on a big project at the Grand Canyon: the new Bright Angel Lodge. Just down the path from El Tovar, it was the company's first attempt at creating a more affordable experience at the South Rim. Bright Angel was a long, low stone-and-log ranch building with thirty-nine hotel rooms and fourteen separate cabins around it. Most of the complex was fairly utilitarian and remarkable only in its small touches, but the entrance had two memorable Colter creations: The main lobby was a Tinkertoy maze of interconnecting logs, and in the adjoining room she crafted a particularly ingenious fireplace. It was built from rocks carefully chosen layer by layer to mirror the various types of stones found along the walls of the canyon. In its ten feet from floor to ceiling, Colter provided a brilliant geology lesson about the Divine Abyss—which could be seen in all of its splendor through large picture windows on either side of the fireplace.

Bright Angel Lodge was the last of the major projects that Ford Harvey had envisioned before his death—finally meeting the challenge he raised at those early Interior Department meetings to make sure the national parks equally served visitors from all walks of life. It was also a showcase for Freddy's growing abilities as a leader. While John Huckel had been doing a fine job holding the Kansas City operation together after Ford's death, he was now well into his sixties, and his health was becoming unsteady, in part because of a drinking problem. While he and Freddy were both on-site during the Bright Angel construction, it was Freddy who was sent to Washington to discuss the project with the Department of the Interior, and to lobby for an exemption to the new hotel tax being contemplated as part of the New Deal programs. He was talking to the same politicians who had been close to Ford, many of whom had watched him and Kitty grow up at the canyon's edge.

Aunt Minnie and Uncle John had high hopes for their nephew as the next leader of the company. Freddy was well liked and he had inherited his father's and his grandfather's gift for making staff members feel part of a family, remembering names and faces and telling details about employees all along the line. One reporter noted the way he "took a special interest in the younger men with whom he worked. If they were in any sort of personal difficulties they instinctively turned to Mr. Harvey and his sympathetic counsel was at their service." He may not have focused enough on the day-to-day particulars of the business, but he clearly had the politicking down. With his natty double-breasted suits, trim mustache, and charm, brimming with enthusiasm, he was becoming more and more presidential.

Even Freddy's obsession with the passenger airline industry looked as if it might finally become more than an expensive hobby. Transcontinental Air Transport had gotten off to a rocky start, and the business had unfolded differently than expected. But planes could now fly at night, and they were fast enough to carry passengers from either coast as far as Kansas City in a single day, so TAT no longer needed trains to supplement its air services. Also, a scandal had rocked the industry in the early 1930s—after the government encouraged the passenger airlines to merge with the airmail companies, the Roosevelt administration came in and declared the deals suspicious. But that was behind them at last. TAT had merged with postal carrier Western Air, and then reorganized again under a new name: Transcontinental & Western Air became TWA.

The new airline chose Kansas City as its national headquarters, and Freddy was named to the board of directors. When the TWA board, led by Henry DuPont, met for the first time in Kansas City in May 1935, the Harveys invited them all to their home for an elegant soiree. It was heady company for the young executive, and got even headier several months later when the controlling shares of TWA were sold to Lehman Brothers brokerage firm and the Atlas investment trust. The deal was negotiated by Lehman Brothers partner John D. Hertz, who had already made two fortunes recognizing unique transportation needs: He started the Yellow Cab Company in Chicago, franchising it nationwide, and then created the "Hertz Drive-Ur-Self System," which became "Hertz Rent-a-Car." As a broker, he had recently helped finance the reorganization of Paramount Pictures.

People like Hertz intrigued Freddy. He couldn't help but wonder if the family business might outgrow its Santa Fe eating house roots when the economy turned around. For that to happen, Fred Harvey would probably have to borrow a lot of money—something both Fred and Ford had always been reluctant to do—or the company would have to go public, with the help of a large national investment banking house such as Lehman Brothers. With that kind of capital, they could think about a variety of bold strategies for the future.

Fred Harvey could open multiple locations in cities where the company was well established—signature full-service family restaurants, diners, or coffee shops. It could also enter the promising "roadside" market as the highway system expanded. With financing, Fred Harvey could consider expanding into other union stations and other national parks, and could make sure it controlled the business of caring for air travelers as it had for train passengers—starting in the West, and perhaps expanding across the country. Not only could Fred Harvey serve food on more and larger planes—the original male stewards replaced by flying Harvey Girls—but it could also run the restaurants and hotels that would eventually spring up in and around airports.

IN LATE JANUARY 1936, Freddy flew his wife and a whole lot of luggage to New York so he could see her off at the pier. Betty had more bags than usual because she had been shopping for baby clothes and toys for weeks. She was about to become an aunt.

Her brother had recently married, and her new sister-in-law was seven months pregnant. Betty had been unable to get to England for their wedding or, several months later, for the funeral of her father. But she was not going to be deprived of the chance to be part of this Drage family event. She intended to stay in England until she was able to hold that little baby—the next generation of her family.

On her arrival, Betty went directly to Somerby Grove, Leicestershire—deep in horse and hunt country about a hundred miles northeast of London—where her brother, Charles, and his wife, Rowena, lived on a large horse farm. She immediately connected with her new sister-in-law, an English country girl amazed by the urbanity of this Kansas City socialite who overwhelmed her with expensive gifts.

Early in her visit, Betty wasn't feeling well, and Rowena asked her family physician, Dr. Harold Furness, to make a house call. When Betty told him about her epic fertility problems, he said he knew someone who might be able to help her—an old medical school friend in London, Dr. Gertrude Dearnley.

An eminent obstetric surgeon in her early fifties, Dr. Dearnley had set up the first fertility clinic in England at the Royal Free Hospital in London. It was a full-service clinic, but Dearnley was known among her colleagues for championing one procedure there that some considered too risky—an abdominal myomectomy, in which benign fibroid tumors were removed from the uterus without compromising fertility. The operation was Betty's last hope to have a child, and she wanted it done immediately. Four days after hearing about it, she was sitting in Gertrude Dearnley's office in London being prepped for surgery. Everything went smoothly, but the first month of recovery was extremely difficult. The incision was painful, and the bleeding was so heavy that it was almost more dangerous than the operation. To slow the blood flow, patients were given regular injections of ergotamine, a milder form of the active ingredient in LSD (without the hallucinatory effects). Betty had six injections over the next month.

To deal with the discomfort, she indulged herself. She twice had a manicurist from Elizabeth Arden sent after hours to her hospital room. And after she returned to her brother's home to convalesce, she had Norah Crampton, a top London fashion designer who had a store in London's Berkeley Square, bring clothes to her so she could shop from her sickbed. In the first weeks after Betty's surgery, Crampton traveled the hundred miles up to Leicestershire twice—once with a selection of tea gowns (Betty bought one green and one gold) and the second time with handbags.

When Betty had just about recovered, her sister-in-law went into labor, and on March 2, 1936, delivered a baby girl. As Betty held her new niece in her arms for the first time, she was told the baby was being named for her, Elizabeth.

Giddy with excitement about the baby—and the possibility that she and Freddy could finally have one of their own—Betty went to London on a shopping spree, buying lovely things for her sister-in-law and herself. In one day at Norah Crampton's shop she bought a black wool dress with a floral top, a black chiffon evening dress, and a violet evening dress; a gray tweed cardigan suit, a mauve tweed jumper suit, and a black and white tweed suit; a mauve tweed swagger coat, a gray coat, and a brown coat with two matching skirts; a white satin blouse, a white shantung blouse, a brown jumper, a black scarf, and a strand of pearls. The next time Betty returned to the shop, she bought bags and hats—four felt sports hats, three leather bags, three tweed bags, and three evening bags—and then evening wear: a blue georgette dress with a cape, a blue tweed dress and coat, a tea gown with a blue lining, a blue-and-white-checked dress, and, just as an indulgence, a fox cape. Over the next two weeks, Betty bought thirteen more dresses, ten more hats, fourteen pairs of stockings, a parasol with a rose quartz and enamel handle, and a mink stole. Her bill was $4,484.09 ($69,656), and that was just at Norah Crampton.

Betty also shopped for the baby, buying exquisite clothes and elaborate prams and cribs. And she bought a few other things that she needed, including riding clothes and, of course, a new puppy. It was an Australian terrier, a breed of tiny working terriers that was becoming popular in England but had yet to catch on in America.

But most of the time she spent in Somerby, playing dress up with her new sister-in-law and baby niece. She hadn't felt this happy, this hopeful, in years.

BACK HOME, FREDDY was doing some shopping of his own. He decided to buy the plane that every private flyer coveted, the Beechcraft Staggerwing—the first aircraft ever designed specifically for the rich aviator market, the progenitor of today's Gulfstream and Learjet planes. The Staggerwing was considered the most beautiful plane ever built (and still is today, with a model hanging in the Smithsonian). It was named for its elegant and unusual wing design: The top wing was staggered farther back than the bottom, for better visibility, and the two were joined by a sculptured piece of metal that curved out dramatically on either end. Each Staggerwing was custom-built with interiors of rich leather and mohair, and the planes had the first-ever pneumatically retractable landing gear, which explained the exorbitant price of $17,000 ($264,000). The Staggerwing was the ultimate aviator status symbol, and Freddy bought the fastest one they made: the B-17 model with the special nine-cylinder, 420-horsepower engine that could fly over two hundred miles per hour, nearly twice as fast as his old plane.

His uncle was predictably upset about Freddy's new toy. At age seventy-two, John Huckel was approaching his fortieth anniversary with the family business and knew his health wouldn't allow him to remain the day-to-day leader much longer. He had lived much of his career in the shadow of Ford Harvey—who had spent a lot of time deliberately hiding in the shadow of Fred Harvey. So Huckel had never really received the credit he deserved for being the driving force in the company's retail operations and hotel management, the overseer of the Indian art and crafts business, and both enabler and babysitter to Mary Colter and Herman Schweizer. His wife, Minnie, had tried to get him a little attention on his last birthday, sponsoring an Indian art show in his honor that displayed for the first time his amazing collection of watercolor reproductions of Navajo sand paintings. But overall, Huckel was an underappreciated force within Fred Harvey.

In mid-March 1936, as Freddy anxiously awaited delivery of his plane, John Huckel was stricken with the flu. Eleven days later, he was dead.

Byron came in for the funeral, which he hoped might mark the end of Fred Harvey being run from Kansas City. In fact, he had already told his sons he planned to move all operations to Chicago. But his sister Minnie made it clear that the main office would be moved only over her dead body. To her, it was high time for Byron, who was about to turn sixty, to officially pass the torch to Freddy.

CHAPTER 40

TAILSPIN

〓〓

FREDDY LOVED HIS NEW PLANE, WHICH HAD A BRIGHT RED FUSE-lage with Cadillac blue wings. To test it out and show it off, he flew to California to see Kitty, who had spent the winter with Mary Perkins at her family's horse farm and was now back at Arequipa, where her friend Harriet McLaughlin was visiting.

Once his sister got a look at his shiny new toy, Freddy turned around and flew the plane back to Kansas City, and then on to New York, bringing along a college chum and fellow flyer, William Read Jr.—yet another rich kid torn between his family business and his love of aviation. His father owned the prominent New York investment banking firm that became the legendary Dillon, Read & Company, which William had fled after the stock market crash. He was now running the trust department at Central Hanover Bank, and trying to find a way to make flying his career.

Freddy met Betty's boat when it arrived early on Thursday morning, April 16, 1936; she came off the S.S. *Manhattan* smiling broadly for the cameras that often greeted prominent overseas passengers, wearing her new mink stole and one of her smart new hats, clutching her fuzzy little puppy to her chest. She and Freddy stayed over in New York—long enough to do some shopping and register the puppy at the Tail Waggers Club—and on Saturday, he spent the afternoon at the Racquet Club with William Read and a bunch of their old college friends. They drank and recounted stories of Freddy's youthful exploits.

The next morning, the Harveys took off in the Staggerwing from New York. The sky was clear, with temperatures in the forties, but as Freddy piloted the plane across northern Pennsylvania and approached the Allegheny Mountains, he ran into icing conditions and decided to land for lunch. He put down at the Duncansville Airport, which served the old railroad town of Altoona—home of the Logan House, the nation's first great trackside restaurant in the years before Fred Harvey. The chic couple with the snazzy plane and the adorable dog enchanted the staff at the small airport.

Freddy called the TWA control tower at Pittsburgh airport, on the other side of the Alleghenies, to ask about the weather ahead. It was one of the perks of being a board member. He was told that the skies were treacherous: dense fog and icing conditions up to seven thousand feet. The TWA staff at Pittsburgh airport strongly recommended that he wait before trying to fly over the mountains.

This wasn't just because the weather was terrible and he was their boss. The tower staff was being hypervigilant in the aftermath of one of the worst commercial plane crashes in the nation's history, which had taken place—on their watch—just twelve days earlier. In fact, federal air safety officials were still in nearby Uniontown, Pennsylvania, sifting through the wreckage of the Douglas DC-2 in which twelve passengers on a flight from Philadelphia to Pittsburgh had lost their lives. The U.S. Senate had been screaming for an investigation of air safety for some time, ever since one of their colleagues, New Mexico Senator Bronson Cutting, had been killed in a private plane in May 1935—followed just three months later by the death of Will Rogers, who crashed in Barrow, Alaska. Then seventeen people died in a commercial airliner accident in Goodwin, Arkansas, that some investigators believed was caused by a suicidal passenger who shot the pilots. And now there was the Uniontown crash, which was front-page news every day in Pennsylvania.

But Freddy was impatient to get home, so he asked for other options. He was told that if he absolutely *insisted* on flying, then he could try backtracking northeast and take the long way through the Newark-to-Cleveland airway. Or he could try taking off and rocketing pretty much straight up in the air until he got above the clouds. That's what the larger commercial planes in the area were doing, but they had deicers and vacuum-driven instruments, equipment that was not available even on the poshest of private planes.

Hearing the same advice from the Pittsburgh tower, another pilot who was waiting along with the Harveys elected to stay on the ground until conditions cleared. But Freddy believed his new Staggerwing was up to the challenge.

"It looks bad," he told one of the grounds crew, "but I'll try it."

Freddy had stopped wearing parachutes when he flew, but when Betty heard about the weather warnings, she put one on. They took off at 2:00 p.m. into what appeared to be an open spot in the clouds above the Duncansville Airport. The red and blue single-engine plane, with "NC281Y" painted in white beneath the wings, climbed three thousand feet and disappeared into the gray cloud bank.

According to expert analysis and reconstruction done at the time—and recent interviews with contemporary pilots with Staggerwing experience—the four wings of Freddy's plane began to ice very quickly. He kept pushing the plane to ascend but was unable to find the top of the clouds, where the visibility would be better and the icing would stop—since moisture doesn't freeze onto the plane in colder air at higher altitudes.

In the meantime, Freddy's instruments were becoming sluggish and unresponsive. And because of the low visibility in the cloud bank, he had to rely on gyroscopic gauges to know which direction he was going—even to determine if the plane was still right side up. But the gyroscopes were powered by air pressure from a "venturi"—an hourglass-shaped metal tube mounted on the outside of the plane—and it was clogging with ice. So the gauges couldn't be trusted.

After ten minutes airborne, Freddy was only twenty miles from the airport but already ten miles off course, lost in the middle of a mountain range. He tried to circle back down—or what *seemed like* down—to find an opening for an emergency landing. But as he circled, the ice on the wings kept getting heavier, increasing the drag on the plane's 420-horsepower engine.

There is a moment in a troubled flight when the plane is no longer really flying *on* the air but falling down through it. There's nothing the pilot can do to maintain altitude, and almost anything he tries will cause the plane to drop faster and faster, until it starts breaking up.

The Harveys hadn't been in the air more than fifteen minutes when the plane's instruments started failing and its shiny blue wings began cracking and shattering. Freddy knew exactly what was happening, but was powerless to do anything to stop it. He was still pulling on the controls, and Betty clutching her puppy, when the plane hit a span of electrical wires, sparking chaotically. Seconds later, they smashed into the side of a mountain. The fuel tank, which had just been refilled, exploded on impact, sending rivulets of burning gasoline streaming down the mountainside.

The crash site was just outside the coal town of Dunlo, Pennsylvania, and as miners from the nearby Henrietta Shaft came running to the scene, they passed pieces of clothing strewn on the ground—a woman's black evening dress, a tuxedo jacket—before reaching what was left of the plane's cabin. It was burning so intensely that they couldn't get close. One miner dashed to a nearby stream, filled his hard hat with water, and ran back to try to douse the flames. He and his co-workers kept this up until local farmers arrived with buckets and formed a brigade, concentrating their efforts on the area where two bodies appeared to be lying facedown on the ground, still strapped into what was left of their leather seats.

After an hour of fighting the fire, and still no sign of a rescue squad, the miners and farmers were able to approach the bodies and turn them over. The seats had provided some protection for their torsos, as had Betty's unopened parachute. So, her arms were intact and still cradling her lifeless dog; her wristwatch still clearly read 2:18, and the pink nail polish on her right hand wasn't even chipped. But her skull had been smashed and burned to ash, as had her feet. Freddy's legs were incinerated at the knees. All that was left of his head was a charred skull.

The front-page stories in all the nation's major newspapers the next morning did their best to be somewhat tasteful about the disturbing condition of the bodies. But the local *Johnstown Democrat* showed no such tact.

"Plane Crash Nightmare," the banner headline read. "Kansas City Rail Leader and Wife Burned to Crisp."

AT THE FAMILY'S REQUEST, there were no eulogies at the funeral in the jam-packed St. James Catholic Church in Kansas City. There was no sermon, no hymns. Just two identical caskets, blanketed with white lilies. There was Mass and absolution for the deceased, and a single reading from the book of John, chapter eleven, concerning the death of Lazarus and the mourning of his sisters.

"Martha said to Jesus, 'Lord, if you had been here, my brother would not have died,' " Monsignor Keyes read to the standing-room crowd. " 'But even now I know that whatever you ask from God, God will give you.'

"Jesus said to her, 'Your brother will rise again.' "

In keeping with the Harvey family tradition, Freddy's casket was carried by his closest colleagues within the company. Betty's was carried by their closest friends, including William Read, who was the last to see them alive. "One Sweetly Solemn Thought" played on the church organ as the sixteen pallbearers brought the caskets to twin hearses. Church bells rang "Abide with Me" as hundreds of car doors closed to begin the long procession to Mount Washington Cemetery.

Like his father before him, Freddy Harvey was eulogized only in the newspapers. Perhaps the most touching piece came from Howard Vincent O'Brien, who wrote the popular "All Things Considered" column in the *Chicago Daily News*. O'Brien received a postcard from a friend visiting the Grand Canyon only days after the plane crash, which immediately caused him to flash back to

> my epochal ride on muleback down Bright Angel Trail, with Fred Harvey leading. Alas that such a fine gentleman, such a blade of Damascus as he was, should be no more; though his end was as he would have willed it—one swift flight out of the skies, and oblivion.
>
> Among the memories I shall always treasure is that of an hour of twilight I spent with him on the tower of a Hopi *khiva*, overlooking the sun-reddened walls of the canyon. We talked of many things, but mostly of religion, and I had a glimpse into a truly clean heart.
>
> I shall never forget it.

It was Kitty, of course, who took Freddy's death the hardest. They had become closer than ever after their father died, handling his estate and sharing big dreams for the company's future. Freddy was finally turning into the businessman she had always hoped he would be, but without losing the carefree spirit and courage of that young man in the photo she kept on her nightstand, her little brother dangling from the edge of the Divine Abyss.

Kitty's closest friends, Mary Perkins and Harriet McLaughlin, had accompanied her on the train from California and stayed with her in Kansas City for several weeks after the funeral. But they couldn't assuage the existential shock of being the last one left alive in her immediate family. Even worse, the moment that her brother died, Kitty was thrust into the middle of a legal nightmare.

CHAPTER 41

KITTY BLINKS

꒐꒑

FREDDY'S WILL HAD ANTICIPATED THAT HE AND HIS WIFE MIGHT die together. In that case, he left his sister everything. But no sooner had his will been read than Betty's mother, Lucy Drage, sued Kitty and the estate.

While Freddy's will forgave the loan he had made for Lucy Drage's interior decorating shop, Betty had died without a will, and since all her marital assets were in her husband's name, her mother, her brother, and her baby niece in England had inherited nothing. So the Drages improvised a uniquely outrageous legal strategy that instantly riveted Kansas City society.

Lucy Drage filed papers in the Circuit Court of Jackson County, Missouri, demanding half of Freddy's estate—which was worth well over $1 million ($15.5 million). She claimed she could prove that Freddy had died in the plane crash minutes before Betty had. And in those last few moments of life, Betty had inherited half of the Frederick Harvey estate—because, according to his will, if he died first, his wife and his sister were to "share and share alike."

If the lawsuit sounded crazed, it was probably because Lucy Drage was out of her mind with grief. This was, in fact, the second time she had lost a child to the recklessness of the rich. Her son David had died in a single-car accident five years earlier—the passenger of Washington socialite Elizabeth Walter Converse, the estranged third wife of powerful New York financier and AT&T heir James Vail Converse, who ran her touring car into a telephone pole. And now Freddy Harvey had taken away her precious daughter. So even though she and Kitty had been friendly for decades—long before they were relatives, they had appeared together in amateur plays (including *Trelawney of the "Wells"* at Westport High School) and washed dishes together at the Tip Top Cafeteria—Lucy insisted on suing her.

Judge Ben Terte ordered an immediate public hearing in the case and signed an order stating that Freddy had outlived his wife, so the claim had no merit. But Lucy Drage's attorney, Frank Sebree, convinced an appeals court that the case law concerning simultaneous death was ambiguous, and they deserved a trial. Courts recognized several theories. There was the "weaker sex" theory, which held that if a man and a woman died together, the woman certainly would die first. But there was also a common-law theory concerning couples of differing ages—in which a younger wife was considered likely to outlive her older husband—and a standing U.S. Supreme Court ruling which held that the physical condition of each spouse before the accident could be used to determine the order of death. So Lucy Drage started hiring experts to do an independent investigation into the crash that killed her daughter and the man who was flying the plane.

THE LAWSUIT WITH Freddy's in-laws was a mortifying public spectacle for Kitty. But it was nothing compared to the horror show taking place within her own family business.

At the age of forty-three, Kitty suddenly found herself owning *all* of her late father's stock in Fred Harvey—the controlling shares of every aspect of the hospitality empire, which even in that year of economic recovery grossed nearly $10 million ($155 million). This was her Uncle Byron's worst nightmare. Not only was control of the company still in Kansas City, but it was now in the hands of a *woman*. Moreover, Kitty had every intention of putting on the armor and playing Joan of Arc again, stepping in for her brother and assuming a leading role in the future of Fred Harvey.

She relished the idea of the nation's first major employer of women finally being run by one. And while she had not spent any time in the boardroom, her desire to be the next Fred Harvey was not necessarily the pipe dream of a rich dilettante. She had the unqualified support of one of Kansas City's most powerful and accomplished financial minds—E. F. Swinney, the elder statesman of the First National Bank of Kansas City and a legendary frontier banker who had first made a name for himself when, as a cashier in 1898, he put up the bail when his friend Jesse James Jr. was arrested for train robbery. A former president of the American Bankers Association and adviser to Presidents Taft and Hoover, Swinney had put together the deal for Kansas City Union Station, and he still sat on the boards of several major companies. The aging banker had been a friend and close colleague of Ford Harvey—who sat on his board and worked with him on the rebuilding of Kansas City's streetcar system. He had also known Byron for years.

So, when E. F. Swinney said that he held Kitty Harvey's business intelligence in high esteem—and that, in fact, he thought she had a better business brain than her uncle—people listened.

Of course, Swinney had his own civic reasons for keeping Fred Harvey in Kansas City. But he also had spent a lot of time with Kitty as she and Freddie worked at investing the money from their father's estate. He was impressed with her. She was an agile, creative investor. Besides stocks and bonds, she would invest in the work of inventors and sell at just the right time. Her large art collection wasn't just a labor of love—it showed genuine business acumen. She had taste, intelligence, wit, and sound instincts, she had confidence without any of her brother's recklessness, and she could move effortlessly between the world of society balls and hunting, fishing, and camping trips.

Swinney had been saying for years that the Harvey System had missed a great executive when Kitty was not born a man. Her time, he believed, had finally come.

But Byron wouldn't hear of it. The last thing he wanted was his opinionated niece, along with his oldest sister, Minnie, ganging up on him, second-guessing him, telling him what to do. Besides, he had already decided that the company should move to Chicago.

Byron told Kitty it would be absolutely inappropriate for her to own a controlling share of Fred Harvey stock, because she did not—and could not—hold an executive position with the firm. He invoked the family tradition that women not get involved with the business, noting how in 1911 her own father, Ford, had forced his sisters and mother to sell their shares. He demanded that she sell him all the shares she controlled, immediately.

According to him, it was the Fred Harvey way.

Kitty refused. She didn't give a *damn* what her father had said in 1911—it was 1936, and the world had changed. Women were in the workforce, they were even starting their own companies. She was perfectly capable of being on the board of her family's business. In fact, given her stock holdings, perhaps she should be *chairman* of the board.

Nor was it just a matter of whether she could help influence the company's future. Kitty also knew that if her uncle bought her out, it would be bad for the business. The amount of cash required to purchase her shares would put Fred Harvey into debt—the first major debt in its sixty-year history—just as the company was finally making some headway after the Depression years in which, for the first time, they had actually lost money. The stock Kitty controlled could be worth more than every penny of profit that the Harvey System had generated over the past few years.

It was unclear if Byron could *make her* sell her controlling shares. Although private companies often had buyback provisions for their most closely held voting stock, Kitty held what she inherited from Ford for eight years with no problems. Yet Freddy had signed a buyback agreement, and the company had a life insurance policy on him for $433,749 ($6.7 million) to pay for the shares. And it is possible that once Kitty inherited controlling shares, the bylaws gave the company the ability to prevent a non-employee from having that much power (although bylaws are easy to amend).

A bit of hurried, stealthy corporate paper-shuffling several months after the crash could have played a key role. Probably as a way to protect company stock from the Drage lawsuit, some of Kitty's voting shares and some of the voting shares in Freddy's estate were quietly reissued by the firm as non-voting shares. That measure, obviously designed to shield the family business, may have balanced the playing field between Kitty and Byron. But, still, if she decided to sell, she could demand much more than the book value of her shares in the harsh economy of that time. She could ask for so much money that maybe her Uncle Byron would realize it made no sense to cut her—and the Kansas City Harveys—out of their own business.

DRAGE V. HARVEY WAS a gruesome lawsuit. The winner had to prove it was her relative who had lived the longest in that carnage, and had more time to suffer the most horrible death made possible by modern technology.

Lucy Drage's lawyer, Frank Sebree, worked for months building a case. His team took new affidavits from anyone who had been at or near the crash site in Pennsylvania. They did their own analysis of all the forensic evidence. And they blew up photos of the cabin of a Staggerwing, as well as the devastating shots taken at the crash site. They planned to make a judge and jury feel as if they were actually inside the plane as it went down. And they believed they could prove that there was at least a minute, and maybe even two minutes, when Freddy was already dead but poor Betty was still alive and conscious, clutching her dog in her arms.

On the day of the crash, some eyewitnesses claimed they saw or heard the plane hit the side of a mountain and lose a wing before nose-diving. The local coroner had even highlighted this in his initial findings. While the government report later disagreed with that assessment, Drage's attorney felt the local farmers and miners who had tried to save the couple would be more sympathetic than the government's expert witness: In the small world of aviation, the safety investigator on the case turned out to be Eugene Vidal, whom President Roosevelt had appointed director of the Bureau of Air Commerce. Since Vidal and Freddy had known each other for years, there was some speculation the government was helping TWA withhold certain facts about the crash. "It was important that airline officials keep their mouths shut," one family member recalls, "because [Freddy's] insurance might be in some jeopardy."

The trial started in April 1937 on the one-year anniversary of the crash. But just as the proceedings were getting under way, the judge was informed by the lawyers that their clients had settled.

Kitty had blinked.

She agreed to pay Lucy Drage about $100,000 ($1.5 million) just to put an end to the grotesque spectacle. Part of the money went into annuities that would give Lucy an annual income of $3,000 ($43,300); the rest she took in cash. Kitty also agreed to pay all the bills Betty had run up buying clothing over the past couple of years. Besides the London shopping spree, there was her tab of $7,347.56 ($110,000) at the posh Marion Dwyer dress shop in Chicago. Her five-page bill included charges for an ermine and velvet wrap, a silver muskrat coat, a Lanvin coat with nutria fur trimming, fourteen gowns with tailored slips for each, assorted designer suits, coats, skirts, blouses, handbags, and evening bags, and twenty-three pairs of gloves.

Kitty let it be known that she had always planned to give the Drages part of the estate, and that suing her had not been necessary at all. Yet Lucy and her lawyers considered the settlement a great victory over difficult odds. In Kansas City, it was rare for anyone to beat the Harveys at anything.

With the case settled, Freddy's estate could finally be probated. It was valued at $750,000 ($11.2 million), on which Kitty had to pay inheritance tax of $105,217 ($1.6 million). She kept the family home in Kansas City, where she expected to be spending more time, and the houses in California. And when all the estate paperwork was finally finished, she turned her attention to becoming more involved at Fred Harvey.

At the same time, her uncle turned his attention to forcing her out.

Byron and Kitty did their best to keep their conflicts out of the newspaper and away from other family members, but their arguments apparently went on for over a year. Daggett Harvey, the only child of Byron's who was not in the business at that time—he was a thirty-two-year-old corporate attorney—would always remember a screaming phone conversation he once overheard between the two of them. In Daggett's later years, after his father was gone and he had joined the family business himself, he would sometimes bring up the incident to his son with a troubled tone in his voice. He said he remembered telling his father, Byron Sr., that he sympathized with Kitty. If his father insisted on forcing her to sell, Daggett wanted to make sure "it was done the proper way."

Apparently, Byron was willing to pay almost anything to make Kitty back down. Family members who discussed this with her, or later had access to the records of her estate, estimate she got at least $1 million in cash for her stock, and more likely as much as $3 million ($45.8 million). And this was during the second wave of the Great Depression. While the secret deal was being negotiated, the slowly rebounding American economy actually took another nosedive in 1937 and went into another recession.

Kitty was crushed to give up her chance to run the family business, although she would never explain why she did it. "She didn't like to speak about painful things," recalled her closest nephew. When asked about difficult family matters, she often told him, "If it were true, I wouldn't want to talk about it." She was a little more direct years later when another of her nephews brought up the subject during lunch at the Ritz in Paris. "Not that it's any of your business," she said, "but I didn't have any choice." Perhaps Byron or his attorneys promised a gloves-off battle, which she knew would hurt the business and the family at a time when they could least afford it. Or maybe she came to believe that Byron had an iron-clad option to buy her shares, and the only fight left was over the price.

But while she never fully explained her decision, it haunted her. Kitty Harvey was not one to let her emotions rule her. She had little tolerance for weepy women. But whenever the subject of how it ended with her Uncle Byron came up, and how she had been forced to sell the company because she was the wrong sex, she always confessed that she was "in tears."

Not long after Kitty sold her shares, the company's oldest and longest-tenured staff member reached his fiftieth anniversary at Fred Harvey. Tim Cooper had been Ford's original assistant back in 1888 and the company's first black office employee. He had worked his way up over the years to become the chief shipping clerk at the Kansas City headquarters—which was soon to be dismantled and moved to Chicago. Byron, who had known Cooper since they were both teenagers, started planning a big banquet in his honor, which the entire family and many work friends would attend. But Cooper reportedly told Byron he "simply refused" to be part of such an event. Instead, he chose to celebrate with the remaining members of the Kansas City Harveys. He and his wife, Helen, had a private dinner just with Kitty and Minnie, in the very formal, very English dining room at Ford's old house.

AS THE FAMILY SIMMERED, a husky thirty-eight-year-old former cigar salesman set out to make himself as famous across the country as Fred Harvey. His name was Howard Johnson.

Back in 1924, Johnson had quit his father's New England cigar business and opened a small store in the Wollaston section of Quincy, Massachusetts, where he sold ice cream made from his mother's recipes at the soda fountain. Within two years, he was wholesaling ice cream to stands all over Cape Cod, and had added spicy frankfurters and addictive tender fried clams to his take-out menu. In 1929, he opened his first restaurant in Quincy, which became unexpectedly popular because of a scandal in the American theater. Eugene O'Neill's experimental play *Strange Interlude* had been banned in Boston because of its frankness about sex, abortion, and mental illness, and the production was mounted instead in Quincy. In addition to its challenging subject matter, the play ran four hours—such a long day's journey into night that it was performed with a dinner break. Howard Johnson's was the closest restaurant to the theater. A family-food star was born.

Despite the Depression, the business did well enough that in 1935, Johnson was ready to expand. He didn't have enough money, however, so he sold a franchise to a sea captain in nearby Orleans, Reginald Sprague, who agreed to peddle the company's signature ice cream, as well as the franks and clams. Sprague's Howard Johnson restaurant had a sit-down dining room attached to a soda fountain where patrons could swivel on stools or order takeout—like a Harvey eating house but more middlebrow, with seashore food and a more East Coast version of Americana.

The new restaurant was so popular that Johnson agreed to sell dozens of franchises. He handpicked the franchisees, working with them closely to choose locations and build to his specifications. He also held their hands through every step of the way, setting up centralized ice-cream-making facilities and contracting for frankfurters and clams so he could completely control the quality of the food served in his name. In 1936, Howard Johnson opened thirty-nine new roadside family restaurants in New England. That was more eating houses than the dwindling Fred Harvey chain still had in the entire Southwest.

Within two years, Johnson had eighty franchises, and his ads proclaimed, "The Howard Johnson vogue is sweeping the country!" By 1940, there were more than one hundred Howard Johnsons, extending from New England down through New York (where he built a restaurant near the world's fair site) and New Jersey, as well as pockets of new franchises around Washington, D.C., and in Florida. The new king of family dining also landed the contract to control all the restaurant stops along what would become America's first major toll-road system, the Pennsylvania Turnpike. It was one more way for Howard Johnson to establish himself as the next Fred Harvey for the nation's most modern form of transportation.

He did so with almost no resistance from Fred Harvey itself. After spending so much time and money getting control of the family business, Byron didn't really have the ambition or the capital to expand into this obvious new market. And after Freddy's death, Byron withdrew the company from all its airline contracts as well—just as Howard Hughes was taking over TWA and the commercial aviation business was having its second wind. Byron decided that Fred Harvey would stick with what it knew—union stations, what was left of the trackside hotels and eating houses, La Fonda in Santa Fe, and of course the Grand Canyon, which, amazingly, now made more money than everything else in the company put together.

CHAPTER 42

PRIVATE PRINGLE TO THE RESCUE

IN THE MIDDLE OF THE HARVEY FAMILY TUMULT, A LETTER FROM Hollywood arrived at Byron's office. It was from Bing Crosby's production company with Paramount, Major Pictures, which had just finished *Pennies from Heaven* with Crosby and Louis Armstrong and *Go West, Young Man* with Mae West and Randolph Scott. They were going to make a movie set at a Fred Harvey eating house in New Mexico in 1900, about a woman who comes west to be a Harvey Girl.

The letter came from William Rankin, who had written the screenplay—which he said treated the Harvey restaurants "with the greatest respect, attempting to show that they were greatly responsible for the development of the Southwest." He wanted to know whether Fred Harvey could help them make their film authentic. Rankin even offered to submit the final shooting script to Byron for his approval. The project, originally called *Susannah Was a Lady* and then *Parade to Empire,* was expected to star Janet Gaynor and Fred MacMurray.

Byron Jr. quickly checked out the production company with a friend in Hollywood, a young costume designer at Paramount, Edith Head. Once she assured him that any film they produced would be "perfectly legitimate and worthwhile," he told his father that Fred Harvey should assist the producers in any way they could. Byron put John Huckel's old assistant Harold Belt on the case. Belt would devote much of the next ten years to the project, for the Harvey Girls movie, like Fred Harvey itself, spent the better part of that decade in turn-around.

TO THE TRAVELING PUBLIC, Fred Harvey was still a western power-house: While many smaller locations had closed, its major hotels, restaurants, and union station operations still appeared to be going strong. Increasingly, the company was known for its Santa Fe dining car service, especially on the Super Chief—its first all-diesel service between Chicago and California, the fastest and classiest train ride ever. The glistening, modern, all-steel Super Chief was the transportation of choice for business and Hollywood types still anxious about flying. In fact, they became so reliant on the train, after its 1936 debut, that it was not uncommon to hear people use "chief" as a verb, as in "I just chiefed in from the coast."

While the Super Chief had the same excellent Fred Harvey dining car service as its predecessors, it had an extra touch inspired by the sensibilities of the Kansas City Harveys in the "good old days." Mary Colter designed a revolutionary china pattern, called Mimbreño, just for its dining cars. She based her design on the whimsical pottery made by Indians in New Mexico's Mimbres valley during the thirteenth century, so all the pieces were decorated with blood-red paintings of stylized, floating animals: amusing fish chasing each other's tails, genuflecting parrots, leaping quail, wrestling birds, and all manner of funny bunnies. The dishes were almost too enchanting to sully with food. They were used in an exclusive dining car space called the Turquoise Room.

The only downside to the Super Chief was that its terminus in Los Angeles was the antiquated Santa Fe Le Grande station on East First Street. But that changed in 1939 when the Santa Fe, Union Pacific, and Southern Pacific finally completed construction of the new $11 million ($171 million) Los Angeles Union Station. Considered the last great railroad station in America, it was also the last for which Fred Harvey was hired to run all the restaurants and retail stores. While Mary Colter did not design the entire majestic station complex, she did create a remarkable space for the Fred Harvey eateries. It had a spectacular arched ceiling that brought to mind the inside of Jonah's whale, spacey Deco fixtures, and a dazzling floor, which appeared to be random zigzags and geometrics until you stepped back and realized it was actually a block-long Navajo blanket made of linoleum tiles.

Colter also designed a marvelous Deco cocktail lounge. Gossip columnist Hedda Hopper immediately dubbed it the "newest rendezvous in town . . . so pleasant there it's a joy to miss your train. No one wants to catch one."

Unfortunately, Hedda was right—a lot of people didn't want to catch the train anymore. The Super Chief itself was successful. So was a new economy train called the Scout, which even had a car for women and children traveling alone, with a Santa Fe "Courier-Nurse" to help out. (It quickly became known, in the words of one corporate historian, as "a rolling nightmare of diapers, midnight feedings and a constant parade of women moving back and forth to the diner seeking warm bottles of milk.") But in general, passenger traffic was falling, along with the prices that passengers were willing to pay. The Santa Fe tried getting into buses, which also stopped at the remaining Harvey eating houses. Fred Harvey even opened its first bus-only restaurant and lounge in the new Santa Fe Trailways bus terminal in Hollywood, on Cahuenga Boulevard. But in general, the railroad's business was flat— just when new investment was needed for more speedy diesel trains to keep up with the times.

BY MOVING FRED HARVEY's main office to Chicago, in the same building as the headquarters of the Santa Fe, Byron had brought the family business closer to the railroad than ever before. So much so that Fred Harvey actually lost its long battle with the Interstate Commerce Commission over whether dining car employees really worked for the Harveys or for the railroad when it came to qualifying for union membership. In a decision the company fought hard, railroad workers were allowed to unionize the Fred Harvey dining cars, which eventually led to unions in other parts of the operation.

At a time when Fred Harvey was under intense economic pressure, it was the last thing the company needed. Every page of the annual report was pockmarked with red ink. Their retail business was so disastrous that Byron urged Herman Schweizer to start liquidating the Indian art.

Schweizer resisted, and somehow managed to keep most of the best pieces hidden in his vault and on his inventories so his priceless collection would not be sold off at bargain prices. But it was hard for him to believe how much American tastes had deteriorated. Where he once had bought pieces that museums fought over, the "Harvey ethnographer" was now handling only the cheap stuff he originally had commissioned for the least discriminating tourists. Instead of stocking handsome shops, he was selling turquoise and silver trinkets through a mail-order catalog.

The Harvey chain was on life support—there were only twenty-nine restaurants left, and half of them were consistently losing money. Byron even had to close the historic first eating house, in Topeka. And when he did, journalist William Allen White was already writing the obituary for Fred Harvey, and for a way of life in America:

> The newspaper announced yesterday that the . . . oldest surviving Harvey house on the Santa Fe system, the one at Topeka, had closed . . . For 50 years and more, Harvey Houses . . . were beacons of culinary light and learning, chiefly because they broiled steak instead of frying it and also used French dressing on head lettuce. Before that, sugar and vinegar were regarded as proper dressing for lettuce in these latitudes. Also, the Harvey houses introduced au gratin potatoes and rare roast beef. Small things these, but devastating to the cook who fried her steak and her potatoes and regarded floating island as the acme of all desserts.
>
> Being centers of good cooking, the Harvey restaurants . . . became centers of good fellowship. When a man wanted to give a stranger or a fellow citizen a good meal, he took him to the Harvey house. When a lady wanted to throw a luncheon party, the swellest thing she could do was to go to the Harvey house. And this custom prevailed through two generations.
>
> The revolution in railroading which has taken off the local trains that stopped for meals, the revolution that has made the railroad the long distance carrier and turned the local traffic over to the bus, made the Harvey house a symbol of the ancient days and olden times. If any Harvey House survives this decade it will be a collector's item, strange, weird, inexplicable in the commerce of tomorrow.
>
> Evidence that we are passing through a great social, economic and political revolution is none the less convincing because the revolution is bloodless. The Harvey house in Topeka

was bombed in the mop-up of that revolution. It might well be marked by a tablet. The tablet should display these lines: "Here, for sixty years, women who put water in the skillet to fry beefsteak rolled in flour learned of their sins, repented and were saved unto full culinary salvation!"

WORLD WAR II began in Europe in September 1939, and even though the United States was still watching and waiting, preparation for war was like an antidepressant for the U.S. economy. This was especially true for the railroads, which were rediscovered as the only dependable way to transport large numbers of troops and heavy munitions long distances. After years of moribund business, the empty seats in the Fred Harvey dining cars and restaurants were starting to be filled again by men in uniform, and while the economy was hardly robust, the worst appeared to be over.

In Hollywood, there suddenly was renewed interest in the Harvey Girls movie. It had fallen through the cracks at Paramount, but the project was then sold to Louis B. Mayer at MGM, who envisioned it as a straight-up Western with Clark Gable and Lana Turner. The film headed into preproduction in the fall of 1941, and MGM was so high on its prospects that Mayer reached out to his friend Bennett Cerf, the forty-three-year-old editor and co-owner of Random House publishers, to have a novelization done of the new screenplay so it could be released with the film.

Cerf called a writer he had always admired but never managed to work with: Samuel Hopkins Adams. The prolific Adams had first made a name for himself at the turn of the century with a shocking series of investigative articles about the pharmaceutical and patent medicine business in *Collier's,* "The Great American Fraud." From then on, he published a book a year, as well as hundreds of magazine articles and short stories, everything from hard-core investigative reporting to biography, mainstream fiction, erotic fiction (under a pen name), and literary criticism. His work had spawned eighteen feature films, including Frank Capra's immortal *It Happened One Night,* with Clark Gable and Claudette Colbert, based on a short story Adams published in *Cosmopolitan.*

Now seventy, Samuel Hopkins Adams looked like W. C. Fields on a late-in-life fitness kick, and showed no signs of slowing down, which is why Cerf was so excited when he agreed to do the novelization. "I have a hunch that Adams is going to do a story that will be really important both for us and for you," Cerf assured Louis B. Mayer.

Before Adams could get started, however, the Japanese attacked Pearl Harbor on December 7, 1941, and America finally joined the war. The author assumed this would derail the project; instead, several weeks after the attack, he was told to get writing, the book was due in five months. He was brought to Hollywood to take a few meetings with executives brimming with plot points and ideas, all of which he found worthless. The highlight of his trip was a conversation he had with a waitress who served him lunch at the MGM studio commissary. She had been a Harvey Girl for seventeen years, and had lots of wonderful stories he could use.

Adams was then sent to Chicago to meet Byron, whose ego he was instructed to massage as heavily as possible. MGM had signed a deal giving Fred Harvey approval rights on the book and the movie. The studio didn't want any legal hassles over the use of actual company names, and Bennett Cerf at Random House was respectful of the powerful Harvey bookstores and newsstands. To woo support, Adams told Byron Sr. and Jr. that he was writing an epilogue to the book—and it would feature *them*. The novel was set in the late 1890s, when Fred was still living, but the epilogue would be set decades later, at a reunion of Harvey Girls, and they would be characters. They loved the idea.

Retreating to his winter home in Beaufort, South Carolina, Adams banged out the first two chapters, over six thousand words, in just two days. He went on to briskly weave everything he had heard from the Harveys, and from that waitress at the MGM commissary, into a story so convincing—if not always consistently compelling—that it would later be quoted as if it were historical nonfiction. He told the tale of three women coming to the imaginary New Mexico town of Sandrock to become Harvey Girls, where they are viewed as fresh meat by the local cowboys, and prissy little busybodies by the only other single women in town, the morally casual waitresses at the Alhambra saloon. Much drama and hilarity ensue as the cowboys and showgirls resist the civilizing impact of the Harvey House, stealing its revered steaks and even trying to burn the place down. One Harvey Girl falls in love with a local rancher with a checkered past, but he turns out to have a heart of gold and they live, of course, happily ever after.

Adams finished the first draft of *The Harvey Girls* well ahead of schedule. He got the revisions done in a month and then held on to the manuscript until the day before his June 1, 1942, deadline, so Bennett Cerf would think he had been working hard on it up until the last minute.

In the meantime, MGM decided to put the movie on hold yet again, and was reportedly trying to dump it off on 20th Century Fox. But Cerf decided Random House should publish *The Harvey Girls* book anyway—and much to everyone's surprise, it was a big seller, immediately going into a second and then a third printing, no doubt helped along by the marketing might of the Fred Harvey bookstores. It sold 8,354 copies in standard hardcover and another 50,589 copies in the less expensive Forum Books hardcover with no movie to support it at all—just the nation's continued nostalgic attachment to Fred Harvey.

AS THE WAR ESCALATED, not only was the entire Fred Harvey system mobilized to feed the troops, but its long-shuttered restaurants were recalled to active duty. Dining rooms were converted into mess halls, the handsome carved-wood tables lined up end to end and supplemented by long banquet tables, so each Harvey House could serve as many as three thousand soldiers a day. The company set up eight large sandwich-making operations in Chicago, Kansas City, Newton, Clovis, Albuquerque, Gallup, Williams, and Los Angeles, which produced tens of thousands of sandwiches a day. Some of them were served in the eating houses, but many others were passed up to soldiers through train windows and doors, since the dining cars could not possibly keep up with demand.

It was a herculean undertaking—much larger than anything the company had experienced during World War I—and the Harvey System was initially unprepared: After so many years of downsizing, the firm hadn't needed to train many new Harvey Girls. So when the government leaned on the Santa Fe to increase the number of servicemen it could transport, and urged Fred Harvey to dramatically increase its capacity to feed them, the company had to go on a major hiring spree, quickly adding two *thousand* workers. Luckily, Dave Benjamin's old system of maintaining records on all employees, current and former, was still in place. Every old Harvey Girl who could still stand up and carry a tray was called back into service.

Still, that didn't produce nearly enough servers for all those soldiers. So, in 1943, the sixtieth anniversary of the hiring of the first Harvey Girls in Raton, the vaunted Harvey System of carefully training young women and dispatching them to live in chaperoned dormitories finally gave way to expedience. Harvey Girls hired in Chicago and Kansas City were sent out into the field before they were ready, some Harvey Houses hired local women—which they had never done before—as waitresses or "troop-train girls," and many other regulations were relaxed.

"It really changed the Harvey standard . . . They were really desperate. They took anybody," recalled Margaret Reichenborn, a Kansan who became a Harvey Girl in Las Vegas, New Mexico, just before the hiring spree:

> When I first got to the Castañeda, there were about eight to ten Harvey Girls. When the troop trains started coming through, there were about twenty-five Harvey Girls. They were mostly local girls. They didn't have to meet the old contracts— no promise not to marry, and they weren't strict about the rules . . . During the war, we couldn't even wear the same uniforms. We couldn't get white hose, then we couldn't get any hose at all. We had long-sleeved white shirts, and we had to keep those clean. But it got so difficult we finally cut off the sleeves to make it easier . . . We often had a lot of very inexperienced waitresses working under very difficult circumstances . . . We all did the best we could.

Yet for many women in the Southwest, who previously would not have considered applying to work for Fred Harvey because they were Hispanic or Indian, this change in Harvey hiring was a civil rights breakthrough. They burst with pride to be the first Harvey Girls of color. There was something deeply powerful about walking into El Navajo in Gallup and seeing that all the Harvey Girls were Navajo. (Troops of color were always fed the same way as white troops. Still, while Fred Harvey was never known to refuse black patrons, it was sometimes guilty of seating them together in less desirable tables—and blueprints for some Harvey Houses in New Mexico and Texas did

specify "colored" seating areas. But any such vestiges of what race reformers called "Jim Crow seating" disappeared during the war.)

These newer, more multicultural Harvey Girls rejected the notion
that they were somehow lesser. "Although they hired a lot of local girls,
there were still many they turned away," recalled another wartime waitress. "Working as a Harvey Girl, even during the war, was a privilege.
I felt lucky to have the job."

The troops on their way to war were just happy for the female attention. "The men were always real friendly," this Harvey Girl continued:

> They were often very lonely and they asked for our names and
> addresses. Each of us received hundreds—literally hundreds—of
> letters. We couldn't even remember who the boy was who had
> written it. I had a milk carton full. One train came through with
> French troops on board. We couldn't understand them and they
> couldn't understand us. Still, they wrote us lots of letters.

But, proud though he was of his company's war effort, Byron was
clearly mortified that Fred Harvey could no longer "maintain the standard." Not only was service slipping, but the food itself suffered because so many ingredients were rationed. So he did what many
executives of service-related companies were doing. He ordered a series
of ads in national magazines to apologize—and also to explain why
civilian patrons were being asked to get up and leave Fred Harvey
restaurants whenever a troop train approached. The campaign began
with a generic ad showing a Harvey Girl holding a chair for a service-
man, with the headline "Sit Down Sergeant, Mr. Harvey's Saving This
Place for You," followed by copy about the company pitching in for the
war effort (and a small plug for El Tovar).

As tourism ground to a halt and even El Tovar became primarily a
rest stop for furloughed soldiers, Fred Harvey unveiled its "Private
Pringle" campaign. It revolved around—but never actually showed—a
ubiquitous private who became the company's symbol for the American fighting man.

One Private Pringle ad showed a large potato being peeled, with
the line "K.P.? Not for Private Pringle!" while another showed a "Do
Not Disturb" sign and a shushing bellhop, with the line "Shhhh! Private Pringle's Asleep!" The ads ran in *Life* magazine and other major

publications, and as the war worsened, they included patriotic asides about how many Fred Harvey employees had "joined Private Pringle" in the armed forces, and admonitions such as "Victory will come SOONER if we: Conserve food in our households, Refuse to buy from black markets, Pay necessary taxes uncomplainingly, Buy War Bonds instead of luxuries, Kill rumors that aid our enemy."

The ad campaign took on a life of its own—especially when it turned out there was a Private Pringle, who wrote from Africa to inform the company that he was now Corporal Murray Pringle, and hoped that upon his return they might help him arrange to have dinner with Lana Turner. But while the Pringle ads helped a little, they could not assuage the feeling within the company that although they were doing their duty, they were also allowing Fred Harvey's sacred standards to slip away.

A HANDFUL OF DEATHS severed even more links to the company's founder. Minnie Harvey Huckel died in July 1943 at the age of seventy-two. She left a large estate to Kitty and to Byron's sons—even to her housekeeper of twenty-three years—because she had no children of her own. Three weeks later, her sister, Sybil, died. Married late in life and widowed, Sybil was still living in the original Harvey family home on Olive Street in Leavenworth, which was donated to a local hospital to be used as a dormitory for nurses.

Later that same year, Herman Schweizer died in Albuquerque at the age of seventy-two. In his later years he had become active at his local synagogue, Temple Albert, and with the B'nai B'rith, and spent more time with his sister and her daughter in Chicago. But he never married, and his legacy was the Fred Harvey art collection—which he had spent his entire career amassing, and the last five years of his life successfully protecting from philistine bean counters at the Chicago office. The company collection would remain intact, under Harvey family ownership, for decades after his death, and was eventually donated to the Heard Museum in Phoenix.

Schweizer's own personal collection of blankets, however, was consigned to one of the local traders in Gallup with whom he spent so many of his fondest hours haggling. Nelson Rockefeller bought one of the fine Saltillo blankets, while several of the institutions Schweizer helped get off the ground—such as the Laboratory of Anthropology in Santa Fe and the Museum of Northern Arizona in Flagstaff—also acquired pieces.

William Randolph Hearst did not buy anything, because he had long ago lost interest in Indian art. While he had originally planned that his castle in San Simeon would primarily be a showplace for his Navajo textiles, the project and his collecting of other styles of art had spiraled out of control. The blankets he had begged Schweizer to sell to him years ago were sitting in warehouses with the Fred Harvey tags still on them—an image conjured perfectly by Orson Welles in *Citizen Kane*.

CHAPTER 43

THE SPIES AT LA FONDA

⊐⊏

W HILE FRED HARVEY MADE MUCH OF HOW MANY TROOPS IT was feeding, the company's most notable contribution to the war effort was top secret. In the spring of 1943, Dr. Robert Oppenheimer came to New Mexico—where he had once visited as a sickly teen—to establish a hidden laboratory on a secluded mesa above Jemez Springs canyon, thirty miles northwest of Santa Fe, at the site of the old Los Alamos Ranch School for boys. It would be the new home of the "Manhattan Project"—so named because it had briefly been located in New York City before scientists realized they needed a more secure location to develop the first atomic bomb. But while some of the world's greatest physicists would work on "the Hill"—as they referred to the mesa lab—their social lives and family time were spent in Santa Fe, more often than not at Fred Harvey's La Fonda hotel.

The Manhattan Project had an office in Santa Fe just a block from the hotel, in an adobe storefront at 109 East Palace Avenue. When Oppenheimer and his family first came to town, they stayed at La Fonda and ate all of their meals there, starting a pattern that continued through the project. For this reason, the government immediately infiltrated the hotel staff, and many of the bartenders and cocktail waitresses in La Cantina—the hotel's main watering hole—were undercover agents. So were several of the front desk clerks and various other staff members. At the Alvarado in nearby Albuquerque, the staff also had its share of G-men.

Oppenheimer hired a local woman named Dorothy Scarritt Mc-Kibbin, a fortyish widow from Kansas City, to run the office in town. She and her family had been social friends of the Harveys. McKibbin handled all the logistics for the Manhattan Project scientists and their families, who primarily traveled on Santa Fe trains, many of them from Chicago (where work was being done at the Metallurgical Lab at the University of Chicago) and California (where radiation research was being done at Berkeley). Since there was still no direct train service into Santa Fe, McKibbin would arrange to have the scientists picked up in Lamy and brought to town, where they would eat at La Fonda before heading up to the Hill, and sometimes spend a night or two there, if there was room, as a reprieve from the spartan accommodations at Los Alamos. La Fonda was usually very crowded, since servicemen stayed there on furlough, sometimes creating a rowdy atmosphere that seemed out of place in laid-back Old Santa Fe.

As the main nexus between the Manhattan Project and the real world, La Fonda served many roles—everything from a lunch spot for shopping Hill wives to a secret rendezvous point. In July 1943, the first physics experiment was completed at Los Alamos—counting the number of secondary electrons emitted by a speck of plutonium-239. Afterward, the speck, which was virtually all the plutonium that existed in the world then, needed to be returned to the University of Chicago. So physicist Robert Wilson drove it down from the Hill before dawn in a pickup truck, armed with his deer-hunting rifle.

He brought it to La Fonda, where Chicago physicist Glenn Seaborg, whose team had discovered the rare element (and would later win the Nobel Prize), was staying with his family. Seaborg was handed the plutonium while a Harvey Girl served him breakfast.

"I just put it in my pocket," he later recalled. (It's unclear what kind of container it was in, but it may not have been anything elaborate—he had originally kept it in a wooden cigar box.) After finishing his meal, he transferred the plutonium to his suitcase for the ride back to Chicago on the Santa Fe.

Once Oppenheimer even tried to use La Fonda as a gossip laboratory to spread disinformation. After reporters were found snooping around town asking about government weapons research, Oppenheimer chose Charlotte Serber, the very chatty wife of his protégé, theoretical physicist Robert Serber, to go spread some rumors at La Cantina that their research was *electromagnetic* in nature, not nuclear—so journalists and foreign spies would be thrown off track. She decided to make an evening of it, dragging along her husband, another physicist, and Oppenheimer's secretary as they ordered drinks and then talked loudly and obnoxiously about bombs equipped with some kind of "electromagnetic gun." They felt ridiculous doing it, and nobody seemed to be paying much attention to them—except for all the U.S. government spies.

"Every once in a while there would be some young loudmouth who would go down to the La Fonda bar and shoot his mouth off," recalled physicist Joseph Hirschfelder. "There would be detectives from the Manhattan Project with notebooks taking this all down; and they would build up a book on the indiscretions of a particular guy. The young loudmouth wasn't warned, but once they had the book on him enough so they could salt him away, he just disappeared."

The bar at La Fonda also saw its share of stealthy arrests. One day a mechanic from the Hill managed to steal a large piece of equipment, a turret lathe, which he unscrewed from the floor of the shop, lifted onto an army truck with a portable crane, covered with a tarp, and sneaked off the compound. He arranged to meet at La Cantina with his buyer, who turned out to be an undercover agent, and was arrested on the spot.

Between the spies and the rowdy servicemen on leave, tensions at La Fonda could run high. Monte Chavez, the maître d' in the hotel's main dining room, would never forget the night a big fight broke out in his dining room between army and navy men. Not knowing what else to do, he walked up to the bandleader and whispered into his ear, "Play 'The Star-Spangled Banner.'" In a moment right out of *Casablanca*—which was still playing in theaters around the country—all the servicemen in La Fonda immediately came to attention, long enough for military police to arrive and restore peace.

CHAPTER 44

BIG HOLLYWOOD ENDING

⑨⑫

M GM DECIDED THE TIME HAD FINALLY COME TO MAKE *THE Harvey Girls.* While cultural historians would later speculate that the studio wanted to distract Americans from their troubles with a tale of frontier life gone by, or portray a world of working women that was a frilly counterpoint to "Rosie the Riveter," the truth was that the decision was prompted by the runaway success on Broadway of *Oklahoma!*— which opened in the spring of 1943 and was playing to packed houses. The first collaboration between Richard Rodgers and Oscar Hammerstein, *Oklahoma!* was a huge stylistic step forward for musical theater— the first "integrated" musical, in which the songs were sung more operatically and used to propel the story forward. It was also a pitch-perfect popularization of the all-American compositions of Aaron Copland, echoing the sound and vernacular vibe of his ballet music for *Billy the Kid.*

MGM believed that if its Harvey Girls Western could be retrofitted as a perky movie musical, it could be the next *Oklahoma!*—but, this time, with big stars, since the Broadway show had used unknowns. Judy Garland was hired to be the solo lead, and she was reunited with her *Wizard of Oz* producer Arthur Freed and co-star Ray Bolger— along with a very young Angela Lansbury in just her fourth movie and dancer Cyd Charisse in her first credited film role.

Johnny Mercer, the lyricist and singer, was hired to write the score with songwriter Harry Warren. Together and separately, they were responsible for a large array of hit songs, from "Jeepers Creepers," "Chattanooga Choo Choo," and "I'm an Old Cowhand (from the Rio Grande)," to "Skylark," "I'm Old Fashioned," and "One for My Baby (and One More for the Road)." When they sat down to start writing, Mercer told Warren he remembered seeing the entire name of the Santa Fe railroad on a boxcar and thinking that the Atchison, Topeka & Santa Fe had "a nice, lyrical quality to it." It reminded him of a poem by Stephen Vincent Benét that begins, "I have fallen in love with American names" (but is much better known for the way it ends: "Bury my heart at Wounded Knee").

They started writing lyrics against a simple trainlike stride-piano line:

> *Do you hear that whistle down the line?*
> *I figure that it's engine number forty-nine*
> *She's the only one that'll sound that way*
> *On the Atchison, Topeka, and the Santa Fe.*

The song took them less than an hour to write, ending with:

> *And they'll all want lifts to Brown's Hotel*
> *'Cause lots of them been travelin' for quite a spell*
> *All the way from Phila-del-phi-ayy*
> *On the Atchison, Topeka, and the Santa Fe.*

It was extremely catchy, if a bit factually challenged. Mercer had added an extra syllable, a beat, to the already long name of the railroad: "the Atchison, Topeka, and *the* Santa Fe." He also added about 750 miles of track, extending the Santa Fe to Philadelphia. A real nitpicker—and train people are sticklers for detail—would also note that while the Santa Fe once had an engine 49 (a number Mercer likely chose only because it rhymed with "line"), that 0-4-0 locomotive, built in 1876 and nicknamed "the Vulcan," was long out of service and scrapped by the year the film was set; also, steam engine whistles were all pretty much the same, so one couldn't "sound" any particular way.

But none of that mattered: It was pure pop poetry. Even the *woo-woos* of the train whistle they used in one verse—echoing the way Mercer's mother used to imitate the trains from nearby Savannah station as she rocked her babies—seemed inspired.

A new screenplay was written, and then producer Arthur Freed had to convince Byron to let them make a musical about Fred Harvey, instead of a drama. It didn't hurt that Freed had just produced the blockbuster *Meet Me in St. Louis,* which was set at the 1904 St. Louis world's fair and featured the Garland hits "The Trolley Song" and "Have Yourself a Merry Little Christmas." Still, Byron was wary. He and other Fred Harvey executives felt the Adams book was under-researched and overwritten. They hadn't paid much attention to the novel until it was already out, and they weren't going to make the same mistake with the film. They planned to oversee the picture the Fred Harvey way—by "concentrating on it."

MGM began by sending Byron a list of all the films the studio had made that had moments of strong religious faith. Then associate producer Roger Edens, one of the studio's top musicians, was dispatched to the Fred Harvey offices in Chicago to actually perform the score for Byron, his son, and their Hollywood liaison Harold Belt, as well as walk them all through the new script.

Before granting the company's approval, Byron had several demands. He didn't want Fred Harvey himself to appear as a character in the picture—it's unclear why—and he said that even though the Harvey House was fictional, it should still display a sign that the Interstate Commerce Commission would have mandated back then, to keep the government happy. He wanted a prominent credit at the beginning of the film, acknowledging their cooperation and the crucial role Fred Harvey played in the development of America.

Byron also insisted that the lyrics to the theme song be fact-checked and corrected. He asked for numerous changes, including the deletion of the reference to passengers going to "Brown's Hotel" since Fred Harvey had its *own* hotels. However, he succeeded only in getting one fix. The train that had been coming "all the way from Phila-del-phi-ayy" would instead be *going* "all the way to Cal-i-for-ni-ayy."

Still, while Byron had his concerns, he was pleased with how seriously the filmmakers had taken the Harvey traditions. One of the highlights of the score was "The Train Must Be Fed," which took what "Mr. Fred has said" about the Harvey Girl mission and turned it into an Americanized version of a Gilbert and Sullivan number. Written by Harry Warren with Roger Edens, it was sung by the eating house manager, the head waitress, a chorus of Harvey Girls, and the newbie waitress Susan Bradley, played by Judy Garland.

The Harvey system, I must say, primarily pertains
To the absolute perfection in the way we feed the trains
Perfection in the dining room, perfection in the dorm
We even want perfection in the Harvey uniform

And the chorus chimed in: "The apron must be spotless and must have the proper swirl, that's the first requirement of a Harvey Girl!" And from there, much rhyming, primping, and synchronized table-setting ensued.

In the fall of 1944, the imaginary town of Sandrock was built on an MGM lot in Chatsworth, California, using the Castañeda and other settings in Las Vegas, New Mexico, as a model. Judy Garland arrived for her first day of production on December 29. The twenty-two-year-old actress was still wondering if she had chosen the right film since Arthur Freed and her fiancé, Vincente Minnelli, were making a musical at the same time with Fred Astaire called *Yolanda and the Thief,* which she had reluctantly turned down. But for the most part, Garland gave the Harvey Girls film her all and put aside any concerns she had that the script had been run through so many typewriters over ten years that the story no longer made a whole lot of sense. (At a private screening years later with her London fan club, she would ask, "Does anybody understand what this picture is *about*? Did you see all the writers? Seven writers . . . and they couldn't come up with *one plot.* We had seven plots . . . one plot per person.")

It was a physical shoot, and a number of actors were injured. At the end of the first day of rehearsal, many of the Harvey Girls reportedly passed out while their costumes were being removed; they had been wearing very tight, heavy corsets that, when unlaced, sent blood rushing to their heads (at least that was the diagnosis in the film's production notes). Ray Bolger was burned by the steam from an antique engine used for the big production number; the male lead, John Hodiak, got hurt doing a fight scene; and Garland fled one day when a spooked horse spooked her.

Johnny Mercer visited the set in early 1945 to watch them shoot "On the Atchison, Topeka, and the Santa Fe." It didn't go well. In order to create one of the most ambitious and complex numbers in film history, director George Sidney devised an extended montage that cut back and forth between the townspeople of Sandrock anxiously awaiting the new Harvey Girls and the girls themselves getting to know each other on the train. Without consulting Mercer, the director had hired Hollywood songwriters to add several new verses to "On the Atchison, Topeka, and the Santa Fe," clumsily establishing certain plot points and characters.

Mercer went ballistic when he heard what they did to his song. "They're going to make me look like an *idiot*," he yelled. "Everybody's going to think I wrote that junk!"

Besides his offended artistic temperament, there was a practical concern. Mercer was also a well-known singer and producer—he had recently started the first major West Coast record label, Capitol Records—and he had already recorded the original version of the tune himself. Bing Crosby had recorded it for Decca, too. Both recordings were kept on hold so they could be released several months before the premiere to pump up interest in the film. But now there would be two different versions of the tune they hoped would be as big as Garland belting out, "Clang, clang, clang went the trolley."

For the Harvey family, the highlight of the filming was Byron Harvey Jr.'s cameo. It served two roles—to keep the family happy, and to fulfill his childhood dream of being an actor, a dream he had put aside to work with his father. Byron was cast as a Santa Fe brakeman, and he and his father spent a day on the set, getting their pictures taken with the cast.

THE FILMING OF *The Harvey Girls* took the better part of six months, and they happened to be six months that changed the world. While the cast and crew spent their days on a soundstage or the outdoor set, President Franklin Roosevelt—who had just been elected to an unprecedented fourth term—met in February with Winston Churchill and Joseph Stalin at Yalta to discuss the possible end of the European war. Then, on April 12, 1945, Roosevelt died of a stroke at his retreat in Warm Springs, Georgia. When she heard the news, Judy Garland broke down sobbing.

As a grieving nation mourned its extraordinary leader—and the more than 200,000 Americans who had died in the war—Harry Truman was sworn in as president. He was sixty years old and had been vice president for only eleven weeks; most Americans knew little about him, except that he had been a U.S. senator from Missouri for a decade and had recently chaired a high-profile commission ferreting out waste and fraud in the military. As people became quickly familiar with their new president, they realized he was the ultimate Middle American. And his idea of America had been imprinted from early on by the Atchison, Topeka, and the Santa Fe.

Truman's early life was like one of those countless plots from *The Harvey Girls*. As a teenager at the turn of the century, he had worked for the Santa Fe as a construction timekeeper when the railroad was building tracks between Kansas City and Chicago. His family lived in Independence—the next major city east of Kansas City—and each morning he would get on a handcar and pump his way out to the construction site between Sheffield and Courtney, to keep tabs on a crew of four hundred. On Saturdays he was responsible for paying the Santa Fe crew, which he was instructed to do in a local bar, all but guaranteeing the workers would drink most of their wages and therefore need to show up for work again on Monday.

When Truman got into politics as an adult in Kansas City, with the help of the Pendergast political machine, he always sought his comfort food at the Fred Harvey restaurants in Kansas City Union Station. He and his family had eaten there often; he was known to be especially fond of the cream of Wisconsin cheddar cheese soup. Ironically, just after Fred Harvey headquarters had left town, the nation would rediscover some of the company's Kansas City ethos through Truman.

Filming of *The Harvey Girls* continued through May, when Allied forces finally declared victory in Europe even as the war with Japan and China escalated. The film wrapped in early June, and Judy Garland, who celebrated her twenty-third birthday on the set, proceeded to marry forty-two-year-old director Vincente Minnelli in Hollywood, at a ceremony where Louis B. Mayer gave her away. After the wedding, they boarded the eastbound Super Chief, where they were given special accommodations in private car 181, including their own compartment and drawing room.

Both Byron Harvey and the top brass at the Santa Fe deluged the Super Chief staff with memos about how absolutely crucial it was that the celebrated couple's journey go perfectly. All meals and cocktails for the couple, and any of their guests, were comped—some by the railroad and the others by Byron. But no matter who was paying, Byron swore that "there will be no slip-up" in any of the service.

When the train pulled in to Dearborn Station in Chicago, and the celebrity newlyweds and their bags were transferred to the New York Central train "Century" for their trip to New York, there was a collective sigh of relief from the Super Chief staff.

AS MIDNIGHT APPROACHED on Friday the 13th in July 1945, a small convoy of slow-moving military trucks from Los Alamos neared the city limits of Santa Fe. When they reached town, the trucks turned their sirens *on*—to warn away any motorists who might dare drive near them. Some hotel guests at La Fonda were awakened by the sirens and wondered what was happening, but the convoy moved on without incident and cut the sirens once they were out of town. The guests went back to sleep.

The trucks continued south until they reached Trinity Site, where Oppenheimer and his colleagues were going to test the first functional atomic bomb. Over the next two days, they were joined by other Manhattan Project staff, including physicist Joseph Hirschfelder, who had to stop at La Fonda on his way down to the test site to pick up the Geiger counters from a Manhattan Project detective.

At 5:29 on Monday morning, the first atomic bomb was detonated, transforming one of the most beautiful sights in America—the predawn sky over White Sands, New Mexico—into the most terrifying image yet conceived by man. When some of the scientists gathered at La Fonda that night to toast their labors and drown their fears, they were changed men. Oppenheimer thought Trinity director Kenneth Bainbridge had summed it up best. After congratulating him, Bainbridge said, "Now we are all sons of bitches."

About three weeks later, on August 6, physicist Otto Frisch was working in the laboratory at Los Alamos when he heard the sound of running footsteps and people yelling. Someone opened his door and shouted, "Hiroshima has been destroyed!" He never forgot the nausea he felt as he watched his friends rush to the telephones to book tables at La Fonda to celebrate.

The second bomb was dropped on Nagasaki three days later, and when Japan still did not capitulate, plans were discussed for dropping a third on Tokyo. Finally, on Tuesday, August 14, the emperor surrendered. World War II, the second war to end all wars, was finally over.

There was jubilation in every city and town throughout the country. Yet the radio soundtrack to that celebration was not songs about war and peace, or patriotic anthems. The #1 record in America on V-J day was a song about the Santa Fe railroad and the heyday of Fred Harvey and his girls. Not only was Johnny Mercer's rendition of the tune the nation's top seller, for the third week in a row, but it was joined at the top of the *Billboard* charts by Bing Crosby's version, Tommy Dorsey's version, and Judy Garland's version. The sheet music alone sold over three-quarters of a million copies.

"On the Atchison, Topeka, and the Santa Fe" was America's audio comfort food—the nostalgic sound of the most powerful nation in the world finally at peace.

EPILOGUE

WHEN *THE HARVEY GIRLS* WAS FINALLY RELEASED IN JANUARY 1946, the premiere was held at New York's Capitol Theatre, on Broadway and 51st Street, and the line to get in circled an entire city block. The location was perfect, since the movie was being hyped as "an original Broadway musical for the screen." It was also ironic. Just a few blocks to the east, at 50th and Madison near the Waldorf-Astoria, was the first Howard Johnson's restaurant in Manhattan.

To assuage Byron Harvey, the film opened with a somber foreword, the language of which had been negotiated for weeks. It read:

> When Fred Harvey pushed his chain of restaurants further and further West along the lengthening tracks of the Santa Fe, he brought with him one of the first civilizing forces this land had known—The Harvey Girls.
>
> These winsome waitresses conquered the West as surely as the Davy Crocketts and the Kit Carsons—not with a powder horn and rifle, but with a beefsteak and a cup of coffee.
>
> To these unsung pioneers, whose successors today still carry on in the same tradition, we sincerely dedicate this motion picture.

And then the singing and dancing began.

The Harvey Girls was a smash hit. It became one of the top-grossing films of all time—even during a year when it was competing with both *It's a Wonderful Life* and *The Best Years of Our Lives*—and it won an Oscar for best original song. The film brought amazing national press attention to both Fred Harvey and the Santa Fe. And besides selling many more copies of the Samuel Hopkins Adams book, Bennett Cerf's Random House published the first popular history of the AT&SF: *Santa Fe: The Railroad That Built an Empire.*

Byron decided this was the perfect time to launch his sons into the next generation of the family business. Only weeks after the movie premiere, he announced he was kicking himself upstairs to be chairman of the board; Byron Jr. was named president, and his brothers Stewart and Daggett were named vice presidents.

Unfortunately, neither the railroad nor Fred Harvey could capitalize on all the publicity. One news story even pointed out that the Santa Fe made less money in 1946 than the song about it had earned.

Once all the troops had come home, there was precious little peacetime business left for the Fred Harvey eating houses and hotels. In late 1947, Byron Sr. left Chicago on a private business train with just one other passenger: Santa Fe president Fred Gurley. Their goal was to inspect all the remaining depot hotels and eating houses from Kansas to California and talk frankly about the future. They got as far as Gallup, New Mexico, and by the time they returned, almost every Harvey House on the Santa Fe was slated to be closed. Only the hotels in major Santa Fe junction points—in Newton, Kansas, and Albuquerque— were considered crucial. A handful of others in the West were kept open because they were popular with some West Coast travelers—especially La Posada in Winslow, Arizona, which remained a favorite of aviators, Howard Hughes in particular, who was there so often they kept a regular room for him, No. 225.

None of the hotels were making much money, if any at all. Fred Harvey's profits came primarily from the Grand Canyon operation, which picked up where it had left off before the war. The firm did steady though diminishing business at its union stations in Cleveland, Chicago, Kansas City, St. Louis, and Los Angeles, its newsstands in Santa Fe stations, La Fonda hotel in Santa Fe, and the railroad dining car service.

But the original Fred Harvey company, which had invented the chain restaurant business, the chain hotel business, and the chain bookstore business—and had demonstrated how a chain could not only connect a nation but actually help hold it together—was no more. The chain had been broken.

ALTHOUGH THE COMPANY was never the same, the Fred Harvey saga and ethos did not lose their ability to inspire. In 1948, Walt Disney fell into a deep depression. His firm had barely survived the war and a crippling strike—it had been six years since his last successful feature, *Bambi*—and he was suffering from arthritis in his neck and shoulders. Hazel George, the studio nurse who gave him treatments for his pain every afternoon, told him he needed a vacation. Everyone around Disney knew the boss had a thing for trains, although they really didn't know why, since he was a fairly taciturn, distant man. So when Hazel heard there was going to be a railroad fair in Chicago, celebrating the centennial of the first trains in America, she told Walt he should go and take Ward Kimball with him. Kimball, one of his top animators, was obsessed with model railroading—a true trainiac.

Disney booked adjoining compartments on the Super Chief, and two days later they boarded the Santa Fe train in Pasadena. They had dinner in the Fred Harvey dining car. Kimball, who had never been on the fancy Super Chief, wanted the beef stew, which he had heard about from other railroaders: They said the Harvey chefs actually seared the beef before mixing it with the vegetables.

"Beef stew? For God's sake!" Disney exclaimed. He ordered them both filet mignon.

The next morning, the engineer sent back word that if Disney and Kimball wanted, they could come ride in the engine. Giddily, the two middle-aged men climbed up into the locomotive when the train was stopped at Winslow. Walt was given the job of manning the air horns, which had to be sounded well before the train approached even the smallest rural crossing. Each time he heard the horn, his face exploded into a smile that his longtime colleague hadn't seen for years. Whenever they passed one of the electronic line-side signals, the engineer would "call the aspect"—for a green light, yelling out "Clear," which the others in the engine had to repeat, mantra-like. It was a way to ensure the engineer was always alert and never took his eye off the rails ahead.

The panoramic view from the engine was much more dramatic than what they could see from their compartment—there was a big difference between passing things and watching an entire world unfold before your eyes. Hawks hung lazily in the air, animals large and small scurried away from the tracks, as the train passed along miles of untouched landscape.

"I can't figure out why in the hell everybody lives in the city," Disney said. "Why don't they come out here where they have this great empty land, filled with opportunity and silence?"

They were allowed to stay in the engine all the way to Albuquerque, more than 250 miles. After getting a bite to eat in the dining car, they retreated to Disney's compartment, where he pulled out the small cut-glass decanter and two shot glasses he always kept in his suitcase and poured them a couple of whiskeys. He then proceeded to reveal to Kimball the real inside story of Mickey Mouse, Walt Disney, the Santa Fe, and Fred Harvey.

It turned out that Disney had spent his early childhood in the Santa Fe town of Marceline, Missouri, where his uncle was an engineer for the railroad and Walt loved to put his ear to the Santa Fe tracks to listen for oncoming trains in the distance. When he was a teenager, the family moved to Kansas City, where he and his older brother Roy took summer jobs as "butcher boys" selling newspapers, sandwiches, and candy on westbound trains. Roy Disney actually worked for Fred Harvey as a butcher one summer; the next summer, Walt took a job with the competing Van Noy news service—and probably wished he had worked for Harvey, because he was often given rotten fruit to sell and ended up losing money on the job. But both brothers were working for the railroad out of Kansas City in the all–Fred Harvey Union Station.

The Santa Fe and Fred Harvey had a huge impact on Disney's image of America, and the kind of business he intended to run. It was no coincidence that Walt Disney used his name alone to brand his company, just as Fred Harvey had. Nor was it surprising when Snow White, the subject of his first feature-length film, turned out to be a combination of a Brothers Grimm princess and a Harvey Girl.

In fact, as he explained it to Kimball, Mickey Mouse had been created on a Santa Fe train ride—along the very same route they were traveling. Disney and his wife, Lilly, were on their way back to California from New York, where he had just learned that because of his business naïveté he had lost control of his first major cartoon character; Oswald the Lucky Rabbit was being swiped by his distributor, Universal Studios, together with all the animators who worked with him on it. Walt brooded and doodled all the way from New York to Chicago, where they boarded the Santa Fe train. And not long after they passed Toluca, Illinois, he started telling his wife about this mouse character he was thinking about. It was based on an actual mouse that Disney had befriended and fed scraps to at his original Laugh-O-Gram Studio on East 31st Street in Kansas City.

He had come up with a really great name for the new mouse character, "Mortimer." And somewhere in America's heartland—Disney wasn't sure where exactly, but he knew it was before they reached the La Junta Harvey House—his wife said the magic words: "Mortimer is too pompous for a cartoon mouse. How 'bout Mickey?"

By the time the Super Chief reached Chicago, Walt Disney had told Ward Kimball much of his life story, in a way and to an extent that none of his employees and few of his friends had ever heard.

The highlight of the Chicago Railroad Fair—besides all the marvelous old, restored engines and train cars—was a pageant called "Wheels a-Rolling," which showed the entire history of railroading from a stage larger than a football field. Walt was delighted when the pageant director invited him to play a small part in the production, portraying a passenger on an old Santa Fe railroad train who stops at a depot restaurant to be served by Harvey Girls. He wore a stovepipe hat and a black frock coat, and he improvised his lines from Harvey House stories he had heard as a child in Marceline and his own experiences as a young man in Kansas City.

After the train fair, Disney and Kimball spent two days at Henry Ford's museum and historical village in Dearborn, Michigan—which also had old trains, as well as re-creations of other aspects of transportation history—and then they caught the Super Chief home. On the way back, Disney started formulating the plans for what he called "Mickey Mouse Park," which became Disneyland, the venture that saved his company from bankruptcy, repurposing all his cartoon characters and launching the empire we know today.

When the original Disneyland opened, it had a replica of an old Fred Harvey restaurant, and the engine of the mini-train ride circling the complex was called the E. P. Ripley. When Disney World opened years later, the Fred Harvey idea of staging authentic Native scenes trackside—like those Disney had seen during so many stopovers in Albuquerque—was used to create a wonderful world's worth of "Indian Buildings" in Orlando, Florida.

BUT WHILE OTHERS continued to be inspired by the Harvey story, Fred Harvey itself was now history. Byron and his sons made the very wise decision to buy the Grand Canyon hotels from the Santa Fe in 1954 for $2 million ($16 million), since the railroad had completely lost interest in owning them. This meant that Fred Harvey would continue to make money, and there would always be a place that retained the original feel of the company's headiest days. But the Byron Harveys never shared the big dreams of Fred, Ford, and Freddy. They had no interest in using the well-regarded Harvey name to build a new chain directed at the sensibilities of postwar America—quality fast food, family dining, or both—in part because they had, in the words of one Harvey great-grandson, "an almost destructive hatred of debt." They simply wanted to run what was left of the company, and perhaps open a few higher-end restaurants around their hometown of Chicago or in Los Angeles. The union station restaurants would continue to link people in St. Louis, Chicago, Kansas City, Cleveland, and Los Angeles to the great old days of railroads and Harvey Girls and comfort food. But the mass marketing of American cuisine and Americana was left to other family businesses—and Fred Harvey's America went on without Fred Harvey.

Kitty Harvey fled Kansas City, where she donated the family home to the French Institute of Notre Dame de Sion, and moved full-time to Arequipa in California, where she made a small fortune investing the millions her uncle Byron had paid for her shares in Fred Harvey. She spent it expanding her amazing art collection, traveling, working with her gardeners to create award-winning floral displays, and making myriad charitable contributions to worthy causes. The best-known result of her charity was the discovery of the oldest human remains in the Western Hemisphere, the "Arlington Springs Man," which was found on Santa Rosa Island in California by an archaeological expedition she funded. Scientists later thought the Arlington Springs Man might have been a woman, and then changed their minds back again, in a controversy Kitty would have found endlessly amusing.

Kitty died of Hodgkin's disease in 1962 at the age of seventy, leaving the bulk of her estate to her family—especially to Byron Harvey III, "Ronny," her favorite—as well as to Mary Perkins and her gardener.

(She also funded the Katherine Harvey Fellows program at the Santa Barbara Foundation, which to this day trains young professionals to get involved in nonprofit work.) She ordered her life's collection of correspondence burned, but arranged for various items in the house to be sent to certain people with notes she had written. Her nephew Stewart Jr. had spent his honeymoon night in 1956 at Arequipa, where he and his bride broke one of the cherrywood beds in the guest room. Kitty had teased him about it, saying she would leave it to him in her will, and days after she died, the bed arrived at Stewart's Boston home, with a note from Kitty advising him to have a furniture craftsman "shore it up in anticipation of more *labor d'amour.*"

Byron Harvey died of colon cancer in 1954 at the age of seventy-eight, and his children ran Fred Harvey through the 1950s and 1960s. They made any number of attempts to reignite the spark of the company. In Chicago, there were the Harlequin Room and other restaurants in the Palmolive Building, the Bowl & Bottle and others in the Continental Companies Building, the Kungsholm and the Old Spinning Wheel in Hinsdale. In Southern California there was the Victor Hugo Inn in Laguna Beach, El Adobe de Capistrano in San Juan Capistrano, and the Pavilion and Curtain Call restaurants in the Los Angeles Music Center. They tried the airport food business in Albuquerque and Grand Rapids, institutional food service at General Motors, Packard Bell, Douglas Missiles & Space Systems, and the First National banks of Kansas City and Memphis. There was even a last-ditch attempt at the turnpike business, with modern restaurants over the Illinois Tollway. All had their fans and their moments, but none were terribly successful or resonant.

In 1966, what was left of Fred Harvey—the Grand Canyon and smaller national park facilities at Painted Desert and Death Valley, La Fonda, a handful of remaining union station and institutional contracts, and a hodgepodge of postwar eateries and theme restaurants—went public, with 162,500 shares selling at an opening price of $17.75, for an initial capitalization of $2.9 million ($19.2 million). But within two years, as Byron's grandchildren were planning to take their places at the top of the company, they were shocked to learn that their fathers had decided to sell the family business to a large Hawaii-based conglomerate called Amfac. Before long, there were no Harveys left at Fred Harvey, and the ninety-two-year relationship between Fred's company and the Santa Fe finally was over.

It wasn't long before the railroad stopped carrying passengers altogether. In May 1971, what was left of America's long-distance rail passenger business was taken over by a quasi-governmental body known as Amtrak. The only remaining Santa Fe line on Amtrak was the Chief, which ran from Chicago to Los Angeles along the very same route that Fred Harvey always rode.

Mary Colter had it right. When she was eighty-seven years old, the grandmother of American architecture was told some troubling news. The last of the great trackside hotels—her masterpiece, La Posada, in Winslow—was going to be shuttered.

"There is," she said, "such a thing as living too long."

APPENDIX I

THE GRAND TOUR OF FRED HARVEY'S AMERICA

At 3:15 every afternoon, the train Fred Harvey took across America still departs from Union Station in Chicago. While run by Amtrak, the train retains its old Santa Fe designation as the number 3 to Los Angeles, and it is still called the Southwest Chief.

Today, my wife, Diane, and I begin our journey: "chiefing" across the country in search of what is left of Fred and Ford's inspiring enterprise. While the company did, in its later years, extend east to Cleveland, Fred Harvey's roots were always in the America that began in Chicago and headed west by southwest by rail. We are here to do the same.

Like many big-city union stations, Chicago's is a massive structure with great architectural bones, but its most dramatic spaces have largely been wasted for years. There are plans to restore the station to its former grandeur—a process that is happening to depots all over the country, thanks to federal funds earmarked for preserving transportation buildings. But until these ambitious plans become reality, most of Chicago Union Station's busiest areas—the underground concourse and food court—pass for what was considered eye-catching in the 1970s, when Amtrak took them over. (The Santa Fe did continue as a freight line until 1996, when it merged with the Burlington Northern, creating BNSF.) The station's lower-level waiting area is so disheartening that our highlight is chatting with a guy in the food court who works as a traveling casualty-notification officer, a specialist in giving military wives the bad news.

When we board the Chief, however, we immediately feel much happier. Even though the days of Pullman luxury are gone, Amtrak does offer first-class sleeper compartments on its long-distance trains, and they are well worth the extra money. They're a bit shabby, but in a cozy, comfortable way, with couch-like seating and a big picture window all to ourselves.

The cabin was advertised as having a private bathroom with a shower, which is technically true. Actually what it has is what Diane refers to as a "shoilet"—a cramped metal closet about the size of an upended coffin that serves both purposes. George Pullman would have appreciated the ingenuity of the shoilet—which has a showerhead suspended over the toilet seat, and almost enough room to wash half-crouched—although he would probably have insisted on marble walls and a porcelain, self-heating seat.

As the Chief picks up speed beyond the city and suburbs, we sit and stare as northern Illinois passes by. Not everything we see is beautiful, yet somehow it is mesmerizing—fields of corn that appear to be blowing over as we pass, the backs of ramshackle houses with burnt-out cars on blocks, the shadows of planes flying toward O'Hare, depots that were once centers of town and now don't even merit a stop of the train. As journalist William Allen White lamented when the first fast Santa Fe train sped past his hometown of Emporia, "This new blue streak gives us the royal run around, the grand bounce, the dirty look—and brushes by like a movie queen! The whistle gives a toot . . . a dark smudge crosses the dawn and it's over."

We are reminded just how much more pleasant the train is than driving. That's especially true for me, since I'm always the one behind the wheel, so I see everything and nothing at the same time. Diane also likes the train for another reason. Whenever she opens the door and sticks her head out of the cabin into the corridor, everything resembles an unfolding scene from a Hitchcock movie.

As we cross through Fort Madison, Iowa, and into northern Missouri, there is still nothing of Fred Harvey for us to see. While some of these small stations once had Harvey newsstands, this section of the Santa Fe was the speedy "airway" to Kansas City. It was where Fred Harvey had its original dining cars, so it seems appropriate that we go visit the rolling Amtrak diner to see what kind of standard is being maintained.

There aren't enough tables for couples to dine by themselves, so we are forced to buddy up with another couple—initially somewhat irksome, but they turn out to be terrific conversationalists, reminding us that before cars and planes travel was once a much more pleasantly social proposition. I recall the words of a Fred Harvey busboy from Emporia, Kansas, lamenting the rise of the automobile: "When the railroad connected towns and was the only reliable way to travel, I think people were friendlier. The country lost something when the railroad went; it seems a lot of history was left behind—the pioneer history and feeling . . . There was a lot of connection between people on the trains."

But connecting with charming people doesn't make unexceptional food delicious. The meal is a little better than the Amtrak snack-bar fare on the eastern-corridor trains, but far from noteworthy. I keep expecting the ghost of Fred to appear and yank the tablecloth—except there are no tablecloths.

Kansas City is the first major Fred outpost on the Chief. Union Station itself is majestic, its restoration in the late 1990s remarkably successful. The main Fred Harvey dining room in Kansas City, which was renamed the Westport Room in the 1940s and remained extremely popular well into the 1960s, is now a fine private restaurant called Pierpont's, with good steaks and seafood. Next to it is the old Harvey lunchroom space, which has been well preserved— the ceilings and walls pretty much intact—and currently houses the "Harvey House Diner." The old Fred Harvey offices on the second floor are now used by a law firm that has kept much of the original wood paneling. Ford Harvey's old corner office is still there, its Indian-head mantel intact and the old National Regulator thermometer on the wall.

Fred's hometown of Leavenworth isn't far from Kansas City—unless you use the MapQuest directions as we did, which take you along the same old, crooked country road Fred's horse-drawn carriage probably used in the 1860s. By highway it's just half an hour or so away, and worth visiting because so much of Fred's stuff is there. The Harvey mansion itself is being lovingly and meticulously restored by local folks who have been slaving away at the job for years. In the restored stables, they have started a modest museum, which includes a real Harvey Girl uniform and a small collection of artifacts. As I've learned over years of research (and eBay surfing), there are an enormous number of collectible items with Fred Harvey's name on them: multiple patterns of signature dishes, silverware and stemware, books, postcards, photographs, playing cards, Indian curios, bottles, coffee cans, candy tins, liquor bottles, Harvey Girl statuettes. But so far, many private collectors have more and better stuff than this museum in progress.

Down the street, however, is the best collection in the country of Fred and Sally's actual housewares—kept at the Leavenworth County Historical Society in the old Carroll Mansion for safekeeping until the Harvey House has been fully restored. Fred's rolltop desk is on display, along with his shotgun and a lot of the dishes and silver from the house. Tucked away in file cabinets is an extensive collection of family photographs and many of the moving letters that Ford received from Fred during his declining years.

For Fredophiles, this is a thrilling collection—although its highlight is also its biggest tease. They have three of the Edison Cylinders Fred used to communicate with his family from England, hand labeled "Father's Voice." Unfortunately, two of the cylinders are cracked like Turkish Taffy, and the third one plays with so much surface noise that you can't hear his voice. I know this because I once carried the cylinder, by hand, from Leavenworth to a highfalutin lab in New York City specializing in incredibly old-tech transfers. They couldn't get a sound off it except crackling.

Back on the train, our Amtrak first-class porters have literally turned down our beds while we were eating, transforming our cabin into a bunk-bed cocoon for two. My wife insists she will never be able to get to sleep with all the train's rocking and rolling, but within minutes those very movements have lulled us both into deep, rewarding slumber. We pass towns in the night that could make the unabridged, director's-cut Fred Harvey–tour itinerary. In Topeka, there's not much left to see of the depot, but the state historical society holds all that is left of the corporate files of the Santa Fe railroad. In Florence, part of the old Clifton Hotel building still stands, and the local historical society puts on periodic Harvey Girl reenactment dinners that are reportedly quite tasty. For this trip, however, we decide to stay on the train until morning and get out at Dodge City.

You can't rent a car at the Dodge City station (which is true at too many western train stations, unfortunately, and makes train travel more challenging than it ought to be). So we remain in our compartment until the next stop, Garden City, where you can arrange to have a rental car waiting: It's the same little depot where Truman Capote and Harper Lee disembarked when they visited Holcomb while researching *In Cold Blood.* We get a car, take the long, flat drive back to Dodge, and realize we made a mistake. Everything in the charming little town is so close to the depot we probably could have done the visit on foot.

Dodge City's main street has been nicely preserved—a little touristy, but it has its charms. The Boot Hill Museum is a hoot. I'm not sure how authentic the cemetery is, with the toes of plaster boots sticking out of the ground, but it does cause all those old cowboy movie images to stir in our minds. Inside the museum there is some amusing vintage furniture for which a great many cows and buffalo gave their lives, and a small collection of Fred Harvey memorabilia.

But the cornerstone of the Boot Hill Museum complex is the Hardesty House, which was the actual home of Fred's in-laws: rancher Jack Hardesty, his wife, Maggie (Sally Harvey's sister), and their daughter. It appears as if nothing has been moved since they died in the early 1900s: It is a little eerie, actually, with the rooms sealed off behind plexiglass walls. But these are probably the last rooms left that look exactly as they did when Fred and Sally Harvey and their kids last visited.

The highlight of Dodge City, however, is the old Fred Harvey hotel, the El Vaquero, which has been brilliantly restored, albeit in a rather surprising way. It is now a dinner theater; probably America's most historically significant dinner theater. For a town with such an outlaw reputation, Dodge City is actually quite friendly and progressive, with a robust arts community. A local theater maven was able to get $5 million from the federal government to turn most of the El Vaquero into a state-of-the-art theatrical facility, with a full digital recording studio. The Depot Theater Company also restored the original hotel lobby space to its absolute Mary Colter–ish perfection: Every piece of her original handmade furniture has been rebuilt from scratch. The juxtaposition of the old hotel lobby and depot with the new dinner theater is a little odd, but it beats the alternative: In many Fred Harvey cities, the old hotel buildings have been torn down.

We board the train the next morning for the long ride into New Mexico, but separate at the La Junta, Colorado, station because I have an opportunity I can't pass up—an invitation to ride with the engineer. One thing about writing a book about Fred Harvey is that you meet a lot of "trainiacs"—an affectionate term for the locomotively obsessed, whether they are historians, modelers, or actual railroad employees. One of the most helpful and generous trainiacs is Brenda Thowe, a longtime personnel executive with the Santa Fe (and now BNSF) and a Harvey Girl enthusiast. Because Brenda has pulled some strings, I climb up into the engine car in La Junta and ride with the engineer, his assistant, and a BNSF supervisor (who is there to make sure I don't hijack the train) all the way through Colorado, up through the Raton Pass, and into New Mexico. It is a thrilling ride, with fascinating running commentary about railroad accidents and all the celebrity ranches we're traversing: "Oh, this is Ted Turner's land, and then down past here is Don Imus . . ."

There's nothing much to see at the old Raton depot, where the Harvey Girls made their debut, but at the next stop in New Mexico, Las Vegas, there are major blasts from Fred Harvey's past. The first is bittersweet: The Castañeda, the Santa Fe's original Mission Revival Fred Harvey hotel and the site of the Rough Riders' reunion, is still there, but just barely. The building and its surrounding structures have been featured in many Hollywood films, going back to old Tom Mix Westerns and, in the color-film era, everything from the parade scene in *Easy Rider* to exteriors for the Oscar-winning 2007 Coen Brothers movie, *No Country for Old Men*. But no matter how sturdy the construction of the graceful Castañeda, its shell—one of the nation's top endangered landmarks—can't survive forever.

Just six miles outside of town, however, is one of America's most astonishing preservation miracles. The shell of the Montezuma—which was used as a seminary from 1937 to 1972, and then sat vacant for nearly a decade—was purchased by billionaire Armand Hammer's foundation in 1981. It became a hulking Victorian backdrop for the new buildings of the American campus of Hammer's pet project, United World Colleges (UWC), an ambitious international program for high school students, now prominently supported by Queen Noor of Jordan, Prince Charles of England, Nelson Mandela, and other world leaders. Then in 2001, the UWC spent $10.5 million to dramatically restore the old building and make it the cornerstone of the educational retreat. You can arrange to tour the hotel's luxurious public spaces, although the creaky third-floor turret, which offers a breathtaking view of the Sangre de Cristo Mountains, is off-limits to anyone but the staff and the occasional student who sneaks up there. After the tour, we wander to the outskirts of the campus to dip our feet in the hot springs, which bubble up in small outdoor pools (and the occasional hot puddle) in several places near the hotel building. It's a popular place for students from the nearby New Mexico Highlands University to come on dates.

Back on the train, we continue on to Lamy station, where we disembark for our short trip to Santa Fe. While there is a daily train, we take the shuttle bus service to the city—or, in our case, to a rental car center.

Our first stop is La Fonda hotel, which has been in continuous use since the company first opened it in 1926. La Fonda is still very much part of the center of town, although it looks a little different than in its heyday. It was run by Fred Harvey until the 1960s, when it became so unprofitable that the company sold it to a colorful, wealthy, menschy New Yorker named Sam Ballen. He rescued La Fonda financially—and helped Santa Fe through its growing pains in the 1960s and 1970s, just as Fred Harvey did in the 1920s, 1930s, and 1940s. But in the process, Ballen allowed parts of the hotel's elegant first floor to be hacked up to create retail spaces. Some of Mary Colter's finest public rooms didn't survive—the famous bar, La Cantina, is now a crepe shop—but the skylighted main dining room is still there, and many of the guest rooms still have the furniture and wall hangings Colter put there. Ballen and his wife, Ethel, both died in 2007, but their daughter now runs La Fonda. I'm pleased to report that the hotel's main dining room, La Plazuela, is still one of the best in Santa Fe—which, considering how many amazing eateries the city has, is quite a testimony to maintaining the standard. Chef Lane Warner's soups are particularly scrumptious (especially the classic sopa de tortilla and the white bean soup with roasted garlic), and the menu still includes New Mexican favorites originally adapted by chef Konrad Allgaier starting in the 1940s.

For years, the only other major repository of Fred Harvey–ana in Santa Fe itself has been the Museum of International Folk Art, which holds all the Spanish colonial art collected by Herman Schweizer and John Huckel. The Harvey collection there includes over four hundred paintings, sculptures, silver pieces, textiles, bells, and furniture, some dating back to the early 1500s. But the long-awaited New Mexico History Museum, which opened in the spring of 2009 right in the middle of downtown Santa Fe, has a small but growing Fred Harvey display and collection, to which several prominent family members have already pledged their substantial holdings.

Visitors to Santa Fe still take pretty much the same day trips as they did when Fred Harvey began the Indian Detours in the 1920s. You go to see Taos—driving along the "High Road," a scenic, curvy highway that was once the *only* road to the pueblo. (For some, the drive is more fascinating than the destination—especially if you stop for lunch, as we do, at Rancho de Chimayo, which has life-altering fresh sopapillas and New Mexican favorites.) And you go to see the Anasazi cliff dwellings at nearby Bandelier National Monument, which is just below Los Alamos (which you can't really "visit," except for its small, intriguing Bradbury Science Museum). The forests around Bandelier are growing back after the wildfires in 2000—triggered when government workers lost control of a planned burn—but the dwellings were spared; the more rugged ruins nearby at Puye, where Ford's wife, Judy, had her stroke, are still closed.

Visitors also continue to go to the active Indian pueblos nearby to watch the dances, shop for arts and crafts, and indulge in the sweet Indian fry bread. Some also drive to Abiquiu, where Georgia O'Keeffe lived and fans still make pilgrimages to her studio and Ghost Ranch—a sprawling retreat and conference center where O'Keeffe had a small home. But the true highlight, honestly, is just motoring along the highway and being constantly blown away by the geologic formations that clearly inspired O'Keeffe's paintings. It's like driving through God's early sketches for the Grand Canyon.

After a few days in Santa Fe, we drive an hour and a half southwest to see one of the last intact Fred Harvey depots in New Mexico, in tiny Belen (although you can now actually get there on the convenient new Rail Runner regional train). Local residents have done a terrific job restoring their tiny Fred Harvey eating house and turning it into a charming Harvey and Santa Fe museum. It's a little trainiac treasure, leaving us with almost enough warm feeling to counteract the existential nausea of then driving to one of the more depressing sites in Fred Harvey's America—the Albuquerque parking lot where the Alvarado Hotel and Indian Museum used to be.

Preservationists fought like hell to keep the Alvarado from the wrecking ball in the late 1960s—in fact, it was one of the first highly publicized historical preservation fights in the country—but they failed, and on February 13, 1970, it was demolished. Amtrak built a modest wooden train station that burned down and was replaced in 2002 by a new transportation center, which, ironically, mimics the Alvarado's facade. The new building is mostly for buses and regional rail lines. The only Amtrak train that stops here is the Chief, which arrives once a day in each direction and, even today, is still greeted by Indians trying to sell their crafts.

The sunset view from the Chief as it heads west from Albuquerque is amazing—especially if you take it in from Amtrak's special observation car, which features extra-high arching windows, a glass ceiling, and comfy swivel seats. (For kids immune to nature's charms, the observation car also has TV screens playing children's movies nonstop.) As the solar light show ends and the stars begin to shimmer, the Chief pulls in to Winslow, Arizona, just in time for a late supper—and we get our first glimpse of Mary Colter's masterpiece, La Posada, the way it was meant to be seen: from trackside. It is one of the most welcoming experiences available in American travel. While Colter may have been right about people living too long—she died in 1958 at the age of eighty-nine—she would be thrilled to know that her artfully miscellaneous hacienda, shuttered for nearly forty years, is enjoying a marvelous second life.

In 1997, a thirtysomething couple from L.A.—entrepreneur Allan Affeldt and his wife, artist Tina Mion—bought the crumbling La Posada complex, which the railroad had been using as a block-long storage closet. Affeldt's thoughtful restoration has been remarkable considering that he did not have Armand Hammer's dollars. He brought La Posada back to life one room at a time—and when it was partially done, he reopened, allowing the first customers to enjoy (and fund) the work in progress. All the guest rooms have now been restored, and named after the most famous guests who stayed in them—although it is unlikely that Truman's or Einstein's quarters originally had Jacuzzis.

La Posada's Turquoise Room restaurant comes as close to capturing a modern vision of Fred Harvey's gourmet comfort food as any place in the country. If I could eat chef John Sharpe's Arizona Green Chile Eggs (with creamy polenta, tomatillo sauce, roasted corn salsa, and warm corn tortillas) every day for breakfast, or start every dinner with his signature paired potage (cream of corn and black bean soup side by side in the same bowl), I'd be a very happy man. (He recently published a Turquoise Room cookbook.)

From Winslow you can take the train to Williams—where some restoration work has begun at the old Fred Harvey Fray Marcos hotel—and then catch the train to the Grand Canyon, which runs once a day. We want the freedom of driving, because this part of Arizona has several treasure troves of Fred Harvey–ana not so easily accessible by rail. So we rent a car in the hip little college town of Flagstaff. Two hours to the north is the Grand Canyon, the nation's best-known Harvey location. But two hours in the opposite direction is Phoenix, which not many people realize is now home to the priceless Fred Harvey company Indian art collection.

Over four thousand pieces originally collected by Herman Schweizer and others—the very best of the Indian Museum textiles, pottery, and silver—were donated by the family trust to the Heard Museum in downtown Phoenix, which features Native American art in an educational setting. While the Heard, a small gem of a museum, has the entire collection, at any given time you can see only those pieces culled from the private storerooms for the themed shows and placed in the ten handsome exhibition spaces. (Kitty's art, including what she inherited from Ford and Freddy, is not part of the family collection: She donated most of it, along with some personal photos, to the small Museum of Northern Arizona, and a few other pieces to the Nelson-Atkins Museum of Art in Kansas City.) The Heard also has a Harvey-esque little restaurant, the Arcadia Farms café, which has outdoor tables in a restful courtyard.

It's a four-hour drive from Phoenix to the Grand Canyon, and we're tempted to stop over in Sedona at our favorite hotel, Enchantment—the same kind of luxe oasis that the Harvey hotels were in their heyday. But we continue on. It's highway driving up to Flagstaff, and then we get on Route 180, the main thoroughfare through the Coconino Forest to the canyon—and a road that may very well have inspired more utterances of "Are we there yet?" than any other in American tourism.

While plenty of people do the canyon as a day trip, they are missing what Fred Harvey employees have always known is the best part—which is being at the canyon after all the day-trippers leave. This means staying over at least one night in one of the Fred Harvey hotels on the South Rim, which can generally be accomplished only with a good bit of advance planning—especially if you want a room at El Tovar (which, trust me, you do). At any time, El Tovar is taking reservations up to thirteen months in advance—so there are people who know to call precisely at 11:00 a.m. mountain time on the first day of the month, exactly thirteen months from when they want to go, because that's when all the rooms for that month are released (including the three corner suites with canyon-view balconies, and all the other most desirable rooms). Many people plan entire southwestern or cross-country trips around room availability at El Tovar because space is so limited, the rooms are so surprisingly reasonable (the rates are controlled by the National Park Service, not the marketplace), and the experience is so worth the wait. You can also make dinner reservations at El Tovar up to six months in advance, and should. While the food can occasionally be a little too inventive for its own good, what they do well at El Tovar (steaks, fish, southwestern dishes) they do really well, and the room is redolent with history. In keeping with the Fred Harvey tradition, the best meal there is breakfast, for which they don't take reservations: It's first come, first served starting at 6:30 a.m., after the early birds like me have been out watching the sun rise over the canyon.

Fred Harvey's operation at the Grand Canyon is now run by a company with a name like an eco-friendly planet on *Star Trek*—Xanterra, which manages food and lodging for many western national parks. The company was created in the 1990s when Amfac, which bought out Fred Harvey, merged its South Rim holdings with a firm that controlled concessions at Yellowstone, Bryce Canyon, Zion, Mount Rushmore, and others. For years, Xanterra didn't do much with its Fred Harvey heritage, much to the chagrin of Grand Canyon employees who still remembered the Harvey glory days. But Xanterra has recently started exploring its roots. The corporate Web site now boasts about the company's "Fred Harvey Legacy." And the signage around the South Rim now pays more homage to the founders of the feast—primarily to Fred Harvey himself (who didn't live to see the hotel, but I have to believe visited the canyon in the 1890s) and to Mary Colter.

At the canyon, we explore all the extraordinary Colter buildings. From El Tovar, it's a short walk to Hopi House, Lookout Studio, and Bright Angel

Lodge, where they have a fine little Fred Harvey museum in the lounge with Mary Colter's famous geological fireplace. It's an excellent collection of Harvey memorabilia, including obscure silver, plates, and stemware, menus, Harvey Girls outfits, and gold service pins. (See it while you can; I've heard from company officials that the room will become a coffee shop.)

Hermit's Rest and the Watchtower are both miles away, in opposite directions. We take the free bus the park service runs to Hermit's Rest, where Colter's marvelous live-in fireplace still elicits gasps (as do the squirrels around the building, which are so tame and accustomed to entertaining tourists that I was surprised they didn't offer to take our picture). But we drive to Desert View to see the Watchtower, allowing us to stop at all the vistas along the way that, over the years, were named and made accessible by Fred Harvey and the park service. The main attraction is still the view from the Watchtower. We are lucky enough to arrive just as the weather is getting "bad"—Colter's faux lookout point being one of the few tourist attractions on earth where you hope for thunderstorms, which swirl dramatically down the canyon, leaving in their wake miraculous rainbows.

My wife is not what you'd call a "camper," so I'm surprised one night when she announces that we should "sleep out"—until I realize that by "out" she means out on our spacious and very private canyon-view balcony. At bedtime, she pulls a couple of blankets and pillows off the cushy bed, wraps herself in the thirsty hotel robe, opens a bottle of room-service wine, and goes out on the balcony to nest on one of the chaise longues. We lie out there looking up at what appears to be every star in the universe—you can see the whole northern celestial hemisphere in panorama, like a planetarium, with no impediments or light pollution.

Taking a sip of wine, Diane turns to me and says, "Now, *this* is my idea of *camping!*"

After four days of such "camping," we reluctantly leave the South Rim and drive back to Flagstaff to catch the Chief. When it arrives, many hours late, it's nearly midnight, and the beds in our cabin have already been turned down. The train goes through the hottest part of California at night, so we miss the handful of cities where the old Fred Harvey/Santa Fe buildings are still in use. The one all the trainiacs are watching with great interest is El Garces in Needles, which Allan Affeldt, who did over La Posada, is helping restore. In Barstow, Casa del Desierto is now a museum and transportation station, and in San Bernardino, the restored Santa Fe depot also houses a police substation.[*]

---

[*] There are several restored Santa Fe depots on the route from St. Louis south into Texas. Besides the gorgeous Art Nouveau St. Louis Union Station itself—now a hotel and shopping mall—there's Waynoka, Oklahoma, and, in Texas, Gainesville, Brownwood, Temple, Slaton, and Galveston. See Appendix III for a complete list of the Harvey locations.

As the sun comes up, we are deep in Southern California, approaching Los Angeles Union Station, the last of the great American train depots. The interior of the station still looks like a 1940s movie set, but the only vestige of Fred Harvey's large operation here is the empty side building Mary Colter designed. All her handmade wood restaurant furniture is gone, but Colter's curved ceilings, her light fixtures, and that amazing faux-Navajo-rug tile floor are in immaculate condition, as are the circular red leather booths and the curved copper bar in the upstairs cocktail lounge. The space is no longer open to the public, but justifies its existence by being rented out for bar mitzvahs, weddings, and film shoots. (It was used as the police station set in *Blade Runner*.)

Because the train arrives many hours late in Los Angeles, we are forced to dash through Union Station because we have a plane to catch. We get a cab to LAX and begin the cycle of rushed indignities that are modern air travel: the lines to get boarding passes, then the lines to get into the queue for security check, all so we can finally board the plane, take a crammed seat less comfortable than the one in the train "shoilet," breathe pre-used air, and eat stale mini-pretzels from tiny, shiny bags.

As we ascend, I attempt to recline my seat but am stopped by two large knees digging into my back. And I think to myself: It really is sad that Freddy wrecked his fancy new plane before he and his company had a chance to teach the fledgling airline industry how to set a Harvey standard for passenger care.

How is it that we can travel faster than ever before, but when it comes to comfort, we are back to a time before Pullman, before Fred Harvey, when people were treated only slightly better than freight?

I turn to my wife, who is only 5 '1" but is still smushed into her allotted seating space—a carry-on bag jammed where her feet would like to be. She looks up at me, with the plaintive eyes of a traveler who has just spent two weeks traversing half the country at a leisurely, life-affirming pace, only to be made weary by a flight that has barely reached cruising altitude.

"I miss Fred," she says.

Me too.

APPENDIX II

MEALS BY FRED HARVEY

FRED HARVEY CHEFS WORKED FROM LARGE HANDMADE "COOKbooks" that assembled typed-out sheaves of recipes sent from the main office in Kansas City as well as their own swapped handwritten recipes, kept for years and handed down from cook to cook in each Harvey location. The recipes were generally in paragraph form, and included not only basic cooking instructions but also advice on presentation and occasional social commentary. Below are some of my favorite Fred Harvey recipes, many of them previously unpublished and copied directly, with all colloquialisms intact, from three actual "cookbooks": one recovered from the family of dining car chef Roy Palmer Jr., who cooked on the Chicago to Kansas City train in the 1920s; another recovered from Otis Thomas, the manager of the Harvey House at the Galveston, which closed in the late 1930s; and a third, a cache of a year's worth of menus and corresponding cooking instructions for the meals served at one Harvey restaurant in 1930, discovered mislabeled in the bowels of an archive. I've also included some of the best of the recipes that appeared in the Santa Fe employee magazine from 1910 to 1913, a few from pamphlets the company published, and a couple that Harvey chefs shared with local newspapers. All of them maintain the standard (even the Bull Frogs Provencal). And they start, as most Harvey meals did, with perfect coffee.

HOW TO MAKE COFFEE

It is a violation of our instructions to use less than eight ounces of ground coffee per gallon. Coffee should be ground medium fine, but not so fine as to contain a flour dust. Your water must be boiling hot, and the water urn should show evidence of the boiling by the steam popping off through the top. When you can see the steam coming out under pressure from the top of the water urn, that is a sign that the water is right for making coffee. If you make four gallons of coffee, pour four gallons of water over rapidly, keeping the urn covered between each pouring so as to retain all the heat. Let this four gallons of water percolate over and through the coffee thoroughly and when the entire four gallons of water have run through, then start to pour over again. If everything is right, at the end of the second pouring the coffee should be finished and be up to the standard. If you do not allow all the first pouring to run through before you start the second, you are very apt to spoil the coffee because when drawing off the second pouring, the stream comes out thin and gets cooled between the faucet and the vessel, with the result that the quality of coffee is immediately adversely affected.

BREAKFAST DISHES

...

HARVEY GIRL SPECIAL LITTLE THIN ORANGE PANCAKES

Combine one-quarter cup diced orange sections and juice (half an orange), one teaspoon grated orange peel (also from half an orange), one cup pancake mix, and about one cup orange juice. Bake small pancakes on hot griddle, using one tablespoon butter for each pancake. Serve with maple syrup, honey or jelly.

FLANNEL CAKES

Combine one pound flour, one quart water and one small yeast cake. Set to raise and work in three beaten eggs, one ounce melted butter, a pinch of salt and two ounces of maple syrup. Let raise again and cook very thin, flannel-like pancakes on hot griddle iron.

RICE GRIDDLE CAKES

Mix two and one-half cupfuls of flour, two tablespoons of sugar, four teaspoonfuls of baking powder and one-half teaspoonful of salt. Work in one-half cupful of cold cooked rice with the tips of the fingers, then add one and one-half cupfuls of milk, one egg well beaten and two tablespoonfuls of melted butter. Drop mixture by spoonfuls on a hot griddle; by the time the last one is on the first one should be cooked on one side and ready to turn (when it should be puffed, full of bubbles and cooked on edges). Turn and cook the other side. By the time the last one is turned, if the work is done quickly, the first one is ready to remove and serve. Care must be taken if the finished products are to be regular in shape, of the same size and evenly browned. It must be remembered that the center of the griddle is usually the hottest part. A soapstone griddle needs only to be heated. The ordinary griddle or frying pan which is frequently used must be first heated and then rubbed over with the freshly cut part of half a raw turnip.

FRENCH PANCAKES FILLED WITH
APRICOT MARMALADE OR COTTAGE CHEESE

Mix well two eggs, one-half cup cream, one tablespoon flour, one teaspoon of sugar, vanilla extract to taste and a pinch of salt, place small amount of dough in a hot buttered skillet and brown on both sides. Fill with marmalade or cottage cheese, roll and sprinkle lightly with sugar. **Cottage cheese filling:** Four ounces of dry cottage cheese pressed through a sieve and mixed with the yolk of one egg, one tablespoon sugar, a pinch of salt, a little grated lemon and vanilla. Work to a smooth paste and spread over pancakes.

FRENCH TOAST À LA SANTA FE

Place one-half cup cooking oil in skillet, heat to hot. Meanwhile, cut two slices white bread three-quarters of an inch thick diagonally to form four triangles, and set aside. In a small bowl, combine two eggs, one-half cup light cream, and salt. Beat well. Soak bread thoroughly in egg/cream mixture. Fry soaked bread in one-half cup hot cooking oil to a golden brown on both sides, about two minutes per side. Lift from skillet to clean paper towel and allow to absorb excess cooking oil. Transfer to baking sheet and place in oven. Bake four to six minutes, until bread slices have puffed up. Serve sprinkled with powdered sugar and cinnamon and apple sauce, currant jelly, maple syrup, honey or preserves.

OLD VIRGINIA SOUR MILK BISCUITS

Stir into two cupfuls of loppered milk or buttermilk, a day old, one rounded teaspoonful of soda (no more). Whip into this with a few swift strokes one tablespoonful of melted (not hot) butter. Have ready in your mixing bowl one quart of flour twice sifted. Measure after sifting. Make a hole in the middle of this and pour in gradually but quickly the frothing milk, stirring the flour down into it with a wooden spoon. The dough should be very soft. Mix, roll, cut out very rapidly with as little handling as possible, and bake in a quick oven.

HUEVOS RANCHEROS, LA FONDA

Wash one cup pinto beans, cover with one-quarter cup cold water, and let soak overnight. In the morning, heat to boiling, reduce heat and let simmer, covered, until beans are tender—three or four hours. Cool. Add one tablespoon red chili powder, which may be obtained from Mexican grocery store, to the cold water and let soak one hour. Sauté four tablespoons minced onion and one-half to one tablespoon very finely minced green chili pepper in one tea-spoon butter very slowly until tender but not browned. Add beans which have been broken up coarsely with a fork and heat through. Add one-quarter to one-half cup hot water if beans are too dry. Transfer heated beans to a well-buttered stirred egg or individual casserole. Make two depressions on top of beans using back of tablespoon, and drop an egg in each depression. Pour two tablespoons soaked red chili powder over the top and dot top of eggs with butter. Bake in a moderate oven (three-hundred-fifty degrees), twenty to twenty-five minutes or until eggs are set sufficiently. (This is one of many Americanized versions of classic Mexican recipes popularized by La Fonda chef Konrad Allgaier.)

SOUPS

...

CREAM OF WISCONSIN CHEESE SOUP

Place twelve saltine crackers in oven to warm. In a saucepan heat two cups of beef broth over medium heat. Add three cups grated sharp Cheddar cheese, stirring constantly as it melts. Add remaining quart of beef broth and simmer until smooth. Meanwhile, in a small skillet over medium heat, make a roux with three tablespoons butter and three tablespoons all-purpose flour. When smooth, add to first mixture. Continue stirring as you slowly add one cup light cream, one tablespoon Worcestershire sauce, and one-quarter teaspoon white pepper. Stir constantly at simmer for fifteen minutes. Serve with toasted crack-ers. (This was a favorite of Harry Truman's, originally at St. Louis Union Sta-tion and later at Kansas City Union Station.)

ALBONDIGAS SOUP

Cut up four onions and three or four seeded green peppers; put them on the fire in a copper pot with two ounces of lard or butter. (Mexicans do not use butter for cooking.) When onions are done or melted, add two gallons of white bouillon and let boil. Have one pound of mixed beef and veal passed through a meat chopper. Add two eggs, one soupspoonful of marjoram, parsley, one half-cupful of cornmeal and a little salt; mix well. Make some small meat balls about half an inch in diameter; drop them into the broth; let simmer for half an hour. (Mexican cooks will press the meat through their left hands over the simmering soup, using the forefingers of their right hand to give the albondi-gas the correct shape.) Skim off the fat, season if necessary, and serve. (This classic Mexican dish was re-created by a Harvey chef in Las Vegas, New Mex-ico—with cultural cooking observations.)

VIENNAISE CHICKEN SOUP WITH HOME MADE NOODLES

Boil one hen, four to five pounds, in one gallon of water with three branches celery, one bay leaf and two tablespoons of salt. When hen is done, strain broth, take four ounces of home made noodles (below) and cook in boiling broth. Before serving, add some finely chopped chives. **Noodles:** Mix two cups of flour, the yolks of two eggs, one ounce of cold water and a pinch of salt and work through for ten minutes. Cover with a dry cloth, and let rest for twenty minutes. Roll dough very thin, again rest until dry on both sides, cut into two-inch strips, place on top of each other and cut very fine, dry again and cook in boiling broth for five minutes.

CREAM OF ONIONS

Melt three ounces of butter in casserole, add one cup of flour and moisten with one quart chicken broth and one pint milk. Stir with egg whip, season with salt and pepper and add six sliced onions. Cook until tender and rub through fine sieve. Place back on fire again and finish soup with hot cream and sweet butter. Serve with small bread croutons browned in butter.

CHICKEN

...

FRIED CHICKEN CASTAÑEDA

Fry an onion, chopped very fine, in butter, add flour, mix and pour in one quart chicken broth and one-half pint cream. Stir and let come to a boil. Let it cook about ten minutes. Add two egg yolks and parsley, and remove from the fire. This sauce must be quite thick. Dip thin slices of one three-pound hen in the sauce so that it adheres to both sides. Lay them in a pan sprinkled with bread crumbs and also sprinkle the chicken with bread crumbs. When cold, dip them in beaten egg and crumbs and fry in deep hot grease. Serve with tomato sauce and French peas as garnish. If handled properly, one three-pound hen will make ten to twelve fair-sized orders.

CHICKEN MACIEL

Preheat oven to broil (or four hundred degrees, if casserole is glass). Dice one pound cooked chicken breast meat into one-inch squares. In large skillet over medium heat, melt one-quarter pound butter and stir in two teaspoons curry powder and one-quarter cup sherry wine. Add chicken to this mixture and sauté five minutes. Meanwhile, cook two cups boiled rice. Using a two-quart saucepan, heat one quart cream sauce. Carefully blend chicken and cooked rice into hot cream sauce. Stir carefully until well mixed. Place in casserole, top with three-quarters cup grated Swiss cheese, and place under broiler until browned, about four minutes, or bake in glass dish at four-hundred degrees until browned and bubbly, about ten minutes. (This was the signature dish of the Kansas City Union Station dining room, named for its longtime manager Joe Maciel.)

CHICKEN LUCRECIO

Unjoint and quarter a six pound hen chicken. Salt and roll in a mixture of two tablespoons chili powder and six tablespoons flour. Roast chicken to a nice brown. Add more of the chili powder–flour mixture and sprinkle with finely chopped garlic and a teaspoon of Camino seed. Add two quarts of water or stock and place in moderate oven for three and one-half hours. When done, remove gravy and stir in one-quarter pound melted butter. Pour gravy over chicken and sprinkle with toasted almonds. (This is another La Fonda favorite from Chef Allgaier, which went nationwide on the Associated Press wire, offered as a treat for "housewives looking for a meal to warm Fall-chilled throats as well as the cockles of the heart.")

BEEF

...

BEEF RISSOLES WITH MASHED POTATOES

Boil two pounds of lean beef, seasoned with salt and pepper. Mix meat with one chopped green pepper, one small chopped onion, a cup of boiled rice, one-half ounce of summer savory, and season with nutmeg and grated lemon peel. Grind this all together in your hash machine. Then form in balls about the size of small hen eggs, bread and fry. If necessary to have more moisture, add a little beef stock. Serve with a mound of mashed potatoes in the center of the dish, a rissole at each end and side, with some thickened roast beef gravy poured around. **Mashed potatoes:** Peel and chop five potatoes and place in pot of salted water. Boil until tender, drain liquid and mash. Add butter and small amount of canned milk and whip. Stir in desired amount of salt and pepper. Garnish potatoes with parsley. This dish may also be served with kidney beans, green peas, French string beans or mixed vegetables. If the above is compounded according to directions it makes a very nice dish and gives you another outlet for that part of your beef which you cannot serve as steaks or roast. We have tried this at several houses with good results.

BEEF TENDERLOIN STROGANOFF

Sauté two pounds of beef tenderloin tips, cut into two-inch pieces with one onion, finely chopped over a fast fire, but not too brown. Sauté one-half pound mushrooms, cut in thick slices, separately, adding one-half clove garlic, mashed with salt, at the last minute. Now put all ingredients together, adding one cup sour cream and one cup white wine, let simmer for five minutes, season with salt, pepper and a pinch of cayenne, and serve.

PLANTATION BEEF STEW ON HOT BUTTERMILK BISCUITS

Place one and one-half pounds beef, cut into one and one-half-inch cubes, and one quart of hot water in saucepan, and bring just to a boil. Reduce heat and simmer for one and a half hours. Add one cup of diced potatoes, cover, and continue cooking thirty to sixty minutes, until the potatoes are mushy. Add another cup of diced potatoes, one-half cup diced onions, six chopped green onions, one-quarter teaspoon black pepper, one clove garlic, minced, and seasonings. Cook until vegetables are tender, about twenty minutes. When ready, split a hot buttermilk biscuit and ladle stew over bottom half. Replace top and add more stew to suit. You can substitute chicken, veal, pork, or ham for beef to make this stew. (This pre–Civil War recipe from a Harvey chef's grandmother was upgraded by using prime beef.)

HUNGARIAN BEEF GOULASH WITH POTATO DUMPLINGS

Sauté one and one-half pounds of chopped onions to a golden brown, add paprika and one clove of garlic, mashed with salt to a puree, mix well and add one and one-half pounds of lean beef, cut in two-inch pieces. Cook for one and one-half hours, stirring frequently to prevent meat from sticking to sauce pan and adding once or twice a half cup of water; season with salt to taste. **Dumplings:** Mix two pounds of grated potatoes, three tablespoons of flour, one teaspoon of corn starch and a pinch of nutmeg and salt, add the yolks of two eggs, form into dumplings the size of a golf ball, roll in flour and drop into boiling hot salt water. Cook slowly for ten minutes (do not cover pot). Before serving, roll dumplings in buttered browned bread crumbs.

CHOPPED BEEF STEAK MARCIA

Pass one pound trimmed beef through meat chopper. Add, finely minced onions sautéed in butter, chopped parsley; season with salt and pepper; mix with one egg, and form into round steaks. Fry slowly in butter until medium done and dish up on platter. Place fried egg on top, and garnish with fried zucchini.

SEAFOOD

...

ANGELS ON HORSEBACK

Dry large oysters with towel, season with salt and cayenne pepper. Wrap in parboiled strips of bacon and tie with toothpick. Dip in flour, eggwash, and fresh breadcrumbs. Place on skewers, and fry in hot lard a golden brown. Serve on toast, and garnish with quarter lemons and parsley.

MOUNTAIN TROUT AU BLEU

Clean a fresh-killed trout, ten inches or more, removing entrails but leaving on head and tail. Be careful not to remove the slime covering the fish, as it is important to the flavor. Place trout in fish pan and set aside. Prepare court bouillon by bringing two cups of fish stock to a boil and adding one sliced onion, one bay leaf, three whole cloves, two tablespoons of vinegar and the juice of half a lemon. Stir, reduce heat and simmer 30 minutes. Strain before using. Pour bouillon over trout to cover. Return pan to burner, reduce heat to slow boil and cook for ten to twelve minutes. Remove trout from pan and serve with drawn butter and horseradish cream, made by mixing one-half cup of heavy cream, one teaspoon of sugar, two drops of white vinegar and one teaspoon freshly grated horseradish. (This dish was served opening night at the Montezuma, and later adapted by a Fred Harvey dining car chef.)

MACARONI AND OYSTERS

Cook macaroni in salted water, without breaking it, till it is soft. Butter a covered mold or small pail quite thickly, and, beginning in the center of the bottom, coil the macaroni around. As it begins to rise on the sides put a layer of oysters, only half cooked, mixed with a thick cream sauce, and then add more macaroni, and so on until the mold is full. Put on the cover and cook in a kettle of boiling water for half an hour. Turn out on a hot platter and surround with cheese balls made by adding melted butter and chopped parsley to grated American cheese and molding into shape. Pass a bowl of cream sauce with this. (This recipe from Harvey Girl B. P. O'Dowd of Kansas City was published in a private Harvey Girl cookbook.)

FINNAN HADDIE DEARBORN

Simmer one pound finnan haddie (smoked haddock) in one and one-half cups milk for ten minutes. Place in two individual shallow casseroles or shirred egg dishes. Arrange potato slices, made from two medium potatoes, at one end of casserole. Brush potatoes with melted butter. Sprinkle with salt. Pour one cup cream over fish and potatoes, sprinkle with paprika. Bake in moderate oven (three-hundred fifty degrees Fahrenheit) for fifteen minutes. Sprinkle with parsley if desired. Cover casserole to retain the wonderful aroma, and serve immediately, hot and bubbly. (This was one of the earliest dishes on the menu at Dearborn Station in Chicago.)

CRABMEAT AND SHRIMPS IN RAMEKINS

Simmer three diced fresh mushrooms in butter with one cup cleaned fresh shrimps. Add one cup cream sauce and one-half cup pure cream, season with salt, cayenne pepper and sherry wine. Let cook for a few minutes, adding one-half cup picked fresh crabmeat. Fill into buttered ramekins, sprinkle with grated Parmesan cheese and bread crumbs. Dot with small piece of butter, and brown in oven.

BAKED HALIBUT WITH LOBSTER SAUCE

Preheat oven to four hundred degrees. Cut two pounds halibut steaks in eight ounce portions. Season with salt, pepper, one ounce bread crumbs, one-half cup soft sweet butter and one-half cup of white wine. Bake in baking dish for twenty minutes and put aside. Cover with aluminum foil to keep moist. For the sauce, melt one-half cup lobster butter (below) and one tablespoon sautéed shallot, one-quarter pound fresh sliced mushrooms, and eight ounces lobster meat for two minutes. Add one-half cup of white wine and reduce by half. Add one cup whipping cream and brandy reduced for five minutes, finish the sauce off the heat by stirring the sweet butter to thicken. Season with salt and pepper. Reheat gently over slow heat till simmer. Pour over baked fish and serve immediately. **Lobster butter:** Place one and one-half cups dry white wine, one-half cup cognac, Kosher salt, one tablespoon freshly crushed black peppercorns, and two pounds lightly salted butter in saucepan. Strain the mixture through a fine sieve pushing down on four and one half pounds crushed lobster heads to extract all the juices. Chill in the refrigerator. When the mixture is cold lift off the butter. Wrap it securely in plastic and keep in the refrigerator or freeze. Makes about one pound.

BAKED CODFISH

One pint of finely shredded codfish; one pint of mashed potatoes; two tablespoonsful of butter; two-thirds of a cupful of cream; three eggs beaten separately, the whites to be added the last thing before baking. Beat the whole mixture hard and long, then bake in a buttered pudding dish. Pour out on a platter and then pour over it the sauce, made as follows: three tablespoonfuls of butter, creamed with one of flour, added to one and one-half cupfuls of boiling water; cook until smooth. Add half a teaspoonful of salt, three shakes of white pepper and two hard-cooked eggs chopped fine.

CODFISH BALLS

One pint of minced cooked codfish; one pair of calves' brains, chopped fine, one cupful of mashed potatoes, one egg and salt and pepper to taste. Cook the brains in water containing a tablespoonful of lemon juice. When tender, drain, blanch and drain again. Chop fine and mix with the codfish, potatoes, eggs and seasoning. Form into small balls, flour lightly, dip in beaten egg and roll in cracker crumbs. Fry in deep fat and serve hot. (These two cod recipes are "lenten delicacies" from the Santa Fe employee magazine.)

SAUTÉED SHRIMP & SCALLOPS

Heat four tablespoons butter in heavy skillet, add one pound of medium shrimp, shelled and deveined, and sauté for three to five minutes or until pink and cooked. With a slotted spoon, remove the shrimp to a dish. Keep warm. Add one pound of bay scallops and four tablespoons of butter to the same skillet. Sauté the scallops for several minutes until cooked. Remove with slotted spoon and add to the shrimp. Over high heat, reduce the skillet cooking juice, then stir in two tablespoons brandy, one tablespoon of tarragon puree (below), two cups of fish veloute (below) and one-half cup heavy cream. Cook over high heat, swirling in the pan, for thirty seconds, lower the heat and stir in the accumulated juices from the shrimp and scallops, fold in the scallops and shrimp. Season to taste with kosher salt and freshly ground black pepper, then reheat gently. Serve with steamed rice. **Tarragon puree:** Heat four tablespoons butter in a skillet, add one cup of fresh tarragon leaves and stir to coat well. Cover the pan and let the tarragon cook gently for thirty minutes. Pour the mixture into a food processor or through a sieve. **Fish veloute:** Melt four tablespoons lightly salted butter in a saucepan and stir in one-quarter cup of all-purpose flour. Gradually stir in two and two-thirds cups of fish stock and stir until sauce is smooth. Bring the mixture to a boil. Lower the heat and let the sauce simmer for twenty minutes, whisking often.

FILLET OF FLOUNDER GLORIA

Remove fillets from fish and flatten with cleaver. Spread finely chopped, well seasoned spinach, mix with minced shallots and bind with egg. Roll fish fillets and place in buttered pan. Season, poach in lemon juice and Bercy wine for about ten to twelve minutes. Remove and dish up on platter with fancy border of Duchesse potatoes. Garnish each fillet with cooked cup mushrooms filled with diced fresh shrimp. Reduce essence in pan, add one cup of well-prepared Newberg sauce, seasoned with salt and cayenne pepper. Pour sauce over fish, glaze quickly under gas flame and garnish with thread of tomato sauce.

DEVILED LOBSTER

Take the meat from the claws of the lobster and pull out all the creamy part from the head and chop it up perfectly fine; mix with it a dust of paprika, a dessert-spoonful of chopped chutney, an ounce and a half of warm butter and one peeled raw tomato chopped fine. Put all these together in a stew-pan and stir over the fire till the mixture boils; then add a tablespoonful of mixed English mustard and the same of French mustard. Stir all together, turn out onto little square pieces of hot buttered toast and serve with a little sprinkling of chopped parsley and lobster coral or paprika. This should be served very hot. The body of the lobster can be used up in the same way or kept for a mayonnaise or other dish.

BULL FROGS SAUTÉ PROVENCAL

Remove skin, dismember bull frog, cut into desired pieces, season with salt and pepper, dip in flour and sauté in butter and one crushed garlic kernel, a few minced shallots, one chopped onion and three sliced fresh mushrooms. Add a few fresh tomatoes, peeled and diced. Let simmer until frog legs are tender, season with salt and pepper and finish sauce with chopped parsley and olives. Serve in chafing dish.

VEGETABLES
...

HARVEY COLE SLAW

In a large bowl, combine one medium head cabbage, shredded, and one small onion, finely minced. Spread one-third cup granulated sugar over it, toss with fork. Next, bring to boil one teaspoon sugar, one and one-half teaspoon salt, one-half teaspoon dry mustard, one-half teaspoon celery seed, one-half cup salad oil, one-half cup apple cider vinegar. Pour over cabbage, toss thoroughly and refrigerate for at least four hours. Serves five to six, lasts beautifully.

GERMAN POTATO SALAD

Boil twelve potatoes. While hot, cut into thin slices, cover with finely sliced onions and add one teaspoon of salt and one-half teaspoon of pepper. Mix the yolk of one egg with three tablespoons of olive oil and four tablespoons of vinegar. Pour the well-mixed dressing over the potatoes, then pour a half-cup of boiling water or broth over the whole mixture and stir well. Sprinkle with chopped parsley; cover and let stand a few hours. This salad will never be dry.

POTATO SOUFFLÉ

Boil four good-sized mealy potatoes; pass them through a sieve. Scald in a saucepan half a teacupful of sweet milk and a tablespoonful of butter; add to the potatoes with a little salt and pepper and beat to a cream. Add, one at a time, the yolks of four eggs, beating thoroughly; put a small pinch of salt into the whites and beat them to a stiff froth, then add them to the mixture, beating as little as possible. Have ready a well-buttered baking dish, large enough to permit the soufflé to rise without running over; bake twenty minutes in a brisk oven, serve at once in the same dish in which baked.

CAULIFLOWER GREENS RESTELLI

Sauté two tablespoons chopped onion and three strips of bacon, diced, in two teaspoons of olive oil until tender but not brown. Add one-half cup chopped tomatoes, one-half cup tomato puree and one-half clove garlic, minced. Simmer until amount is reduced by half, about twenty minutes. Wash one cauliflower (one and one-quarter pound), including the good leaves and stems; chop fine. Cook five minutes in boiling salted water and drain. Add to tomato sauce and serve. Sprinkle grated Parmesan cheese over each serving if desired. (This was created by a sous chef at St. Louis Union Station for the droves of new immigrants passing through.)

MRS. FORD HARVEY'S BAKED EGG PLANT

Egg Plant is very popular in the south and Mrs. Ford Harvey thinks it is finer when baked than cooked in any other way. Her method is to take one medium sized egg plant, cut it in halves, remove the pulp and mix with it one cup bread crumbs, one-fourth cup stock or cream, one-half cup chopped mushrooms (canned). Season with butter, pepper, salt. Fill the two halves with the mixture and sprinkle bread crumbs over the top, with a little butter. Bake twenty minutes and serve with hot tomato sauce. (Judy shared this recipe with the *Kansas*

City Star, for a dish she may very well have brought to serve at her Tip Top Cafeteria.)

BELL PEPPER, FORD HARVEY STYLE

Remove the skin from six bell peppers (enough to make twelve orders) by dipping them into hot grease. Peel three or four eggplants and cut and dice a quarter of an inch thick. Cut the peppers in two lengthwise, remove the fleshy part adhering to the seeds, chop it and add to the eggplant. Cut two or three onions and one green pepper fine; put on the fire with three ounces of olive oil or butter and let cook for ten minutes. Add a handful of fresh bread crumbs, one crushed clove of garlic, eggplant, and a little salt, and stir frequently until done. Add one tablespoon flour, mix well; pour in one-half pint milk; let come to a boil and keep stirring. Add two whole eggs and a little chopped parsley. Mix well, season if necessary, and remove from the fire. Stuff the bell peppers with this mixture. Sprinkle with grated cheese; put a small lump of butter on each one, and leave them in a hot oven long enough to produce a nice golden brown color. (This was known as a favorite dish of Ford's.)

GUACAMOLE MONTEREY

Mash one avocado, add one tomato, chopped fine, one-half cup cottage or cream cheese, two tablespoons chopped green onions, one tablespoon lemon juice, one-half tablespoon chopped chives, one-half tablespoon salt, dash of pepper, dash of Worcestershire. Mix thoroughly and chill. Serve on lettuce with peeled, chilled tomato wedge or use as dunk mixture.

STUFFED ONIONS

Parboil in salt water for twenty minutes some large white onions; drain and let cool. Take out the inner parts of the onions with a tablespoon or large vegetable scoop. Add to these two handfuls of bread crumbs and two of mushrooms. Chop the whole fine, put it in a saucepan with a ladleful of drawn butter and tomatoes chopped fine, parsley, salt and pepper. Mix well. Stuff the onions, then put them in a flat saucepan and sprinkle with bread crumbs and a little butter. Bake for about half an hour until a light brown color. (This was a favorite recipe of Chef Geyer, who cooked for the Coyote Special.)

RISOTTO PIEMONTAISE

Sauté one small onion, chopped fine, in butter to a golden brown. Add one cup uncooked rice and continue heating until rice is browned lightly, about ten minutes, stirring constantly. Add about one-half teaspoon salt, and two-and-a-half cups of boiling chicken broth, cover, reduce heat to low and cook slowly for eighteen to twenty minutes or until rice is tender and excess liquid has evaporated. Serve hot, topped or mixed with grated Parmesan cheese. (This is an Americanized version of the classic Italian dish from chefs at Los Angeles Union Station—and perhaps a precursor of Rice-A-Roni.)

CHILI SAUCE

Take ten ounces of dry red chili, free from seeds and veins. Set in the oven for five minutes to make them crisp, being careful not to burn them. Soak in plenty of water for two hours, drain and put them on the stove, with one sliced onion, one clove crushed garlic, two ounces of sugar, a little salt and one quart of water. Let boil fifteen minutes. Dissolve about a tablespoonful of cornstarch in a little water, add it to the boiling chili and strain until every particle of pulp is forced out of the chili. Mix well and season to taste. The foregoing is a Mexican dish, but the average American prefers a somewhat milder sauce, which can be produced by one quart or more of tomatoes instead of water.

DESSERT

...

BAKED APPLE

If the skin is thin and of a deep red color it is not necessary to pare the apple, but the core at all times should be carefully removed, especially every bit of the lining of the seed cells. The apples should be baked in granite or earthen vessels—never in tin, as tin gives them an unpleasant flavor and dingy color. Fill the core cavities with sugar, heaped or scant according to the tartness of the apples; add also a few grains of salt and sufficient water to half cover the apples. Bake in a quick oven and baste frequently.

HOT STRAWBERRY SUNDAE

Marinate one pint of strawberries, cut in half, in four tablespoons Jamaican rum for one hour. Bring three-quarters of a cup of strained honey, four tablespoons of lemon juice and the rind of one orange, cut into strips to boil; remove orange rind and combine flavored honey with strawberries. Serve over vanilla ice cream immediately. (Inspired by a sundae that a Harvey restaurant manager had at the Chicago world's fair—which combined hot maple syrup and strawberries—this became the favorite dessert at Kansas City Union Station.)

ECONOMICAL LAYER CAKE

Put into the mixing bowl one cupful of flour, one cupful of sugar, a pinch of salt, one level teaspoonful of baking powder. Mix well together, dry. Melt in the measuring cup a piece of butter the size of an English walnut; break into this an egg (without beating) and fill the cup with milk. Pour into the mixing bowl and beat all together rapidly for a minute. Flavor to suit taste and bake in a hot oven. With one-quarter the amount of sugar it makes fine muffins or gems, can be used for steam batter pudding, or cottage pudding, and, with the addition of nuts, raisins and spice, makes delicious "hermits." (This penny-wise recipe came from "an experienced and economical housewife" whose husband was "in the Harvey Service.")

PLUM PUDDING WITH BRANDY SAUCE

Mix one pound of raisins, one pound of currants, one pound of chopped suet, one pound of grated bread, one-half pound of flour, one-half pound of "C" sugar, one ounce of candied citron, one ounce of candied lemon peel, one ounce of blanched almonds, chopped fine, three grated nutmegs, five eggs, a little salt, and the rind and juice of one lemon. Mix with sweet cream until a spoon will stand up in the middle. Boil five or six hours. Add two wine glasses of brandy, if desired, and serve with brandy sauce. (This dish was served on the inaugural run of the Fred Harvey–George Pullman dining car.)

BUTTERSCOTCH PIE CHANTILLY

Boil one pound of sugar with a little water until brown and add four ounces sweet butter. In the meantime heat two quarts of milk in double boiler, add caramelized sugar and bind with fifteen egg yolks combined with four ounces corn starch. Whisk with egg whip and make a smooth cream. Fill into baked pie crusts and let cool. Garnish with vanilla flavored, sweetened whipped cream, using pastry bag with star tube.

NEW ENGLAND PUMPKIN PUDDING

Mix one pint cream, six ounces melted butter, ten eggs and one-half pound sugar together. Add three pounds pumpkin pulp, one-half teaspoon each of cinnamon and nutmeg. Fill in buttered pudding mold, place in bain-marie and bake in oven for about thirty to forty minutes. Unmold and serve with lemon sauce.

OATMEAL COOKIES

Two cupfuls granulated sugar; one and one-third cupfuls butter, four eggs: Stir these until light and creamy. With four cupfuls of sifted pastry flour, mix one and one-third teaspoonfuls soda, two teaspoonfuls cinnamon. Stir into butter, sugar and egg; then add four cupfuls of rolled oats (not cooked), two cupfuls shredded raisins and two cupfuls chopped nuts. Mix well; drop into tins and bake in a slow oven.

RICH RAISIN CUP CAKES

Put together and boil for a few minutes—two cupfuls of seeded raisins and two cupfuls of water, one and one-half cups of sugar and two teaspoonfuls of shortening, allow to cool then add one teaspoonful of cinnamon, one-half teaspoonful of nutmeg, one quarter teaspoonful of cloves, one teaspoonful of soda, one-half teaspoonful of baking powder, one cup of chopped nuts and one cupful of flour. Drop the mixture into cup cake pans one tablespoonful to each tin. This makes two dozen cup cakes or one large loaf cake if desired.

BRANDY FLIP PIE

In a small bowl, pour one tablespoon unflavored gelatin over cold water and let stand five minutes to soften. In double boiler over slow-boiling water, combine four egg yolks, lightly beaten, one-half cup sugar, and scalded milk. Cook until mixture coats spoon, then remove from heat. Add softened gelatin and stir until dissolved. Chill in refrigerator until mixture is slightly thickened. Meanwhile, beat egg whites stiff with one tablespoon sugar, nutmeg, and brandy. In a large mixing bowl, gently fold egg-white mixture into chilled mixture and pour into cooled, baked pie shell. Return to refrigerator and chill until firm. Before serving, top with one pint whipped cream and garnish with chocolate curls. Shave chocolate curls from one pint slightly warmed bitter or semisweet chocolate, using the blade of a potato peeler.

FRENCH APPLE PIE WITH NUTMEG SAUCE

Pare and slice eight cups tart apples and place in the saucepan with one-half cup water to cover. Bring to a boil and cook until tender, about five minutes. Add one-half cup sugar, mixing gently to avoid damaging apples. Using slotted spoon, arrange apples in pie tin lined with pastry. In a small bowl, stir to mix one cup graham cracker crumbs, one-half cup flour, and one-half cup sugar. Add one-third cup butter and a few drops vanilla and stir thoroughly with a fork until mixture has a coarse, crumbly texture. Sprinkle the graham cracker topping evenly over apples. Place in oven preheated to four-hundred-fifty degrees for ten minutes, then reduce temperature to three-fifty degrees and bake for thirty minutes, or until pastry turns light brown. **Nutmeg sauce:** In small saucepan, beat one egg yolk, one-half cup sugar, and one cup milk together well. Heat to just boiling and remove from heat immediately. Add one teaspoon nutmeg and stir thoroughly. (This classic eating house comfort-food dish was tarted up by the head Fred Harvey baker at Los Angeles Union Station.)

LA FONDA PUDDING

Beat three egg yolks until thick and lemon-colored; gradually add one cup sugar, beating constantly. Fold in one cup finely crushed graham crackers, one-half cup chopped nuts, one teaspoon baking powder, one-eighth teaspoon salt, and one-half teaspoon vanilla. Fold in three egg whites, stiffly beaten. Bake in a buttered eight-by-eight-by-two-inch pan in moderate oven (three-hundred-fifty degrees) for forty-five minutes. Cool in pan for ten minutes. Remove from pan. Cut in squares and serve topped with whipped cream and extra chopped walnuts if desired.

ALMOND SOUFFLÉ PUDDING

Boil one quart milk and four ounces butter, add four ounces flour and stir on fire until dry. Remove and add ten egg yolks, one by one, beating with wooden spoon and mix in four ounces finely chopped or ground almonds. Whip ten egg whites real stiff, add sugar and combine with rest of ingredients. Fill in buttered pudding molds and bake in bain-marie for about twenty-five to thirty minutes. Serve with Sabayon or vanilla sauce. **Vanilla sauce:** Melt three-quarters cup butter; blend three tablespoons cornstarch and one and a half cups sugar. Add three cups boiling water, stirring constantly, and cook until thickened. Add three teaspoons vanilla just before serving.

CHOCOLATE PUFFS

Boil together one cupful of flour, one cupful of water and half a cupful of butter. Remove from fire and beat in an ounce of melted chocolate and (one at a time) three eggs. Bake in a gem pan, and when done cut off the top and put into each cake a teaspoonful of strawberry preserves. Cover with whipped cream, sweetened and flavored.

APPENDIX III

FRED WAS HERE:
A MASTER LIST OF
FRED HARVEY LOCATIONS

A WORKING MASTER LIST OF ALL FRED HARVEY OPERATIONS from 1875 to 1948 (based on company records, although there were so many Harvey operations that even the company records don't agree on where they all were and when they opened and closed). **Boldface** means building still exists; *bold italics* means Harvey spaces restored, being restored, or still functioning; L = Lunchroom, D = Dining Room, N = Newsstand, H=Hotel, which just means some kind of lodging was available, anything from modest guest rooms to full hotel service—names and opening dates for more modern and noteworthy hotels are in the Notes; all locations ATSF except: * = St. Louis & San Francisco Railway, # = Kansas Pacific Railroad, @ = Southern Pacific Railroad (? = date in dispute or opening and/or closing year not verifiable with known Fred Harvey or ATSF archival materials).

	OPENED	CLOSED	FACILITIES	NOTES
ALABAMA				
Birmingham*	1896	1930	L, N	
ARKANSAS				
Fayetteville*	**1896**	**1930**	N	
Fort Smith*	**1896**	**1930**	N	
Jonesboro*	1896	1930	L, N	
Rogers*	1896	1930	L, D, N	
ARIZONA				
Ash Fork	1895	1948	L, D, N	Escalante 1906
Del Rio	1898	1956		Dairy Farm

Grand Canyon	*1905*	*open*	*L, D, N, H*	*El Tovar 1905; Phantom Ranch 1925; Bright Angel Lodge 1935*
Holbrook	1884	1886	L, D, N	
Kingman	1901	1938	L, D, N	
Painted Desert Inn	*1947*	*1949*	*D*	*reopened 1963 as Painted Desert Oasis gift shop, restored in 2006 adding museum*
Peach Springs	1884	1889	L, D	Dairy Farm
Phoenix	1896	1946	N	
Prescott Junction	1890			
Seligman	1895	1948	L, D, N	The Havasu 1913
Williams	*1887*	*1954*	*L, D, N*	*Fray Marcos 1908*
Winslow	*1887*	*open*	*L, D, N, H*	*La Posada 1930, closed 1957, restored and reopened 1997*

CALIFORNIA

Bagdad	1887	1908	L, D	
Bakersfield	1902	1948	L, D, N	
Barstow	*1887*	*1959*	*L, D, N*	*Casa del Desierto 1911*
Fresno	**1900**	**1923**	**N**	
Hollywood	1939	1952	L, D, N	Bus terminal restaurant
Los Angeles	1893	1939	L, D, N	Santa Fe Le Grande Station
Los Angeles UPT	*1939*	*1967*	*L, D, N*	
Merced	1902	1934	L, D, N	
Mojave@	1887	1933	L, D, N, H	
Needles	*1887*	*1948*	*L, D, N*	*El Garces 1908*
San Bernardino	*1887*	*1940*	*L, D, N*	
San Diego	**1897**	**1936**	**L, N**	
San Francisco	**1901**	**1938**	**L, N**	**Ferry Building**
Ocean Wave	1900	1911	D	Ferry steamship
San Pablo	1900	1933	L, D, N	Ferry steamship
San Pedro	1911	1933	L, D, N	Ferry steamship
San Francisco	1938	1968	L, N	Bus terminal
Stockton	**1900**	**1923**	**N**	

COLORADO

Colorado Springs	**1899**	**1938**	**L, D, N**	
Hugo#	1875	1879	D	
La Junta	1879	1948	L, D, N, H	El Otero 1895
Palmer Lake	1899	1902	L	
Pueblo	1887	1889	L, D	
Trinidad	1895	1933	L, D, N, H	Cardenas 1903

ILLINOIS

Chicago	**1899**	**?**	**L, D, N**	**Dearborn Station**
Chicago	?	?	L, D, N	Englewood Station
Chicago	**1925**	**?**	**L, D, N**	**Union Station**
Chicago	1933	1941	L, D, N	Straus Building
Chillicothe	1889	?	D	
East St. Louis	after 1896	?		Dining car commissary
Galesburg	1895	?		
Streator	1895	?		

IOWA

Fort Madison	1889	?		

KANSAS

Arkansas City	1883	1933	L, D, H	
Augusta	?	1887	N	
Chanute	**1896**	**1931**	**L, D, N**	
Coolidge	1880	1888	L, D, H	Moved from Lakin
Dodge City	*1888*	*1948*	*L, D, N*	*El Vaquero 1896*
Elk Falls	1888	1895		
Emporia	1888	1937	L, D, N, H	
Florence	*1878*	*1900*	*L, D, H*	*Clifton 1879*
Fort Scott*	1896	1930	L, N	
Halstead	?	1888		
Hutchinson	1883	1946	L, D, N	Bisonte/1906
Kinsley	1887	1896		
Lakin	1879	1880	L, D, H	Moved to Coolidge
Lawrence#	1875	1879	D, H	ATSF newsstand 1896–?
Lyons	1886	1888		

Madison	1885	1889		
Manchester	1888	1904		
McPherson	?	1888		
Newton	**1883**	**1957**	**L, D, N, H**	**Arcade 1901, bottling plant, poultry farm**
Ottawa	1887	1904		
Pittsburg	1896	?	N	
Rush Center	1888	1889		
Sawyer	?	1904		
Spivey	?	1893		
Syracuse	1890	1933	L, D, N	Sequoyah 1908
Topeka	1876	1940	L, D, N	
Wallace#	1875#	1879	L, D, H	
Wellington	1881	1939	L, D, N, H	
Wichita	**1914**	**1935**	**L, D, N**	**Union Station**
Winfield	?	1895		

MISSISSIPPI

Amory*	?	?	N	

MISSOURI

Cape Girardeau*	1896	1930	N	
Joplin*	1896	1930	L, N	
Kansas City	*1914*	*1962*	*L, D, N*	*Union Station 1914*
Kansas City	1937	?	D	KC National Bank
Lexington Junction	1889	?		
Marceline	1889	1895	L, D	
Monett*	1896	1930	L, D, N, H	
Newburg*	1896	?	L	
Springfield	1896	1930	L, D, N	Commissary
St. Louis	*1896*	*1970*	*L, D, N*	*Union Station*
Tower Grove*	1886	1930	N	

NEW MEXICO

Albuquerque	1883	1968	L, D, N	Alvarado 1902
Albuquerque Airport	1949	?		
Belen	*1903*	*1935*	*L, D, N, H*	
Clovis	**1899**	**1948**	**L, D, N, H**	**Gran Quivira 1900**
Coolidge	1887	1889		
Deming@	**1881**	**1929**	**L, D, N, H**	**Union Station**
Gallup	1895	1957	L, D, N	El Navajo 1923

Lamy	1881	1938	L, D, N	El Ortiz 1910
Las Cruces	1896	?	N	
Las Vegas depot	**1881**	**1948**	**L, D, N, H**	**Castañeda 1899**
Las Vegas resort	*1881*	*open*	*D, H*	*Montezuma 1882, Harvey management ended 1884, owned by AT&SF until 1903, restored by United World College in 2001*
Raton	1881	1903	L, D	
Rincon	1883	1933	L, D, H	
San Marcial	1883	1929	L, D, N, H	
Santa Fe	*1926*	*open*	*L, D, N, H*	*La Fonda, expanded 1929, sold 1968*
Vaughn	1883	1936	L, D, N	Las Chavez 1910
Wallace	1882	1886	L, D	

OHIO

Cleveland	**1930**	**1968**		**Union Station restaurant/shops**

OKLAHOMA

Afton*	1896	1930	N
Antlers*	1900	1910	L, D, H
Ardmore	?	1899	N
Bartlesville	?	?	N
Claremore*	?	?	N
Enid	?	?	N
Francis*	1896	1930	L, N
Guthrie	*1895*	*1930*	*L, N*
Henryetta*	?	?	N
*Hugo**	*1896*	*1930*	*L, N*
Madill*	1896	1930	N
Miami*	?	?	N
Muskogee*	?	?	N
Oklahoma City	1899	1960	N
Okmulgee*	1896	1930	N
Purcell	1899	1935	L, D, N
Sapulpa*	1896	1930	L, D, N, H
Snyder	1896	1930	L, N
Talihina	1893	?	
Tulsa	1896	1930	N
Vinita	1896	1930	L, D, N

Waynoka	*1910*	*1937*	*L, D, N*	
Woodward?	1880	?		

TENNESSEE

Memphis*	1896	1930	N	

TEXAS

Amarillo	**1910**	**1940**	**L, D, N, H**	
Beaumont	?	?	N	News agency
Bovina	?	1904		
Brownwood	*1915*	*1944*	*L, D, N*	
Canadian	1910	1939	L, D, N	
Cleburne	1899	1931	L, N	
Dallas	1901	1923	L, D, N	Union Station
El Paso	1906	1948	D, N	
Fort Worth	**1913**	**1933**	**L, D, N**	
Gainesville	*1901*	*1931*	*L, N*	
Galveston	*1897*	*1938*	*L, D, N*	
Houston	1911	1948	L, N	
Kingsville	1911	?		Hotel Casa Ricardo
Panhandle	1896	1899	D	
Paris	*1896*	*1930*	*N*	
Rosenberg	1899	1923	L, D, N	
Silsbee	1905	1923	L, D, N, H	
Slaton	*1912*	*1942*	*L, D, N*	
Somerville	1901	1940	L, D, N, H	
Sweetwater	1911	1933	L, N, H	Cottages
Temple	1899	1933	L, D, N, H	Dairy farm

Sources: Fred Harvey corporate files, Heard Museum; Fred Harvey year-end P and L volumes, Jere Krakow Collection; James David Henderson, "Meals by Fred Harvey"; *Harvey House Cookbook*, Michael McMillan; Fred Harvey Yahoo! group.

ACKNOWLEDGMENTS & OUTSHOUTS

"Some day a book will be devoted to a detailed description of the Harvey system, its hotel, dining room, and the extraordinary features of a management which allows a traveler to dine on brook trout in the middle of the desert, and on the rarest fruits in vast reaches of the country where nothing is raised but cactus and sage brush. [It is] worthy of the study of the artist, the epicure, the student of Indian life, and of the many men in the United States who lay claim to the title of 'hotel manager.'"

—*Phoenix Republican,* July 1911

This book has been an adventure in learning a new form of nonfiction writing—an emerging genre I think of as "history buffed," which dares journalists to bring their investigative and storytelling skills to tales once told only by academics. It has also been an adventure in rediscovering America—my version of a life-changing road trip, across the nation and across time. I thank everyone who got sucked into the vortex of this project over the past five years, and all who assisted with the journey.

My addiction to all things Southwestern began in 1991, when my wife, Diane, and I visited Santa Fe for the first time—thanks to our friend, trauma psychiatrist Sandy Bloom, who had just bought a perfect little cabin in the mountains outside of Pecos. I was hooked on New Mexico's big sky the moment we pulled onto the highway outside Albuquerque airport in our very white rented SUV. But I wasn't exposed to the Fred Harvey story until we got back to Philadelphia—and our friends Kim and Tom Moon insisted that the next time we went west, we see the Grand Canyon from the vantage point of a room at El Tovar. We could only get a room there for one night in the fall of 1993, but those twenty-four hours made a big impact—a rush of Americana and archaeological rapture, topped off when I bought Diane a set of toy six-guns in the lobby gift shop (the pictures I took of her twirling them with delight still hang in my office). By the time we had finished driving the five hundred sun-drenched miles from the canyon to Sandy's cabin (stopping at the Fred Harvey souvenir shop at Painted Desert), I had decided to start "saving string" (as editors say) on a project concerning Fred Harvey and the West.

I saved string for ten years, until a life-changing lunch in early 2004 with my longtime editor at Bantam, Ann Harris. She asked me what books I planned to write during my career, besides the one I was then researching. And after hearing me talk about Fred, she dispatched me to write her a proposal for an epic historical biography about all things Harvey. I've been researching, writing, and "Frediting" ever since.

I was very fortunate in the earliest phases of this book to receive the full co-operation of all the branches of the Harvey family—in Boston, Chicago, and Santa Fe—each of which is the keeper of one part of the legacy. I'm especially indebted to Stewart Harvey Jr., who was the family member most immersed in Harvey history and most interested in passing on the whole story—and not just the PR-department legend. Stewart and I have had an epic email correspondence over the past five years.

Daggett Harvey Jr. and his wife, Ellie, have also been extraordinarily kind, hospitable (they let me work in their Chicago carriage house), and trusting, since they allowed me to borrow most of their priceless Harvey artifacts (and the files of Daggett's father, the Harvey historian of his generation). Joy Harvey and her late husband, Byron "Ronny" Harvey III—with whom I corresponded often, and who I interviewed once, at length, before his death in 2005—were also very generous with their time and insights. So was Ronny's sister, Helen Harvey Mills, who shared her extraordinary and lovingly curated collection of family photos. Later in the book, I got to know Kay Harvey (the widow of Stewart's brother Fred) in Santa Fe; she shared her collection and insights, and then made a generous gift to the new Museum of New Mexico so it could one day house and care for all the disparate collections. And my wife and I spent one evening of fine-wining and revelry in San Diego with Harvey cousin Victoria Vanderbilt after a Harvey Girl reunion, where we learned that the Harveys know how to party.

I was also helped by David Benjamin's living relatives in Kansas City, Ann Kander and Judge Howard Sachs, who shared valuable family information, documents, and photos. And at the very end of my journey I tracked down, in England, Elizabeth Drage Pettifer, who shared recollections of the last days of Betty and Freddy Harvey. (Elizabeth still has some clothes from Betty's last shopping spree, which were delivered to her home after the crash.)

I owe a huge thanks to Dr. Jere Krakow, the recently retired director of trails for the National Park Service, who in his previous life as a historian had planned to write a corporate history of Fred Harvey, and during his research was able to save many original corporate documents that otherwise would have been thrown out. If he had only saved them, I and other researchers would already owe him a debt of gratitude. But, when I started this project, he also allowed me to come to Santa Fe and borrow not only materials he had saved, but his own actual research files. His generosity and sense of academic camaraderie know no bounds, and I owe him at least another dinner at the Pink Adobe for his help with this project, and his patience with me.

Like many authors interested in the Harvey saga, I was also given extraordinary assistance by Brenda Thowe, the queen of the Harvey Girls (and, in her day job, a personnel specialist with the Santa Fe, now the BNSF, railroad). Brenda keeps track of all the nation's living Harvey Girls, and also has an amazing collection of files from the railroad, which she copied for me and then brought to Philadelphia. Her interest in this book, and the subject, is unflagging.

My special thanks to those who answered my truly endless queries at the major repositories of all things Harvey and Santa Fe: Karen Underhill, Bee Valvo, Richard David Quartaroli, and the amazing research staff at Northern Arizona University's Cline Library; Lin Fredericksen, Nancy Sherbert, and so many others at the Kansas State Historical Society; Mario Nick Kliamades and LaRee Bates at the Heard Museum; Michael Quinn and Colleen Hyde of the NPS archive at Grand Canyon; Mary Beveridge at the Kansas City Public Library's Missouri Valley Special Collections; Roger Myers, Veronica Reyes, and Erika Castaño, University of Arizona Special Collections; the staff of the Leavenworth County Historical Society (including curator Joanie Kocab and former director Mark Bureman); the staff of the Old Trails Museum in Winslow, Arizona (especially former director Janice Griffith); Sandie Olson at the Waynoka, Oklahoma, Historical Society; Wanda Landrey, Beaumont, Texas, historian who shared her wonderful collection of old Harvey recipes; Jim Sherer and Dave Webb at the Kansas Heritage Society in Dodge City; Tomas Jaehn and Daniel Kosharek at the Chavez Library in Santa Fe; Roy Zarucchi and Carolyn Page, who shared their research on Montezuma doctor William Page; David Phillips, keeper (and master printer) of all the greatest photographs of Leavenworth and the Old West; the late Russell Crump, an eccentric trainiac who lived with his amazing Santa Fe railroad collection; Dennis Northcott of the Missouri Historical Society; Tammy Dicke, assistant director of the Kearny County Library; Kelli Proehl, Emporia Public Library; Karen Beal in alumni relations at the University of Missouri-Kansas City; Cynthia R. Miller, curator of visual culture, the Henry Ford museum; Matthew Fernandez, news researcher at the *St. Louis Post-Dispatch;* Alexandra Shadid, graduate research assistant, Western History Collections, University of Oklahoma Libraries; Ann Barton, Texas Women's College Cookbook Collection; Linda Gegick, museum administrator, City of Las Vegas Museum and Rough Rider Memorial Collection; the folks from the Kansas City legal community who helped me piece together the Harvey/Drage lawsuit (Stephanie Murphy and Stephen Mitchell at Lathrop, Gage; Frank Sebree II, Sam Sawyer Jr.); Mary Goodman and her daughter Wendy Waldock; Cambria

County Library; Ori Siegel for his help with New York Central Railroad history; staff of the New Mexico State Library; Miranda Lewis, secretary at the vestry of St. Marylebone's church in London; Maureen McMillan at the Belen Harvey House museum.

Also thanks to Ted Steele, the president of the St. Louis Genealogical Society; MaryAnne Widel of the North West Missouri Genealogical Society; Judy Garland historian John Fricke; Kim Walters, associate director, Institute for the Study of the American West at the Autry National Center, and her research associate Manola Madrid for finding and translating Charles Lummis's letters (and later finding his photos of his trip with Ford). Also thanks to those lured in at the end for photo research and last-minute fact-checking: Coi Drummond-Gehrig at the Denver Public Library; Jackie S. Robinson from the Florence, Kansas, Harvey House Museum; Wanda Fixsen and Thelma Jennings at the Fort Wallace Museum; Stephen Priest; Mary Colton (who not only helped me track down the amazing Harvey Girl pictures of her grandmother Margaret Becker, but also shared two of her handwritten diaries); Glenn Fye at the Albuquerque Museum; Katherine Degn at the Kraushaar Galleries; Keith Sheridan; and Wallace Dailey at the Theodore Roosevelt Collection at Harvard College Library.

Special thanks for logistical and other support for our cross-country train trip to Bruce Bossman and Bill Johnston of Xanterra's Grand Canyon operation; Allan Affeldt, who with his wife, Tina Mion, saved La Posada; George Shaw, the Canyon Diablo bridge enthusiast who works away in the basement archive of La Posada, pausing only to give desperate strangers rides to Flagstaff; Dick Babcock at *Chicago* magazine; and Marc Magliari at Amtrak.

Like many long-form nonfiction writers, I rely on the kindness of researchers. First and foremost, thanks to Jason Schwartz, a fine journalist and history buff, who as an undergraduate at Penn was my primary researcher for this project and without whose engagement, hard work, and "where's Fred" newspaper reading this book might never have taken shape. Thanks to Heather Paxton, who after we met over the phone through Kansas City's society magazine, *The Independent,* volunteered to be my one-woman Midwestern research staff and made inestimable contributions to this book. And thanks to Andy Hines, who did an amazing job overseeing the fact-checking and keeping track of the blue files.

Thanks also to two of my former Columbia J-School students, Amanda Zafian in New York and Maria Ahmed in London, who made many research breakthroughs (and to John Tofanelli, of Columbia's Butler Library research staff, who helped with database searches). Thanks to Lauren Gilger for last-minute photo and menu research in Arizona, and to Jason Wesco, who assisted me in Topeka. My other research assistants on this project (in the order of their servitude in the Fred-mines): Dan Kaplan, Jennifer Machiaverna, Maria

Popova, Nick Barr, Jess Feurst, Elizabeth Slavitt, Matt Rosenbaum, Anthony Campisi, Jessica Haralson, Tali Yahalom, Maggie McGrath, Khanh-Anh Le, and Jonathan Wroble.

I am honored but also saddened that *Appetite for America* turns out to be the last book edited by Ann Harris in her amazing sixty-year publishing career. We did four completely diverse and wonderful book projects together over fourteen years, and also energized each other's lives and work in many different ways. I will miss working with Ann, but am glad to still have her as a friend. (The same is true for several others from the Bantam family who nurtured me and my books, but have since moved on.)

Thanks to my bright, intuitive new editor, John Flicker—who has quickly embraced Fred (and me)—for his brainstormery and good humor, and his assistant Jessie Waters for all her hard work. I'm especially grateful for the ongoing support of Nita Taublib, the executive vice president, publisher, and editor-in-chief at Bantam Dell, and I'm pleased to be working again with Gina Centrello, the president and publisher of the Random House Publishing Group, who published my first book in paperback.

Loretta Fidel, my smart, empathic, supremely patient agent, has been an especially wonderful proponent of this book, through a writing and editing process that had more than its share of challenges. She has also been a fount of Harvey puns, and I truly appreciate all her Fredilections.

Thanks to my family, especially my mother-in-law, Joan (who not only read the manuscript but tried some of the recipes for the holidays); my brother, Dan, who actually shlepped to California to film a Harvey Girl reunion (how did we get home that night?) and always gives good website; and my beloved kiddos: Jake, Emma, Anna, Eli, and Miranda. Thanks to my hoop buddies for keeping me grounded, elbowed, and amused.

I always thank my wife, Diane, last, because nothing I do could be accomplished without her. This book took more out of her—out of both of us—than the others, so I owe her even more gratitude than usual for her endless hours as my editor, and her endless love and support as my wife of twenty-two years. There are times when those two roles get too intertwined, but she is always there for me in all ways. In life, love, work, and play, she doesn't just maintain the standard—she exceeds it every day. Thank God for her.

FREDITOR'S NOTES & SOURCES

In RE-CREATING THE STORY OF FRED HARVEY AND THE AMERICA his family business helped build, I relied first on the surprisingly large cache of Fred's own datebooks, business correspondence, personnel letters, and artifacts—as well as those of Ford, Freddy, Byron, Minnie, and Kitty Harvey and Dave Benjamin—which have been held privately for decades by disparate branches of the families, some of whom never realized their true significance. In many cases, I was allowed to borrow the original materials and bring them back to my office in Philadelphia, so I could really spend time with them— which made a huge difference (and made me, temporarily, the curator of the world's best Fred Harvey museum). I had access to the fruits of two private family history projects undertaken by Fred's grandsons: a dogged fact-finding mission by Daggett Harvey Sr. in the 1960s, when he was still an executive with the company; and a voluminous, rambling oral history by the retired Stewart Harvey Sr. in the 1980s, which fills over thirty ninety-minute cassette tapes. And I was the first writer ever allowed to use the remarkable private Fred Harvey archive of Dr. Jere Krakow, a treasure trove of corporate documents, ledgers, and microfilmed records.

In addition, I interviewed at length six Harvey family members with direct personal knowledge of the main characters and events in this book: Stewart Harvey Jr., Byron "Ronny" Harvey III, and Daggett Harvey Jr., who all worked for the company with their fathers; Joy Harvey, Ronny's wife and a historian in her own right, who provided special insight into the Harvey women; Helen Harvey Mills, the keeper of the family photo archive; and Kay Harvey, the widow of Frederick Huckel Harvey and the only Harvey left in Santa Fe—as well as David Benjamin's living relatives in Kansas City, Ann Kander and Judge Howard Sachs, and even Freddy and Betty Harvey's niece in England, Elizabeth Drage Pettifer.

All this allowed me even greater insight into the large repositories of original Fred Harvey and Santa Fe railroad corporate material spread across the breadth of the Harvey System. In every place they operated, the Harveys were considered local celebrities. So there are literally dozens of archives around the country where the Harvey saga is viewed through a unique local prism, which made my job both easier and harder.

As a key to these chapter notes, here's a simple view (which took me five years to see simply) of the world of what's left of Fred, and the abbreviations used to reference it. There are seven major private collections. Stewart Harvey Jr. maintains one in Boston, but many of Stewart's holdings were donated to the Leavenworth County Historical Society collection to assist in the Sisyphean effort to turn Fred's original house into a museum. The Daggett Harvey Collection is held privately in Chicago—and includes Fred's original datebooks, scratchpads, and ledgers, as well as a scrapbook put together in the 1940s with many of his original papers, and most of Ford and Byron's correspondence—as is the Helen Harvey Mills Collection. Some of the Byron Harvey III Collection is held privately in Boston by his widow and children. The Kay Harvey Collection is held privately in the old family compound in Santa Fe. David Benjamin's papers are in the Ann Kander Collection, held privately in Kansas City. And Dr. Jere Krakow's collection is held privately in Albuquerque.

Most of the existing files from Fred Harvey's corporate offices are spread across Arizona. Material from the main Chicago office is now in Phoenix at the Heard Museum, which is also the final resting place of the company's Indian art. (This collection includes the Harvey clipping file, an excellent resource with only one problem—it includes the dates of stories and where they were printed, but generally no page numbers.) Other Fred Harvey corporate files—largely those originally held at the Grand Canyon offices, including materials concerning the Harvey Girls movie—ended up at the Cline Library at Northern Arizona University and the National Park Service archive at the Grand Canyon. The Kansas State Historical Society Collection includes the Santa Fe railroad's corporate files, which document the railroad's side of its dealings with Fred Harvey and its own, sometimes revisionist version of Harvey history. The Missouri Valley Special Collections department of the Kansas City Public Library is one-stop shopping on local history, and since many K.C. papers aren't yet fully digitized, I sometimes relied on their bound in-house clipping collection (which, unfortunately, has no original page numbers or story titles). Many of the other newspapers from Kansas and New Mexico—especially Leavenworth and Las Vegas—had to be read on microfilm, but I was always extremely grateful to have access to the historical *New York Times, Chicago Tribune, Los Angeles Times, Wall Street Journal,* and others through ProQuest; to census and immigration information through ancestry.com; to academic articles through JSTOR; and to some papers through Newsbank's "America's Historical Newspaper" database, as far as it goes (which is, unfortunately, only up to 1922).

I went through nearly a thousand books and academic papers on the way to telling this story—just ask my researchers, whose library management abilities and sheer strength were constantly tested—but a handful of them were particularly helpful, and are often cited below.

The canon of underappreciated scholarship on all things Fred begins with a quirky 1942 master's thesis by Harold L. Henderson, an ambitious graduate student of history from the University of Kansas City (now the University of Missouri–Kansas City), who was the first to spend significant time with family members (he interviewed Fred's daughters Minnie and Sybil), employees, and some corporate files. Oddly enough, the next major academic study of Fred was done by an unrelated young scholar with the same last name: "Meals by Fred Harvey: A Phenomenon of the American West," by James David Henderson at the University of Arizona in 1965. This second thesis was later published as the slim book *Meals by Fred Harvey*, which is still in print. (Another thesis I found very helpful was "Harvey Girls Then, Now, and Forever," by Judith Ann Stoll, for her 1995 degree from Emporia State University.)

For the most part, Fred's story has been relegated to chapters in books about other subjects, starting with *Food and Flavor* in 1913 by prominent New York critic Henry Finck, who viewed Fred as a "food missionary" out to save "ungastronomic America," and, in 1940, *Our Southwest* by Erna Fergusson (who worked for the Harveys in Santa Fe during the Indian Detours, interviewed many key employees, and reportedly had her manuscript fact-checked by the company). The Harvey legend is also featured, in compact form, in the major books about the Santa Fe railroad on which I relied: James Marshall's *Santa Fe: The Railroad That Built an Empire*, which was written in the 1940s (and, judging from what I saw in the company's files, heavily informed by, and edited by, officials from the railroad and Fred Harvey); *Steel Trails to Santa Fe* by L. L. Waters, in the 1950s; and Keith L. Bryant Jr.'s very solid *History of the Atchison, Topeka & Santa Fe Railway* in the 1970s.

Several contemporary books deserve special note. The two books produced by the Heard Museum for the 1996 show of art from the Fred Harvey collection are in many ways the culmination of a century of academic research and writing about Harvey and the railroad: the more user-friendly *Inventing the Southwest* by Kathleen Howard and Diana Pardue; and the dense and rewarding *The Great Southwest of the Fred Harvey Company and the Santa Fe Railway*, edited by Marta Weigle and Barbara Babcock. Arnold Berke's biography, *Mary Colter: Architect of the Southwest*, is splendid visually and narratively. And I should make special note of *The Harvey Girls: Women Who Opened the West* by Lesley Poling-Kempes, a smart feminist academic book published in 1989, which grew out of an oral history project Lesley did with Harvey Girls and their relatives in the early 1980s. I will always regret my failure to convince Lesley to let me listen to the original tapes of her Harvey Girl interviews. But because she decided not to share them (which is, of course, an interviewer's prerogative), I relied on the myriad, and often quite wonderful, quotes in her book, all of which are cited below.

I also found inspiration and factoids in the train writings of Lucius Beebe—whose books are wonderful, exuberant, manic, and, in places, almost delightfully unintelligible. Now, *that* guy must have been amazing company on a long train ride.

ABBREVIATIONS FOR FREQUENTLY QUOTED SOURCES

AKC:	Ann Kander Collection
BHC:	Byron Harvey III Collection
CLC:	Cline Library Collection, Northern Arizona University Library
CT:	*Chicago Tribune*
DHC:	Daggett Harvey Jr. Collection
HHMC:	Helen Harvey Mills Collection
HMC:	Heard Museum Collection
Htapes:	Stewart Harvey Sr. tapes
IND:	*The Independent (Kansas City)*
JKC:	Jere Krakow Collection
KCJP:	*Kansas City Journal-Post*
KSHSC:	Kansas State Historical Society Collection
KCStar:	*Kansas City Star*
KCT:	*Kansas City Times*
KHC:	Kay Harvey Collection
LAT:	*Los Angeles Times*
LC:	*Leavenworth Conservative*
LCHSC:	Leavenworth County Historical Society Collection (donated by Stewart Harvey Jr.)
LT:	*Leavenworth Times* (also *Daily Times*)
LVO:	*Las Vegas Optic*
MVSC:	Missouri Valley Special Collections (Kansas City Public Library)
NPSGC:	National Park Service archive, Grand Canyon
NYT:	*New York Times*
SFMag:	*SantaFe Magazine* (also Santa Fe employee magazine)
SHC:	Stewart Harvey Jr. Collection

NOTES

PROLOGUE

xiv So when "Red John": The earliest and best iteration of this often-told Fred story appears in "The Rise of the Harveys" by William Curtis, *Los Angeles Times,* May 7, 1911, page V19, which features an interview with Charles Brant, the original maître d' at the Montezuma.

xvi "a food missionary": This term for Harvey was coined by the New York critic Henry T. Finck in "Ungastronomic America," *Century Magazine,* Nov. 1911, and was later expanded into his 1913 book *Food and Flavor,* pp. 5–7.

xvii years before Coca-Cola: Coca-Cola was invented in 1886, almost a decade after Fred's chain started, and wasn't sold outside of Atlanta or bottled on a wide scale until the mid to late 1890s.

xix Most of the Indian: I have chosen to use the word "Indian" throughout the book—instead of "Native American"—even though there continues to be debate about its political correctness. It is the term that was used during the time I am writing about, and it has certainly come back in style, which is why the new Smithsonian museum is called National Museum of the American Indian.

xix "More than any single": Frank Waters, *Masked Gods,* p. 109.

CHAPTER I: POT WALLOPER

3 legal notice appeared: "Law Notices," *Times* (London), July 12, 1843, p. 7.

3 where Fred was baptized: Records at All Souls Church, St. Marylebone, London, show the baptism—number 272 for the year—took place on July 12, 1835. The family's address was listed as 15 Great Marylebone Street (which is now called New Cavendish Street and the numbers are different).

3 "with a coachman": Htapes, no. 5, side B, SHC.

4 living with his widowed Aunt Mary: 1851 U.K. census, London, Tottenham Parish, p. 15; they lived at 63 High Street.

4 in the late spring of 1853: All biographies of Fred claim he arrived in 1850, but I have come to the conclusion they're incorrect. The 1851 U.K. census says he was still in England then, and his entry in the 1900 U.S. census—the only one that asks what year he arrived—clearly says that he first came to America in 1853. Also, Fred became a U.S. citizen in 1858, under a rule that allowed expedited naturalization, after only five years, for people who entered the country before the age of eighteen. Since Fred was always in a hurry, it is more logical that he applied for expedited citizenship as soon as he could, which would have been five years after an arrival in 1853.

4   avoid being drafted: Author interview with Stewart Harvey Jr., who said he was told this by Fred's longtime employee Herman Schweizer.

4   Washington Street Market reeked: Information on the market comes from *The Stranger's Guide Around New York and Its Vicinity*, pp. 21 and 53; and from "How New York Is Fed," *Scribner's Monthly*, Oct. 1877, pp. 729–31.

5   Smith & McNell's: Information on Smith & McNell's is from *NYT* stories: "Old Hotel to Change Hands," Sept. 27, 1899; "Market Men's Inn Has to Raise Prices," Oct. 4, 1907; "High Prices Down Smith & M'Nell's," Dec. 4, 1914; and Topics of the Times, Aug. 11, 1948, p. 22.

5   "pot walloper": This was Fred's own phrase, passed down through family lore, author interview with Stewart Harvey Jr.

6   photography innovator R. A. Lewis: Author correspondence with John S. Craig, who maintains Craig's Daguerreian Registry at www.daguerreotype.com.

6   dying in August 1855: Death certificate from Wolverhampton District, Aug. 31, 1855, HHMC, originally discovered by Fred's great-granddaughter Helen Harvey Mills and great-great-granddaughter Natalie Bontumasi.

6   "concerned about trying": Author interview with Stewart Harvey Jr., who said he heard this directly from his great-aunt Minnie, Fred's daughter.

7   his friend and mentor: Fred's naturalization papers are among the many original items pasted into the Fred Harvey scrapbook in DHC. Hitchcock is listed as a witness on the form.

7   William Doyle: While Fred himself told the story of his Merchants Dining Saloon partner, no published account has ever mentioned his partner's name. Based on my examination of the 1860 U.S. census, for the Fifth Ward of the city of St. Louis, p. 293, Doyle is the most likely candidate. He and his family are reported as living in the dwelling directly next to Fred's; more telling, Doyle is listed as a "saloon keeper," and in the next entry Fred is listed as a "restaurant keeper." They also both reported similar assets. Doyle's name does not appear in any of the city's commercial directories for this time period, so it is possible this is a coincidence and Fred's partner was someone else, not listed in the census. But best available evidence points to Doyle.

7   "Negroes Bought Here": Bancroft, *Slave-Trading in the Old South*, p. 141; the sign was in front of Bolton, Dickins & Company.

7   on the steamship *Africa:* His departure was noted in the *New York Herald*, Oct. 27, 1859.

7   brought his father: Fred's father and sister appear in the 1860 U.S. census as living with him in St. Louis.

7   blond Dutch woman: Little is known about Ann Harvey because she was later written out of Fred's life story. But she clearly appears, by name, as his wife in the 1860 federal census, and she is referred to in the St. Louis city census done later that same year. Her hair color is assumed based on color photos in LCHSC of the children she had with Fred.

8   "I'm for whoever wins": This quote was related by Fred's daughter Minnie to Harold L. Henderson in "Harvey," p. 55.

CHAPTER 2: THE LAST TRAIN STOP IN AMERICA

10   Captain Rufus Ford: Biographical information comes from 1860 and 1870 U.S. censuses; Gould, *Fifty Years on the Mississippi*, p. 421; and Petersen, *Steamboating on the Upper Mississippi*, p. 267.

10 "Horrible & Slow-Jolting": Marshall, *Santa Fe,* p. 97.

11 "young, skinny, wiry": Cullinan, *United States Postal Service,* p. 79.

12 photo taken of him: Photo in DHC was sent to Byron Harvey Jr. in 1958 by Ralph R. Richardson, a descendant of one of Rufus Ford's partners.

12 nation's first traveling post office: Details of this episode come from a letter Fred wrote, June 26, 1884, as part of an effort to make sure his boss got credit for the invention, published in U.S. Railway Mail Service, *History of the Railway Mail Service* (Washington, D.C.: Government Printing Office, 1885), copies in DHC.

13 "it simply rained hogs": Details in this paragraph are from a June 15, 1962, press release from the Chicago, Burlington & Quincy Railroad, "Centennial of First U.S. Railway Car," DHC.

13 became part of those tragic: Almost everything about Ann Harvey's existence has to be inferred from other facts, including her death: We know when she gave birth and when Fred remarried, so we must assume she died in between from some complication of childbirth. While there has always been family gossip about her (author interview with Stewart Harvey Jr.), the only time she was acknowledged in print was in the *KCJP,* April 20, 1936, in an article that claimed that "after the death of his first wife, the bride he brought with him from England, the original Fred Harvey married again." According to Harold L. Henderson, "Harvey," p. 55, the family requested a correction on that article—primarily because it went on to suggest, incorrectly, that Ford and one of his younger siblings had different mothers, both "facts" apparently copied from a *Who's Who* entry at the time. A note was left in the *KCJP* morgue to assure "the same error will not be again committed," and the *Who's Who* entry was changed in the 1938–1939 edition.

14 His new wife was Barbara: Sally's background is re-created from the 1860 U.S. census and Mattas family documents in DHC, primarily those put together when Sally's mother made a claim for a widow's pension on Jan. 17, 1893, National Archives Record MC382408.

14 Harvey family Bible: This Bible was, for many years, in the collection of Daggett Harvey Sr., who in the 1960s extensively cataloged the family holdings in his possession as part of his exploration of Fred's past, in a document called "Diaries and Other Biographical Material Left by Fred Harvey." Almost every item on his list continues to be part of DHC—except this Bible. Since everything else in the collection corresponds exactly to his notes, I have to assume this is accurate as well.

14 marriage record: Book C, p. 19, of St. Joseph marriage records for 1863—discovered by MaryAnne Widel, archivist at the North West Missouri Genealogical Society.

CHAPTER 3: A GENTLEMAN AMONG THE BLEEDING KANSANS

16 "Herds of buffalo": This quotation is from David Benjamin, and is paraphrased in all his obituaries, including *KCT,* May 8, 1933.

17 wide dirt streets: Descriptions of town come from the photos in David Phillips's two excellent books, *The Taming of the West* and *The West: An American Experience,* which feature new prints of the work of Leavenworth photographer E. E. Henry, especially pp. 34–53.

17 "pistol-packin' pencil pusher": Phrase coined by historian Cecil Howes in

"Pistol Packin' Pencil Pushers," p. 116, his essay on frontier journalism; but most information on Anthony comes from "Fighting Words: Pistol Packin' Dan Anthony and Frontier Journalism," the thesis by my primary researcher on this book, Jason Schwartz.

18   "Dr. J. J. McBride": Doctor ads from *LT,* May 11, 1866, p. 2. and *LT,* March 30, 1865.

18   "The men of Leavenworth": *LC,* Apr. 6, 1865, p. 3.

19   died nine days later: The children's death notices are in *LT,* March 31 and April 11, 1865.

19   peculiar item: *LT,* Oct. 28, 1865, p. 2.

20   "three weeks rustication": *LT,* Oct. 7, 1865.

20   a position selling ads: Fred is identified as General Business Agent in the Dec. 2, 1865, edition of the *LC,* p. 2.

20   "large display": *LT,* Oct. 12, 1866.

20   joined a Masonic: A May 26, 1931, letter to Fred's daughter Sybil from the grand secretary emeritus of the Masonic Bodies of Kansas details his joining the Leavenworth Commandery No. 1 on May 27, 1868, DHC.

21   Shakespeare was a favorite: There's an inventory of books from Fred's library that were donated to Stanford University in the 1940s in DHC; many were Shakespeare; other of his Shakespeare books are still in family hands, mostly in KHC in Santa Fe.

21   "High Iron": See Beebe, *High Iron,* p. i.

22   they had *all* fallen apart: To re-create how Leavenworth failed to become a major train town, I relied on Taylor, "Boom Town Leavenworth"; Bob Burton, "Southern Kansas Heritage," from the Santa Fe Railway Historical and Modeling Society, which discusses railway politics; and "Era of Peace, Part 42," in Cutler's monumental *History of the State of Kansas.*

CHAPTER 4: RAILROAD WARRIOR

24   informed the publisher: This, and the details that follow about his travels and negotiations with his bosses at the newspaper and elsewhere, come from the earliest of Fred's datebooks, DHC, which was started in 1867 but used by him during 1868 as well. Pages unnumbered, but some dated.

25   "how to ask for things": Quoted in Fergusson, *Our Southwest,* p. 193.

25   "Once I've sold an ad for you": This dialogue was recounted by Fred in his Sept. 12, 1868, entry, 1867 datebook, DHC.

25   "Fred Harvey was the best": Dan Anthony, who owned the *LC,* which later merged with the *Times,* was quoted saying this in the *LT* obituary of Fred, Feb. 10, 1901.

25   paid him only $40: Harvey, April 12, 1868, entry, 1867 datebook, DHC.

26   "Still in Pittsburgh": Harvey, Jan. 1, 1869, entry, 1869 datebook, DHC.

26   "not for mere pleasure": From a biographical sketch of Fred in *Kansas: A Cyclopedia of State History,* vol 3, pt. 1, pp. 385–87.

26   a silent partnership: Documented in Harvey, Nov. 28, 1868, entry, 1867 datebook, DHC. Background on Ellsworth cattle business is from Streeter, "Ellsworth as a Texas Cattle Market."

26   article about Hickok: "Wild Bill," *Harper's New Monthly Magazine,* February 1867, p. 273.

26 telling the *St. Louis Democrat:* The article appeared in the April 16, 1867, edition. The reporter was Henry Stanley, who went on to his own renown as the journalist later sent to the jungles of Africa to find the lost Scottish explorer David Livingstone; it was he who spoke—or at least *claimed* that he spoke—the immortal words "Dr. Livingstone, I presume?"

27 $4,485.22: Harvey, Nov. 28, 1868, entry, 1867 datebook, DHC.

27 "physical disability": July 1864 draft registry for St. Joseph, Mo., line 14, National Archives and Record Center.

27 "Started out this morning": Harvey, Jan. 7, 1869, entry, 1869 datebook, DHC.

27 "equal parts spirits": Harvey, undated entries, 1879–1880 datebook, DHC.

27 "His nervous disposition": Minnie Harvey in Harold L. Henderson, "Harvey," p. 15.

28 published a study: Beard, "Neurasthenia, or Nervous Exhaustion."

28 "more distress and annoyance": Beard, "Nature and Treatment of Neurasthenia," p. 580.

28 "The miseries of the rich": Beard, *Practical Treatise on Nervous Exhaustion,* 3rd ed., pp. 30–31.

28 "a disease of": Ibid., p. 25.

28 "It cannot be denied": Ibid., p 254.

28 "Americanitis": According to *The Oxford English Dictionary,* the first printed use of this great word was in *Gentleman's Magazine,* Oct. 1882, p. 500.

CHAPTER 5: OPPORTUNISTIC SPONGE

29 decided to take his wife: All the details of this trip are from Harvey, July 5–Sept. 10, 1869, entries, 1869 datebook, DHC; the letters mentioned are from Fred's "Magic Ink" copybook, covering the same period, HHMC.

30 National Peace Jubilee: Details in Jarman, "Big Boom in Boston."

30 "I see you have not yet": Harvey to Wilder & Sleeper (publishers of *LC*), Aug. 18, 1869, in Magic Ink copybook, HHMC.

30 to the New York Central station: Information on the New York Central ride comes from author correspondence with Ori Siegel, a railroad historian I met through the NYC-RR Yahoo! group.

31 The doctor said: From letters Fred wrote home Aug. 16–18, 1869, Magic Ink copybook, HHMC.

31 four-bedroom house: It is still there, 1318 South Second Street.

32 "We accept the proposition": Harvey, early March 1875, entry, 1875 datebook, DHC.

33 "Fred was like an opportunistic sponge": Author correspondence with Stewart Harvey Jr.

33 closest friend: Information about Captain Byron Schermerhorn comes from "Byron Schermerhorn: The First President, Businessman, Poet, Civil War Intelligence Agent," in an undated issue of the Brink's Company annual report, pp. 8–9, LCHSC; author correspondence with Joseph Irwin, a descendant of Schermerhorn's wife, Nellie Irwin; and Schermerhorn, *Schermerhorn Genealogy and Family Chronicles,* p. 245.

34 "The Stale Trout": This illustrated volume of Schermerhorn's poetry is in the Illinois History and Lincoln Collections of the library at the University of Illinois at Urbana-Champaign.

35 "Bubbles Bursting": *CT,* Sept. 20, 1873, p. 1.

36 tracks too slimy: Account in Bryant, *History of the Atchison, Topeka and Santa Fe Railway,* p. 56.

36 "hopper dozers": "Crops," *CT,* May 29, 1877, p. 2.

CHAPTER 6: SAVAGE AND UNNATURAL FEEDING

37 he would re-read a list: This list is still pasted inside Fred's 1872 datebook, DHC.

38 Pullman had grown up: Pullman biographical material is from Leyendecker, *Palace Car Prince.*

39 "the atmosphere was something dreadful": Ibid., p. 37.

39 "varnish": I picked this up from the delicious railroad writing of Lucius Beebe, who uses it in all his books; the first reference I can find is in *High Iron,* p. 190.

40 "freight doesn't complain": I first came across this phrase, which is also sometimes "freight don't complain," in Stoll, "Harvey Girls Then, Now, and Forever," p. 24.

40 first major workforce of free black men: Tye, *Rising from the Rails.*

40 "whom passengers could regard": Ibid., p. 3.

41 "If there is any word": "Railroad Refreshments," *NYT,* June 10, 1857, p. 4.

42 "American cookery is worse": Quoted forty years later by Finck, who felt it was still true, in *Food and Flavor,* p. 28.

43 Logan House hotel in Altoona: See Porterfield, *Dining by Rail,* p. 13.

43 "The Grand Excursion": This is based on the exhaustive eyewitness account of the trip in Seymour, *Incidents of a Trip,* chaps. 7 and 8.

44 The onboard dinner menu: The menu as well as descriptions of the photos are taken from Brey, "Carbutt and the Union Pacific's Grand Excursion to the 100th Meridian."

44 "only too glad to know": Seymour, *Incidents of a Trip,* p. 86.

CHAPTER 7: THEY'LL TRY ANYTHING

46 started a company, Harvey & Rice: This account of the often-mangled story of Harvey and Rice's partnership comes from several sources, some of which don't agree on details, including "How Fame Has Been Won for the Harvey Service by Devotion to a Business Principle," a Fred Harvey company biography in *SFMag,* Feb. 1916; the biographical sketch of Rice in *Portrait and Biographical Record of Leavenworth, Douglas, and Franklin Counties, Kansas,* p. 837; Harold L. Henderson, "Harvey," pp. 19–20; and Stoll, "Harvey Girls Then, Now, and Forever," for which she actually interviewed Rice's great-grandson, Don Phelps.

46 more grueling pace: This is borne out by the entries in Fred's shiny red datebook covering 1875–1877, DHC, as well as reports in local newspapers. Generally, whenever the freight agent for a major railroad arrived in town, it was news.

47 "Shall I make a deduction": This notation and those below it (including "Send Ball some white fish") all from Fred's datebook for 1875–1877 (shiny red), with no dates except the cigar bill, which was for Feb. 1875.

47 They really hated being: The friction between Harvey and Rice has never

been well explained. Some sources suggest Rice's standards weren't high enough; some say Rice was angered because Fred wanted half the profits but didn't do half the work; one source conjectured the problem was the delivery of profits—whichever of them got to a location first had to bring the profits home to split them, and there was distrust that this was working out fairly.

48 a scant 560: All the track lengths and the dates of completion for different Santa Fe lines come from the invaluable resource in the appendix to Marshall, *Santa Fe*. Based on the company's own records, it accounts for every length of track the Santa Fe and its associated roads ever ran on.

48 "They'll try *anything*": Millbrook, "Fred Harvey and the Santa Fe," p. 10.

48 Charlie Morse: Morse wrote a privately published autobiography for his children, *A Sketch of My Life*. His rail career is covered on pp. 32–40. Oddly, he didn't mention Fred at all.

48 superb deal: There is no contemporaneous reporting on this deal, which was never written about during the first decade the companies did business. But it is referenced in a digest of the contractual dealings between the two companies, "Brief History of Santa Fe Fred Harvey Relations," which is dated Aug. 4, 1942, and appears to have been produced using original documents otherwise long lost, pp. 1–4, DHC.

49 When they opened for business: The only eyewitness account of this day comes from "Engineer for 51 Years to Pull Last Throttle Today," *Kansas City Journal*, June 30, 1926, Harvey clipping file, HMC; and "Shepard Smith, a Famous Frisco Engineer for Forty-two Years—Retired June 30," *Frisco Employes' Magazine*, July 1926, p. 8. Interestingly, while every corporate history ever done says the eating house opened Jan. 1, 1876—and it was first mentioned in the Leavenworth paper on Jan. 5—Shep claimed in two separate interviews that his meal was in 1875.

50 nobody wanted to go past Topeka: This fanciful notion came from a May 5, 1905, article in the *Philadelphia North American* by Leigh Mitchell Hodges, which the Santa Fe reprinted two years later during the inaugural year of *SFMag*, starting on p. 271 of its July 1907 edition. It turned out to be the first long, widely disseminated story about the Harvey empire.

50 "the neatest, cleanest dining hall": "All Bran New," *LT,* Jan. 5, 1876, p. 3.

50 some ten million visitors: This statistic, and other details about the fair, are from Rydell, *All the World's a Fair,* p. 10.

51 "Declaration of Rights for Women": Stanton, *Concise History of Woman Suffrage,* pp. 299–303.

51 through Enoch Hoag: Mentioned in Harvey, Feb. 13, 1872, entry, 1872 datebook, DHC.

52 "People were a little disappointed": Quoted in John W. Ripley and Robert Richmond, *The Santa Fe in Topeka: A Book of Nostalgic Recollections About Santa Fe Personalities and Events* (Topeka, Kans.: Shawnee County Historical Society, 1979), p. 14, citing the *Topeka Commonwealth*, Nov. 5, 1876, but the same writing elsewhere cites the *Topeka Daily Blade*, Nov. 6, 1876.

CHAPTER 8: SUITED TO THE MOST EXIGENT OR EPICUREAN TASTE

54 Captain returned the favor: According to author interview with Joe Irwin, descendant of Schermerhorn's wife, an inscription in a Schermerhorn family Bible says Fredericka Harvey Schermerhorn was born and died in 1877.

54   "To hell, I guess": This story about Dodge has appeared in many places, one of the earlier is Wright, *Dodge City,* p. 150.

55   as an experiment: The contract from March 20, 1876, is in Santa Fe railroad file 306, KSHSC.

56   laid out all the money himself: The documents from this transaction are in the Harvey scrapbook, DHC, and show Fred paying $4,275 to the previous owners on Jan. 1, 1878, and $1,000 to the railroad the same day "for furniture and fixtures."

56   ambushing the Raton Pass: This episode is re-created from accounts in Bryant, *History of the Atchison, Topeka, and Santa Fe Railway,* p. 45; and Marshall, *Santa Fe,* p. 149.

58   "has no cards": "Florence Railroad House," *Florence Herald,* Feb. 23, 1878.

58   The effusive chef: Descriptions of Phillips and his background, and the life and food of the hotel (over the next pages), all come from a lengthy article called "Notes from America," in London's *The Field,* by Samuel Nugent Townshend, based on his Oct. 1878 press junket, which was then reprinted in the *Florence Herald* on March 15, 1879, as "An Englishman's View of Florence."

60   share of the profits: In his 1879 datebook on January 22, DHC, Fred wrote, "I have this day arranged with W. H. Phillips to pay him one hundred dollars per month, and two per cent of the net proffits arrisening from the Houses . . . he to devote his intire time for one year in consideration of the above."

60   "Every Tuesday and Friday": *Florence Herald,* June 28, 1879.

CHAPTER 9: COWBOY VICTUALER

61   niece and nephew from England: The U.S. census for 1880 (Kearny County, p. 7) shows them working at the hotel; the story about Annie Baumann's failed marriage is family lore, from author interview with Stewart Harvey Jr., but her visit is recounted on p. 5 of a 1986 Florence Historical Society publication in LCHSC.

61   herd for sale: The documents relating to Fred's purchase of the XY herd are all in the Harvey scrapbook in DHC. And the sale is covered in Blanchard, *Conquest of Southwest Kansas,* p. 205.

62   "the round-up": Strong to Harvey, March 3, 1879, in scrapbook, DHC.

62   invited the entire town out: This July 4 picnic is re-created from Mrs. Carrie E. Davies, "Lakin in 1878," in Kearny County Historical Society, *History of Kearny County, Kansas,* pp. 51–52, as well as a June 26, 1935, letter to Fred Harvey company from a Lakin history buff, C. A. Louks, KSHSC.

62   praying for each of them: This was described in a letter from Byron Schermerhorn's daughter Nell ("Mrs. E. D. Smith") to her childhood friend May Harvey, Christmas 1937, HHMC.

63   one of the richest ranchers: Biographical information on Jack Hardesty comes from the Hardesty House museum in Dodge City; the digested clippings file of the *Ford County Globe* at the Kansas Heritage Center in Dodge City; Fredric Young, *Dodge City: Up Through a Century in Story and Pictures* (1972), p. 117; and Haywood, *Trails South,* pp. 99–102.

64   languishing partnership: According to entries in Fred's 1879 datebook, DHC,

it appears they were now managing only the Wallace and Hugo locations—
it's unclear what happened to Lawrence.

64 So, on a Thursday in early October: Harvey, Oct. 9, 1879, entry, 1879 datebook,
DHC; this entry is also used for the dollar amount of the deposit.

64 told him to close out the account: While there are many versions of this story,
this one comes from p. 9 of an unpublished manuscript by the *Saturday
Evening Post* writer Edward Hungerford, who wrote several articles based on
interviews with company officials at the turn of the century, but possibly intended this forty-page manuscript, "The Dining Room That Is Two Thousand Miles Long," to become a book.

64 "Give me half": While this anecdote about the last gasp of Harvey & Rice
clearly is accurate—it comes from the teller himself, who later became Fred's
most trusted employee—the exact date of the end of Harvey's relationship
with Rice has been the subject of debate. Many sources claim they were in
business together for only a year, and their partnership ended when Harvey
started working with the Santa Fe, which is most likely AT&SF revisionism.
A couple of sources claim they remained in business together until 1882—
citing a biographical sketch of Rice published in 1899. I arrived at this date in
1879 by examining all these materials and cross-referencing them with Harvey's own datebooks, where this 1879 transaction is the last time Harvey ever
mentions Rice.

64 Fred also moved his growing XY herd: Details of the move and the life on his
ranch come from various essays in *History of Kearny County, Kansas,* including one written by Sam Corbett (pp. 446–47), who ran the XY ranch, and
"The Eli Hall Story" (pp. 169–70) in the Deerfield section.

65 He chose Slavens & Oburn: His deal with them is detailed in his 1879 datebook, notation of Jan. 12, 1880, DHC. While it is likely he would have chosen
a K.C. firm anyway, it is interesting to note that he was probably lobbied hard
by the new head of the Kansas City Stock Yards—his old colleague Charlie
Morse, who resigned from the railroad when William Strong got the job he
coveted.

65 "I've seen many": Fergusson, *Our Southwest,* p. 193.

CHAPTER 10: VIVA LAS VEGAS

66 Dr. John Henry Holliday: Details of Doc Holliday's brief stay in Las Vegas
are from Roberts, *Doc Holliday,* pps. 108–14.

67 "Murderers, Confidence Men, Thieves": *LVO,* April 8, 1880.

67 "We are informed that a purse": *LVO,* May 10, 1881.

68 "the worst-looking boxcars": Frank C. Monroe, "Reminiscences of the Santa
Fe Frontier," *SFMag,* Oct. 1931, p. 44.

68 John B. Stetson: I first came across this connection in Brenda Maddock's biography of D. H. Lawrence, *A Married Man;* she found it in Jones, *Health-
Seekers in the Southwest.*

68 Jesse James . . . was reportedly joined: Bowman, *Montezuma,* p. 12. This book
and Sheppard, *Montezuma*—both very hard to find (I borrowed the copies
from the Montezuma's own collection)—were my primary sources on the
hotel, besides the actual clips from the *LVO.*

69 He liked to hop off the train: *Railway Review,* Feb. 29, 1888, p. 568.

70   "You know better than this": This quote, and the scene, come from the re-creation of a Harvey inspection in L. L. Waters, *Steel Trails to Santa Fe*, p. 272.

70   the Uncle Dick: Bryant, *History of the Atchison, Topeka, and Santa Fe Railway*, p. 218.

70   could see sections: Actually, you can still see them; author interview (in mov-ing engine) with current engineer of the Southwest Chief, Randy Decker, Sept. 3, 2005.

71   Ironically, there was *not* going to be a Santa Fe: A good recounting of this can be found in Tobias and Woodhouse, *Santa Fe*, pp. 14–20.

72   tracked down to a house: Covered in the *LVO*, esp. " 'The Kid' Killed," July 18, 1881, p. 2.

72   several books: See Robert N. Mullin and Charles E. Welch, "Billy the Kid: The Making of a Hero," *Western Folklore*, 32, no. 2 (April 1973), p. 106.

72   "Daring Desperados": *LT*, Oct. 28, 1881, p. 1.

73   The Santa Fe had hired a shiny new: Page's challenging time at the Mon-tezuma is documented in his diaries, which are part of the Dr. William H. Page Collection, Hale Library Archives, Kansas State University, Manhattan, Kansas.

73   "I *know* you to be such": Ibid., Sept. 18, 1881.

73   Competing restaurant owners: Two stories in the *Albuquerque Morning Dem-ocrat* capture the friction, one from Aug. 4, 1886, "A Protest," and another from Feb. 3, 1888, which reads, "No thanks, we don't need an eating house. We have a number of enterprising grocers in Albuquerque who are able to furnish our people with canned goods in just as satisfactory a manner as Mr. Fred Harvey."

74   "Eating Establishment Excitements": *LVO*, Sept. 12, 1881, p. 2.

74   "Harvey Heard": *LVO*, Sept. 13, 1881.

75   "a blow on the right temple": Dr. Page, "Physician's Day-Book," Sept. 1881, Page Collection.

CHAPTER 11: WE ARE *IN* THE WILDS, WE ARE NOT *OF* THEM

76   "Papa, when are you": Minnie Harvey to Fred Harvey, Jan. 31, 1882, DHC, which also mentions their new telephone.

76   electric lights: The arrival of the first representative of the Brush Electric Light company in Cleveland, the predominant seller of lighting systems to major cities, made the front page of the *LT*, July 23, 1881: "Electric Light: A Gentleman Here Talking Up the Matter to Our Citizens."

76   It even fell to Sally: Leaf, March 7, 1881, signed by Sally Harvey to Ford Har-vey, in collection of Ford's daughter, Kitty, donated to the Museum of North-ern Arizona in Flagstaff.

76   euchre: One of the earlier books fueling the craze was Meehan, *Laws and Practice of the Game of Euchre*. Sally's euchre playing was covered more and more into the 1880s and early 1890s, especially in the *Leavenworth Standard*'s April 28, 1888, description of a big euchre party thrown by Sally for her visit-ing sister.

77   "Mother, make the girls": Nell Smith to May Harvey, Christmas 1937, HHMC, details this and the holiday anecdotes below.

77   Cherubic, charming: Dave Benjamin's entry into the Harvey world was well documented in the *KCStar*, Oct. 15, 1922 (which includes a sketch of him at

age twenty-one) and again in the *KCStar*, "Turning Point of My Career," Dec. 4, 1932. Information on his brothers' backgrounds comes from Harry's obituary, "Harry L. Benjamin Is Dead," *KCStar*, April 24, 1923, p. 3.

78 J. J. Blower: A letter from Blower, dated Jan. 19, 1882, in KSHSC, explains: "Having resigned my position with Mr. Harvey owing to a misunderstanding between us I find myself without employment." The letter is one of the earliest existing on AT&SFRR Eating Houses stationery: It lists Fred as "Proprietor" and Blower as "Gen'l Accountant"—each of their names at the top of the page on either side. (It may be that their "misunderstanding" was over whether this was Fred's private company or a partnership with the Santa Fe.)

78 Ford was away at college: Ford Harvey to family, Jan. 17, 1880, LCHSC: "I arrived at Racine about eight o'clock Wednesday night and came up to the college on a wagon."

79 "things are now": "Springs 'Snack,' " *LVO*, Feb. 11, 1882, p. 2.

79 list at the top: See A. Conkle to C. Pullen, Nov. 24, 1881, on "General Office Hot Springs Company" stationery, which lists Fred Harvey as "Manager" and includes an analysis by "Prof. F. V. Hayden U.S. Geologist" showing temperatures of up to 130 degrees. Dr. William H. Page Collection, Hale Library Archives, Kansas State University, Manhattan, Kansas.

79 "the waters are especially": "Springs 'Snack.' "

79 favorite coffee purveyors: While the relationship between the companies is well documented—they did magazine ads together, and are in each other's corporate histories—a nice insight into the relationship is a touching Nov. 23, 1908, letter in DHC to Fred's son Ford from a Chase executive, letting him know of the elder Chase's death.

79 And on the morning of Sunday: Re-created from "Gay Guests," *LVO*, April 17, 1882, p. 2, which describes the trip.

80 It was lit by: This is according to the *LVO* coverage on opening day, April 17, 1882, which included a late edition that reproduced the menu for the evening while the banquet "is 'on.' " This re-creation, however, also uses the next-day coverage, including "Banquet and Ball," *LVO*, April 18, 1882, p. 2.

81 "dangerously ill": "Railroad Revelations: The Run of Items Found in the News-Butcher's Train Box," *LVO*, April 19, 1882.

81 Raymond Excursions: Background on their significance is in Marguerite S. Shaffer, *See America First* (Washington, D.C.: Smithsonian Institution Press, 2001), pp. 22–24.

82 had left the Boston area: A Raymond & Whitcomb ad in the *Boston Globe*, Feb. 15, 1882, gives departure dates and times, and complete route.

82 Montezuma porters complaining: Springs Spray, *LVO*, May 1, 1882.

82 "Captain Manners": This scene is re-created from Marshall, *Santa Fe*, p. 164.

83 The entire trip was documented: The junket was described, in glorious detail, in a privately published book, *Che! Wah! Wah!* by George Street, which is the source of all quotations through the end of the chapter.

CHAPTER 12: HARVEY GIRLS

85 "gang of gamblers": See Bryant, *History of the Atchison, Topeka, and Santa Fe Railway*, p. 113, for the entire anecdote.

86 "A colored waiter": *LVO*, May 3, 1882, p. 2.

86 "several darkies": Fergusson, *Our Southwest*, p. 194.

86 "would be satisfied": Harold L. Henderson, "Harvey," p. 42.

86 He was traveling with young Tom Gable: Background on Gable comes from U.S. census for 1870 and 1880; the Linn Street address is confirmed by Gable's entry in the autograph book of young May Harvey in 1882, DHC, which was a birthday present from Tom's daughter Mary.

86 "old Fred lit like a bomb": Gable was interviewed by Erna Fergusson about this incident, for *Our Southwest*, pp. 194–95; quotes from him are adapted from that section of the book.

87 "Don't throw the dishes": This recollection by early Harvey Girl Matilda Thomas was posted on the Web site of the Florence Harvey House Museum: www.florenceks.com/text/local/local_hh-history.htm. Its origin is unclear, but the folks at the Florence museum take their Harvey Girl oral history pretty seriously, so I don't doubt its authenticity.

87 "The Scarcity of Women": This article was reprinted in *LVO*, Nov. 18, 1881.

88 They sent cables back: It is Harvey family lore who picked these first Harvey Girls in Leavenworth. Some sources have claimed Sally was actively involved, which is likely, and remained involved for years, which is pretty unlikely. But since Fred, Dave, and Tom Gable made this decision, it is probable their wives found the first girls.

88 "And that": Fergusson, *Our Southwest*, p. 195.

88 Minnie O'Neal: Minnie's story is pieced together from U.S. census records and an account that her daughter-in-law, Helen Gillespie, gave in Poling-Kempes's *Harvey Girls*, pp. 62–64.

88 Tom Gable laid out the rules: The rules about the Harvey uniforms, woven into Minnie's story, are adapted from Marshall, *Santa Fe*, p. 100.

88 be in bed: Earliest proof of this is a sign printed in 1887 with employee rules, JKC.

89 take a damp cloth: Recollection of a later Harvey Girl, Violet Grundman, about what she was told of the early years, quoted in Poling-Kempes, *Harvey Girls*, p. 55.

89 one other significant female workforce: Noted by Poling-Kempes, Ibid., p. 60.

90 Four new eating houses: Dates of location openings confirmed on datelines in Harvey company files, HMC, and by cross-referencing letterheads on eating house stationery.

90 "in the Harvey Service": This phrase eventually became so popular that it was used as the title of the Harvey section in the *SFMag*.

91 large silver brooch: Some of the oldest service pins have been on display at the small museum off the lobby of Bright Angel Lodge at the Grand Canyon.

91 cramped one-room office: "Brief History of Santa Fe Fred Harvey Relations," Aug. 4, 1942, p. 1, DHC.

91 younger brother Harry: "Harry L. Benjamin Is Dead," *KCStar*, April 24, 1923; also "Personalities in the Hotel Business," *Hotel Monthly*, Aug. 1943, p. 22.

91 not uncommon for each house to generate: Fred did this computation for the Topeka house for the month of May 1877 in his 1875 datebook, DHC.

91 "one of those keen-eyed": "How One Man Conducts Sixty-six Hotels," *Leslie's Illustrated*, Feb. 27, 1913, n.p., HMC.

92 "maintaining the standard": Bryant, *History of the Atchison, Topeka, and Santa Fe Railway*, p. 111.

92 "their secrets of success": "Personalities in the Hotel Business," p. 21.

92   He combined: What Dave did is not really documented well, only its result; a reading of Fred's letters and datebooks makes it clear that he did not do all the writing and codification of the early Harvey ethos. This was Dave's job. He was likely helped by his brother Harry, who was reportedly a better writer, but Harry's role in the business never became very public, so the contribution of the Benjamin brothers was largely credited to Dave.

92   "FUNDAMENTALS": This list, constantly recopied through generations of Harvey paperwork, was found in a xeroxed Fred Harvey Recipe Book compiled by Roy Palmer, who was a Harvey dining car cook in the 1920s, on p. 1. From the collection of Brenda Thowe.

93   sign that hung: 1887 sign with employee rules, JKC.

94   "cup code": I relied on versions of this from Poling-Kempes, *Harvey Girls*, pp. 51 and 217; Bryant, *History of the Atchison, Topeka, and Santa Fe Railway*, p. 114.

95   "We *concentrate* on it": Harold L. Henderson, "Harvey," p. 53.

95   telegraph code: Copies of the company's printed telegraph codes, and Fred's own handwritten codebooks, are in DHC.

95   "sack of potatoes": Author interview with Stewart Harvey Jr.

95   "The Crank": Bryant, *History of the Atchison, Topeka, and Santa Fe Railway*, p. 111.

96   He proposed four time zones: Information about William Allen's standardizing time is in Prerau, *Seize the Daylight*, pp. 43–45.

CHAPTER 13: LIKE A HOUSE AFIRE

98   Fred was amazed: Ford Harvey manuscript, undated but presumed written in the early 1920s, apparently for *American Magazine*, UA, box 3, file 16, p. 6, HMC.

98   His personal profits: The earliest P and L that survives, in the scrapbook, is for 1886, in which his share was $58,725.88; by the time of that P and L, they had the same locations as in 1884 and 1885, when this chapter is set; this conservative estimate is based on $50,000 in 1885.

99   he offered to buy them out: Paperwork concerning this sale is in the Fred Harvey scrapbook, DHC, beginning with the agreement on Aug. 1, 1882, which was then paid out over a period of months.

100   "It was the tenth of May": Song lyrics and anecdote are in Blanchard, *Conquest of Southwest Kansas*, p. 76.

100   had the plumber leave all the pipes: Author interview with Mark Bureman, then director of the Leavenworth County Historical Society, which is housed in that building, now called Carroll Mansion.

100   Fred bought the house from Harvey: The paperwork for the sale, completed Feb. 9, 1884, including the receipts for what the Rushes had spent, is in the scrapbook in DHC.

101   "There are not even 20": Benjamin to Harvey, June 13, 1883, scrapbook, DHC.

101   "men without noses": *LVO*, April 20, 1885.

101   explosion was heard: This recounting of the fire is based on the coverage in the *LVO* for Jan. 18, 19, and 20, 1884, which consumed pretty much the whole newspaper; Kitty's vacation plans from *LVO*, Jan. 14, 1884.

102   "required a whole dictionary": "The Origin," *LVO*, Jan. 28, 1884.

102   One hotel historian: Quoted in Bowman, *Montezuma*, p. 22.

102   Fred did not rush: This retelling of Fred's take on the Montezuma fire is

based more on what wasn't reported than on what was. While many sources claim that Fred was involved with the management of the Montezuma for many years after this fire, I see no evidence for this in any of his records. And the fact that there are no reports in the Leavenworth or Las Vegas papers about him or his people visiting the hotel in the aftermath of the fire convinces me that he had already turned over management of the Hot Springs hotels to the Santa Fe, or used the fire as an excuse to finally do so. In fact, Fred appears to have started pulling back from managing the Hot Springs properties as early as a month after the Montezuma opened, when the May 15, 1882, *LVO* reported that the railroad's superintendent in Las Vegas, Pullen, had taken over management of the bathhouse "in place of Fred Harvey whose frequent absence allowed him no chance to properly attend to that department."

102 "Come to my home": Springs Spray, *LVO*, Jan. 21, 1884.

103 Bill Phillips, decided it was time: This is also based on what *wasn't* reported, since there is no published reporting I know of concerning what happened to Bill Phillips. He simply disappeared from company documents and newspaper coverage.

103 "the best meal on the road": Benjamin to Harvey, June 13, 1883, DHC.

103 Americanizing certain international: This is more my observation of what started happening to the menus after the switch from Phillips to Vizzetti, whose rise is detailed in Fergusson, *Our Southwest*, p. 197.

104 mentoring the founder's son: For background on Schermerhorn's job at Brink's and his move to Harvey's employ, see "Byron Schermerhorn: The First President, Businessman, Poet, Civil War Intelligence Agent," in an undated issue of the Brink's Company annual report, LCHSC; "Railroad Rebates," *LVO*, March 21, 1885; and the 1886 P and L in DHC, where their percentages of the business profits are described.

104 "reigns over all": *LVO*, March 11, 1884, cited in Sheppard, *Montezuma*, p. 27.

104 "the handsomest": Nell Smith to May Harvey, Christmas 1937, HHMC.

104 "your Crass old": May Harvey autograph book, signed Jan. 14, 1882, DHC.

104 award after award: *LT*, July 1, 1883, p. 8.

CHAPTER 14: ACUTE AMERICANITIS

106 "I have been looking": Fred Harvey to Sally Harvey, Feb. 15, 1889, DHC.

106 "general electrization": Beard, "Neurasthenia or Nervous Exhaustion."

107 "the greater prevalence": George Miller Beard, *American Nervousness, Its Causes and Consequences: A Supplement to Nervous Exhaustion (Neurasthenia)* (New York: Putnam, 1881), p. vii.

107 "no precedent": Ibid., p. 65.

107 "it would seem": Ibid., p. 112.

107 "The lank and shriveled Yankee": *Medical News*, Dec. 30, 1882, p. 737.

107 "Many years ago I": Beard, *Practical Treatise on Nervous Exhaustion*, 2nd ed., p. 184.

107 "the character of the friends": Ibid., p. 185.

108 "I doubt whether there is": Ibid., p. 242.

108 special dainty diet: Beebe, *Mr. Pullman's Elegant Palace Car*, p. 355; also Beebe, *Mansions on Rails*, p. 169.

108 he returned feeling just as sick: "Personal," *LT*, Sept. 8, 1883, p. 4.

109   "Fred, time's clock": "A Half-Century Old," June 27, 1885, handwritten poem in Fred Harvey scrapbook, DHC.

109   *Etruria:* Background on ship is from Henry Fry, *The History of North Atlantic Steam Navigation* (London: S. Low, Marston, 1896), pp. 82–85.

109   pulled away from: Time of departure is explained in Fred Harvey to Sally Harvey, July 3, 1885, Gilsey House hotel, DHC.

109   After nearly a decade: Denis Brian, *Pulitzer: A Life* (New York: John Wiley and Sons, 2001), p. 104.

109   Sally had asked Byron: Schermerhorn mentions this to Fred in his letter, which is written on "Office of Fred Harvey, Leavenworth, KS," stationery, and dated June 28, 1885, at "The Harvey House," Fred Harvey scrapbook, DHC.

109   pressed flowers: This letter, from which the pressed flowers still fall when removed from its envelope, is undated but appears to have been from the trip, DHC.

110   "As you read I can see": Schermerhorn to Harvey, June 28, 1885, DHC.

110   "absolutely fireproof": Bowman, *Montezuma*, p. 15, appears to be quoted from Burnham, from a biography of his partner, John Root.

110   "lots of old friends": Springs Spray, *LVO,* Aug. 1, 1885.

111   apparently triggered: "In Ashes Again," *LVO,* Aug. 10, 1885, p. 2.

111   "found a handful of diamonds": Springs Spray, *LVO,* Aug. 11, 1885.

111   "regained much of his failing health": Springs Spray, *LVO,* Aug. 27, 1885.

111   "very much better": Springs Spray, *LVO,* Aug. 31, 1885.

111   sailed in February 1886: We know this because in Fred Harvey to Sally Harvey, Aug. 24, 1886, DHC, he laments that he has been away from home for seven months.

111   each with a manager: Estimates of staffing are based on early staff photos, census materials, and lists of Harvey employees who got free train passage.

112   At a muscular: Descriptions of Ford are from author interview with Stewart Harvey Jr. based on what his father and great-aunt Minnie had told him.

112   "Ford and the children": Undated letter from Fred Harvey to Sally Harvey, Hotel Belle Due, Munich, DHC, believed to be from his first long trip to Europe in 1886.

112   Bulwer-Lytton: In his defense, Sir Edward also coined the less-disparaged phrases "the pen is mightier than the sword," "the pursuit of the almighty dollar," and "the great unwashed."

113   A mile or so: Author interview with the current engineer of the Southwest Chief, Randy Decker, Sept. 3, 2005.

113   Ford did have another mentor: It is clear from later warm correspondence between Ford Harvey and Strong that they had been close for a long time.

114   Cleveland ordered a massive: Background on Cleveland and the trains is from Brodsky, *Grover Cleveland,* p. 148.

114   a legal dispute over $27: *Wabash, St. Louis & Pacific Railway Company v. Illinois,* Oct. 25, 1886, 118 U.S. 557, 7 S.Ct. 4, 30 L.Ed. 244; see sec. 2 for the difference in shipping rates, between $65 and $39.

114   quickly pushed through Congress: See Stone, *Interstate Commerce Commission,* p. 6.

114   pooling: See Johnson and Van Metre, *Principles of Railroad Transportation,* p. 292.

115   to *one dollar:* Bryant, *History of the Atchison, Topeka, and Santa Fe Railway,* p. 104.

CHAPTER 15: TRANSCONTINENTAL FRED

116   always remember going to a parade: Author interview with Byron "Ronny" Harvey III at his nursing home in suburban Boston (which turned out to be the last interview he ever gave), Sept. 2, 2004.

116   "My Dear Son Byron": Copy of leaf from an album kept by Byron in CLC, written on Jan. 20, 1887; the torn-off page is marked "Leaf from an album kept by Byron Harvey Sr., who was 11 in 1887. He was taught horseback riding by a veteran of the Indian Wars."

116   "Well, Ma": Fred Harvey to Sally Harvey, n.d., Munich, DHC.

117   "Meals by Fred Harvey" all the way to California: "The Railroads: Wild Rumors—A. and P. Eatinghouses—the U.P. Coming," *LAT,* May 24, 1887, p. 1.

117   "the people who made": Monroe, "Reminiscences of the Santa Fe Frontier," p. 43.

117   briefly run the eating houses well: Author correspondence with John Sweetser of the California Pacific RR Discussion Group, March 9, 2009; according to digested clippings in his collection, S&L took over the houses on Dec. 1, 1885 (*Mohave County Miner,* Nov. 29, 1885, p. 3), and within six months they were considered almost as good as Fred's (*Albuquerque Morning Journal,* July 6, 1886). But by spring of 1887, there had been fires in Coolidge, Mojave, and Lathrop (*Albuquerque Morning Democrat,* April 17, 1887) that had crippled their business.

117   he had such a severe attack: Described in Fred Harvey, April 12–18, 1887, entries, 1887 datebook, DHC.

118   "With the aid": *SFMag,* Feb. 1916, p. 46, cited in Harold L. Henderson, "Harvey," p. 33.

118   nearly $100,000: This figure was derived by taking the amount Fred claimed he had invested in the company during a lawsuit in 1891 and the amount he recorded as his investment in the company just before adding these new houses. In the P and L dated Feb. 25, 1887 (scrapbook, DHC), he said the investment as of Jan. 1, 1887, was $42,366.68. In the lawsuit, detailed in Resume of the File in the case of *Fred Harvey v. AT&SF RR Co.* in the Circuit Court of Cook County, Illinois, Aug. term, 1891, Bill in Chancery, filed Aug. 6, 1891, DHC, the amount invested was, according to p. 5, "not less than $150,000."

118   joined by his daughter: Their trip is detailed in Fred's 1887 datebook, DHC, starting on June 25.

118   he went shopping: The receipts for most of these purchases are in the Fred Harvey scrapbook, DHC.

119   He was not pleased: His comments on these places are in the entries for Oct. 24–Nov. 6, 1887, 1887 datebook, DHC.

119   face the siege of Chicago: "The Impending Warfare: Atchison, Topeka & Santa Fe Will Soon Reach Chicago," *CT,* May 25, 1887, p. 6.

119   "the handsomest trains": *Boston Globe,* May 5, 1888, p. 4; descriptions of the cars themselves are from "Finest in the World," *KCT,* April 29, 1888, typescript in Santa Fe railroad files, n.p., KSHSC.

120   wood-burning heaters: Schafer, Welsh, and Holland, *American Passenger Train,* p. 74.

120   "vestibules": White, *American Railroad Passenger Car,* p. 450.

121   They said Strong would build: Rumors of Strong coming to New York are in

"A Great Santa Fe Plan: The Road Will Soon Have a Line into New York and Boston," *CT,* May 12, 1888, p. 2.

121   When Ford first started dating: Biographical sketch of Charles Blair and his family is in Cutler, *History of the State of Kansas,* "Part 8, Bourbon County."

121   The courtship of Ford and Judy: Described in detail in Nell Smith to May Harvey, Christmas 1937, HHMC.

122   didn't want to convert: This fact is inferred from their actions: We know he did not convert, and even though the Blairs were lifelong Catholics, Ford and Judy were married in Ford's Episcopal church. For details of the wedding and honeymoon, see "Forever and for Aye," *Leavenworth Evening Standard,* May 21, 1888, p. 1 (copy in LCHSC, which also has the wedding invitation).

CHAPTER 16: BITING THE HAND

123   "a private car and free beer": Marshall, *Santa Fe,* p. 206.

123   "Unless confidence is restored": "To Borrow Ten Millions," *CT,* Oct. 17, 1888.

123   *Times* was reporting: "An Unpleasant Situation," *NYT,* Nov. 15, 1888, p. 1.

124   "I almost wish": Fred Harvey to Sally Harvey, March 9, 1889, DHC.

124   Nearly 100,000 people: This re-creation of the Oklahoma land rush is based on the on-scene reporting of William Willard Howard in "The Rush to Oklahoma," *Harper's Weekly,* May 18, 1889, pp. 391–94.

125   "giant centipedes with hundreds": Oklahoma City 89ers Association, *Oklahoma, the Beautiful Land* (Times-Journal Publishing Company, 1943), pp. 223–24.

125   It also appears: Details of their contract appear in "Brief History of Santa Fe Fred Harvey Relations," Aug. 4, 1942, p. 4, DHC; this secret cash payment is inferred from two surviving Fred Harvey P and L statements in DHC from Nov. 1889 and Feb. 1890, in which there is a line item for "AT&SF Investment" listed under "Resources." The Nov. 1889 balance on this investment from the railroad, from seven months after the deal, was $81,411.90; by Feb., it was down to $79,935.72. The $100,000 is an estimate based on the same computation as explained in the note for page 118.

126   So was George Pullman: "Gossip from the Railways," *Santa Fe New Mexican,* June 15, 1891.

126   George Washington Kretzinger: See his biography in *The National Cyclopaedia of American Biography* (New York: J. T. White, 1904), p. 93.

127   Mostly, he took the long train rides: Tim Cooper's career with Fred Harvey is documented in Hugh Gardner, "Saga of Tim W. Cooper: Guiding Personages of the Nationally Famous Fred Harvey System," *Pittsburgh Courier,* n.d., but appears to have been published in 1939, Fred Harvey scrapbook, DHC.

127   seen in the telegraph codes: Fred Harvey, handwritten codebook, page for letter *Q,* DHC.

128   "a peculiar character": *Herald* story reprinted in *Railway Review,* Feb. 29, 1888, p. 568.

128   "at great risk and loss": Resume of the File in the case of *Fred Harvey v. AT&SF RR Co.* in the Circuit Court of Cook County, Illinois, Aug. term, 1891, Bill in Chancery, filed Aug. 6, 1891, pp. 2–3, DHC.

128   recently bought a second farm: "Old Fred Harvey Ranch House Will Be Razed," *Emporia Gazette,* April 5, 1946; and "Fred Harvey Ranch House to Go," *KCT,* April 9, 1946.

128 five thousand meals *a day:* Amounts are extrapolated from figures in Resume of the File, p. 5.

129 reported annual earnings: *Boston Globe,* Dec. 1, 1891, reported for fiscal year ending in June, net income was $9,899,997; capitalization estimate from Bryant, *History of Atchison, Topeka, and Santa Fe Railway,* p. 160.

CHAPTER 17: THE BIGGEST CATERED LUNCH IN AMERICAN HISTORY

130 in New York, just before heading: According to his notes in a Leavenworth National Bank scratchpad, DHC, that he was using instead of a datebook in 1891–1892, he had just arrived back in the United States and on May 4 traveled to Washington, D.C., to lobby, among others, Senator Perkins of Kansas and Senator Brice of Ohio.

130 collection of Schermerhorn's poems: The only known copy is in LCHSC.

130 birth to a baby girl: Nickname, author interviews with Stewart Harvey Jr. and Joy Harvey, also noted in her photo album of a trip to the Grand Canyon in NPSGC

130 they put in a bid: The planning and execution of these lunches were re-created from "How the Lunches Were Served," *CT,* Oct. 22, 1892, and an item in the *Leavenworth Evening Standard,* Oct. 31, 1892.

131 Ford made a bet with his father: The bet, including the signatures of Fred and Ford and Dave Benjamin as witness, is recorded in the Leavenworth scratchpad 1891–1892 on a page dated Oct. 7, 1892, DHC.

132 they decided to team up: "How the Multitude Will Be Fed," *CT,* Nov. 2, 1891, p. 8.

134 fifteen somber, well-dressed: Re-created from *NYT* coverage of the bankruptcy filing, "The Order of the Court," Dec. 24, 1893, p. 2.

135 "to the frontier the American intellect owes": Turner, "Significance of the Frontier in American History," p. 37.

136 welcomed Fred back: The terms of the new agreement between Fred Harvey and the Santa Fe's receivers are noted in "Brief History of Santa Fe Fred Harvey Relations," Aug. 4, 1942, p. 4, DHC, contract for Jan. 15, 1894.

136 snowball fights on the streets of Tucson: " 'The Last Time It Snowed' in Tucson," *LAT,* Feb. 14, 1894, p. 2.

136 kept rising and rising: "Pueblo Drowned Out: Successive Cloudbursts Cause Havoc, Ruin, and Death," *Washington Post,* June 1, 1894, p. 1.

137 *New York Times* proclaimed: "Greatest Strike in History: Pullman Boycott Will Involve Scores of Industries, Great Commercial Disaster Threatens," *NYT,* July 1, 1894, p. 1.

137 had met at Fred Harvey's: Their excursion was covered in "All Out of Doors," *LAT,* June 10, 1894, p. 16.

138 court ruled against Debs: *In re Debs,* 158 U.S. 564 (1895), 158 U.S. 564, *In re Debs et al.,* No. 11, May 27, 1895.

138 welcome a visit from "mamma": Fred Harvey to Ford Harvey, May 31, 1895, LCHSC.

138 Among Fred's guests: A letter from Fred Harvey to Ford Harvey, July 5, 1895, in LCHSC, written from 23 Carlton Road, describes the entire visit and negotiating points. Details of the agreement they finally made are in "Brief of Supplemental Agreement," Sept. 27, 1895, between A. F. Walker and J. J. McCook, receivers, and Fred Harvey of Leavenworth, copy in DHC.

CHAPTER 18: LET THE BOYS DO IT

141   "massive of head and features": Descriptions of Ripley from L. L. Waters, *Steel Trails to Santa Fe,* p. 343.

141   Ripley was its passenger: Fred actually had his address listed in his 1875 date-book, DHC.

141   "we are under no obligation": Ripley to Aldace Walker (Santa Fe board chairman), Jan. 30, 1896, DHC, describes how Ripley was prepared to sack his old friend; at the end of the letter is typed in Walker's report of the views of the executive committee.

142   Ripley initially dictated: Ripley to Fred Harvey, May 29, 1896, LCHSC.

142   negotiate a new ten-year deal: Fred Harvey to Ford Harvey, June 20, 1896, describes the "memorandum of Ripley's proposition" and says, "I think it is a very fair one"; the power of attorney document, executed on Jan. 9, 1897, is in DHC; details of the deal are in "Brief History of Santa Fe Fred Harvey Relations," Aug. 4, 1942, pp. 5–6, DHC.

143   doubled the number of cities: The lists of new locations come from the company master list and time line in DHC.

144   St. Louis Union Depot: "Secured a Chicago Caterer," *CT,* April 18, 1896, p. 9.

144   serving the dishes: Harvey, *Hospitality Cookbook,* p. 14; information on separate dining rooms, Porterfield, *Dining by Rail,* p. 298.

145   special dining car menu: "The New Santa Fe Flyer," *LAT,* Nov. 5, 1895, p. 9.

145   "interfere with the strictest": Fred Harvey to Ford Harvey, July 5, 1895, LCHSC.

146   "The amount you gave him": Ibid.

146   "Wet clothes": Quote from "Recalls Incident on Fred Harvey Ranch," *Emporia Gazette,* Feb. 1, 1946; other information on farm is from *Emporia Gazette,* April 5, 1946.

146   "fewer white shirts and brains": "What's the Matter with Kansas?" *Emporia Gazette,* April 15, 1896.

147   "The more one sees": "In the Land of the Plutocrat," *Emporia Gazette,* July 6, 1897.

147   "no smirking, tip-seeking negro": *El Paso Herald,* reprinted later in *SFMag,* Sept. 1910, p. 76.

148   "We'll guarantee you": Poling-Kempes, *Harvey Girls,* p. 100.

148   When a new girl cleared: " 'Harvey Girls' Long a Part of Kansas City Scene," *KCStar,* Feb. 17, 1946, p. 1-C.

148   "caused a lot of jealousy": Poling-Kempes, *Harvey Girls,* p. 101.

148   "nearly every single": Ibid., p. 126.

148   "is responsible for a great deal": William Curtis, untitled story, *Chicago Record,* May 9, 1899, HMC.

149   "When my father": Hahn, "Till the Well Runs Dry," p. 184.

CHAPTER 19: ROUGH RIDDEN

150   "un-American": Richard T. Ely, "Pullman: A Social Study," *Harper's New Monthly Magazine,* Feb. 1885, p. 465.

150   a tomb impervious: Details of Pullman's grave from "Lies in Solid Rock," *CT,* Oct. 24, 1897, p. 24.

151   disinherited his twin sons: "Cut Off with Income of $3000 Each," *Boston Globe,* Oct. 28, 1897, p. 3; and "Disinherited," *LAT,* Oct. 28, 1897, p. 1.

151   his personal barber: "Pullman's Barber Shut Out," *NYT,* Dec. 16, 1898, p. 1.

152   Smart, direct, and sometimes stunningly: Descriptions of Minnie Harvey are from the vivid recollections of her great-nephew Stewart Harvey Jr., from author interviews, and from photographs of her in LCHSC.

152   John Huckel: Huckel used his first name, John, but was more often referred to by his middle name, Fred. But since it is hard enough to keep track of Fred, his son Ford, and his son Freddy already, I'm referring to him as John. Biographical information comes from his obituaries: "Death of J. F. Huckel," *KCT,* March 27, 1936; *NYT,* March 28, 1936, p. 15; and "John F. Huckel, Fred Harvey Official, Passes Away," *SFMag,* May 1936, pp. 15–16.

152   a health crisis: Author interview with Joy Harvey, wife of the late Byron "Ronny" Harvey III—she recalled hearing this from Kitty Harvey.

152   whose namesake niece: "Birthday Party," *LT,* July 2, 1881, p. 4.

154   "cowboy cavalry": "Teddy's Terrors: Cowboy Cavalry Regiment Going to Cuba; the Men Who Are Being Enlisted Are Rough Riders, Dead Shots, and Fearless Fighters," *LAT,* April 28, 1898, p. 3.

154   "benevolent assimilation": From McKinley's order to the secretary of war, Dec. 27, 1898, reprinted in *NYT,* Jan. 6, 1899, p. 1.

154   "A splendid little war": Hay to Roosevelt, July 27, 1898 (just before he was named secretary of state). See William Roscoe Thayer, *John Hay: In Two Volumes* (Boston: Houghton Mifflin, 1915), p. 337; the "turkey shoot" quote credited to a Seaman Cross from the battleship *Oregon.*

156   As the Rough Riders' train: Roosevelt's visit is re-created from coverage in the *NYT, CT,* and *LAT,* as well as "Roosevelt There: Rain Ruined Decorations at Las Vegas," *Santa Fe New Mexican,* June 24, 1899, and "Rough Riders Grand Reunion," *Albuquerque Daily Citizen,* June 26, 1899.

156   "almost lifted bodily": "Teddy's Coming," *LAT,* June 25, 1899, p. B1.

156   Harvey Girls wore special outfits: Author interview with Leslie F. Loewe, retired chairman and CEO of Angelica Corporation; and Poling-Kempes, *Harvey Girls,* p. 56.

157   Williams sent the spoon: "Was F. Harvey's Spoon," *LT,* June 13, 1900, p. 4, reprinted from *St. Louis Democrat;* actual letter from Williams is in DHC along with typescript of this article and a Jan. 27, 1900, letter to Fred from John C. Burrowes, the superintendent for dining cars for the Southern Railway, to whom the spoon was apparently first sent.

CHAPTER 20: THE CLUTCHES OF THE GRIM MONSTER

158   "Frederick Harvey Ill": "Frederick Harvey Ill at Streatham," *NYT,* Oct. 15, 1899, p. 1.

158   most renowned medical authority: There have been numerous references to Harvey being treated by "one of the most eminent surgeons" (in the words of Dan Anthony in the *LT*), but nobody named the doctor. It had to be Frederick Treves, who was, at that time, not only the world's most famous surgeon but also the world authority on exactly what was wrong with Fred. Besides this circumstantial evidence, there is one hard fact—just after Fred's surgery, his treatment was transferred to another London physician, a transfer that corresponds to Treves quitting his private practice to go treat soldiers in the Boer War.

159   written the textbook: Information on Treves from Stephen and Lee, *Dictio-*

nary of National Biography, p. 857; and Trombley, *Sir Frederick Treves,* esp. pp. 80–83, from which the quotes are taken.

159 was reporting that Fred: "Railroad Record," *LAT,* Oct. 25, 1899, p. 9.

159 "Fred Harvey Not Dead": *Santa Fe New Mexican,* Oct. 27, 1899, p. 1.

159 tethered permanently: Htapes, no. 7, side B: "He had a colostomy, which my father [Byron Harvey, Fred's son] told me all about and he was scared to death—my father had the same thing."

159 "even a teaspoonful": Fred's graphic descriptions of his pain and physical problems are in letters to Ford Harvey, Feb. 23, March 6 and 10, April 3 and 6, 1900, LCHSC. The March 6 letter is particularly interesting because it has a note at the end written to Ford by what appears to be Fred's sister Eliza (who appears to have also been the actual writer of the letters, presumably dictated to her by Fred).

160 "I think if Mamma": Fred Harvey to Ford Harvey, April 6, 1900, LCHSC.

160 "sometimes I feel hopeful": Fred Harvey to Ford Harvey, Feb. 23, 1900, LCHSC.

160 "The pain, Mother": These Edison Cylinders still exist at LCHSC, but so far nobody has been able to make a modern transfer of the sound on them. This quote is from Michael Quinn, a photo researcher at NPSGC, who is the only living person known to have actually heard what was on the cylinders—from a reel-to-reel tape the company had made decades ago when the cylinders still played. The tape had been lost for years; urged on by me and others, Quinn finally found it mislabeled in the NPS archive, and then various historians at southwestern institutions with an interest in Fred Harvey, led by Karen Underhill at CLC, paid to have a restoration attempted on the tape. It, too, failed, although the restorers did believe they heard Fred croak out the word "Mother." For now, we'll have to rely on Michael's memory.

161 In one of the last pictures: In HHMC.

161 "the first moment": Fred Harvey to Ford Harvey, Aug. 21, 1900, on Chicago Beach Hotel stationery, LCHSC.

161 "Your words and actions": Fred Harvey to Ford Harvey, Aug. 23, 1900, LCHSC.

161 "If you can impress upon her": Fred Harvey to Ford Harvey, Aug. 21, 1900, LCHSC.

162 spontaneous, tax-evading "gifts": Explained in a six-page letter in DHC, dated June 28, 1900, from Leavenworth and addressed to Ford and Dave Benjamin. It notes, "My wife joins me in these gifts to our children and approves of, in evidence of which her signature to these instructions accompanies my own below."

162 "unless mamma and you object": Fred Harvey to Ford Harvey, telegram, Sept. 7, 1900, LCHSC.

162 "The Chinese doctor is not": Ford Harvey to Fred Harvey, Sept. 8, 1900, LCHSC.

163 "Have seen Chinese": Fred Harvey to Ford Harvey, telegram, Sept. 9, 1900, LCHSC.

163 "the most sprightly invalid": Fred Harvey to Ford Harvey, Oct. 3, 1900, Wellington Hotel, LCHSC.

163 "It was a delightful surprise": Visit detailed in Strong to Ford Harvey, Oct. 24, 1900, LCHSC.

164 Dave was riding from Houston: This scene in Galveston is re-created from

"From the Stricken City," *KCStar*, Sept. 15, 1900, p. 1—which I first learned about in Larson, *Isaac's Storm*, pp. 159–63, on which I also relied. Details of the building come from a previous *Galveston Daily News* story, Feb. 14, 1897, n.p.

165   Fred came to Leavenworth: Fred's movements over the last weeks are detailed in "Fred Harvey at Point of Death," *LT*, Feb. 7, 1901, p. 4.

165   headed to Southern California: Details are in "Southern California by Towns and Counties: Pasadena; Rev. Mr. Hobart Accepts Call of Baptists, Wind-Up of Tournament of Roses Affairs," *LAT*, Jan. 7, 1901, p. 11.

165   California had become a major Fred: According to company datelines in DHC, the ferryboat restaurants opened in 1900, and the operation at the Ferry Building in 1901.

165   knew that their leader: This is based on how the company has always operated, letters to Fred from employees wishing him good health (in DHC and LCHSC), and what reportedly happened when other key members of the Harvey family died, particularly Ford.

166   dry, cracking lips: This was a common end-of-life treatment even then, see Thornton, "Treatment of Uterine Fibro-myoma" p. 863.

166   "Fred Harvey lies": "Fred Harvey at Point of Death," p. 4.

167   "Father passed away peacefully": A copy of the telegram sent to William Strong, affixed to a copy of Fred's 1880 portrait, is in DHC. It is unclear if this is actually Strong's copy—returned to Ford after his death—or an extra.

167   "Fred Harvey . . . has done more": William Allen White's obit from the *Gazette* was reprinted in *LT*, Feb. 14, 1901, p. 2.

167   "in many ways": "Fred Harvey Will Probated Yesterday," *LT*, Feb. 16, 1901, p. 4; also copy of will in DHC.

167   "to be greatly in excess": "Fred Harvey's Estate Worth Over a Million," *LAT*, Feb. 16, 1901, p. 1.

168   "will be conducted just as it was": "Fred Harvey Will Probated Yesterday."

CHAPTER 21: A LITTLE JOURNEY IN THE WILDERNESS

173   self-appointed "Apostle": Information on Lummis's background comes from Thompson, *American Character*, and author correspondence with Thompson.

174   Ford met up with the Ripley: This trip is re-created from "Lummis Acted as Guide in Wonderland," *LAT*, Oct. 31, 1901, p. 12, for which Lummis was either the main source or the uncredited author, as well as Lummis's own journal entries about the trip, which are in the Autry National Center of the American West and were translated for me (he wrote in English and Spanish) by research associate Manolo Madrid. Also, Lummis wrote a two-part story about the trip, "A Week of Wonders," in his magazine *Land of Sunshine* 15 (June–Dec. 1901), pp. 315 and 425. His photos from the trip are also in the Autry collection.

175   "a G-string": Lummis, "Week of Wonders," p. 327.

176   controversial relic hunter: Information on Wetherill and the Hyde Exploring Expedition is from Snead, *Ruins and Rivals*, pp. 31–64.

178   "Ours has been": Cited in Hughes and Priehs, *In the House of Stone and Light*, p. 28 n. 16. The Grand Canyon history section is re-created from parts of this book; Stephen Pyne's provocative 1998 book, *How the Canyon Became Grand*, a repackage of his 1982 scholarly book *Dutton's Point*; and Neumann, *On the Rim*.

179   The Santa Fe offered Moran: Moran's relationships with the railroads are re-
      created from Wilkins, *Thomas Moran;* Bryant, *History of Atchison, Topeka, and
      Santa Fe Railway,* p. 120; and also Bryant's article "The Atchison, Topeka, and
      Santa Fe Railway and the Development of the Taos and Santa Fe Art
      Colonies," p. 437.

180   "the Divine Abyss": Quoted in Hughes and Priehs, *In the House of Stone and
      Light,* p. 58, citing John Burroughs, *"The Divine Abyss,"* in *Time and Change*
      (Boston: Houghton Mifflin, 1912), p. 49. Muir himself had actually been fear-
      ful when he first heard the railroad was building a line to the canyon, but later
      changed his mind, writing in 1902, "When I saw those trains crawling along
      through the pines of the Coconino Forest and close up to the brink of the
      chasm at Bright Angel, I was glad to discover that in the presence of such stu-
      pendous scenery they are nothing. The locomotives and trains are mere bee-
      tles and caterpillars, and the noise they make is as little disturbing as the
      hooting of an owl in the lonely woods." *The Writings of John Muir* (Boston:
      Houghton Mifflin, 1918), p. 348.

180   When Ford looked into the Divine Abyss: While some of this interior mono-
      logue is extrapolated from later events and insights from Ford's obituaries, the
      best example of Ford discussing his obsession with the canyon appeared in
      "How One Man Conducts Sixty-six Hotels," *Leslie's Illustrated,* Feb. 27, 1913,
      HMC.

181   "You want to put the hotel": Lummis diary for Oct. 28, 1901, recounts this
      scene.

CHAPTER 22: THE FRED HARVEY INDIAN DEPARTMENT

182   Minnie was thrilled: While Minnie's actions were generally behind-the-
      scenes and undocumented, she is credited for instigating the Indian Depart-
      ment in Bryant, *History of the Atchison, Topeka, and Santa Fe Railway,* p. 120.

182   Ford wasn't sure: Ford explained his unsureness about various retail adven-
      tures that John Huckel pushed the company into in an unpublished manu-
      script dated July 19, 1927, marked "For system" in company files, HMC. "We
      walked around the idea a good many times before we went into the business
      of selling Indian goods and curios."

182   "Once Harvey women": Author interview with Stewart Harvey Jr.

183   Schweizer was like a character: Background on Schweizer comes from
      Howard, " 'A Most Remarkable Success' "; and Fergusson, *Our Southwest,* pp.
      199–201.

183   tiny Harvey House in Navajo: This was first located in Coolidge, New Mex-
      ico, where this incident took place, but the eating house was later moved
      twenty miles west to Gallup.

183   "bald-headed man": Howard and Pardue, *Inventing the Southwest,* p. 12.

184   he was the first to order: Adair described this in his book *The Navajo and
      Pueblo Silversmiths,* pp. 25–26; and Howard quotes a personal interview with
      Adair in " 'A Most Remarkable Success,' " p. 88.

184   He had trouble adjusting: This insight is based on the obvious friction be-
      tween the men in the tone of their career-long correspondence.

184   "America's Orient": This provocatively loaded term was coined by cultural
      historian Barbara Babcock, in "A New Mexican 'Rebecca,' " p. 406.

185   who apparently had been recommended: Grattan, *Mary Colter,* p. 6. Bio-

graphical information on Colter is largely drawn from this book and Berke, *Mary Colter,* and author correspondence with Berke.

185 "An incomprehensible woman in pants": Frank Waters, *Masked Gods,* p. III.

187 "Herman stood in front": Fergusson, *Our Southwest,* p. 201.

187 "He just had room after": Author interview with Stewart Harvey Jr.

187 "Fred Harvey saw the value": Amsden, *Navaho Weaving,* p. 35, quoted in Fergusson, *Our Southwest,* p. 201.

187 "as handsome and inviting": Quoted in Howard and Pardue, *Inventing the Southwest,* p. 16, from Hudson letters dated Feb. 6 and 7, 1903.

188 some five thousand pieces: *Albuquerque Journal Democrat,* May 11, 1902.

188 "staged authenticity": This phrase, used to critique different types of tourist experiences, was coined by sociologist Dean MacCannell in 1973.

188 Elle of Ganado: She and her husband, Tom, are profiled in Howard and Pardue, *Inventing the Southwest,* pp. 60–61.

189 Then text began to emerge: This re-creation of her weaving comes from the photo taken of her during the process. Ibid., p. 60.

189 He was whisked: Coverage of Roosevelt's appearance in Albuquerque, *NYT,* May 6, 1903, p. 3.

190 saddled white stallion: Described in Chappell, "The Railway at Grand Canyon," n.p.

190 "The only word I can use for it": Roosevelt's visit is re-created from "President Visits an Awful Place," *LAT,* May 7, 1903, p. 1 (which includes full text of his speech), and notes from Charles Lummis's diary for this day, from the Autry National Center for the American West collection.

193 "further back from the rim": *Coconino Sun,* June 5, 1903.

CHAPTER 23: TENTH LEGION

194 "the Tenth Legion": This scene is re-created from a later *KCStar* story—one of the first for which a journalist was allowed access to Fred Harvey offices to see normal daily operations—"Taking the Harvey System Apart to See What Makes It Tick," March 29, 1914, which included the dialogue; the "Tenth Legion" reference comes from "Intimate Glimpses of Fred Harvey Personalities: Frank Clough," *SFMag,* Oct. 1936, p. 40.

194 tiny toads found their way: Story recounted years later in Corb Sarchet, "Toads in Coffee Cups Greeted Customers of Harvey House," *Wichita Morning Eagle,* marked "1953," but no date, HMC.

194 was now buying and serving: These statistics, which appear in various turn-of-the-century stories, appear to have originated in Leigh Mitchell Hodges's article in the May 5, 1905, *Philadelphia North American,* but there is also a 1908 internal list, "Estimates of Supplies During the Year 1908 on Entire System," in DHC that reconfirms them.

195 sparked a huge controversy: "Olive Oil—a Manufacturer Claims That the California Product Is Equal or Superior to the Imported Article," *LAT,* July 17, 1903, p. 6.

195 "the multiplication table": "Taking the Harvey System Apart."

196 Samuel Crumbine: This incident is recounted in Crumbine's memoir, *Frontier Doctor,* pp. 74–75.

197 "titular head of the dining car operation": Author correspondence with Stewart Harvey Jr.

197   "My father didn't know": Htapes, no. 6, side B.

197   He teamed with the new American powerhouse: See Stechschulte, *Detroit Publishing Company Postcards*, pp. 333–35.

198   "peculiarly lacking": *IND*, Nov. 27, 1915, p. 5.

198   A handful of eastern entrepreneurs: Background on William and Samuel Childs is from Landmarks Preservation Commission Report, Feb. 4, 2003, for the former Childs restaurant building at 2102 Boardwalk in Brooklyn, p. 2, www.nyc.gov/html/lpc/downloads/pdf/reports/childs.pdf; on Horn and Hardart, see "Meet Me at the Automat," *Smithsonian*, Aug. 2001.

200   In a very cozy arrangement: The Huckels lived at 3530 Locust Street; the Benjamins at 3620 Gillham (where they lived with Dave's bachelor brother, Alfred).

200   "His employees who do their work": "How One Man Conducts Sixty-six Hotels," *Leslie's Illustrated*, Feb. 27, 1913, n.p., HMC.

201   "instruct our people always": Ford Harvey, unpublished manuscript, July 19, 1927, pp. 10–11, HMC, emphasis added.

202   developing a running list: This list is digested from various writings of Ford's meant to help employees understand company ethos, including Ibid.; undated manuscript, presumably written in the early 1920s, apparently for *American Magazine*, UA, box 3, file 16, p. 6, HMC; and "Ideals Applied to Buying at Fred Harvey's," from his address at the National Restaurant Association convention in 1925, published in *Restaurant News and Management*, Nov. 1925, pp. 13–15.

CHAPTER 24: ON THE VERY BRINK OF THE DIZZY GULF

205   the government wouldn't even take it for free: Correspondence is in the Santa Fe collection, box 130, KSHSC.

205   Voth had converted: See Michael F. Brown, *Who Owns Native Culture?* which opens with a scathing indictment (pp. 11–15) of Voth's intrusions.

206   "whittling bows and arrows": "Prisoner of 18 Years: Geronimo, the Bloodthirsty Indian," *Boston Globe*, Sept. 18, 1904, p. SM12.

206   after seeing a Fred Harvey promotional display: For more details on Hearst's collecting, see the introductory essay in Blomberg, *Navajo Textiles*.

206   "My Dear Mr. Schweizer": An undated letter in HMC, presumably from Dec. 1905, includes all these quotations. Interestingly, ten years later Hearst did end up forcing Schweizer to accept newspaper coverage for a $6,861.90 ($154,000) bill he ran up at Hopi House and refused to pay. As detailed in a Dec. 2008 article about Harvey public relations by Patricia Curtin in the *Journal of Communication Management*, both Fred Harvey and the Santa Fe were so mortified by the episode that they made sure the resulting double-page spread on the Grand Canyon in the *San Francisco Examiner* on May 2, 1915, mentioned neither company's name.

207   "I will bet you two huge": Hearst to Schweizer, n.d., early 1911, cited in Blomberg, *Navajo Textile*, p. 12.

208   ultimate Fred Harvey oasis: Details on El Tovar are from the company publication *El Tovar: Grand Canyon of Arizona*, and Berke, *Mary Colter*, pp. 60–70.

209   "to see how the world": Advertisement in *CT*, Nov. 26, 1904, p. 11.

209   one of his father's favorite: Background on Charlie Brant is from his obituary, "Charlie Brant Has Gone," *SFMag*, Jan. 1922, pp. 23–30.

210   "rimming": Ernest Kolb interview tape is GRCA 36063, transcript, p. 55, NPSGC.

210   "Stop your jiggling": Ibid., p. 51.

210   "Reared upon the very brink": "El Tovar, the Magnificent New Santa Fe Hotel on Brink of Grand Canyon," *LAT,* Aug. 18, 1905, p. 116.

CHAPTER 25: TRAINIACS

212   "to let some other man": "Scott Is Making Up Time," *KCStar,* July 10, 1905, p. 5.

212   "dude food": Marshall, *Santa Fe,* p. 281.

213   "Porterhouse Steak": Onboard menu from L. L. Waters, *Steel Trails to Santa Fe,* p. 390.

213   "An American cowboy": Marshall, *Santa Fe,* p. 391.

213   "Any man who can cook": "Scott Is Making Up Time."

214   But in 1905, the nation's railroads: See Roy and Bonacich, "Interlocking Directorates," p. 368.

214   "private varnish": Beebe, *Mansions on Rails,* app. pp. 373–76.

214   "It was a great deal to us kids": Poling-Kempes, *Harvey Girls,* p. 133.

215   "To be 'nice' ": Ripley to Ford Harvey, Oct. 31, 1913, DHC.

216   "are being gradually strangled": Ripley to Colonel William Nelson (publisher of the *KCStar*), Oct. 7, 1910, copied to Ford, in HMC.

217   Dave Benjamin was in San Francisco: "David Benjamin Telephones Calmly as Earthquake Showers Plaster," *KCJP,* March 12, 1933, n.p., HMC.

217   "This is about the only time": "Fought Hard to Save the Ferry," *Washington Post,* April 22, 1906, p. 1.

218   Ford and Dave put the finishing touches: See "Harvey Agreement," Jan. 10, 1911; there are copies in DHC and AKC.

218   heard he had a girlfriend: Htapes, no. 8, side A.

218   "He was a handsome": Author correspondence with Stewart Harvey Jr.

218   personal notes were discovered: Daggett and Ellie Harvey found them, with me, when we went through their Fred Harvey holdings.

219   "I want you so": Judy Harvey to Ford Harvey, Oct. 11, no year, DHC.

219   "I will be thinking of you darling": Judy Harvey to Ford Harvey, n.d., presumably May 1908, Waldorf-Astoria stationery, DHC.

220   its best year ever: This according to two sources in JKC, one an income table from 1896–1912, in the Santa Fe collection, file 31, KSHSC; the other from a company ledger for the Harvey Hotel & Restaurant Company.

CHAPTER 26: KANSAS CITY STARS

223   substantial advances: These are documented, along with the rest of the finances of the estate, in the Final Report by Trustees of Fred Harvey Estate, Jan. 26, 1911, p. 3; May had withdrawn $37,400 ($842,000), copy in DHC.

224   women should not own stock: Htapes, no. 7, side A.

224   *lend him* the money: "Harvey Agreement," Jan. 10, 1911, p. 6, DHC.

225   which made Dave uncomfortable: This insight comes from an unsigned affidavit prepared by Dave Benjamin in Dec. 1920, a copy of which is in AKC. It appears that when Dave started looking into selling his shares after the war, he found they weren't valued as high as he thought they should be.

226 now bring his Airedale: Htapes, no. 2, side A.

226 several of these wannabe firms: "A Fount of Railway Food," *KCStar,* Dec. 24, 1911 (n.p., but p. 174 in MVSC bound volume), details the companies.

227 "there won't be any better": Harry Benjamin to the *St. Louis Star,* Oct. 20, 1912.

228 "Ford is in all things": *IND,* July 4, 1914, p. 7.

228 From the resort town: See stamps on their immigration document "Legation of the United States of America," which also details what Dave looked like (Nose: "Long"), which is in AKC (along with photos from the trip).

229 "incalculable hardship": "Six Ships Relieve Crush of Tourists," *NYT,* Aug. 2, 1914, p. 3.

229 massive humidors: Information on humidors and employees, and long quote about the kitchens in the new station, are from "In Station Cafe, 170 Helpers," *KCStar,* Oct. 29, 1914, p. 2.

230 "Tell Shep to come here": "Shepard Smith, a Famous Frisco Engineer for Forty-two Years—Retired June 30," *Frisco Employes' Magazine,* July 1926, p. 8.

230 an enterprising journalist later: Jeffrey Spivak explores this in *Kansas City Union Station* (Kansas City Star Books, 1999), pp. 57–58.

231 "many Kansas Citians": This and other details of opening day are from *KCStar* coverage, Nov. 2, 1914, p. 22 of the bound clipping volume in MVSC.

231 helped create a national best-seller: Marshall, *Santa Fe,* p. 110.

CHAPTER 27: NATIONAL PARKING

233 "What a *bunker*": From coverage of the billionaire special, "Wealth Visits Grand Canyon," *LAT,* March 29, 1910, p. 19.

234 "It would be exceedingly inappropriate": *Proceedings of the National Parks Conference, 1911,* p. 15.

234 "Gentlemen, you are not": *Proceedings of the National Parks Conference, 1915,* p. 21.

235 "wide, safe, dustless": Quoted in Weigle and Babcock, *Great Southwest,* p. 18.

235 "All classes of people": *Proceedings of the National Parks Conference, 1915,* p. 23.

235 "For the first class": *Proceedings of the National Parks Conference, 1917,* p. 324.

235 "We took a Packard": Ibid., pp. 323–25.

236 "In my opinion": *Proceedings of the National Parks Conference, 1915,* p. 23.

236 "Scenery is a splendid thing": See Albright and Schenck, *Creating the National Park Service,* pp. 51 and 54–55.

237 "You know how": Ben Weller, "West We Go: Canyon Country," *Minneapolis Star Tribune,* Aug. 30, 1998, p. 1G.

237 "From the time a tourist arrives": "Guides Fight for Customers," *Washington Post,* Jan. 7, 1917, p. 8.

238 "You can't imagine": Grattan, *Mary Colter,* p. 26.

238 "the most palatial": "Hearst Seeks Senate," *NYT,* Feb. 10, 1914, p. 1.

238 "variegated vagabondizing": Twain, *Roughing It,* p. 28.

239 "Down a winding footpath": Irvin S. Cobb, *Roughing It De Luxe* (New York: George H. Doran, 1914), pp. 41–44.

240 "Europe is Closed": *SFMag,* n.d., sometime in early 1915, p. 58, KSHSC.

241 budget of more than $160,000: See John Huckel to Schweizer, March 7, 1935, HMC, which includes a breakdown of expenses for San Diego.

241 Although the San Diego fair: Much of my re-creation of behind the scenes at this fair is based on reporting in Bokovoy, *San Diego World's Fairs.*

242 "the color of evil": Post, *By Motor to the Golden Gate,* p. 165.

243 "Stopping at the various Harvey": Ibid., pp. 160–63.

244 over 150,000: Ford actually said 116,000 in his talk, but a forestry official at the canyon said he was only counting those who checked into Harvey establishments and the real number was over 150,000.

244 "I have heard personally": *Proceedings of the National Parks Conference, 1917,* p. 323.

245 "It is true that one finds": "War Has Taught Americans Who Have Traveled Abroad This Is the Land of the Best," *Atlanta Constitution,* Aug. 6, 1916, p. B4.

CHAPTER 28: DARING YOUNG FREDDY & HIS FLYING MACHINES

246 "the funny papers": Freddy Harvey to Ford Harvey, postcard, n.d., etching of Dresden, DHC.

246 "I was very frightened": Shand-Tucci, *Crimson Letter,* p. 228, describing an interview Townsend did with gay activist Randy Wicker.

247 "born flyer": Noted in Bingham, *Explorer in the Air Service,* p. 10.

247 "We lacked men of experience": Ibid., p. xii and p. 10.

248 "with as much calmness": *IND,* Nov. 24, 1911, p. 8.

248 "It's the greatest sport": "Harvey Flies Here Today," *KCStar,* Nov. 18, 1917, p. 3-A.

249 "two leather-rigged, behooded": "Many Watch Big Biplane," *KCT,* Nov. 19, 1917, p. 4.

249 "very expert bird man": *IND,* Nov. 24, 1917, p. 8.

249 "The Three Bombardiers": Collins, *Tales of an Old Air-Faring Man,* p. 6.

251 Ford was summoned: Described by Hines in his memoir, *War History of American Railroads,* p. 89; also Bryant, *History of the Atchison, Topeka, and Santa Fe Railway,* p. 240. This section is also based on McAdoo's memoir, *Crowded Years.*

253 "proven in federal court": See Falconer, "Segregation of Delinquent Women and Girls as a War Problem."

253 "one immoral girl": All material from this study can be found in Purcell-Guild, "Study of One Hundred and Thirty-one Delinquent Girls."

253 "forfeited their claims": See Additon, "Work Among Delinquent Women and Girls," p. 152.

254 powerful tenor voice: Scene recounted in "Indian's Song Wins Red Cross Dollars," *KCJP,* May 27, 1918, p. 8.

255 His squadron's performance: "New York Hosts Stage Greatest Freedom March," *CT,* July 5, 1917, p. 14; and "Airplanes over City Fly in Battle Lines," *NYT,* July 5, 1918, p. 20.

256 His departure was delayed: Details of Freddy's medical procedure and the family's reaction to his orders to ship out are from Ford Harvey to Byron Harvey, Sept. 18, 1918, DHC.

257 "Bring out your dead": Barry, *Great Influenza,* p. 5.

257 "was so greatly appreciated": Bingham, *Explorer in the Air Service,* p. 10.

258 "How are you": Dialogue from story in *IND,* Feb. 22, 1919, p. 8.

258 "greatest living railroad man": "Edw. P. Ripley Dies," *NYT,* Feb. 5, 1920, p. 9.

259 Arequipa: Description of the estate and its background comes from a *LAT*

real estate listing decades later: Ruth Ryon, "Seeing Action in Beverly Hills," May 10, 1998, p. K-1.

259　"a short siesta": "Death Call for Edward P. Ripley," *LAT*, Feb. 5, 1920, p. 11.

CHAPTER 29: SOROPTIMISTAS

260　"Never in their wildest expectations": *IND*, Feb. 15, 1919, p. 4.

261　"emptying garbage": "Society Serves Working Girls," *KCStar*, Feb. 6, 1919, p. 1.

261　"the newspapers never get hold of": *IND*, March 1, 1919, p. 6.

262　twelve hundred had reportedly quit: This comes from "A Shortage of Table Girls," an undated clipping reportedly found in the collection of Flora Alice Steele, a relative of the Harvey personnel manager Alice Steele, according to Stoll, "Harvey Girls Then, Now, and Forever," p. 71.

262　"a girl herself": This is noted in a profile of Steele: Frances L. Garside, "This Woman Hires All Girls for Fred Harvey Restaurants," *Hartford Courant*, May 13, 1923, p. SM6.

262　"The girls at a Fred Harvey Place": This is from a 1905 testimonial written by well-known orator Elbert Hubbard and originally published in his *Roycrofters* magazine—although later published by the railroad as a promotional piece. It is frequently referred to by historians as "Fred Harvey's eulogy," which it was not. In fact, it may have been something of an advertorial since, by that time in his career, Hubbard was taking some commissions for his over-the-top assessments of American phenomena. See Beisner, " 'Commune' in East Aurora."

263　"Today's girl is 'glorifying' ": See the profile of Steele: "Modern Business Girl Less Superficial Than First to Invade Field," *KCJP*, Nov. 20, 1927, n.p.

263　"A girl who is lonely": Garside, "This Woman Hires All Girls."

264　"I was dressed real nice": Stinelichner's story comes from her quotes in Poling-Kempes, *Harvey Girls*, p. 82 and p. 94.

264　"Silver City Millie": Background on Millie's story is from Evans, *Madam Millie*, pp. 13–24.

266　including one who is gay himself: Author correspondence with Arnold Berke.

266　clarity about her sexuality: Several living family members confirmed that Kitty was openly gay, especially the one who was closest to her, Byron "Ronny" Harvey III, who spent the most time with her and her girlfriends.

266　"Living Reproductions": Details from "Society in Picture Poses," *KCStar*, Sept. 17, 1911.

268　She was just a teenager: Many details on the life of Kitty Harvey, who was covered a lot in the society pages for her good works and travels, but almost never for her relationship to the Harvey company, come from the only long story ever published about her, "Publicity Shy Katherine Harvey, After Many Years of Doing Things for City, Now Permanent Resident," *Santa Barbara New Press*, Aug. 5, 1951, n.p., file RC39(11)949, HMC.

268　"We'll warm their trousers": Author interview with Ronny Harvey, Sept. 2, 2004, for this and the quotations about Kitty and Mary Perkins below.

268　linking him romantically: Information about the Drage family comes from myriad small stories in the Kansas City social newspaper, *IND* (most of which don't have titles, but just run as items), and a profile of Betty's mother, Lucy Christie Drage, in the *KCStar* on Sept. 22, 1929, p. 34 in the MVSC newspaper archive for that year.

269 "the rumor of pretty little Betty": *IND*, April 15, 1922, p. 4.

269 "got as far as the door": *IND*, April 29, 1922, p. 4.

269 "failed to cure": *IND*, July 1, 1922, p. 3.

270 "magnificent, with few duplicates": Report on the gifts and the thank-you notes is in *IND*, Sept. 9, 1922, p. 8.

270 "the big white stork": *IND*, Feb. 10, 1923, p. 3.

CHAPTER 30: THE ROAR OF THE TWENTIES

272 If you were a close friend: These parties were documented in a letter from Freddy's friend Frank Baker to Daggett Harvey Sr., March 1, 1976, DHC.

272 two silent pictures: Plot analysis of these two hard-to-see silent films comes from Leah Dilworth's provocative essay "Discovering Indians in Fred Harvey's Southwest," in Weigle and Babcock, *Great Southwest*, p. 159.

273 "The biggest thrill": Quoted in Poling-Kempes, *Harvey Girls*, p. 127.

273 "All the girls knew who he was": Opal Sells Hill, quoted in Ibid., p. 142.

273 "What's that Carole Lombard is wearing": "On the Side with E. V. Durling," *LAT*, Oct. 2, 1938.

274 "Diamond-Studded Toothbrush": The clipping—which is undated but presumably from the early fall of 1924, is in DHC, along with the exasperated letter that Ford wrote to Byron about it on Oct. 2, 1924.

275 company's bizarre battle: Details of Campbell Russell's crusade against Fred Harvey's jacket rule come primarily from coverage in the hometown *Daily Oklahoman* on Sept. 4 and 28, 1921, and the national coverage it generated (clippings of most of which are in HMC).

276 "discrimination": "State Commission Decrees Men May Eat Minus Coats," *Washington Post*, Sept. 16, 1921, p. 3.

276 "Women do as they please": "Man in Shirt Sleeves," *CT*, Sept. 17, 1921, p. 6.

276 "snobbery from England": "The Weekly Grouch," *Frederick (Okla.) Press*, Sept. 29, 1921, n.p.

276 "ruthless warfare": *Daily Oklahoman*, Sept. 4, 1921, p. 7.

276 "take all the dogs": *Hominy News*, Sept. 30, 1921.

276 "Unlike the lower animals": *Fred Harvey et al. v. Corporation Commission*, 1924 OK 716, 229, p. 428, 102 Okla. 266, case number 12963, decided Sept. 16, 1924, Supreme Court of Oklahoma.

277 even historic Delmonico's closed: For details on these closings, see "Delmonico's Ends Its Long Career," *NYT*, May 20, 1923, p. 1; and John Walker Harrington, "Death Marks the Cabarets," *NYT*, June 3, 1923, p. XX2.

277 locked away or sold off: Author interview with Stewart Harvey Jr.

278 innovate with food: For background on how food service changed during Prohibition, see Drowne and Huber, *1920s*, esp. pp. 129–35; Hogan, *Selling 'Em by the Sack:* and Langdon, *Orange Roofs, Golden Arches*.

278 "They're coming tonight": Advertisement in *LAT*, April 17, 1902, p. 5.

279 seven thousand employees: Noted by Ford in undated manuscript, presumably written in the early 1920s, apparently for *American Magazine*, UA, box 3, file 16, p. 3, HMC.

280 "I would rather be Alfred": From obituary, *KCStar*, Dec. 14, 1924, pp. 111–12 of MVSC bound volume.

280 head off to the local airfield: As he did in El Paso on June 21, 1922, as reported the next day in the *El Paso Times* in "Fred Harvey 'Hops Off' in Army Plane

for Sightseeing Trip of El Paso Shortly After Arrival" (which also noted that when he and Betty had dinner, the hotel orchestra "announced the naming of the 'Fred Harvey fox trot' in his honor and the restaurant baron was presented with an author's copy of the piece").

280 Byron had received a patent: It was patent number 1,491,234, issued April 22, 1924; a year later, he also patented a "Transcontinental Car," which was a club car with a central serving area allowing for separate first-class and tourist-class "lounging comfort," which was patent number 1,523,642. The scale model was described in author correspondence with Stewart Harvey Jr.

CHAPTER 31: SANTA FATED

282 "City Different": Tobias and Woodhouse, *Santa Fe,* p. 178.
282 R. Hunter Clarkson: The story of Clarkson and the beginnings of the Santa Fe operation are detailed in Thomas's obsessive *Southwestern Indian Detours.*
283 first practical process for freezing food: After Clarence Birdseye tried to get Fred Harvey and other companies to try his frozen concoctions, his company went bankrupt and was reorganized; it was later bought by the Postum conglomerate, which changed its name to the one Clarence had been using, General Foods.
283 shop for a suitable hotel: Noted in an unpublished family history by the historian Bertha Dutton, who also sat on the board of the Fred Harvey art trust, p. 25, LCHSC.
283 "Pullmans on wheels": Ibid.
284 Before departing: Judy Harvey's ill-fated trip to Detour country is re-created from "Death Comes Suddenly to Mrs. Harvey," *Santa Fe New Mexican,* July 22, 1926; "Late Mrs. Ford Harvey Was Daughter of Pioneer of Kansas; Bishop's Tribute," *Santa Fe New Mexican,* July 24, 1926; and "Mrs. Ford F. Harvey Dies," *KCStar,* July 22, 1926 (n.p., all from corporate clipping file in HMC).
285 to visit the Puye Cliff Dwellings: Published reports did not name the precise location they were visiting when Judy got sick, just that it was "an Indian Village forty miles from Santa Fe." Puye, which was on the Indian Detours, is the most likely site.
286 bleary-eyed: The time of death, and the fact that Ford was with her until the end, were reported in "Death Comes Suddenly to Mrs. Harvey."
286 "was as simple as that": "Mrs. Ford F. Harvey Dies."
287 government's first transcontinental: Route 66 was actually the second transcontinental highway—the first, privately funded, was the Lincoln Highway in 1913, which ran from New York to San Francisco, following the Union Pacific's route through Nebraska, Utah, and Nevada. Details on Route 66 history are from Olsen, *Route 66 Lost and Found,* p. 98. Interestingly, Route 66 was rerouted in 1938, and the new route bypassed Santa Fe, just as the railroad's High Iron had.

CHAPTER 32: A WONDERFUL LIVE TOY TO PLAY WITH

289 "The Southwest is the great": D. H. Lawrence, "Just Back from the Snake Dance—Tired Out," *Laughing Horse,* Sept. 1924, pp. 26–29.
290 "Indian detour couriers are smart girls": W. E. Hill, "The Great Southwest," *CT,* Nov. 24, 1929, p. D11.

291 "It takes so long": This essay appears in slightly different forms in different volumes (the best-known of which was more heavily edited by Edmund Wilson for *The Crack-Up*), but this is from the original typewritten and hand-edited manuscript in *Fitzgerald: My Lost City: Personal Essays, 1920–1940*, app. 1, p. 316 (which is typewritten page 13, first entry for 1927).

291 "Wild buffalo fed": While several historians have used edited recollections of this quote, from a handwritten scrapbook entry by Harvey Girl Opal Sells Hill, it did appear in "Mr. Rogers Waxes Enthusiastic over the Beauties of the West," *NYT*, May 13, 1931, p. 27, and is also in Smallwood and Gragert, *Will Rogers' Daily Telegrams*, telegrams for March 12, 1931, no. 1498, vol. 3, p. 26.

291 "The only test": Fisher, *From the Journals of M. F. K. Fisher*, pp. 167–69.

CHAPTER 33: POISED FOR TAKEOFF

295 Freddy Harvey was one of those: Freddy's day with Lindbergh is described in "Lindbergh 'Drops In' Again," *LAT*, April 12, 1928, p. 1.

295 the *Wall Street Journal* announced: "Form Transcontinental Air Transport Company," *Wall Street Journal*, May 16, 1938, p. 20.

296 "Air travel in the U.S.": "Train & Plane," *Time*, May 28, 1928.

297 first big golf game: "Southerner on Ticket Is Goal of Virginians," *Washington Post*, June 10, 1928, p. M4.

298 their teams finally met: Coverage of the match is in "Will Rogers Leads Team to Win Over Blues," *KCJP*, June 15, 1928, p. 8.

298 "Something *terrible* just happened": Break-in is re-created from coverage in "Detectives Rake Underworld for Harvey Intruder," *KCJP*, Oct. 5, 1928, p. 2-A; and "A Knife Bandit in Home," *KCT*, Oct. 5, 1928, p. 1.

300 frequent house calls: This observation is inferred from the original coverage, which said she was being treated "by a private physician," and observation of later probate records showing frequent house calls. At that time, a private doctor making private calls on a wealthy patient would have been fairly normal.

300 marriage had long been over: While coverage of the Drages never really acknowledged this, it is clear the couple never lived in the same place for the last five years of Colonel Drage's life. Also, author interview with Stewart Harvey Jr. Both the loan and the co-signing are mentioned in probate documents, probate no. 43,282, Probate Court of Jackson County at Kansas City.

300 "the greatest year": Quoted in Klingaman, *1929*, p. 54.

301 had grown astronomically: A conservative estimate was 88 percent growth in the number of restaurant and lunchroom keepers, according to *Recent Social Trends in the United States*, p. 668.

301 he was running: These tallies come from "Byron S. Harvey Becomes Head of the Fred Harvey System," *SFMag*, Feb. 1929, p. 44; details were also confirmed by corporate year-end report ledger books in JKC for 1931.

302 "How large can": Ford Harvey, unpublished manuscript, July 19, 1927, pp. 17–18, HMC.

CHAPTER 34: FORD HARVEY HAS A COLD

303 "Ford Harvey has": This re-creation of the scene of Ford realizing he is sick in his office is based on an author's visit to the office, which still looks very much

now as it did then; descriptions of the office culture from taped interviews with Stewart Harvey Sr. and author correspondence with Stewart Harvey Jr.; details from obituaries, especially "Ford Harvey Dead," *Santa Fe New Mexican*, Dec. 14, 1928; and an authorly nod to the canon of Gay Talese at *Esquire*.

304 "milder variety": "Flu Epidemic Spreading Fast," *LAT*, Dec. 12, 1928, p. 7.

304 He hired nurses: The nurses' names were in the Ford Harvey probate documents, including their paid bills, probate no. 31,671, Probate Court of Jackson County at Kansas City for 1929; which were also used to flesh out many other details of his treatment.

305 "progressing satisfactorily": "Ford Harvey Is Worse," *KCStar*, Dec. 13, 1928, p. D-14.

305 "Ford Harvey Nears Pneumonia": *KCJP*, Dec. 13, 1928, p. D-14.

305 Dr. Griffith recorded: As per death certificate, file no. 40,792, Missouri State Board of Health.

306 "I have lost an old friend": White's reactions to Ford's death, and those below it, are all quoted in "Ford Harvey, Worthy Son of a Worthy Sire, Taken by Death," *SFMag*, Jan. 1929, pp. 33–35.

307 "all forms of petting": "Taboo on Kissing Is Urged While Flu Epidemic Rages," *Washington Post*, Jan. 5, 1929, p. 5.

307 "In as few words": "Will of Ford Harvey," *KCStar*, Dec. 20, 1928.

307 "one of the shortest": "Harvey Children Receive All of $1,000,000 Estate," *KCJP*, Dec. 20, 1928; dollar amounts in the rest of this section are based on Ford Harvey probate documents.

308 the Christmas present Ford had chosen: Handwritten receipt from John Angel, dated Jan. 4, 1929, in the amount of $175 ($2,118), in Ford Harvey probate documents, along with request from Freddy for reimbursement on Jan. 12, 1929, since he paid for the delivery with a personal check.

309 "A Harvey should always be": Gertrude Benjamin Schloss to Amfac (the company that bought Fred Harvey in the mid-1970s), Jan. 10, 1976 (it was later forwarded to the Grand Canyon office and ended up in Amfac file, CLC).

309 Since Freddy and Kitty: The ownership stakes of the lucrative Union Station business are in the Harvey Hotel & Restaurant Company corporate meeting book, p. 79, DHC, which shows the stockholders as of Jan. 14, 1929.

CHAPTER 35: FREDDY SPREADS HIS WINGS

311 "You may not be able": Colter to Hunter Clarkson, Oct. 4, 1926, as quoted in Berke, *Mary Colter*, p. 162, which is also the source of other La Fonda design background.

312 "You never met": Pyle, *Home Country*, p. 76.

312 "the most beautiful hotel in America": De Beauvoir, *America Day by Day*, p. 186. This entry was for March 20, 1947, and went on to describe the scene at the hotel: "Around the patio there are cool galleries paved with mosaics and furnished in the Spanish style. In the lobby an Indian has, for years, been selling fake turquoise and petrified wood to the tourists. This small-time tradesman has a noble face sculpted with deep wrinkles, like an old chief in James Fenimore Cooper. The dining room is Mexican-style in decor, dress, and varied cuisine. And here we are, four French people gathered together by chance,

fraternizing around a table, just as travelers fraternized at roadside inns in old adventure novels."

312 "Airsickness is mental": "Meeting the Food Problems of Travelers Who Go by Air," *KCStar*, June 6, 1929, n.p., HMC.

313 Transcontinental Air Transport finally: Background on TAT from "The Lindbergh Line," *Aviation History*, July 2007, pp. 34–41; daily coverage in the *NYT* and *LAT*; and author interview on Aug. 5, 2008, with author Gore Vidal, the son of TAT executive Eugene Vidal, who provided much useful insight—along with some career advice for me. "Why are you writing about some caterer," he asked, "when my *father* is the real story?"

315 "showed no concern": "Air Passengers Transferred Owing to Mishap to Plane," *Hartford Courant*, July 10, 1929, p. 13.

315 "blood trickling from my tiny lobes": "Love of Flying," *New York Review of Books*, Jan. 17, 1985. Interestingly, the vivid first paragraph of this article—which is all that is available for free on Web searches—leads the reader to believe (and some journalists have rewritten) that Vidal was on the maiden flight of TAT. But a footnote, available only in the full text, appears to suggest that a fact-checker challenged this bit of Vidal family lore and, since the passenger lists for that first flight were widely published, was able to prove his memory false. But the lede of the essay wasn't changed.

316 "American Aviation Shall Be": From dedication book of the Columbus event, *Winged Victory*, p. 5.

316 "the American Century": This was the title of an essay Luce wrote in *Life*, Feb. 17, 1941.

CHAPTER 36: PAY NO ATTENTION TO THAT CRASHING SOUND

317 "Young man, I'm shielding": Collins, *Tales of an Old Air-Faring Man*, p. 110.

318 But the flight never arrived: Re-creation of the search for this plane is based on national coverage at the time but also the excellent two-part series by Richard Melzer in the *Valencia (N.M.) News-Bulletin:* "Greatest Airplane Search in Southwest Touched Off in Western Valencia County," March 25, 2006, and "No One Survived Crash in Rugged Terrain," April 1, 2006, both written with the help of the Valencia County Historical Society.

319 "a Railroad Problem": "Broad Street Gossip: A Railroad Problem," *Wall Street Journal*, Sept. 10, 1929, p. 2.

320 "We had one customer": Quoted in Poling-Kempes, *Harvey Girls*, p. 184.

321 "You've lost a wheel, sir": "F. H. Harvey in a Thriller," *KCStar*, March 16, 1930, n.p., company clipping file, HMC.

322 "homelike and livable": Memos on the Wellington wall debates found in the Santa Fe "Splinters" collection, a copy of which I read in the Russell Crump archive in Kansas City before Russell's untimely death. The memo with this phrase, near the end of the debate, was dated Oct. 12, 1937.

323 "Congratulations on the new": Grattan, *Mary Colter*, p. 67, citing her phone conversation with Harvey executive Harold Belt on Nov. 3, 1977.

324 railroad-rich Van Sweringen: Details on the brothers and their station are from Harwood, *Invisible Giants*.

325 "really the fronts of drawers": "Harvey Comes to Cleveland," *Publishers Weekly*, Aug. 16, 1930, pp. 585–87.

326 "Why does this magnificent applied science": "Einstein Sees Lack in Applying Science," *NYT,* Feb. 17, 1931, p. 6.

326 "What's his business?": "Einstein Is 'Great Relative,' Hopis Decide on His Theory," *NYT,* March 2, 1931, p. 5.

CHAPTER 37: LOAVES AND FISHES

327 "Of course we can": This scene is re-created from Bob O'Sullivan's wonderful piece, "It's 55 Years Late, but Thanks, Mr. Harvey, for the Memory," for the *CT* travel section, Dec. 11, 1988, p. 3.

328 started removing some links: This list of closures was compiled from datelines in the Fred Harvey and Santa Fe corporate archives, but also cross-checked against company ledgers in JKC.

329 "Those were tough times": Quoted in Poling-Kempes, *Harvey Girls,* p. 189.

330 "My waiter informed": Adam C. Powell Jr., "Soap Box: Without a White Massa Trouble Is Negligible," *Amsterdam News,* May 15, 1937, p. 22.

332 The two of them would sit: This scene is re-created from reporting in Kathy Howard's essay on Schweizer, "'A Most Remarkable Success,'" p. 93; and Berke, *Mary Colter,* pp. 190–93.

332 "a balcony-ringed, cave-like": Berke, *Mary Colter,* pp. 199–205, which is also the source for the descriptions below.

333 "the bulkiness of this manual": Colter, *Manual for Drivers and Guides.*

CHAPTER 38: HEIR RAISING

334 "In the 1930s": Author correspondence with Stewart Harvey Jr.

335 "put yourself in my position": Anecdote from Htapes, no. 6, side A.

335 "I am enclosing": Byron Harvey to his three sons, Oct. 15, 1923, SHC.

336 "Trust you will have": Byron Harvey Jr. to Stewart Harvey Sr., telegram, June 2, 1931, SHC.

337 So Minnie and Freddy both: Author email correspondence with Stewart Harvey Jr.

337 he openly defied Minnie: Author interview with Byron "Ronny" Harvey III, at which he produced his original birth certificate.

338 "Mrs. Frederick Harvey Here": *Chicago American,* Jan. 14, 1933, n.p., clipping found in scrapbook in Santa Fe Harvey family compound, which was kept by Mrs. Stewart Harvey Sr., SHC.

339 "to cooperate with other officers": "A Wider Harvey System," *KCStar,* Feb. 27, 1933, n.p., company clipping file, HMC.

339 "I try to follow the teachings": "David Benjamin Is Dead," *KCJP,* May 8, 1933, n.p., family scrapbook file, AKC.

339 "who has had his share": "David Benjamin Telephones Calmly as Earthquake Showers Plaster," *KCJP,* March 12, 1933, n.p., Harvey company clipping file, HMC.

339 clutching his chest: Details of Benjamin's death are in "Kansas City Mourns Loss of David Benjamin," *Kansas City Jewish Chronicle,* May 12, 1933, p. 1.

341 "Let 'em have it": Richetti, "Famous Cases" (based on FBI's own files).

342 "Wild Dash Rouzer": "Harvey Girls," *KCStar,* Feb. 17, 1946.

343 "The thirty-six freight": Quoted in Poling-Kempes, *Harvey Girls,* p. 184.

CHAPTER 39: GREAT EXPECTATIONS

344 "One day while zooming": *Mademoiselle* magazine story quoted in *IND*, Jan. 4, 1936, n.p., Harvey clipping file, HMC.

345 "Be a Tail Wagger": From "Blue-Blooded Tail Waggers Aid 'Poor,' " undated clip from unknown paper, probably fall of 1932, found in Daggett Harvey Sr.'s Frederick Harvey clipping file, DHC.

345 photographed holding her: "Susanna Arrives for Blessed Event," *KCJP,* Feb. 9, 1934, n.p., Harvey company clipping file, HMC.

345 "I always wondered": Htapes, no. 8, side B.

345 "They fought a lot": Author correspondence with Stewart Harvey Jr.

345 "camping and wandering": "Back from a Trip to Remote Country of Cliff Dwellers," *KCStar,* Nov. 22, 1932, p. 4.

346 "Away my knaves": Entire duck press scene is re-created from untitled *KCJP* article, Oct. 31, 1934, n.p., p. 36 of the historical clippings file for "Union Station Restaurant," MVSC.

347 pulled fifty carloads of sugar: Htapes, no. 2, side A.

349 "took a special interest": "Mr. and Mrs. Frederick H. Harvey Killed in Crash of Private Plane," *Santa Fe Magazine,* June 1936, p. 9.

350 On her arrival, Betty went: Betty's trip to England is re-created based on Freddy Harvey probate documents, Probate Court of Jackson County at Kansas City; author interviews with Elizabeth Drage Pettifer, for whose birth Betty went to England; and author correspondence, Aug. 14, 2007, with Mary S. Goodman, the daughter of Harold Furness, the doctor who arranged for Betty to consult with Dr. Dearnley.

351 she had Norah Crampton: Crampton's multipage bill is document no. 43,282 in the Freddy Harvey probate file, Probate Court of Jackson County at Kansas City.

CHAPTER 40: TAILSPIN

354 She and Freddy stayed over: The couple's last visit to New York is re-created from obituaries but especially "Fred Harvey Spent Pleasant Week-End Here," *New York Journal,* April 20, 1936, Daggett Harvey Sr. clipping file, DHC.

354 The next morning, the Harveys took off: Their fateful flight is re-created from obituaries, especially "Blast in the Air," *KCT,* April 20, 1936; and the Bureau of Air Commerce report on the crash, "Statement of Probable Cause Concerning an Accident Which Occurred to a Privately Owned Airplane near Dunlo, Pennsylvania, on April 19, 1936" (report dated June 11, 1936, no. 10,574), signed by Eugene Vidal. I also interviewed several contemporary Staggerwing flyers, including Paul Tollini and American Airlines pilot Bill Plecenik, who were given copies of the government report and eyewitness reports to help create the most probable scenario for what happened in the cockpit.

356 "It looks bad": "Blast in the Air."

357 "Plane Crash Nightmare": *Johnstown Democrat,* April 20, 1936, p. 1.

357 "Martha said to Jesus": "To the Grave Together," *KCStar,* April 23, 1936, reported on what was read at the funeral.

358 "my epochal ride": Howard Vincent O'Brien, "All Things Considered," *Chicago Daily News*, April 29, 1936, n.p., company clipping file, HMC.

CHAPTER 41: KITTY BLINKS

360 Lucy Drage, sued Kitty: The re-creation of this legal action comes from *KCJP* and *KCStar* coverage from when the suit was settled in April 1937 and author interview with Kansas City attorney Frank Sebree II, who recalled his father's representation of Lucy Drage in the lawsuit.

361 nothing compared to the horror show: The re-creation of the internal struggles of the Harvey family over ownership is based on "It Happened in Kansas City," *KCStar*, April 1, 1949, which discussed the situation; taped interview with Stewart Harvey Sr., who discussed the situation in some detail; author interviews with Stewart Harvey Jr. and Daggett Harvey Jr., who shared recollections of what their fathers told them; and author interviews with Byron Harvey III and Joy Harvey, who shared recollections of what Kitty herself told them. Valuations come from corporate ledgers in JKC and Freddy Harvey probate documents.

364 "It was important": Htapes, no. 8, side A.

365 "it was done the proper way": Author interview with Daggett Harvey Jr.

365 more likely as much as $3 million: Estimate based on the money actually changing hands in 1938, which is most likely; Joy Harvey recalled hearing the higher estimate. Some of the paperwork from the final transaction is in a small, five-by-eleven expanding file, with advertising from turn-of-the-century financial firms, hand marked "Valuable Papers B. S. Harvey," in DHC, including an envelope of Fred Harvey stationery containing letters from the summer of 1936 showing preliminary changes in the company stock owned by Kitty.

365 "She didn't like to speak": Author interview with Byron Harvey III.

366 "Not that it's any": Author correspondence with Stewart Harvey Jr.

366 "simply refused": Hugh Gardner, "Saga of Tim W. Cooper," scrapbook, DHC.

367 "The Howard Johnson vogue": Advertisement in *Hartford Courant*, May 28, 1938.

CHAPTER 42: PRIVATE PRINGLE TO THE RESCUE

369 "with the greatest respect": Rankin to Byron Harvey on Major Pictures Corporation stationery, misdated Oct. 22, 1926 (but marked received at Fred Harvey offices in Chicago Oct. 24, 1936). Found in the voluminous files of a lawsuit between Fred Harvey and the owners of a Philadelphia restaurant called Harvey House, JKC.

369 *Susannah Was a Lady:* Original titles and stars from the file of a lawsuit against the film company by the author of a magazine story, who claimed the movie was based on his piece. See *Funkhouser v. Lowe's, Inc.*, United States Court of Appeals, Eighth Circuit, 208 F.2d 185, Dec. 11, 1953. Rehearing denied Jan. 5, 1954, paragraph 5; also, George H. Reed to Byron Harvey, Nov. 7, 1936, Harold Belt file on Harvey Girls movie, CLC.

369 "perfectly legitimate": Head to Byron Harvey Jr., Nov. 11, 1936, and Byron Harvey Jr. to Byron Harvey Sr., Nov. 12, 1936, Harold Belt file, CLC.

370 revolutionary china pattern: Information on Mimbreño from Richard Luckin's exhaustive *Mimbres to Mimbreño.*

371 "newest rendezvous in town": "Hedda Hopper's Hollywood," *LAT,* May 17, 1939, p. 12.

371 "a rolling nightmare": Bryant, *History of the Atchison, Topeka, and Santa Fe Railway,* p. 336.

372 "The newspaper announced": *Emporia Daily Gazette,* Jan. 31, 1940, p. 4.

374 "I have a hunch": Kennedy, *Samuel Hopkins Adams and the Business of Writing,* p. 205, citing Adams's papers and Bennett Cerf's book *At Random* (a memoir that, on p. 170, gives the impression that Cerf conjured the idea of the Harvey Girls book himself, unprompted by the movie project, after a meeting with Byron). Kennedy's book also is the source for material about the writer's dealings with the Harveys.

376 "It really changed the Harvey standard": Quoted in Poling-Kempes, *Harvey Girls,* pp. 198–99.

377 specify "colored" seating: Author interview with Russell Crump as we looked at these blueprints in his archive.

377 "Although they hired": Quoted in Poling-Kempes, *Harvey Girls,* p. 198.

378 "Victory will come SOONER": At bottom of "KP? Not for Private Pringle!" advertisement in *Life,* Dec. 20, 1943, p. 57.

CHAPTER 43: THE SPIES AT LA FONDA

381 "I just put it in my pocket": Quoted in Rhodes, *The Making of the Atomic Bomb,* p. 477.

382 "electromagnetic gun": Conant, *109 East Palace,* p. 131.

382 "Every once in a while": Badash, Hirschfelder, and Broida, *Reminiscences of Los Alamos,* p. 86.

CHAPTER 44: BIG HOLLYWOOD ENDING

384 "a nice, lyrical quality to it": Furia, *Skylark,* p. 156.

385 They planned to oversee the picture: The behind-the-scenes micromanagement of the picture by Byron is re-created from company correspondence and author interview with film historian John Fricke, who also did the excellent liner notes to the 1996 rerelease of the film's complete soundtrack.

386 "Does anybody understand": Quoted in Fricke, liner notes, p. 5.

387 "They're going to make me look like an *idiot*": Furia, *Skylark,* p. 156.

388 "there will be no slip-up": Byron Harvey to "Mr. Wendell," memo, June 1, 1945, CLC.

389 "Now we are all sons of bitches": Quoted in Rhodes, *The Making of the Atomic Bomb,* p. 675.

389 "Hiroshima has been destroyed": Quoted in Rhodes, Ibid., p. 735.

EPILOGUE

392 They got as far as Gallup: This sad trip, the end of the Fred Harvey eating house empire, was recounted by eyewitness Harry Briscoe in my correspondence with him, and also in his book, *Watching the Trains Go By.*

393   "Beef stew? For God's sake!": This quote recounted in Broggie, *Walt Disney's Railroad Story*, p. 62; this book, with in-depth interviews with Kimball, was a primary source for this section, esp. pp. 51–66.

394   "I can't figure out why": Ibid., p. 68.

395   "Mortimer is too pompous": Ibid., p. 67.

395   "Mickey Mouse Park": Ibid., p. 88.

396   "an almost destructive": Author interview with Daggett Harvey Jr.

397   "shore it up": Author correspondence with Stewart Harvey Jr.

398   "There is such a thing": Grattan, *Mary Colter*, p. 111.

APPENDIX I

400   "This new blue streak": *Emporia Gazette*, May 13, 1936.

400   "When the railroad connected": Poling-Kempes, *Harvey Girls*, p. 184.

407   if you want a room at El Tovar: The phone number is 888-297-2757. Start dialing *now*. And don't be discouraged, because for the first hour or two, it's mostly people trying to reserve the handful of rooms at the floor of the canyon at Phantom Ranch. If you get through in the first two or three hours, you'll probably get what you want.

BIBLIOGRAPHY

Adair, John. *The Navajo and Pueblo Silversmiths.* Norman: University of Oklahoma Press, 1944.

Additon, Henrietta A. "Work Among Delinquent Women and Girls." *War Relief Work* 79 (1918).

Albright, Horace M., and Marian A. Schenck. *Creating the National Park Service: The Missing Years.* Norman: University of Oklahoma Press, 1999.

Amsden, Charles A. *Navaho Weaving, Its Technic and History.* Albuquerque: University of New Mexico Press, 1949.

Babcock, Barbara. "A New Mexican 'Rebecca': Imaging Pueblo Women." *Journal of the Southwest* 32 (1990).

Badash, Lawrence, Joseph O. Hirschfelder, and Herbert P. Broida. *Reminiscences of Los Alamos.* Boston: Reidel, 1980.

Bain, David. *Empire Express: Building the First Transcontinental Railroad.* New York: Viking, 1999.

Bancroft, Frederic. *Slave-Trading in the Old South.* Baltimore: J. H. Furst Company, 1931.

Barry, John M. *The Great Influenza: The Epic Story of the Deadliest Plague in History.* New York: Penguin, 2005.

Beard, George M. "The Nature and Treatment of Neurasthenia (Nervous Exhaustion), Hysteria, Spinal Irritation, and Allied Neuroses." *Medical Letter* 12 (1877).

———. "Neurasthenia or Nervous Exhaustion." *Boston Medical and Surgical Journal* 3, no. 13 (1869).

———. *A Practical Treatise on Nervous Exhaustion (Neurasthenia): Its Symptoms, Nature, Sequences, Treatment.* 2nd ed. New York: E. B. Treat, 1888.

———. *Practical Treatise on Nervous Exhaustion.* 3rd ed. New York: E. B. Treat, 1894.

Beebe, Lucius. *High Iron: A Book of Trains.* New York: D. Appleton-Century, 1938.

———. *Mansions on Rails.* Berkeley, Calif.: Howell-North, 1959.

———. *Mr. Pullman's Elegant Palace Car.* Garden City, N.Y.: Doubleday, 1961.

Beisner, Robert L. " 'Commune' in East Aurora." *American Heritage* 22 (1971).

Berke, Arnold. *Mary Colter: Architect of the Southwest.* New York: Princeton Architectural Press, 2002.

"Billy the Kid, Making of a Hero." *Western Folklore* 32, no. 2 (April 1973).

Bingham, Hiram. *An Explorer in the Air Service.* New Haven, Conn.: Yale University Press, 1920.

Blanchard, Leola H. *Conquest of Southwest Kansas: A History and Thrilling Stories of Frontier Life in the State of Kansas.* Wichita, Kans.: Wichita Eagle Press, 1931.

Blomberg, Nancy J. *Navajo Textiles: The William Randolph Hearst Collection.* Tucson: University of Arizona Press, 1988.

Bokovoy, Matthew F. *The San Diego World's Fairs and Southwestern Memory, 1880–1940.* Albuquerque: University of New Mexico Press, 2005.

Bowman, Jon, ed. *Montezuma: The Castle in the West.* Santa Fe, N.M.: New Mexico Magazine, 2002.

Brey, William. "Carbutt and the Union Pacific's Grand Excursion to the 100th Meridian." *Stereo World,* May–June 1980.

Briscoe, Harry. *Watching the Trains Go By: A Narrative of a Santa Fe Railway Man.* Midwest City, Okla.: Santa Fe Railway Historical and Modeling Society, 2005.

Brodsky, Alyn. *Grover Cleveland: A Study in Character.* New York: St. Martin's, 2000.

Broggie, Michael. *Walt Disney's Railroad Story: The Small-Scale Fascination That Led to a Full-Scale Kingdom.* Pasadena, Calif.: Pentrex, 1997.

Brown, Karen A., and Nancy L. Hyer. "Archeological Benchmarking: Fred Harvey and the Service Profit Chain, Circa 1876." *Journal of Operations Management* 25 (2007).

Brown, Michael F. *Who Owns Native Culture?* Cambridge, Mass.: Harvard University Press, 2004.

Bryant, Keith L. "The Atchison, Topeka, and Santa Fe Railway and the Development of the Taos and Santa Fe Art Colonies." *Western Historical Quarterly* 9 (1978).

———. *History of the Atchison, Topeka, and Santa Fe Railway.* New York: Macmillan, 1974.

Cerf, Bennett. *At Random.* New York: Random House, 2002.

Chappell, Gordon. *The Railway at Grand Canyon.* San Francisco: National Park Service, 1986.

Chicago, Burlington & Quincy Railroad. "Centennial of First U.S. Railway Car." Press release, June 15, 1962.

Collins, Paul F. *Tales of an Old Air-Faring Man: A Half Century of Incidents, Accidents, and Providence, the Reminiscences of Paul F. Collins.* Stevens Point, Wis.: UWSP Foundation Press, 1983.

Colter, Mary. *Manual for Drivers and Guides Descriptive of the Indian Watchtower at Desert View and Its Relations, Architecturally, to the Prehistory Ruins of the Southwest.* Grand Canyon National Park, Ariz.: Fred Harvey, 1933.

Conant, Jennet. *109 East Palace.* New York: Simon and Schuster, 2005.

Crumbine, Samuel. *Frontier Doctor: The Autobiography of a Pioneer on the Frontier of Public Health.* Philadelphia: Dorrance, 1948.

Cullinan, Gerald. *The United States Postal Service.* New York: Praeger, 1973.

Curtin, Patricia. "Fred Harvey Company Public Relations and Publicity (1876–1933)." *Journal of Communication Management,* 12, no. 4 (2008).

Cutler, William G., ed. *History of the State of Kansas.* Chicago: A. T. Andreas, 1883.

de Beauvoir, Simone. *America Day by Day.* Berkeley: University of California Press, 2000.

Drowne, Kathleen M., and Patrick Huber. *The 1920s.* Westport, Conn.: Greenwood, 2004.

Dyer, Frank L., and Thomas C. Martin. *Edison: His Life and Inventions.* New York: Harper & Brothers, 1910.

Evans, Max. *Madam Millie: Bordellos from Silver City to Ketchikan.* Albuquerque: University of New Mexico Press, 2004.

Falconer, Martha P. "The Segregation of Delinquent Women and Girls as a War Problem." *Annals of the American Academy of Political and Social Sciences* 79 (1918).

Fergusson, Erna. *Our Southwest.* New York: Knopf, 1940.

Ferrell, Robert H. *Harry S. Truman: A Life.* Columbia: University of Missouri Press, 1996.

Finck, Henry T. *Food and Flavor.* New York: Harper & Brothers, 1913.

Fisher, M. F. K. *From the Journals of M. F. K. Fisher.* New York: Pantheon, 1999.

Fitzgerald, F. Scott, and James West (editor). *My Lost City: Personal Essays 1920–1940* (The Cambridge Edition of the Works of F. Scott Fitzgerald V. 4). Cambridge: Cambridge University Press, 2005.

Fred Harvey Company. *El Tovar: Grand Canyon of Arizona.* 1909.

Fricke, John. Liner notes. *Harvey Girls.* 1996.

Furia, Philip. *Skylark: The Life and Times of Johnny Mercer.* New York: St. Martin's, 2003.

Giles, Frye W. *Thirty Years in Topeka: A Historical Sketch.* Topeka, Kans.: G. W. Crane, 1886.

Gould, Emerson W. *Fifty Years on the Mississippi; or, Gould's History of River Navigation.* Saint Louis: Nixon-Jones, 1889.

Grattan, Virginia L. *Mary Colter: Builder upon the Red Earth.* Flagstaff, Ariz.: Northland Press, 1980.

Hahn, Emily. "Till the Well Runs Dry." *New Yorker,* Oct. 23, 1965.

Harvey, Fred. *Hospitality by Fred Harvey Cookbook.*

"Harvey House History." City of Florence, Kansas. www.florenceks.com/text/local/local_hh-history.htm.

Harwood, Herbert H. *Invisible Giants: The Empires of Cleveland's Van Sweringen Brothers.* Bloomington: Indiana University Press, 2002.

Haywood, C. R. *Trails South: The Wagon-Road Economy in the Dodge City–Panhandle Region.* Meade, Kans.: Prairie Books, 2006.

Heineke, Janelle, and Mark M. Davis. "The Emergence of Service Operations Management as an Academic Discipline." *Journal of Operations Management* 24 (2007).

Henderson, Harold L. "Frederick Henry Harvey." Master's thesis, University of Kansas City, 1942.

Henderson, James D. "Meals by Fred Harvey: A Phenomenon of the American West." Master's thesis, University of Arizona, 1965.

Hines, Walker D. *War History of American Railroads.* New Haven: Yale University Press, 1978.

Hogan, David G. *Selling 'Em by the Sack: White Castle and the Creation of American Food.* New York: New York University Press, 1997.

Howard, Kathleen L. " 'A Most Remarkable Success': Herman Schweizer and the Fred Harvey Indian Department." In *The Great Southwest of the Fred Harvey Company and the Santa Fe Railway.* Edited by Marta Weigle and Barbara A. Babcock. Phoenix: Heard Museum, 1996.

Howard, Kathleen L., and Diana F. Pardue. *Inventing the Southwest: The Fred Harvey Company and Native American Art.* Flagstaff, Ariz.: Northland, 1996.

Howes, Cecil. "Pistol Packin' Pencil Pushers." *Kansas Historical Quarterly* 13, no. 2 (1944).

Hughes, Johnson D., and Timothy J. Priehs. *In the House of Stone and Light: A Human History of the Grand Canyon.* Grand Canyon, Ariz.: Grand Canyon Natural History Association, 1978.

Hughes, J. P. *Fort Leavenworth: Gateway to the West.* Topeka, Kans.: Kansas City Historical Society, 2000.

Hungerford, Edward. "The Dining Room That Is Two Thousand Miles Long." MS.

Ingham, John N. *Biographical Dictionary of American Business Leaders.* Westport, Conn.: Greenwood, 1983.

Jarman, Rufus. "Big Boom in Boston." *American Heritage* 20, no. 6 (1969).

Johnson, Emory R., and Thurman W. Van Metre. *Principles of Railroad Transportation*. New York: D. Appleton and Company, 1919.

Jones, Billy M. *Health-Seekers in the Southwest, 1817–1900*. Norman: University of Oklahoma Press, 1967.

Kansas: A Cyclopedia of State History, Embracing Events, Institutions, Industries, Counties, Cities, Towns, Prominent Persons, etc. Vol. 3. Chicago: Standard Publishing, 1912.

Kearny County Historical Society. *History of Kearny County, Kansas*. Lakin, Kans., 1964–.

Kennedy, Samuel V. *Samuel Hopkins Adams and the Business of Writing*. Syracuse, N.Y.: Syracuse University Press, 1909.

Klingaman, William K. *1929: The Year of the Great Crash*. New York: Harper & Row, 1989.

Kurlansky, Mark. *The Big Oyster: History on the Half Shell*. New York: Ballantine Books, 2006.

Langdon, Philip. *Orange Roofs, Golden Arches: The Architecture of American Chain Restaurants*. New York: Knopf, 1986.

Laroche, Michel, and H. G. Parsa. "Brand Management in Hospitality: An Empirical Test of the Brisoux-Laroche Model." *Journal of Hospitality and Tourism Research* 24 (2000).

Larson, Erik. *Isaac's Storm*. New York: Crown, 1999.

———. *Devil in the White City*. New York: Crown, 2003.

Leavenworth City Directory. 1865–1890.

Leyendecker, Liston E. *Palace Car Prince*. Niwot: University Press of Colorado, 1992.

Loudon, Irvine. *Death in Childbirth: An International Study of Maternal Care and Maternal Mortality, 1800–1950*. New York: Oxford University Press, 1992.

Luckin, Richard. *Mimbres to Mimbreño: A Study of Santa Fe's Famous China Pattern*. Golden, Colo.: RK, 1992.

Marshall, James L. *Santa Fe: The Railroad That Built an Empire*. New York: Random House, 1945.

McAdoo, William G. *Crowded Years: The Reminiscences of William G. McAdoo*. Boston: Houghton Mifflin, 1931.

Meehan, Charles. *The Laws and Practice of the Game of Euchre as Adopted by the Washington, D.C., Euchre Club, by a Professor, One of the Oldest and Most Noted Euchre Players in the United States*. Philadelphia: T. B. Peterson and Brothers, 1877.

Millbrook, Minnie D. "Fred Harvey and the Santa Fe." *The Santa Fe in Topeka, Bulletin of the Shawnee County Historical Society*, no. 56 (1979).

Moore, Henry M. *Early History of Leavenworth City and County*. Leavenworth, Kans.: Samuel Dodsworth Book Co., 1906.

Morse, Charles F. *A Sketch of My Life*. Cambridge, Mass.: Riverside Press, 1927.

Neumann, Mark. *On the Rim: Looking for the Grand Canyon*. Minneapolis: University of Minnesota Press, 1999.

New York City Landmarks Preservation Commission. *Landmarks Preservation Commission Report*. 1994.

Oberholtzer, Ellis P. *A History of the United States Since the Civil War*. New York: Macmillan, 1917–37.

Olsen, Russell A. *Route 66 Lost and Found: Ruins and Relics Revisited*. St. Paul: Voyageur Press, 2006.

Petersen, William J. *Steamboating on the Upper Mississippi*. N. Chelmsford, Mass.: Courier Dover Publications, 1996.

Phillips, David. *The Taming of the West*. Chicago: Regnery, 1974.
————. *The West: An American Experience*. Chicago: Regnery, 1973.
Poling-Kempes, Lesley. *The Harvey Girls: Women Who Opened the West*. New York: Paragon House, 1989.
Porterfield, James D. *Dining by Rail: The History and the Recipes of America's Golden Age of Railroad Cuisine*. New York: St. Martin's Griffin, 1998.
Portrait and Biographical Record of Leavenworth, Douglas, and Franklin Counties, Kansas. Chicago: Chapman, 1899.
Post, Emily. *By Motor to the Golden Gate*. New York: D. Appleton, 1916.
Prerau, David. *Seize the Daylight: The Curious and Contentious Story of Daylight Saving Time*. New York: Thunder's Mouth Press, 2006.
Proceedings of the National Parks Conference . . . 1911, 1912, 1915, 1917. Washington, D.C.: Government Printing Office, 1912, 1913, 1916, 1918.
Purcell-Guild, June. "Study of One Hundred and Thirty-one Delinquent Girls Held at the Juvenile Detention Home in Chicago, 1917." *Journal of the American Institute of Criminal Law and Criminology* 10 (1919).
Pyle, Ernie. *Home Country*. New York: William Sloane Associates, 1947.
Pyne, Stephen. *How the Canyon Became Grand*. New York: Viking, 1998.
Recent Social Trends in the United States: Report of the President's Research Committee on Social Trends. New York: McGraw-Hill, 1933.
Rezneck, Samuel. "Distress Relief and Discontent in the United States During the Depression of 1873–1878." *Journal of Political Economy* 58 (1950).
Rhodes, Richard. *The Making of the Atomic Bomb*. New York: Simon and Schuster, 1986.
Richetti, Adam C. "Famous Cases: Kansas City Massacre: Charles Arthur 'Pretty Boy' Floyd: Consipracy to Deliver a Federal Prisoner." www.fbi.gov/libref/historic/famcases/floyd/floyd.htm.
Roberts, Gary L. *Doc Holliday: The Life and Legend*. Hoboken, N.J.: John Wiley and Sons, 2007.
Roy, William, and Phillip Bonacich. "Interlocking Directorates and Communities of Interest Among American Railroad Companies, 1905." *American Sociology Review* (1988).
Rydell, Robert W. *All the World's a Fair: Visions of Empire at American International Expositions, 1876–1916*. Chicago: University of Chicago Press, 1987.
Schafer, Mike, Joe Welsh, and Kevin J. Holland. *The American Passenger Train*. St. Paul: MBI, 2001.
Schermerhorn, Richard, Jr. *Schermerhorn Genealogy and Family Chronicles*. New York: Tobias A. Wright, 1914.
Schwartz, Jason. "Fighting Words: Pistol Packin' Dan Anthony and Frontier Journalism." Master's thesis, University of Pennsylvania, 2007.
Seymour, Silas. *Incidents of a Trip Through the Great Platte Valley, to the Rocky Mountains and Laramie Plains, in the Fall of 1866, with a Synoptical Statement of the Various Pacific Railroads, and an Account of the Great Union Pacific Railroad Excursion to the One Hundredth Meridian of Longitude*. New York: D. Van Nostrand, 1867.
Shand-Tucci, Douglass. *The Crimson Letter: Harvard, Homosexuality, and the Shaping of American Culture*. New York: St. Martin's, 2003.
Sheppard, Carl. *Montezuma: A Biography of a Building*. San Rafael, Calif.: Patricia H. Sheppard, 2002.
Smalley, Eugene V. *History of the Northern Pacific Railroad*. New York: G. P. Putnam's Sons, 1883.

Smallwood, James M., and Steven K. Gragert, eds. *Will Rogers' Daily Telegrams.* Vol. 3. Stillwater: Oklahoma State University Press, 1979.

Snead, James E. *Ruins and Rivals: The Making of Southwest Archaeology.* Tucson: University of Arizona Press, 2001.

Stanton, Elizabeth C. *The Concise History of Woman Suffrage.* Edited by Mari Jo Buhle and Paul Buhle. Urbana: University of Illinois Press, 1978.

Stechschulte, Nancy S. *The Detroit Publishing Company Postcards: A Handbook for Collectors of the Detroit Publishing Company Postcards Including Checklists of the Regular Numbers, Contracts, Harveys, Miscellaneous Art Cards, the 50,000 Series, Sets, Little Phostint Journeys, Mechanical Postcards, the Panoramas, and Many Others.* Big Rapids, Mich.: N. S. Stechschulte, 1994.

Stephen, Leslie, and Sidney Lee. *The Dictionary of National Biography Founded in 1882 by George Smith.* London: Oxford University Press, 1937.

Stoll, Judith A. "Harvey Girls Then, Now, and Forever." Master's thesis, Emporia State University, 1995.

Stone, Richard D. *The Interstate Commerce Commission and the Railroad Industry.* New York: Praeger, 1991.

The Stranger's Guide Around New York and Its Vicinity. New York, 1853.

Street, George. *Che! Wah! Wah!* Rochester, N.Y.: E. R. Andrews, 1883.

Streeter, F. B. "Ellsworth as a Texas Cattle Market." *Kansas Historical Quarterly* 4, no. 4 (1935).

Taylor, David G. "Boom Town Leavenworth: The Failure of the Dream." *Kansas Historical Quarterly* 38, no. 4 (1972).

Thomas, Diane. *The Southwestern Indian Detours.* Phoenix: Hunter, 1978.

Thompson, Mark. *American Character: The Curious Life of Charles Fletcher Lummis and the Rediscovery of the Southwest.* New York: Arcade, 2001.

Thornton, J. K. "Treatment of Uterine Fibro-myoma." *Lancet,* Nov. 6, 1886.

Tobias, Henry J., and Charles E. Woodhouse. *Santa Fe: A Modern History, 1890–1990.* Albuquerque: University of New Mexico Press, 2001.

Trombley, Stephen. *Sir Frederick Treves: The Extra-ordinary Edwardian.* London: Routledge, 1989.

Turner, Frederick J. "The Significance of the Frontier in American History." *Proceedings of the State Historical Society of Wisconsin* (1893).

Twain, Mark. *Roughing It.* Edited by Franklin R. Rogers. Berkeley: University of California Press, 1972.

Tye, Larry. *Rising from the Rails: Pullman Porters and the Making of the Black Middle Class.* New York: Henry Holt, 2004.

Waters, Frank. *Masked Gods: Navaho and Pueblo Ceremonialism.* Chicago: Swallow Press, 1950.

Waters, L. L. *Steel Trails to Santa Fe.* Lawrence: University of Kansas Press, 1950.

Weigle, Marta, and Barbara A. Babcock, eds. *The Great Southwest of the Fred Harvey Company and the Santa Fe Railway.* Phoenix: Heard Museum, 1996.

White, John H. *The American Railroad Passenger Car.* Baltimore: Johns Hopkins University Press, 1985.

"Wild Bill." *Harper's New Monthly Magazine,* Feb. 1867.

Wilkins, Thurman. *Thomas Moran: Artist of the Mountains.* Norman: University of Oklahoma Press, 1998.

Wright, Robert M. *Dodge City: The Cowboy Capital and the Great Southwest in the Days of the Wild Indian, the Buffalo, the Cowboy, Dance Halls, Gambling Halls, and Bad Men.* Wichita, Kans.: Wichita Eagle Press, 1913.

INDEX

Familial relationships to Fred Harvey appear in parentheses following names.

PHOTO CREDITS

Page iv: Detroit Publishing/Fred Harvey postcard courtesy of Michael McMillan (MM)

Page v: courtesy of Helen Harvey Mills (HHM)

Page xx: Norman Forsyth photograph courtesy of the David R. Phillips Collection (DPC)

Page 1: courtesy of Daggett Harvey Jr. Collection (DHC)

Page 170: Special Collections/University of Arizona Library/Fred Harvey Collection/ Box 5 Folder 5 Print 5-5-1

Page 171: Peyton-Strauss studio, Kansas City; courtesy of Stewart Harvey, Jr. Collection (SHC)

INSERT 1

Page 1: 1: HHM; 2: courtesy of Leavenworth County Historical Society (LCHS); 3: HHM; 4: DHC; 5: DPC

Pages 2–3: 1: LCHS; 2: LCHS; 3: courtesy of Fort Wallace Museum; 4: HHMC; 5: courtesy of Kansas State Historical Society (DSHS); 6: DHC; 7: KSHS; 8: courtesy of Jere Krakow Collection (JKC)

Pages 4–5: 1: Florence Harvey House Museum Collection (FHHC); 2: DPL; 3: Richard Lukin Collection; 4: courtesy Palace of the Governors Photo Archives (NMHM/DCA) #127376; 5: HHM; 6: HHMC; 7: KSHS; 8: KSHS; 9: FHHC; 10: DHC

Pages 6–7: 1: Ann Kander Collection; 2: JKC; 3: HHMC; 4: JKC; 5: Gordon Chappell Collection/Denver Public Library (GCC-DPL; 3: Denver Public Library Collection (DPL); 4: courtesy Palace of the Governors Photo Archives (NMHM/DCA) #14292; 5: HHM

INSERT 2

Page 1: 1: photo by G. L. Rose, Grand Canyon National Park Museum Collection (GCNP); 2: SHC; 3: photo by Charles Lummis, courtesy of Braun Research Library/Autry National Center (BRL); 4: DPL; 5: Charles Lummis Collection, BRL

Pages 2–3: 1: HHM; 2: Fred Harvey Collection GCNP; 3: Mary Larkin Smith Collection GCNP; 4: GCC-DPL; 5: GCC-DPL; 6: Theodore Roosevelt Collection/Harvard College Library; 7: DPL; 8: Fred Harvey Collection GCNP; 9: KSHS; 10: DPL

Pages 4–5: 1: MM; 2: DHC; 3: KSHS; 4: courtesy of Waynoka Historical Society (WHS); 5: WHS; 6: FHHC; 7: HHM; 8: Kitty Harvey Scrapbook GCNP; 9: MM

Pages 6–7: 1: Nancy Tucker Collection; 2: Fred Harvey logo used by permission of Xanterra Parks & Resorts, Inc.; 3: SHC; 4: Kay Harvey Collection (KHC); 5: KHC; 6: HHM; 7: WHS; 8: courtesy of Gordon Chappell; 9: El Tovar Studio, Fred Harvey Collection GCNP; 10: HHM; 11: courtesy of Elizabeth and David Pettifer; 12: DHC
Page 8: 1: Joy Harvey Collection; 2: GCC-DPL; 3: KSHS; 4: KHC; 5: MM; 6: DHC

About the Author

STEPHEN FRIED is an award-winning investigative journalist and essayist, and an adjunct professor at Columbia University Graduate School of Journalism. His acclaimed first biography, *Thing of Beauty: The Tragedy of Supermodel Gia*, inspired the Emmy-winning film *Gia* and introduced the word "fashionista" into the English language; he is also the author of the widely praised books *The New Rabbi, Bitter Pills: Inside the Hazardous World of Legal Drugs,* and *Husbandry*. A two-time recipient of the National Magazine Award, Fried has written frequently for *Vanity Fair, GQ, The Washington Post Magazine, Rolling Stone, Glamour, Ladies' Home Journal,* and *Philadelphia* magazine. He lives in Philadelphia with his wife, author Diane Ayres.

www.stephenfried.com

About the Type

This book was set in Caslon, a typeface first designed in 1722 by William Caslon. Its widespread use by most English printers in the early eighteenth century soon supplanted the Dutch typefaces that had formerly prevailed. The roman is considered a "workhorse" typeface due to its pleasant, open appearance, while the italic is exceedingly decorative.

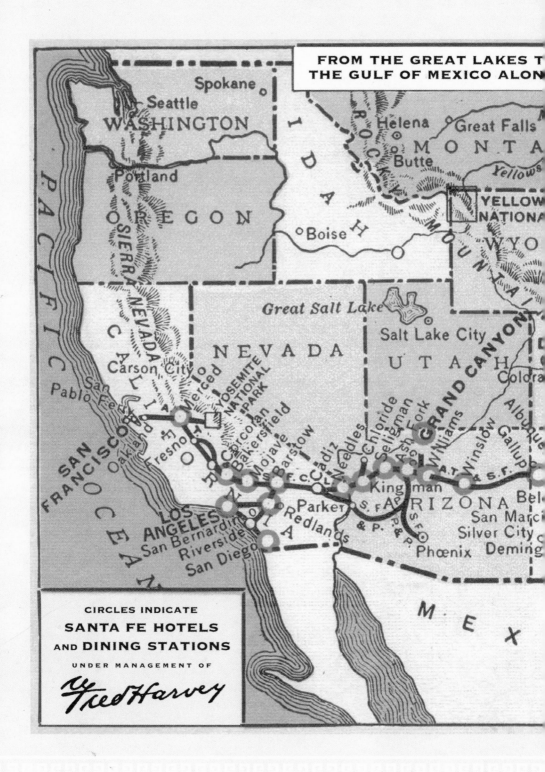

FROM THE GREAT LAKES T
THE GULF OF MEXICO ALON